خواهی که داوت بردرد صد سلسله بیدا را
منتکش گردن بند زنجیر استبدادرا

MIDDLE EAST
PAST AND PRESENT

Muhammad, by an anonymous Persian painter, probably of the late 19th century. The panels around the painting identify the prophet: "Muhammad ibn-Abdullah, may the blessing and peace of God be upon him."

MIDDLE EAST PAST AND PRESENT

YAHYA ARMAJANI

Macalester College

PRENTICE-HALL, INC., ENGLEWOOD CLIFFS, NEW JERSEY

13-581579-7

Library of Congress Catalog Card Number 77-76315

Printed in the United States of America

Current printing (last digit) :
10 9 8 7 6 5 4 3 2

PRENTICE-HALL INTERNATIONAL, INC., *London*
PRENTICE-HALL OF AUSTRALIA, PTY. LTD., *Sydney*
PRENTICE-HALL OF CANADA, LTD., *Toronto*
PRENTICE-HALL OF INDIA PRIVATE LIMITED, *New Delhi*
PRENTICE-HALL OF JAPAN, INC., *Tokyo*

FOR RUTH

حقیقت نه بررنگیست که ازو بپرستی
دوستـ نهانی است که جان دل پرستی

PREFACE

This book is a result of twenty years of teaching Middle East history in a liberal arts college. It is written for students and general readers who do not have knowledge of the history and culture of the area, and for teachers who may or may not be experts in the field themselves. The materials found in this book have been discussed and sifted in the classroom year after year and only those appear which have helped students to appreciate the past and present problems, accomplishments, and contributions of the peoples of the Middle East.

The Middle East is presented in four parts. Part One deals with the advent and spread of Islam, Part Two with the Ottoman and Safavid empires, Part Three with western imperialism and the Middle East, and Part Four with the modern period during which the Middle East was divided into many nation states. Those who have a year-long course on the Middle East may profitably use the first two parts in the first semester and the last two in the second.

Many peoples have contributed to the formation of the culture described in this volume, but no adequate understanding of Middle East history is possible without a discussion of at least three groups. These are Arabic-speaking peoples, Persians, and Turks. Any survey which neglects any one of the above is bound to present a distorted picture of the area. Without counting lines or words, I have tried to give each group its proper place in the history of the region as a whole.

This book, like any other history book, has a point of view. Its viewpoint is that of a native. I hope that my Persian birth and upbringing has not prevented me from presenting, insofar as the main issues are concerned, the Arab and Turkish points of view. My aim has been to write it in such a way that those who read it will be looking from the inside out and not from the outside in. This is not to say that foreign appraisal of a culture is not valuable or necessary. But it helps us gain that quality of human perception which we call "understanding" if we study the Middle East not because its oil is essential to the United States, but because the virtues and vices, wisdom and follies of its people have influenced the destiny of the people of the world and might do so again.

In preparing this volume I have used the works of Arab, Persian, Turkish, and western scholars. I wish it were possible for me to mention them all, but their number, scattered over the years, is so large that listing them would fill pages. Without their scholarship I could not have written this book and my gratitude to them is deep and sincere.

For the past fifteen years the Louis W. and Maud Hill Family Foundation of St. Paul, Minnesota, has helped four colleges of the city to carry on area study programs cooperatively. As coordinator of the Middle East area, I have received grants from the foundation to travel in the countries of the Middle East for study and research. In a real sense this volume is a result of their faith in our program and is offered as a token of my gratitude for their interest.

My thanks are due to Mr. Kenneth Holmes, Emeritus Professor of History at Macalester College, who read most of the manuscript and offered useful suggestions. I do not know what I would have done without the aid of Boyd C. Shafer, James Wallace Professor of History at Macalester, who read the whole manuscript. His knowledge of history and his ten years' experience as editor of the *American Historical Review* made his numerous suggestions invaluable. I am grateful to Professor Nikki Keddie of the University of California in Los Angeles, who also read the whole manuscript. This volume has been enhanced by her keen and penetrating criticism and suggestions. My thanks go also to my students, Allen Gibas and James Polzin, who read half and all of the manuscript, respectively, and offered suggestions. If, despite the efforts of these people, there are still mistakes and shortcomings, I assume full responsibility for them and for interpretations and conclusions.

Finally, I want to thank my patient and long-suffering secretaries, Katherine Cross and Nancy Nielsen, who typed the manuscript again and again, enough to have gained them each full credit for a course on Middle East history. My wife and family, who have lived with the preparation of the manuscript for at least three years, do not need to be told that I am grateful—they know it.

YAHYA ARMAJANI

St. Paul, Minnesota

CONTENTS

II. THE HEIRS OF THE ISLAMIC EMPIRE

III. IMPERIALISM AND AWAKENING

MIDDLE EAST
PAST AND PRESENT

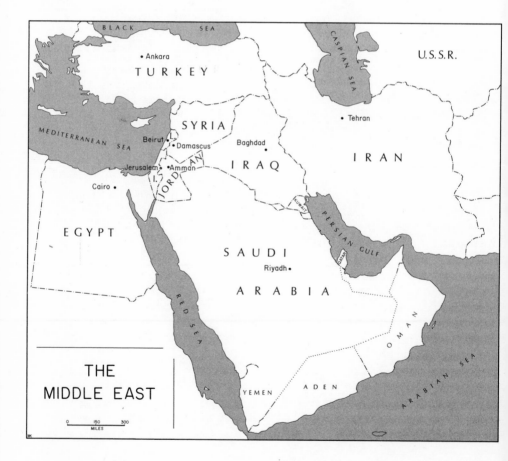

THE
MIDDLE EAST

0   150   300
      MILES

INTRODUCTION
TO THE MIDDLE EAST

The names of the area under consideration are nearly as controversial as the many issues and problems besetting the region. Before World War I, most of the region was part of the Ottoman Empire and was referred to, from the vantage point of Europeans, as the "Near East." Iran, Afghanistan, and occasionally India were sometimes called the Middle East. The rest of Asia was called the "Far East" and also the "Orient."

With the dismemberment of the Ottoman Empire after World War I and the creation of many independent states, especially in the Balkans, the term "Near East" fell into disuse. It has been kept alive, however, by such organizations as the Near East Foundation, the Association of Near Eastern Colleges, and by some modern authors who prefer "near" to "middle."

During World War II, the whole area from eastern Iran to the western borders of Egypt came to be regarded as a single unit for military and lend-lease purposes. Consequently, the military, unencumbered by academic considerations, christened it the "Middle East." By the end of the war the term was used by so many local and international agencies that it became customary. After World War II some authorities seeking accurate geographical identification, and others motivated by nationalism and resenting the words "near," "middle," and "far" because of their European orientation, have referred to the area as "West Asia" or "Southwest Asia." Two other terms must be mentioned—the "Nearer East" used by Hogarth, and the "Hither East" used by Kahn.

Unfortunately, the majority of those who use the term "Middle East" do not agree about the area it covers. At one extreme is the Middle East Institute, which considers the whole "Islamic World" from Morocco to Indonesia and from Sudan to Uzbekistan as "Middle East." At the other extreme are such modern books as *There Goes the Middle East*, in which the name refers only to

the Fertile Crescent[1] and Egypt. In between the extremes are the Royal Institute of International Affairs (British), for whom "Middle East" encompasses
Iran, Turkey, Arabia, and the Fertile Crescent, Egypt, Sudan, and Cyprus;
and other books (including this one) for whom "Middle East" means the same
areas except Sudan and Cyprus.

From A.D. 635 to roughly the year 1000, Egypt, Arabia, the Fertile Crescent,
and Iran had a common history. From about 1300 to 1920, Turkey and the
above areas minus Iran shared a common history. Consequently, the choice
in this volume of a limited area, namely Egypt, Turkey, Iran, Arabia, and the
Fertile Crescent, is not as arbitrary as it might seem. For over 1,300 years the
above area was the main arena for cultural, political, and economic activities
which in turn influenced the outlying regions. An understanding of the movements in this area will serve as an important means towards understanding the
life and culture of the surrounding regions.

The whole territory is as large as the United States and is roughly a square
surrounded by intruding bodies of water—the Persian Gulf, Red Sea, Mediterranean Sea, Black Sea, and, in a way, the Caspian Sea. Except for southern
Egypt and Arabia, the area is outside the tropics.

THE LAND

Geographically, the Middle East is divided into three zones.

1. *The Southern Zone* comprises all of Egypt, stretches northward on the lower
curve of the Fertile Crescent, and includes all of the Arabian Peninsula. It is
an extension of the African Sahara, including the Arabian plateau, and has
an average elevation of from 2,000 to 3,000 feet. The highlands of this plateau
are in Hijaz, the eastern coast of the Red Sea. They have an elevation of 9,000
feet, and go higher in a southeasterly direction towards Yaman, where they
reach 14,000 feet. This range prevents the scant moisture of few clouds from
reaching the land in central Arabia, thus creating one of the most awesome
deserts in the world, the *Rub al-Khali* (empty quarter) on the southeastern part
of the peninsula.

2. *The Northern Zone* comprises the northern tier of the Middle East. Geological disturbances have created three extensive mountain ranges: the Tarus in
Turkey, the Zagros in western Iran, and the Alborz in northern Iran. In these
rugged ranges Mount Ararat (17,000 feet) in Eastern Turkey is well known to
westerners as the landing place of Noah's Ark. Another well known mountain,
Mount Damavand (19,200 feet) is situated in northern Iran and is snowclad
all year round. It is the highest peak west of the Himalayas and is mentioned
in the legendary lore of the Persians.

Most of Turkey is on the Anatolian plateau. The average height is between
3,000 and 5,000 feet with the upland ranges reaching 6,000 to 8,000 feet above

---

[1] "Fertile Crescent" is used to define a territory covered by Iraq, Syria, Lebanon, Jordan,
and Israel.

sea level. The average rainfall is between 10 and 17 inches and the temperature ranges from 30°F. in January to 86°F. in July.

Over half of modern Iran is on the Iranian plateau which stretches outside of the political limits of the country into Pakistan and Afghanistan. Its elevation is between 200 and 8,000 feet above sea level. Unlike the Anatolian plateau, the Iranian plateau is surrounded by mountains with no outward drainage of any sort. Consequently, the inner region of the Iranian plateau is almost rainless and contains two deserts. One, on the north, is Dasht-e Kavir made up of salt swamps, and the other, Dasht-e Lut, to the south, is made up of firmer sands like a normal desert. The average rainfall on the outer rim of the plateau is 9.2 inches and the temperature range is 35°F. in January to 85°F. in July.

3. *The Intermediate Zone* is between the north and the south. This curves upward from southern Palestine to the southern foothills of the Tarus and then down to the Tigris-Euphrates Valley through the Persian Gulf to Oman. On the west there are two small ranges of mountains which run parallel to the Mediterranean. They are the Lebanon and the Anti-Lebanon. The elevation is from 5,000 feet in the south to 16,000 feet at Maronite Center in the north. This zone between the mountains of the north and east and the rifted region of Egypt and Arabia to the south and west sheltered the deposits of marine life which, through tectonic disturbances, resulted in the great oil fields on both sides of the Persian Gulf.

By far the most important geographical phenomenon common to all of the Middle East is aridity: it is estimated that 90 per cent of the area of the Middle East is arid. Water is the most important human and economic factor, for where there is no water there is no life. Indeed, the Persian word for desert is *bi-aban*, "without water." Five to six per cent of the Middle East area is cultivated and of this one-fifth needs water. To preserve water the ancient Assyrians, Babylonians, and Romans built cisterns and viaducts and ancient Persians built *qanats* or underground conduits which brought water for scores of miles from the mountains to the plains. To this day the Bedouin women in both Arabia and the Sahara wash their hair with camel urine in order to save water for human and animal consumption. One can stand at the foot of the Sphinx outside Cairo and look down the Nile River and see that where water comes there is vegetation. One inch beyond the reach of water nothing grows.

Consequently, geographers describe the Middle East in at least six different categories.

1. The desert, in which nothing grows, such as the land east and west of the Nile, the Rub al-Khali in Arabia, and the Kavir and the Lut in Iran.
2. The arid steppe south of the Fertile Crescent, where during the spring the camels can find some scrub and thorn and the Bedouins go from one temporary water hole to another.
3. The less arid steppe of south Turkey, west Iraq and east Iran where land is uncultivable but good enough for grazing sheep and goats.

4. The oasis with permanent water and therefore dwellings and, sometimes, major towns.
5. The mountain region of Turkey and Iran with cultivated green valleys, terraced hillsides, and numerous villages nestled against the mountains.
6. The coastal areas of the Black Sea, Caspian Sea, Red Sea, Mediterranean Sea, and the Persian Gulf. The abundance of these waterways has made it possible for every one of the Middle Eastern countries to have a sea outlet.

This area is fed by only two river systems. One is the Nile River, which is fed by the Blue Nile rising from the highlands of Ethiopia and by the White Nile flowing from the highlands of Central Africa. They join in Khartoum and flow northward to the Mediterranean Sea, thus completing a journey of 4,145 miles. The Nile River has divided the Libyan Desert by the creation of Egypt, the cultivated portion of which is an oasis of about ten miles on both sides of the river. Egypt then is truly the "gift of the Nile." The Nile is doubly life-giving, for not only does it bring water, but also in its annual flooding it deposits some 100 million tons of extremely rich sediment to replenish the soil.

The other river system in the Middle East is the Shat al-Arab which, in part, forms the boundary between Iraq and Iran. It is formed by the junction of the twin rivers Euphrates and Tigris, some 60 miles before reaching the Persian Gulf. Both rivers rise in the highlands of Turkey and take a circuitous journey southward until they join. Shat al-Arab is in turn joined by the Karun, a river in Iran which comes down from the Zagros Mountains and is navigable as far north as Ahvaz. Worthy of mention in this parched area are Kizel Irmak (Red River) in northern Turkey, and Sefid Rud (White River) and Karkhe in north and south Iran respectively. Of less significance geographically but explosive politically are the Jordan, Litani, and Orantes Rivers, which irrigate portions of Syria, Lebanon, Jordan, and Israel.

With the exception of the Caspian littoral in northern Iran and parts of northeastern Turkey, rainfall is not only inadequate but also what little there is is limited to the spring and winter seasons. Drought in the summer is the general rule. Usually one can expect hot summers and warm winters in Arabia, the Fertile Crescent, Egypt, and parts of Iran, and cold winters and cool summers in the mountainous regions of Turkey, Iran, and Lebanon.

There is ample evidence that perhaps millennia ago there were large forests in the area, but thanks to war, neglect, and goats, with very few exceptions the Middle East is now a deforested region. On the southern shores of the Caspian and Black Seas, and on the mountains of Lebanon, there is an abundance of pine, oak, and juniper. In the rest of the area the one tree present everywhere is the poplar.

Wheat, barley, rye, beans, lentils, onions, pomegranates, pears, and plums are harvested in most countries of the Middle East. Citrus fruits grow in Lebanon, Israel, and Iran; apples in Lebanon; figs and nuts in Turkey and Iran; olives in Israel, Jordan, and Iran; and grapes in most parts of the area.

Persian peaches and melons are world famous and so are the dates of Iraq. This latter fruit is a food staple for the majority of peoples in the Persian Gulf area. Its pit is used as animal fodder, the fiber of the tree is woven into rope, and its wood is used for fuel.

Chief among the industrial crops are cotton in Egypt, flax and hemp in the Fertile Crescent, coffee in Yaman, and tea in Iran and Turkey.

It is quite likely that many animals, such as the dog, sheep, goat, pig, and ass, were first domesticated in this area. Owing to the scarcity of grazing lands, the number of cattle is insignificant and milk yield is quite low. Horses and camels, it is believed, were brought from the East. Notwithstanding the fame of Persian cats and Arabian horses, the most distinctive animal in the area is still the camel. As a beast of burden, it has not yet been fully replaced by modern means of transportation. The camel is so essential a part of the Bedouin life that in Arabic there are scores of words to denote the various stages of its growth. The camel provides milk and meat for the nomad, its hair is turned into tents and cloaks, its dung into fuel, and its urine into hair wash. In addition to being the "ship of the desert," it turns the water wheel and pulls the plow.

Sea food abounds in the area even though its use by the inhabitants is limited because of the dietary laws of Islam and Judaism. The sardines of the Persian Gulf, the caviar of the Caspian Sea and the tuna of the Black Sea are world famous.

Not only is the Middle East limited in its agricultural production, but it also has scant mineral resources other than oil. Indeed, the vast resources of oil have made the area one of the richest in the world as well as marked it as a prime target for international intrigue and power politics. It is estimated that by A.D. 2000 the demand of the world, except the Soviet Union and China, will be for 1,650 million tons of oil annually. It is quite likely that half of this amount will then come from the Middle East. Moreover, the supply of oil there is so extensive that it will not be exhausted for a long time. Practically all of the oil lies in Iran, Iraq, Saudi Arabia, and Kuwait. The oil resources of the other Middle Eastern countries are negligible.

Another factor contributing to the importance of the area is its strategic location. It connects the three continents of Africa, Asia, and Europe. Located on the eastern end of the Mediterranean, the "Middle Sea," it touches the three major oceans of the world. It has often been referred to as the "Bridge to the East," and from the earliest times it has served as the land route to China and India from the West.

The three narrows or straits of the Middle East make it an important maritime route connecting different parts of the world. The 16-mile long Bosporus and the 25-mile long Dardanelles, or the Hellespont, are joined together by the Sea of Marmora and link the Black Sea with the Mediterranean. These straits have witnessed untold numbers of conquerors. Long before Xerxes flogged it in anger and down to the present it has been a center of political and economic controversy in the history of the world.

The other famous waterway is the Strait of Bab al-Mandab at the southern end of the Red Sea. It links the Mediterranean Sea, through the Suez Canal, with the Arabian Sea and the Indian Ocean.

The third is the Strait of Hormoz, which links the region drained by the Tigris and Euphrates to the Indian Ocean through the Persian Gulf.

In more modern times, the advent of railroads has made a deep impression on the Middle East. As evidence of this, one might mention the Berlin-Baghdad Railway which became the *cause célèbre* of the nineteenth century "Eastern Question." More recently, by way of air travel, one cannot go very far without landing at one or more of the modern airports of the Middle East.

In addition to its economic and strategic importance the Middle East is the birthplace of some of the earliest human civilizations and the cradle of three of the most important religions of the world, namely, Judaism, Christianity, and Islam. Consequently, the historian and the theologian, as well as the economist and the political scientist, find the area a fertile ground for study and investigation.

The Middle East as a whole may be likened to the early architectural pattern of houses in the region—four wings and a central patio. One wing is Turkey on the northwest, the second Iran on the east, the third Saudi Arabia on the south, and the fourth Egypt on the southwest. The central "courtyard" is the Fertile Crescent, which at present contains Lebanon, Syria, Israel, Jordan, and Iraq. Each one of these wings has an entrance to the central courtyard. Turkey and Iran, in addition to their front doors, each have back doors. Turkey's opens toward Europe and Iran's toward Asia. In history, whenever the front entrance of either of these countries to the central courtyard has been closed, the country involved has been concerned though it has not necessarily believed itself to be threatened. Hence, throughout history the peoples of Asia Minor, first the Byzantines and then the Turks, have afforded liaison between Europe and the Middle East, while the Persians have performed the same role between the peoples of China and India and the West.

On the other hand, the other two wings, namely Saudi Arabia and Egypt, have not had back doors to other areas, or at least they have not used them. Traditionally, the flow of the economic, cultural, and manpower movements from Arabia and Egypt has been toward the Fertile Crescent. Consequently, each time the front door of either of these two countries to the central courtyard has been closed, the country has felt itself threatened. Furthermore, it can be stated with some justification that throughout history, the many powers that gained control of all of the Fertile Crescent usually were able to conquer Egypt and the Arabian Peninsula, but not necessarily Turkey and Iran. Hence, this, in addition to the modern phenomenon of "Arabism," accounts for the extreme interest of Saudi Arabia and Egypt in the twentieth century in the affairs of the Fertile Crescent as opposed to the relative indifference of both Turkey and Iran.

THE PEOPLE

Most of the inhabitants of the Middle East, such as Egyptians, Lebanese, Turks, and Persians are Caucasian people of the same general type as the Greeks, Italians, Spanish, and Irish. There are Negroid types scattered in the area, particularly in the Sudan. There are also some Mongoloid people, especially the Turkman of northeast Iran. With the exception of a few isolated pockets, however, the Middle East has been a crossroads area for so long that racial mixing has made it literally impossible to separate the people from the point of view of physical differences.

What differentiates the peoples of the Middle East more than any other factor is language.

A. The Indo-Europeans. The dominant group in this category are the Persians, who have linguistic and cultural ties with the Persian-speaking peoples of Afghanistan, Tajikistan, and parts of Turkmanistan and Uzbekistan as well as of Pakistan. There is linguistic affinity between Persian and most of the languages of India and Europe. In the Middle East, the Armenians and the Kurds are related linguistically to the Persians. Religiously, however, they are apart both from the Persians and from each other. The Armenians are scattered in most of the countries of the Middle East as well as of the world. Their major concentration is, of course, in the Soviet Republic of Armenia. The Kurds, on the other hand, are less cosmopolitan and most of them live in a region which comprises parts of Turkey, Iran, and Iraq. Both groups have nationalistic aspirations.

B. The Turkic Peoples. The dominant group in the Middle East in this category is the Turks. They have linguistic ties with the Turkmans and Uzbeks in the east and the Hungarians and Finns in the west. As we shall see in this study, the Turks are relative newcomers to the Middle East.

C. The Semites. Those who speak the Semitic group of languages live in a relatively small contiguous area and are not as scattered as the Indo-Europeans or as separated as the Turkic. The dominant group in the Middle East in this category are the Arabic-speaking peoples. These do not comprise a "nation" for there are regional, nationalistic, and religious differences among them. There are linguistic and cultural ties between the Arabic-speaking peoples of the Middle East and those of the Sudan and North Africa as far west as the Atlantic Ocean.

Linguistically related to the Arabs are the Israelis who speak Hebrew and who comprise a separate state in the Middle East. Another related group are the Assyrians, also called Chaldeans, who speak Syriac. The Assyrians are Christians and live mostly in Iran and Iraq with small numbers in Syria and

Lebanon, and much larger numbers outside of the Middle East in the United States.

RELIGIOUS GROUPS

The diversity of linguistic groups is confounded by religious differences and the latter are, at times, more serious. The majority of the people of the Middle East are Muslims, who are divided into Sunni and Shi'i sects. Most of the Muslims of the world belong to the former group. They consider themselves the adherents of the *Sunna*, or "practices," of the Prophet. They believe themselves to be orthodox Muslims, but their orthodoxy is questioned by Wahhabism, which is the state religion of Saudi Arabia. The main divisions of the Shi'is are (a) Ja'fari, or Twelvers. Theirs is the state religion of Iran and they are scattered in other countries of the Middle East; (b) Ismaili, or Seveners, are scattered throughout the world of Islam; (c) Zaydis, whose faith is the state religion of Yaman; (d) Alawis, who live in northern Syria. Within the Islamic community are the Sufis, who have not separated themselves to form a sect, but whose mysticism is suspect by the ulama, or the "clergy" of Islam. More will be said about these groups in the discussion of the development of Islam.

No introduction to the Middle East will be complete without some knowledge of the non-Muslim religions of the area. As these will not be discussed in the following pages, each receives a brief description here.

The largest religious minority in the Middle East is Christianity. The Christians of the Middle East are divided into four communions.

A. EASTERN ORTHODOX CHURCH. Historically, this church grew out of the four original Eastern Patriarchates—Constantinople (now Istanbul), Alexandria, Antioch, and Jerusalem—which separated from the western Church in 1054. Later the church became divided along national lines such as Greek Orthodox, Russian Orthodox, and so forth. Each group is independent, autocephalous, and has its own Patriarch. The Patriarch of Constantinople is, however, first among equals. The adherents of the Patriarchate of Constantinople are mostly Greek, while those of the Patriarchate of Alexandria, with their headquarters in Cairo, are Arab and Greek. The majority of Christians in the Patriarchates of Antioch and Jerusalem are Arab. Damascus is the center for the Patriarchate of Antioch.

B. ORIENTAL CHURCHES. This communion has several branches.

1. *The Coptic Church of Egypt.* This church, whose Patriarch resides in Cairo, rejected the decision of the Council of Chalcedon and became Monophysite, that is, emphasized the single nature of Christ. It is similar to the Ethiopian Church except that in Egypt the liturgy is in Coptic and Arabic. It must be noted that the language of the Copts is Arabic. Coptic is used in parts of the liturgy only.

2. *The Syrian Church,* sometimes called "Jacobite." This church is also Monophysite and was organized under the Patriarch of Antioch with residence in Homs, Syria. Its liturgy is conducted in Syriac.

3. *The Armenian Church.* Usually referred to as "Gregorian," this church is within the

Eastern Orthodox tradition. Its most important Patriarch is the Catholicos of Etch-mizdzin in the Soviet Republic of Armenia. It has been a national church since the Armenians had a national existence in the Caucasus. During their long history the Armenians were caught between the Byzantine-Persian wars and later between the Ottoman-Persian wars. Consequently, in recent centuries they have been vassals to both the Ottomans and the Persians and later to the Russians. One of the results of the Russian Bolshevik Revolution was the formation of the Armenian Soviet Republic with Erivan as its capital. Outside the Republic there are Armenian communities scattered in most of the countries of the Middle East.

4. *The Nestorians.* As a church the Nestorians believe in the dual nature of Christ. Before the advent of Islam they were the main propagators of Christianity through-out Asia. From their bishoprics in Iran they sent missionaries as far as China. As a "nation" they are called Assyrians and speak Syriac, which belongs to the Semitic family of languages. Their Patriarch, the Mar Shimmun, is a temporal as well as religious ruler. For centuries the agricultural Syrians lived under the suzerainty of Iran, while the highlanders, known as the Jeeloo, lived under the domination of the Turks. During World War I both groups became pawns in international rivalry. In the Middle East the largest Assyrian settlements are in Iran and Iraq.

C. ROMAN CATHOLICS. They are divided into two groups. One follows the Latin rite, and is composed of Roman Catholic Europeans who have settled in the Middle East and individual converts from the various Orthodox and Oriental churches. The other and by far the larger group is the Uniate Church. This is the term applied to the Orthodox who accept the supremacy of the Pope but who in turn are allowed to use the Oriental rite in worship and whose clergy have permission to marry. On the whole, the Uniates have held to their original national traditions and have their own Patriarchs. These are the Greek Catholic, Syrian Catholic, Armenian Catholic, Chaldean Catholic (Nestorian), Coptic Catholic, and Maronite Catholic. This last is the largest subdivision and, by custom, the President of the Republic of Lebanon is chosen from its ranks.

D. ANGLICAN AND PROTESTANT. The Anglicans serve the British communities in the Middle East as well as the converts from the Oriental churches and a few from Islam and Judaism. The Protestant churches have evolved principally from the missionary activities of American churches in the nineteenth and twentieth centuries. Their members are converts from the Oriental churches as well as from Islam, Judaism, and Zoroastrianism.

A second non-Islamic religion in the Middle East is, of course, *Judaism*, which is the raison d'être for the establishment of the state of Israel as well as the state religion. All of the original Jewish inhabitants of the Middle East are Sephardim, while the Ashkenazim, who all reside in Israel, are newcomers from Europe. Most of the countries of the Middle East, with the exception of Saudi Arabia, Jordan, and Yaman, still claim small Jewish communities.

A third non-Islamic religion native to the Middle East is *Zoroastrianism*, the religion of the Persians until the Arab conquest. As a religion, it has profoundly influenced Judaism, and, more especially, Christianity and Islam. Two of its offshoots, Mithraism and Manicheanism, rivaled Christianity for the allegiance of the people of the Roman Empire. After the Arab conquest a large number of those who were not killed or converted fled to India to form the present Parsee (Persian) communities of India and Pakistan. A small number of Zoroastrians still live in Iran.

Among the other non-Islamic religions in the Middle East, the following must be mentioned:

The Druzes. This religion, whose adherents live in the mountains of Lebanon, Syria, and Israel, is an offshoot of the Ismaili subdivision of the Shi'a, who accepted the Fatimid Caliph Hakim (996–1021) as the incarnation of Deity. The name is perhaps derived from its first missionary who was called Darazi (1019). Theologically, they drew from many other religions and beliefs, and in time became a distinct people refusing to accept any converts.

The Yazidis. Even though they deny the existence of the devil in their religion, their neighbors refer to them as "devil worshippers." Yazidism is also a radical offshoot of Shi'a Islam and is a mixture of Muslim, Jewish, Christian, Manichean, and Shamanistic beliefs. There are some 25,000 believers and they live in northern Syria and Iraq.

The Sabians. Not to be confused with Sabaeans of pre-Islamic Arabia, the Sabians (or Mandeans) are more popularly but perhaps erroneously called "The Christians of St. John the Baptist." Their religion is of Judeo-Christian orientation and is mentioned three times in the Koran. Perhaps because of this the Muslims gave them the status of the "people of the book." The Arabs, impressed by the fact that these people washed themselves frequently as a religious ritual, referred to them as *mughtasilah* (those who wash themselves)— hence their possible connection to the disciples of John the Baptist. Today they live mostly in Iraq and are recognized for specialization as silversmiths.

The Bahais. This religion is an offshoot of the Shaykhi sect of Shi'a Islam, started in Iran in 1844, and was known as "Babi." In 1863 the Bahais split from Babis and organized a religion of their own. During its century and a quarter of turbulent existence, Bahaism has veered away from the major original tenets and has become syncretistic, embracing all religions of the world. The majority of Bahais live in Iran, though unrecognized, but their headquarters is in Haifa, Israel, and they have "assemblies" in many parts of the world.

DIVERSITY AND UNITY

Superimposed over these religious communities, which have also enjoyed varying degrees of communal and political autonomy for centuries, are 11 modern states and some seven Shaykhdoms each with varying degrees of independence and development. Since no state, with the possible exception of Saudi Arabia, is made up of one religious community, the transcendent religious and communal loyalties often clash with the more limited national loyalties. Consequently, in all of the states of the Middle East it has become customary to identify each person according to his religion, and more often than not members of the minority religions feel that they are second-class citizens. To avoid this, Lebanon has devised a formula in which religious communities have been given political power commensurate with their number. A Maronite Catholic is always President, a Sunni Muslim the Prime Minister, a Shi'a Muslim the Speaker of the Parliament, an Orthodox Christian in one ministry, a Druze in another, and so on. This is precarious, to say the least, but is more conducive to peaceful coexistence than the situation in Iraq, where the Shi'a majority are more or less governed by a Sunni minority. Also, in their midst they have the Kurds, whose religion is Sunni but whose language is related to the Persians; and the Armenians and the Assyrians who neither speak the same language nor profess the same religion as the rest of the Iraqis.

Even from the brief description above it is evident that there is much cultural diversity in the Middle East and the danger of overgeneralization about the peoples and cultures of the area is great. Throughout the Middle East, group identifications are still strong. Individuals find themselves with conflicting loyalties sometimes on linguistic grounds such as Arabic, Armenian, Hebrew, Kurdish, Persian, Syriac, or Turkish; sometimes on religious levels such as Bahai, Druze, Jew, Orthodox, Protestant, Roman Catholic, Sabian, Shi'a, Sunni, Yazidi, or Zoroastrian; and sometimes on national grounds when loyalty is expressed in terms of nation-states. This last form of loyalty is strongest among the Israelis, Persians, and Turks, and, to a lesser degree, among the citizens of the various Arab states. It is this diversity which has led anthropologist Carleton Coon to suggest that the Middle East is a mosaic of peoples, a kind of patchwork quilt of different cultural groups.

Nevertheless, in this patchwork quilt there are threads that run through the whole so that one can discern similar patterns and observe a unity. One of these patterns is the community life of the people. It is safe to say that all over the Middle East there are three types of community life: the nomad, the village, and the town.

Probably fewer than five per cent of all the peoples of the Middle East are now nomadic. There are almost no nomads in Lebanon, while in Saudi Arabia perhaps they number as high as 25 to 30 per cent. The main concern of the nomad is to follow grass, and therefore water, but depending on the locale, his main activity may be the herding of sheep, goats, or camels. The nomads of the Fertile Crescent and Arabian peninsula who look for water on a virtually flat landscape are called "horizontal," while the nomads of mountainous Iran and Turkey who live higher in search of grass during the summer are called "vertical." But whether "horizontal" or "vertical" their communities are all organized along similar lines and they are governed by a leader, usually hereditary, who is called "Shaykh" among the Arabs and "Khan" among the Persians and Turks. The nomads are practically self-sufficient and to acquire the few necessities which they cannot produce they sell sheep, milk, butter, cheese, and wool to the townsmen. They all live in tents and can move at a moment's notice with their meager possessions. All of them are loyal to the tribe rather than to the central government. They do not understand, or find them unacceptable if they do understand, such modern notions as the income tax, parliaments, military service, or national frontiers. In earlier centuries the tribes were considered to be the backbone of the kingdoms. They were given autonomy in their region and in turn they supplied the king or caliph with troops in time of war. The regularity of their paying tribute varied directly with the power of the ruler. In these days of national budgets, national armies, and national education, however, the tribes are fighting a losing battle and they and their nomadic ways of life will someday disappear.

Estimates are that between 75 and 80 per cent of the people of the Middle East live in the second type of community, the agricultural village. Farming is the main economic activity, supplemented by crafts. The village, the center of the community life, is a cluster of houses built close together. In most of the Middle East these houses are build of sun-dried brick. With the exception of northern Syria and some parts of Arabia, where the homes are built like inverted cones, village homes throughout the area are usually one or two story rectangles. In the mountainous regions the villages cling to the hillside and, as nearly all of them are away from the main highways, they go almost unnoticed. Many of the farmers use methods which have not changed in thousands of years. Others use somewhat improved practices, while still others have begun to use modern farm machinery. Ignorance of scientific farming, illiteracy, disease, and absentee landlordism leave the farmers of the area little economic surplus and, with few exceptions, they lead lives of grinding poverty.

The villagers' clothing is quite simple and ranges from the "nightgown" of the Egyptian to the long shirt and trousers of the Persian. Bread, supplemented by vegetables, is the staff of their life. The village women do not suffer the general seclusion of their sisters in the towns nor enjoy the freedom of the tribal women. The villager is, on the whole, as docile and content as the tribesman is proud and restless. Most of the modern states of the Middle East have inaugurated long-range and far-reaching programs to improve the life of the peasant. These range from division of land to introduction of education and establishment of cooperatives. One of the most advanced programs is in Iran, where thousands of educated young men are enlisted in "literacy corps," or "health corps," or the like, and work for two years in villages throughout the country in lieu of their military service obligation.

Urban community life has always existed in the Middle East. Indeed, Damascus boasts of being the oldest continuously inhabited city in the world and other cities such as Baghdad, Beirut, Cairo, Esfahan, Istanbul, Jerusalem, and Mecca are old by any standards. It is difficult to generalize about the cities and towns of the Middle East except to say that they contain the most extreme contrasts. Modern apartment buildings stand next to a thousand-year-old mosque or homes build of sun-dried bricks. The richest men in the country live in cities and so do the poorest. Illiterates rub shoulders in the streets with the most educated. A few women wear the latest gowns from Paris and dance to the most recent tunes, while only blocks away their less fortunate but more numerous sisters live the secluded life of old.

The governments of the Middle East have been city governments for centuries and to this day they usually operate in the interests of the city dwellers. The rising middle class of the Middle East lives in cities and it is here that political parties are formed, new constitutions are drafted, and political demonstrations are staged to make or break governments. At the same time, farmers are increasingly attracted to the cities because of jobs in commerce and industry. Hence, the population explosion is everywhere apparent in the cities as dislocated villagers are crowded into slum dwellings. The city dweller of the Middle East is the individual in transition between the established patterns of the past and the unaccomplished hopes of the future. He is caught between the placid villager who does not want to go any place and the satisfied European who feels that he has already arrived. At best, he carries the burden of the whole country on his shoulders. At worst, he is the shrewd opportunist who profits by the confusion of his fellow countrymen.

In the villages as well as the urban centers the family has been the most important unit. The traditional Middle Eastern family gives status and self respect to the individual. City life and institutions have not, as yet, disrupted this. Without his family the Middle Easterner is nothing. The kinship group provides economic and political security. Even if one leaves the village or the nomadic tribe, he retains his identity with the family.

The smallest unit in the social structure of the Middle East is the household. In many cases this is an extended family household, in which the senior male is the patriarch and represents the family in all matters. In modern times political loyalties are often based on family ties.

The nuclear family is now widespread in the Middle East, especially in the city. Whether the family will be extended or nuclear depends upon such factors as economic productivity, patterns of land tenure, and urbanization. While it is true that the family provides security for the person, contact with western culture has created many tensions within families and, occasionally, conflicts within the household and within larger groupings become extremely serious.

With the glaring exception of the nomads, the sexes have been traditionally segregated and women have been markedly subordinate to men. The veil, covering the faces of women, became the prime symbol of Muslim conservatism with regard to the status of women. Even though the veil has been lifted in many parts of the Middle East there is much resistance to the changing status of women, and the Middle East is still a man's world.

There are many evidences of class awareness in the Middle East and usually three class levels are identified in the cities and villages. These are the elite, the small middle class, and the vast mass of poor people. There is relatively little stratification among the nomads except for hereditary nobility. Social status influences speech habits, gestures, and other aspects of daily behavior, and one can readily discern class levels in a community if he spends a little time there. Some of the major factors in the determination of social status are loyalty to family, size of family, age, land holdings, wealth, political power, religion, education, and artistic knowledge.

For many centuries the economic differences between the ruling elite and the masses have been great. Socially they were not entirely separated and ideologically they shared similar goals and values. The landlord and the peasant all slept on the floor, sat on the floor, ate similar food, wore a similar style of clothing, and kept themselves warm during the winter in the same way. They were both practicing Muslims, believed in Islamic institutions, and had similar ideas of right and wrong. To be sure, the economic differences were apparent in that the landlord's food was more plentiful and his clothing and bedding were of better material. Westernization, however, has radically changed this situation. Not only has it widened the economic gap, but it has also created other gaps where the illiterate poor man does not feel as comfortable in the presence of his wealthy master as his father once did. The ruling elite, whose education has given him knowledge of the West and whose wealth has enabled him to adopt Western ways, has separated himself from his poorer compatriot. He does not live in the same type of house as his father did, nor does he sleep and sit on the floor, nor eat similar food. He has all of the gadgets of comfort enjoyed in the West, whereas the villager's life has changed very little. More often than not a member of the new elite is not a practicing Muslim and does not hold to the values of the past. Even his daily speech has so many western words in it that the illiterate poor man has difficulty understanding his language.

Today, the social structure of the Middle East is undergoing vast change. There has been land reform and there will be much more. Even where there has been little reform, the all-powerful position of the landlord is giving way. One can improve his social class position if he has sufficient education. A certain amount of wealth is always helpful, but some observers believe that a military career, coupled with education, is an excellent means of acquiring influence and power. With the improved means of communication and the increase in the number of schools, the illiterate masses of today will provide the skilled workers of the society of the future and will grasp a good share of the political power in the process.

NATIONALISM

Nationalism is another sentiment which is common to practically all the peoples of the Middle East. Nationalism in itself is divisive. Even though it sets the Egyptians against the Syrians and the Iraqis against the Persians, nevertheless, the ingredients of this nationalism are common to all.

(1) One of these ingredients is pride in the glory of the past. The Middle Easterner, whether he be Arab, Persian, or Turk, wants everyone to know about his past and appreciate it. The past gives him reason for his boastful pride. If the greatness of any nation is in the power of its armies and its ability, by brute force, to impose its will upon others, then the people of the Middle East can claim this greatness. There were times when Middle Eastern nations

such as the Egyptians, the Babylonians, Assyrians, Persians, Arabs, and Turks had the "atomic" weapons of their day. By brute force they built great empires and imposed their will on more territory and more people than some of the great empires in the West. In the following pages appear great generals such as Khalid ibn-al-Walid, Sa'd ibn-Waqqas, Mahmud of Ghazna, some of the Ottoman Sultans, Chengiz Khan, Tamerlane, Nader Shah, and a host of others, any of whose military exploits and shrewd imperial strategy overshadow many a famous counterpart in Europe. The "Pax Romana" imposed by the Roman Empire was quite insignificant as compared to the "peace" imposed by the descendants of Chengiz Khan in Asia. In the latter part of the thirteenth century Marco Polo could travel from either western Russia or the eastern Mediterranean over the length of Asia, north and central, to the capital of Kublai Khan in Peking on well established roads without fear of molestation.

There are those who believe that greatness is not measured in terms of brute force alone, but in terms of qualities of intellect, which make lasting contributions towards the betterment of civilization. In this too the peoples of the Middle East can take pride. A typical day in the life of a Western man is enriched by many contributions from the Middle East. His year is determined by the birth of a Palestinian, and the month, the week, the day, and the hour are based on a system of reckoning and calendar started by the Egyptians and Babylonians and perfected by the Persians. He washes himself in a "bath" introduced into Europe by the Turks and dries himself with a "Turkish" towel.

At breakfast he may drink coffee "qahwa" (Arabic). He drives to his work on wheels, a discovery by someone in the ancient Middle East. During the day he may use scientific and business words such as algebra "al-jabr" (Arabic), alcohol "al-kohl" (Arabic), or tariff "Ta'rifa" (Arabic). His books are named after "Biblos"—hence Bible and bibliography—a town in Lebanon where the idea of a book was first conceived. His post office is an institution of the Persians reported by Herodotus; he writes on paper brought to the West by Muslims; and he uses "Arabic numerals," devised in India and brought to Europe by the Arabs.

At home he may relax on his divan "deevan" (Persian) or sofa "suffa" (Arabic) and read a magazine "makhzan" (Arabic). Later he puts on his pajamas "pa-jameh" (Persian) and lies down on the mattress "matrah" (Arabic). Indeed, more and more western historians acknowledge the great debt which the Renaissance owes the Muslims of the Middle Ages who preserved and built upon all the important learning of the Greeks and the Romans and passed it on to Europe.

Long before the Renaissance the Muslims from diverse nationalities in the Middle East collected books on all subjects in Latin, Greek, Syriac, Persian, Sanskrit, Chinese, and any other language they could find and brought them to Baghdad. The Caliph, Ma'mun, established a "Bureau of Translations" under the leadership of the Christian Hunayn ibn-Ishaq (809–873) and had these manuscripts, mostly Greek, translated into Arabic, which was considered a holy language just as Latin was considered holy in Europe.

Later Muslims studied these and built upon them and produced philosophers such as Averröes (ibn-Rushd) to whom St. Thomas Aquinas was indebted; and mathematicians such as Omar Khayyam who devised the Jalali calendar still used in Iran today, which is more accurate than its Gregorian counterpart in use in the West. In medicine Muslims produced a host of famous physicians, among them Razi, and Avicenna, whose writings were the standard textbooks of medicine in Europe until the eighteenth century and whose "portraits adorn the great hall of the school of medicine at the University of Paris." In the following pages appear scientists, philosophers, geographers, historians, men of letters, and artists whose contributions to civilization are unquestioned.

There are still others who believe that true greatness implies a spiritual basis, to make it humane and constructive. In this also the people of the Middle East have contributed much. The three great monotheistic religions of the world have their origins in the Middle East. There is Judaism given form by Moses, born in Egypt; Christianity founded by Jesus, born in Palestine; and Islam founded by Muhammad, born in Arabia. Every one of these religions is in turn indebted to the less known Zoroastrianism, founded in Iran. To these religions of the Middle East, western civilization owes its most cherished values and goals and its concepts of God and man, and of life and afterlife.

(2) Indeed, the memory of former physical strength, intellectual attainment, and spiritual contribution is so vivid in the mind of the Middle Easterner that he is often in danger of living in the past without any thought of the present or the future. Whenever, on the other hand, he is conscious of the present, he is overwhelmed by a feeling of inferiority. This sense of inferiority is the second ingredient in his present-day nationalism. He is dependent not only upon the technology of the West, but he is also overtly (in the case of a Turk) or covertly (in the case of the Arab and Persian) working hard to become like the European. He wears western-style clothes, eats western food, enjoys western music, lives under western law, reads western philosophy, and likes western institutions.

Whenever Middle Easterners are together they talk about the long distance they have to go to catch up with the West and their frustration with a society which is not moving fast enough. Whenever they face a westerner their pride intervenes and they become defensive and, sometimes, belligerent. On the one hand, they feel that they have to borrow from the West in order to survive, and on the other hand, they resent having to do so. Yet there is no precedent for this guilt feeling about borrowing in the Islamic Middle East. When Islam emerged from the Arabian desert, it was a new, vigorous faith without a set of traditions and within the context of a primitive culture. In general, it delighted in satisfying an insatiable curiosity and widening its horizons without hesitation. Islam became fascinated with Hellenistic thought, adopted the Persian method of administration, and did not hesitate to borrow heavily from any culture within reach. The question arises, then, why this hesitation to borrow now?

For one thing, there is the pride of a religious society which replaced Christianity in many areas and is now hesitant to learn from a civilization which goes by the name of Christian. Perhaps the more important reason is that the countries and cultures from which Islam borrowed were either decadent or had just been defeated. Consequently, a victorious Muslim army took over ideas just as it confiscated war booty. The situation is radically different now. In the modern encounter with the West, the Muslims are not confident of their own position and any borrowing is out of weakness rather than strength. Furthermore, the leaders of Islam are afraid that those of their coreligionists who adopt western ways do not do so with the idea of enriching their heritage, but with the idea of replacing it with the superior institutions of the West.

(3) A third ingredient of modern nationalism is secularism. The influence of modern scientific civilization is uniformly great in all the countries of the Middle East although it is more advanced in some countries than in others. Islam is going through the same kind of struggle that Christianity did during the eighteenth and nineteenth centuries. Like Christianity, Islam has to react one way or the other to modern science, ideas, and institutions. There are at least two types of reactions. In his *Civilization on Trial*, Arnold Toynbee says that "whenever one civilized society finds itself in this dangerous situation *vis-à-vis* another, there are two alternative ways open to it of responding to the challenge." One is "zealotism" which "takes refuge from the unknown in the familiar," and in a struggle against superior tactics and new weapons the society "responds by practicing its own traditional art of war." The other he names "Herodeanism," which "acts on the principle that the most effective way to guard against the danger of the known is to master its secret," and in the struggle against superior tactics and new weapons "responds by discarding its traditional art of war and learning to fight the enemy with the enemy's own tactics and weapons."

In the Middle East the "zealots" are, for the most part, headed by religious leaders who are fearful of the western institutions and the encroachment of western ideas. They want to go back to the purity of Islam, "when it was pure and unadulterated with foreign ideas." Precisely, they mean the time of the first four caliphs when the Koran was the only book and the Sunna the only law. Some of the more "progressive" in this group, to minimize any idea of borrowing, have gone so far as to claim that the Koran was the first to predict most of the modern scientific and technological advances from electricity and telephones to jets and space rockets.

The "Herodeans," on the other hand, react differently. They are, for the most part, headed by the young progressives who see salvation in total modernization. These modernizers are, in turn, divided into three groups. One is still oriented toward the western European form of political democracy. They are imbued with ideas of the "Enlightenment" and those forces which brought about the American and French Revolutions. A second group of modernizers follows the ideas of democracy which have been "purified" and "fulfilled" by the Communist revolutions in the Soviet Union and, more recently, in China. They are attracted by the dialectics of Karl Marx and the meteoric rise of Communist power. A third group of modernizers, while favoring the West over the Communist world, calls itself neutral and tries to supplement the political democracy of the West with social reform, while at the same time being attracted by the "one party democracy of the Communist world." With the exception of those who are doctrinaire Communists and, therefore, antireligious, the majority of the modernizers are secularists who, while they do not oppose religion, do not find Islam or any other religion relevant to the problems of the day.

Islam is going through the same inner struggle in adjusting to modern conditions that Christianity experienced in the nineteenth century. Since Islam does not distinguish between the "secular" and the "religious," the laws of Islam drawn up in the seventh and eighth centuries are religiously binding in the twentieth century and make the problem of adjustment more difficult. On the other hand, the student of the modern movements in the Middle East must always bear in mind that the identification of culture and religion has always been looked upon with favor by Islam even though such identification has been generally decried by Christianity.

(4) A fourth ingredient in nationalism is suspicion. A modern nationalist, whether he be Arab, Persian, or Turk is ashamed not to be suspicious of Europe. At best he will be considered "gullible" and at worst "Communist" or "imperialist," depending upon his circle of friends. The Middle East may be compared to a campfire. There was a time when its flames went high and illuminated the surrounding areas. Its lights and warmth attracted many people and, in that fellowship, much was learned and shared. However, as will be seen in these pages, the people went into a deep slumber and the ashes of time covered their huge fire. Now they have awakened and want to push away the ashes and, with the use of embers, start a new fire. In this attempt they are confronted with two problems. The first problem is that every time, especially in the past century and a half, they have attempted to push the ashes away, they have been prevented by hands from the outside. These hands have been British, Russian, French, German, and American. Consequently, Middle Eastern nationalists are suspicious of the policies of Europe, and have come to believe that the countries of the West, Communist and non-Communist, do not approve of their awakening. The simple remark of a tourist expressing sorrow over the disappearance of the camel or the covered bazaar is not taken as an innocent comment but rather as an ominous design to discourage progress. This xenophobia often based on reality and sometimes on imagination, is an important element in the thought processes of the people of the Middle East.

(5) The second problem caused by the attempt to build a new fire is one of choice. It is difficult to know which log to use. This causes confusion, which is a fifth ingredient of nationalism. As the heir of an ancient culture, the Middle Easterner has a problem about what to keep and what to discard. As a people facing the aggressive culture of the West yet desiring change, their problem is what to accept and what to reject. These decisions are not easy, and as a result there is sharp disagreement between mother and daughter, father and son, friend and friend. Take, for example, the question of music. There are those who reject western music and there are those who despise their own traditional eastern music. Among those who love the western music there is a sharp disagreement between those who love classical western music and those who admire jazz. In this conflict one should not overlook those who want to combine the two! This confusion is typical of every aspect of life, be it food, dress, education, politics, or even religion.

ISLAM

The general and vivid pattern that unifies the patchwork quilt known as the Middle East is, of course, Islam. Even though there are many sects and schools of thought in Islam, reputedly some 72 of them, it is still the strongest common experience of the peoples of the area. Many writers are in the habit of saying that "Islam is not only a religion, but it is a way of life." Of course, in a sense, every religion is a way of life. By this statement they mean that Islam attempts to regulate the whole of life. Hence, it not only sets up spiritual goals, but also provides the institutions, laws, and the general environment in which those goals should be attained. It leaves little to the individual. Islam tells him when and how to pray, how many times and in what direction; it has laws about marriage and divorce, property, and inheritance; it has rules for the art of war and the maintenance of peace. These are practically the same in all Islamic countries. For over 1,300 years Muslims have fought others and each other, built institutions, written books, organized revolts, and erected edifices, all in reference to Islam—either for it or against it or under its aegis. Consequently, Middle Eastern history cannot be understood without a knowledge of Islam. Therefore, this study will begin with Islam.

Before we begin, a word of explanation is necessary. The civilization now under study was triggered by the initial Arab conquest, and hence is sometimes called "Arab" civilization. Unfortunately, the modern states which go by the name of "Arab" consider themselves the sole heirs of that culture and boast of "Arab" contributions to the civilization of the world. This is as confusing as it is untrue. Originally, the Bedouins of Arabia, when they conquered Syria, Mesopotamia, Egypt, and Iran, were conquering non-Arab countries. In the process these sons of the desert brought with them not only Islam, but also the Arabic language which they believed to be the" language of angels." Furthermore, they imposed this language upon the conquered people, to the extent that it became the medium of instruction as well as that of official communication. Consequently, all of the scholars within a certain period wrote in Arabic, irrespective of their national origin. A vast majority of these scholars were not Arabs. Indeed, a number of them, such as the celebrated Ibn Khaldun of North Africa, did not even think very highly of the Arabs.

Later, some of the people who had been conquered by the Arabs in the seventh and eighth centuries, such as the Syrians, Egyptians, and North Africans, adopted Arabic as their language. Others, however, such as the Persians, Turks, and Indians, who had never adopted Arabic as their spoken language, discontinued the use of it in their writing in the same way that many Europeans gave up the use of Latin.

Indeed, until the emergence of Arab nationalism, in the twentieth century, the term "Arab" was applied almost solely to the inhabitants of the peninsula of Arabia. Even after World War I the Egyptians would not accept the idea advanced by some of the leaders in the Fertile Crescent that "everyone who speaks Arabic is an Arab." This pan-Arabistic formula failed to attract many followers until after World War II.

The desire to unite all who speak Arabic in one "Arab" nation is understandable and may be quite legitimate even though it has many opponents within the Arabic-speaking community. But this is hardly justification for calling everyone in the Middle Ages who wrote his works in Arabic an "Arab." To add further confusion, some scholars in the United States, in an attempt to reserve the now-coveted word "Arab" for those who wrote in Arabic in the Middle Ages, have applied the word "Arabian" to the early conquerors from the desert. This is not only arbitrary, but it has even resulted in such absurd claims as that the Persian Gulf should be called "Arabian Gulf."

The map of the Middle East has been revised so many times since the conquest of Islam that these problems plague other peoples as well. Today the people of the Soviet of Uzbekistan claim Avicenna, the great physician and philosopher of the eleventh century, as "Uzbek" because he was born in Bokhara, which is now located in Uzbekistan. Persians claim him as their very own because his mother tongue was Persian and he lived and died in Iran. The office of information of the League of Arab States considers Avicenna as the "contribution of the Arabs" to the world simply because he wrote his scientific works in Arabic. To whom does Avicenna belong?

To avoid confusion we will not consider the period under consideration either Arab, Persian, or Uzbek and will admit that it had a character of its own. Perhaps the best name for it is "Islamic," despite its limitations, because Islam was the only common denominator of the whole area and because Islam made Arabic a holy language, such that all learned works were written in it. Even though some of the contributors to this civilization were not Muslims themselves, there is no question that they did their work under the aegis of Islam.

PART ONE

THE RISE AND FALL
OF THE
ISLAMIC EMPIRE

حضرة امير المؤمنين على عليه السلام

PRECEDING PAGE: *A Persian rug portraying "His Reverence, the Leader of the Faith-ful, Ali, upon whom be peace."* TOP TO BOTTOM: *The Mosque of Azhar University in Cairo* (COURTESY OF THE ARAB INFORMATION CENTER). *Muslim pilgrims face the Ka'ba in the Sacred Mosque in Mecca* (COURTESY OF ARAMCO). *The interior of a mosque, with a pool for ablutions before prayer.*

CHAPTER 1

MIDDLE EAST BEFORE ISLAM

Muhammad was born in A.D. 570. He formed the first Islamic government in 622. By 633, it was poised for conquest, and nearly ready to launch aggressive campaigns which, even in their initial stages, did not stop until they had reached Iran to the northeast and Egypt to the southwest. During this period, peoples in different parts of the world, ignorant of Muhammad and his ideas, were busy with their own problems.

Europe had just begun to recover from the shock of the fall of Rome and the destruction of the western section of that once mighty empire. Different tribes, such as the Franks, the Merovingians, the Visigoths, the Ostrogoths, and others, had fought against each other, but none had been able to impose its will upon the rest. The Church was the only major institution recognized by the masses even though large numbers of peoples in Europe were still pagan. This was the era of Pope Gregory the Great, who began his reign in 590, when Muhammad was 20 years old, and died 14 years later. The last of the four great Latin Fathers and the first of the Medieval Popes, he can be said to have ushered in the "Middle Ages." Although he was made Pope against his will, he became most active once he assumed office. He spent the wealth of the Church for charity, fed the poor, and redeemed the captives of war. He launched a great missionary activity and promoted the construction of monasteries in the remote regions of Europe. He was instrumental in the conversion of England to Christianity. This monk, the first ever to become Pope, referred to himself as "the servant of the servants of God." Yet he claimed that the Bishop of Rome, as Pope, should be acknowledged as the supreme master of all Churches, East and West. He felt that in the absence of an emperor in the West, the Church should fill the vacuum. It is said that he "mourned every minute he had to give to earthly concerns," but considered it necessary to assume the powers of a temporal prince. In this, as will be seen, he was in agreement with Muhammad.

To the east, in India, the golden age of the Gupta, with its achievements in

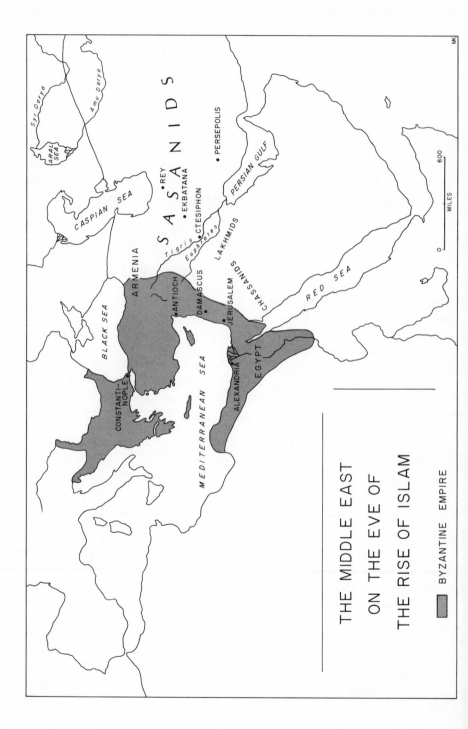

THE MIDDLE EAST
ON THE EVE OF
THE RISE OF ISLAM

BYZANTINE EMPIRE

literature, science, and technology had come to an end. Now, after a century of bondage to the Huns and the internal struggle for power, Harsha-Vardhana, a scion of the house of Gupta, carved a kingdom in northern India and began to rule in 606. He survived Muhammad by 15 years, dying in 647. In those 42 years he restored peace and security to the land and his capital, Kanauj, became a center of art and learning. Although reared in the worship of Shiva, Harsha-Vardhana was converted to Buddhism and emulated the Great King Ashoka (274–236 B.C.). Hsüan Chuang, the famous Chinese Buddhist traveler, relates that Harsha proclaimed a great feast of charity every five years to which all the needy of all religions were invited. On them he bestowed all the surplus of the treasury, a ceremony climaxed by divesting himself of his jewelry and princely attire and giving them away. However, all this was centered around one man and, as such, was quite precarious. After his death the subcontinent reverted to confusion and warfare. This lasted until the arrival of the followers of Muhammad.

In China a revival was also in progress during the lifetime of Muhammad. The T'ang dynasty, one of China's most illustrious, had replaced the rule of the nomadic invaders and had ushered in the golden age of China. One of China's greatest emperors, Tai Tsung (627–649), ascended to the throne five years after the flight of Muhammad from Mecca to Medina and ruled until A.D. 650. After several years of cruel warfare Tai Tsung devoted his days to the ways of peace by encouraging commerce, building canals, rehabilitating prisoners, and establishing schools. It is related that when someone suggested to him that he be severe with criminals, Tai Tsung replied in the best tradition of Confucius, whose disciple he was, "If I diminish expenses, lighten the taxes, employ only honest officials, so that the people have clothing enough, this will do more to abolish robbery than the employment of the severest punishments." These were also the days of the travels of the famous Chinese Buddhist pilgrim Hsüan Chuang, who went to India and translated some 75 Buddhist books into Chinese. It is further maintained that block printing was invented in China at this time. China at the time of Muhammad was most likely the world's best governed state.

Farther east, Japan was going through cultural and religious ferment. A contemporary of Muhammad in Japan was the country's first empress, Suiko (592–621), who during the regency of Prince Shotoku Taishi built Buddhist temples and established Buddhism. Later the Prince issued a "constitution," which was an amalgam of centralized government, Confucian ethics, Chinese political theory, and Buddhist religious thought. These movements, strengthened by the example of China's T'ang dynasty, led to the Taikwa reform of 646 in which the emperor was elevated to high authority and divine eminence. All Japan was said to belong to him and everyone lived in order to obey his command. While the followers of Muhammad were emerging from the desert of Arabia, Japan was ending its life of tribal feudalism and beginning an era of closely-knit imperial state.

Nearer home, the territory north of the Arabian Peninsula was dominated by two great and proud powers. To the west was the Byzantine Empire which controlled all of the Balkans and Asia Minor, the eastern shores of the Mediterranean, Egypt, and parts of North Africa. It was the heir of the Roman Empire and its capital was at Byzantium or Constantinople. The official religion of the Empire was Eastern Orthodox Christianity and its language was Greek. To the east were the Persians, ruled by the Sasanids, heirs of the ancient Achamanean Empire. The Sasanids controlled both sides of the Caspian Sea, the eastern part of the Fertile Crescent, and the whole territory between the Tigris and Indus Rivers. Their winter capital was at Ctesiphon on the banks of the Tigris, and their summer capital at Ekbatana, the modern Hamadan. Their religion was Zoroastrianism and their language was called Pahlavi or middle Persian. Both the Persian and Byzantine empires were autocratic and both used religion as a tool of the state. Linguistically and culturally, however, the Persians were the more homogeneous and therefore were much more proud of their heritage. These two empires were constantly at war, neither side being strong enough to subdue the other for any length of time.

A few years before the birth of Muhammad, the two empires were ruled by two great contemporaries. In Byzantium the emperor was Justinian (527–565) and in Persia the Shahanshah was Khosro Anushiravan (531–571), whom the Greeks called "Chosroes" and the Arabs referred to as "Kasra." Both rulers were active, ambitious, and believers in absolute power. Both were reformers and law givers. The two "brothers," as they called one another, concluded an "eternal peace." Justinian paid 11,000 pounds of gold for it because he wanted to be free to attack Italy. However, the peace lasted not even a decade. By A.D. 540 the armies of Anushiravan were poised outside Antioch. Justinian was desperate. He bought a five-year truce in 545 for a reputed 2,000 pounds. Finally, in 562 Justinian agreed to pay an annual tribute of 30,000 pieces of gold for a 50-year peace, but hostilities were resumed almost as soon as he died. War between the two empires had become a habit.

One must not assume, however, that the Persians and the Byzantines spent all of their time in warfare. In peacetime there were diplomatic and commercial as well as cultural exchanges. Brisk trade went on in spices, stones, ivory, and silk. The Byzantines had time to develop art, illuminate manuscripts, build magnificent churches, and immerse themselves in deep theological questions. The Persians, in their territories, were enlightened patrons of letters, carried on trade with India and China, built beautiful edifices, developed a complete administrative organization and established the educational Institution of Gundi Shapur which became "the greatest intellectual center of the time." Interchange in trade, art, and thought continued in spite of war.

But war also continued. The empires produced two other giants: Khosro Parviz (583–628) in Iran and Heraclius (610–641) in Byzantium. Khosro Parviz who, ironically enough, was reinstated in 589 by the Byzantine Emperor

Maurice, declared war on Phocas, the centurion who had revolted against Maurice and had killed him in 603. For 19 years the Persians swept everything before them. By 613 the Persians had captured Dara, Antioch, Aleppo, and Damascus. In 614, Khosro Parviz sacked Jerusalem and carried away to Iran the "True Cross," a most cherished Christian possession, believed to be the actual cross on which Jesus was crucified. In 616, Khosro marched in to Alexandria. By 619, Persian troops once again, for the first time since Darius II, occupied Egypt. In the meantime, another Persian army had overrun all Asia Minor and, after capturing Chalcedon in 617, was poised across the Bosporus from Constantinople.

In 610, the same year that Muhammad received the call from Allah to be His Messenger, Heraclius became the Emperor of Byzantium. For twelve years he suffered defeat at the hands of the Persians and spent his time preparing for war. In 622, the same year that Muhammad assumed the role of the Prophet-King in Medina, Heraclius struck back at the Persians. He won victory after victory against the vain and tired Persian army. In 628 he stood at the gates of Ctesiphon. Khosro Parviz was killed by one of his own sons and Heraclius got back all that he had lost including the "True Cross." But it was an empty victory, for Iran and Byzantium had bled each other to exhaustion. Death was not long in coming. The blow was dealt by the Arabs, the inhabitants of the Arabian Peninsula to the south, who were vassals of both.

The wars between Iran and Byzantium did not reach Arabia. It was considered an inhospitable territory by the civilized empires of the north. Moreover, the roaming Bedouins, who comprised five-sixths of the population, proved uncontrollable. To protect themselves from periodic raids from the deserts, the two empires had given autonomy to two strong tribes who were supposed to keep the raiders in check. Thus, the Persians had allowed the Ghassanid tribe to be under the "protection" of the Byzantines, while the Byzantines, in turn, had accepted the same relationship between the Lakhmids of Hira and the Persians. South Arabia, however, especially Yaman, because of its milder climate, settled culture, and proximity, was most of the time under the suzerainty of Iran. In Persian inscriptions one finds the names of Hamir, Aiden, Yaman, and other places in south Arabia as tribute-paying regions. However, the Byzantines also had contact with them through Ethiopia and the Red Sea.

The central and northern part of the Arabian peninsula such as Hijaz and Najd, was mostly barren desert. The oases were few and far between. The Bedouin dwellers of this vast wilderness alighted from their camels where there was water and tarried while it lasted. The nomad, according to Ibn Khaldun, a later celebrated Muslim historian (1332–1406), was illiterate, did not care for crafts, and was destructive to civilization. "The Arabs use stones to set them up as support for their cooking pots. So they take them from buildings which they tear down to get the stones and use them for the purpose. . . . They tear down the roofs to get wood" for burning. Brigandage, or *razzia*, was one of the pillars of the Arab's economy and was his way of life. He raided for food, camels, and women throughout his life.

There were few settlements in this area. One of them was Mecca in Hijaz, about 50 miles from the Red Sea, which owed its continuous existence to a well, *Zamzam*, its economic prosperity to the fact that it was on the spice route from south Arabia to the Mediterranean ports in the north, and its prominence to the existence of the Ka'ba, the ancient shrine which was at the center of the religion of the inhabitants of the peninsula.

Probably more than a thousand years before Christ the Arabs of the area saw a meteor fall from the heavens and, because of this, regarded it as holy. They took this black stone *hajar-ul-aswad* and built it into a cubic structure called *Ka'ba*. Neighboring tribes began to come every year to worship the Ka'ba. In the course of centuries a pantheon grew around the Ka'ba and its worship became universal among the pagan Arabs of the peninsula and an annual pilgrimage took place, usually in the month of Dhu'l-Hajja, the twelfth of the lunar calendar. By an unwritten law, at this time and also during two other months all raiding was forbidden and tribes could come and go unmolested. The pilgrim changed his clothing for the *ihram*, that is, two pieces of white cloth without seams. Then he went to the great square in the center of which was the Ka'ba. He kissed the black stone and went around it seven times, three times running and four times walking, each time kissing the black stone. He then recited a prayer in a location which in Islamic times came to be known as the "Place of Abraham," based on the tradition that it was Abraham who had built the Ka'ba in the first place. Then he went outside the city gate and approached two hills, one called Safa and the other Marwa. After climbing Safa and then running down the hill and up Marwa seven times repeating prayers each time he reached the summit of each hill, the pilgrim returned to Mecca and walked around the Ka'ba, kissing the black stone.

Then followed about six days of rest in which the pilgrim perhaps engaged in business transactions, games and contests, and listened to poetry. On the eighth day he walked to the nearby village of Mina and spent the night there. The next morning he walked to Mount 'Arafat and from there to Muzdafila to spend the night.

The tenth day was the high point of the pilgrimage, for it was the day of sacrifice followed by *Id-al-Kabir*, or the great feast. On this day the pilgrim went to Mina and approached a temple with three huge pillars. This temple was probably the place of sacrifice for the appeasing of evil spirits and represented the *Shaytan-al-Kabir*, the great devil. Then he acquired an animal commensurate with his wealth and sacrificed it on the spot. This done, he put on his regular clothes and went to Mecca for another round of barter before returning home.

Except for raiding and searching for water, this was the sum total of the

Arab's religious, economic, and cultural life. The religious ritual at Ka'ba is performed to this day by the Muslims without much change.

Mecca grew as a metropolis and the Arabs who made the pilgrimage annually brought their tribal gods and placed them in the enclosure around the Ka'ba. After the rituals of pilgrimage, the Arabs bartered goods, took part in athletic contests, including camel and horse racing, and recited their prowess in poetry. The poet was at once a bard, an oracle, an historian, a moralist, and a man of mysterious power. He vilified the rival tribes in satire and malediction and reminded his own clansmen of courage, honor, and bravery. But few samples of poetry have survived from pre-Islamic Arabia. Legend says that they were prize-winning poems which had been hung on the entrance to the Ka'ba. Hence, they are called *mu'alliqat*, "the suspended ones." From the content of the surviving poems we may assume that at least three things were dear to the heart of the Arab—dark wine, a rushing charger, and a long day spent with a lovely damsel in a black tent in the desert.

Mecca became hence the economic and cultural center of central and north Arabia. The political control of the city was in the hands of the Quraysh tribe. Indications are that at the time of Muhammad the Quraysh tribe had passed the zenith of its power and was losing its prestige and control. There was disunity among the clans which invited rival tribes from neighboring settlements to challenge their prestige. Nevertheless, the Quraysh were still in a position of power and influence. When the season for pilgrimage was over, the tribes on the one hand scattered over the peninsula and engaged in the time-honored custom of raiding for water, wealth, and women. On the other hand, the leaders of the Quraysh tribe sent well-protected caravans north to Syria, Egypt, and Iran to sell their goods and replenish their stock for the business of the next season. Consequently, the curious among the Quraysh were not ignorant of the outside world. No doubt they were affected by the frequent wars between Byzantium and Iran and had learned how to play one against the other. As there were Jewish and Christian tribes and settlements in Arabia, the pagan Arabs, no doubt, knew something about their beliefs. Among the gods, the Arabs knew the name of Allah (the same as El-loh or Elohim of the Old Testament) and in Mecca there was a small group of people, known by the name of *Hanif*, who seem to have had monotheistic beliefs.

CHAPTER 2

MUHAMMAD, THE MESSENGER OF ALLAH

In the setting briefly described above, and probably in the year A.D. 570, Muhammad was born in the neighborhood of Mecca. He belonged to the Quraysh tribe, member of the minor and apparently less prosperous clan of Hashim. His father, Abdullah, died before he was born and his mother, Amina, died when he was a child of six. He was cared for by his granduncle, Abdul Muttalib, and after the latter's death by the boy's uncle, Abu Talib.

The life of Muhammad, like the lives of other prophets, has probably been fictionalized by his adoring followers who attempted to write a biography a century or so after his death. There is no record of the life of Muhammad until he reached the age of 24, and even then the information is meager. Sifting and putting together the many stories about his early life, one may safely assume that he got a job with one of the business enterprises in which the Quraysh tribe was engaged. He probably travelled as a caravan boy to the Fertile Crescent, Egypt, and perhaps to Iran. Many a night he must have listened to the conversation between his masters and Christian and Jewish merchants. He must have had a feeling of frustration as he heard the Jews and Christians back their arguments by referring to a book while his own people had no book to quote. Early in life he must have wished his people also had a book. More than once we read in the Koran, "Now you have a book in Arabic," as though this were a most important thing.

In any case, whatever Muhammad did, it is fairly certain that it must have been in the field of business transactions, for he became familiar with all aspects of trade. In the year 594, when Muhammad was 24 years old, a rich widow by the name of Khadija was looking for a man who knew enough about business to be employed as "manager." Khadija had lost her second husband and had decided to personally supervise his commercial activities. The fact that she could do so shows that in pre-Islamic Arabia women did not have such a lowly position as is often claimed. To be sure, for economic reasons some of the tribes practiced female infanticide, but nevertheless, women could not only hold property but could also be self-supporting if they so chose. A friend of the family recommended Muhammad for the job. He was honest, experienced, and also of the Quraysh tribe. Khadija employed him and a year later they were married—she being 40 years of age and he only 25. Since she was wealthy, had a superior social position, and was his employer, perhaps the tradition is correct in stating that it was she who proposed marriage.

Overnight, as it were, Muhammad was catapulted from a caravan boy to head of a prosperous business concern and became a man of influence in the Quraysh tribe. For 25 years he enjoyed a blissful life with Khadija. Two sons and four daughters were born, but unfortunately the sons died in infancy. He had a happy life at home and a prosperous business. Like other rich men of Mecca, he also had acquired and furnished one of the volcanic caves, *ghar*, at Hira on the outskirts of Mecca and would go there to escape the heat and noise of the city in order to meditate.

In the year 610, toward the end of the month of Ramadan, while Muhammad was resting in the cave, it seemed to him that he heard a voice, which he later described as the "ringing of the bells." Ramadan was a month of fasting in pre-Islamic Arabia, as it is now in the world of Islam, and Muhammad, being a religiously inclined person, was very likely fasting. This voice said to him, *Ikra bismi rabbika . . .* , "Recite in the name of the Lord who created, created man of a blood clot. . . ." He was frightened. According to tradition, Muhammad thought he had become "possessed" just like the poets he despised, so much so that he even thought of committing suicide. He must have been puzzled also. In the name of which lord should he speak? After all, there were over 300 of them around the Ka'ba.[1] He told his wife about this experience and Khadija thereupon went to her cousin Waraqa, who was a Christian, and related Muhammad's experience. Waraqa is supposed to have exclaimed, ". . . and lo, he will be a prophet to this people. Bid him to be of good heart." Muhammad had received his call. Later the night of this momentous day was celebrated as "The Night of Power."

When, after a brief interval, Muhammad heard the voice again bidding him to "arise and warn" there was no question in his mind that he was chosen by Allah to be His messenger. Khadija was one of the first to believe in him as the Prophet of Allah. From then on the revelations came to him at more frequent intervals and the "voice" was identified by him as the voice of Angel Gabriel who dictated the words of Allah to him.

For nearly ten years Muhammad preached the unity of God as opposed to the polytheism of the city of Mecca.

Say: He is Allah, the One!
Allah, the eternally Besought of All!
He begetteth not nor was begotten.
And there is none comparable unto Him. (K. 112)

[1] See above, p. 28.

Muhammad's concept of Allah and the latter's habit of revealing Himself to prophets had come from the Jews and Christians. It was quite natural, therefore, for Muhammad to consider himself a prophet in the Judeo-Christian tradition and speak about Adam, Noah, Abraham, Moses, Jonah, the Children of Israel, Mary, and Jesus. Like the prophets of old, he spoke against idolatry and preached the one living Allah who had power over all life. Allah was interested not only in the Jews and Christians, but also in the Arabs. It was He who had saved the Ka'ba from destruction at the hand of Abraha, the Abyssinian ruler of Yaman who had used elephants in his attack on Mecca. Since this had taken place around the last decade of the sixth century, it was still vivid to his hearers.

Hast thou not seen how the Lord dealt with the owners of the elephant? Did he not bring their stratagem to nought, and send against them swarms of flying creatures, which pelted them with stones of baked clay, and made them like green crops devoured [by cattle]? (K. 105)

He took advantage of the months of pilgrimage when thousands came to Mecca. He preached Allah the Compassionate and the Merciful; Allah who had sent Muhammad to dissuade them from idolatry and to warn them about the Day of Judgment and the resultant punishment or reward awaiting them in afterlife. It was in these warnings that he waxed eloquent. He warned them about the time

When the sun is overthrown,
And when the stars fall,
And when the hills are moved,
And when the camels big with young are abandoned,
And when the seas rise,
And when souls are reunited. . . . (K. 81)

He assured them that ". . . When the trumpet shall sound one blast and the earth with the mountains shall be lifted up and crushed with one crash. Then, on that day will the Event befall. . . . On that day ye will be exposed; not a secret of you will be hidden. . . ." (K. 69)

Not many followed him. His wife, his cousin Ali, and his servant Zayd were among the first. There were a number of slaves who heeded his warning, but they did not have any influence. About the only man of consequence who accepted his message was Abu Bakr, a man of great stature among the Quraysh. The rest either ignored him or, worse, ridiculed him and said he was mad and possessed, as the following passages indicate.

"By the Star when it setteth,
Your comrade erreth not, nor is deceived;
Nor doth he speak of his own desire. . . ." (K. 53)

And, ". . . Thou art not, for thy Lord's favor unto thee, a madman." And again, "By the morning hours and by the night when it is stillest, thy Lord hath not forsaken thee nor doth he hate thee . . ." (K. 53).

However, the Quraysh did not look with pride at having a prophet in their midst. Muhammad's fellow businessmen saw in his preaching their own economic ruin. The spread of the new faith would destroy the pantheon around the Ka'ba and, indeed, the Ka'ba itself. Consequently, pilgrimage would be abandoned, and without pilgrimage, Mecca would cease to exist and the Quraysh would lose their economic prominence. As a matter of fact, until the discovery of oil in the third decade of the twentieth century, the greatest source of income of Arabia had been from pilgrimage. Thus the old struggle between prophetic demands and business profits manifested itself. No doubt Muhammad understood that the prosperity of the Quraysh was at stake, but there was nothing he could do about it. He continued to preach his message with conviction and simplicity.

To escape persecution, a number of Muhammad's followers decided to migrate to Ethiopia, but this did not prove very successful. The temptation for Muhammad to gain success by compromise must have been great. At one time he agreed that perhaps three of the deities in the pantheon, Lot, Manat, and Uzza, all female, were genuine even though inferior to Allah. Later, however, he renounced this statement and proclaimed only Allah.

In this struggle, the life of Muhammad was not in danger. He belonged to the clan of Hashim and its leader, Abu Talib, was his uncle. Even though the old man never accepted the claim of his nephew, he nevertheless protected him. Instead, the brunt of the persecution was borne by the slaves who accepted Muhammad. According to the laws of pre-Islamic Arabia, the slaves did not enjoy any protection. Perhaps it was to persuade the opposition to leave these slaves alone that the following revelation was received by Muhammad:

Say: O disbelievers! I worship not that which ye worship; nor worship ye that which I worship; and I shall not worship that which ye worship, nor will ye worship that which I worship. Unto you your religion, and unto me my religion. (K. 109)

The darkest year in the life of Muhammad was 619. In that year Abu Talib, his foster father, uncle, and protector, died. His place was taken by Abu Lahab, a fanatical foe of Muhammad's message, a person whom Muhammad had cursed through a revelation:

The power of Abu Lahab will perish, and he will perish. His wealth and gains will not exempt him. He will be plunged in flaming fire, and his wife, the wood carrier, will have upon her neck a halter of palm-fibre. (K. 111)

To make matters worse, his beloved Khadija also died in that year. The loss of Khadija to Muhammad was like the loss of an anchor to a ship. From then on the tide of life tossed him to and fro. He had not married a second wife for 25 years while Khadija was alive. During the ten years after her death, he married about as many wives. He married some of the women in order to protect and support them, for their husbands had given their lives for his cause and custom demanded that he should marry them. Others he married for political reasons, to cement relations with other tribes. One gleans from the Koran and from tradition that he was never again as happy in his home life after Khadija's death.

For the first time, Muhammad thought of leaving Mecca and seeking his fortune elsewhere. He tried to explore the possibilities in the neighboring settlement of Taif, but the anger of the inhabitants of Taif towards him was much greater than he had imagined. He was nearly stoned to death and had to go into hiding. Only the intercession of some of the tolerant leaders of the Quraysh assured Muhammad enough protection for him to return to Mecca.

Fortunately for Muhammad, the city of Yathrib, some 200 miles to the north of Mecca, had developed problems which, in the end, proved beneficial to his cause. Yathrib was originally settled by three Jewish tribes of Banu Nadir, Banu Qurayza, and Banu Qaynuqa. Later the city was invaded by two heathen tribes of Aws and Khazraj, who claimed to have come from south Arabia. They usurped land from some of the Jews, reduced others to slavery, and made alliances with the rest. Later, differences arose between Aws and Khazraj over leadership and they fought each other. The insecurity resulting from this internecine struggle became so intense that no one felt it safe to go about his business. No doubt the more level-headed among the two tribes felt that the dissension should be ended, but no one had enough prestige to do this. Clearly this was the work for an arbiter, who would come from outside. Muhammad became the much-needed arbiter. The choice of Muhammad was not entirely accidental. In the first place the Yathribites were familiar with the message of Muhammad. Their fellow townsmen, the Jews, had told them about Moses and their prophets and had assured them of the coming of a Messiah. Consequently, Muhammad's words did not fall on unfamiliar ears. Furthermore, it must be recalled that Yathrib was located on the trade route between Yaman and Damascus, and that the city was the economic rival of Mecca. The Yathribites knew about the feud between Muhammad and the other leaders of the Quraysh. They saw in Muhammad not only a new prophet, but also a man of ability, familiar with the inner councils of the Quraysh, who could lead them in their rivalry against the city of Mecca.

In 620, six Khazrajites met Muhammad and carried on a preliminary conversation. The next year they appeared with more converts to the new faith. By 622, a substantial number from Yathrib, both Aws and Khazraj, invited Muhammad to come to their city. Under the circumstances, Muhammad had no real choice, reluctant as he must have been to leave the city of his birth. He sent a number of his followers in small groups, among whom were such wealthy Quraysh men as Umar and Uthman. He himself, together with Abu

Bakr, his father-in-law, Ali, his cousin and son-in-law, and his two wives, slipped out of Mecca unnoticed and arrived in Yathrib about September 24, 622. This was called *Hijra*, or the emigration. Some 17 years later Umar, as the Caliph of Islam, designated this year as the year one in the Muslim calendar. Even though Muhammad had concluded a treaty with the Yathribites, known as the Treaty of Al-Akaba, it took courage for the Meccans to take their wealth, women, and children and settle among strange and enemy tribes. Henceforth, these people were called *Muhajirun* or emigrés, while the members of Aws and Khazraj tribes who had welcomed Muhammad became known as *Ansar*, or helpers. In time the city was no longer called Yathrib, but *Madinat al-Nabi*, the City of the Prophet, or simply Medina.

Three major problems faced Muhammad in the new city. The first was that in Medina he was not only a prophet of Allah, but also the head of a state. He had to see to the welfare of the community, act as judge, legislate, and organize his followers. It has been suggested that in Medina his role as Prophet was overshadowed by his duties as a political leader. Perhaps it is nearer the truth to say that in his mind and in the opinion of his followers, the two offices were combined. According to the Old Testament, when Moses spoke, regardless of the subject, it was not Moses but rather Yahweh who was actually speaking. In the same way, the legislation of Muhammad as the political leader, and his various judgments and declarations, were considered not merely the declarations of the man Muhammad, but also the solemn commands of Allah. In his person, as Prophet-King, government and religion merged and the spiritual and the temporal became one and inseparable. Islam became a theocratic institution and has remained so, at least in theory, to this day.

Consequently, the revelations of Muhammad in Medina do not have the simplicity nor the poetical beauty of those in Mecca. They tend to be repetitious and verbose. Whereas the revelations in Mecca warned and beseeched, those in Medina have a tendency to command and threaten. Going through an index of legislation in the Koran, one finds such subjects as ablutions, adultery, almsgiving, arbitration, booty, contracts, divorce, drink, fighting, forgiving, general conduct, good, idolatry, justice, marriage, orphans, parents, war, women, worship, and a host of other rules, spiritual, moral, and temporal. All of these are commandments of Allah for the regulation of life in the Islamic community. Throughout the centuries, believers from diverse nationalities have had to struggle with these laws by interpreting them time and again, but change them they could not. In a theocracy, the religion and the state are inseparable. The modern Muslim is caught on the horns of a dilemma. On the one hand, as a Muslim he has identified his nationality with his religion. On the other hand, as a modern, he wants a society in which religion and state are separate. The choice is a difficult and a revolutionary one. Even in Turkey, where the choice has been made and a "secular" state has been established, it has been difficult for the people to adjust themselves to the new concept. The modern claim is that a "Turk" may be a Muslim, a Christian, a Jew, an agnostic or even an atheist, but in the consciousness of the people a "Turk" is still synonymous with a Muslim. All the non-Muslim citizens of Turkey are in a class by themselves and are not really Turks. Consequently, a modern-day young man who calls himself a "Muslim" may or may not be a religious man. In his mind, religion and nationality are so intermingled in the concept of "Islam" that he may be loyal to Islam as a political institution without having any purely religious loyalties.

The second problem which confronted Muhammad in Medina was what might be termed the "Jewish Question." It has been mentioned that the city of Medina had a large Jewish population. It has also been mentioned that Muhammad considered himself a Prophet in the Judeo-Christian tradition.[2] Historians agree that Muhammad had every expectation of being welcomed among the Jews and the Christians. He felt somewhat closer to Judaism than to Christianity, and in Mecca he had already adopted many of the Jewish practices, such as observance of fast days, prayer toward Jerusalem, and so forth. When he arrived in Medina he expected the Jews to accept him as a Prophet and help him root out paganism. In this he was sorely disappointed. Not only did the Jews of Medina refuse to accept him as a prophet, but they mocked him as pretentious, and ridiculed his lack of knowledge of the Old Testament. They accused him of garbling the Scriptures and refused to accept an Arab as the Messiah. Muhammad, nevertheless, persisted in his hope.

Oh ye who believe, Be mindful of your duty
to Allah and put faith in His Messenger.
He will give you twofold of His mercy. . . . *(K. 57)*

He also reminded the Jews that they did not have a monopoly of the blessings of God. "That the People of Scripture (i.e., Jews and Christians) may know that they control naught of the bounty of Allah, but that the bounty is in Allah's hand to give to whom He will." (K. 57)

When these and similar pleas were met with stubborn resistance, Muhammad retaliated by accusing the Jews of perverting the word of God and later resorted to massacre and banishment. It is difficult to determine from this distance in time whether the Jews of Medina and its environs remained neutral in the struggle which was going on between Muhammad and the Meccans[3] or resorted to "fifth column" activities. It is certain, however, that Muhammad accused them of "siding with the confederates" (that is, Meccans and Bedouin tribes). In about 625, Muhammad banished the Jewish tribe of Banu Nadir from Medina. Two years later some 600 of the Banu Qurayza were slaughtered and the rest sent into exile. In 629, the Jews of Khaybar, an oasis north of Medina, were expelled. In each case their lands were given to the increasing number of outsiders who had flocked to Medina to join Muhammad.

[2] See above, p. 32.
[3] See below, p. 38.

It was perhaps because of his experience with the Jews that Muhammad decided to chart an independent course and organize an Arab religious community. He did not reject the Judeo-Christian tradition, but instead claimed that the Jews and the Christians had disobeyed the commandments of God, and, in some instances, had garbled the Scriptures. He who, according to Jewish custom, used to pray facing north toward Jerusalem one day abruptly turned south toward Mecca. Since that time all Muslims pray facing Mecca with the conviction that the Ka'ba was built by Abraham at the behest of Allah. As the Ka'ba had been defiled by the presence of the gods and goddesses, the mission of Muhammad was to destroy the idols and restore the worship of Allah. Saturday and Sunday being Jewish and Christian holy days, Muhammad chose Friday. The Jews used to call the people to the synagogue for prayer by the blowing of a horn, and the Christians by the ringing of a bell. Muhammad instituted the *adhan*, or use of the human voice. He introduced enough changes in prayer, fasting, dietary laws, and other rituals to constitute a separate and distinct religious community.

The third and the most important problem which Muhammad had to solve was his dealing with the Meccans. Perhaps the thought had occurred to him in Mecca, but certainly very early in Medina he had decided that he was not going to be like Jesus and some of the other Prophets who had preached but left the fate of the message to their followers and God. Like Moses, he decided to establish the rule of Allah on earth in the form of an independent state with laws handed down by Allah Himself. This could be done only through diplomacy, war, and conquest. During the ten years in Medina, from 622 until his death in 632, Muhammad engaged in war practically every year. He personally participated in most of them. These wars were explicitly for the purpose of imposing the rule of Islam on the Arabs. Since the most powerful antagonist was the city of Mecca, Muhammad gave this city his special attention.

Almost immediately after his arrival in Medina, Muhammad had to provide for the welfare of his followers from Mecca as well as for his supporters in Medina. For this he had ordered sorties against Meccan caravans. In 624, the second year of the Hijra, in Ramadan, the month of truce, he learned about a rich caravan led by Abu Sufyan headed for Mecca, and decided to attack it. Abu Sufyan, who had heard about the plan, had sent to Mecca for aid. Some 900 Meccans and 300 Muslims met at Badr, about 20 miles southwest of Medina.

The battle was short, small, and desperate, but Muhammad won. Some European historians have emphasized the fact that, as battles go, this was quite insignificant, with a total of only some 60 casualties on both sides. But Muslim historians have called it "the battle, *ghazwat*, of battles." It was indeed one of the most important engagements in the history of Islam. If Muhammad had lost, very likely Islam would have been nipped in the bud. The victory, however, confirmed Muhammad's leadership, and "proved" that he was fighting for Allah. "Allah had already given you the victory at Badr," says the Koran. The victory was believed to be a miracle and the new straveled across the desert from tent to tent. The Muslims in subsequent battles were convinced that they were fighting for Allah. They believed that if they died they had "witnessed" and would go to paradise; if they lived they could partake of the booty. This first battle became the pattern for the future in which the soldiers of Allah would repeat the *shahada* ("witness") and go into battle with contempt for death.

The Meccans, however, could not let the defeat go unavenged. The next year Abu Sufyan marched at the head of 3,000 men. In most of the desert battles, the women would come along to encourage their men in battle. Muhammad, it is reported, would choose one of his wives by lot to accompany him in each campaign. The two sides met at Uhud and Muhammad got a sound beating and was wounded. Apparently the defeat was caused by disobedience of one of the Medinese tribes. In any case, the Meccans, for reasons which are not clear, did not pursue their victory and Muhammad recovered from both the wound and the defeat.

Muhammad could not succeed in unifying the Arabs under Islam without Mecca and the Meccans could not afford to have Muhammad's soldiers raiding their caravans. Once more, in 627, Abu Sufyan came toward Medina with a large army. Muhammad decided to stay in the city and defend the one access to it. Even this would have been most difficult had it not been for the advice of Salman the "Persian," probably an Arab orderly of a Persian officer, to dig a trench. This Muhammad did, to the disgust of his followers. The Meccans, who had had no experience with this type of warfare, were equally disgusted with such a cowardly method. Cowardly or not, it was effective, and after a week of reciting poetry derogatory of Muhammad, the Meccans lifted the siege and went home. This battle has been called the battle of *Khandaq*, or the "Trench."

The war was costing the Meccans a great deal of money, not to mention the disruption and loss of trade. Muhammad, on the other hand, did not have much to lose and felt that time was on his side. Furthermore, his shift of the *qibla*, direction of prayer, from Jerusalem to Mecca and his respect for the Ka'ba had made it evident that Muhammad regarded Mecca as holy and had incorporated pilgrimage to Mecca into his new religion. Thus, Mecca continued to retain its economic predominance as a place of pilgrims and with this assurance, the Meccans did not have any reason to continue the warfare. Muhammad, on his part, used good judgment and allowed diplomacy to take the place of the sword. In 628, he concluded the peace of Hudaybiyah, which put the Muslims and the Meccans on an equal footing and won permission for the Muslims to make the pilgrimage to Mecca.

This treaty ended the war between the two cities. A number of important people from the Quraysh, among them Khalid ibn-al-Walid and Amr ibn-al-As, who were destined to become two of the famous generals of Islam, submitted to Muhammad's leadership. Two years after the treaty of Hudaybiyah, which was to have lasted for ten years, Muhammad found an excuse to approach Mecca with his army. He probably had assurance that the Meccans would not oppose him. The new religion, with its veneration for the Ka'ba, enhanced the economic position of the Quraysh. Abu Sufyan himself came and offered his allegiance. Others followed and Muhammad entered his native city as a victor. He ordered the destruction of all the idols around the Ka'ba and proclaimed it as *haram*, forbidden to pagans. He was magnanimous to his defeated fellow tribesmen and, much to the relief of the Medinese, he decided to go back to Medina and continue it as his political capital. Mecca, however, remained the religious capital of Islam.

Muhammad's work was not finished. It was his purpose to unify Arabia. He continued his wars of conquest. Soon delegations from all parts of Arabia— Oman, Hadramut, and even Yaman—came to accept Islam. The ceremony was simple—a verbal confession and the payment of *Zakah*, poor tax, were sufficient to initiate a whole tribe into the new religion. Whether they came out of conviction or expediency is difficult to judge.

In 632, the tenth year of the Hijra, Muhammad made what became his last pilgrimage to Mecca. He was the acknowledged Messenger of Allah and the Lord of Arabia. It is said that he made a speech so moving that it remained in the memory of his hearers and has come to be known as his "Farewell Address."

In this speech he told his followers that every Muslim is a brother unto every other Muslim. Thus he abolished tribal loyalty and substituted loyalty to Islam. He also admonished his followers to consider ties of faith more binding than ties of blood. He virtually abolished raiding, by forbidding his followers to appropriate anything which belonged to their brother unless willingly given to them. Three months later (June 8, 632) he died in the arms of his favorite wife, Ayisha, and was buried where he died, under the floor of her room.

Muhammad left behind a religious community which was at the same time an armed encampment. Its house of worship was also a court of law as well as headquarters for military command. He established a religion without a hierarchy or clergy; where every believer was also a military conscript, and the leader in worship was also the commander in battle. Tradition says that he wrote letters to the potentates of his time and invited them to Islam. There is no evidence, however, that Muhammad intended his message to go beyond Arabia. He did what he set out to do: now the Arabs also had a Prophet and a Book. He tried to establish a brotherhood of Muslims and was not interested in the brotherhood of all the peoples of the world, unless the whole world would accept Islam. He said, "I am a man like you," and as a man he had his strengths and weaknesses. He had such an inspiring personality that, years later, his followers studied every detail of his conduct and every word which he had uttered. His life served as a model for personal piety and governmental policy for all generations.

CHAPTER 3

ISLAM, THE MESSAGE OF ALLAH

The chief designation for Muhammad is *Rasul Allah*, the "Messenger of Allah." The Muslims have always considered the message to be of greater significance than Muhammad the Messenger. Muhammad is not central to Islam as Jesus is to Christianity. Strictly speaking, Muslims are not the people of Muhammad in the way that Christians are the people of Christ. Rather, they are the people of the Book—the Koran, which is the message of Allah.

This message is called *Islam* and those who accept it are called *Muslims*. The word "Islam" is derived from the three-consonant root *slm*, which means "submission." Another meaning of the word is *peace* because peace follows the surrender (submission) of the enemy in war. Hence the Arabic greeting in Islamic countries, *salam alaykum*, means "Peace be unto you." Some ultra-modern Muslims of the twentieth century claim that the meaning of Islam is "the religion of peace." Historically, however, the meaning of Islam has been "the religion of submission"—submission to the will of Allah. The grammatical construction *Islam*, based on the root *slm*, means "the submitting." *Muslim* means "he who has submitted," *muslima* means "she who has submitted." In non-Arab Islamic countries the term *mosalman* is used instead of muslim.

By this definition, anyone who has submitted to the will of God is a Muslim, for the word simply means that he has submitted. According to Islamic tradition, the first person who submitted was Abraham. In one sense, for example, a Jew is a "muslim" and so also is a Christian. This broad definition of Islam is perfectly legitimate and may, someday, become an instrument of ecumenicity. Up to now, however, only a small number of individuals throughout the history of Islam, mainly the Sufis, have thought in such inclusive terms. The narrower definition of Islam is the more historically accurate one. Islam, therefore, is surrender to the will of Allah as revealed to Muhammad the Messenger of Allah and the head of the state.

The religion which goes by the name of Islam contains the terms of the surrender of the individual to the will of Allah. Man agrees to live under the jurisdiction of Allah as revealed through His Messenger, which means that all his actions are regulated by the laws promulgated by Allah. Before Islam became involved in theology and philosophy, it dealt with law. As a theocracy, Islam has always considered law as the most important factor in religion.[1] The study of the laws of Allah, *Shari'a*, is the most important discipline in the world of Islam. In the beginning, a simple theology provided a background for the law. The outlines of the simple theology and rules of conduct had taken shape before the death of Muhammad and may be found in the pages of the Koran.

The terms of the "submission" contain at least ten articles. Five of these are articles of belief, or *iman*, and the other five are articles of practice or religious duties, *ibadat*.

ARTICLES OF BELIEF, "IMAN"

1. Doctrine of the Unity of God. The first and the greatest dogma of Islam is *la ilaha illallah*, there is (absolutely) no god save Allah. The unity of God is the cornerstone of Islamic faith. Without this everything falls apart and is devoid of meaning. The Koran (chapter 112, cited above)[2] rejects the Christian Trinity as blasphemy. Indeed, *shirk*, or the idea that God might have a partner, is considered the unforgivable sin. Allah is the supreme creator, lawgiver, judge, sustainer, provider, and ordainer. Allah has many attributes, *sifat*. He is compassionate and merciful, but these seem to be overshadowed by his majesty, might, and power. Allah is best known through His names, *asma al-husna*, which seem to be synonymous with His attributes. The Muslim rosary has 99 beads which represent as many names of Allah. Some of these names are *nasir* "victor," *fattah* "opener," *qahhar* "subduer," and *wahhab* "bestower." There is no doubt that this uncompromising belief in one powerful and transcendent God is the main source of the strength of Islam. The Koran, like the scriptures of other religions, contains its share of contradictions about God. Later Muslim theologians wrestled with these problems and they still do. In Islam, however, such discussions have been considered as intellectual pastimes and are not so vital to everyday life. The believer, no matter how intellectually alert, has a sense of resignation (Islam) and is content with things as they are, or appear to be.

2. The Doctrine of Prophethood. Islam is basically dispensational. It believes that in each era (dispensation) of human history God has sent someone to teach the people and to warn them of the impending judgment. These men are usually referred to in the Koran as *nabi* "prophet," or *rasul* "messenger." It is significant to note that since Allah is the same as the "Yahweh" of the Jews and the "Heavenly Father" of the Christians, the prophets whom He sent are all in the Judeo-Christian tradition, beginning with Adam and ending with

---

[1] See below, p. 103.
[2] See above, p. 31.

Muhammad. Similarly, the history of mankind is considered within the context of the Judeo-Christian tradition. The rest of humanity is not considered at all in the history except for those who have already or will in the future attach themselves to the last phase of this "real" history, namely Islam. Neither are their prophets and sages genuine messengers of God nor are their books valid texts of God's will.

God sent prophets from time to time. Adam is the first. Abraham is not only a prophet, but also the first Muslim, for he submitted to the will of God and went to where he was commanded. Similarly, Moses, David, Jesus, and all the prophets of the Old and New Testaments are prophets in the Islamic sense. Of the scores of prophets, however, only 28 are mentioned in the Koran, four of whom are Arabs not mentioned in the Bible. One, curiously enough, is "the two-horned one" whom the commentators believe to be Alexander the Great! The latter's exploits in the Middle East have made him a legendary figure with superhuman attributes.

Muhammad is considered to be the last of the Prophets. He is sometimes referred to as the "seal," or more commonly as the *khatim ul nabi'in*, the "finisher of the prophets." After him there will be no other prophets. Assuming that God sent so many prophets at short intervals for the guidance of man, it seems rather odd to conclude that He would not send another one for over 1,300 years. This assumption has presented problems to the Muslims. The Shi'a sect, even though professing the finality of Muhammad, believes that there are twelve *imams* who are both temporal and spiritual successors of Muhammad.[3] The modern Bahai faith, which is an offshoot of the Shi'a sect, has picked up the basic dispensational character of Islam and has rejected the idea that Muhammad is the last of the prophets.

Perhaps most Muslims believe Muhammad to be the greatest of all prophets. Such a belief, however, has no scriptural basis in the Koran. Muhammad repeatedly disclaims any superhuman powers, or even a miracle save that of the Koran, and is told to ask forgiveness for his sins. He has the same position as Abraham, Moses, and Jesus, who with him are considered to be the major prophets. Being the last, he is the most important simply because he has the latest message from God. In the Koran, the four major prophets have special titles. It speaks for the personal humility of Muhammad in that his title is the most modest. In the Koran Abraham is called *khalilullah*, "the friend of God"; Moses is called *kalimullah*, "the spokesman of God"; Jesus is called *ruhullah*, "the spirit of God" and *kalimatullah*, "the word of God." Muhammad is called *rasulullah*, "the messenger of God," and sometimes simply *nabi*, "prophet."

3. The Doctrine of the Book. Next to the doctrine of the unity of God, this is by far the most important doctrine in Islam. In Christianity, the New Testament is important mainly because it contains the biography of Jesus Christ who is at the center of the faith. On the other hand, in Islam Muhammad is

[3] See below, p. 100.

important mainly because he is the bearer of the Book (Koran) which is at the center of the faith.

When God sent prophets He gave each one a Book. Each book contained practically all that man needed to know for his guidance in that age. Sometimes God had one of His angels dictate the book to the prophet. It is believed that the Angel Gabriel dictated the last Book of God, the Koran, to the last prophet, Muhammad. The Koran, according to orthodox Muslims, is the uncreated word, *kalam*, of God. In other words, the Koran existed before God created the universe, and in this sense the Muslims believe that the Book is the uncreated word of God. Being the incarnate Word of God, the Koran cannot be duplicated, either in the perfection of its contents or in the excellence of its language. Indeed, about the only miracle attributed to Muhammad is the *i'jaz*, the miracle of the Koran. According to orthodox Islam, the Koran may be studied but not investigated critically. It must be followed without reservation or criticism. As *shirk*, "polytheism," is a mortal sin, so is *bida'*, "revision," of the laws of the Koran or deviation from them, a capital crime.

All ideas and institutions, beliefs, and practices, must conform to the Koran. The Muslims speak of the Koran as having "descended," *nazala*, to Muhammad from time to time. Muhammad, therefore, is not the author of the Koran. God is the author and Muhammad, as it were, is the recorder. The importance of Muhammad is only a reflection of the Koran. The Muslims are followers of the Koran, the Book, in which the terms of Islam, the submission, are inscribed. They are not followers of Muhammad and, in that sense, do not like to be called Muhammadans. Since the Koran was dictated to Muhammad in the Arabic language, the orthodox have always frowned at the idea of translating it. The vast majority of the Muslims of the world do not understand Arabic. But since almost all of the Muslims have adopted the Arabic alphabet for their language, they are at least able to read the Koran even though they don't understand most of it. It is believed that there is merit in repeating the actual words of Allah.

According to Muslims, the Old and New Testaments also have "descended" from Heaven and were given to Moses, the prophets, and Jesus. Inasmuch as the Koran is the last and the latest Word of God, it supersedes all others and is more relevant to the problems of modern man.

The Doctrine of the Book has contributed to both tolerance and rigidity in Islam. It made the Muslims tolerant of Jews and Christians and, later, of other religions. According to this doctrine, Islam has divided all humanity into two categories—people with a book and people without a book. Jews and Christians are *ahl al-kitab*, "people of the book." These people are not to be forced to accept Islam. If persuasion does not avail, they should be allowed to remain in their own faiths under the protection of Islam. As a result of this doctrine, Jews and Christians have lived among Muslims with a good deal of religious freedom. In fact, whenever Jews were persecuted in Christian Europe, they went to the Muslim countries and there lived in peace. The Doctrine of the Book is the

basis for what became known as the "millet" system, or a system of autonomous "communities" in the Ottoman Empire. It must be noted that "millet"
is a term applied to religious groups, although among non-Arabs it is sometimes
used to denote political nationality.

Furthermore, this doctrine has allowed a certain degree of accommodation.
Zoroastrians of Iran used to be regarded as "people without a book." As such
they did not have a place in the Islamic hegemony. When it became evident
to the early conquerors, however, that all could not be converted, killed, or
banished, some accommodation had to be made. Accordingly, Zoroastrians were
also regarded as "people of the book." Although such recognition has not been
officially extended to the adherents of Hinduism and Buddhism, Muslim kings
of India, such as Akbar (1556–1605), and countless ordinary individuals have
stretched the point and treated Hindus and Buddhists as though they were
"people of the book."

For the modern Muslim, however, the millet system has been vexing as well
as a source of embarrassment. It is rather evident that the idea of "nationality,"
imported from the west, is political in nature and makes it possible for people
of different religions to belong to the same nation, but it also clashes with the
Islamic idea of religion as the base of nationality. The Muslim countries of the
twentieth century which, on the one hand, want to be democratic and extend
equality to all citizens, and at the same time be Muslims, have found themselves tangled in inconsistencies. For example, in a number of Muslim countries
the millet system is preserved side by side with a modern constitution which
declares equality for all. Indeed, in some countries non-Muslims cannot aspire
to high positions and, even with all the good intentions of the modern Muslim,
the non-Muslim groups are second-class citizens.

It was stated above that the Doctrine of the Book has also contributed to the
rigidity of Islam. The Koran, being the uncreated Word of God, has become a
closed book. No one may question its authority or study it critically. Any attempt to try to trace the development of religious and legal ideas in the Koran
is considered sacrilegious. Nevertheless, it is doubtful that all of the Koran was
written during Muhammad's lifetime. Moreover, there is no certainty that all
of the Koran was originally contained in one volume. In 651, there were enough
variations of the different sections of the Koran to induce the then Caliph
Uthman to appoint a commission to produce an authorized version. The result
was that Uthman canonized one version and reputedly destroyed all others.
Apparently he was not successful in destroying all, for by 933, which is the date
of the last canonization, there were admittedly seven different readings. Furthermore, one may legitimately doubt whether a people of such a meager cultural
background as the Arabs were conversant with some of the concepts recorded
in the Koran. The only pieces of pre-Islamic literature (which are believed, by
some, to be of doubtful origin) do not contain any theological or philosophical
concepts. Indeed, the first grammar for the Arabic language was written over a
century after the death of Muhammad and that by a non-Arab. Given these

considerations, one wonders what would happen if the Koran were studied as critically as the Bible has been. It would be interesting to discover whether or not scholars would reach the conclusion presently held, in the absence of such a critical study, that the words of the Koran as we have it today were all recorded by Muhammad.

4. The Doctrine of the Final Judgment. The most eloquent verses of the Koran deal with eschatological topics such as heaven, hell, day of judgment, resurrection, and also a faint idea of purgatory and limbo. In these concepts the Muslims have practically the same views as the Christians. It must be noted, however, that Muhammad is not considered as an intercessor. Only "those who repent and believe and are righteous in act" and those who are martyrs for the faith will go to paradise.

5. The Doctrine of Angels and Jinns. These are mentioned in the Koran as populating heaven and earth. Angels are creatures of God who continuously worship Him and do His bidding. Their duties are to record men's actions, be witnesses on the Day of Judgment, hold God's throne, and generally be useful to those whom God favors. Jinns are also created by God and some of them are believers. There are some jinns who have rebelled and have turned into *shaytans*, "satan." In this form they try to lead people astray and to oppose the Prophet. Their leader is Iblis, who was an angel but fell from grace by refusing to pay homage to Adam.

ARTICLES OF PRACTICE, "IBADAT"

To the Muslim, these are more important than the articles of faith. Although the above articles, especially the unity of God and the Book, set the tone, the articles of practice are considered the *arkan*, or pillars of Islam.

1. The Witness. Every Muslim must make a profession of his faith or bear witness, *shahada*, to his beliefs. This, in fact, is the creed of Islam in one sentence: *la ilaha illallah, Muhammadun rasulullah*, "There is no God except Allah; Muhammad is the Messenger of Allah." This states the unity of God and is a reminder of the terms of submission brought by the Messenger of Allah. This is the most oft repeated sentence in the world of Islam. It is whispered in the ear of the newborn child, it is repeated by him throughout his life, and it is the last sentence uttered when he is laid in the grave. It is used to call the faithful to prayer and it has served as the battle cry of Muslim soldiers in all the wars of Islam. The utterance of this sentence will admit a nonbeliever into the fold of Islam.

2. Prayer. A Muslim, male or female, must pray five times a day—morning, noon, midafternoon, sunset, and night. The prayer must be in Arabic and it must be performed toward Mecca. The prescribed prayer from beginning to end is called a *rak'ah*. The noon, midafternoon, and night prayers have each four rak'ahs, while the sunset prayer has three and the morning prayer two. The muezzin calls the faithful to prayer five times a day from the minaret of the mosque. In modern times a loudspeaker from the minaret sometimes plays a tape recording of the call. The person who prays must be clean, the act for

which has been ritualized by washing the hands and face in the prescribed manner. This is followed by anointing the head and feet with water. In the absence of water the whole ritual may be performed with sand. There are certain postures which the individual assumes during prayer, such as standing erect, bowing with hands on knees, sitting on haunches, and prostrating one self. It is preferable to pray in a mosque, but it is not mandatory. In the early Islamic period women would attend the mosque for prayer, but this is no longer the custom. One has to pray wherever convenient, at home, place of work, or mosque. Most of the prayers in mosques are performed individually There is very little corporate worship in Islam. There is no such thing as "mem bership" in a mosque. Islam does not have a priesthood, there is no ordination rite, nor is there a well-defined hierarchy. The religious leaders who perform marriage, conduct funerals, and sometimes preach are called *imam* in Arabic speaking countries, *mullah* in Iran, and *hojja* in Turkey. The more educated ones are called *ulama*, "learned." They usually teach in schools and theological seminaries. In the Muslim world seminaries train not only preachers, but also lawyers and teachers of Arabic, the language of the Koran.

3. Giving. "Giving," not specifically almsgiving, as *Zakah* is commonly translated, is the third pillar of Islam. There are two types of giving in Islam The first is *Sadaqa*, the voluntary almsgiving which is common to all religions The other is *Zakah*, an obligatory offering tantamount to a tax levy. During the time when the Islamic supranational state was in power, this tax was collected from all Muslims. It was used by the government both for war and peace. Customarily, two and a half per cent of a person's income was expected though this was never uniformly enforced.

Zakah was an obligation imposed only on the Muslims. The "people of the book" paid a different type of tax called *jizya*, or poll tax. This was paid for protection. Since all wars in Islam were theoretically for the expansion and propagation of Islam, non-Muslims would not be recruited for the army. In place of military service the non-Muslims had to pay this special tax. In the absence of any mosque organization or community, all voluntary giving was collected by the government. These offerings which were collected in the form of real estate as well as cash, were and still are kept in a special account called *waqf*, "religious endowment," by the government. All modern Muslim states have a bureau or a ministry of religious endowments, *awqaf*.

4. Fasting. This is carried out during the month of Ramadan, the ninth of the Muslim calendar, which was holy for the Arabs before Islam and continued as such perhaps because Muhammad received his call in this month. The fasting begins at dawn usually after a meal and ends at dusk every day when the fast is broken. The nights should be spent in keeping vigil and in the reading of the Koran. In most Muslim countries all offices are closed in the morning during this month and sometimes no restaurants are permitted to remain open.

5. Pilgrimage. Every Muslim is enjoined, if he can afford it, to go to Mecca

t least once in his lifetime. The person who has made the pilgrimage or *hajj* s given the title of *al-hajj* and in non-Arab countries, *haji*. The rituals of pilgrimage in and around Mecca are the same as they used to be long before slam.[4] Hundreds of thousands of Muslims from all parts of the world make this pilgrimage every year. There is no question that the experience is very uplifting for the faithful and the spectacle very impressive. Furthermore, the *hajj* has given and continues to give a sense of solidarity to the Muslims of the world.

6. Holy War. Some Muslims, especially the adherents of the *Kharijite* sect, have elevated holy war, *jihad*, as the sixth pillar of Islam. There are numerous references in the Koran to war and the Muslim's duty to fight. "Warfare is ordained for you, though it is hateful to you; but it may happen that ye hate what is good for you." (K. 2: 216) "Then when the sacred months have passed, slay the idolaters wherever ye find them, and take them [captive], and besiege them, and prepare for them each ambush. But if they repent and establish worship and pay the poor-due, then leave their way free. Lo! Allah is forgiving, merciful." (K. 9: 5) To these and other verses like them Islam owes its great expansion. Indeed, all land not within the domain of Islam, *dar al-salam*, was considered *dar al-harb*, or the domain of war. In more recent years, however, the faithful have not responded to the call. The last time it was invoked was in the fall of 1914, when the Ottoman Sultan who was also the Caliph of Islam, proclaimed a jihad in all its solemnity against the British and the French. Not many paid attention to it. Indeed, the Muslim Arabs fought against the Caliph himself. The word jihad means "striving" and many a modern nationalist uses it in the sense of striving against poverty, disease, ignorance, as well as colonialism and imperialism.

Good Works. In addition to the above articles on faith and practice there is a general category in Islam called *ihsan*, which may be translated as "good works." There are laws against gambling, usury, using alcohol, and eating pork. Muslims are enjoined to take care of the orphans, to be kind, to deal honestly, and to forgive. In general, a Muslim is encouraged, wherever he is, to do that which is *halal*, "permitted," and to refrain from that which is *haram*, "forbidden," and leave the rest to "Allah the Compassionate and the Merciful."

[4] See above, p. 28.

CHAPTER 4

THE BEGINNINGS OF THE ISLAMIC STATE

The First Four Caliphs

Abu Bakr   632–634
Umar   634–644
Uthman   644–656
Ali   656–661

PROBLEM OF SUCCESSION

Muhammad died on June 8, 632. As long as Muhammad was alive, he fulfilled the duties of prophet, judge, king, religious leader, and commander. No one questioned his right to do so. The death of Muhammad was the passing of at least two "persons," one, the Prophet of Allah and the other, the Head of the State. The Prophet, as the last sent by God, could not have a successor. The Head of the State, however, with his corollary duties as commander-in-chief, law-giver, judge, and so forth, had to have a successor, who was called Caliph.

Even before Muhammad's body was interred, a bitter struggle arose over succession. There was more than one claimant for the position of Caliph. This struggle continued for centuries and has colored the history of Islam. The argument which began around the body of the Prophet-King sometimes erupted in war and has not, in a sense, ended even yet. According to an eminent Muslim historian of the twelfth century, "No other issue in Islam has caused more bloodshed than the caliphate."

One of the great transformations wrought by Muhammad was the replacement of the tribal or national brotherhood by a religious one. He preached the brotherhood of Muslims rather than the brotherhood of man. The modern concepts of nationalism and internationalism do not find a ready home in Islam. Muhammad sought the creation of a supranational state with himself as its Prophet-King.

As far as is known, Muhammad, not having a male heir, had not designated anyone to be his successor. Perhaps he was following the tribal custom in this matter. The Arabs, like their cousins the Hebrews in the period of "Judges," were in the habit of electing their leaders for life. The qualifications for the office were perhaps judged by the need of the community at the time in question. There were those, however, who claimed that Muhammad had, indeed, appointed Ali as his successor but that the enemies of the heir-designate had destroyed the will. In any case, the issue was so joined with Muhammad's death that no one thought of burying the Prophet until the successor was chosen.

When Ayisha announced the death of Muhammad, the leaders of the tribes of Aws and Khazraj, who were the Medinese supporters of the Prophet and were called "Ansar," were the first to act. They were the traditional enemies of the Meccans and did not like the economic and social encroachment of the latter in their city. They reasoned among themselves that the Quraysh should be satisfied with the honor of giving a Prophet to the Arabs. They felt that the Medinese, who had aided the Prophet, should be given the honor of supplying the head of the state. Their difficulty, however, was in deciding whether this person should be from Aws or Khazraj.

While the Ansar were jockeying for position among themselves, the Muhajirun, that is, the leaders of the Quraysh who had accompanied Muhammad to Medina, were not idle. They had gathered in the Prophet's Mosque to discuss the matter. When they heard that the Ansar had almost reached a decision, Abu Bakr, Umar, and several of the other leaders rushed to the meeting place of the Ansar. There, in that room, a struggle ensued which calls to mind the proverbial smoke-filled caucus room of an American Presidential Convention. Umar, who eventually became the second caliph, was present, and told the story a few years later.

Abu Bakr told the Ansar in no uncertain terms that the Arabs as a whole would "recognize authority only in the Quraysh." The truth of this statement must have shaken the Ansar. The Quraysh had been the most prominent tribe as custodian of the Ka'ba, and everything Muhammad had done had strengthened rather than weakened their position. The Ansar then suggested a confederation of tribal leaders as a council. This was impractical and would dissipate the unity which Muhammad had imposed on the Arabs. By this time, everyone's feelings were aroused and they were about to come to blows. At this point, according to a prearranged plan, Umar nominated Abu Bakr and swore allegiance, *baya'h*, to him. The Muhajirun followed and then the not-too-solid ranks of the Ansar broke and they did the same. Umar ends his narration by saying, "We jumped on Sa'd ibn-Ubada (the man whom the Ansar were about to elect) and someone said that we had killed him. I said, 'God killed him!'"

There was a third group, almost forgotten in the struggle for leadership. This was the immediate family of the Prophet, about the only people interested enough to attend the body of the dead leader. Around the deathbed were Ayisha, his wife, in whose arms the Prophet died, Fatima, the Prophet's only surviving daughter, her husband Ali, who was also Muhammad's cousin, and a few others. Apparently they had taken it for granted that Ali, as cousin and son-in-law of the Prophet and as the consort of the only descendant of Muhammad, would be the natural and rightful successor. Later it was claimed that an alleged will of Muhammad was "destroyed" which had mentioned Ali as successor. It is reported that Fatima made a moving speech on behalf of her husband, and Ali refused to pay allegiance to Abu Bakr for six months, but both efforts were to no avail.

ABU BAKR

Among the Quraysh, Abu Bakr was one of the oldest Muslims, both in age and in conversion to Islam. He was a close friend of Muhammad and was also his father-in-law. He became the first Caliph, *Khalifat Rasul Allah*, "the regent of the Messenger of Allah." His short rule of a little over two years was spent in reunifying Arabia under Islam. The allegiance of Arab tribes to Muhammad was superficial and he had not lived long enough to strengthen his hold over them. With the Prophet gone, the tribes began to follow their old ways. They severed the strongest bond that tied them to Islam, which was the paying of the Zakah tax. For a people who were not used to paying taxes, Zakah was an economic burden which hampered their freedom. Some of the tribes chose to forget what little they had accepted of Islam. Other tribes, not to be outdone by the Quraysh, claimed prophets of their own. To Abu Bakr and his advisors this was intolerable, and they decided to meet the challenge with force.

The Meccans who, under the canopy of Islam, had virtual control of Medina, waged war on the rest of Arabia. Khalid ibn-Walid was the commander in these wars. His brilliant generalship was such that one by one the tribes were subdued. By the time Abu Bakr lay on his deathbed in 634, the victorious army of Khalid had followed some of the belligerent tribes into Syria and had defeated a detachment of the Byzantine army.

UMAR

To make sure that no struggle would arise over the succession, Abu Bakr, before his death, named Umar as his successor. Umar had been Abu Bakr's closest advisor, if not the actual power behind the Caliph. This ambitious and energetic man, who had reached the top position at the age of forty-three, was not only one of the early believers but was also a father-in-law of the Prophet. His full name was Umar ibn al-Khattab. Under his inspired leadership, the Arabs of the desert erupted like a volcano and consumed everything before them. In the course of a decade they defeated the Byzantine Empire and spread westward to the Mediterranean and southward to Egypt. At the same time another branch of their armies conquered the Persian Empire and advanced to central Iran. This spectacular and speedy victory by a subject and uncultured people over two of the largest empires of the time has baffled historians and has, therefore, been the subject of much speculation. And yet, Rome was destroyed by the Huns, and the Chinese were conquered by the Mongols. The reasons are not difficult to find.

Muhammad's vision of empire, so far as can be determined, did not extend beyond the Arabs. Abu Bakr had his hands full most of the time he was Caliph, so that actually he was quite reluctant to order Khalid to go into Iraq and Syria. But Khalid had already penetrated into Syria, and Abu Bakr acquiesced to that which had already been accomplished. Umar, however, consciously planned and led the eruption.

Perhaps this was not the first time that the Bedouins of the Arabian peninsula had marauded the Fertile Crescent to the north. It is probable that the Assyrians, Babylonians, Chaldeans, and the Phoenicians—all Semites—had emerged from the peninsula and had built great empires. The Hebrews also had come and had left a religious imprint. The Arabs came now in their wake, destined to establish an empire and impose a faith as well.

Umar, who did so much to spread the new faith, was the St. Paul of Islam. But unlike St. Paul who appealed to Rome for protection, Umar challenged and defeated the empires of Rome and Iran. Umar was an Arab, a devout follower of Islam, and a confirmed believer in the theocracy for which he was *Amir al-Mawminin*, "Commander of the Believers." As such he had a threefold purpose. One was to establish an Arab Empire with Arabia as the center of power. To implement this purpose, Umar banished all non-Muslims, even Christians and Jews, from Arabia so that Arabia would be a completely Muslim land. The second purpose was that Islam become the dominant, if not the sole, religion of the empire. The third was that Arabic, the language of Allah and of the Koran, become the language of the Empire. Umar and his associates were not the first people in world history nor the last to have such plans, but he and his followers were more successful than most.

Fortunately for Islam, Umar was not alone. Khalid ibn-Walid and Amr ibn-al-As, two of the most talented generals in the history of warfare, were as young as Umar and equally enthusiastic. Aside from their personal faith in Islam, they saw in it the means for a great adventure. Furthermore, Umar and his lieutenants were impelled to lead a campaign outside of Arabia. The restless Bedouins who had followed the banner of Muhammad had shown their fickleness by abandoning the new religion after the Prophet's death. Abu Bakr had to subdue them again but they were still restless. As Muslims, they were not allowed to fight each other nor raid each others' tents. Raiding had been the habit of generations and could not be given up so easily. So Umar encouraged them to fight non-Muslims outside Arabia, thereby ridding himself of Bedouin intransigence at home and affording the new government the prospects of victory abroad. Moreover, it was not difficult to induce the tribesmen to fight outside Arabia, for the wealth of Iran and Byzantium was proverbial. The prospects of such a rich economic reward strengthened with the faith that he was fighting for the cause of Allah, made the Arab soldier a formidable foe. The Muslim Bedouins believed that if they were killed, they would go to Paradise; and if not, they would share in the booty. Few soldiers went to war expecting to be killed. One of the Muslim historians writes that Abu Bakr called the people to *jihad*, holy war, and reminded them of the booty they could capture from the Greeks!

In addition to the individual desire for booty, the desire of the insolvent government of Medina for tribute must not be overlooked. "Fight against such of those who have been given the Scripture . . ." says the Koran, "until they pay tribute. . . ." Experience had shown the first two caliphs that they could not collect the Zakah from the tribes in Arabia without the use of force. So they tried to use the tribes to collect tribute from the "people of the book" outside Arabia. They must have been surprised by their own success. Shortly afterward, they had simplified their demands into three words, "Islam, tribute, or sword."

Most Muslim historians emphasize the religious motivation in the advancement of Islam. Most of the modern interpreters of Islamic history have tried to minimize it. If the former exaggerated, as they did, the latter read history poorly. It is impossible to conclude that Islam did not play an important role. It was the battle cry of every soldier and the rallying point of every tribe. Without Islam there could not have been a cohesion of the various tribes, and without this unity they would not have been much more than raiding parties. In the mind of every Arab from Umar down to the lowliest soldier, Allah, Muhammad, war booty, tribute, martyrdom, and paradise were all part of the same indivisible package.

The reasons for victory, like everything else, are not all based on the initiative and ability of the aggressor. The two giants in the north, Byzantium and Iran, had been fighting each other for centuries. Even as the Arab bands were marching northward, Heraclius, the Byzantine Emperor, was flushed with victory over the Persians whom he had pushed back. He was tired, and Khosro Parviz, the Persian Shahanshah, was dead. The throne of Iran, from the death of Parviz in 628 to 634, when young Yazdgerd III became Shah, had changed hands several times. Both the Byzantines and the Persians, tired and bleeding, expected a few years peace. After all, they were the only real adversaries. They did not expect anyone to attack them, and least of all the bedraggled Bedouins of the desert.

Wars cost money and money comes from taxing the people. The peoples of Byzantium and Iran were burdened with heavy taxes to defray the great expenses of the war and to provide the high level of living to which the leaders of both countries were accustomed.

Moreover, the early vigor of both Christianity and Zoroastrianism had given way to endless theological divisions in Byzantium and priestly oppression in Iran. Among the Christians, there was a bitter fight going on between the Monophysites who believed in only one nature for Christ and those who accepted two natures, divine and human. The attempt of Heraclius to compromise by ignoring Christ's nature and substituting his one will, did not please either party. Indeed, it created a third faction.

In Iran, the Mobeds of Zoroastrianism had become intolerant and had used the power of the state to advance their aims. Religious revolts such as Manicheanism and Mazdakism had been started to lighten the burden of the state religion. To these people, the simple and theologically uncomplicated belief in Allah must have been like a breath of fresh air.

It must be remembered, too, that there were many Arab tribes in the Fertile Crescent, north of the Arabian peninsula. Some of them were kinsmen of the tribes to the south. They must have welcomed the opportunity to be rid of their Greek and Persian overlords.

The conquest of civilized people by nomadic armies is not a new phenomenon in history, but it is always hard to explain. In this case, the power of both the Byzantines and Persians was reputedly so great that Abu Bakr was reluctant to send his troops, and Umar was also cautious. The commanders in the field, however, were uninhibited and they, more than anyone else, should be credited with the advance of Muslim arms.

By 634, Khalid ibn-Walid, after a series of forced marches, attacked eastern Syria. He could not have done this had it not been for the assistance of the Ghassanids, who were Arabs and had treaty agreements with the Byzantines. By February 635, Khalid laid seige to the city of Damascus. He gave the inhabitants three choices which became standard in subsequent wars of Islam. These choices were to accept Islam, pay tribute, or fight. Damascus surrendered in September 635. The decisive battle was fought a year later in August 636 in Yarmuk, between Heraclius and Khalid. The Arab victory forced the Byzantine emperor to leave all of Syria and Palestine to the Muslims. Syria fell in 637 and Jerusalem in 638. Thus, in four short years, the Arabs had become masters of the best Byzantine provinces in the Fertile Crescent.

With Syria as a base, the Arabs probed the mountainous regions of Armenia, Georgia, and northern Iraq, but found penetration difficult. Amr ibn-al-As, who apparently was familiar with Egypt, led a detachment there with the reluctant permission of Umar. By 639 he reached the border and pushed on to Pleusium and Heliopolis. After receiving reinforcements he moved down the Nile to the famous city of Alexandria and received its surrender in September 642.

While these campaigns were going on in the west, Sa'd ibn-Waqqas, a third general of Islam, with some 6,000 troops, moved toward Iran. In three major battles, the fate of the Persian Empire was sealed. The first took place on a hot, windy day in June 635 at Qadesiya, in which the Persians, under the command of Rostam, were defeated. Two years later, with the aid of Arab tribes along the Euphrates, Sa'd laid seige to Ctesiphon, the capital of the Sasanids. The famed capital fell in 637. The wealth of the city must have been beyond the imagination of the Arab soldiers, and they looted Ctesiphon to their heart's content. It is reported that they used camphor for cooking and exchanged the "yellow pieces" or *safra* (gold) which they had not seen before with the "white pieces" or *bayda* (silver) which was somewhat familiar! A remnant of Yazdgerd's army met the Arabs at Nahavand, near modern Hamadan, and was defeated in 641. The Shah himself was murdered by a greedy miller somewhere in the region of Marv, thus bringing to an end the Sasanid rule which had started in A.D. 226.

Thus, in the course of some eight years, the Arabs from the desert had overrun a territory extending from western Egypt to central Iran, and from the southern borders of Asia Minor to the Arabian Sea. Even though they had not conquered it entirely, the victory was nevertheless very impressive. What Iran and Byzantium could not do to each other, the Arabs did to both.

For an understanding of the modern Middle East it is essential to note that the peoples of Syria, Palestine, and Egypt have all but forgotten the battles of Yarmuk or the surrender of Damascus, Jerusalem, and Alexandria. But if they do remember it, they do so with pride for the victory of Islam. A vast majority of them became Muslims and they all adopted the Arabic language and took pride in being part of an Arab Empire.

Not so the Persians. They still remember with bitterness the battle of Qadesiya and the subsequent defeats at the hands of the Arabs. The peoples of the Fertile Crescent and Egypt were under a foreign power, the Byzantines. The victory of the Arabs over Byzantium was regarded as a change of masters for the people. Very likely they had cause to welcome such a change. The Persians, on the other hand, were no subject people and had strong nationalistic feelings. The victory of the Arabs changed the position of the Persians from that of a master to a servant and they could not accept it. As soon as the Persians recovered from the shock of defeat, they consciously tried to destroy the Arab hegemony. They succeeded in breaking up the unity of the Arab Empire in A.D. 750. They refused to speak Arabic and, as soon as they could, they stopped writing it. They profess Islam, but since 1500 belong to a sect which sets them apart from the majority of the Arabs.

Three hundred and fifty years after the battle of Qadesiya, the Persian poet Ferdosi immortalized it in his book, *Shahnameh*, "Book of Kings," which depicts the history of Iran in poetry from mythological times until the conquest of the country by the Arabs. There has hardly been a Persian school child who has not memorized all or parts of the story. On the eve of the battle *sepahbod*, "general" Rostam has the premonition of defeat and he writes a moving letter to his brother in Ctesiphon.

Drinking camels' milk and eating lizards' meat
Have caused these Arabs, bedraggled and bare feet!
To want the Crown of Kiyan upon their pate.
A thousand curses be on thy head, O fate!

The Persians did not forget their defeat. Indeed, the Persians used to use the "Yazdgerdi Calendar" in which year one was the death of the last Sasanian king. Neither did the Persians forgive Umar. Until the second decade of the twentieth century it was customary in Iran, on a special day, to burn Umar in effigy. Umar, the second Caliph of Islam, met a violent death. It was perhaps no accident that his assassin was a Persian by the name of Abu Lolo Firooz, who killed Umar on November 23, 644.

CHAPTER 5

PROBLEMS OF EXPANSION AND ADMINISTRATION

The rapid expansion of the Islamic arms had resulted in many problems of logistics, administration, and justice that the Koran had not foreseen. Abu Bakr's method of administration was similar to Muhammad's in its simplicity and personal application. Like the Prophet, his place of work was the Mosque in Medina. There he led the faithful in prayers, judged the disputes between parties, and directed the army. The community was still relatively small and the problems were both familiar and simple. According to the time-honored custom of the tribes, the warriors did not receive any pay. Each soldier shared in the booty and acquired the belongings of the person whom he killed. The income of the state was still largely from Zakah and from one-fifth of all booty, as established by Muhammad.

With the acquisition of vast territories, the administrative problems connected with them could not be handled as before. New policies were needed and Umar was equal to the occasion. The fact that he is regarded as the "second founder" of Islam is due as much to the success of his administrative policies as to his conquest of new territories for Islam. It is very difficult to determine whether all the policies attributed to Umar were his, or whether they belonged to his great-great grandson, the Umayyad Caliph, Umar II (717–720), or whether they belonged to others who used the name of Umar for prestige.

It may be safely assumed that, given Umar's devotion to Muhammad, he would follow the latter's principles as closely as possible. Indeed, among the policies attributed to Umar can be distinguished those which mirror Muhammad. It was the first time that the new Islamic community was confronted with the problem of having conquered non-Arab peoples and seeing some of these non-Arabs accept Islam. The problem of what to do with the non-Arab conquered peoples was not as difficult as the problem of how to deal with the non-Arabs who became Muslims.

To guide him, Umar had a number of principles and facts which had been taught by the Prophet. He knew that Muhammad was an Arab, sent by Allah with a message for the Arabs. He also knew that this message could not be withheld from the non-Arabs. He believed that the Islamic community, *umma*,[1] was a brotherhood of all Muslims, not of all mankind. Furthermore, with the vast territory under his control, Umar saw the necessity of establishing a solid base, preferably in Arabia, where nothing would prejudice the solidarity of this brotherhood. With the above principles in mind, Umar interpreted Islam to be a brotherhood of Arabs who had accepted the message of Muhammad. The non-Arab Muslims could join the Muslim umma, but would not be part of its inner circle—an honor which would remain the prerogative of the Arab.

The Jews also, in the days when they had their Temple and some degree of autonomy in Jerusalem, faced a similar problem. There were many pagans who were attracted to Judaism and accepted the religion without any attempt at conversion on the part of the Jews. But this did not mean that these converts would partake of the blessings of the "seed of Israel." In the Temple the Jews had provided a place called "the court of the proselytes" and converts could proceed into the Temple that far and no farther. In somewhat the same way, Umar interpreted Islam (and perhaps Muhammad would have approved) to mean a brotherhood of Muslims led by a privileged inner circle of Muslim Arabs. To this end he issued orders and these orders can be better understood in the light of the above analysis.

In the first place he drove all non-Muslims out of Arabia. To this day, non-Muslims are not considered permanent residents of the country. Secondly, he prevented the Arabs from obtaining land in the conquered territories. Without a land of their own, "home" would always be Arabia. In the third place, he frowned on intermarriage, even with converts, in order to keep the blood pure and the Arab military aristocracy intact. In the fourth place, to prevent the Arab warriors from fraternizing and mingling with the conquered peoples, he ordered the establishment of military cantonments. Those familiar with British imperialism in India will recall British military cantonments on the outskirts of main cities. Among Muslim encampments, some of which became cities later on, were Fustat in Egypt, Ramlah in Palestine, and Kufa and Basra in Iraq.

Consequently, the work of cultivation, trade, and the local administration of districts was left in the hands of the inhabitants who, theoretically, were laboring for the "benefit of Muslims," and were referred to as *ra'iya*, which means "herd." In Christian territories the local bishop was in charge of affairs, while in Iran the *dehqan*, country squire, had the administrative responsibilities.

One of the cardinal principles of Umar was that all immovable property

---

[1] The reader should become familiar with the term *umma*, community. At first it referred to the Muslim-Arab community. But soon it was used by all the writers to include all of the Muslims of the world. In this sense it is also used in modern times.

and land in conquered territories belonged to the Muslim-Arab community, umma. The income of the state, in cash and in kind, came from different sources. One was *Khums*, or one fifth of the booty, which had been instituted by Muhammad. Another was the *jizya*, poll tax levied on non-Muslims. A third source was the land tax levied on all non-Arab cultivators. The total income was so large that the Arabs were exempt from paying Zakah. Since all proceeds belonged to the umma, whatever remained after defraying the expenses of war, administration, and public welfare was distributed among the Arabs. For this, Umar ordered a census taken and established a bureau, which he called *diwan*, after the Persian institution of the same name, *divan*, for the purpose of distribution. The above policy strengthened the Arabs, all of whom were members of the inner circle of the Muslim umma. All Arabs were elevated to the rank of the privileged class and, only because they were Arabs, they received an annual stipend in addition to exemption of payment of Zakah.

As a result of the census, all Arabs were classified according to rank based on the length of their faith in Islam, service to the Prophet, position in the tribe, etc. At the top was the family of the Prophet whose favorite wife, Ayisha, received an annual stipend of 12,000 dirhams (about $3000). The next in rank were the fellow emigrés of Muhammad from Mecca, followed by his Medinese companions, each of whom received an average annual stipend of about 5,000 dirhams. Then came the members of the different Arab tribes, men, women, and children, all classified according to the length of their faith in Islam. The lowest soldier could collect an annual stipend of 600 and nonfighters of at least 200 dirhams. Contrary to the claims of a number of modern historians, the Arabs did indeed use Islam to bolster their position. Arabism was identified with Islam, at least by Umar and his followers if not (and this is by no means certain) by Muhammad himself.

This policy of Arab superiority, however, could not stand the test of time. Sooner or later the large number of non-Arabs who, for whatever reason, had accepted Islam would insist on the broader interpretation of the Koran as meaning Muslim brotherhood rather than Arab-Muslim brotherhood. Before long, scores of non-Arab Muslims "passed" as Arabs, some to escape degradation, others to receive stipend, and a few to attain prestige. This was going on while hundreds went a step farther and "passed" as descendants of Muhammad himself! These "descendants" of the Prophet, who enjoy all the privileges and prestige of this relationship, are legion in all of the Muslim world, especially the non-Arab!

UTHMAN

If the policies of Umar disintegrated sooner than expected, it was because his successor was one of the worst administrators in the annals of Islam. When Umar knew that he would not recover from the wound which the Persian assassin had inflicted on him, he appointed a committee of six to choose the next caliph. Both Ali and Uthman were members of the committee. To the disappointment of Ali, no doubt, Uthman was elected Caliph. Uthman ibn-Affan was past 70, and, like Ali, was a son-in-law of Muhammad. He belonged to the aristocratic Umayyad clan of the Quraysh whose leader at the time of Muhammad, Abu Sufyan, was bitterly opposed to the Prophet. After the capitulation of Mecca to the religious and political demands of the Prophet, the Umayyads, thanks to Muhammad, had emerged unscathed.

The Umayyads settled in Medina and exerted leadership in different aspects of the Islamic state. Perhaps it was through their efforts that Uthman was elected. As it turned out, it was the Umayyad family rather than Uthman who actually took over the reins of the state. The mild-mannered, unenergetic old man preferred reading the Koran to public affairs and trusted the administration of the state to the members of his family. Soon his Umayyad relatives replaced old and tested warriors as governors of conquered provinces. He even deposed the conqueror of Egypt, Amr ibn-al-As, from the governorship and instead appointed his foster brother, who had been denounced by the Prophet. Uthman pretended not to notice when his kinsmen began to acquire land in conquered territories in spite of Umar's ruling against such a practice. Other Arabs, outside of the Quraysh, who did not like this law but nevertheless were too afraid of Umar to oppose it, were encouraged by Uthman's indifference.

Not through the initiative of Uthman, but mostly because of the momentum of the movement, the military campaigns continued. By 646 Alexandria was recaptured, having been lost to the Byzantines through an attack from the sea. The Muslim armies advanced through the Berber territory in North Africa and captured Tripoli and ancient Carthage. Uthman permitted the Berbers to have the privileges of the "people of the book." By 652 the Muslims began to have treaty relationships with the Nubians. The campaign in Syria was under the leadership of Mu'awiya, another member of the Umayyad family. Muslims under his leadership won their first naval battle in the capture of Cyprus and later pushed on to Rhodes. In the north, the Muslims took Azarbaijan and parts of Armenia, and in the east, they advanced to the neighborhood of Kabul, the capital of modern Afghanistan.

More and more, however, the attention of the leaders of Islam was turned inward, especially to the mismanagement of Uthman. He had appointed his half-brother, who had spat upon the Prophet, as governor of Kufa, and his cousin as the head of the treasury. In addition to widespread nepotism, it was reported that Uthman had become so corrupt that he would sell governorships for cash or gifts of beautiful slave girls. Many of the close companions of the Prophet were against him. It was an open secret that these feelings were encouraged by Ali and his supporters.

Ironically enough, the only lasting achievement of Uthman, namely the canonization of the Koran, was the act which instigated an uprising against him in Kufa and which culminated in his death. He was becoming increasingly unpopular in all parts of the Muslim world, especially where the followers of Ali were strong. The scholars in Kufa accused Uthman of tampering with the text of the Koran by suppressing verses which were against the Umayyads. The uprising, started in this tumultuous city, encouraged the friends of Ali in Egypt to rise in protest against Uthman. The Egyptians went a step farther and sent a detachment of 500 soldiers to Medina in 656 and surrounded the Caliph's house. Apparently Uthman was oblivious to these events. It is reported that he was reading the Koran when the soldiers broke into the house and killed him. According to Muslim historians, his assassin was Muhammad, the son of Uthman's friend Abu Bakr, the first Caliph of Islam. Thus did the second of the Caliphs meet a violent death.

ALI

A week after the murder of Uthman, Ali assumed the office of Caliph. He was the cousin and the son-in-law of Muhammad, and the only one of the old companions of any importance. It is not correct to say that he was "elected." He was simply proclaimed by his supporters as the fourth Caliph to the satisfaction of all those who believed that he was the "only" rightful heir to the Prophet. The caliphate, which had been "wrested" from him three times had at last, so it was claimed, been conferred upon the right person. But unfortunately for Ali and his followers, the position of caliphate had, by this time, found many aspirants.

Twenty-four years after the death of Muhammad, a new generation had grown to manhood which had experienced almost continuous victory, traveled far and wide, had tasted power, had partaken of new pleasures, and had inherited great wealth. The days of the simple life of the desert were gone and with them the awe and respect formerly held for those who had been close to the Prophet. Ali's caliphate was hardly begun before two of his closest associates, Talha and Zubayr, refused to acknowledge him.

In the course of three decades, interested Muslims had brooded over the problem of succession. Three opinions had emerged. One group believed that the successor of the Prophet must be from the Quraysh tribe. This was a development of the original argument between the Meccans and the Medinese immediately after the death of the Prophet. The first three caliphs had held this opinion. Abu Bakr had been chosen by an unpremeditated gathering of some of the leaders from rival parties. Umar had been appointed by his predecessor and Uthman had been elected by a committee appointed by Umar. Apparently these methods were acceptable. Since all members of the Quraysh tribe were eligible for the caliphate, there was a good deal of rivalry among the different families.

The second group, commonly called the "legitimists," believed that the caliphate was a divine office and the appointee had to assume office by divine ordinance. Since no one questioned the fact that Muhammad was Prophet-King by divine ordinance, they argued that successorship would legitimately belong, by divine designation, to the family of the Prophet. According to this theory, Ali, as the son-in-law, cousin, and adopted son of Muhammad, was the legitimate successor and after him, leadership would go to his sons, i.e., Muhammad's grandsons, and so on down the line. The legitimists were known as *Shi'at Ali*, or "partisans of Ali," and later on as simply *Shi'a*.

The third group, which comprised a minority of Muslims, believed that the caliphate did not belong to a particular family. They believed in the dictum of the Koran that greatness was based on piety and not on blood. They went so far as to say that even a slave could become a caliph. In their social ideals and personal life they were puritans and loved the simplicity of the prophetic message. At first they sided with Ali, very likely because of his piety, against his enemies. Later they left him and became known as *Kharijites*, "seceders." They became the self-appointed warriors for the purity of Islam and were thorns in the flesh of all caliphs.

Very likely Ali's associates, Talha and Zubayr, were afraid that the position of Ali would establish the caliphate in his household to the exclusion of the rest of the Quraysh. Ayisha, the young wife of Muhammad, who had a personal hatred for Ali, joined the insurgents at Basra.

Thus the first civil war in Islam, which was by no means the last, was fought outside of Basra on December 9, 656, 24 years after the death of Muhammad. On the one side there was the son-in-law of the Prophet and on the other side the Prophet's favorite wife. In the Battle of the Camel, so called because Ayisha rode on a camel and aroused the warriors, Ali was the victor. He was quite magnanimous to Ayisha and sent her to Medina.

With this crisis out of the way, Ali began to rule with Kufa as his capital. He dismissed most of the appointees of Uthman from office and inaugurated reforms which favored the more simple pattern of the Prophet. He had not reckoned, however, with a more formidable foe. Mu'awiya, governor of Syria and a relative of Uthman, refused to acknowledge Ali. One Friday Mu'awiya exhibited the blood-stained shirt of the murdered Caliph, Uthman, and accused Ali of being an accomplice in the murder. In this way the Umayyads challenged the succession of Ali.

The struggle, however, was over other issues as well. By the time of the caliphate of Ali, the Muslims had created a large empire. The contact of the uncultured, ill-clad, but zealous Arab Muslims with the cultured and sophisticated peoples of Syria and Iraq had tremendous effect on the Muslims. They were dazzled by so much wealth and by so much learning. Moreover, in a very practical way, they needed the help of the conquered peoples to administer the vast new empire. Thus the ostensibly inter-Arab war was, in a real sense, also a rivalry between the former dependencies of the Byzantines and the Persians. Should Syria, representing the Greco-Roman culture, be supreme, or should Iraq, representing the Persian culture? It should be noted that Medina, as the center of the Muslim-Arab empire, had already lost its preeminence.

The two armies, Ali with his Iraqis and Mu'awiya with his Syrians, met at Siffin on the Euphrates in July 657. The Syrians averted certain disaster by lifting the copies of the Koran on their lances and asked for arbitration. Ali, whose valor and piety overshadowed his political acumen, accepted arbitration based on the Koran!

The arbiters took their time in arriving at a verdict. In the meantime, a large number of Ali's followers were disgusted with him for accepting arbitration. They seceded with the slogan, "There is no arbiter except God." Ali fought and defeated these Kharijites in 659 on the banks of Nahravan Canal.

It is difficult to ascertain what went on in the arbitration meetings. There are charges and countercharges. Whatever the facts, Ali, the acknowledged Caliph, had wittingly or unwittingly questioned his own right to the caliphate by accepting arbitration. Mu'awiya, only a governor, had won by appearing to have a legitimate claim to the caliphate. It is said that the arbiters "deposed" both, which in reality meant that they deposed Ali, for Mu'awiya was not a caliph. They did not, however, propose means of electing a new one. In May 660, Mu'awiya had himself proclaimed Caliph in Jerusalem. For the first time there were two caliphs in Islam. In January 661, Ali was wounded by a Kharijite while on his way to the mosque and died two days later.

The downhearted followers of Ali proclaimed his eldest son, Hasan, as Caliph. Hasan, however, did not relish the inevitable struggle ahead. Mu'awiya prudently agreed to pay him a royal pension and protection if he would retire to his villa near Medina. This Hasan did and Mu'awiya became the undisputed ruler of Islam with Damascus as his capital.

Thus ended the period of the "Orthodox" Caliphs. This is the period which has been idealized as the time of pure theocracy, when the law of Allah was the law of the land and the *sunna*, "way of the Prophet," was the path which everyone tried to follow. Most of the religiously oriented Muslims of the twentieth century always refer to this period as the best illustration of Islam at work and yearn to go back to it. Some European historians of Islam have called this period both "republican" and "democratic." Republican it may have been in that there was no attempt, except in the case of Ali, to establish a family dynasty. Democratic it certainly was not. At best it was an oligarchy. In theory, the caliphate was a prerogative of the Quraysh, but in practice it was decided by a very small and powerful group within the tribe.

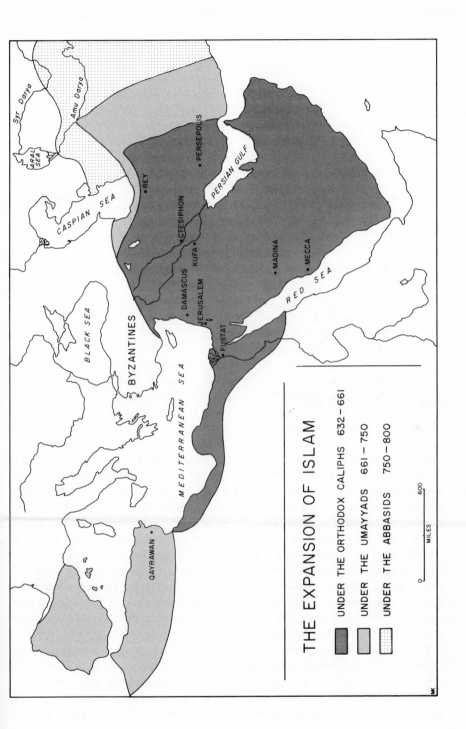

THE EXPANSION OF ISLAM

UNDER THE ORTHODOX CALIPHS 632–661

UNDER THE UMAYYADS 661–750

UNDER THE ABBASIDS 750–800

0   600

MILES

SYR DARYA

AMU DARYA

ARAL SEA

CASPIAN SEA

REY

PERSEPOLIS

PERSIAN GULF

CTESIPHON

KUFA

MADINA

MECCA

DAMASCUS

JERUSALEM

FUSTAT

RED SEA

BLACK SEA

BYZANTINES

MEDITERRANEAN SEA

QAYRAWAN

CHAPTER 6

THE UMAYYAD DYNASTY, 661-750

The Sufyan Branch
Mu'awiya I (661–680)
Yazid I (680–683)
Mu'awiya II (683)
The Marwan Branch
Marwan I (683–685)
Abd al-Malik (685–705)   Hisham (724–743)
Walid I (705–715)   Walid II (743–744)
Sulayman (715–717)   Yazid III (744)
Umar II (717–720)   Ibrahim (744)
Yazid II (720–724)   Marwan II (744–750)

With the establishment of Mu'awiya in the caliphate, a new era came into being in the world of Islam. He organized the dynasty after the manner of the Byzantines and the Persians, abandoning the "republicanism" of the Medinese period. For the sake of placating the traditionalists and preserving appearances, however, Mu'awiya took his son, Yazid, around to different tribes in Arabia and let them acknowledge him as his successor. But, this practice was soon abandoned and the succession went to the oldest son or to whoever was the strongest in the family. Even so, no caliph was undisputed and the Umayyad dynasty, as a whole, was not stable. As is apparent by the list of the Umayyad Caliphs, the average length of a caliph's reign was only six years. Only four ruled for over ten years while the rest ruled less than five. Among the latter there were three who did not last even a year.

Our information concerning the Umayyads comes almost entirely from Abbasid historians who were prejudiced against that dynasty and depicted its rulers as nothing but pleasure-loving and hard-drinking usurpers of the caliphate. True as this description may be about a number of them, it is evident that not all of them were hard-drinking and pleasure-loving. Even some of those who were did much to strengthen the empire and advance its frontiers. The Umayyad caliphs were confronted with a vast empire with diverse elements in religion and culture and with manifold problems of administration. Given the circumstances, the Umayyads did not do badly.

It took Christianity and Buddhism each about 300 years of struggle and development before a "Christian" state was established under Constantine or a "Buddhist" state came into being under Ashoka. This was not so with militantly aggressive Islam. Even during the lifetime of Muhammad, people joined it for diverse and sometimes contradictory motives. There were, to be sure, those whose acceptance of Islam was a total conversion of their life and attitude. They formed the nucleus of the believers and their number grew with the passage of time. They were zealously on guard to protect the purity of the faith. The early Kharijites were among them and sided with Ali for the preservation of the faith proclaimed by Muhammad.

There were also those who accepted the message of Islam for purely opportunistic reasons. The Meccans under the leadership of Sufyan, the scion of the Umayyads, certainly belonged to this group. When they found fighting against Muhammad futile, they joined him and remained in political and economic control of the new movement. They observed the laws of Islam and performed its rituals, but they were not converted men and would not think of sacrificing their personal gain for the sake of the faith.

There were still others who were brought into the realm of Islam by coercion. Most of these were the Bedouin tribes of Arabia, who were subdued by Muhammad but who had had to be reconquered by Abu Bakr. They were interested in fighting and booty and, as long as they were kept busy fighting the outsiders, they did not hamper the authorities in Medina. The Umayyads, like their predecessors, employed these tribesmen in wars of expansion and also used them against their rivals for the throne. The puritans of Islam hated the Umayyads and considered them a disgrace to the Islamic umma. These zealots for the purity of Islam took advantage of every opportunity to destroy the power of the Umayyads. The Umayyads, on the other hand, had control of the government and were able to win successive struggles against the claimants to the caliphate.

STRUGGLE AGAINST BYZANTIUM

The unfinished job of conquest, as far as the Arabs were concerned, was still the Byzantine Empire. Its riches beckoned the fighters of Islam. Mu'awiya, when he was governor of Syria, had been victorious against the Byzantines on land and on sea. But he was unable to take advantage of the victory, perhaps because of the civil war caused by the assassination of Uthman. During his struggle against Ali, Mu'awiya had even consented to buy peace by paying tribute to the Emperor Constans III (642–668).

Soon after he secured his position as Caliph, Mu'awiya opened hostilities against the Byzantines. One of his generals, later aided by Mu'awiya's son, Yazid, reached Chalcedon (modern Kadikoy) across the Bosporus from Constantinople in the winter of 668. The next spring they laid siege to the capital itself. The fortifications, however, proved impregnable and the Emperor, Constantine IV, too energetic for the Arabs to make any headway. The siege was discontinued but the expedition turned out to be of political value to the Caliph. Yazid was recognized as the hero of the siege, which made it easier for Mu'awiya to proclaim him the heir apparent to the caliphate.

The Umayyads, however, did not abandon their designs on the Byzantine Empire. In addition to a few engagements by sea, the raids over the borders of Asia Minor constituted a regular summer activity on the part of the Arabs.

The second assault upon Constantinople came during the reign of Caliph Sulayman (715–717). His brother, Maslama, occupied both sides of the Bosporus and laid siege to the capital from August 716 to September 717. Accounts of this engagement are plentiful. They speak of naphtha and special siege artillery used by the Arabs, as well as the chain across the Bosporus and the "Greek fire" used by the Byzantines against them. In the end, the new Emperor, Leo, a Syrian from Marash and the founder of a new dynasty, saved the capital. He was aided by famine and disease in the Arab camp, as well as by an exceptionally severe winter. Maslama, however, would not give up until ordered to do so by the new Caliph, Umar II.

The Arabs made still another attempt to capture Constantinople many years later, in 782, under the Abbasid Caliph Mahdi. This time, the Empress Irene hastened to ward off the danger by agreeing to pay tribute. Despite all these attempts, the Arabs were never able to gain a foothold in Asia Minor. The Byzantine Empire lasted, one way or the other, until 1453, when it was wiped out by the Ottoman Sultan Mehmed the Conqueror.

EXPANSION IN NORTH AFRICA AND SPAIN

In 670 the Arabs had built the garrison city of Qayruwan in Tunisia as a base for the conquest of North Africa, which they called *Ifriqiya*. In the ensuing 30 years the Arabs tried to oust the Byzantines from the region and to subdue the rebellious Berber tribes. By the end of the seventh century, the Muslim capture of Carthage terminated the Byzantine rule. Under the leadership of Musa, who was appointed governor in 708, all of North Africa from Egypt to the Atlantic came under Arab rule and was governed directly from Damascus instead of from Egypt as had previously been done.

The Berbers of North Africa belonged to what is known as the Hamitic branch of peoples and were probably akin to the Semites. Those living in coastal cities had become Christians and had produced a number of early Christian scholars, one of the most famous being St. Augustine. For the majority of the Berber tribes living in the hinterland, Christianity did not seem to offer an attraction. Even though the Berbers resisted the penetration of

Muslim Arabs, in the end they became adherents of Islam and joined the Arab armies for further conquest.

In 711, Tariq, one of Musa's Berber lieutenants, crossed into Spain at the head of an all-Berber raiding party. Tariq established his base near a rock which bears his name, Jabal al-Tariq, "Mount of Tariq," now known as Gibraltar. His adventure reveals the confused state of affairs in that country. What started as a raiding party in the spring of 711 resulted in the conquest of half of Spain by the end of the summer.

Jealous of the spectacular success of his henchmen, Musa crossed into Spain with 10,000 Arab-Syrian troops and conquered some of the cities Tariq had bypassed. He overtook Tariq in Toledo and roundly scolded him and put him in chains for acting without orders. From then on, the advance of the Muslims in Spain resembled a triumphant parade more than a war of conquest. In 713 Musa's army reached the Bay of Biscay.

By order of the Caliph Walid I, Musa left his son, Abd al-Aziz, in charge of the conquered territory and started back to Damascus together with Tariq. It was a triumphal procession with hundreds of captured Visigothic princes, maidens, slaves, and enormous amounts of booty. Soon after he arrived in Damascus, a new Caliph, Sulayman, attained the throne and gave Musa a taste of the same medicine the latter had given to Tariq. Musa was put in chains for "insubordination," his wealth was taken from him, and it is said that he died a beggar in an obscure corner of Hijaz.

In the meantime, the Muslims finished the conquest of Spain, which they called Al-Andalus (perhaps "the land of Vandals"). By 718, the Muslims crossed the Pyrenees and raided the French countryside and churches. It was not until 732, the hundredth anniversary of the death of Muhammad, that the Muslim army under Abd al-Rahman was defeated in the celebrated battle of Tours by Charles Martel. Despite later Muslim raids and occupations of French cities such as Avignon and Lyons, the Muslims were not henceforth considered a permanent threat to the security of western Europe.

The Muslims stayed in Spain for nearly 800 years. In 755, the Umayyads ousted from Damascus established a rival caliphate in Spain with their capital in Cordoba. For centuries, Spain was the channel through which Islamic influence flowed to the West. Spain is the only country conquered by the Arabs the majority of whose inhabitants did not become Muslim. It is also the only country which was reconquered totally by the Christians and the only country in which no Muslim community has remained. The story of Islam, mostly Berber and Syrian (Moorish), in Spain is a fascinating one which is outside the scope of this volume.

ADVANCE IN ASIA

The Umayyads, in addition to their struggle against the Byzantines and their conquest of North Africa and Spain, were able to pacify, at least for a time, the rebellious inhabitants of Iraq and Iran. They also got a foothold beyond the river Sir Darya (Jaxartes) in modern Uzbekistan, and made contact with the Turanians. This campaign was started during the caliphate of Abd al-Malik and concluded in the reign of Walid I. The mastermind behind these expeditions was Hajjaj ibn-Yusuf, the schoolmaster from Taif near Mecca. He is depicted as a bloodthirsty tyrant by the Persian historians and as a defender of the faith by the Arabs. He was fearless, cruel, and blindly loyal to the Umayyads. He destroyed the pretender to the throne who controlled Mecca for nine years. As viceroy of the East he saw many "heads ripe for cutting" and, according to all accounts, harvested 120,000 of them!

After pacifying Iran, he sent several thousand Arabs under the leadership of Qutayba who, after taking Marv and Balkh (in modern Afghanistan), crossed the Amu Darya (Greek, "Oxus"; Arabic, "Jayhun") and in a series of campaigns between 705 and 712 took Bokhara and Samarqand and Kharazm (Khiva), all in the modern Soviet Republic of Uzbekistan. Later he crossed the sister river to the north, Sir Darya (Greek, "Jaxartes"; Arabic, "Sayhun") into Turkish-Buddhist strongholds and exacted tribute from them.

Another general, Muhammad al-Thagafi, a son-in-law of Hajjaj, went south toward India and between 710 and 712 took Mokran, Baluchestan, Heydarabad, and went north along the Sind River to Multan in the Panjab. This part of India was gradually wrested from Hindu religious domination and became Islamic. In 1947, it became the core of the Muslim state of Pakistan.

With the downfall of the Umayyads the almost continuous expansion which had been started by Abu Bakr came to an end. The result was an immense empire extending from the Amu Darya to the Sudan. Remarkable as this achievement was, the empire started to disintegrate almost as soon as it reached this immense size. By the time the Abbasids came to power, the vast empire had already been divided. It was fragmented still more in the course of centuries, leaving behind only a dream of a united Islamic empire.

CHAPTER 7

INTERNAL DEVELOPMENT UNDER THE UMAYYADS

The almost continuous wars of expansion and the acquisition of enormous booty kept the Bedouin tribesmen both occupied and happy. By the middle of the eighth century, however, the tribes had spent their vigor. A large number of them had returned to their old haunts in the desert to enjoy their wealth. The rest had scattered to the four corners of the vast empire and had been assimilated by the people among whom they had settled.

The ruling dynasty, nevertheless, was beset by many problems, not the least of which was administration of the vast empire. Since the Arabs, in general, considered agriculture beneath their dignity and had little concern for the complexities of settled life, Mu'awiya and his successors had little choice but to use the conquered peoples, mainly Persians and Greeks, for purposes of administration. For example, it is said that Hisham (724–743), one of the three effective caliphs of the dynasty, had the political methods of the Sasanian kings translated for him from Pahlavi (middle Persian).

ADMINISTRATION

The empire was divided into five provinces: (1) Kufa, which was the base for Iraq, Iran, and the east; (2) Hijaz, for the Arabian peninsula; (3) Jazira, for Syria and the north; (4) Egypt; and (5) Ifriqiya, for North Africa and Spain. Each province had a viceroy called *amir* or *sahib*, who was appointed by the caliph. The viceroy had complete control of the affairs of his province. He appointed agents and judges and was responsible for the fiscal administration of the province, sending the surplus taxes to the capital in Damascus. More often than not the caliph sent his own tax collector, but toward the end of the Umayyad period the caliphs were so weak that the viceroys were de facto rulers. The viceroys amassed great wealth and the only indication that they were under the authority of the caliph occurred every Friday when the name of the caliph was specially mentioned in prayers.

The judges held court only for the Muslims. The non-Muslims held separate courts according to their religious laws. The judges also administered the affairs of the religious charitable foundations, *waqf*, which were financed by the faithful, in addition to the estates of orphans.

For decades the Umayyads continued using the Byzantine and Persian coins. This was perhaps because these coins were adequate in quantity. Furthermore, they were too busy fighting to pay attention to such matters. There must have been some reluctance on the part of the early caliphs to ignore the iconoclasm of Islam and to engrave an image on a coin. Abd al-Malik (685–705) was the first to mint new coins which bore his own image and verses from the Koran. The Persians under the Sasanid king, Khosro Anushiravan, had a comparatively simple tax system. The nobles, knights, scribes, and servants of the king were exempt from taxation. All males who had come of age, other than the above, paid a head tax. The cultivators and merchants paid a certain percentage of their income in kind or cash. The early caliphs thus used a Muslim version of the Persian system of taxation. Ordinarily the Arab Muslims, like the Persian nobility, were exempt from taxation. The non-Muslims or the "people of the book" paid the regular poll tax. The status of cultivators, who during the Umayyad period were almost all non-Arabs (Umar had forbidden the Arabs to own land), was not changed at all. They continued to pay the same tax which they had been paying to the same Persian or Byzantine agents. Consequently, the Arabs, or Islam for that matter, did not change the land tenure system prevalent in the Byzantine and the Persian Empires and it remained substantially the same until modern times.

This system of land holdings, however, did not remain as simple as the Arabs thought it would. In the first place the law prohibiting Arabs from holding land outside of Arabia was both impractical and unpopular. Uthman looked the other way when members of his own family began to acquire land. The practice continued to increase so much so that during the Umayyad period Arabs not only acquired land of their own but "leased" public domain from the government and sold it to others as private property. Being Arabs and Muslims, they did not pay taxes on their private property.

In the second place, the early Arab leaders were caught between the demands of Islam for egalitarianism among all Muslims regardless of nationality, and their own nationalistic feelings. They could not make up their minds whether all Muslims should be exempt from taxation or whether only Arab Muslims should be so privileged. Umar, as has been noted, took the chauvinistic approach, while Ali believed more in the egalitarian Islamic approach. The early Umayyads believed in the theory of the superiority of the Arabs and tried to secure special privileges for them. As long as the advancing Muslim armies continued to send booty back to the capital, it did not make much difference who paid taxes and who was exempt. The ruling class had enough wealth, with some to spare. But during the first quarter of the eighth century, when expansion slackened and economic conditions were stabilized, the government began to feel the pinch.

Umar II (717–720), the most devout caliph among the Umayyads, believed that God had appointed him caliph, and that a caliph's primary responsibility was to call people to Islam, not to collect taxes. Consequently, he exempted all Muslims from taxation. The status of the poll tax, however, remained in a state of flux for some time. This state of affairs left the non-Muslims and non-Arab gentry in a precarious economic situation, for they did not know from one caliph to another how they would be taxed. Dissatisfaction was rampant in many parts of the empire, especially in Iran, and contributed in no small way to the downfall of the Umayyads.

LIFE AND LEISURE

Emerging from the harsh and barren life of the desert into the glitter and sophistication of Byzantine and Persian urban centers; falling, as it were, into the lap of luxury from the tent of poverty; being the recipients of so much wealth; and becoming masters of so many slaves, male and female: all this could not but leave its imprint upon the manners and mores of the Arabs. The simple virtues preached by Islam as practiced by Muhammad and the Orthodox Caliphs were too confining to be practical for these affluent Arabs. Accordingly, they satisfied themselves by paying lip service to these virtues and, while observing the outward rituals of piety, immersed themselves in their newly found paradise of pleasure. Beginning with Uthman, who was not inattentive to the demands of the good life, and especially the Umayyad caliphs and their lieutenants, these conquerers of the vast domain could have paraphrased a statement attributed to Pope Leo X (1513–1521) to read, "Allah has given us the empire, let us enjoy it."

Abul Faraj al-Isfahani (897–967), who claimed lineal descent from Marwan II, the last Umayyad caliph, wrote a book called *Kitab al-Aghani* (*Book of Songs*), which became a veritable "best seller." People enjoyed reading the book as much as the author must have enjoyed writing it. Painstakingly, if not perhaps in a scholarly fashion, he went about collecting anecdotes, songs, stories, poems, games, pastimes, habits, jokes, and anything about the Arabs of the Umayyad and Abbasid periods which "entertained the hearers." He was a mixture of an anthropologist, literary and musical anthologist, and a keyhole observer. Ibn Khaldun, the great Muslim historian, regards the book as the "social register of the Arabs."

No one, be he a caliph or a commoner, escaped Isfahani's scrutiny. He relates how Mu'awiya entertained himself in the evenings by listening to stories and poems and drinking rose sherbet. Isfahani, as well as others, describes the wine drinking habits of the caliphs. It is said that Yazid drank every day; Walid I, every other day; Hisham, every Friday after prayers; Abd al-Malik, once a month; and the champion of them all, Walid II, used to swim in a pool of wine gulping at every stroke!

The wealthy Arabs loved to hunt and race horses, as both sports were native to Arabia. Yazid I had hunting dogs with gold anklets and each dog had a special caretaker. The less wealthy used to enjoy cockfights and games of dice.

The games of chess, originally from India, and backgammon were brought from Iran. The modern Arabs playing backgammon (Persian, *nard*; Arabic, *tawla*) always count in Persian. Later both of these games were introduced in Europe where the word "rook" is Persian *rokh* and "checkmate" is Persian *shahmat* (the king is confounded). Somehow the piece called *Fil* (elephant) in Persian, Arabic *al-fil*, and Spanish *elalfil*, had become "bishop" in English, while the Persian *vazir* has turned in English into "queen."

The most revealing information given by the author of *Kitab al-Aghani* is the transformation of the holy cities of Mecca and Medina into centers of leisure, pleasure, and vice. A large number of Arabs who received very lucrative pensions went "home" to the central cities of Arabia to enjoy themselves. There were clubs and cabarets, houses of ill-repute and elegant salons, belly dancers, serious musicians, and songsters, from all parts of the empire. Slave girls by the scores waited to entertain their masters, who reclined on cushions and drank wine from silver or golden goblets—all within a stone's throw of the Ka'ba and the tomb of the Prophet.

No less a personage than Sukayna (Sakineh to non-Arabs), the daughter of Imam Husayn and the great-granddaughter of the Prophet, was the center of attraction in Medina. Her dazzling beauty attracted numerous husbands, all on her terms; her charms captivated many; and her wit and practical jokes were the talk of the town. She was the patroness of music (a profession denounced by the Prophet) and an arbiter of fashion. Her hairdo was imitated by the ladies of the realm.

Not to be outdone, the summer resort of Taif, near Mecca, had its own attraction in the person of Ayisha, whose father was a companion of the Prophet and whose mother was the daughter of Abu Bakr, the first caliph. She did not marry as often as Sukayna but she did the unusual by refusing to veil herself on the grounds that people should see her beauty and praise the handiwork of Allah.

Thousands of pilgrims who poured into the two cities both contributed to the gaity and enjoyed these pleasant opportunities. There were, no doubt, those who gaped in bewilderment at the shocking spectacles and shook their heads in disapproval.

CLAIMANTS FOR THE CALIPHATE

Underneath the glittering appearance of leisure and gaity there was trouble. Among other things, the Umayyads were beset by two primary problems. One of them was the perennial question of succession to the caliphate, complicated by rival claimants to the high office. The death of Ali and the subsequent accession of Mu'awiya to the caliphate had settled the question in the mind of the majority of the Muslims that only a member of the Quraysh could aspire to the high office. The Kharijite notion that anyone with proper spiritual and moral qualifications could become a caliph regardless of his lineage had been rejected. The legitimist notion that the caliphate was the sole prerogative of the house of Ali had only a minority of followers. The fact that a majority upheld the Quraysh claim did not solve the problem, for there were rivals among the Quraysh, each of whom considered himself best suited for the position. It was generally agreed among the Quraysh tribesmen out of power that the Umayyads were the least deserving to occupy the caliphate. It was the Umayyads who had ousted the Prophet from Mecca, who had fought against him, and who had accepted Islam as a last resort.

Added to this animosity towards the Umayyads was the resurgence of the native Arab tribalism. This had been temporarily replaced by loyalty to Islam, although it had been allowed to reassert itself by Uthman and had come to full bloom at the time of the Umayyads. In the new society this tribal loyalty took the form of a bitter rivalry between the north Arabs and the south Arabs. The northerners were usually called the Qaysites and the southerners the Kalbites or Yamanites. The struggle between the two was long and bitter, and is considered one of the causes of the downfall of the Umayyads. The Sufyanid branch of the dynasty came to power with the help of the southerners, whereas Marwan I asserted his supremacy with the aid of the northerners. The later Umayyad caliphs went to one side or the other, depending upon which side their mothers belonged, and generally acted as heads of feuding families rather than as leaders of an empire.

The death of Ali did not end the claim of his partisans, namely that the caliphate belonged to the descendants of the Prophet through his daughter, Fatima. Consequently, the two sons of Ali, Hasan and Husayn, were possible rallying points for the opponents of the Umayyads. Hasan, the older brother, who seemed to have been more interested in maintaining a harem than in claiming an empire, was persuaded by Mu'awiya to retire for life to a villa outside Medina with an annual stipend of 5,000,000 dirhams. It is said that he contracted and broke some one hundred marriages which won him the title of *mitlaq*, "the divorcer." He was allegedly poisoned in 699, probably on account of some harem jealousy. The Shi'is, however, believe that he was killed by Mu'awiya and consider Hasan as an Imam and a martyr.

The younger brother, Husayn, was of a different mettle. He was ambitious and gave vigorous leadership to the opposition which had its center of strength around the town of Kufa at the head of the Persian Gulf. In 680, when Yazid became caliph, Husayn refused to acknowledge Yazid and secretly left Medina to join his own followers in Kufa, who had already proclaimed him caliph. Unfortunately for Husayn, the plot was discovered and the small band, including women and children, was ambushed in Karbala, an oasis south of modern

Baghdad. Most of the men were killed; Husayn, the grandson of the Prophet, was beheaded; and the women and children were taken captive.

This was the culmination of a series of unsuccessful political moves on the part of the partisans of Ali to secure the caliphate. Very likely in any other situation the event of Karbala would have been recorded as another political failure. Indeed, the incident at the time did not create much excitement. In the subsequent history of Islam, however, the ambush at Karbala assumed important religious significance. Ali and Husayn became more formidable foes of the established caliphate through their deaths than through their lives. Husayn came to be considered the prince of the martyrs and the anniversary of his death on the tenth of Muharram (680) became a rallying occasion for the opponents of the caliphate. The religious processions commemorating the event are reminiscent of similar processions and self-mortifications which were carried on in Mesopotamia for the death of the god Tammuz. With a cause and three martyrs, the followers of Ali separated themselves from the main body of Islam and formed a religio-political community with a theology and philosophy of their own.

The house of Ali was not the only claimant of the caliphate. It will be remembered that one of the persons disputing the caliphate with Ali was Zubayr, who died in this attempt. His son, Abdullah (the nephew of Ayisha, the wife of Muhammad), at first sided with Husayn. After the latter's tragic death, he claimed the office for himself.

Yazid sent an expedition against Abdullah to Medina and Mecca in 683, two cities in which the latter had strong support. Mecca was besieged and bombarded, causing the Ka'ba to be burned to the ground and the Black Stone to be split into three pieces. In the meantime, Yazid died, and the expedition was inconclusive. Abdullah was acknowledged as caliph in Hijaz, Iraq, and Egypt. To the population, tired of the bloody feuds, Abdullah ibn-Zubayr was a happy compromise between the unpopular Umayyads and the extremist claims of the house of Ali. Furthermore, the death of Yazid had sparked rivalry within the Umayyad camp. Had Abdullah been willing to remove his capital from Medina to Damascus, he would have been acknowledged even in Syria. He belonged, however, to that group of Muslims who believed that Mecca and Medina should remain as the spiritual and political centers of Islam. He was not willing to move the center of power to Damascus, which was a non-Arab city.

In the meantime, Marwan, the founder of the Marwanid branch of the Umayyads, had come to power in Damascus with the help of the southern Arabs and had defeated the nothern Arabs who supported Abdullah at Marj Rabit in 684. Abdullah, however, continued as caliph in Hijaz until 692, when the notorious Hajjaj defeated him in the second siege of Mecca. Hajjaj sent Abdullah's head to Damascus. With the death of Abdullah, the influence of the old-school Muslims came to an end, and with it the supremacy of the Arabian peninsula, "the Cradle of Islam."

ARAB VERSUS NON-ARAB MUSLIMS

At the bottom of the Muslim society in the newly formed empire were the slaves—white, black, and yellow—who were brought from territories extending from Turkistan to central Africa and from Iran to Spain and France. Islam did not abolish slavery. Although Islamic law forbade the enslavement of other Muslims, apparently those who adopted Islam in slavery were not set free. Judging by the number of slaves mentioned by historians, even allowing for exaggerations, one has to conclude that Muslim society was based, to some degree, on a slave economy. Even a private in the army is said to have had slaves to wait upon him.

Slave trading was very active and lucrative and remained so until the nineteenth and, in some parts of Arabia, the twentieth century. Legal marriage between Muslims and slaves was forbidden but concubinage was allowed and was very popular. The children of such a union were the master's and were considered free. It should be noted, however, that Islam considered the liberating of slaves efficacious for gaining reward in after-life, and the pious freed their slaves now and then.

The next level above the slaves was occupied by the *dhimmi*, members of the tolerated religions which were Jews, Christians, and Sabians, as mentioned originally in the Koran. Later when the Arab leaders realized that they could not possibly kill all those who were not considered "people of the book" by the Koran, the privilege of being considered "people of the book" was extended to cover the Zoroastrians of Iran and Berbers of North Africa[1] Since a *dhimmi* was not permitted to join the Muslim army because the army fought for the propagation of Islam, he paid *jizya*, a poll tax. The *dhimmi* was judged in his own religious court and was allowed to practice his religion. On occasions some *dhimmi* held important public offices, but they were the exceptions rather than the rule. In general, however, the non-Muslim was a third class citizen who was restricted in his dress, hairdo, manner of riding, and holding of public office. His witness was not admitted in a Muslim court. Pious caliphs like Umar II tried to force the conversion of the *dhimmi* through imposing very stringent regulations and even persecution. Large numbers, in the course of time, became Muslims to escape such humiliations.

Next above the *dhimmis* were the non-Arab Muslims called *mawali*, or clients. It was their status *vis-à-vis* the Arab Muslims which became the bone of contention and the source of so much discontent and rebellion. The primary burden of being non-Arab Muslims was borne by the Persians, for they constituted the most important group among the *mawali*. *Ajam*, the Arabic word for "non-Arab," as used by historians, almost always refers to a Persian. Another name for Iran among the Arabs even to this day is "the country of the Ajam."

These people, who had accepted Islam out of either conviction, force, or expediency, naturally placed the broadest interpretation on the egalitarian

[1] See above, p. 44.

statements of the Koran. The Arabs, on the other hand, following the leadership of Umar I, were inclined to interpret the Koran from a more limited point of view. Ummayyad society was based on the supremacy of the Arabs, and the new plutocrats hardly wanted to share their new privileges with the converts. That the Arabs could not manage without the converts in anything except perhaps in military matters caused them to have a feeling of inferiority. They tried to compensate for this inferiority by asserting Arab national superiority and by forcing the notion on the conquered peoples. The non-Arabs were taxed heavily, forbidden marriage with the Arabs, humiliated in many ways, and were called "clients" of the Arabs.

The most chauvinistic of the Umayyad caliphs was perhaps Abd al-Malik, who with the effective help of his henchman, Hajjaj, the viceroy of Iran, ordered that all the books of the administration be henceforth written in Arabic rather than in Persian and Greek. He issued new coins with Arabic inscriptions and forced the people to use Arabic in their correspondence. It is said the Hajjaj beheaded thousands who continued to write in Persian. In the *Aghani* we read that the caliphs tortured any Persian who praised his own country. The author of the *History of Bokhara*, reports that Persians who knew too little Arabic to pray in that language lined in rows and repeated the words of the prayer after an Arab. This seems to indicate that in early times the converts were allowed to say their prayers in their own language.

These humiliations, of course, were bitterly resented by all the *mawali*, especially the Persians. As a result, the Persians espoused any cause, be it Shi'a or Kharijite or whatever, provided it was against the Umayyads. The heavy hands of Hajjaj secured peace for a few years but the Umayyad Dynasty was beset with too many problems to last long.

Around 740 the Abbasids, descendants of Abbas, an uncle of the Prophet, claimed their right to the caliphate. In a short while, the Shi'is, the Persians, and all others who, for one reason or another, were dissatisfied with the Umayyads, rallied to the Abbasids. In 747, the legendary young Persian, Abu Muslim Khorasani, unfurled the black flag of the Abbasids. Black had also been the color of the Prophet's flag. Khorasani headed an army made up of Persians which took Marv, the capital of Khorasan. Two years later, Iraq was taken and on Thursday, October 30, 749, Abul Abbas, the great-great-grandson of Abbas, was proclaimed caliph in Kufa. Marwan II, the last of the Umayyads, met the insurgents on the banks of the Greater Zab in January 750 and was decisively defeated. In April of that year, Damascus fell.

Members of the Umayyad Dynasty, and their relatives and friends, were hunted and put to the sword. However, at least one prince, Abd al-Rahman, the grandson of Hisham, escaped and reached Spain after a series of harrowing experiences. Here he established the Umayyad caliphate of Spain with Cordoba as his capital.

The coming of the Abbasids ushered in a new era. The dream of Umar I to create a United Arab Empire had failed. The victory of the Abbasids resulted in the creation of two rival empires. Even the Muslim umma had been broken by war and strife. The center of gravity moved from Syria to Iran. The new capital was Kufa on the border of Iran. Non-Arabs felt a sense of liberation and Persians occupied the chief positions in the new government. The idea of Arab supremacy receded to the desert with the Arabs, not be heard of again until in the more inclusive form of "pan-Arabism" in the twentieth century. The Arabs went but Islam remained, and under the guise of Islam marched many ideas and systems, sometimes Persian, sometimes Ottoman, and sometimes Indian.

CHAPTER 8

THE ABBASID GOVERNMENT
AND SOCIETY

The history of the Abbasid Caliphate may be divided into two parts. The first extends from 750 to 842 and the second from 842 to the sack of Baghdad by the Mongol, Hulagu, in 1258. Two of the greatest caliphs in the Abbasid line, Harun al-Rashid and Ma'mun, belong to the first period. The other six caliphs, while not so illustrious as Rashid and Ma'mun, were at least masters of their own empire and had control over the affairs of the state. For all practical purposes it may be claimed that the Abbasid line, insofar as power was concerned, ended in 842. The caliphs after this date were mere figureheads who were neither in control of the empire nor masters even of their own immediate households. Some of these caliphs were so degenerate and weak that even in the capital city of Baghdad they were no more than exalted prisoners under the control of strong men. These strong men sometimes were Persians but most of the time were Turks who elevated and dethroned the caliphs at will and ordered almost every aspect of their lives. Outside of Baghdad and farther away from the seat of authority, the empire was so divided that sometimes not even the strong men who controlled the caliphs had any influence, let alone the weak caliphs themselves. There arose, both east and west of Baghdad, increasing numbers of small and large principalities that functioned like independent states without regard to the existence of the caliph.

When he was proclaimed caliph, Abul Abbas made an inaugural speech in the mosque at Kufa and in the course of the ceremony gave himself the title of al-Saffah, popularly translated as "blood-letter." In doing so, he started two trends. Every one of the subsequent Abbasid caliphs also gave himself a title, such as Mansur, Mahdi, Rashid, etc. Indeed, the caliphs are known mainly by their titles. The second trend was that the executioner standing beside the caliph became a permanent fixture of the Abbasid court.

THE EARLY ABBASIDS AND THEIR RELATION
WITH MUHAMMAD AND THE QURAYSH TRIBE

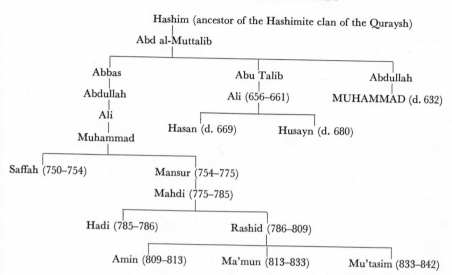

Hashim (ancestor of the Hashimite clan of the Quraysh)
Abd al-Muttalib

Abbas — Abu Talib — Abdullah

Abdullah — Ali (656–661) — MUHAMMAD (d. 632)

Ali

Hasan (d. 669)   Husayn (d. 680)

Muhammad

Saffah (750–754)   Mansur (754–775)

Mahdi (775–785)

Hadi (785–786)   Rashid (786–809)

Amin (809–813)   Ma'mun (813–833)   Mu'tasim (833–842)

It will be remembered that the Abbasids originally came to power by utilizing the discontent of the different segments of the empire such as the Shi'is, the Kharijites, the religiously orthodox, the Persians, and other malcontents. To each group, the Abbasids promised the right thing so that each group helped them to come to power in order to achieve its own ends. The stakes were high and there were no holds barred.

No sooner was the new caliphate established than Saffah and the more unscrupulous Mansur, who was the real founder of the Abbasid Dynasty, began to rid themselves of those who had been their allies against the Umayyads. In typical style, the Abbasids sided with one group to get rid of the others. One of the last and most important of these allies of the Abbasids was the legendary Abu Muslim Khorasani. The real name of this remarkable Persian was Behzadan. He outwardly professed Islam but was accused of being a Zoroastrian. In any event, he decided to side with the Abbasid claimants and so unfurled their black flag. Apparently, his soldiers wore black uniforms and were known as "Black Shirts." Historians agree that the Abbasids owed their success in a large part to Abu Muslim and his Persian troops. It is quite likely that he wanted to get rid of the Abbasids after using them to destroy the Umayyads. Apparently the Abbasids had a similar plan. They wanted to rid themselves of Abu Muslim after they had used him to defeat the Umayyads. The Abbasids moved faster to implement their plan. Mansur invited Abu Muslim to his own house for a feast in 754 and had him put to death. This treachery caused such an uproar in Iran, especially in Khorasan, that it took the Abbasids nearly a century to put the upheaval down.

One of the most important issues which won the Abbasids the support of the orthodox segment of the population was the alleged lack of religious zeal on the part of the Umayyads. The Abbasids promised a more theocratic Muslim state as opposed to the worldliness of the Umayyads. This promise they proceeded to fulfill. To be sure, the Abbasids were not any less worldly than their Umayyad cousins, but they did keep the pretense of religiosity. They catered to the wishes of the religious leaders, imposed Islam upon the masses, became dogmatic and were the first in Islam to organize an inquisition. As a token of their religiosity, the Abbasid caliphs used to wear the mantle of the Prophet on ceremonial occasions and for Friday prayers. The weaker the Abbasid caliphs became politically the more pretentious they became religiously. True to the practice of empty piety, the caliphs from Mu'tasim added on the word *Allah* at the end of their names, such as *al-Mu-tasim Bi-Allah*, (pronounced Billah).

At the time of the shift in power from the Umayyads to the Abbasids, a large segment of the population of Iran, especially in the rural areas, was still non-Muslim. With few exceptions, the Umayyads believed in Arab supremacy and their policies conflicted with the interests of the upper-class Persians. On the whole, the masses had been left alone. The Abbasids, however, having put aside Arab supremacy, emphasized religion and began to impose it upon the masses of the population. The various groups who had helped the Abbasids to come to power were thwarted in their aims and they all turned against the established order. The strongest and the most numerous among these groups were the Persians who became one of the chief opponents of the Abbasids, as they had been of the Umayyads. Persian opposition took three forms—religious, political, and literary—but the central aim remained unchanged: namely, freedom from Arab rule.

The first form of Persian opposition was religious. Since the religious policy of the Abbasids uprooted the life and mores of the masses, the common people protested through the only means at their disposal. They engaged in different religious uprisings. Soon after the murder of Abu Muslim, Sinbad the Magian,' a good friend of the deceased, set out in 755 to destroy the Ka'ba. The caliph had little difficulty in destroying him. In 767, however, another individual by the name of Ostadsis claimed to be a prophet and a reincarnation of Abu Muslim. Ostadsis was followed by several other prophets, all of whom found ready adherents among the frustrated and resentful population and who led armed uprisings against the caliphate. The most famous of these prophets was a man by the name of Muqanna, the "Veiled Prophet of Khorasan," who rebelled against the caliph in 776. His followers, who numbered in the thousands, wore white garments and were called the "White Shirts." They robbed caravans, destroyed mosques, and killed those who gave the call to prayer and those who responded to the call. Muqanna claimed that Abu Muslim was god and had been reincarnated in himself, the Veiled Prophet. His rebellion was so destructive that the Caliph Mahdi had to send several expeditions against him. Most Muslim historians devote pages to the Veiled Prophet.[1]

If the uprising of the Veiled Prophet was bizarre and confused, the rebellion of Babak Khorramdin was orderly and serious. Even though some sixty years had passed since the murder of Abu Muslim, Babak used this incident to arouse his own followers. Babak's religion was a mixture of Zoroastrianism and Mazdakism called Khorramdin, "good religion." His followers were called "people of good religion" and more popularly "red shirts" because of their uniform. His movements was also anti-Islamic and for over twenty years he was a thorn in the flesh of two caliphs, Ma'mun and Mu'tasim.

Babak was originally probably a shepherd from Azarbaijan. The caliphs sent many expeditions against him. It was not until 840 that Afshin, a Persian general in the service of Mu'tasim, captured Babak and brought him to Samarra, the residence of the Abbasids. Babak was placed on an elephant and paraded in the city. The caliph ordered him decapitated. After one arm was cut off, Babak smeared his face with the blood of the stump. He explained that loss of blood would make him pale and he did not want the onlookers to see him in that condition lest they think that he became pale from fear. Thereupon he was cut to pieces.[2]

The second form of Persian opposition to the Abbasid power was political. Afshin, the Persian general who captured Babak, was typical of this group. As a Persian aristocrat, he was anti-Arab but did not like the popular uprisings of the masses. Indeed, the upper class Persians were not in the habit of caring for the masses. They felt that they could accomplish their anti-Arab aims subtly from within and through political control. Such popular uprisings as Babak's would only confuse the issue as far as the Persian aristocrats were concerned.

The aristocrats were quite successful in their scheme and penetrated every aspect of the Abbasid government and society. In stark contrast with the Umayyads, the Abbasids were so immersed in things Persian that some have referred to the early Abbasid caliphs as "Sasanid kings with Arab blood." When one considers that Persians occupied positions of power and responsibility, and Persian culture, customs, and even costume became the vogue, the above statement is not too much of an exaggeration.

---

[1] In St. Louis and Kansas City, Missouri, there is a fraternal organization called "The Veiled Prophets of Khorasan." They believe that the "Veiled Prophet" was a mythical figure in the "never, never land of Khorasan." Perhaps this organization gets its name from Thomas Moore's story "Lalla Rookh," whose hero is the Veiled Prophet of Khorasan.

[2] Ironically, not long afterwards, Afshin himself was tried and executed for heresy. In the court he was accused of beating two Imams; of having Zoroastrian scriptures in an honored place in his house; and of not being circumcised. He admitted all these charges.

At the very beginning Saffah instituted the office of the grand vazir. The grand vazir acted in all matters for the person of the caliph and had practically unlimited power. A dictum of the Abbasids said that he who obeys the vazir has obeyed the caliph and he who obeys the caliph has obeyed God!

The first occupant of the office of grand vazir was Khalid ibn-Barmak, the head of a remarkable family which held the grand vazirate for over half a century. Khalid was a Persian from Balkh whose father was a priest, *barmak*, in a Buddhist monastery. Though Persian and a Shi'i, Khalid, his son Yahya, and Yahya's sons Fadl and Ja'far were successive vazirs under the first five caliphs. The power of the Barmakids, and their generosity, wealth, and sumptuous living, are part of the stories of the *Arabian Nights*. They had charge of the civil and military affairs and appointed and deposed governors and generals at will. Even candidates for the position of chamberlain to the caliph had to meet their approval. Allegedly, Harun al-Rashid could not withdraw money from the treasury without their approval. A caliph of Harun's temperament, however, could not share power with anyone. Harun, his sister Abbasa, and Ja'far, the son of Yahya, had grown up together and were boon companions. Nevertheless, the power of the Barmakids and their Shi'a faith, coupled with a probable scandal involving Abbasa and Ja'far, brought an end to their house. Ja'far was executed and Yahya and Fadl died in prison. However, this was not the end of the Vazirate or of the Persian influence.

The third form of Persian opposition to the Abbasid power was literary. It is called the *Shu'ubiya* movement. It was started during the Umayyad Dynasty by non-Arab Muslims (Persian and non-Persian) to combat the claims of national superiority on the part of the Arabs. Most of the proponents of the movement were the non-Arab secretaries in government offices. They wrote both negatively against the Arabs and also positively extolling the achievements of their own nationality.

Under the Abbasids, the Shu'ubiya had become a Persian literary movement whose purpose was, through original writing and especially translation of Persian books, to revive the spirit of the Persian culture and to reestablish the Persian social structure and tradition. They were *avant-garde* literary critics who encouraged the spirit of skepticism in religion and morals and espoused heretical causes. There is not much doubt that some of them were anti-Islamic in subtle ways. Two of their members, the literary genius ibn-Muqaffa and the blind poet, Bashshar ibn-Burd, were executed for heresy by the caliphs Mansur and Mahdi, respectively.

GOVERNMENT AND ADMINISTRATION

Neither Saffah nor Mansur felt secure in Kufa. Saffah moved to nearby Hashimiya and Mansur decided to build a new capital on the site of a little Persian village on the Tigris named Baghdad, "God-given." This city, with its numerous parks, beautiful gardens, spacious palaces, thousands of mosques and public baths, became world famous as the center of power, learning, commerce, and leisure, as well as the scene of the stories of Scheherazade (Shahrzad) in *The Thousand and One Nights*. All roads led to Baghdad and one could literally see people from all parts of the known world of the time in the streets of Baghdad. The city was rich and gaudy and the caliphs and their vazirs spent money in unprecedented quantities. For example, Zubayda, the wife of Harun al-Rashid, would not serve food except on gold plates and would not wear shoes unless they were studded with precious stones. Once she spent three million dinars for a pilgrimage to Mecca. At the wedding of the heir presumptive, Ma'mun, and his bride, Puran, a thousand matched pearls were showered upon the couple as they sat upon a bejewelled golden divan. Gifts of several slave girls at a time and thousands of gold pieces to poets, jesters, and other flatterers were quite common.

Abu Nuwas, the libertine poet and close friend of Harun was telling the truth when he sang:

> *"Youth and I, we ran*
> *a headlong race of pleasure*
> *No recorded sin*
> *but soon I took its measure."*

Very likely Harun was present when his comrade sang:

> *"Come, Sulaiman, sing to me*
> *And the wine, quick, bring to me!*
> *Lo, already dawn is here*
> *In golden mantle clear.*
> *Whilst the flask goes twinkling round,*
> *Pour me a cup that leaves me drowned*
> *With oblivion, how'er, so high*
> *Let the shrill muezzin cry!*

Harun had also his critic in another poet, Abu al-Atahiya, who saw doom in all that glittered and warned the Caliph:

> *"Live securely as you wish;*
> *the palace heights are safe enough.*
> *With pleasure flooding day and night,*
> *and the smooth proves sweeter than the rough.*
> *But when your breath begins to clog*
> *in sharp contractions of your lungs,*
> *Then know for certain, my dear Sire,*
> *Your life was vain as idle tongues."*[3]

Foreign dignitaries seeking audience with the caliph were so dazzled by the

---

[3] The three poems are found in *Anthology of Islamic Literature*, ed. by James Kritzeck, pp. 86–88.

wealth and beauty of the rooms that often they would mistake the office of the chamberlain as the audience hall! In such surroundings did the early Abbasids govern their far-flung empire.

The country was administered by a council presided over by the grand vazir. The members of the council were the heads of different administrative departments, sometimes called vazirs; the chief justice, and the commander of the army. One of the most important departments of the administration was the Department of Taxation. Since there was no booty from conquest the state had to have revenue from land which had been conquered. Theoretically all land belonged to the Muslim community, *umma*, but in practice there were six types of land. (1) Land which belonged to the caliph personally. He paid no tax to the state except the religious Zakah or tithe (ushr). (2) Land which was given to soldiers in return for military service. These paid a land tax to the state. (3) Uncultivated land which was under the direction of the caliph and could be given by him to anyone. (4) Land, the original owners of which had been driven away and which had been given to Muslims. They did not pay taxes but only Zakah. (5) Land, the original owners of which had come back or had not been driven away. They had to pay a land tax even after conversion to Islam. (6) Land belonging to persons having a special treaty relationship with the state, who paid a stipulated sum.

There was also a special tax on business profits but it is difficult to ascertain the proportion. Quite characteristically, the merchants complained that "one third" of their wealth went to the government. Other sources of revenue were the poll tax from non-Muslims, tribute, and sometimes booty. The practice of extortion was quite common. Indeed, there was a Bureau of Confiscations. Each official from the caliph down would confiscate the property of a person below him who was guilty of some charge or who had fallen out of grace. Theoretically, the public treasury, *bayt al-mal*, had two accounts, one for the caliph and one for the state, but in reality the caliph had control of both. In theory also, all taxes received from Muslims were to be spent for the benefit of Muslims such as the poor, orphans, strangers, and war. According to information available, when the first Abbasid caliph died he left "four shirts and five pairs of trousers," but when Mansur, the second caliph, died he left 600,000 dinars. In the early Abbasid period the budget was balanced, but by 908 such was not the case, and it got worse as time passed.

Two of the most important items of expenditure were the royal household and the royal bodyguard. The precarious position of the caliph is shown by the fact that in 867 the cost of the bodyguard was 200,000,000 dinars, or twice the annual land tax of the whole empire. The wealthy citizens were made to pay the difference. Other items of expenditure were the care of the Holy Cities, frontier posts, stipends for members of the Hashimite clan, and salaries for personnel.

Another important department was the postal service, *barid*, an institution nherited from the Sasanids by Umayyads and enlarged by Yahya Barmaki to erve the public. Trunk roads connected important centers of the empire, aravanserais dotted the roads, and a postal timetable was kept in Baghdad or the whole realm. Interestingly enough, one of the functions of the Post Office was intelligence service. Then as now, the service used merchants, ravelers, venders, etc., for espionage, internal and foreign. Perhaps the only difference was that the Abbasid chief of the intelligence used a large number of old women in his service!

Other departments of administration were audit, chancery, and police. One of the functionaries of the Police Department was the *muhtasib*, who was n charge of public morals and religious observance. The courts were under the upervision of the Chief Justice in the capital, whose representative in every ity was the judge, *qadi*. The qadi was versed in Islamic canon law, *shari'a*, nd presided in the local courts. He also was in charge of the religious endowments, settlement of property for orphans and minors, marriage and divorce ontracts, and inheritance. In connection with the Department of Justice there vas a Bureau of Inspection which was concerned with matters such as the yranny of officials, complaints on taxes, enforcement of court decisions, and the are of public worship.

The Abbasids, like the Umayyads, were confronted with the everpresent problem of succession. The Umayyad practice of appointment by the caliph ontinued, but it did not help the Abbasids any more than it had the Umayads. The most serious incident occurred after the death of Harun al-Rashid. He had designated both of his sons to succeed him in order of age, first Amin and then Ma'mun. Ma'mun, whose mother and wife were both Persians, claimed the caliphate with the full support of the Persians. He marched to Baghdad and assumed the caliphate after killing his brother. Four years later, however, he shocked the capital by raising the green flag of the Shi'is and by designating Ali al-Rida, the eighth Shi'i Imam, as heir to the throne. He was forced to leave the capital and after two years of struggle recanted. He egained the caliphate and, reputedly, ordered the death of the Imam Rida n Khorasan. He then sent his trusted general Tahir back to Khorasan to quell he rebellion caused by the death of the Imam. Tahir went to his native Khorasan and established the first independent principality in the East and dropped the name of the caliph from Friday prayers.

COMMERCE, INDUSTRY, AND AGRICULTURE

Arabs disdained agriculture but not business. The Prophet himself was a uccessful merchant and Islam has always had a high regard for merchants. With ports like Baghdad, Basra, Siraf, Alexandria, and Cairo, there was brisk business activity within the empire as well as with the outside world. Chinese hips were not an uncommon sight at the wharves of Baghdad. Caravan routes onnected the four corners of the empire, distributing products from one section o another. Processions of caravans carried goods such as rice, linen, silk, wine, brocades, pearls, glass, metal, fruit, perfume, marble, carpets, tables, cushions, frying pans, trays, bowls, drugs, and countless other commodities. Foreign trade with all parts of the world, with the exception of south Europe, was brisk and profitable. Muslims established a colony of merchants in China from where they brought porcelain and silk. From India they imported spices and dyes. They dealt in fur with Russia and in ivory with Africa. The discovery of Abbasid coins in Russia and Germany attests to the existence of an international trade.

Industry had to produce in order to keep pace with such a flourishing commerce. Pearls from Bahrain, steel swords from Yaman, wine from Shiraz, tiles from Kashan, and rugs from all parts of Iran were world famous. Papermaking had been learned from the Chinese and the Abbasids had several paper mills in operation in Iran, Iraq, and Egypt. The economy of the empire as a whole, however, was agrarian. The early Abbasid caliphs and more especially the Barmakids built dams, canals, and irrigation ditches in Iraq, Khorasan, and other parts of the realm. The whole region was more fertile then than it is now. It produced and distributed more wheat, rice, dates, cotton, fruits, nuts, oranges, melons, and vegetables. Also, one must not forget that one of the most lucrative institutions of the empire was slavery.

FOREIGN RELATIONS

By the time the Abbasids came to power the vigor of the Arab conquest had spent itself and the Arab warriors had either gone back to the desert or had been assimilated. The Abbasids added very little to the territory they had inherited. Except for the bodyguard which remained in Baghdad, they did not even maintain a standing army. Consequently, most of their foreign relations depended upon the sending of emissaries and in the giving and receiving of gifts.

An exception to this general situation, however, was their relation with Byzantium. The riches of Constantinople were still inviting and the conquest of Asia Minor had become a challenge. Emperor Constantine V (741–775), taking advantage of the civil war between the Abbasids and the Umayyads, had pushed back the Arab invaders all along the southern borders of Asia Minor. In 782, Mahdi sent an expedition under the command of his son, Harun, which advanced to the Bosporus. Queen Irene sued for and concluded peace with the payment of tribute. The Byzantine Empire was weak enough to excite the expansionist tendencies of the Arabs, both Umayyad and Abbasid, but strong enough to withstand their attacks. Consequently, the Arabs were happy to receive money and make peace which in turn gave the Byzantines a breathing spell.

Later Emperor Nicephorus I (802–811) broke the treaty. Harun was so enraged at hearing the news that he wrote the famous letter quoted by practically every historian of Europe. "From Harun, the Commander of the Faithful, to Nicephorus, the dog of a Roman . . ." Harun sent an expedition which, true to form, exacted the tribute and returned. Arabs were not destined to master Asia Minor. Islam, however, conquered it through the instrumentality of the Turks.

European writers have made much of the fact that Harun al-Rashid and Charlemagne were contemporaries and have recorded that Charlemagne's envoys brought gifts from "Aaron, the King of Persia." The Muslim writers, however, are all silent about such a relationship. It is quite plausible that the Abbasid caliph would want the friendship of Charlemagne against the Umayyad Caliphate of Spain, and that Charlemagne could profit from the hostility between Baghdad and Constantinople. Nothing substantial, however, came of it except the exchange of gifts.

ABBASID SOCIETY

One of the most important transformations during the Abbasid period was the fact that Arab segregationist policies were discarded and society became international. Thanks to the vastness of the empire and the existence of good communications, and more especially, thanks to slavery and concubinage, Arabs, Persians, Syrians, Egyptians, Berbers, Turks, and Indians became mixed, at least in urban centers. Muslim writers like the author of *Aghani* describe mainly the life and leisure of the caliphs and upper classes. As for the common people, we know that they had ample opportunity to use the numerous public baths and, as in modern times, even small towns and larger villages claimed such accomodations. Strangers were cared for in hostels and, if they were too poor, they could always sleep in the mosque. The women were segregated and their duty was in the home and in the rearing of children, except slave girls who would amuse men by their song and dance. Polygamy was permitted to the extent of four legal wives. It being a slave society, we may assume that the men of the upper and middle classes availed themselves of the opportunity and had at least half a dozen slave concubines if not four wives. Tables and chairs were never in use in the Middle East. The upper classes sat on raised divans covered with mattresses and cushions and the lower classes on mats. Food was served in large circular copper trays. Families which could not afford individual plates would sit around a common tray and eat.

A large part of the population, especially in the rural areas and among the lower classes, had not become Muslims. During the early Abbasid period the majority of the non-Muslims were Zoroastrians and next in number the Nestorian Christians. The number of Jews was quite small. The Abbasids were wont to keep the pretense of religiosity and, to please the Muslim theologians, persecuted the non-Muslims. Caliphs such as Harun al-Rashid, Mutawakkil, and others were especially harsh. The dhimmi could not build places of worship and all that were built after the Arab conquest were ordered demolished. They had to wear special attire and some were even branded on their foreheads. Their homes could not be taller than those of the Muslims and their testimony against the Muslims was not admitted in court. Away from the capital where everyone was at the mercy of the local governor, the dhimmi were required to pay the poll tax in a prostrate position, and in lieu of a receipt were given a seal which they hung around their necks. Under such circumstances, conversions to Islam were numerous. Notwithstanding all this, there was tolerance in Islam. Many Christians and Jews held positions of honor as businessmen, court physicians, philosophers, and even vazirs. We do not, however, know of any occasion that a Zoroastrian as such was so honored or tolerated. It is safe to assume, therefore, that the brunt of the persecution was borne by all Zoroastrians and the lower-class Christians and Jews. The Arab supremacy preached by the Umayyads caused resentment among the aristocrats and intelligentsia of Iran and Syria, while the religious zeal of the Abbasids persecuted the majority of the rural population. Perhaps it was their cry which the author of *Aghani* recorded:

"*Oh, that the tyranny of the Umayyads would return
Oh, that the justice of the Abbasids would go to hell.*"

CHAPTER 9

PERIOD OF PRINCIPALITIES

The house of the Abbasids was built with propaganda and bricks of empty promises on a soil which was basically hostile to it. The different segments of society, some of which had based their hopes on the ascendency of the Abbasids, were now disgruntled. Their hopes had been changed into resentment.

The Arabs were dissatisfied for having been cast aside; the Syrians for having lost their power; the Shi'is for having been deceived; the Persians for having been disinherited; and the non-Muslims for having been humiliated. The Kharijites had all but become nihilists and were constantly against the official establishment. During nearly a century of "honeymoon" which the caliphs enjoyed, they did not use their enormous wealth and power to keep the empire intact, let alone to weld a nation. Most of the credit for public works should go to the Barmakids and other vazirs rather than to the caliphs. The "Golden Age" was ushered in by the natural historical process rather than by a conscious effort on the part of the caliphs. To be sure, there were some exceptions, as for example Ma'mun for a short while, but on the whole the caliphs were interested in power and pleasure and maintained themselves with the aid of the executioner and the bodyguard.

The caliphs felt ever more insecure with the passing of time. Their Khorasan bodyguards had been weakened or had left in disgust. The north and south Arabs, who had continued their feuding, were not inclined to save the caliphs from the obvious designs and machinations of the Persians. To protect himself, Mu'tasim (833–842) brought in Turks to act as his bodyguard. The Turks were as brave and obedient as they were uncouth and unlettered. They could be used as a lever, so the caliph hoped, to let the Arabs and Persians destroy each other. The fact that Mu'tasim's own mother was a Turkish slave may have contributed to the move.

In any event, the stalwart Turks who replaced the Khorasanis as the caliph's bodyguard, proved to be a Frankenstein monster. In a few years their rowdyism and debauchery caused so much trouble in Baghdad that the caliph moved his capital to nearby Samarra, and took his bodyguards with him. The caliphs did not return to Baghdad until fifty years later. But whether the capital was in Samarra or in Baghdad the difficulty continued.

A few years after the Turks entered the service of the caliph, they began to take control of affairs of the state. By 861 they felt strong enough to kill Mutawakkil and replace him with his son. From then until 941 the Turks made and unmade caliphs and became virtual rulers of whatever was left of the empire. Soon their leader became the grand vazir with the title of *amir al-umara* (commander in chief) and the hapless caliphs were not even left alone in their insignificant status. Three of them were blinded and were seen begging in the streets of Baghdad! With such a situation in Baghdad it is not surprising that governors in practically all parts of the empire should carve out principalities for themselves and become independent of the capital.

THE PRINCIPALITIES OF THE WEST

One of the first regions to separate itself from the authority of the Abbasids was Spain. Six years after the fall of the Umayyads, one of their princes, Abd al-Rahman, established an independent state in far-off Andalusia. Even though Spain is outside of the scope of this study, it is important to note that the Umayyads established a strong caliphate there with Cordoba as capital. Either as a centralized power or as principalities, the Muslims stayed in Spain until 1609 when they were finally ousted by Philip III. The notable contribution of the Caliphate of Spain was in fact that it acted as the main channel through which Muslim philosophy, science, art, and architecture found their way to Europe.

In North Africa, Idris ibn-Abdullah, a great-grandson of Imam Hasan who had escaped because of his involvement in a Shi'a uprising, established himself in Fez, Morocco. This Shi'a principality lasted from 788 to 974 and has the distinction of being the first Shi'a state.

Another principality is known as Aghlabids (800–809) after Ibrahim ibn-al-Aghlab, a governor appointed by the Caliph Harun. He set up an independent Sunni kingdom in Tunisia. His equally energetic successor built a fleet and took Malta and Sicily and raided the coast of Italy.

Two short-lived principalities followed one another in Egypt. Both were Turkish. The first, Tulunids, was started in 868 by a son of a Turkish slave, Ahmad ibn-Tulun, who was sent to Egypt to assist the governor. He took advantage of the confusion and announced his independence of Baghdad. Later he took over control of Syria. His successors were not so strong and the family had lost the leadership by 905. The second dynasty, known as Ishkhidids, ruled in Egypt from 935 to 969. They also ruled, for a while, in Syria and Palestine before being defeated by the Hamdanids. This latter was another small dynasty which raised the Shi'a flag in North Syria with centers in Aleppo and Homs. They lasted from 929 to 1000. Their claim to fame was the fact

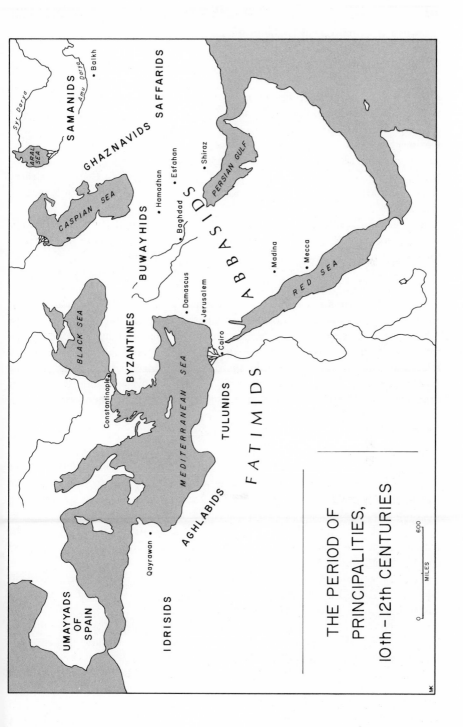

THE PERIOD OF
PRINCIPALITIES,
10th – 12th CENTURIES

that they were patrons of Isfahani, the author of *Aghani*, and of two celebrated poets, Mutanabbi, and Ma'arri.

The most important principality, which in time assumed the proportions of a strong state, was the Shi'a dynasty known as the Fatimids. The founder, Ubaydullah, who established himself on the ruins of the Aghlabid Dynasty in 909, was a descendant of Abdullah ibn-Maymun, the Ismaili leader in Iran.[1] The Ismaili Shi'is, who had a network of missionaries in all parts of the Muslim world, chose North Africa as the best place to establish a beachhead. By 969 they controlled all Egypt. There they chose Cairo as their capital and claimed the caliphate. Thus, by the second half of the tenth century there were three rival caliphates in Islam, the Abbasids, the Fatimids, and the Umayyads of Spain.

The Fatimids, like the other Islamic dynasties, reached the zenith of their power soon after they had begun, and then went into a decline. Fortunately for them, their decline coincided with the decline of their other two rivals and they were allowed to survive until 1171, when they were defeated by the Saladin (Salah al-din) of Crusade fame.

As a Shi'a caliphate, the Fatimids had a definite Persian orientation, though their method of administration was much the same as that of the Abbasids. Their main concerns were the propagation of Ismaili doctrine and the expansion of Shi'a power. The Fatimids established the famous Azhar University in 972, and throughout the Fatimid period it was one of the centers of Shi'a learning. Later, Azhar was taken over by the Sunnis and has remained in operation to this day, claiming to be the oldest university in the world.

THE PRINCIPALITIES OF THE EAST

The rebellion against the central authority of Baghdad in the east started much later than in the west. The first leader to declare independence was Tahir, the son of a Persian slave from Khorasan. He was a trusted general of Ma'mun, given the governorship of Khorasan and sent there to quell the uprising after the murder of Rida, the eighth Shi'a Imam.[2] Almost as soon as he arrived in Khorasan, Tahir omitted the caliph's name in the Friday prayer, a sure sign of independence. His successors ruled with Nishapur as their capital until 872, or only 52 years.

The first consciously Persian principality was the kingdom of the Saffarid (867–903), started by Ya'qub Saffar (coppersmith). His center of activity was Sistan in eastern Iran, though he had control of all Iran for a time. He was the first to conduct a campaign (unsuccessful) against the Caliph Mu'tamid (870–892). He also reestablished the Persian language in all official correspondence and was a patron of Persian literature.

A second Persian principality, that of the Samanids (874–999), claimed

---

[1] See below, p. 101.
[2] See above, p. 85.

descent from Saman, a Persian nobleman. They had control of central and northern Iran and the vast territory in Transoxiana with their capital in Bokhara. Under the Samanids, Persian literature came into its own. Their court attracted such eminent Persian scientists and poets as Razi, Avicenna, Rudaki, Bal'ami and others.

The stream of Turks that started moving toward Baghdad in 830 grew in volume and by the middle of the century some of them had started kingdoms of their own in the east. One of the most important of these was the Ghaznavids (962–1186). The founder, Alptigin, was a slave of the Samanids who rose in importance and in time carved out a kingdom in the region covered by modern Afghanistan and the Panjab. The greatest among the Ghaznavids was Mahmud (999–1030) who assumed the title of sultan and was the acknowledged suzerain of the region from western Iran to northern India and the confines of Transoxiana. The Ghaznavids were the first of the many Turkish warriors to establish kingdoms in Iran. Turks though they were, all of them were Persianized and became great patrons of Persian art and literature. The celebrated Ferdosi dedicated his famous *Shanameh* (*Book of Kings*) to Mahmud.

Contemporaneous with the Ghaznavids in the east were the Buyids of northern Iran. Their home was the Daylaman highlands on the southern shore of the Caspian sea. After working their way southward and capturing Esfahan and Shiraz, their leader, Ahmad, was invited to Baghdad in 945 by the beleaguered caliph, Mustakfi, who wanted to be delivered from his Turkish bodyguards. Ahmad assumed the title of *amir al-umara* and his name was both mentioned in Friday prayers and engraved on coins.

The caliph did not fare much better at the hands of this Persian Shi'a than he had at the hands of the Sunni Turks. The new strong-man blinded Mustakfi and appointed Muti' (946–974) whose name, ironically enough, means "obedient." They established Shi'a practices and for over a century of their rule (945–1055) governed from Shiraz rather than Baghdad which, by now, had lost its luster. To emphasize their Persian origin, they used the title of *shahanshah* (king of kings). The Buyids were replaced by a new and more notable group of Turks, known as the Saljuqs.

This new group of Turks belonged to the Ghuz tribe of Kirkhiz Turks in Central Asia. Very likely they had been influenced by Nestorian Christians[3] who had sent their missionaries in previous centuries. They appear on the scene of Middle East history, however, as devout Sunni Muslims. Their warlike and aggressive nature, coupled with the weakness of the contending principalities, made it possible for them to fight their way south and west. By 1037 they had occupied Khorasan, Ray, and central Iran, and 18 years later (1055) their leader, Tughrul, entered Baghdad and was made *amir alumara*, by Caliph Qa'im (1031–1075), a process which must have become monotonous!

The early rulers of most principalities were both aggressive and constructive.

[3] See above, p. 9.

In the case of the Saljuqs, the rulers were Tughrul, his nephew Alp Arsalan and the latter's son, Jalal al-Din Malekshah. In the span of half of a century (1037–1092) these three subdued their rival principalities and ruled using the caliphs as puppets. The Saljuqs, however, could not hold the empire as a unit. Eventually, they were divided into three groups. One known as the Saljuqs of Iran with their capital in Maragheh (1037–1194); another known as the Saljuqs of Asia Minor with their capital in Konya (1071–1299); and the third known as the Saljuqs of Syria with their capital at Aleppo (1094–1117). Of these, the Persian Saljuqs became famous through their celebrated Persian vazir, Nizam al-Mulk, who served Alp Arsalan and Malekshah for over forty years. He established institutes of higher learning in different cities, the most famous of them being the Nizamiya in Baghdad. Under his patronage Omar Khayyam, the Persian astronomer-mathematician who became world famous for his rubayiats, helped to revise the calendar. The outcome was the "Jalali" calendar, which is in use in Iran today. Nizam al-Mulk was a learned man himself and the most famous work attributed to him is *Siyasatnameh* (Treatise on Government) which he wrote for the guidance of Malekshah.

In 1194 the Saljuqs of Iran were overwhelmed by the Turks of Kharazm who, contrary to the regular pattern, were Shi'is. Their dynasty is known as Kharazmshah. One of its princes, Ala al-Din Muhammad (1200–1220) decided to end the Sunni caliphate in Baghdad. The aged and desperate Caliph, Nasir (1180–1225), who had heard of a new band of "Turks" who were on the march, asked their aid against his Kharazmshah enemies. He got more than he bargained for. The strange tribesmen turned out to be Mongols under Chengiz Khan![4]

Looking back over the period of principalities, which lasted some 300 years, it may be noted that on the whole the petty kingdoms of the west were established for dynastic and religious reasons. Some like the Aghlabids and the Tulunids were motivated by personal glory and ambition while others, principally the Fatimids, were established for religious reasons. In the east, however, religion did not play a great part. The motivation there, in addition to personal ambition, was primarily Persian patriotism. The Persians were consciously anti-Arab and did much to revive Persian domination. The population of the Fertile Crescent, Egypt, and North Africa, partly because some of the groups were of Semitic origin and partly because they were subject peoples at the time of the Arab invasion, had adopted Arabic as their spoken and written language. To be sure there were pockets of resistance, but these were not so strong. In the east, however, the Persians resisted the pressure of Arabization and refused to speak Arabic. The Turkish tribes who were scattered on the Iranian plateau, some of whom established dynasties, learned to speak Persian rather than Arabic. Because of the central location of Baghdad and the attraction it had for the intelligentsia, Arabic continued to be the language of learning almost to

[4] See below, p. 130.

the advent of the Mongol era. But Persian, which had always remained the spoken language, became also the language of administration, even of the Turkish principalities, from the time of the Saffarids in 867.

The question may be asked, "How was it then that the Abbasid caliphs lasted so long?" As a matter of fact, the caliphate, as an institution, was intentionally kept alive, from at least 850 to 1225, by a succession of strong men or "princes." The principal reason for this was the prestige of the office and its high position in the mind of the Muslim population. It was customary for these princes to receive an order of "investiture" from the caliph. This was probably to placate the populace and especially the religious leaders. Such letters of appointment were readily given by the caliphs mostly out of fear and sometimes for a price. One of the few who did not have such an official "appointment" was Ya'qub Saffar. The anonymous author of the *History of Sistan* relates that the religious people asked Ya'qub whether he had a permit from the caliph and he answered in the affirmative. He then invited them to see it. When they were all gathered, he asked his aide to bring the "permit." To the consternation of the visitors, the aide entered holding a cushion on which there was a naked sword. Ya'qub brandished the sword menacingly a few times and asked the divines whether Saffah (the founder of the Abbasids) had any other permit but a sword such as this. The assembled company was speechless both from fear and also from the force of the logic. Whereupon Ya'qub said, "Now that you have seen the permit, you can go home!"

Another reason that the caliphs were allowed to survive was the concern for legitimacy. The majority Sunni party believed that the caliph should be a member of the Quraysh tribe. The warring princes could not possibly make such a claim. Some of them did try, through marriage, to connect themselves with the house of Abbas. Even the Shi'is, who did not believe the Abbasids were legitimate caliphs, were afraid of popular sentiment. The Fatimids did actually take Baghdad in 1058 and forced Qa'im to renounce his right to the caliphate in favor of the house of Ali, but Tughrul the Saljuq saved the imprisoned caliph. Another Shi'i to threaten the caliph was Mohammad Kharazmshah but he was destroyed by Chengiz Khan and never had the opportunity.

Thus the members of the house of Abbas survived, even after the destruction of Baghdad, until 1517. At that time the Ottoman Sultan Selim put an end to the pretense when he defeated the Mamluks and took the "caliph" prisoner.

CHAPTER 10

RELIGION, LAW, AND ETHICS

Culturally speaking, the Arab conquest of the Fertile Crescent and Iran was a barbarian invasion of the advanced civilizations of the Byzantine and Persian empires. In the history surveyed thus far, four significant periods of this cultural movement may be distinguished. The first two have already been discussed.[1]

1. The period of the "Leading Caliphs,"[2] when the chief activity was the consolidation of the military conquest and the preaching of the simple faith brought from the desert.
2. The period of the Umayyads which was still very close to the primitive Bedouin culture and was plagued by civil wars. It nevertheless brought the faith in contact with the Byzantine and Persian cultures and raised many questions concerning faith and conduct in the community of Islam.
3. The period of borrowing of the early Abbasids in which the best available writings of the non-Islamic world were collected and systematically translated into Arabic.
4. The period of creativity during the decline of the Abbasids and the rise of principalities when Muslim theologians, scientists, philosophers, and others produced original works built upon the knowledge which they had acquired.

A brief discussion of the period of translation or borrowing is necessary in this rather topical approach to Islamic culture, because without it, the creative contributions of scores of Muslim scholars would not have been possible. Furthermore, it serves to remind the student of the Middle East that this culture was an amalgamation of Egyptian, Greek, Persian, Syrian, Indian, and Chinese sources and was a far cry from the original simple faith brought out of the Arabian peninsula. It will be seen, however, that this original simple faith was never discarded. All knowledge, contradictory as this may seem, was related to the central faith.

It will be remembered that the Umayyad, Abd al-Malik, ordered the transla-

---

[1] See above, pp. 48 and 64.
[2] The Muslim historians have always applied the adjective "Rashidin" to the first four caliphs.

tion into Arabic of the Sasanian method of administration. No doubt aid was sought by the Arab rulers from diverse sources for the problems at hand. The bulk of translations was done during the reign of the early Abbasids, especially Harun al-Rashid and Ma'mun. It was the latter who established *bayt al-hikma* (House of Wisdom) whose principal activities were the collection and translation of works from all parts of the world. It should be said, to the glory of the early Abbasids, that even though they squandered large sums of money on extravagant pleasures, they also supported intellectuals. Some of the caliphs did not hesitate to ask their enemies, the emperors of Byzantium, for books. As the records indicate, members of the Bureau of Translations were some of the highest paid intellectuals in the history of the world.

They translated all kinds of works, without bothering to be selective, from Greek, Pahlavi, Latin, Sanskrit, Chinese, Syriac, Nabatean, and other languages. Going over a list of scores of translations, it is possible to generalize that from Greek they translated works of philosophy, logic, medicine, and mathematics; from Persian, history, government, medicine, and literature; from Sanskrit, mathematics, medicine, and astronomy; and from Nabatean, agriculture and magic.

Practically all of the translators were non-Arabs and some were non-Muslims. Three of the most important translators, each from a different faith, who left an imprint on Islamic culture in different fields are, in chronological order, Ibn-Muqaffa (d. 757), a Zoroastrian; Hunayn ibn-Ishaq (809–873), a Christian; and Thabit ibn-Qurrah (d. 901), a Sabian.

Ibn-Muqaffa's real name was Ruzbeh Parsi but he was better known by his derogatory Arabic nickname, which means "son of a shriveled man," because his father's hand was shriveled through torture. The sincerity of his conversion to Islam was doubtful. For a time he acted as secretary in the court of the last Umayyad caliph and then continued with the Abbasids, though not for long. One of his most important translations is *Khodaynameh* (Book of Lords), which was rendered into Arabic as *Siyar al-Muluk al-Ajam* (Attributes of the Kings of Iran). This became a model of historical writing for later Muslim historians. The most famous of his translations, however, is the ancient Sanskrit classic, *Panchatantra*, which had been rendered into Pahlavi as the "*Fables of Bidpay.*" Ruzbeh translated it into Arabic as *Kalila wa Dimna*. This is a delightful animal story in which the animals take on the characteristics of humans and discuss all sorts of philosophical and moral ideas. Each idea is introduced by a parable involving even more animals. This has become a classic in the literature of most of the nations of the world. Inasmuch as both the original Sanskrit and the Pahlavi version are lost, the debt to the gifted translator, Ruzbeh, is the greater.

The book, *Kalila wa Dimna*, introduced the Persian style in the writing of Arabic in which new similes, satire, and prose were expressed in simple and familiar words. This polished the Arabic language to such a degree that it remained the norm until recent times. Ibn-Muqaffa was a Shu'ubiya[3] leader and is reported to have claimed that his Arabic was much better than that of the Koran. He was suspected of being a Zoroastrian at heart, which he probably was, and was burned to death by the order of Mansur, the second Abbasid caliph.

The second eminent translator was Hunayn ibn-Ishaq. He was a Nestorian Christian who had training in medicine but became famous as a translator. As a Nestorian Christian, his mother tongue was Syriac and he did not know Arabic very well. But he must have improved tremendously, for Ma'mun used to pay him in gold the weight of the books he rendered into Arabic. Among his translations are Galen, Hippocrates, Plato's *Republic*, Aristotle's *Categories*, and others.

He served four caliphs and was the personal physician of Mutawakkil. He never became a Muslim, saying, with perhaps a twinkle in his eyes, that he wanted to be where his fathers were, whether it be in heaven or in hell.

The third luminary in the field of translation was Thabit ibn-Qurrah, a Sabian[4] (836–891). He belonged to the star-worshipping Sabians and, together with his subordinates of the same faith, translated most of the then known works in mathematics and astronomy from Greek. Among his translations are works by Archimedes, Apollonius of Perga, Euclid, and others. He established a school of translators most of whom were, like that of Hunayn, members of his own family. In about the second generation, the family was converted to Islam, as seems to have been the case with the family of Hunayn.

THEOLOGY AND RELIGION

The simple creed of Islam, "There is no God but Allah and Muhammad is His Messenger," together with a few rituals and rules of conduct, seemed adequate enough for life in the desert. Catapulted into the mastery of an empire and drawn into close relation to and in competition with other religions, and involved in a variety of questions about life and eternity, the old faith seemed shamefully naked. Furthermore, the turbulent history of the period with its bloodshed, civil wars, assassinations, disputes over succession, Umayyad worldliness, and a host of other problems, raised theological questions which rocked the new religious society of Islam.

One of the first groups to form definite opinions and separate themselves from the main body were the Kharijites.[5] These seceders were most liberal in their interpretation of the Koran and adamant in their belief that the office of the caliphate, the burning question of the time, was open to all Muslims no matter what their racial origin. "Even a slave can be a caliph," they insisted, provided he was righteous, honest, and went about doing good. They developed the

---

[3] See above, p. 82.
[4] See above, p. 10.
[5] See above, p. 61.

doctrine of salvation through works and gradually came to the view that anyone could be saved through good works regardless of his faith. As has happened so many times in history, the Kharijites went about with drawn swords killing those who would not agree with their liberal ideas. By the tenth century they had become virtual nihilists and were recruited by a number of the founders of principalities against the established regime in Baghdad. Ya'qub, the founder of the Saffarid principality, had a large contingent of Kharijites in his army.

On the other side of the theological controversy were those who believed in salvation through confession. They believed in the suspension of human judgments concerning the acts of men and left it to God. Hence, they are known as Murji'ites. It was an attempt to accomodate the reality as well as the worldliness of the Umayyads to Islam. They said that once a man confessed his faith in Islam, as certainly the Umayyads did repeatedly, he was a true Muslim no matter what his actions. In between these two views came that of the Mu'tazilites, who formed a dominant school of religious thought for some time. They believed that when a major sin is committed by a Muslim he has separated himself from the community, umma, but has not become an infidel. They also believed in free will, which was a doctrine espoused by the Qadarites, against Jabrites who followed the predestinarian pronouncements of the Koran.

The main interest of the Mu'tazilites, however, was in other questions which Greek rationalism had raised in the mind of the Muslims. One of these had to do with the names of Allah. Traditionally, there were some 99 of them. To the Mu'tazilite rationalists, the anthropomorphic connotations of these names were disturbing. Furthermore, they believed that such names negated the unity of God emphasized in the Koran. Consequently, they separated the name of "Allah" from divine attributes, and, to preserve the unity of Allah, said that God and His attributes were not coexistent. The other question of great importance had to do with the Koran itself. The orthodox notion was that the Koran was the uncreated word of God and coexistent with Him. The rationalist Mu'tazilites could not accept this and announced that the Koran was created and, therefore, not eternal. Many of these rationalists were executed by the Umayyad Hisham (724–743) for teaching the creation of the Koran and believing in free will.

During the reign of the Abbasids, however, the Mu'tazilites became strong and Ma'mun himself joined them. Under their influence he made a special proclamation of the dogma of the creation of the Koran. This caused a great deal of turmoil among the orthodox, but the Mu'tazilites had the upper hand. These former champions of freedom of thought induced Ma'mun and two of his successors to set up an inquisition to persecute anyone who would not subscribe to the new dogma.

It was not until the middle of the tenth century, however, that orthodoxy found its champion in the person of Abul Hassan Ali al-Ash'ari. He rejected free will and instead claimed that man was responsible for his actions only because God willed it. He declared the eternal nature of the Koran. As to God and His names, he said that every name attributed to God has a meaning which is different from the meaning of the same name when applied to man. Consequently, God is removed from the knowledge of man and the two have nothing in common.

Greek and other systems of thought continued in Islam, and the scholastic school which Ash'ari founded tried to reconcile Islam with these. This task was accomplished to the satisfaction of the orthodox by the prince of Muslim theologians, Abu Hamid al-Ghazali (1058–1111). He was born in Tus, Khorasan, and after a tumultuous life died in his birthplace. He studied every philosophy and religious thought and was converted to some of them in turn. His autobiography reads like the confessions of St. Augustine and, in much the same way as the Christian Saint, Ghazali taught orthodox Islam in the Nizamiya College in Baghdad, and then quit to spend his days in contemplation. In his famous book, *The Revival of the Sciences of Religion*, he has tried to bring together Islam, Greek rationalism, and Persian mysticism into one harmonious unit. According to Ghazali, knowledge is of two categories—knowledge connected with theology and knowledge which is not connected with theology. Of the latter, he recommends medicine, mathematics, and crafts, and permits the study of poetry and history. His works were translated into Latin and he is considered to be one of the important influences on Saint Thomas Aquinas who also attempted to bring together Christian revelation and Greek rationalism in harmony. Whereas medieval Thomism was challenged by the Protestant Reformation and subsequent philosophical systems, the medieval house in which Ghazali and others placed Muslim orthodoxy has remained intact. In this sense it is not correct to talk about the "end of Medieval Islam," for the so-called medieval scholasticism of Islam was not even challenged until the beginning of the twentieth century and remains unchanged.

SHI'ISM

The theological movements discussed so far, and many others, did not cause permanent rifts in Islam. The movement, however, which eventually separated Islam permanently into two camps was Shi'ism. It will be remembered that the partisans (Shi'a) of Ali banded together on the question of the caliphate.[6] Failing to establish their claim by politics or by war, the Shi'is separated permanently from the majority and founded a religion of their own, complete with theology, philosophy, government, and ethics. Religiously, Shi'ism has Zoroastrian, Nestorian, and other overtones, and has supplied Islam with mysteries, saints, intercessors, belief in atonement, and a spirit of high cult, all of which are repugnant to the majority of Sunnis. The Sunnis consider the Koran infallible, while the Shi'is place infallibility in a man, the Imam who is sinless and has been considered as man-God. The martyrdom of Husayn, the

[6] See above, p. 60.

third Imam, at Karbala has afforded the Shi'is the opportunity to pour out their religious feelings in processions, all sorts of self-mortifications, passion plays and poems, depicting his death as vicarious for the sins of the world.

Ali, the first Imam and the "rightful heir" to the Prophet, claimed to have received the light of prophecy from Muhammad and to have passed it on to his descendant-successors. This enables the Shi'is to claim that Muhammad is truly the last Prophet, whose mission is perpetuated in his descendants through Ali. They believe in this so strongly that they are not satisfied with the witness of Islam, "I believe that there is no God but Allah, and Muhammad is the Messenger of Allah." To this they always add a third sentence, "I believe that Ali is the regent [*Wali*] of Allah."

This doctrine of the Imamate forms the heart of the political theory of the Shi'is, which is purely theocratic. No Muslim, Sunni or Shi'a, questions that Muhammad was the head of the state as agent of Allah. Since, according to the Shi'is, his powers both spiritual and temporal have passed on to Ali and successively to the other imams, then it follows that the legitimate government belongs to the imam. All other governments not under the imam or his agents, including all Sunni caliphs, are usurpers. Consequently, the first three caliphs of Islam, Abu Bakr, Umar, and Uthman, are considered "usurpers" by the Shi'is.

The Shi'is believe in the doctrine of the Return. This has many things in common with the return of the deliverer in Zoroastrianism, the coming of the Messiah in Judaism, and "second coming" of Jesus in Christianity. The majority of Shi'is believe that there were twelve imams and that the twelfth, the Mahdi ("messiah") has disappeared and shall return at the end of time when he will bring the whole world under the jurisdiction of Shi'i Islam. The twelve imams are shown below.

```
                      1. Ali (d. 661)
       ┌──────────────────┴──────────────────────┐
2. Hasan (d. 669)                        3. Husayn (d. 680)
                                         4. Ali Zayn al-Abidin (d. 712)
                       ┌─────────────────────────┐
                      Zayd              5. Muhammad al-Baqir (d. 731)
                                        6. Ja'far al-Sadiq (d. 765)
              ┌───────────────────────────┐
       Ismail (d. 760)          7. Musa al-Kazim (d. 799)
                                8. Ali al-Rida (d. 818)
                                9. Muhammad al-Jawad (d. 835)
                               10. Ali al-Hadi (d. 868)
                               11. Hasan al-Askari (d. 874)
                               12. Muhammad al-Muntazar
                                   (The Mahdi) (d. 878)
```

Another division is called Zaydi for they stop with Zayd, the grandson of Husayn and regard him as their leader. They don't believe in the doctrine of the return and are quite close to the Sunnis.

Another and more important sect among the Shi'is is the Ismaili or the Seveners. The sixth imam had two sons, Ismail and Musa. He first appointed Ismail but because of the latter's alleged drinking habits, he later transferred the succession to Musa. Ismail predeceased his father. Nevertheless, this sect considers Ismail as the seventh imam. They introduced esoteric occult mysteries around the number seven and had the best organized missionary activity in all Islam. One of their leaders founded the Fatimid caliphate.[7] It was one of the Fatimid caliphs, Hakim, who claimed deity and had a following called Druze, who may be found in Lebanon and Israel today. Another offshoot of the Ismaili was the Qarmatians. They were accused of practicing communism even to the sharing of wives. This was a fraternal organization with secret mysteries. They caused havoc among the Muslims. In 930 they succeeded in taking away the sacred black stone of the Ka'ba which was not returned until twenty years later.

A better known branch is called Assassins (Arabic, *hashishiin*) because, reputedly, they caused their volunteers to smoke hashish before going on their murderous missions. Their founder Hasan Sabbah (d. 1124) established his headquarters in the high and inaccessible redoubt, Alamut, in the Alborz mountains northwest of Qazvin. Sabbah's activities were basically political and apparently anti-Sunni. Indeed, even collaborators of the Sunnis were opposed. Nizam al-Mulk was a strong Sunni and he established several Nizamiya Colleges especially to teach Ash'ari doctrine. Naturally, he was one of the targets of the Assassins. Sucessive expeditions against Alamut failed and is was left for Hulagu, the Mongol conqueror of Baghdad, to destroy Alamut also.[8]

SUFISM

Sufism or Islamic mysticism is yet another development in the field of religion. It is so called because the adherents used to wear a garment made of wool (*suf*). Sufism flourished among Arabic-speaking peoples and one of the earliest Muslim mystics was Rabi'a (d. 801), the celebrated lady from Kufa. According to some scholars of Islamic religious history, Sufism is the "supreme manifestation of the Persian mind in the religious sphere." Celebrated Persian mystics such as Ghazali, Attar, Rumi, Hafez, and a score of others bear the claim. Practically every religion has produced its particular form of mysticism. In Islam, Sufism was also a reaction to the Ash'ari theology of the separation of God and Man. According to the Sufis, the world is a manifestation of God and there is a true resemblance between the attributes of God and man. The Christian monastic orders and the mystical nature of the Gospels impressed the Sufis. Rumi says that "the monastery of Jesus is the place for the people of the heart." With Hafez, the "church" is replete with joy and openness while the "mosque" is dark and harsh. Orthodoxy, so the Sufis believed, had placed Islam in a shell. The Sufis broke the shell (*qishr*) but thought it a necessary evil.

The Sufis, like the early Christians, called themselves "people of the way." The idea is built around the claim that the soul of man has been separated

---

[7] See above, p. 92.
[8] See below, p. 131.

from its Maker and has a longing to return and be lost in Him. Attar in his exquisite allegory called "The Conversation of the Birds" tells the story of the birds (humanity), who went out to seek *simorgh* (God), who was their king and lived beyond the mountain, *qaf*. They had to pass seven valleys (conditions) of (1) search, (2) love, (3) understanding, (4) detachment, (5) communion, (6) wonder, (7) union and/or extinction. Of the thousands who flew to seek the king only 30 birds, in Persian, *si* (*30*) *morgh* (*bird*), arrived. The rest perished on the way and many even killed each other to save themselves. The bedraggled 30 birds who arrived were severely tested by the vazir of the king. Having passed the test, the portals opened and the veil was rent asunder. They entered and found peace. But when they looked at each other they realized that they were the *simorgh* [God] and that *simorgh* was none other than they the *simorgh*, 30 birds. Detached from the outer world they saw themselves as they were in the beginning!

Jalal al-Din Rumi (1207–1273) of Khorasan, who lived and died in Konya, Asia Minor (hence his name, *Rumi*, "Roman") is considered the prince of all the mystics. His book of poems, *Masnavi*, is full of anecdotes taken from everyday life to show the way to union with God. A pure and polished heart can reflect more clearly the beauty of God. He founded the order of the Molavi (Turkish, *Mevlevi*), whose habit of dancing to music gained for them the name of "whirling dervishes."

Hafez of Shiraz, a more joyous and cheerful mystic than Rumi, used wine, roses, and love both as an allegory and as aids to spiritual life. To him life was supremely joyous and, like the wine which he enjoyed, also bitter. He could see the "light of God in the Magian house of worship," and the "countenance of [his] beloved in a cup of wine." Like all the Sufis he believed in the supremacy of the heart over the mind. "The stage of love is much higher than that of the intellect. He can kiss the [former's] threshold who is ready to endanger his life."

It was Ghazali (1058–1111), however, who had tried Sufism and later became a theologian, who gave the mystics a place in the orthodox scheme so that they were tolerated. Consequently, the Sufis never separated from the Islamic community. They organized orders and had their own hierarchy of leaders but remained within Islam, both Sunni and Shi'a. One of these orders was *Bektashi*, to which all of the Ottoman sultans belonged. Another was a Shi'a fraternity, the *qizilbash*, "red heads," of which the Safavid shahs of Iran were leaders.[9] Most of the Sufi orders, however, did not have anything to do with politics and war.

LAW

It is difficult to say which is more important in Islam, faith or law. Muslims on the whole have spent more time and thought on the ramifications of law than on religion. Actually, law and religion are two sides of the same coin. Law

[9] See below, p. 163.

is the will of God, and Islam is the term of submission to it. It is the Muslim belief that Jews and Christians had corrupted and complicated the law of God and Allah sent Muhammad to clarify the confusion. In the medieval period, Judaism, Christianity, and Islam were closer together than at any other time in history. All three had the same conception of God as one who was the ruler of the universe, who demanded obedience, and who had given mankind the law. In Judaism, He had given it to Moses and the priests; in Christianity to the Church of Christ; and in Islam, to Muhammad and the community, "umma," of believers.

The most important foundation of Islamic law is the Koran. But, the expanding community soon discovered that the Koran did not contain all the situations and questions which came up for decision and judgment. Furthermore, the political and religious controversies led Muslims to ask, "What would Muhammad have done?" or "What did the Prophet do?" In the early years there were many who had known the Prophet personally and they narrated (*haddatha*) the practice (sunna) of the Prophet. Thus, *hadith*, or tradition, was used to make a difficult decision, to settle a religious or moral controversy, to solve a delicate legal problem, to advocate a new idea, and to do a thousand and one other things. The practices of the Prophet in all matters, from weighty and legal questions to the way he brushed his teeth or ate watermelon, became the norm.

The farther in time the Muslim community moved from Muhammad, the greater became the number of hadith, so that by the middle of the ninth century there were some 600,000 traditions in circulation. The science of hadith became one of the most important branches of learning and was the forerunner of Muslim historiography. Every hadith has two parts: an authority or a chain of authorities (*isnad*) and a content (*matn*). A typical hadith is the following taken from the collection by Bukhari:

> *Abdullah ibn al-Aswad told me; Al-Fadl ibn al-Ata told us; Isma'il ibn Umayya told us on the authority of Yahya ibn Abdullah ibn Sayfi that he heard Abu Ma'bad, the freedman of Ibn Abbas, say, "I heard Ibn Abbas say: 'when the Prophet, the blessings of Allah be upon him, and peace, said Mu'adh to the Yaman, he said to him . . .' "*

There are three categories of creditability: authentic, fair, and weak. The basis of examination is the creditability of the chain of authority and not the nature of the content. The theory is that if the chain of authority is strong then the content is correct.

There are six authoritative collections of hadith but by far the most important is the one by Muhammad ibn-Ismail al-Bukkari (810–870) from Bokhara, as the name indicates. Of the 600,000 traditions he collected in the span of 16 years, he chose about 7,500 of them to be of genuine authority. These collections are second only to the Koran and their authority cannot be questioned. The Koran and the hadith formed the totality of the law of God, shari'a, which became the foundation of Islamic jurisprudence.

Islam, however, expanded very quickly and there were civil, criminal, fiscal, and other cases which varied in different countries and raised problems. To solve those problems two other principles were added. One is *qiyas* or analogy, which is used when the principles established by the Koran or hadith are no longer applicable. The other is *ijma* or consensus of the community, which became an excellect expedient for introducing novel ideas and institutions. The jurists resorted also to private judgment *ra'y*, but it never received authoritative sanction. It must be pointed out that analogy and consensus were resorted to only when the Koran and hadith could not be of any assistance.

SCHOOLS OF LAW

Different interpretations of the Koran and the hadith together with varying circumstances both in time and place led to the formation of at least seven schools of law, four of them among the Sunnis and three among the Shi'is.

1. The Hanafite School (Sunni). It is named after Imam Abu Hanifa who was born in Iran about 699, and was a textile merchant. He was against the Umayyads and later turned against the Abbasids also. He was arrested and died in prison in 767. Even though he did not write a book, his ideas, transmitted through his students, are accepted by more than half of the Sunni Muslims in the world. He emphasized analogy and the principle of equity, which is based on natural law. His is the most tolerant of the legal schools of Islam. It is said that he believed that the Koran should be translated into the vernacular and that prayers should be conducted in other languages than Arabic. The Hanafite system was used by the Ottoman Turks and is prevalent in India, Afghanistan, and Central Asia.

2. The Malikite School (Sunni). This school was founded by Malik ibn-Anas of Medina (715–795). His book, codifying some 1,700 legal traditions, introduced the formula of consensus of the community (*ijma*) for the first time. It is more conservative than the Hanafi school and is followed by the Muslims of North Africa, exclusive of Egypt.

3. The Shafi'i School (Sunni). Between the conservatism of the Malikites and the liberalism of the Hanafites, came the Shafi'i school. Muhammad ibn-Idris al Shafi'i (767–820), its founder, was a member of the Quraysh and lived mostly in Baghdad and Cairo. He was a mean between the two extremes and is believed to have influenced all schools. He wrote a book entitled *Sources of Law*, which is based on the critical examination of hadith. His rite is followed in Indonesia, Egypt, East Africa, and Lebanon.

4. The Hanbali School (Sunni). The founder of this school was Ahmad ibn-Hanbal (c. 780–855), who became the champion of Islamic fundamentalism. He rejected consensus, analogy, private judgment, and in fact anything that was outside the letter of the Koran and the hadith. He was caught by the inquisition inaugurated by Ma'mun and continued by two of his successors. Ibn-Hanbal was beaten, chained, and imprisoned, but he would not recant.

Too conservative to be popular, this rite has only about 3,000,000 followers. They are among the Wahhabis of Arabia.

5. The Ja'fari School (Shi'a). It is also known as the Imami school. It is the most important Shi'a system of jurisprudence. It rejects *qiyas, ijma,* and *ra'y.* The Sunnis believe that their four schools have said all that needs to be said about law and do not need any new opinion or deviation. The Ja'faris, however, believe that the hidden imam is the true head of the state. In his absence he rules through his spokesmen who are called *mujtahids,* that is, interpreters of the will of the imam. There are usually three or four of these mujtahids at a time. They are not chosen but simply acknowledged by the consensus of the community to be learned, pious, and qualified to issue opinion, *fatwa,* which is as binding to the faithful as a Papal bull is to the Roman Catholics. All the Shi'i Twelvers follow this school.

Because of the fact that Shi'ism is a minority religion in Islam and was persecuted by the Sunnis for a long time, the Imami school permits concealing one's faith if revealing it is dangerous to life. This is called *taqiyya.* It allows temporary legal marriage (*mata'a*) from a few days to 99 years. The children of such unions belong to the father and do not receive equal share with the children of permanent marriages.

6. The Ismaili School (Shi'a). This is named after Ismail, son of the sixth imam. The difference between this school and the Ja'fari is that there is only one spokesman for the imam, in whom there is an indwelling spirit of the imam, and in whom is reflected the light of the imam. Consequently, it is as liberal or conservative as the leader. The office is hereditary. The most famous leader is the recent one, the Agha Khan (1877–1957), who traced his lineage to Hasan Sabbah. He appointed his grandson, Karim Khan, as the new leader. The Ismailis are scattered in India, Iran, and East Africa.

7. Zaydi School (Shi'a). This is named after Zayd, the son of the fourth imam. They do not believe is a hidden imam and are closest to Sunni Islam. They are dominant in Yaman.

ETHICS

Ethics is connected with law (Shari'a), and Shari'a regulates the life of the Muslim in all its aspects. Everything which is not governed by the Shari'a is left for man to decide for himself according to the mores of his society. For the Muslims all conduct falls in one of five categories:

1. Obligatory (*wajib*). The performance of these acts has reward in heaven and neglect brings punishment.
2. Meritorious (*mustahab*). Acts which are recommended. Commission is rewarded but omission is not punished.
3. Permissible (*mubah*). Acts which are legally neutral, being neither rewarded nor punished.

4. Reprehensible (*makruh*). These are acts which are disapproved but not forbidden. Omission is meritorious but commission is not punished.
5. Forbidden (*haram*). These are acts for which the culprit is punished.

Some moralists in Islam believe that it is possible for the same act to go through the above categories. For example, lying and killing are forbidden within the Islamic community and yet become increasingly permissible until they are obligatory in war with the infidel.

CHAPTER 11

PHILOSOPHY, SCIENCE, AND HUMANITIES

To the early Muslim mind, philosophy was a "foreign science" and as such it was a challenge to Islamic theology. The Muslims, however, were forced to take up the challenge of philosophy because a large number of the neo-Muslims who were familiar with Greek philosophy began to think of Islam in philosophical terms. Some of the manifestations of this type of thinking among groups such as the Mu'tazilites have already been discussed. What interested the Muslims most was, of course, the Shari'a, which could not be enforced without a state, and the state could not be held together without a caliph. As has been noted, it was the caliphate that was the main problem of the new community and this problem became more difficult as caliphs became weaker and rival caliphs appeared. Consequently, Muslim philosophers have interested themselves in *political* philosophy. To be sure, they have dealt with other branches of philosophy, but their main concern was government. Plato's *Republic* and Aristotle's *Politics* have had more fascination for them than other works. Even Islamic theology is political in nature and expression.

For the purpose of better understanding the succeeding centuries of the history of the Middle East including the contemporary period, it should be stated here that Muslim political and historical philosophy is derived from four streams. One is the Koran and the "political theology" incorporated in it. The second is the contributions of Muslim political philosophers. The third is what might be called "practical precepts" written for the guidance of princes, which might or might not include the two above. The last source is the Irano-Turkish theories which are, more or less, secular in nature. All Muslim governments of the later periods reveal varieties of combinations of two or three or all four of the above sources. The Koran and the theological-political problems related to it have already been discussed.[1] What follows is a brief discussion

---

[1] See above, pp. 42–43.

of Muslim political philosophy and a few words about the "practical precepts."

Ya'qub ibn-Ishaq al-Kindi, who lived during the last half of the ninth century, was the first philosopher the Arabs produced. As he was the only one throughout the medieval and early modern periods, he has certainly earned the title "the Philosopher of the Arabs." Unfortunately, however, most of his works have been lost and there is not much that can be said about him except that he combined the views of Plato and Aristotle.

One of the foremost political philosophers of Islam was Abu-Nasr al-Farabi (870–950), a Turk from Transoxiana who gained the reputation of being the "second teacher," Aristotle being the first. He set out to try to resolve the dilemma created among the learned Muslim community by the challenge of Greek philosophy.[2] Some aspects of Greek thought were congenial with Islam but others were not. The Greeks wanted a philosopher for a king while Islam had already a prophet. To the Greek, law was the product of man's mind, while to the Muslim, law was the will of God.

In his book, *Opinions of the Citizens of the Virtuous City*, Farabi resolves the dilemma between philosopher and prophet by combining the two. Only a prophet-philosopher with imagination (function of prophecy) and intellect (function of philosophy) can create a state and promulgate law.

Farabi was followed by Abu Ali Husayn ibn-Sina (980–1037), a Persian from Bokhara. Commonly known as Avicenna, he was undoubtedly one of the great geniuses of all time. He was familiar with Farabi's work and admits indebtedness to him. In his encyclopedic work, called *Shafa*, he collected and classified, with copious notes, all that was known of Greek philosophy up to his time. In political philosophy he was a synthesizer. He linked the ideal state of Islam with Plato, modifying Farabi's position by stating that prophecy was the result of the highest human intellect. It is the function of prophecy to promulgate laws which men obey. He agreed with Farabi, however, that in the absence of a prophet, it was still possible to develop a good society.

These individuals, their contemporaries, and those who followed them were influenced by the social and political movements of their time. It will be remembered that the most important political reality in this period was the decline of the caliphate and the rise of rival principalities, especially those of Shi'a persuasion, among which the Fatimids were the most important and aggressive. During a century of Umayyad and Abbasid power and affluence, there had grown up a string of large cities throughout the empire from Cairo to Transoxiana. The merchants, artisans, and entrepreneurs, of these urban centers were affluent, cosmopolitan, and fascinated by new ideas. The masses, as usual, bore the brunt of the extravagances of the weak caliphs and were extremely dissatisfied.

The Shi'is in general, and especially the Ismailis, had a well-conducted

[2] See above, p. 98.

missionary organization fanning the grievances of the masses against the caliphs. Furthermore, in order to reach the intellectuals, they established schools in urban centers and encouraged the integration of Islam with Hellenic and Persian cultures against the Orthodox Sunnis. The Fatimids actually took over Baghdad and, had it not been for the power of the Saljuq leader, Tughrul, who cast his lot with the Sunnis, the history of the Middle East might have been different.[3] Farabi flourished under the Shi'a Hamdanids in Aleppo. Avicenna was perhaps a Shi'i and was brought up in an Ismaili home.

The secularization of Islam which was started by Farabi and Avicenna on the philosophical level was carried on by an already flourishing semisecret fraternity called the "Brethren of Sincerity." These philosophical "study clubs," mostly encouraged by the Ismailis, were established in urban centers and carried on semipolitical activities against the government.

Avicenna inaugurated a sociological dimension within the process of secularization. He incorporated the old Persian system of social classification in his scheme. He divided society according to professions, such as rulers, administrators, artisans, farmers, etc., as against the division of society according to lineage which was preferred by the Arabs. It must be emphasized here that both Farabi and Avicenna were believing Muslims who had been influenced by Greek thought and also by Sufism. They had to find a tenable and rational basis for their faith and also a political philosophy which would take note of the rise of men who were eager to be declared "legitimate" rulers and who were stronger than the caliphs. The order of society reintroduced by Avicenna gave the aura of legitimacy to the powerful men who considered it their profession to rule even though they were not remotely related to the Prophet.

Not fifty years after the death of Avicenna there appeared a number of books written to teach the princes the ways of government. These books are generally referred to as "Practical Precepts" or "Mirrors to Princes." Among these, the most important are *Qabusnameh* written for the Ziyarid principality in about 1082, and *Siyasatnameh*, written for the Saljuqs[4] in about 1092. In these books, the art of government is taught through anecdotes, maxims, and examples, all taken from Sasanian kings. These books are regarded as still another influence in the shaping of Muslim political philosophy, which is neither Greek nor Islamic. In *Qabusnameh*, for example, we read that it is the duty of the prince to improve cultivation because "good government is secured by an army; an army maintained with gold; gold is acquired through taxation of country squires (*dehqan*); and dehqans are sustained through justice and fairness to the peasantry."

Quite obviously the conclusions of Farabi and Avicenna were not acceptable to the orthodox. To both, prophecy, rather than being a gift of God through revelation, was a natural phenomenon attained through imagination and/or the "active intellect." According to them, it was possible to establish the

[3] See above, p. 93.
[4] See above, p. 94.

"virtuous city," without a prophet or, particularly, without Islamic revelation. Sustained through the power of the Saljuqs, the orthodox bestirred themselves against these heretical ideas, the Shafi'is started schools like that of the Ismailis. Nizam al-Mulk, the most effective champion of orthodox theologians, placed orthodox civil administrators in all departments of the government. These orthodox bureaucrats were in an excellent position to apply the Muslim shari'a, to every aspect of the machinery of government and society. It was for his activities in the cause of Sunni orthodoxy that Nizam al-Mulk was murdered by an agent of the Assassins, who belonged to the Shi'a Isma'ili sect.

The Orthodox, however, could eradicate, neither the influence of the philosophers nor the realities of the situation. Even Nizam al-Mulk incorporated the non-Muslim Persian tradition and ethics in his book. Ghazali, who taught in the Nizamiya College at the time of the Saljuqs, in his attempt to keep the unity of the umma intact, stated that piety was the only qualification for the office of the caliphate. Consequently, power may legitimately be placed in the hands of the sultan who rules for the caliph. The fact that the caliph's name is mentioned in Friday prayers and engraved on coins, insures, according to Ghazali, the unity of the umma.

Later on, Ibn-Taymiyya (1263–1328), who belonged to the fundamentalist Hanbali school but lived under the Mamluks when there was no caliph at all, offered an even more dangerous compromise. He said that anyone who had the power to coerce and seize the government was a legitimate ruler, provided he obeyed the Shari'a. To him, "religion without a sultan, army, and money is as futile as a sultan with army and money but without religion." From this there was only a short step to the claim that a sultan (not caliph) rules by the authority of Allah. The Ottomans took that step.

SCIENCE AND HUMANITIES

True to the tradition of learning in the medieval period, the Muslim scholar had a wide variety of knowledge. For a philosopher to be a famous physician, able to solve mathematical equations and write learned treatises on music and astronomy (to name only a few), was quite common. Some of them, like Omar Khayyam, wrote poetry for relaxation. The Muslims considered science to be of two categories—"religious sciences" and "physical sciences." The humanities were commonly called *adabiyyat*, which included poetry and prose, the latter being mostly moral stories. In between these two categories were geography and history.

MEDICINE

The field of medicine in early Islamic history was dominated by Persian Christians. The great Sasanid medical center and hospital in Gundi Shapur in Iran was in operation during the Arab occupation. The hospital built in Baghdad by Harun was after the Persian model and was called by its Persian name, *bimarestan*. Both the physicians and the pharmacists had to pass special examinations. There is evidence that physicians were bound by an oath. The head of the hospital in Gundi Shapur was Jibril ibn-Bakhtishu, a Christian. He and his family served as court physicians for the Abbasids. Among translators of Greek and Persian medical works into Arabic, as well as being distinguished physicians in their own right, were Hunayn ibn-Ishaq (809–73), Yuhanna ibn-Masawayh (777–857), an ophthalnologist, and Tabari, only to name a few.

The most original work in medicine, however, was done by two Persians, Razi and Avicenna. Muhammad ibn-Zakariya al-Razi (865–985) was born, as his name shows, in Ray, near Tehran, the capital of modern Iran. Most of his life he lived under the patronage of the princes of the Samanid principality and, for a time, was the chief physician at Baghdad. He was a very prolific writer and some of his works, including his major one, *Al-hawi* (Comprehensive Work in Medicine), were translated into Latin and later into French, German, and English. He invented the seton in surgery, and reported his clinical studies on the kidney stone, smallpox, and measles. For his philosophical writing on the side of rationalism, he was maligned by the orthodox and had to defend his own philosophy and private conduct.

Avicenna, who has already been introduced as a great philosopher, was also a very distinguished physician. He also wrote on mathematics, art, and music. He is one of the very few among Muslim scholars who has left behind a partial autobiography. At ten he had mastered the Koran and was well-versed in literature. By 16 he was a full-fledged physician and was called upon to treat the Samanid prince. There, he was given admission to the prince's well-stocked library and spent "the next eighteen months" in reading. At 18 he "had exhausted all these sciences," meaning philosophy, logic, mathematics, medicine, and the like. This man, who claimed that medicine "was not a difficult science," wrote his famous encyclopedia on medicine called *qanun*. This replaced all other works in medicine and was used as a text in the schools of Europe until well into the seventeenth century. He wrote about contagion and the spread of diseases by water and earth. He had a volume on *materia medica* in which he has classified and commented on hundreds of drugs.

His life was a tumultous one as he was forced to go with the princes to their wars. He never left Iran but was on the move most of the time. He also came under attack for his lack of orthodoxy. Unlike Razi who took time to defend himself, Avicenna wrote the following poem:

You cry that I have cast my faith away
And point a pious finger; yet I say
That unbelief in such a man as I
Would shake the very pillars of the sky.
The prayer of all men in the Prophet's name
Are my prayers—yet my own are not the same:
No thought of mine, no act that I control

But bears the precious difference of my soul.
Is this, then, he that you call infidel?
Say on, accuser, but consider well:
If I have turned from Him who blessed my birth,
There's no true Moslem left in all the Earth.[5]

He died in Hamadan and was buried there in 1037.

MATHEMATICS AND ASTRONOMY

In the field of mathematics and astronomy the Muslims drew from Greek and Indian sources. The most important contribution of the Muslims in mathematics is the "Arabic numerals," which they learned from the Indians. Indeed, they were quite slow in adopting them themselves. One of the giants in the field of astronomy was Muhammad al-Kharazmi, the translation of whose work introduced the "Arabic" numerals, and algebra. "Algorism" is named after him. Another scholar in astronomy and mathematics was Abu Rayhan Biruni (973–1048) who worked for the princes of the Ghaznavid principality. On the basis of the rotation of earth on its axis, he figured the latitude and longitude of many cities in the Middle East. Omar Khayyam's great contribution in revising the calendar has already been mentioned.[6] Hulagu, the Mongol victor of Baghdad, built an observatory in Azarbaijan where Nasir al-Din Tusi of Khorasan, one of the last of the famous astronomers, invented intricate astronomical instruments such as the armillary sphere, mural quadrant, and solstitial armil. His astronomical tables were standard for many centuries. There were many observatories, in different centers. Most of the astronomers assumed the earth was round and measured the size and circumference of the earth with astonishing accuracy.

Muslim scholars were also interested in chemistry (*alkimya*), physics, biology, zoology, and botany. They had laboratories for experimentation. One of the important chemists was Jabir Ibn-Hayyan (Gebir to medieval Europeans), who experimented in 776. He described calcination and reduction and knew of evaporation, sublimation, melting, and crystallization. The Arabic origin of such words as chemistry, alcohol, antimony, and others shows the degree of indebtedness of the Europeans to medieval Muslim scientists.

GEOGRAPHY

Muslim conquests and commerce brought an awareness of the world. The Abbasid period produced a number of globetrotters, merchants, and scientific geographers who wrote their observations. Theoretically, they were under Ptolemy's influence, but in their travels they saw things differently and produced a mass of descriptive material about India, Ceylon, China, and Russia.

[5] Translated from Persian by the author and put into poetic form by John Lewin.
[6] See above, p. 94.

Kharazmi drew a map of the world which was in use until the fourteenth century.

Ibn-Khordadbeh, whose name shows that his father was a Zoroastrian, was postmaster of western Iran about 848. His book on "roads and countries" described in detail the four main commercial routes of the period, among other things. One went from Spain, southern Europe, and Asia Minor to the Caspian. Another connected north Africa with India through Syria and Iran; the third went along the eastern Mediterranean to the Persian Gulf; the fourth was a sea route, through the Red Sea and the Indian Ocean, to Ceylon and China. Ya'qubi of Khorasan, who flourished in the ninth century, wrote a book in 891 called the *Book of Countries* which discusses topography and especially economic geography.

Two other geographers of the period were Estakhri of Persepolis (c. 950) and Muqaddasi of Jerusalem (c. 980). The former produced probably the first colored map of the world and the latter wrote his original geographical observations from more than twenty years of travel in most of the Muslim world. A more famous geographer, who lived in Sicily in the twelveth century, was Idrisi (d. 1166), who sums up the contributions of Muslim geographers before him. He believed that the earth was a sphere and his maps are remarkably accurate. To him the lands north of China and Russia were lands of Gog and Magog. His maps are the reverse of modern maps in that north is at the bottom and south at the top of the page. This account of geography should not be concluded without mentioning that remarkable Greek slave, Yaqut (ruby) (1179–1229) who, after being given his freedom, roamed around where fancy took him, supporting himself by copying and selling manuscripts. His copious notes resulted in his famous *Dictionary of Cities* in which names are arranged alphabetically.

HISTORY

Islam is a revealed religion and revelation involves time, place, person, and event—all of which form the stuff of history. In Islam, as in other revealed religions, history was a divine plan closely tied up with the umma. Furthermore, Muhammad's claim that he was the last Prophet in the Judeo-Christian tradition called for a knowledge of the lives of Prophets in the Old and New Testaments. Perhaps, preoccupation with conquest on the one hand and lack of qualified persons on the other postponed formal history writing to the Abbasid period. A good deal of material, however, had been prepared during the Umayyads.

As has already been mentioned,[7] the Arabic translation of the book on Persian Kings by Ruzbeh (Ibn-Muqaffa), became a model for history writing as well as for other forms of literature. There were, however, two deviations

[7] See above, p. 97.

from the pattern. One was in content. Muslim historians, on the whole, were interested only in the accounts of the Bible and the religio-political events of Islam. They were not interested in the history of China, Rome, or any other nation not dealt with in Biblical history. Even in their "universal" histories, which normally started from the creation of the world until the author's time, they ignored non-Biblical and non-Islamic activities and did not deviate from the stereotyped pattern. The second deviation from the Persian model was that, having been trained in the science of hadith, they wrote history chronologically with direct quotations from the usual chain of authorities.

The names of historians who wrote from different points of view, Arab, Persian, Sunni, and Shi'a, are too numerous to mention here. All that a large number of them did was to repeat what was written before, usually starting from Adam and bringing it up-to-date. Later, during the period of principalities, the writing of local history gained ascendency, a practice which was a relief from the norm and which left posterity a wealth of local historical material. The stereotype, however, did not die. Even in the twentieth century "history" books have been published which start from Adam.

Of the two historians of the Arab conquest, one is the Egyptian, ibn-Abd al-Hakam (d. 870), who described the conquest of Egypt; and the other is the Persian, Ibn-Yahya al-Baladuri (d. 892), who wrote a comprehensive narrative of the Arab expansion. Of the two most important writers of "universal" history, one is Muhammad al-Tabari (838–923) from the province of Tabarestan on the south coast of the Caspian Sea. In addition to a standard commentary on the Koran, he wrote the *History of Apostles and Kings*, in which he has arranged his carefully collected material complete with chains of authorities, year by year from the creation of the world until A.D. 915. This work became the standard for later historians.

Another person equally famous as a historian and geographer was Abul-Hasan Ali al-Mas'udi (d. 956), the globetrotter from Baghdad. He is one of the few who deviated from the stereotype. His famous book, *The Golden Meadows and the Jewel Mines*, is a topical history of civilization. He deviated even farther from the norm by writing about the Indians, Persians, Romans, and other heathens. Furthermore, his book abounds in historical anecdotes, which he, no doubt, collected in his travels.

LITERATURE

In the field of literature, the Prophet Muhammad disliked poets and poetry but did not have any objection to storytelling. As it turned out, his followers throughout the centuries did not produce much fiction but may have written more poetry than the writters of any other culture in the world.

It has already been mentioned that the ornate and refined method of expression, common in the Persian literature of the Sasanids influenced the Arabic language permanently. The writings of the Shu'ubiya both in the original and in translation have already been discussed.[8] These later developed into a style of writing called *maqama* (assembly) which criticized the social and political life in a subtle and delicate manner. The *maqamat* of Hariri (1054–1122) of Basra are the most famous of this type.

Aside from the *Book of Songs*, with which the reader is familiar, there was not much serious literary production in prose. The most famous on the lighter side, however, is *A Thousand and One Nights*. This was prepared by one Jahshiyar (d. 942) from the Persian original called *hezar afsaneh* (A Thousand Tales). The translator added a few stories of his own, using the original plot and the same heroes and heroines, including Shahrzad. In the course of centuries, as individuals copied the book they added more stories from all parts of the world, but always keeping the same plot. It apparently took final form in the late Mamluk period in Egypt and is known in English as *The Arabian Nights*. It has probably been translated into most languages of the world.

The nature and content of pre-Islamic Arabic poetry has been discussed.[9] It suffices here to say that the Umayyads perpetuated the pre-Islamic content of Arabic poetry. One of the most famous desert love stories sung by Arab and Persian poets repeatedly is the love story of Layla and Majnun.

During the Abbasid era, Persian influence crept in and although the main trend of Arabic poetry did not change very much, Persian style came into vogue. The reader is already familiar with the Shu'ubiya poet, Bashshar ibn-Burd, with the profane poet Abu Nuwas, and with the serious Arabic poet, Abu al-Atahiya.[10]

The period of principalities saw the resurgence of the Persian language. It has been shown that the patriotic Saffarids and Samanids used Persian as a medium of literary and official expression. Even the Turkish principalities were Persianized and used the language in their correspondence and became patrons of Persian literature. The language has come to be called "new Persian," as distinct from Pahlavi or "middle Persian."

In the discussion of Sufism a number of Persian poets such as Rumi, Attar, Hafez, and others have been mentioned. The greatest epic poet of Iran was Abul Qasem Ferdosi who wrote the history of Iran in poetry from the mythological times through the conquest of the country by the Arabs. *Shahnameh* or the *Book of Kings* is one of the most stirring poems in Persian literature. Nezami, another poet, wrote the love story of Layla and Majnun. Three other love stories which were repeatedly sung by poets were Joseph and Zolaykha (Potephar's wife), Vis and Rameen, and Farhad (a stonecutter) and Shirin (a queen). Even this scanty discussion of Persian literature should include another luminary of Shiraz, the city of poets: Sa'di, whose collection of short anecdotes in prose and poetry, *The Rose Garden* (*Golestan*), is a textbook in every Persian school.

[8] See above, p. 82.
[9] See above, p. 29.
[10] See above, p. 83.

It must be noted here that poets were supported by the patronage of caliphs and princes who were more interested in flattery than in science or literature. Consequently, the bulk of Persian and Arabic poetry contains a great deal of bombast and the clever use of words for flattery. The poets had to do this in order to make a living and some of the better ones became very rich indeed. Every poet sought a patron and it became customary for each prince to have his own coterie of poets. Some of the princes in the period of principalities vied with each other in attracting certain able poets. Writing poetry became a means of lievlihood and every occasion—be it birth, death, marriage, war, victory, construction of a palace, or a successful hunt—became a suitable subject for poetry. It was customary for nobles to commission poets for suitable verses. Sometimes the poets sent the same poem to more than one patron and received a fee from each. If a proper fee or suitable gift was not forthcoming, the poet ridiculed the patron with satire and maligned him, always in exquisite poetic form. The power of the word in possession of poets was sometimes as potent as the power of the sword in the hands of princes. Nevertheless, some of these same poets who wrote so much sweet flattery and sometimes bitter satire also worte—on their own time—some of the lasting poems which take the reader's soul to heights of artistic experience.

ARCHITECTURE AND THE ARTS

Some of the modern Middle East artists have stated that the term "Muslim Art" is misleading, for Islam as a religion forbade some arts and frowned on others. While this is true, it is also a fact that the followers of Muhammad did not obey him in this any more than they did in the reciting of poetry which the Prophet had disliked or the drinking of wine which he had expressly forbidden. The Arabs did not bring much else into the arts besides a wealth of tribal melodies which later were incorporated by composers and singers in their works. But, coming as they did into the midst of the Christians of Byzantium and the Zoroastrians of Iran, two religious groups who used the arts as handmaidens, the Arabs could not long remain aloof. Consequently, the arts developed outside the inner religious circle of Islam and have never had its support.

Architecture is a possible exception to the above generalization, for Islam needed mosques and mosques had certain needs which were peculiar to Islam. Hence, the artistic talents of the new converts were directed into the construction of mosques. The architectural needs of Islam were few and simple. A fountain or pool was constructed outside the mosque for the purpose of ablutions. Consequently, the normal approach to a mosque from the street is not to the inside of the building but to a large courtyard provided with pools and fountains. Also, the Muslims needed a preferably high place from which the muezzin could give the call to prayer. For this they constructed tall circular or square columns, attached to the mosque. These were called *minarets* from the Hebrew, *minora*.

Islam had two requirements for the inside of the Mosque. One was the direction to Mecca which is called *qibla*. The mosque had to be built so that the worshipper could face Mecca for prayer. As this had to be exact, it became customary to build a prayer niche called *mihrab*, from the Persian *mehraveh*, meaning the niche or dome of Mithra, of which the mosque mihrab was an exact copy both in shape and name. The other requirement was a pulpit, *minbar*, a staircase-like construction, often portable, from which the preacher spoke while sitting on the top step.

Most of the mosques and palaces built during the Umayyad and Abbasid periods have been destroyed. The best examples of Umayyad architecture which have survived are the Umayyad mosque at Damascus and the Dome of the Rock at Jerusalem. Of the Abbasid buildings, nothing is left except the ruins of the mosque in Samarra and the better preserved Friday mosque at Esfahan, built around 760. It is the opinion of the authorities that, in general, the Umayyad architecture shows Byzantine influence, while the Abbasid architecture shows Persian influence. The Sasanids had developed ovoid and elliptical domes, and arches and spiral towers, which were copied by the Muslims.

Because of the interdictions against the painting of pictures, mosques were decorated with colored tiles, *kashi*, from the town of Kashan, Iran. The decoration on the tiles would sometimes be intricate geometric or floral designs of great beauty. Talented artists expressed themselves through calligraphy, a branch of the arts which had the support of religion, in copying the Koran or writing Koranic verses on tiles for the decoration of the mosques. Even though Islam forbade the representation of animate objects, painting was patronized by the caliphs and one of them, Mu'tasim, had the walls of his palace at Samarra decorated with nudes. During the period of principalities, artists illustrated books. Ferdosi's *Book of Kings* with its myths and stories was a fertile ground for artistic expression. This was the beginning of miniature art for which the Persians became famous.

The only branch of music which received approval from Islam was the chanting of the Koran. This however, became so stereotyped that it has not changed for centuries. Scholars, in imitation of the Greeks, wrote on the theory of music, but there was very little development of serious music. There were composers, singers, instrumentalists, and dancers but, as has already been noted, they were used mostly for merrymaking.[11]

The paradox that the foregoing survey of culture reveals is that the period of greatest creativity occurred during the period of principalities (c. 900–1200), when the caliphs were weak and princes driven by diverse motives were fighting against each other. The reasons for the continuity of progress, despite war and strife, are not hard to find. In the first place, the Arab conquest acted as a catalyst to tired societies that had been in a rut for some time. Neither did the religion which the Arabs brought with them have a new elixir for the produc-

---

[11] See above, p. 72.

ion of thought which the existing religions of the Middle East did not have, nor did Arabic as a language have a hidden capacity for the expression of culture which other languages did not possess. The fact remains, however, that it was Islam and Arabic which became the instruments of the awakening and, in the process, were themselves renovated and enriched. The peoples of the Middle East, who were thrown out of their rut and revitalized by the conquest, started again where they had left off and continued in spite of instability and war.

In the second place, the weakness of the central government in Baghdad was an indirect aid to the process of creativity. As we have seen, the Abbasids were committed to upholding religious dogma and did not shun persecution and inquisition to carry out their purpose. The weakness of the caliphs freed the philosophers and scientists in their investigations, without which they could not have been creative. The independent princes who either did not understand the dogmas or did not care, vied with each other in patronizing the intellectuals whom the religious divines in Baghdad continued to accuse of heresy. It is doubtful whether a strong caliphate would have allowed such creativity, and this is borne out by the fact that after the Saljuqs restored the power of orthodoxy and Ghazali wrote his book, scholarship and creativity began to languish. The "Middle Ages" of the Middle East started with the restoration of the power of orthodox Islam. Its "Renaissance" started perhaps during the first decades of the twentieth century and the "Reformation" has yet to occur.

A SELECTED BIBLIOGRAPHY

Andrae, Tor, *Mohammed: The Man and His Faith*. New York: Harper and Brothers, 1960.

Arberry, A. J., *The Holy Koran: An Introduction. With Selection*. New York: The Macmillan Company, 1953.

Arnold, Sir Thomas, and Alfred Guillaume, eds., *The Legacy of Islam*. London: Oxford University Press, 1931.

Browne, E. G., *Arabian Medicine*. Cambridge, England: Cambridge University Press, 1921.

Cragg, Kenneth, *The Call of the Minaret*. New York: Oxford University Press, 1956.

Creswell, K. A. C., *Early Muslim Architecture: Umayyads, Early 'Abbasids and Tulunids* (2 vols.). Oxford: Clarendon Press, 1932–1940.

Donaldson, Dwight M., *The Shi'ite Religion: A History of Islam in Persia and Irak*. London: Luzac, 1933.

Faris, Nabih A., *Arab Heritage*. Princeton, N. J.: Princeton University Press, 1944.

Gibb, H. A. R., *Arabic Literature: An Introduction*. London: Oxford University Press, 1926.

————, *Mohammedanism, An Historical Survey*. London: Oxford University Press, 1949.

Hitti, Philip K., *History of the Arabs* (7th ed.). New York: The Macmillan Company, 1961.

Jeffery, Arthur, *The Qur'an as Scripture*. New York: R. F. Moore, 1952.

Jurji, Edward, *The Middle East: Its Religion and Culture*. Philadelphia: Westminster Press, 1956.

Khadduri, Majid, *War and Peace in the Law of Islam*. Baltimore: Johns Hopkins Press, 1955.

Le Strange, Guy, *Baghdad During the Abbasid Caliphate*. London: Oxford University Press, 1924.

Lewis, Bernard, *The Arabs in History*. London: Hutchinson's University Library, 1950

Morgan, Kenneth W., ed., *Islam—The Straight Path*. New York: The Ronald Press, 1958.

Nicholson, Reynold A., *A Literary History of the Arabs*. Cambridge, England: Cambridge University Press, 1962.

Pope, Arthur Upham, *An Introduction to Persian Art Since the Seventh Century A. D.* New York: Charles Scribner's Sons, 1931.

Robinson, J. Stewart, ed., *The Traditional Near East*. Englewood Cliffs, N. J.: Prentice-Hall, 1960.

Rosenthal, E. I. J., *Political Thought in Medieval Islam*. Cambridge, England: Cambridge University Press, 1962.

von Grunebaum, Gustav E., ed., *Unity and Variety in Muslim Civilization*. Chicago: University of Chicago Press, 1955.

Watt, W. Montgomery, *Muhammad, Prophet and Statesman*. London: Oxford University Press, 1961.

PART TWO

THE HEIRS
OF THE
ISLAMIC EMPIRE

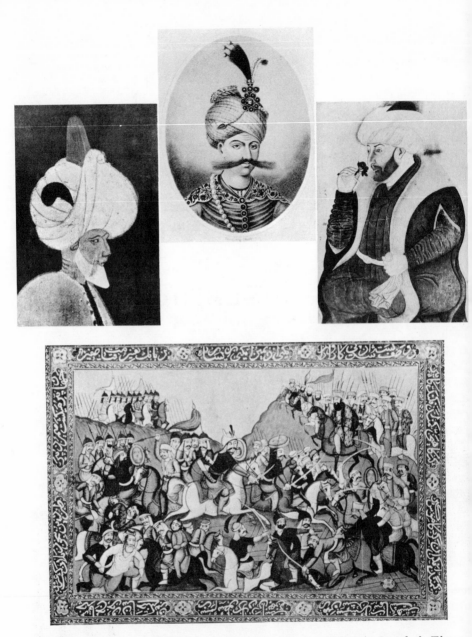

PRECEDING PAGE, TOP TO BOTTOM: *The Blue Mosque (1616) in Istanbul. The Shah Mosque and the Shah Square.* ABOVE, CLOCKWISE FROM TOP: *Shah Abbas the Great (1587–1629),* an engraving from a Persian painting (COURTESY OF IRANIAN PRESS AND INFORMATION). *Sultan Mehmed the Conqueror (1451–1481),* in a 15th-century miniature by Sinan (COURTESY OF THE TURKISH INFORMATION OFFICE). *The Battle of Chaldran (1514),* a mural in Chehel Sotoon Palace, Esfahan (COURTESY OF IRANIAN PRESS AND INFORMATION). *Sultan Suleyman the Magnificent (1520–1566),* in a 16th-century miniature by Nigari.

CHAPTER 12

ISLAM ON THE DEFENSIVE

One of the most striking differences between Islam and other religions such as Christianity or Buddhism is the fact that Islam, unlike the other two major religions, was founded upon conquest and for nearly a thousand years drew its lifeblood from war and expansion. To be sure, both Christianity and Buddhism became imperialistic and perpetrated wars; but the fact remains that both were minority communities for 300 years and both experienced persecutions which have left indelible marks upon each. Islam, on the contrary, did not know persecution and did not experience the feelings of a minority community, but rather experienced victory over other societies. These facts have left indelible marks upon it.

The attempts of some historians, mostly Europeans or Europeanized Middle Easterners, to divide the Islamic movement into "religion," "empire," and "culture" as three distinct entities and then to state or to imply that "Islam the religion" was not dependent upon the expansion of the empire is to distort the whole history of the period. To be sure, the historians' intentions are good. For centuries Islam and its Prophet were maligned by the West; the tendency of modern western historians is to make amends and to right the wrong. Since in their own minds the idea of a religion being propagated by war of expansion is repugnant, they have tried to imply that the wars of conquest in Islam were not for the propagation of the "Islamic religion" but rather for the establishment of an "Islamic empire."

The Muslims, be they theologians or historians, do not share this view. To them the empire and religion were one, the wars of expansion were ordered by Allah, and the soldiers were fighting for His cause. The early Muslim writers, as well as later historians, described in detail and with great pride the battles in which the Prophet himself had participated. The picture of Muhammad with a sword in his hands is not at all incongruous to a Muslim, whereas the painting of Christ or Buddha handling a sword will shock even a Christian or Buddhist soldier on his way to war.

From the battle of Badr (624) in which Muhammad participated, until the last years of the eleventh century, the armies of Islam did not suffer major defeats and the advance of Islam was not effectively checked. The Saljuqs and the other Turkish tribes who gained supremacy over the Arabs came as devout Muslims and helped to strengthen orthodoxy and the unity of the umma under the caliph of Allah. Every victory convinced the Muslims that Allah was with them and every conquest made them feel more invincible. Even though Asia Minor proved too high a wall to scale, they never gave it up. When in 1071 the Saljuqs defeated the Byzantine army in the battle of Manzikert and established a kingdom in Asia Minor, hopes ran high. In the same way that Muhammad the last Prophet had proclaimed Islam the last religion, the Islamic empire under the caliph would be the first to bring all the world under the aegis of Allah and his Prophet.

THE CRUSADES

The first attack on such a psychological and spiritual buildup came from Europe in the form of the Crusades. Europeans defeated the armies of Islam on their home ground and produced such a shock among the Muslims of the Fertile Crescent that the event still arouses strong emotions of resentment and disgust. As a matter of fact, the Crusades in themselves were only a passing phase in the history of Islam. They only momentarily halted the advance which was later begun again with the Ottomans. Nevertheless, in the mind of most of the Arabic-speaking Muslims, the Crusades remained a blemish on the body politic of Islam.

The Crusades joined the history of Europe with that of the Middle East. Naturally, they affected these two regions differently. The Crusades were caused by many factors. In the first place, they may be considered as a reaction of the Christian West to the persistent aggression of Muslim Middle East. Second, the continuous strife between the Sunni Saljuqs of Syria and the Shi'a Fatimids of Egypt had made it very dangerous for Christian pilgrims to visit the holy places in Palestine. Third, the destruction of the Church of the Holy Sepulchre by the Fatimid caliph, Hakim, did arouse genuine religious concern in Europe. Fourth, the growing power of the Saljuqs in Asia Minor threatened the lucrative trade which cities like Genoa, Pisa, and Venice had been carrying on with the East. These trade centers helped the Crusaders in the expansion of their commerce. Fifth, Islam had already shown signs of weakening in Europe. In 1050, Castile and Aragon had taken Andalusia from the Muslims of Spain. In 1060, the Normans had taken Sicily. By 1080, the Muslims had all but lost command of the Mediterranean. Furthermore, the reports of the pilgrims about weakness and dissension in the Muslim camp spread through Europe and did not fall on deaf ears. Sixth, there was genuine religious motivation among the Crusaders. They wanted to free the birthplace of Christ and to convert the "infidels." That they were doing it with the sword bothered only a small handful, like St. Francis of Assisi. Seventh, there were many landless

Constantinople

SALJUQS

ARMENIA

EDESSA

Tigris

ANTIOCH

Euphrates

JERUSALEM

• Damascus

• Jerusalem

• Cairo

FATIMIDS

Nile

THE
CRUSADER STATES
Ca. 1140

0   150   300
MILES

MK

knights, princes, and nobles who wanted domains of their own. Eighth, there were many who went for the adventure of seeing the world and perhaps gaining part of the fabled riches of the East. Ninth, there were the masses who were oppressed and bored and wanted change. Finally, when Emperor Alexius Comnenus, who was beleaguered by the Saljuqs of Asia Minor, sent his appeal in 1094 to Rome for help, things began to happen: Pope Urban II made his famous call to arms in 1095 and most of Europe responded as though they were waiting for such a summons.

In the first crusade, which was the most important of all, some 150,000 men (not all soldiers) gathered in Constantinople under the leadership of Godfrey of Bouillon, Baldwin of Lorraine, and Raymond of Toulouse. In the spring of 1097 they marched southward and took Nicaea, Eski Shehir, and Tarsus. From there a column under Baldwin occupied Armenia while another took Antioch and without too much difficulty went southward, hugging the coast of the Mediterranean. On July 15, 1099, the Crusaders stormed Jerusalem and massacred Christans and Muslims indiscriminately. Godfrey became king of Jerusalem. The other territories along the coast north to Antioch and east to Edessa were organized, along European feudal lines, into small kingdoms.

Victory won, most of the Crusaders went home. Those who remained, reinforced by a flow of knights from Europe and the vigilance of the fleets of the merchant cities, lived in comparative peace for almost 50 years. The Crusaders were never able to extend their power east of the Jordan River. In the south they went as far as Aqaba and in the northeast to the headwaters of the Tigris. In a region already torn by petty principalities, the creation of a few new ones did not change the general picture. In time the Christian kingdoms, following the example of their Muslim neighbors, started fighting among themselves. Sometimes, Muslims and Christians went so far as to seek each other's aid against their own coreligionists.

In the meantime, a new star had arisen among the Muslims of the Fertile Crescent in the person of a former slave by the name of Imad al-Din Zangi who founded the short-lived Zangi Dynasty in 1127. He was strong enough to capture Edessa from the Cusaders in 1147. His able son, Mahmud, took Damascus and Aleppo and sent his Kurdish lieutenant, Shirkuh, against the tottering Fatimids in Egypt. In 1171, this Kurd's nephew, a young man by the name of Salah al-Din Yusuf ibn-Ayyub (Saladin), simply stopped mentioning the Fatimid caliph's name in prayers and that was the end of the Fatimids. Being a good Sunni, he substituted the name of the Abbasid caliph, who probably did not know Saladin existed and cared even less. In 1175 he declared his independence in Egypt and formed the Ayyubid principality. He gained fame in defeating the Crusaders in the battle of Hittin on July 4, 1187, and soon after that retook Jerusalem, Antioch, Tripoli, and Tyre.

The fall of Jerusalem signaled the third Crusade (1189–1192). The fact that three powerful monarchs of Europe, Frederick Barbarossa of Germany, Richard the Lionhearted of England, and Philip Augustus of France, led this one, added more luster than achievement. They took Acre after a siege of two years and made peace in 1191. Soon after this, Saladin died and his kingdom was divided among the members of his family, who fought against each other, a pattern which had become characteristic of all these dynasties. The Crusaders took advantage of the situation and by 1229 they had Jerusalem as well as the coastal cities.

The weakness of the Ayyubids set the stage for the rise of another principality. This was accomplished in Cairo by a slave, Aybak, who founded the Mamluk (slave) Dynasty of Egypt in 1252. The fourth slave king, Baybars (1260–1277), started a series of campaigns and took several cities in Palestine and captured Antioch in the north. His successors continued the pressure and by 1291 the last of the Crusaders were driven out.

The Crusades, which spanned nearly 200 years, were only a phase in the history of the Middle East. They did not change the pattern of the era of the principalities. The periods of peace were more numerous than times of war, and in peace there was much social contact between the Christians and the Muslims. The Crusaders who had come with a definite feeling of superiority over the infidel Muslims were forced to change their minds quickly. The Franks, as they were called by the Muslims, soon recognized the higher culture of the Muslims and emulated them in practically everything but religion.

As the Crusaders went home with these newly acquired tastes, traders took advantage of the situation and soon the market places of Europe displayed such exotic merchandise as sugar, pepper, cloves, ginger, rugs, tapestries, muslin, velvet, satin, mirrors, rosaries, and perfumes of many kinds. In the art of war the Franks learned the use of carrier pigeons from the Muslims and the latter learned the use of crossbows and the wearing of heavy mail from the Franks.

Two hundred years of intermittent warfare built a reservoir of ill will on both sides, and war propaganda was rampant. A good deal of misinformation about Islam in Europe dates from this period. And yet there were also people of good will—scholars who translated manuscripts, Muslim physicians who cured the sick among the Franks wondering all the while at the latters' superstitious concept of medicine. There were also people like St. Francis of Assisi and Raymond Lull who believed in approaching Muslims in love rather than in war. There were also intermarriages, as is evidenced by a large number of blue-eyed blonds in Lebanon, Syria, and Palestine.

THE MONGOLS

While the Muslims of the western Middle East were struggling against the Crusaders, the Muslims of the east were attacked by a new force which was more destructive and cruel than any in the annals of history. The Mongols who roamed in the uplands of Outer Mongolia around Lake Baikal and who had penetrated the Great Wall of China and overrun that civilization, had spread themselves westward until they had come to the eastern-most boundaries of the Muslim principality of Kharazm. Muslim historians, both in Arabic and Persian, use the terms Turk, Turkoman, Tatar, and Mongol quite indiscriminately. While all of the above were related to each other linguistically, it is important to note that there already were Turks living on both eastern and western sides of the Caspian Sea long before the coming of Islam. Uzbeks and Turkomans were among the important tribes in the east, while the Khazars and Bulgars were among the better known in the west. The Saljuqs, for example, were Turkomans. The Saljuqs of Asia Minor were joined by the Turks of the western side of the Caspian. The Mongols, however, were entirely newcomers, appearing in the thirteenth century. Because of the great importance and fame of the Mongol leader, Chengiz Khan, many Turks have tried to attach themselves to the Mongols and ultimately to Chengiz Khan.

Ti Mu Chin, who later assumed the title Chengiz Khan was born between 1155 and 1162 to a minor clan leader among the Mongols who inhabited Outer Mongolia. By courage and cunning he rose to prominence, united the different tribes and stormed the Great Wall which the civilized Chinese had built against such marauders from the north. Chengiz became the founder of an important dynasty in China and did not destroy the civilization which he conquered. As heir to the Chinese empire, his rule extended to Tibet and Sinkiang in the west. That was the natural boundary of China and it is doubtful whether Chengiz, who had his hands full with such a large empire, had any notion of coming west in force.

It is not quite certain why he ordered the westward move so far from his base. According to one report, Caliph Nasir of the Abbasids invited his aid against Kharazm.[1] Modern research has cast doubt on this, and it should not be regarded as a primary reason. According to another, and probably a truer account, Chengiz sent a trade mission to the west where a brother-in-law of the Shah, who was governor of the border town of Utrar, killed the merchants and confiscated their rich merchandise. This act and the subsequent unwillingness of Muhammad Shah of Kharazm to deliver the culprit so infuriated the great Khan that he called a council of tribal chieftains who decided to attack the kingdom of Kharazm. It is also likely that Chengiz as an emperor of a settled and civilized China had difficulty controlling his restless and warring Mongol tribesmen and had to keep them busy fighting, which was about the only occupation they relished.

In any event, the avalanche started in 1219 in Sinkiang and by the time its initial fury was over about 1224, the Mongols had overrun the Iranian plateau and were approaching Kiev in the Ukraine. In its wake the chain of cities on the plateau, such as Balkh, Bokhara, Samarqand, Marv, Harat, Nishapur, and Ray were looted and burned, and the majority of the inhabitants were slaughtered. Not one of these cities has ever been rebuilt to its pre-invasion size. The city of Ray (ancient Rages), with half a million people, was literally leveled to the ground. Today nothing remains of the metropolis except a village of the same name south of Tehran. One eyewitness, not finding words to describe the horror which he experienced, writes of the Mongol invasion: "They came, they looted, they killed, they burned, and they left." That after such a destruction the Persians were able to rise again and exert their cultural heritage and absorb the Mongols is one of the remarkable phenomena of history. According to some historians, had it not been for the spread of Sufism among the Persians with its qualities of patience, fortitude, and contemplation, they could not have survived the senseless butchery in their midst. It may also be true that the

[1] See above, p. 94.

holocaust enhanced the practice of Sufism with its spirit of self-abnegation and withdrawal so that succeeding Persians did not care for political power and continued to live in a detached attitude until the twentieth century.

Chengiz Khan died in 1227, having conquered and organized the largest empire the world had ever known, from the Vistula to the Pacific. There is hardly any doubt that Chengiz Khan was one of the greatest military geniuses of all time. His army was held together by strict discipline. As the whole army was entirely made up of cavalry, it was very mobile. Each soldier had one, and sometimes two spare horse(s). As a Mongol, he had perfected the art of surprise and of feigning retreat. Perhaps from the Chinese he had learned the use of explosives and had organized a demolition corps for the purpose of destroying fortifications. He usually asked the cities to surrender before each attack. If a city surrendered without fighting, a tenth of all property was confiscated and a tenth of the population taken into slavery. The rest were put at the mercy of the Mongol governors. If a city resisted, then the looting and slaughter were more indiscriminate. A Persian historian, who was understandably biased, characterizes Chengiz Khan by attributing the following saying to him: "The greatest joy is to conquer my enemies, to pursue them, to take their property, to witness the weeping of their kinsmen, to ride their horses, and to possess their daughters and wives."

After his death, the empire of Chengiz Khan was divided into three parts. First was the mother region with its capital in Peking, whose ruler had the title of Khaqan with titular authority over the whole empire. The second part was in Russia, with its capital at Kazan on the banks of the Volga. In Russian history the Mongols are known as the "Golden Horde." The third part was in Iran, with its capital in Maragheh in Azarbaijan. In Persian history the Mongols are known as "The Ilkhan."

The founder of the Ilkhan dynasty was Hulagu, the grandson of Chengiz Khan who started, in 1252, to unite what Mongol generals of Chengiz had conquered and held after his death. The most tenacious resisters of the Mongols were the Assassins whom the earlier Mongol avalanche had not consumed. In 1238 the Grand Master of the Assassins in Alamut had sent emissaries to the kings of England and France and had asked for aid against the Mongols. From both he had received noncommittal responses. In 1256, however, Hulagu, the grandson of Chengiz, destroyed the strongholds of the Assassins and captured their famous redoubt, the fortress of Alamut. Two years later, Hulagu and the Mongols were at the gates of Baghdad. There was nothing that the weak and beleaguered caliph, Musta'sim, could do except to ask for mercy. His predecessors had saved themselves by bestowing honors on such strong men, but Hulagu, being a pagan, was not moved by such considerations. Neither was he impressed by the warning that the killing of the caliph would "disturb the natural order of the universe." The caliph and his retinue were put to death and the city was given over to plunder. Compared to the destruction of Persian cities, Baghdad did not fare badly at all.

Thus ended the reign of the Abbasids who had 37 caliphs, about eight of whom had ruled in reality and most of the rest had reigned as puppets for 508 years. Some Middle East historians have overrated the significance of the fall of Baghdad, as some European historians have done in the case of the fall of Constantinople some 200 years later. Each was an anticlimax and did not greatly alter the existing situation.

Hulagu advanced into Syria but was checked by the Mamluks, a feat which saved Egypt from the ravages of the Mongols. The Ilkhanid territory extended from the Caucasus to the Indian Ocean and from the Euphrates to the Amu Darya. The immediate descendants of Chengiz Khan became patrons of civilization and learning. The Persians, who influenced the Turkish principalities, began to educate the Mongols in the arts of government and culture. The Ilkhans surrounded themselves by Persians in every aspect of their administration. As part of a large empire, Iran was linked with China by well-traveled routes kept open and safe by a peace which was imposed by the Mongols. There were commercial and cultural exchanges between Iran and China. The famous Persian miniatures which were developed in this period show definite Chinese influence. Marco Polo, who traveled through Iran to Peking around 1272, speaks of the thriving industries of Tabriz, of the silk of Kashan, and the embroideries of Kerman.

The Mongols were pagans and for a time the Ilkhans of Iran seesawed between Christianity and Islam. Indeed, as early as 1245, Pope Innocent IV sent an embassy under the Franciscan, Jean Plavo de Caprini, all the way to Karakorum in Mongolia for the purpose of opening religious missions in their domains. Actually, from the Ilkhanid period, Iran has attracted embassies from European countries for political, religious, commercial, and cultural purposes continuously to the present time.

In the contest between Christianity and Islam for the allegiance of the Ilkhan kings, Islam was the victor. Ghazan Khan (1295–1304) became a devout Muslim and severed his relation with the Khaqan in China. He was one of the greatest of the Ilkhans, and restored peace to war-torn Iran. Under him the abused and downtrodden peasantry began to prosper. Ghazan Khan instituted an equitable tax system, proclaimed rules of conduct for government officials, and strengthened internal communications. Ghazan was a Muslim with Shi'a leanings. He forced many of the Mongols to follow him and with the zeal of a convert destroyed not only "heathen" temples but also Christian and Jewish houses of worship. He did much to strengthen the Shi'a dervish orders which influenced the social and religious life of Iran and out of which came the Safavid Dynasty.

After such an utter destruction wrought by the Mongols, it is surprising that any kind of initiative was left in Iran. And yet, the fascinating result of the Mongol invasion was that it produced one of the most culturally productive eras in Persian history. It is a tribute to the Persians that they not only restored their own culture, but also civilized the Mongols and, indeed, used their conquerors to improve their own lot. The struggle for survival on the part of the Persians was purely individualistic and was carried out in three ways.

In the first place, as they had done in the case of the Arabs, the Persians influenced the Mongols and assimilated them into the Persian culture. During the Umayyad and the Abbasid reigns the Persians organized political revolts, fomented religious uprisings, joined forces with rival Arab factions, and used personal sacrifice in order to gain their ends. During the Mongol period, however, there was no sign of collective revolt or uprisings and no manifestations of personal bravery. Indeed, there was every sign of abject submission. Individual Persians in perhaps all walks of life, by the use of their talents and cunning, worked their way into the confidence of the Mongols and led them toward cultural rebirth of Iran rather than political domination for themselves.

Two of the best examples of this type of individual attempt in the cultural conquest of the Mongols are Nasir al-Din Tusi and Rashid al-Din Fazlullah, the former associated with Hulagu and the latter with Ghazan. Nasir al-Din, the great astronomer and man of science, exercised great influence over Hulagu Khan. He advised the Mongol conqueror to occupy Baghdad but persuaded him to save the library and bring the books to Maragheh, the Ilkhan capital in Iran. He also persuaded Hulagu to build a magnificent observatory which became the base for astronomical studies for both the Chinese and the Persians. Rashid al-Din was a philosopher, historian, and physician in the court of Ghazan Khan and later became his vazir. Both of the above individuals, and perhaps many others, were eventually executed, but they had learned to enjoy the opportunities which life offered and were resigned to the rest. Although the Persians did not fully recover from the invasion, they retained their individual and cultural pride. It must be stated that the assimilation of the Mongols was made easier because of the vast distance which separated them from their native base in Mongolia. Lacking knowledge of a sedentary life, the Mongols had no one from whom to learn except the people they had conquered.

The second way used by the Persians for survival during the Mongol period was artistic creativity. The first wave of Arab invasion suffocated the artistic sensitivity in the Persians. Islam destroyed the values which the Persians cherished and its strict iconoclasm forbade representational art and put the artist under severe limitations. The artist was alienated from his surroundings and was pushed into seclusion. Later he expressed himself in abstract art through geometric designs and calligraphy. But he always created a border on his canvas or rug and shut himself up, as it were, in the central medallion. The Mongols also destroyed values but, not having any religious dogmas of their own, they did not impose any restrictions. The artist could indulge in representational or any other form of expression to his heart's content. It was indeed the power of the once-barbaric Mongols which freed Persian culture from the limiting influences of Islam and brought Iran into contact with the cultures of Asia and Europe. The famous Persian miniature painting is a mixture of

Chinese and Persian. The artist was free to choose for illustration any of the numerous episodes in the books which the copyist handed to him. It is interesting to note that the Persian artist painted borders around the miniatures but sometimes the pictures inside protrude the borders at different points, reflecting the artist's freedom to move about.

The third way in which the Persian spirit withstood the onslaught of the Mongol invasion was through Sufism, by which he minimized the significance of the real world which had crumbled about him. Sufism played a part in enabling the Persian to avoid the rigors of Mongol domination, and also gave rise to some of the greatest Persian creative talents. Sufism was a reaction to the Persians awareness of the transitory nature of life—an awareness which was heightened by Mongol destruction—so that the mystic experience, i.e., union of the self with God, became a means by which to free the soul. Some of the greatest Persian poets and writers, such as Rumi, Hafez, Sa'di, and others, belong to this period.[2] The western mystic of the thirteenth and fourteenth centuries, having experienced the transitory nature of the world as a whole, decided that he could not enjoy any part of it and became an ascetic. The Persian, on the other hand, kept on disavowing the world as a whole while at the same time enjoying the parts which were within his reach.

By the time the Crusaders were driven away and the Mongols had been absorbed, a pattern emerged in the Middle East which had been forming since the decline of the Abbasids at the beginning of the tenth century. The pattern was not new, but was quite traditional to the Middle East.

In the first place, Iran was separated from the Fertile Crescent along the general line of the Tigris, Shat-al-Arab, and Persian Gulf. Such had been the case during the Sasanid rule. Even though the people on both banks of the rivers had gone through the experience of a common history and intermingling of cultures, neither side felt attached to the destiny of the other. This tendency had already started in the last decades of the ninth century and was subsequently strengthened. During the Crusades, the Saljuqs of Syria repeatedly asked the aid of their kinsmen the Saljuqs of Iran, but their plea fell on deaf ears. Similarly, when both the Persians and the Turks in the east were attacked by the Mongols, the powers in the Fertile Crescent did not come to their aid. The same division, which was the pattern before the coming of Islam, continued after the coming of the Mongols. Apparently, the common confession of faith does not make any more difference in the Muslim world than it does elsewhere among different nations that have the same religion.

In the second place, during the Ilkhan period and afterward, the Persian language replaced Arabic in everything except the saying of prayers and the reading of the Koran. It has been mentioned how the Saffarids and the Samanids started the revival of the Persian language. Throughout the period of principalities Persian came to be used more and more, but still the learned

[2] See above, pp. 102ff.

wrote their serious works in Arabic. After the coming of the Mongols, however, Persian came to its own in every field. All writing, poetical, philosophical, or scientific, was done in the Persian language. The vast majority of the Persians, however, continued to say their prayers and read the Koran in Arabic without understanding them. Consequently, the history of Iran from the Ilkhans to the present is an independent one. Including it with the rest of the Middle East is about as difficult as dealing with the history of England in a survey of European history.

It must be observed in this connection that the Mongol invasion was a mixed blessing for Iran. It was detrimental because it engendered so much individualism and political submissiveness that the development of political national unity was inhibited. In the midst of lawlessness, the Persian became a law unto himself. He usually declined from espousing any cause, especially if it was political and nationalistic. The great poet, Sa'di (d. 1292) wrote: "It's all proper to talk about love of country, but it's senseless to die for the place of one's birth." On the other hand, the Mongol invasion proved a blessing in that it freed the Persians spiritually and created a form of cultural unity. They were not bound by laws of religion nor inhibited by a sense of inferiority to the Arabs. A new cultural "nationalism" replaced the old political struggle for supremacy. Once a cultural identity was established, political unity followed a century and a half later in the founding of the Safavid dynasty.

In the third place, after the Crusades, the Fertile Crescent, Arabia, and Egypt also fell into the traditional patterns of the past. The Arabian Peninsula, which began to lose its importance with the advent of the Abbasids, had long been isolated. Its inhabitants had gone back to their traditional desert life as readily as they had come out of it. The relationship between the Fertile Crescent and Egypt also fell into a pattern which is familiar to students of the ancient Middle East. Somehow Egypt and the Fertile Crescent could not get along on equal terms and they are not able to do so now. Either one had to rule the other or both be ruled by a third power. At the end of the Crusades, it was Egypt under the Mamluks that ruled the Fertile Crescent.

The history of the Middle East from the fall of Baghdad until the middle of the nineteenth century, however, is the story of neither the Arabic speaking peoples nor of the Persians. The main actors were actually the Turks. These were the Ottoman Turks, who replaced the Byzantine empire, and the Persianized Turks in Iran, who established the Safavid empire. The development of Iran, as has been stated, was retarded because of havoc wrought by the Mongols. The Ottomans, therefore, had a head start and to them we shall now turn.

CHAPTER 13

THE OTTOMAN SULTANATE

Osman I (1299–1326)   Murad I (1360–1389)
Orhan (1326–1360)   Bayezid Yilderim(1389–1402)

It has already been noted that in the almost continuous struggle between the Muslim caliphate and the Byzantine empire the Turkish soldiers proved to be an effective advance guard for Islam. It was they who won the Battle of Manzikert north of Lake Van in Armenia and took the Emperor Diogenes prisoner in 1071. This victory opened Asia Minor to Muslim settlement, and enabled the Turkish tribesmen to penetrate westward as far as Smyrna. The Saljuq Turks who had accomplished this feat were eventually separated from their kinsmen in Iran and organized the Saljuqs of Asia Minor or "Rome" as the Muslims called the region. Through a series of wars the Saljuqs occupied most of Asia Minor and ruled in reality or in name until 1302. During most of this time their capital was in Konya (Iconeum). During the last half of the thirteenth century and the first half of the fourteenth century, the Turks had a number of effective princes who attracted the Muslim intellectuals to their capital and were strong enough to provide safety for commerce. Perhaps the most important change wrought during the 300 years of Saljuq rule was the Turkification of a large segment of Asia Minor. Some of the nomadic Turks influenced by the influx of the Turks of the western Caspian had become settled farmers in the villages of Asia Minor.

With few exceptions, the Turkish tribes who came into contact with Islam accepted the Sunni faith and were fanatically loyal to its tenets and institutions. Their attachement to Islam was mostly emotional rather than rational, more out of a sense of loyalty than from understanding. Under the circumstances, it is not perhaps surprising to see the rapid growth of Sufi Orders among them, because Sufism did emphasize loyalty and extol devotion. Sufism, which started as the attempt of an individual to attain union with his God, took on a social aspect among the Turkish tribes. Mainly to practice their devotion the adherents to Sufism banded themselves into brotherhoods. These brotherhoods grew among both the Sunnis and the Shi'is. The loyalty of the individual to the person of the leader was more acceptable to the Turk than loyalty to an abstract idea.

These groups, which later came to be known as "dervish" orders, gave a sense of solidarity and belonging to the Turks, who found themselves among strangers. Into these orders they brought the tradition of their tribes, such as strict discipline, loyalty to the leader, and patience in privations. There were numerous orders and each one had a leader who had attained to that position through his spiritual insight, discipline, piety, and wisdom. Each order, *tariqa*, had a headquarters called *khaneqah* and each headquarters had a leader, called *shaykh* (Arabic), *dada* (Turkish) or *Peer* (Persian)—all of which mean "elder." The novice, *murid*, shaved his head and followed a life of rigid self-discipline, study, prayer, and night vigil until he was pronounced "enlightened." At religious services they sat in a circle and repeated loudly a phrase of the Koran until overcome by emotion. In some orders there was music and the singing of Sufi poems until, in their state of ecstasy, the dervishes would dance and lose themselves in God. Upon "enlightenment," some let their hair grow long and engaged in missionary activities.

Attached to these orders were also "lay brothers" who had an association called *akhi*, which resembled an economic guild. They accepted the leadership of the Elder and adhered to the virtues preached by the order, even though they were engaged in business. Another group of laymen attached to the order was a militant one, *ghazi*. Their purposes were war against the "infidel" non-Muslims and the capture of booty and slaves. In much the same way that the discipline of the contemplative order of Zen Buddhism encouraged the growth of the Samurai warrior in Japan, the rigid self-discipline of the Sufi orders produced the *ghazi* warrior who followed a set of rules and virtues, "futuwa," as earnestly as he blindly obeyed the wishes of the leader. Members of orders were recognized by a special badge which they wore on their turbans or by a special article of clothing. In the absence of a strong central government, these orders offered political and economic security and religious satisfaction and motivation. In these orders religion, commerce, and war were joined together and societies bound by a set of rules and obedience to the leader were established. The founders of both the Ottoman Dynasty of Turkey and the Safavid Dynasty of Iran belonged to Sufi orders, the former Sunni and the latter Shi'a. Whether the ghazi warriors were influenced by a similar group among the Byzantines, called *skritoi*, is not certain. It is certain, however, that the coming of the Mongols and their subsequent settlement strengthened the ghazi tradition.

The origin of the Ottomans is mixed with legend. They belonged to the Oghuz Turks of Central Asia. A certain Ertoghrul was given a reward of a fief in northwest Anatolia for helping the sultan of Konya against the Mongols in 1251. His son, Osman (Uthman) was a ghazi leader fighting for the cause of Islam. While these events which subsequently challenged the destiny of Europe were going on in Asia Minor, in Europe itself Emperor Frederick II of the Holy Roman Empire had died in 1250, the Moors were being pushed out of Spain, England was ruled by Henry III, the Muscovite princes were rising against the Mongol domination, and the Crusaders had been driven out of Jerusalem.

Osman began around 1300 and in 26 years he had carved out a little principality for himself in Asia Minor in the region of modern Eski Shehir. Before he died, he had declared himself an *amir* independent of the sultan of Konya. Similar small ghazi principalities had been established in like manner, only to lose strength after the first or second generation. The house of Osman, however, was destined to be an exception. Thirty-seven of his descendants ruled one of the largest empires of the world for 622 years. His descendants never forgot him. They were proud to call themselves Osmanlis—hence, Ottomans —and each one upon ascending the throne was girded with the sword of Osman as a symbol of power.

One is tempted to search for the causes of such a long existence, but here one is confronted with one of those intangible aspects of history where there are no satisfactory answers. Certainly one reason is the fact that the warrior ghazis had an economic base in the *akhi*, and they together with the spiritual section of the order were all one closely knit group loyal to each other and to the leader. Another reason frequently mentioned is the general disarray in the world of Islam and the crumbling domain of the Byzantines. Although this weakness contributed to the ascendency of the Ottomans, one must not conclude, however, that the Ottoman victories were easy. The city of Bursa was under siege for almost nine years. A unique aspect of the Osmanlis, however, and one which certainly contributed to their power, is the fact that for over eight generations one after the other of Osman's descendants over a span of 200 years were men of resolution, good administrators, and leaders in their own right. By the time the sultans began to show signs of weakness, the empire was so large that it took another 200 years for it to disintegrate. During these last years the "sick man of Europe" was kept alive because it was in the interest of the rival powers of Europe to let him live.

The important city of Bursa was taken by Orhan while his father Osman was dying in 1326. Orhan made the city his capital and continued the expansion of the principality. The ghazi brotherhood was not based on ethnic grounds but on loyalty and action. Consequently, they accepted all comers provided they became Muslims and were loyal to the leader. With this spectacular success, other smaller ghazi bands joined Orhan and his power grew. Furthermore, Orhan quite wisely changed the prevalent ghazi tradition of destroying the enemy after he was defeated or forcing him to become a Muslim. He adopted the Muslim tradition of permitting Christians and Jews to live as "people of the book" and pay the usual head tax. This policy brought stability rather than destruction, and urban centers as well as rural areas which under the weak Byzantines or warring bands had had a precarious existence found new security.

Before his death in 1360, Orhan ruled a principality of considerable size, with flourishing cities such as Bursa, Iznik (Nicocaea), Izmid (Nicomedia), and Bergama (Pergamum). At least three events came to his aid. One was the rivalry between two Byzantine claimants, John Cantacuzemus against John Palaeologus. Orhan allied himself with the former and found access to Europe. He then let loose the restless ghazis in Thrace and along the Black Sea coast for looting and plundering. Orhan also married Theodora, the daughter of Cantacuzemus. The second aid was the Black Death, a plague that began in 1347, and which spread all over the Balkans and disrupted everything. If there was any chance of the Crusaders coming to check the advance of the Ottomans, the Black Death ended that. The third aid was an earthquake in 1354 which struck the European side of the sea of Marmara and destroyed Gallipoli.

Murad I succeeded his father in 1360 and two years later Edirne (Adrianople) fell into his hands and it served as the capital of the enlarged state for a century. This big-voiced illiterate son of Orhan, who used to sign his orders with prints of his thumb and three fingers, loved learning and established schools and alms houses. He also pushed westward into the Balkans. He was shrewd enough to ally himself with one Christian prince against others and in the end, finish them all. He conquered Bulgaria, Macedonia, and parts of Serbia. In Asia Minor he used diplomacy aided by show of force and captured Ankara. Perhaps his greatest battle was that of Kossovo (1389) which subdued Serbia and opened up southeastern Europe. Murad was killed in battle and it fell to his successor, Bayezid I, to finish the victory.

Bayezid (1389–1402) was the first Ottoman to put on the airs of a monarch. In addition, he was shrewd, cruel, vain, and ambitious. One of his first acts was to have his brother, Ya'qub, strangled in order to rid himself of a possible rival. He forced the religious leaders to justify the act through the Koran. This practice gradually became a regular procedure among the Ottomans for nearly three centuries. His ruthlessness and quick action caused his subordinates to call him Yilderim (thunderbolt).

Under him Constantinople was completely blocked by land, but the Ottomans did not have enough sea power to close the city from the sea. Bayezid started a navy in 1390, with the help of seafaring ghazis who had joined him. By 1396 his navy was raiding the shores of the Adriatic and his army was advancing by land into Nicopolis. These victories alarmed Sigismund, King of Hungary, and he organized a crusade of knights from England, France, Germany, and other parts of Europe. In the famous battle of Nicopolis (1396), the Europeans were routed and hundreds of their nobles fell into Bayezid's hands. This was probably the last attempt at organizing a "crusade" but was not the last in checking the growth of the Ottomans. The victor, however, pursued his campaign not westward into Europe, but southward into Greece.

Bayezid, however, had his heart set more on Asia Minor than on Greece. He wanted to be the recognized ruler of a Muslim state. Even though he and his father referred to themselves as "sultan," he wanted official sanction from the puppet caliph in Cairo. After the fall of Baghdad the Mamluk rulers, to give outward prestige to their own position, had taken a member of the Abbasid family who had escaped death at the hands of Hulagu's soldiers and proclaimed him caliph. The subduing of Asia Minor, however, was against ghazi tradition. The ghazis were not willing to fight against fellow Muslims, especially against ghazis of brother orders. Murad had advanced to Ankara mostly through diplomacy, but Bayezid did not have such patience. He had to bring Christian mercenaries in order to fight against Muslims, and this embittered the ghazi states of Asia Minor. To save themselves from Bayezid some of them appealed to the Mamluks of Egypt and others sought the aid of a new conqueror Timur, who had appeared on the eastern horizon.

THE MAMLUKS

This strange and unique oligarchy of slaves ruled Egypt from 1250 to 1517. During this long period, only a few rulers brought a semblance of tranquility to the people of Egypt. Otherwise, the Mamluk domination brought destruction to the country and misery to the masses. Indeed, the people of Egypt have perhaps had the longest history of domination by other peoples. From the fall of the Pharaohs to the middle of the twentieth century, Egypt has been ruled by diverse and always alien peoples. Among these, the Mamluks were the worst.

The Mamluks were not a dynasty, for seldom did a son succeed his father. It was an oligarchy of slaves in which the average reign was not more than five years. At the death (often violent) of the strong man, the remaining slaves in the oligarchy fought each other for the top position. To remain in power, the slave sultan gave land and privileges to the amirs who were slaves themselves and who owned slaves of their own.

The series of Mamluk sultans is usually divided into two groups. One is called the Bahri (sea) who ruled from 1250–1390. They were mostly Turkish and Mongol slaves. The other is Burji (citadel) whose rule from 1382 to 1517 slightly overlaps that of the Bahri. They were mostly Circassian slaves, with the exception of two who were Greek. Each Mamluk knew that his life as a sultan was short. So he lived lavishly and did what his heart desired. The fact that there are some beautiful edifices left from the Mamluk period shows that at least some desired the nicer things in life.

Two of the most famous Mamluk sultans were Baybars (1260–1277) and Qalawun (1279–1290). Baybars checked the advance of the Mongol Hulagu and dealt a crushing blow to the Crusaders. Qalawun controlled Syria and built one of the most advanced hospitals of the period in Cairo. It is a strange paradox that in the midst of so much bloodshed and turmoil, Egypt became an important center of learning in the world of Islam. Cairo was also a thriving commercial center for the East-West trade which brought goods to the Red Sea and then by caravan to the Mediterranean. Some of these slave sultans who did not take the trouble to learn Arabic apparently encouraged the development of literature and art. Perhaps to perpetuate their own memory, they fell into the habit of constructing mausoleum-mosques and in this way contributed to the architectural development of the Islamic world. One of the most exquisite of these mausoleums is the one built by Kaitbay who died in 1495.

In order to add prestige and, at least, an appearance of legitimacy to his rule, Baybars found an uncle of the fallen Abbasid caliph who had escaped death at the hand of the Mongols and installed him with great pomp and ceremony as Caliph al-Mustansir. Later he set out with the new caliph to conquer Baghdad. Apparently Mustansir was killed by the Mongols. Undaunted, Baybars found another scion of the Abbasid family and installed him as Caliph al-Hakim. Hakim and his descendants were puppets of the Mamluks in Cairo. Their duties were to administer the religious endowments and to crown each succeeding Mamluk sultan. One of these "caliphs" invested Bayezid I with the authority to be sultan.

TIMUR (1336–1404)

Timur was born in Transoxiana in 1336. An arrow in one of his earlier battles wounded his leg and made him lame (Persian, *lang*) and so he was known as Timur Lang which in European annals became Tamerlane. He was one of those adventurers who enjoyed cutting pretentious princes down to size. He fought and destroyed and was seldom defeated. It is doubtful whether he had any plans for founding a dynasty, let alone a stable empire. He, like most of the post-Mongol sovereigns, did not have much regard for human life. Some were more sadistic than others. Timur liked to build pyramids from human heads, a practice which was imitated by a few who followed him. Nevertheless, he was a patron of art and literature, and was magnanimous at times even to his enemies. He probably had one great love; and that was the city of Samarqand. He wrought destruction practically everywhere else but built Samarqand and neighboring Bokhara. His tomb is still in Samarqand but not much else has survived.

Unlike Chengiz Khan and a number of Turkish war lords, Timur was literate and had a fair knowledge of literature. Two volumes of autobiography are credited to him. Although there may be doubts as to his complete authorship, the volumes reveal his character and that of his time. He writes about himself: "And from the twelfth year of my age I travelled over countries, and combated difficulties and formed enterprises and vanquished armies, and I hazarded my person in the hour of danger; until in the end I vanquished kingdoms and empires, and established the glory of my name."

Timur heard about the exploits of the Muscovite princes against the Golden Horde. In 1388–1391 he led a campaign to the north against the Golden Horde, the Lithuanians, and the Muscovites. He approached the suburbs of Moscow and received tribute from Vasily (1389–1425), the son of Dimitri Donskoy who was the first Muscovite prince to defeat the Golden Horde. From there he went to Iraq, sacked Baghdad, and wrested all of Syria from the Mamluks of Egypt. He was then in a position to aid the ghazis against Bayezid.

Timur's last campaign was against Bayezid. It was perhaps his greatest campaign, for in all others from Central Asia and India to Iran and Syria, Timur had not met such a strong state as the Ottomans had established. The engagement took place on July 21, 1402, and Bayezid was defeated and taken captive. Timur overran all of Asia Minor, going as far west as Smyrna. Then he went to Samarqand, taking his famous captive with him in an iron-barred litter to prevent Bayezid's further attempt to escape. Bayezid died on the way and it is not known if his body ever arrived in Samarqand.

The establishment of the Ottoman Turks in Asia Minor and in the Balkans was a political and economic threat to the kings and merchants of Europe. From the beginning, the European states tried to check the advance of the Ottomans by seeking alliance with the enemies of the Ottomans to the east. Henry III of Castile (1390–1406), who wanted to check the advance of the Ottomans and at the same time extend the fame of Spain, sent embassies to Timur. Two of his envoys were present at the battle of Ankara. After the battle, Timur dismissed the envoys and sent an ambassador of his own along with them to Spain. Timur also sent a letter to Henry IV of England (1399–1461), proposing commercial relations. This letter and Henry's reply were conveyed by an English Friar known as "Archbishop John" who was residing in Tabriz.

Perhaps the most famous of the early European ambassadors to Iran was Ruy Gonzalez di Clavijo who travelled with Timur's envoy back to Samarqand. This man wrote his experiences and described his observations. He set out from Spain in 1403 and after harrowing experiences arrived in Tabriz. Following the regular caravan route he went to Tehran, Nishapur, Mashhad and on to Samarqand, which he found "larger than Seville."

The Ambassador and his party stayed in Samarqand as the guest of Timur. There were also other ambassadors from Babylon, Egypt, and China. One of the food items which Clavijo mentions frequently is horsemeat, which must have been quite a delicacy among the Turkomans. Eating horsemeat is definitely forbidden in Islam, but apparently the Turks of Central Asia could not give up the habit of a lifetime. Clavijo describes the beautiful gardens and suburbs of Samarqand, enumerates the merchandise of the bazaars, such as linen and skins from Russia, silk and musk from China, and spices from India. Clavijo returned to Spain the same way he had come and arrived at the court of Henry III on March 24, 1406, but Timur was dead by then.

Before the battle of Ankara, while Timur was still in Syria, he met the celebrated Muslim historian of North Africa, Ibn-Khaldun. His introduction to history is more famous by far than the contents of his history. The lengthy introduction, *muqaddima*, antedates the best of the social and political histories of the West by about 500 years. He discusses the importance of social and psychological factors in history, and his historical methodology in research and interpretation won him a place among the major historians of the world. Arnold Toynbee, the twentieth-century English historian, believes that Ibn-Khaldun's prolegomenon is "the greatest work of its kind that has ever yet been created by any mind in any time or place."

Ibn-Khaldun was in the service of the Mamluk Sultan, Faraj, who had been defeated by Timur and was now seeking peace. Timur, who apparently did not lose many opportunities to meet men of skill and learning, had several meetings with Ibn-Khaldun. The celebrated historian has recorded these meetings, which picture Timur to be somewhat knowledgeable about North Africa. Later he asked Ibn-Khaldun to prepare a detailed written report about Egypt and North Africa. Ibn-Khaldun prepared the report but was very eager to expound to the conqueror his philosophy of history, which was built around the concept of "asabiyya." This concept has been translated by some as "nationalism," by others as "group solidarity," and by still others as "social solidarity." Civilizations rise and fall in direct proportion to the strength of this solidarity among the people who govern. Group solidarity is the most important factor in laying the foundation of a civilization. The same civilization, however, is an important cause of the weakening of this solidarity and, therefore, is a cause of the decline of that civilization.

Ibn-Khaldun probably thought that since "social solidarity" existed among the primitive Turks, Timur was the best person to revive the empire of Islam. But Timur did not show any interest in this, even though he allowed the historian to give his lecture.

Ibn-Khaldun must have been greatly disappointed to find out that Timur was fascinated not by the historian's theory of "group solidarity" but by his mule. In their last meeting Timur admired Ibn-Khaldun's mule which prompted the historian to present it to the conqueror. Ibn-Khaldun, who was reluctant to leave Egypt for Syria now seemed somewhat eager to accompany Timur, perhaps still hopeful of exciting the conqueror with his pet theory. Indeed, Ibn-Khaldun suggested that he had no desire to go to Cairo. Nevertheless Timur dismissed him.

Timur died in 1405, three years after the battle of Ankara. The dream of Bayezid to rule the Muslim world was shattered and it seemed that the house of Osman had come to an abrupt end. The sons of Timur, however, could not control Asia Minor. The serveral sons of Bayezid fought against each other. Some of the ghazi amirates declared their independence and others supported the warring sons of Bayezid. Mehmed, however, won the throne and continued the house of Osman.

The descendants of Timur were unlike him in that they did not engage in wars of conquest, but they were like him in that they were poor administrators. His son, Shah-Rokh, was the good and virtuous ruler of Khorasan. A grandson, Ibrahim, encouraged literature in Shiraz. Another grandson, Hosein, was patron of learning in Herat and discussed history and literature with such men of letters as Jami and Mirkhond. Another grandson, Ulugh Beg, who ruled in Samarqand, was a famous astronomer whose astronomical tables were translated into Latin in 1650 and are considered to be the most accurate and complete contribution of this field to the West.

Nevertheless, the death of Timur ushered in a century and a half of feudal wars and postponed Iran's resurgence. By the middle of the fifteenth century, two groups, both Turkish, emerged in northern Iran. One was the Qara Qoyunlu or Black Sheepmen (1378–1469), whose territory was overrun by Timur and who were forced to pay tribute to him. They, however, recovered their losses after the conqueror's death, established themselves in Tabriz, and gained control of Baghdad. The other was Aq Qoyunlu or White Sheepmen (1378–1502), whose great leader Uzun (tall) Hasan (1453–1478) carved a kingdom. By this time Constantinople had fallen and Europe had become more than ever fearful of the menace of the Turks. They were still looking for allies who would attack the Ottomans from the east. What the Europeans had planned to do with the help of Timur, they tried to achieve with Uzun Hasan. Venice took the initiative in this case and sent an embassy to Uzun Hasan. The leader of the embassy was Caterino Zeno, whose mother-in-law was the sister of Theodora, the wife of Uzun Hasan. Zeno was received very favorably and Uzun Hasan started hostilities against the Ottomans in 1478 but nothing came of it. Lack of rapid communication and fluctuating circumstances did not permit a concerted attack on the Ottomans both from the east and the west. About the only result of this embassy was that a number of Persian metal workers settled in Venice where they produced specimens of their craft. Later, in centers such as Nuremberg and Augsburg, these patterns were published in books and were copied by gold- and silversmiths all over Europe.

CHAPTER 14

THE OTTOMAN EMPIRE

Mehmed I (1412–1421)	Selim I (1512–1520)
Murad II (1421–1451)	Suleiman (1520–1566)
Mehmed II (1451–1481)	Selim II (1566–1574)
Bayezid II (1481–1512)	Murad III (1574–1595)
	Ahmad I (1595–1603)

The capture and death of Bayezid[1] was the signal for warfare among his sons and the disintegration of Ottoman control in Asia Minor. For ten years the struggle for supremacy continued among four sons of Bayezid; Musa, Isa, Mehmed, and Suleiman. The ghazi amirs of Asia Minor either took sides or went their own independent way. Isa was eliminated early in the struggle. For a time it seemed that Suleiman had the upper hand, as he was supported by the courtiers in Edirne, the capital. Musa and Mehmed, however, did not acknowledge his leadership and, joining together, slew Suleiman. The surviving two brothers then fought against each other. Musa was acknowledged in Europe and Mehmed remained master in Asia Minor. It was a fight to the finish and in the end he who was more sympathetic to the basic foundations of the Ottoman power won the day. Musa had revolutionary ideals and had come under the influence of Bahr al-Din Simawna, whom he appointed as chief qadi in Europe. Simawna had come under the influence of Manichean syncretism and wanted to unite Judaism, Christianity, and Islam into one religion. Socially and economically he harbored ideas beneficial to the masses. Indeed, Bayezid himself had played with the idea of uniting the religions and nationalities of his domain and probably named his sons as symbols of this union: Musa (Moses—Judaism), Isa (Jesus—Christianity), Mehmed (Islam), Kasimir (Balkan), Ertoghrul (Turkish). Such ideas were too complicated for the majority of the Turks. Furthermore, the privileged classes who had won

---

[1] See above, p. 142.

their fiefs and wealth could not countenance giving them up in favor of the masses.

Mehmed, on the other hand, was everything a good Turk desired. He had revived the ghazi tradition and the virtues of war which lay at the foundation of Ottoman power. With the help of the powerful ghazis and the feudal lords, Mehmed defeated his brother in 1413 and was installed in Edirne as the sultan of the Ottomans. In retrospect, the coming of Timur was only a disturbing interlude in the forward movement of the Ottomans. Timur had not destroyed the Ottoman army and Mehmed used it to come to power. The Ottomans had started as a military state and Mehmed strengthened that tradition.

THE OTTOMAN ARMY

Mehmed's work was not finished. The Turks of Asia Minor would not accept subservience to a centralized state. The ghazi amirs were interested, first and foremost, in their own independence of action and were loath to fight fellow Muslims. Had it not been for the corps of Janissaries that Orhan had started and the organization of the army that had subsequently developed, there would not have been an Ottoman Empire.

At the heart of the Ottoman Army was the corps of Janissaries (Turkish, *yeni cheri*, "new army"). This became the most important fighting force and was a dread to all the foes of the empire. It has already been noted that the ghazis took all comers who espoused their cause and accepted Islam. Gradually, in battle they took slaves and forced them to be Muslims and soldiers. Orhan expanded the practice and later, with the sanction of the religious leaders, the Christian population of the kingdom was made to contribute a certain percentage of its male population as tribute. These were taken as children, completely severed from their Christian parents, and were brought up as Muslims. They were not allowed to marry and their loyalty was to the person of the sultan. Those more able were trained as pages for the court and educated to become administrators. The rest were given military training in the Janissary corps, which may have been the first well trained standing army of Europe. These, being slaves of the sultan, were under his personal command and he could deal with them as he pleased without reference to the religious leaders.

All of the Janissaries were invested into the Baktashi order of dervishes, as was the sultan himself. Their uniform was like that of the Baktashis. Their headgear was white felt with a piece of white cloth hanging from the top of the hat to the shoulder. A spoon was embroidered on this cloth as a symbol of the fact that their livelihood came from the sultan. Each prized his food ki and its loss to the enemy was considered a disgrace. Their commander was called *agha*.

The Janissaries were always infantry troops and were supplemented by an irregular infantry called *azab*. The cavalry was divided into three groups. The most important was *sepahi*, who were provided by the feudal lords to whom land had been given as reward for service or bravery in battle. The second group, *akinji*, was reserve cavalry called in time of war and its duty was to scout and to pursue the enemy. Each cavalryman was provided with two horses. The third group was the royal cavalry which always surrounded the sultan. There were usually 12 commanders of infantry, cavalry, and artillery who formed a council called *birun aghaleri* (outside commanders), while the officers guarding the court were called *anderun aghaleri* (inside commanders). As the empire grew in size two important commanders in chief (beylarbey) were appointed, one for Europe and one for Asia. The weapons for the infantry consisted of bow and arrow, dagger, rifle, and a short sword for man-to-man fighting. The cavalry carried spears and clubs.

With the aid of this strong fighting machine, Mehmed was able to subdue the independent leaders of Asia Minor and reunite the kingdom. His untimely death in 1421 was kept a secret until his successor Murad II had a chance to come to Edirne and assume control. Murad laid siege to Constantinople but had to abandon his plans because of revolt in Asia Minor. Compared with his forebears and in contrast to his son, Murad II was a peaceful sultan. He abdicated twice in favor of his son but had to return to meet emergencies which had developed. He devoted a good deal of time to the development of the Turkish language and the education of his children.

The Turkish language belongs to the Altaic family of languages. When the Turks came to the Muslim world they did not bring with them any written works. They spoke Turkish but the official medium of communication was Persian and almost all the Turkish rulers of principalities were bilingual. When the Saljuqs came to Asia Minor they brought with them a Turkish grammar which a certain Muhammad Qashqai had prepared in 1074. Even the Saljuqs, however, kept their records in Persian and considered it the language of culture. The destruction of Iran by the Mongols isolated the Oghuz Turks of Asia Minor and they gradually came to have a written language of their own. It had many words borrowed from Arabic and Persian. Rumi, the Persian Sufi poet, who had made his home in Konya in the thirteenth century, wrote exclusively in Persian. But his son, Sultan Veled, also a poet, wrote in both Turkish and Persian.

Murad encouraged the writing of chronicles of his Ottoman ancestors in Turkish. He himself was a poet and wrote in both Persian and Turkish. Throughout the fifteenth and sixteenth centuries, Arabic was the language of religion, Persian the language of poetry and decreasingly that of communication, and Turkish the lingua franca and the language of military command.

Mehmed II ruled for 30 years and was engaged almost incessantly in war. He experienced one famous victory and two defeats. He is known, however, for his one great victory and has been given the title of *fatih* (conqueror) for taking Constantinople. Almost as soon as he became sultan, he started preparing for the capture of the city. The siege began on April 6, 1453, and lasted for 53 days. Great balls of stone were hurled against the city walls to no avail. The entrance to the Golden Horn was chained and the Turks could not enter. Repeating a method which the Varangians from Kiev had tried in 908, Mehmed ordered some 70 ships to be pulled on greased runways up the hill, and slid down into the Horn behind the chains. The city had not foreseen such an eventuality. On May 29, 1453, the Turkish columns entered the city through a breach in the wall. Emperor Paleologus, who had incurred the wrath of the citizens by agreeing to become Catholic if the Pope would send him aid, was slain, and on the same afternoon Mehmed entered the city and went straight to Hagia Sophia, the great Cathedral, and ordered it changed into a mosque.

Mehmed must have decided to make Constantinople his capital for he did not allow the customary pillage to last very long. It is said that he saw a soldier removing a stone mosaic from Hagia Sophia and killed him, saying: "I have given the captives and movables to my followers, but the buildings are mine." Most of the churches were converted into mosques. He caused the city to be settled by Turks and Christians. Since the Patriarch of the Orthodox Church had died, he ordered the election of a new Patriarch and gave him a jeweled cross as the Byzantine emperors used to do. As has been pointed out, the fall of Constantinople, like the fall of Baghdad, was an anticlimax. The Turks felt that they had to take it, but not because it blocked their commercial or military or political interests. Like the well-known reason for climbing a mountain, the Ottoman had to take the city because it was there. The city had been so depopulated for lack of business and industry that the sultan had to resettle it.

Europe did not lose anything except a symbol of Christian power in the East, but the Turks gained a beautiful and famous capital. The Muscovite princes of Russia perhaps gained most of all by the fall of Constantinople. Ivan III (1462–1505) married Sophia, the niece of the last Byzantine emperor, who had been the ward of the Pope, and added the crest of the Byzantine emperors to his own shield. His grandson, Ivan the Terrible (1533–1584), assumed the title of Tzar as heir to the Byzantine emperors, and the Russian Orthodox Church called Moscow "the third Rome which would never be destroyed."

Mehmed pushed his conquest in Europe to Bosnia, Herzegovina, and Wallachia and subdued the Tatar Khan of Crimea. In Asia Minor he destroyed his perennial rivals, the Khans of Karaman, and put an end to the hopes of the White Sheepmen.[2] The Black Sea had become a Turkish lake. He built a strong navy and by 1470 had gained control of the eastern Mediterranean. Venice was forced to make peace. His two setbacks occurred in his failure to take Belgrade or Rhodes. He died in 1481.

In the now-familiar struggle for power and the bloodbath which followed the death of the sultan, the Janissaries supported Bayezid II, and he became sultan. His rival and brother, Jem, sought the aid of Pope Innocent VIII and King Charles VII of France, but could not gain the throne and died in 1495. By Ottoman standards, Bayezid was not a warlike individual, though as long

[2] See above, p. 144.

as Jem was seeking aid in the courts of Europe, Bayezid was hampered in his movements. After the death of Jem, however, the Ottomans in a great naval engagement in Navarina defeated the Venetians and put an end to the latter's hopes of supremacy in the Mediterranean. Bayezid was troubled by border disputes with the Mamluks of Egypt and more importantly with the rising star of Esma'il, the founder of the Safavid dynasty of Iran.[3] It was left to Bayezid's successor, however, to deal with both.

The sickly Bayezid could not cope with his three sons, who started fighting him and each other while he was still alive. The Janissaries had become a real power behind the throne and sided with the most warlike of the sons, Selim, who became sultan in 1512. As a warrior, he was nicknamed *Yavuz* (inflexible) and in his short reign of eight years he added more territory to the empire than any other sultan. He was happy in the company of scholars and he himself wrote poetry in three languages. He was also a terror to his subordinates and got rid of so many vazirs that the statement, "May you become the vazir of Sultan Selim," was not considered a compliment.

The activities of Shah Esma'il in Iran, his use of the many Shi'is of Asia Minor against the Ottomans, and his alliance with the Mamluks forced Selim to act. He defeated Esma'il in August 1514 but the result was not conclusive. What was more significant, and what gained the Ottomans territory and prestige, was his victory over the Mamluks of Egypt two years later at Marj Dabiq.

Aside from the fact that Selim was bent on conquest in the east, he had a good excuse for war because Mamluk Sultan, Qansawh al-Ghuri, had allied himself with Shah Esma'il. Ghuri, therefore, had no choice but to fight the Ottoman Selim. A famous battle took place at Marj Dabiq, north of Aleppo, on August 24, 1516. The Mamluks were routed and all Syria fell to the Ottomans. The Turks entered such cities as Aleppo, Damascus, Beirut, and Jerusalem more as deliverers from the excesses of the Mamluks than as conquerors. Selim continued his victorious advance southward and in January 1517 met the new Mamluk Sultan Tuman, and defeated him outside Cairo. All Egypt, as well as the holy cities of Arabia, now fell into his hands. The Ottomans became heirs of both Byzantine emperors and the Abbasid caliphs, with a vast empire to match their new position. Selim took the last puppet caliph, Mutawakkil, with him to Constantinople and later allowed him to return to Cairo, where he died. Even if the story is true that the last caliph transferred his "authority" to the Ottoman sultans, the latter were not in a hurry to assume the title. Their subordinates referred to the Ottoman sultans as caliphs and met with no objection. Gradually everyone took it for granted. So far as is known, the title was first mentioned officially in the Treaty of Kuchuk Kainarji between the Turks and the Russians in 1774.

Suleiman, the only son of Selim, became sultan in 1520 and ruled for 46

---

[3] See below, p. 163.

years. Under him the Ottoman Empire reached its pinnacle of power and glory, and he has been called the "Magnificent" by the Europeans. In Ottoman history he is known as Qanuni (Lawgiver). Suleiman decided to carry out the plans of his great-grandfather, Mehmed the conqueror, and take Belgrade and Rhodes. Europe was then much stronger than at Mehmed's time, but Suleiman's contemporaries, Charles V, Frances I, and Henry VIII, were fighting each other and were too involved in the Reformation to have time to deal with Suleiman. Belgrade fell on August 8, 1521. The following year Suleiman attacked the strongly fortified island of Rhodes. The battle was costly to both sides. Suleiman promised that, with surrender, all the knights who wanted to leave would be given safe conduct with their movable possessions. All who remained would have religious liberty and exemption from taxes for five years. Only then did the island surrender. Suleiman fulfilled both of his promises.

Four years later, Suleiman started out with 100,000 men toward Vienna. The Janissaries had been getting restless from inaction. On August 31, 1526, the sultan won a major battle at Mohacs, Hungary, which enabled him to capture Buda and Pest on both sides of the Danube. He did not have enough men, however, to take Vienna and had to return to Istanbul.[4] Suleiman tried it again in 1529 but his march was impeded by rains and he did not reach Vienna until the end of September. On October 12 the Ottomans breached the wall of Vienna and launched a strong attack, but were beaten off. The Janissaries were not interested in continuing the war because of the approaching winter. A council was held in the field and the Ottomans retired on October 15. Suleiman let it be known that since Ferdinand was not in Vienna, the sultan had lost all interest in taking the city. This was the farthest advance of the Ottomans in Europe. It is doubtful whether the Europeans realized that they had been saved from a catastrophe, for they kept on with their own quarrels. Luther wrote a halfhearted pamphlet, "On the War Against the Turks," but apparently he thought that Rome was more dangerous than the Turks. In about the same spirit, the chief religious leader of the Ottoman Empire at the time of Selim had issued a statement that there was more "merit in killing one heretic Persian [Shi'a] than seventy Christians."

Suleiman's rule was the most glorious in Ottoman history, and its length gave it an aspect of permanence and luster. The entrance to the royal palace in Istabul was called *aliqapu* or the Sublime Porte,[5] and the halls were always crowded with officers, guards, sepahis, and Jannisaries. Even though Suleiman's income was far more than that of his European contemporaries, he never seemed to have enough. His source of revenue was regulated by religious law and it was composed of the tithe from the Muslims, poll tax from non-Muslims, and tax on conquered territories. These taxes were augmented by import and

---

[4] Shortly after the Ottomans captured Constantinople, they renamed it Istanbul. Sometimes it was also referred to as Islambul.

[5] It became customary for the Europeans to refer to the Ottoman government itself as the Porte or Sublime Porte.

export duties, levies on mines and markets, and fines and confiscation of property. His annual income was estimated by Venetian visitors to be between ten to twelve million ducats (about $10,000,000).

The Ottoman sultans maintained large harems made up of slaves who were practically all Christians, and who were guarded by eunuchs headed by *kizlar aghasi* (head of the women's bureau). Suleiman had some 300 women in his harem. According to custom, the girls lined up every day and the sultan, after reviewing them, gave his handkerchief to the one he desired. Girls who failed to attract the attention of the sovereign by the time they reached the age of 25 were usually married to the sepahis of the Sublime Porte.

According to written observations of European visitors, the trade routes were kept in good repair and there were caravanserais along the route. In large cities, there were public baths for men and women, and for a mere four aspers (about one cent) any Turk could spend an hour in the bath. Then, as now, the food of the common citizen consisted of black bread, rice, fruit, and sometimes mutton. There was not much wine drinking in the home out of deference to the Islamic law, but there were taverns which were managed most likely by the non-Muslims, where the "Turks go in and drink all day long." It is reported that card playing was unknown among the Ottomans, but this is very doubtful, for in Iran of the same period the game was well known. Apparently, all European visitors were impressed with the policing of the cities and some declared that Istanbul was safer than any other capital in Europe.

Suleiman's reign marks the beginning of a long decline. Powerful as he was, Suleiman could not cope with the greed of his own retinue or the ambitions of his own officers. The Janissary corps had grown too large to be manageable and increasingly was taking active part in the political affairs of the state. The old ghazi virtues were things of the past. Suleiman himself broke the time-honored tradition of promotion by merit and made his boon companion, Ibrahim, the grand vazir. Ibrahim happened to be an able administrator, but it soon became customary for the sultans to appoint their own favorites without regard to ability.

It was customary also that the sultan preside over the meetings of the Divan (Council). Suleiman delegated this important duty to his grand vazir and spent the time in the harem with his beloved Khurrem (Roxelana to the Europeans), the Russian slave girl who had become his legal wife. She meddled in the affairs of state in favor of her sons and caused Suleiman to order the execution of his oldest son by another woman. Later, the sultan ordered the death of his second son, Bayezid. In the end, the only one left to assume power, Selim, was debauched and a drunkard. Selim's short rule of eight years did not arrest the disintegration of the Empire. After him, most of the sultans preferred the harem to the halls of government. The Ottoman empire was based on the principle of absolute monarchy. The glory of the empire was a reflection of the ability, courage, and wisdom of the supreme ruler. Such an empire could not last long with uninterested and weak monarchs.

CHAPTER 15

OTTOMAN INSTITUTIONS
AND CULTURE

The Ottoman Empire was primarily an army encampment (*urdu*). Fighting
was a most important business. The sultan accompanied the army and he took
his pay as a Janissary, his name being first on the roll. The old formula which was
written in "Mirrors to Princes"[1] was repeated over and over again by Ottoman
counselors: "No government without an army, no army without money, no
money without subjects." In true Mongol fashion the absolute commander of
this military encampment was the sultan. Unlike the Mongols, however, the
Ottomans were Sunni Muslims, and as such, their government was a theocracy.
This meant that the power of the sultan was limited by the law of Allah. The
Ottoman empire was dedicated to the advancement of Islam. It was the land
of Islam and soldiers fought for the cause of Islam. Even the capital was sometimes called Islambul. This naturally limited the power of the sultan. He had
to share it with the Shaykh ul-Islam, the highest religious dignitary in the land.
The balance between an absolute monarch and an absolute God was very
delicate. It always wavered. It is safe to say that all Ottoman institutions and
laws were attempts to find a balance between the two.

Already a good deal of work had been done on determining this delicate
balance during the time of the Abbasids and the period of principalities. By
force of both circumstance and the writings of persons like Ghazali and Ibn-
Taymiyya, anyone with sufficient might could legitimately rule over the
Muslims provided he was with the Shari'a.[2] The natural step to believing in
the divine right of kings was taken by Jalal al-Din Dawwani (1427–1501)
who in his *Akhlaq-e Jalali* (*Ethics of Jalali*) wrote: "The sultan is a person
distinguished by divine support . . . sovereignty itself is a gift of God and his
[the sultan's] divine right will not be affected by his conduct." The Ottoman

[1] See above, p. 110.
[2] See above, p. 111.

Sultans tried to use their prerogatives as much as they could without doing away with the Shari'a. They certainly used titles: "Vicar of God on Earth," "Successor of the Prophet," "Pontiff of the Muslims," "Refuge of the World," "Shadow of God," and, in unbecoming modesty, "Servant of the Two Sanctuaries," (i.e., Mecca and Medina).

The Ottomans tried to keep the balance between theocracy and absolute monarchy, first by using the Irano-Turkish tradition, which gave law-making authority to the sultan. This, however, could be done only with the consent of the *ulama* (religious leaders) who had to make sure that there were no similar laws in the Shari'a. More importantly, however, the sultans used the Islamic law concerning slavery to their own advantage. Since they did not have control over free Muslims except within the limits of the Shari'a, the sultans filled the administrative offices of the state with slaves, over whom they had absolute control without reference to the Shari'a. Consequently, the two institutions grew side by side. One is generally called the "Muslim Institution" and the other the "Ruling Institution." It must be noted that in such a vast empire, comprising diverse peoples, and lasting for centuries, institutions shifted from time to time. The above classification should not be taken too strictly but they should serve as a useful guide to a general understanding of the Ottoman culture.

THE MUSLIM INSTITUTION

The members were drawn from the Muslim population who were, of course, free. They had studied in special schools, *medresseh*. The curricula of such schools consisted of subjects on Islamic religion, Islamic education, and more importantly, Islamic law. Out of these schools came the future preachers, mosque scribes, muezzins, dervishes, teachers in both lower and higher schools, readers of the Koran, qadis, and muftis. Since Islam theoretically has neither a priesthood nor a hierarchy, the above offices would generally correspond, in Christian traditions, with ministers/priests, monks, schoolteachers, and lawyers. All scholars studied the Shari'a and, with the possible exception of some of the dervishes, were devoted to it and believed in the social and political institutions which were based upon it.

Of the above, those who came directly into contact and sometimes into conflict with the members of the ruling institution were lawyers, usually called *qadi* or *mufti*. The Ottoman courts from the lowest to the highest were run by these people. As in their administrative organization, the Ottomans had two chief judges, one for Anatolia (Asia Minor), and one for Rumeli (Europe). True to the military nature of the Ottoman empire, each of the chief judges was called *qadi askar* (Chaplain of the Army). At the pinnacle of this vast religious organization was the Shaykh ul-Islam who was as close to the sultan and his chief advisor as to the intricacies of the Shari'a. In the history of the Ottoman empire these men were sometimes very powerful individuals.

One of the responsibilities imposed by the Institution was the administration of the *Vaqf,* religious endowment. It had complete charge of the expenditure of funds and managements of land and other properties which had been given by the pious for charitable and religious purposes. The chief duty of the judges, however, from small-town mufti to the Shaykh ul-Islam was to study each case, determine its relation to the Shari'a and give an opinion, *fetva.* The issuance of an opinion usually settled the case. The *fetva* of the Shaykh ul-Islam had, of course, national importance. At least eleven sultans were deposed by *fetva.* On all matters the Shaykh ul-Islam, representing the Shari'a, had veto power over the decisions of the sultan. He usually said "olur" (can be) or "*olmaz*" (cannot be) and the sultan had to obey. In practice the implementation of such an arrangement depended upon the power of the sultan and the courage of the Shaykh ul-Islam. In some cases the religious leaders showed courage, and good judgment as when the Shaykh ul-Islam vetoed Sultan Selim the Grim's decision to kill the Christians who refused to learn Arabic. At other times these leaders went along with the wishes of the sultan, such as giving religious sanction to the practice of fratricide whenever a new sultan ascended the throne. All the members of this Muslim Institution were called the *ulama,* learned men. As a class they were extremely reactionary, and were almost always opposed to change.

THE RULING INSTITUTION

Parallel to the Muslim Institution was the Ruling Institution. This group comprised the sultan and his family, the grand vazir and officers of the government, members of the court, and the standing army. Usually everyone except the sultan and his children was of Christian descent and a slave. Elevation to high office such as grand vazir did not change the slave status of the person holding office. Most of these slaves were acquired through the *devshirmeh,* or the practice of taking Christian boys as tribute. The bulk of them were trained as Janissaries. The brighter ones were trained as page boys at the court and received rigorous training in administration. At the age of 25, they were sent away as minor officials in the provinces. Some rose to positions as prominent as the grand vazirate. Indeed, all of the officers of the empire save the members of the Muslim Institution were slaves. All of the boys brought through the devshirmeh were given Muslim education and converted to Islam. Unlike the Janissaries, the members of the administration were allowed to marry. Their children, being born Muslims, could not be slaves. Since they were free, these children could not hold office in the Ruling Institution. As slaves, members of the Ruling Institution were under the direct control of the sultan and not under the Shari'a. In this way the sultan had absolute control of the army and administration without interference from the ulama.

The decision-making body of the administration was the divan or council, presided over by the sultan. The usual members were the grand vazir, the two beylarbeys (commanders) of Rumeli and Anatolia, the two qadi askars, the two *defterdars* (treasurers) and the *nishanji* (chancellor). Each of these vazirs had his own appointees on the provincial, county, and city levels. Later the admiral of the navy (*qapundan pasha*) and the commander of the Janissaries (*agha*) were also members of the council. The whole civil administration was created to support the army. In time of war the provincial governors joined the standing army with their levies.

There were naturally clashes of interests between the Ruling and Muslim Institutions. Since the Shari'a had not foreseen all the problems of a large and complex empire, and could not be expanded, the Ruling Institution resorted to at least three other devices to meet new problems. These were *adet, urf,* and *qanun.* Adet was the custom of each community, which was different among the varied nationalities of the empire. Urf was the nonreligious law which might have emanated from the will of the sultan and/or the judgment of the leaders of the community. Urf was usually introduced when Shari'a did not find a solution. Qanun was the official decree of the sultan which superseded adet, urf, and other qanuns. The ulama were against all three because these did not emanate from the Shari'a. Furthermore, these devices gave more power to the sultans who were tempted to contravene the Shari'a even more. During the period of reform in the nineteenth century, the ulama and the constitutionalists became allies (even though they were opposed in ideology) against the power of the sultan and the Ruling Institution.

NON-MUSLIMS

As a Muslim state, the Ottomans early gave up the ghazi practice of forced conversion to Islam and instead adopted the toleration allowed to the "people of the book" by Islam. The Turks referred to the non-Muslim religious communities as *millet,* and the whole practice became known as the *millet system.* Since the Christian subjects of the Ottomans were almost all members of the Orthodox Church and as such had national ecclesiastical organizations, the Ottomans considered each of them a separate millet. Each millet, whether it be Armenian, Syrian, Greek, or Serbian Orthodox, or Jewish, was under the jurisdiction of its own religious organization and was subject to its laws. This had two effects. One was that these religious communities under this system were freer than under most Christian rulers. As ecclesiastical bodies they became prosperous and powerful. Secondly, members of the top echelons of these millets, who had privileged positions, became as reactionary as the ulama and they also were against change in the empire. It was only after the interference of European nations in the affairs of the Ottomans and their use of the Christian minority as a tool of their imperialism that the Ottomans became suspicious of these millets and ceased to be tolerant as they had previously been. The institution of the millet system should not be taken to mean that non-

Muslims were the equals of Muslims in the eyes of the law. Eventually all non-Muslims were referred to as *rayet* (servile), while the Muslims were *taba'a* (subjects) of the empire.

ARABIC-SPEAKING REGIONS

On the whole, the Turks were not colonizers, and certainly they did not try to colonize Syria and Egypt. The Arabic-speaking peoples were the largest single component of the empire. Either because the Arabs were their co-religionists or for other reasons, the Turks did not bring the Fertile Crescent and Egypt under the direct administration of Istanbul. Under Selim, who conquered the area, and subsequent sultans, local amirs continued to rule and paid tribute to the Sublime Porte. The Ottomans were content to send a governor general just to keep an eye on the affairs. For nearly 400 years, Ottoman rule gave Syria a tranquility which it had not enjoyed since the Umayyad period.

The Arabic-speaking Muslims were never slaves and they reached high positions, especially in the Muslim Institution. Indeed, the Ottomans treated the Arabs much better than they did the Anatolian Turks who were called "*eshek* Turk" or donkey of a Turk. The myth generally circulated by modern Arabs to the effect that 400 years of Ottoman rule suffocated Arab progress cannot be maintained by evidence. The Turks honored the religion of the Arabs, the language of the Arabs, and the laws which the Arabs had established. Certainly in these and other fields the Arabs were freer than some Turks, and the fact that Arabic-speaking peoples did not show greater progress should not be blamed wholly upon the Ottomans.

The situation in Egypt became intolerable not because the Ottomans wanted it that way but because their policy of leaving the local authorities in power continued the despicable Mamluk rule. The Ottomans were interested only in tribute and in not much else. So, the old Mamluk sultans stayed on as Shaykh al-Balad (head of the province) and Amir al-Haj (head of pilgrimage). The last was actually the military commander. The appointments of both of these officials had to have the approval of the Divan in Istanbul. These local officials and their underlings confiscated property and looted the country as before. The Turkish governor generals (pasha) were helpless. Some of the pashas who could not overcome local amirs joined them in the plunder. The pashas were ousted at the will of the Mamluk amirs. In about 250 years of direct Ottoman rule, there were more than 100 pashas. Quite often an emissary of the local amir came, riding on a donkey, to the residence of the pasha at the citadel and cried out, "Descend, O Pasha," and this was usually enough for the pasha to pack his bags and go home to Istanbul.

The Mamluk amirs became so strong that in 1769 the Mamluk Ali Bey took Mecca and proclaimed himself sultan. The Mamluks were not eliminated until the coming of Napoleon and the rise of Muhammad Ali.[3]

[3] See below, pp. 211ff.

CULTURAL LIFE

First and foremost, the Turks were soldiers and, more specifically, soldiers of Islam, whose aim was to propagate the faith and advance its power. In this role they felt their important tasks were to uphold the Shari'a as judges and to maintain law and order as administrators. The wealth of the Turk consisted of land, either as farmer or landlord, or the salary he received for his services. The Christians and Jews were left with the more lucrative tasks of conducting the domestic and foreign commerce of the empire.

Islam owes a great deal to these soldiers and it is difficult to imagine what would have happened to the faith had the Turks not appeared on the scene. The Saljuq Turks saved the Abbasids from the Shi'a Fatimids and the Christian Crusaders. They were the first to establish Islam in Asia Minor and it was they who advanced the banner of Islam as far as the gates of Vienna.

As soldiers, the Turks, perhaps lacked originality in cultural fields, but they were great admirers and patrons of learning. Since Islam and the Shari'a were transmitted to them in Arabic, they continued to regard the language as "holy" and used it as a medium of religious and legal expression. In all other fields, be it literature, art, philosophy, or mysticism, the favorite language was Persian. Their assimilation of Persian lore was so great that in their correspondence with their perennial enemies, the Safavids of Iran, the sultans likened the Safavids to the dastardly "Turanians" who were reputedly the ancestors of the Turks!

The Turks excelled in many branches of learning. Mulla Khusrev was a distinguished jurist under Mehmed the Conqueror, and his works became standard. During the reign of Suleiman the Magnificent, Ibn-Kemal was considered the greatest scholar in Islam. Perhaps because of the needs of war, the Turks produced a large number of eminent physicians. They were famous in central Europe for their surgery and ophthalmology. While in medicine they used Turkish, in historiography the more popular language was Persian. Turkish historiography began with official chronicles and includes accounts of campaigns and conquests. Most of the historians, in imitation of their Abbasid predecessors, wrote comprehensive histories. A few, however, wrote monographs on biography, method of administration, palace life, and even on causes of the decline of the empire.

In literature, the Turks followed the Persians in both style and language to such an extent that, as one writer has said, "Turkish literature has become a true depository of ideas from Islamized Iran." There were talented poets who wrote in Turkish like Fuzuli (d. 1556) and Ahmed Nadim (d. 1730). The masses who frequented coffee houses listened to the professional and itinerant story tellers, *meddah*, who regaled their audiences with the stories in the vernacular, interspersed with lines of poems. The influence of Europe in the nineteenth century and the need to have the participation of the masses, forced the writers to use simple Turkish rather than the Persianized Turkish which had been in vogue.

Perhaps the only works of art which can be recognized as definitely "Turkish" are in the field of architecture. The early Ottoman monuments were mostly Saljuq style which use numerous low cupolas covered with Persian decoration. After the conquest of Constantinople, the Ottomans built not only mosques but palaces and caravanserais. In all these, especially mosques, one can see a graceful blending of Byzantine architecture and Persian decorative designs that produced a style and beauty all its own. The most famous architect of the Ottoman empire was a slave by the name of Sinan who lived during the reign of Suleiman the Magnificent. The edifices erected by this talented man include mosques, schools, palaces, hospitals, and public baths. But the most celebrated of his buildings is the Suleimaniyeh Mosque. Built in the proximity of the Saint Sophia Church in Istanbul, it does what it was designed to do—it eclipses the Byzantine edifice.

OTTOMAN DECLINE

It has already been noted that the latter part of the reign of Suleiman the Magnificent marks the beginning of the decline of the Ottoman empire. As a military organization, the vitality of the Ottoman state depended upon warfare and its economy was based on loot and tribute from the conquered nations. Because of both the rise in power of the nations of Europe and Asia and of the long distances involved, military conquest became more expensive and more difficult. By the end of the sixteenth century, conquest had virtually stopped and the army became restless in having to perform defensive duties. The whole machinery of government, which was oiled and fueled by war, gradually came to a grinding halt. The process of decay took some 300 years but the signs had already appeared in the seventeenth century.

The sultan was the supreme ruler and as such presided over the meetings of the Divan and personally led the campaigns. Suleiman, however, delegated this duty to his grand vazir. For a time the fiction of the sultan's participation was preserved by the building of a marble latticed window in the divan chamber behind which the sultan was believed to be listening. Later the sultans did not bother to carry on the pretense and did not know what was going on. Suleiman also broke the established procedure that only after years of service and demonstration of ability could promotion to higher positions take place. He promoted his friend, Ibrahim, from court page to grand vazir.

Furthermore, as conquest stopped and income from that source dwindled, the sultans tried to pay for the huge expenses of the court by selling offices to the highest bidder. This was a departure from the prevalent custom of training officials from the *devshirmeh*. Beylarbeys, provincial commanders, rich individuals, and groups bought and sold offices at the expense of the masses. The sultans, however, continued to live in luxury and debauchery. In the absence of rules for a peaceful transfer of power sometimes the best of the princes were eliminated. Even the education of the princes was discontinued. They were brought up in the harem and had as their companions eunuchs and women of no education. From Murad III (1574–1595) on, the best that can be said about the Ottoman sultans is that some were not as bad as others.

The grand vazirs who ruled in the name of the sultan became corrupted by the system. Having bought his way up to that position, the grand vazir was not a free agent. He was usually indebted to the women of the harem, or eunuchs, or the army, or the ulama, or a combination of these, who wanted him to exploit the population for their own benfit. Since his life was in the hands of the sultan who, in turn, was influenced by groups with vested interests, it was more prudent for the grand vazir to join the groups in plunder. It must also be said that were it not for the courage and ability of some of the grand vazirs the empire would not have lasted as long as it did.

Among the more famous of the strong grand vazirs are the Koprulus who, like the Barmakids during the time of the Abbasids, ruled as a family for nearly 50 years. Mehmed Köprülü was appointed by the mother of Mehmed IV (1648–1687) to save her son from the carnage that was going on. It is reported that in five years as grand vazir he killed over 30,000 people who were members of both the Muslim and Ruling Institutions. He tried to revive the military spirit of the Ottomans and organized military campaigns. His son, Ahmed, continued as grand vazir with distinction until his death in 1676. Sultan Suleiman II appointed a younger brother of Ahmed, Mustafa Köprülü, in 1689. But these strong grand vazirs, no matter how able, were very few in number and came at long intervals. All they could do was prolong the life of the empire rather than cure its disease.

In searching for the causes of decline, the corruption of the army stands out in bold relief, for the power and weakness of the empire was in relation to its military strength. The Janissaries, once the heart of the army, had been weakened by being allowed to marry. This had caused the soldiers to give first loyalty to their families rather than the sultan, who had commanded their sole loyalty when they did not have families of their own. Under Murad III, the members of the organization were permitted to enlist their sons in the corps. Later on, when need arose, unemployed Muslims were admitted. By the beginning of the seventeenth century, devshirmeh had been abandoned and the Janissaries were engaged in trade on the side. Since they were no longer slaves, they had become a powerful caste over whom the sultan did not have much control. They increased in number and became a great burden to the economy of the country. By the middle of the eighteenth century the Janissary pay ticket was bought and sold in the open market. By the time they were disbanded in the 1800's, of the 150,000 on the roll, only 2,000 had had military training.

The other important branch of the army, the sepahis, who were the feudal cavalry, did not fare much better. At the time of Murad III, the feudal lords and members of the court entered their servants, slaves, eunuchs, and others on the roll of the sepahis and pocketed their pay. By the middle of the eighteenth century, the Ottoman cavalry had ceased to exist as an important force.

Direct taxation had been replaced by the sale of the taxes of a district to the highest bidder. Taxes were not high, but the manner of collection was oppressive to the masses. The taxes of a district were traded in the market and the buyer had to make his profit at the expense of the villager. Since offices of the administration could be held by the giving of "presents," each had to make enough to be able to give a portion to the person above him and so on up to the sultan.

The ulama, the ruling classes, the leaders of the millets, and the businessmen (who were mostly Christians), were all involved and were equally reactionary and opposed to change. They liked the system which had given them the privileges and did not want strong men at the helm. They wanted the system to work for their own benefit and not for that of the people. When the system was in danger, they banded together to protect it. But, once the danger was passed, they continued their plunder.

Two more factors must be mentioned in relating the process of the decline of the Ottoman empire. One is economic. The discovery of the New World and the emergence of mercantilism in Europe had shifted trade centers. Mediterranean trade ceased to be important and land routes were replaced by sea routes. This wrought havoc to the Ottoman economy and there was not much incentive for investment.

A second reason is that the decline of the Ottoman empire coincided with the resurgence of Europe as a whole and as a continent of independent nations. European merchant adventurers were going every which way in search of markets and raw materials, and a declining colossus such as the Ottoman empire was bound to be affected. Countries such as Russia, Austria, Germany, France, and England expanded at the expense of the Ottomans. The Treaty of Karlowitz (1697), in which practically all Europe was represented, was the beginning of the end of Ottoman supremacy in Europe and the start of European imperialism in the Middle East.

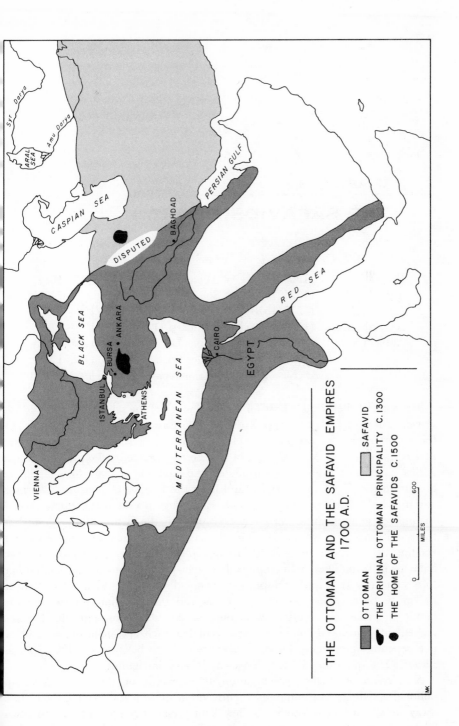

THE OTTOMAN AND THE SAFAVID EMPIRES
1700 A.D.

OTTOMAN

THE ORIGINAL OTTOMAN PRINCIPALITY C. 1300

SAFAVID

THE HOME OF THE SAFAVIDS C. 1500

0   600
MILES

SYR DARYA

AMU DARYA

ARAL SEA

CASPIAN SEA

DISPUTED

BAGHDAD

PERSIAN GULF

BLACK SEA

BURSA • ANKARA

ISTANBUL

ATHENS

MEDITERRANEAN SEA

RED SEA

CAIRO

EGYPT

VIENNA •

MK

CHAPTER 16

THE SAFAVIDS OF IRAN

Esma'il I	(1500–1524)	Abbas II	(1642–1667)
Tahmasp I	(1524–1576)	Soleimam	(1667–1694)
Esma'il II	(1576–1578)	Hosein	(1694–1722)
Khodabandeh	(1578–1587)	Tahmasp II	(1722–1731)
Abbas I	(1587–1629)	Abbas III	(1731–1736)
Safi	(1629–1642)	Nader Shah Afshar	(1736–1747)
		Karim Khan Zand	(1747–1779)

The map of the Middle East for the beginning of the seventh century is not so very different from the map of the Middle East a thousand years later. In the seventh century two powers dominated the area. The Byzantine empire had control of Asia Minor, most of the Fertile Crescent, Egypt, and North Africa, and ruled from Constantinople. The Sasanids of Iran dominated the area from the Tigris to the Indus and from the Persian Gulf to the Caucasus and the Urals. These two empires fought each other to a standstill and weakened themselves so much that they fell easy prey to the Arabs of the desert. A thousand years later we find the Middle East again dominated by two powers residing in the same areas as before: the Ottomans in Asia Minor and the Safavids in Iran. These two empires, like their predecessors, fought each other to a standstill. It is quite tempting to conclude, as some have done, that as the mutual weakening of the Byzantines and the Sasanids played into the hands of Arabs, the mutual weakening of the Ottomans and the Persians played into the hands of Europeans. Whether such a conclusion is valid or not depends upon many imponderables which are beyond the scope of this survey. The question in itself, however, is very intriguing.

As a result of the Mongol invasion, the Persians, on the whole, gave up political activities, and immersed themselves in Sufism and whiled their time away in all sorts of eclecticism. They kept their language and culture alive. Though they were not interested in political and dynastic activities, they influenced those who were. The Mongols and diverse Turkish tribes who formed principalities in Iran took on the culture of the Persians and, with few exceptions, adopted the Persian language and institutions.

From the Mongol invasion until 1502, Iran did not enjoy a unified and stable government. The Ilkhans, after vacillating between Christianity and Islam, accepted the latter and, like the Turks of Anatolia, attached themselves to Sufi orders. Ghazan Khan settled the question of religion and became a Muslim. He came under the influence of a Sufi by the name of Shaykh Safi Gilani (d. 1334) who had organized an order in Rasht, a provincial capital near the Caspian Sea. By the fifteenth century, the Safi order of Sufis had joined the Shi'a sect and like the Sunnis, had laymen who engaged in business activities and soldiers who were zealous to advance the cause of Shi'ism by the sword. The military followers of the Safavids had red headgear and were called "red heads," *qizilbash*.

The members of the qizilbash were known for their absolute devotion to their leader, which office, in good Shi'a tradition, was hereditary. They were in constant war with Sunni ghazi states and later with the Ottomans ruling in Asia Minor. There were large numbers of Shi'a sympathizers in Asia Minor who were thorns in the flesh of the Ottoman body politic. Esma'il, the direct descendant of Safi, was a boy living in Iran where his father, Shaykh Haydar, was the leader of the order and was killed in 1490. With a number of his father's followers, Esma'il went to Ardabil in 1500. He was then 13. In two years this remarkable boy conquered all of Shirvan, Armenia, and Azarbaijan, and declared himself Shah.

The Safavids claimed that they were *sayyids* (descendants of the Prophet) on their father's side and descendants of the Sasanid princes on their mother's side. That they were either is unlikely. They were probably members of a Turkish or Kurdish tribe in Azarbaijan and their early followers were Turkomans. Esma'il's mother tongue was Turkish and he also wrote poetry in that language. Indeed, when the Ottomans gloried in using Persian, Esma'il's court used the Turkish language. The Safavids, however, were Persianized at a rapid pace, and, like the heads of other principalities, assumed the title and culture of the Persians and were known by outsiders as Persians.

Esma'il conquered all of Iran and forced the inhabitants to become Shi'i. He was the bitter enemy of all Sunnis and encouraged the Shi'is of Asia Minor to revolt against the Ottomans. Shi'ism became the state religion of Iran and this thwarted the ambition of the Ottomans, especially of Sultan Selim, who wanted to be the supreme ruler of the Muslim world. Also, Shi'ism prevented Iran from being swallowed up by the Ottomans. Even though the Safavids were Turks, they identified themselves with Persians and the Safavid Dynasty certainly brought about a national Persian independence.

In any case, Shah Esma'il at the age of 20 was master of most of Iran and caused a number of revolts against the Sunnis of Asia Minor. Bayezid II and Selim I were contemporaries of Shah Esma'il. Selim I, who was suspicious of

Esma'il, decided to follow a conciliatory course. After all, the Ottoman sultan was not interested in taking Iran, and Bayezid would be satsified if Esma'il were to direct his conquest eastward and let Asia Minor alone.

In at least two letters which he wrote Esma'il, both in Persian and Turkish, Bayezid congratulated him on his victories and offered "fatherly" advice. He asked that Esma'il cease the destruction of the graves and mosques of the Sunnis and refrain from the use of religion as a means of grasping political power. He also hinted that Esma'il would find his position very insecure because "Persians are a people who won't obey a king who is not one of them." Esma'il, however, responded by intensifying his persecution of the Sunnis. Bayezid forbade the Ottoman subjects from going to Iran but did not molest visitors from Iran. In the meantime, Shah Esma'il won a resounding victory against the Uzbeks and captured their leader, Shaybak Khan. The blind religious obedience of the Sufi warriors to the command of Esma'il was so great that at the Shah's order, the qizilbash actually ate the victim's raw flesh! Esma'il ordered Shaybak's skull to be rimmed with gold and used it as a drinking goblet throughout his life. He ordered his rival's body to be skinned and stuffed with straw and sent it to Bayezid. Selim, the son of Bayezid, was not as conciliatory as his father had been. He developed a hatred for Esma'il and many Persian and Turkish historians consider this to be the immediate cause of war between the two. Actually, the growing power of Esma'il was a direct threat to Asia Minor, especially with the large number of Shi'i sympathizers who were living there. Furthermore, as defenders of Sunni orthodoxy, the Ottomans could not remain indifferent.

When Selim became sultan, Esma'il did not send him a congratulatory message, and continued his devastation of Sunni property. Selim, as defender of Sunni orthodoxy, had no choice but to lead a campaign against Esma'il. Selim had a long way to go and Esma'il, by following a scorched earth policy, tried to draw the Ottomans to the interior of Iran. The Ottoman soldiers were not happy in eastern campaigns. Perhaps the heat, the inhospitable terrain, and the fact that they had to fight Muslims had something to do with it. Even the Janissaries were unhappy. The sultan, however, persisted in his march and in killing Shi'is wherever he could find them in his own domain. It is estimated that he destroyed some 40,000 Shi'i Sufis. The first engagement took place in Chaldran, west of Lake Urmia (Rezayieh) on August 24, 1514. The victory of the Ottomans was definite though not conclusive. Selim occupied Tabriz for a time. Shah Esma'il, who was 28 years old, became rather despondent at the defeat and took to wine. The battle of Chaldran is important in the history of the Middle East because it was the first of the engagements between the two protagonists, namely, the Ottomans and the Persians, for over a period of 200 years. Secondly, it convinced the Safavids of the importance of modern weapons. The tendency of both Turkish and Persian historians to exaggerate makes it difficult to ascertain the number of troops involved. What is certain, however, is that the Ottomans had cavalry and infantry with muskets and the all important artillery. The Safavid army was made up entirely of qizilbash cavalry with spears, bows, and swords. They were all religious devotees of Shah Esma'il and fought bravely with the encouragement of their women, who, apparently, accompanied them. But they found out that fanatical courage was no match for guns and it was the Turkish artillery that won the day for the Ottomans at Chaldran, as well as at Marj Dabiq two years later against the Mamluks. The Safavids purchased firearms and were able to avenge Chaldran in later years.

Shah Esma'il died at the young age of 37 but, in spite of the Chaldran defeat, had laid the foundation of an empire based on two principles. First, it was Shi'i, and second, it was Persian. Shah Esma'il and his son, Shah Tahmasp, were more interested in the former while Shah Abbas and the later Safavids emphasized the latter.

Having become masters of all of Iran, shah Esma'il and his qizilbash devotees enforced conversion to Shi'ism at swordpoint and created a centralized state based on Shi'i doctrine. The Persians, who had become tired of wars and bloodshed, accepted the suzerainty of the Safavids and the Shi'i sect without much resistance. Shi'ism separated the Shi'i Turks of Iran from the Turks of Asia Minor who remained Sunnis, and the gap has not been breached to this day. Shi'ism also separated the Sunnis of the Ottoman Empire from the Sunnis of Central Asia and defeated the hope of the Ottoman sultans to rule as caliphs over a unified Islamic world.

From the death of Shah Esma'il in 1524 until the accession of Shah Abbas the Great in 1567, the Safavids under three shahs, Tahmasp I, Esma'il II, and Mohammad Khodabandeh, turned their eyes eastward and carved out an empire which stretched from the Persian Gulf to both sides of the Caspian Sea and from the Tigris to Transoxiana. They held their own against the Ottomans, reoccupied Tabriz, and fought back and forth against the Ottomans over Baghdad in the south and Armenia in the north. It was their aim to establish a Shi'i theocracy with the Shah as the sole leader. The fighting order of the qizilbash was the backbone of the state. The country was divided into districts and each district was under a leading qizilbash who ruled it as a fief. In return, he provided the Shah with soldiers in time of war and with a portion of the revenue. Otherwise, he was free to do as he pleased. It was through these qizilbash feudal lords that the whole country was forced to become Shi'i. In towns and villages all across the land people were asked to curse the first three caliphs, that is, Abu Bakr, Umar, and Uthman. Those who refused were summarily executed.

Because of the facts that the Safavids controlled a large territory in the east and that Tabriz, their capital, was too close to the Ottoman border to be safe, Shah Tahmasp moved the capital to the city of Qazvin, in north central Iran. The qizilbash leaders became so rich and powerful that they tried to interfere in the question of succession, which had generally become the most acute and perennial question in the whole Islamic world, Arab, Ottoman, or Persian.

The qizilbash fought each other over the succession and gradually revolted against the "most perfect leader" of the qizilbash order, the Shah himself. Very much like the Boyars of Russia, the qizilbash lords preferred an oligarchy in which they wielded power collectively rather than a centralized government under an autocratic shah. They became especially troublesome at the time of the mild-mannered ascetic shah, Mohammad Khodabandeh, and tried to influence him to choose a weak successor. To insure the success of their scheme, they executed most of the Safavid princes, including the heir apparent and his mother.

A younger brother of the crown prince, however, was rescued and taken secretly to Khorasan. Some years later, this young prince, with the help of the more loyal qizilbash, defeated the quarrelsome leaders and assumed the throne as Shah Abbas (1587). Under Shah Abbas, Iran reached its zenith of power politically, economically, and culturally. After the passage of a thousand years, a territory as extensive as during the time of the Sassanids was, once again, called Iran. It is no doubt for this reason that the Persians remember Shah Abbas with pride and affection and have given him the title of "the Great." Fortunately for Shah Abbas, he ruled during the time when the Ottomans were at their weakest. He was a contemporary of no less than five sultans. Russia to the north was going through its "time of troubles" after the death of Ivan the Terrible. Shah Abbas was the contemporary of Ivan the Terrible, Boris Godunov and Michael, the latter being the first in the line of the Romanovs. Consequently, Shah Abbas extended his territory at the expense of both the Ottomans and the Muscovites and had little difficulty in penetrating into Transoxiana to the north and the Indus valley in India.

One of the first things Shah Abbas did in asserting his power was to curb the power of the qizilbash feudal lords. His enmity toward them was both personal, in that they had killed his mother and brother, and political, in that they desired an oligarchy rather than a strong central government. He had them executed without mercy. He still maintained a qizilbash corps but they were armed with the traditional antiquated weapons. To offset their prestige, he organized two armies, one made up mostly of Christian subjects from Georgia and Armenia, and the other composed of Persians. He equipped these two with modern muskets and artillery.

The destruction of the qizilbash also weakened militant Sufism. Shah Abbas was not a fanatical Shi'i like his predecessors. While Shah Tahmasp would not allow Christians to come to his court because, as "infidels," they would defile it, Shah Abbas went out of his way to welcome foreigners and to be good to his Christian subjects. No doubt, as will be seen, he was politically motivated in his dealing with Christian nations; but, nevertheless, he could not have done all that he did without some liberal convictions.

To his new capital in Esfahan he brought a large number of Armenians from their home in Jolfa. Across the Zayandeh Rud (river) in Esfahan he built the New Jolfa and settled the Armenians there. More Armenians migrated voluntarily to all parts of Iran. Perhaps Shah Abbas brought the Armenians with the idea of using them as hostages to keep the Armenians in Asia Minor under his control. Nevertheless, once there, the Armenians were given freedom and had a liberalizing effect on their Muslim neighbors. They could own their own houses, could ride on a horse, and could wear any kind of clothes they pleased, a privilege which non-Muslims did not have before or for long after Shah Abbas until modern times. Silk, which was one of the most important exports of Iran as a trade, became a monopoly of the Shah, and Armenian merchants administered it for him. In being kind to the Christians and giving permission to Catholic missions to establish themselves in Iran, he hoped to ally himself with Europe against the Ottomans, to take advantage of the presence of so many Eurpoean ships in the Persian Gulf, and to take trade away from the Ottomans. Indeed, by subtle remarks and hints, he had led some of the Christian monks from Rome to believe that he was just about ready to become a Christian. At one time, he even let it be known that any Muslim in his realm could become Christian if he so desired.

Shah Abbas, of course, was a Shi'i Muslim and continued the policy of strengthening that religion in Iran as a counteraction to the Sunnism of the Ottomans. In the course of years, the nationalism of the Persians took on a religious flavor and Shi'ism and Persian nationalism became one and the same thing.

Shah Abbas built a beautiful mausoleum over the tomb of the eighth imam Ali al-Rida in Mashhad and made a vow to walk from Esfahan on a pilgrimage at the completion of the edifice. He fulfilled his vow, and pilgrimage to Mashhad became about as important as the pilgrimages to Mecca and to Karbala, the tomb of Husayn. The honorary title of "Mashhadi" was bestowed on anyone who had gone to Mashhad and became as important as *haji* for going to Mecca, and *karbalii* for going to Karbala. Safavid kings, to show their subservience to the first imam, Ali, referred to themselves as the "dog of the threshold of Ali."

Shah Abbas did much to revive commerce and industry. He built numerous caravanserais and guest houses all along the trade routes. He was most harsh in his treatment of dishonest government officials in all parts of the country and, no doubt for this reason, was very popular among the common people. His habit of going among the people in disguise to inspect their condition of life has given rise to a fund of stories that Persian grandmothers still tell their grandchildren. Like most sovereigns of his period, he was also a tyrant and had many executioners at his command. He had five sons. Of these, two died naturally and of the remaining three, one was executed and two blinded by his order, all on baseless charges. Like his contemporary Ivan the Terrible, when Shah Abbas died in 1629, there was no worthy successor left, for he had killed them all.

The Shi'i theocracy, like that of the Sunni, was championed by the Persian ulama. Corresponding to the Shaykh ul-Islam of the Ottomans, the Safavids had the *Molla Bashi*, who was the chief of all the clergy. He, together with three or four others, was a *mujtahid;* that is, they had the right to give their opinions as representatives of the hidden Imam, who was the true head of the state. In this way the Shi'is, unlike the Sunnis, were not limited by the Shari'a, though this did not make them any less conservative. Shah Abbas was strong enough to limit the ulama to the field of law and preaching and did not let them interfere with his political and international affairs. When foreign ambassadors arrived, the ulama did not usually attend the reception given in the ambassadors' honor. Sometimes they did attend such meetings but usually left the banquet before wine was served or musicians had begun to entertain the guests. But the descendants of Shah Abbas gradually lost their power to the ulama. Shah Sultan Hosein was so superstitiously religious that he would not move without the advice of the ulama. This weak and indecisive Shah lost most of his empire to the Afghans. Tahmasp II was not much better, and were it not for the rise of Nader, the soldier of fortune, who is referred to as the "Napoleon of Iran," the whole empire would have disappeared. Even though Nader's accomplishments did not last very long, they came at an opportune time to give Iran a continued existence and bring it to the eighteenth century still with a strong government.

Nader was a Turk related to the Afshar tribe, which was one of the Turkish tribes loyal to the Safavids. He was born in 1688 and was an officer in the Safavid army. The weakness of the Safavids caused the Ottomans to encourage the Sunni Afghans to attack Iran. Their success whetted the appetites of both the Russians under Peter the Great and the Ottomans under Ahmed III. The Russians stopped their plans because of the death of Peter in 1725, but the Ottomans continued the hostilities and it was Sultan Mahmud I who defeated Shah Tahmasp II in 1731. In the peace treaty of 1732, Iran gave up five cities in the Caucasus.

Nader did not like what was going on, so he led a revolt against the Shah and chose the latter's infant son, Abbas III, as Shah with himself as regent. He then tore up the treaty and fought against the Ottomans. The infant Shah died in 1736 and Nader, instead of assuming power himself, gathered together the leaders of the tribes and representatives of the population from all walks of life and caused them to request him to become Shah.

The great assembly took place in Dasht-e Moghan in Azarbaijan. An eye witness, the Armenian Catholicus, who had been invited to attend, gave a detailed description of the gathering. He estimated that a thousand delegates were present. Nader announced that now that he had rid the country of foreign aggressors, he was "old and tired" and wanted to retire to Khorasan. He was then 48 years old. It was incumbent upon the delegates to choose a suitable person to become Shah. The next day the delegates assembled in front of his tent and reported that they had discussed the matter and could find no one more suitable than himself. Nader then came to the main reason for which he had put on such a spectacle. He said that he would accept the throne under three conditions:

1. That they would agree not to help the members of the Safavid family;
2. That they would accept his own son as his legal successor;
3. That they would not curse the first three caliphs, and would not molest the Sunnis.

These were accepted and he was crowned Shah on March 6, 1736.

Nader Shah was neither a Shi'i nor a Sunni, but a freethinker. His main purpose was to break the power of the Shi'i ulama and to protect himself, at least temporarily, from the Ottomans while he was busy in the east. In 1738, he led a campaign against the Moghul empire of India. He took Ghazneh, Kabul, and Lahore. On March 20, 1739, he defeated Mohammad Shah of India and entered Delhi. In this campaign, in addition to gaining two fabulous thrones, one of them the famous peacock throne, he brought with him the famous diamond Kuh-e Nur and so many other riches that it was possible for him to exempt the Persians from paying taxes for three years. He led successful campaigns against the Russians and the Ottomans, but these did not last long, for his character had also changed and he became suspicious and ruthless. He blinded his own son. He was assassinated on June 20, 1747.

Ironically enough, the cause of his assassination was not his change of character but his religion. Nader Shah was a freethinker and wanted to unite all religions. He ordered that the Old and New Testaments be translated into Persian. He also had the Koran translated into Persian. He gathered the representatives of all religions in Iran and told them that if there was only one God, there should be only one religion. He offended the Shi'is and other Muslims by saying that he was as good as Muhammad and Ali. "Their greatness," he said, "was because of their success in war and I have reached this position by war."[1] He was interested in uniting Islam. To achieve this goal he made a five-point proposition to the Ottoman Sultan, Mahmud I:

1. That Shi'i doctrine be recognized officially as the fifth school of thought in Islam;[2]
2. That the Shi'is should have special accommodations in Mecca;
3. That every year there should be a special leader of pilgrimage, *Amir al-Haj*, from Iran;
4. That Ottomans and Persians should exchange prisoners of war;
5. That Ottomans and Persians should exchange ambassadors.

The Shi'i leaders in Najaf were greatly perturbed over this news. They opposed these measures and led a revolt against Nader Shah which culminated in his assassination. The failure of Nader Shah shows how deeply committed to Shi'ism the Persians had become.

[1] See above, p. 95.
[2] See above, pp. 105ff.

The death of Nader Shah was the signal for more confusion and warfare. For a brief period it seemed that a Persian dynasty in Shiraz under Karim Khan Zand might save the situation, but his untimely death gave the opportunity to the Turkish Qajar tribe from the north to take control under Agha Mohammad in 1779. The history of Iran during the Qajar rule belongs to the period of European imperialism in the Middle East and will be treated later.

CHAPTER 17

TWO CENTURIES OF
INTERNATIONAL RELATIONS

The Mongol invasion and the subsequent fall of Baghdad ended the isolation of Iran and brought her into contact with Europeans of all types, priests, merchants, diplomats, and adventurers. The Crusaders became conscious of the differences existing between Iran and the rest of the Muslims to the west and they tried to cultivate the rulers of Iran against Syria. The Ilkhans and the Timurids were approached by the Europeans in order to seek allies against the Ottomans. The relations became mutually profitable and were intensified by Shah Abbas the Great.

This is not to say that there were no trade or diplomatic relations between the European countries and the Ottomans. Many countries of Europe had vied with each other to trade with the Ottomans. This attitude, however, changed when the Turks became more belligerent and threatened the independence of western European countries. In peacetime there were diplomatic relations and exchange of embassies. Venice continued trade relations with the Ottomans the longest, in spite of frequent wars. These relations, however, either were broken by war or were always in danger of being broken. Usually the ambassadors from the countries against whom the sultan had commenced hostilities were thrown into prison. Furthermore, the Ottomans were always conscious that they were commissioned by Allah for the propagation and expansion of Islam. Consequently, whatever relations existed were precarious and were not on mutual terms.

In the case of Iran, however, the situation was quite different. The Safavids, even in their most fanatical mood, never had the idea that they were commissioned by Allah to convert the infidels. On the contrary, if they felt commissioned at all, it was for the conversion or the destruction of Sunnis. It did not make any difference to them who destroyed the "heretical" Ottoman power, they or the "infidel" Christians. Since the aim of the Europeans was also the destruction of Ottoman power, the Persians and the Europeans approached each other on a basis of equality. The Europeans needed Iran, or at least thought they did, to counteract the pressure of the Ottomans. The Persians needed Europe to engage the Ottomans in war and, more importantly, to monopolize the commerce of the Middle East.

The spectacular victories of the pagan Mongols over Islam encouraged Europeans to seek a rapprochement with them both to counteract the aggressive nature of Islam and also to make an attempt to convert the Mongols to Christianity. Pope Innocent IV sent two embassies to the Mongols. The leadership of one of them was with an Italian monk, Giovanni de Piano Carpini. He arrived in Mongolia in 1246 and was present when Ogatai was chosen to succeed his father, Chengiz Khan. Saint Louis (1226–1270), the king of France, was friendly to the Mongols and sent them an embassy.

After the fall of the Abbasids, Europeans felt welcome in Iran and they came in great numbers for religious and commercial purposes. One of the most famous of these was Marco Polo (1254–1324), the record of whose adventures did much to stimulate more Europeans to make the journey eastward. In the formative years of the Ottoman empire, the Europeans were wary of this new antagonist and preferred to do business with Iran. During the reign of Ghazan Khan (1295–1304) Iran, rather than the blockaded Constantinople, was the center of commercial exchange between Asia and Europe, and Tabriz was an important center of business.

The embassy of the Spanish rulers of Castile to the court of Timur has already been mentioned.[1] They arrived when Timur was leading a campaign against Bayezid in Ankara. They witnessed the battle and later went with the victorious Amir to Samarqand. The accounts of the experiences of this and other embassies are excellent sources for studying the life and culture of the Middle East of that period.

The Safavid policy was based on animosity to the Ottomans. In Iran the national spirit had become weakened, mostly because of the destruction wrought by the Mongols, and the people were more interested in religion. The Safavids used this trait and made Shi'ism the state religion of the newly created empire. The Safavids separated Iran from the rest of the Muslim world and courted the friendship of Europe. Shah Abbas was especially helpful to the Christian Armenians whom he had brought to Esfahan. He built churches for them and gave them commercial privileges and religious freedom. They were free from paying import and export duties. Portuguese, Spanish, Dutch, English, Russian, French, and Indian merchants did business in Iran. Even the Ottoman merchants found it more profitable to carry on commercial activities in Iran during peace periods.

Economically, it was an opportune time for the Persians because trade routes had shifted from the Mediterranean. Europeans were seeking other routes.

[1] See above, p. 142.

Henry the Navigator of Portugal was using the Cape route to capture the trade of West Africa from the Muslims and establish trade with India. It was not long before the Portuguese were bringing spices from India and had established themselves in the Persian Gulf.

In 1507, during the reign of Shah Esma'il, the Portuguese fleet under Admiral Albuquerque landed at Hormoz on the Persian Gulf. They set up trading posts in Hormoz, Bahrain, and Muscat. By the middle of the sixteenth century, Hormoz was one of the most famous marts of the world. Milton has recorded its glory in his *Paradise Lost*. The Mamluks of Egypt and the merchants of Venice who had profited by the overland trade to the Mediterranean were indignant at being passed by. The Abbot of St. Catherine's Monastery at Mt. Sinai was sent to Rome as a result of this. The Mamluks together with Venice tried to persuade the Pope to prevent the Portuguese from trading in the Persian Gulf. The Mamluks even threatened to destory the Christian holy places.

Even though neither the delegation nor the threat bore any results, one must not conclude that the overland trade to the Levant was inactive. Throughout most of the sixteenth century, Aleppo still remained an important business center as the main caravan depot for silk, spices, dyes, and drugs from the East. This, however, did not last. By the end of the sixteenth century and throughout the seventeenth century, the main trade route was by water and the eastern Mediterranean experienced an economic decline.

Shah Esma'il also opposed the Portuguese capture of Hormoz but after a year of negotiation signed a treaty with Albuquerque in 1508. In return for the Persian recognition of the Portuguese establishment in the Persian Gulf, the Portuguese offered to help Iran in the occupation of Bahrain, and in subduing piracy on the shores of Baluchestan and Mokran. They also agreed to help each other against the Ottomans. In 1551 and 1574 the Portuguese sent embassies and gifts to Shah Tahmasp I and Shah Esma'il II, respectively. Both these monarchs were fanatical Muslims and did not like close personal contacts with the "infidels." Good relations and business, however, continued.

Even after Portugal was eclipsed by Spain, the trade installations and factories on the Persian Gulf continued. Philip II of Spain (reigned 1556–1598) sent an embassy to Iran under the leadership of Pere Simon Morales, who knew Persian. Philip made three requests: (1) that Iran give religious freedom to the Catholics; (2) that Iran give special privileges to the Spaniards; and (3) that Iran not make peace with the Ottomans. Apparently, all of these were in accord with the Safavid policy. A Persian ambassador was sent back with the same monk but, unfortunately, the ship, *Bon Voyage*, was lost on the way.

In 1598 two Portuguese monks, one a Franciscan, Alfonso Cordera, and another a Dominican, Nicolo di Melo, arrived in Esfahan and were received by Shah Abbas. To the latter the Shah gave a jewel-studded cross. These monks were allotted land for building a church and parish house, and continued religious work for many years. Spain was especially anxious to incite Iran against the Ottomans and Shah Abbas wanted Spain to harass the Ottomans from the sea. He also asked Philip to send a consul to mediate differences among the Christians. He also was willing to export all of Iran's silk by way of Hormoz under certain conditions.

During the reign of Elizabeth I of England, the British, seeing that the Cape route was monopolized by the Portuguese and the Spaniards, tried the northern route via Russia. The advantage of this route was that it would take them to Iran and would also open the way to the cold regions of China where there would be better market, so they hoped, for the English woolens. Having made contact with the court of Ivan the Terrible, the British formed the Muscovy Company in 1553. In 1561 the English representative of this company, Anthony Jenkinson, went by way of Moscow, Astrakhan, and the Caspian Sea to Qazvin, the capital of the Safavid Shah Tahmasp I. Jenkinson was not well received by the Shah, who felt reluctant to give audience to infidels at his court. More importantly, the route from Moscow to the Caspian was dangerous and costly and the company could not realize profits. Furthermore, they discovered that the Mongols were not interested in using English woolens. By 1591, the British also began using the Cape route.

There came to Iran at the time of Shah Abbas two young Englishmen, Anthony Sherley and his 18-year-old brother, Robert. They were adventurers with military training and knowledge who were not connected with any business enterprise. Shah Abbas was attracted to them as persons and, no doubt, saw in them means of improving his army and getting closer to the Europeans. They were employed by the Shah as military advisors and both took part in battles against the Ottomans. Robert Sherley married a Persian Christian girl and spent all his life in Iran.

In 1599, Shah Abbas sent a large embassy to Europe. The Persian ambassador, Hosein Ali Bayat, accompanied by Anthony Sherley, had letters to the rulers of Russia, Poland, Germany, France, Spain, and England, and also to the Pope. In the letters the Shah introduced Anthony as a "dear brother" who had come to Iran voluntarily and with whom "we ate food from the same plate and drank wine from the same cup." The whole party included one *molla* (Shi'i clergyman), two or three Catholic monks, five interpreters, fourteen servants, four guards, and thirty-two camel loads of gifts.

It took them a month to travel the 500 miles to the Caspian Sea and another two months to cross the sea. In Russia they were guests of Boris Godunov and, after six months of unpleasant experiences, went to Europe via Archangle. In the fall of 1600 they reached Prague and were received by King Rudolph II. The king accepted the Shah's proposal of war with the Ottomans and did not want the embassy to go any farther. The suggestion, however, was not accepted and the delegation proceeded to Italy. Venice did not receive them because they had made peace with the Ottomans and were entertaining a delegation from Istanbul. In Rome, Sherley and Bayat quarreled and were received by Pope Clement VIII separately. Apparently, Sherley promised the Pope that the Shah would cooperate in forcing the Orthodox Christians of the Caucasus to become Roman Catholics.

Bayat and Sherley separated there. Sherley went to Spain and from there o England, and never returned to Iran. Bayat went to Spain and planned to eturn to Iran by ship. Prior to leaving Spain, however, a fanatical Christian tabbed the Muslim molla to death. Worse than this, in the minds of the 'ersians, three members of the embassy became Christians. One was Ali Qoli, he nephew of the Ambassador, who was baptized with King Philip as a god-ather, and given the name of Don Philip. The second was the chief sercretary f the embassy, Uruj Bey, who was baptized with the Queen as his godmother, nd became known as Don Juan of Persia. The third was Bonyad Bey, who vas baptized as Don Diago. What happened to the Ambassador and the rest f his party is not certain. Very likely, being sure that he would be put to death r such a miserable record, he prudently decided not to return to the Shah. ▲ Persian historian, however, relates that in 1613 a Persian envoy returned rom Europe together with a Spanish ambassador, and the envoy was summarily ▶ut to death. Later Shah Abbas explained his action to the Spaniards by saying hat the Persian ambassador had "behaved so ill towards the attendants who ccompanied him, and vexed them so much, that several of them adopted the ℃hristian faith and remained in Europe in order to escape from his [the executed mbassador's] tyranny. . . ."

Having had no results from the first embassy, Shah Abbas sent Anthony's ▶rother, Robert Sherley, in 1608. The main objective was England. The talians and Spaniards, who did not like the British entry into the commercial ompetition, did not treat Robert's embassy with favor. Anthony Sherley ʻas employed by these governments to cause trouble for his brother. The ritish, however, who had formed the English East India Company in 1599, ʻere set to expand their trade and responded favorably to Shah Abbas. In ̇616 English ships came to the Persian Gulf and the Company established ̇eadquarters in Esfahan. By 1622, an Anglo-Persian force expelled the Por-̇uguese-Spanish traders from Hormoz and Bahrain and later from Muscat ̇nd Basra as well. The English also tried to enter the Levant trade but, as ̇e French had the upper hand there, they established a branch in Baghdad. ̇n Iran, Hormoz was replaced by Bandar Abbas, a new port built by Shah ̇bbas, and the English did most of their business there, with branches in ̇sfahan, Shiraz, Basra, and Baghdad.

In the meantime, the Dutch had appeared on the scene in 1581 and by 1602 ̇ad federated their various enterprises into one, the United East India Com-̇any. In 1623, the Dutch also opened a trading house in Bandar Abbas. Their ̇rrangement with the Shah was to barter Dutch merchandise with Persian ̇gs, wool, silk, and brocade. This affected the English trade unfavorably, ̇ausing a great deal of rivalry between the English and the Dutch merchants. ̇y the time of the death of Shah Abbas in 1629, there were a number of foreign ̇ores in the bazaars of Esfahan and Shiraz. In the reign of Shah Safi (1629–̇642), Dutch business was flourishing and the Dutch had practical control of ̇e Persian trade. By the time Shah Abbas II ascended the throne, the Dutch ̇ad a virtual monopoly of the trade in Iran. They were exempt from paying import duties but instead had to buy 600 loads of silk annually. In addition to silk, they exported Persian rugs, fruit, and wine. The Persian merchants however, did not like to deal with the Dutch. The complaint was that the Dutch dickered and the Persians, past masters of the art themselves, did not want to deal with wary and knowledgeable competitors!

The Safavid hospitality toward Europeans attracted the Germans also In 1523, Shah Esma'il sought the alliance of Charles V against the Ottomans Two years later, when Charles' reply finally reached Iran, Shan Esma'il had died. In 1600, emperor Rudolph II of Germany (1576–1612) received Antony Sherley, and in return sent an embassy to Iran. Apparently the German ambassador brought Boris Godunov into the alliance and arrived in Iran with letters from both rulers. When the letters arrived, Shah Abbas was already engaged in a successful campaign against the Ottomans. In the meantime Boris Godunov had troubles of his own in Russia and nothing came of the alliance.

During the Safavid period, a large number of Europeans worked in Iran and received high wages. Shah Abbas, consistent with his policy of attracting the Europeans, was lavish in his entertainment of foreign ambassadors. More often than not he himself went out of the city to welcome them. The visitor were received by a guard of honor with full dress uniforms and military bands Slaves were also around with wine and ice water for the guests. To impress the Europeans with his tolerance of non-Muslims, the leaders of the Christian Jewish, and Zoroastrian communities were invited to the receptions. Most unusual of all, 25 women were trained to entertain the foreign guests. These ladies, contrary to custom, were all unveiled. Shah Abbas went so much out of his way to be friendly to the monks that they thought he was ready to become a Christian, and the Shah did not do anything to discourage them. One year when Christmas fell in the fasting month of Ramadan, the Shah, as was his custom, went to the Armenian quarter of Esfahan for a reception. There he drank wine and then whispered in the ear of the Spanish Ambassador, who is the narrator in this case: "When you see the Pope in Rome, tell him how in the month of Ramadan in the presence of the qadi and the mufti and the head of government I served wine. Tell him that even though I am not a Christian, I am worthy of praise."

In addition to the social amenities, the Europeans enjoyed special trade privileges. All the provincial governors and administrators had strict orders to facilitate travel arrangements for the *frangi* (European) businessmen. The Europeans were also given the courtesy of being subject to their own law while in Iran. The Safavids were not alone in giving such privileges to the Europeans. The Ottomans also extended them to the French. These privileges given by Sultan Suleiman the Magnificent, recognized the jurisdiction of th French Consul over all the Frenchmen. It must be noted that such privilege were given as a courtesy and on the basis of equality. In their minds it wa the extension of the millet system to the "people of the book." Later it wa used as a means of European imperialism in all of the Middle East. This practice, later called "capitulations," continued until the second decade of the twentieth century.

Beginning with the last decade of the seventeenth century, trade in the Persian Gulf began to slacken. For one thing, the European traders had found greener pastures and better profits farther east in Asia. Furthermore, the political situation in Iran was worsening and the weak Safavid shahs could not maintain peace and security. The Afghan invasion of Iran in 1722 ended the Dutch trade in that country. The war with England and France had also weakened the Dutch. Nader Shah was not pleased with the English because they had not helped him in his Ottoman campaign, while the Dutch had. After he became Shah, however, he changed his attitude and renewed the past agreements with the British without signing new ones. Karim Khan Zand had difficulty with the English in 1769 over the control of ports and customs on imported goods. As a result the port of Bushahr on the Persian Gulf was closed and Basra became the port. By the middle of the eighteenth century any semblance of equal relationship between the Europeans on the one hand, and the Persians or the Ottomans on the other, came to an end. In 1780 the English helped Suleiman Pasha to secure his Pashalik in Basra and in 1789 helped determine the fate of Bushahr (Bushire) in the same way. The era of European imperialism had begun.

It is significant to note that two centuries of contact with Europe had not created much intellectual reaction either in Iran or in the Ottoman Empire. Both the Turks and Persians copied from the West the technique of making cannons and mortars, but that seems to be about all. As early as 1481, in the reign of Bayezid II, the Jewish refugees from Spain wanted to set up a printing press but were refused permission. The Shaykh ul-Islam ruled against it for fear that the Koran might be printed. Later, in 1493, however, the Jews were allowed to have one provided they printed in Hebrew only. In the middle of the sixteenth century, the Armenians were permitted to have a printing press under the same conditions as the Jews, and in 1627 the same type of permission was granted the Greeks. It was not until 1721 that the sultan allowed anything to be printed in Turkish. All other things from Europe were forbidden, including clocks, as they were deemed to interfere with the work of the muezzin, the individual who called the faithful to prayers.

Even though the Persians were more liberal in such matters than the Ottomans, there was not much to show for it. Shah Abbas imported a printing press, but there is no evidence that he used it at all. Shah Safi, in addition to having European gunmakers, had a watchmaker, a goldsmith, a diamond cutter, and a painter. Shah Abbas II brought two painters named Lokar and Angel from Holland, and some portraits of the monarchs are still in existence.

Intellectually, both Turkey and Iran remained impervious to the West. Islam as a religion of successive dispensations believed itself to be the last and, therefore, the most complete. Consequently, the Muslims, be they Shi'i or

Sunni, did not think that they could learn anything from a religion such a Christianity, which was believed to be less complete than Islam. In the Ottoman empire the Shaykh ul-Islam and the bulk of the ulama never had any intellectual relationship with the Europeans and did not allow any. In Iran the Shi'i religion had been mingled with Persian patriotism and had formed such a fanatical and dogmatic shell that not much could penetrate it. Furthermore, the European intellectuals who had come to the Middle East were mostly monks. These individuals, on the whole, had a medieval mentality and were both unaffected by and opposed to the Reformation that was going on in Europe. They, like their Muslim colleagues, had closed minds and did not have much to offer to medieval Islam. Hence, neither side felt inclined to approach the other. The subsequent interaction between Middle East and Europe went over the heads of most of the leaders of Islam and did not begin to show effect until the second half of the nineteenth century.

CHAPTER 18

SAFAVID INSTITUTIONS AND CULTURE

The Safavid religious, social, and administrative institutions are similar to those of the Ottomans insofar as they are Islamic and Turkish. They are different in that they are Shi'i and Persian. Unlike the Ottomans, the Safavids did not organize an armed encampment (although they did, of course, maintain an army), and their institutions were not tied to the military. Inasmuch as a number of the institutions started by the Safavids in Iran lasted until World War I, it is important that these be explained. As far as the Turkish elements are concerned, the Safavids, being Turks themselves, used the same names such as Beylarbey, Shaykh ul-Islam, etc., but not for the same positions. Perhaps for the purpose of belittling the Ottoman officers, the title of the highest personages in the Ottoman empire were given to lower functionaries in the Safavid governmental organization. For example, among the Persians, sultan was the name given to the lowest provincial administrator and Shaykh ul-Islam and Beylarbey were not anywhere near as important offices among the Safavids as they were among the Ottomans.

Concerning Islamic Shari'a, the Safavid Shahs were free agents compared to the Ottoman Sultans. With the Sunnis, the Shari'a was meticulously defined by the four orthodox schools.[1] Deviation or innovation which went beyond the limits of the four schools was frowned upon. The Ottoman ulama gave their opinions based on the Hanafite school of religious law and the sultan was bound by those decisions which were published as *fetva*. Even though the Shi'is considered the Shari'a of great importance, the spokesmen of the hidden Imam, who was the true ruler of the empire, could interpret the law according to the needs of the time. There was the belief that these spokesmen, *mujtahids*, were inspired by the hidden Imam to make the interpretation. This procedure

---

[1] See above, pp. 105ff.

identified the opinion of the mujtahid with that of the Imam and made it binding.

Two factors saved Shi'i society from undue rigidity. In the first place, there was usually more than one spokesman at a time. Sometimes there might be four or five, and these men naturally did not always agree with each other in their opinion of a certain case in point. In the second place, there was no hierarchical organization to appoint these spokesmen. Anyone aspiring to be a mujtahid had to study Shi'i theology and law, but not all of them reached the coveted position. In addition to proper academic training, they had to have a reputation for piety, wisdom, and common sense. Under ordinary circumstances, a given individual among the ulama with the proper reputation was considered a mujtahid by unofficial and popular consensus. Sometimes the Shah or other high officers of society helped a person along by repeatedly and openly asking his opinion, and in this way built his reputation as a mujtahid. Consequently, if the mujtahids in a Shi'i society agreed to issue unanimous opinions, the result might be quite rigid and reactionary. On the other hand, a king or government clever enough to set one mujtahid against the other could get by with a great deal of innovation and deviation, both of which are anathema in Shi'i and Sunni Islam alike.

From the time of the Safavids until the middle of the twentieth century, there existed in Iran three types of relationships between the king and the Shi'i ulama. In the first place there have been kings like Shah Abbas the Great (1587–1629), and Naser al-Din Shah Qajar (1848–1896), who have been more or less friendly with the ulama. There has been a certain amount of give and take. Sometimes they were able to divide the clergy and impose their will upon them and sometimes they were checked by the ulama. In the second place, there have been kings like Nader Shah (1736–1747) and Reza Shah Pahlavi (1924–1941) who have imposed their wills on the clergy and have destroyed the latter's influence. Both of these Shahs were powerful enough to expropriate the religious endowments (waqf) which have traditionally been the source of income for both Shi'i and Sunni religious institutions. When the ulama told Nader Shah that such funds should be spent for religious schools and mosques where prayers are said for the success of the shah, he tersely replied that apparently their prayers were ineffective, for in the past 50 years the country had declined. He added that since the soldiers in his army had checked this decline, they were the true "students of religion," and should receive their share from the endowments.

In the third place, the majority of the later Safavid kings, such as Shah Sultan Hosein (1694–1722), through the Qajar period have been under the domination of the Shi'i clergy.

It is quite apparent that any society under the second and third situation would become rigid and reactionary either by the dogma of the clergy or by the will of the dictator. In the first situation, society is more likely to be free because of the existence of two more or less equal powers which might neutraliz each other to the benefit of the common man. A most famous example of this is the well-known tobacco monopoly given by Naser al-Din Shah to the British (1892). The mujtahids issued an opinion against it and there was such a complete strike against smoking that the Shah himself could not procure tobacco for his *qalyan* (hubblebubble) and was forced to cancel the concession.

Furthermore, among the shahs of Iran, only the Safavids occupied a special position as the *murshed-e kamel* or the most perfect leader (that is, of the Sufi order). As the alleged descendants of the Prophet, and the actual leaders of the Sufi order, they exercised a certain religious power. The Safavid shahs, especially the early ones, combined in their persons not only kingship but also religious leadership. As such, they had religious as well as political power and the more liberal among them followed an independent course. Consequently, the Safavid governmental organization was not divided into "Muslim" and "Ruling" institutions like that of the Ottomans. In a sense, all power belonged to the Imam whose spokesmen were the mujtahids. In the early Safavid period, however, the Shah, as the "perfect leader," assumed religious power and acted as the spokesman for the Imam. Later, when the power of the Shah declined, the mujtahids assumed more and more power. Furthermore, in Iran the religious organization had complete charge, under the Shah, over justice and religion; but, unlike the Ottomans, did not have a voice in the administrative councils of the government.

The highest Shi'i clergyman in the realm was *Molla Bashi* who was usually the most learned individual and acted as "chaplain" to the Shah. He did not have any adminstrative or judicial duties. His influence was in indirect proportion to the power and personality of the Shah.

The judicial process in the empire was the exclusive prerogative of the ulama and was administered by a "Divan of Justice." It met four days a week and was composed of six members:

1. The *sadr-e khass*, who had charge of justice in the north and in important cities.
2. The *sadr-e amm*, who had charge of justice in the rest of the country.
3. The *qadi* of Esfahan, who held court at his own house.
4. The *shaykh ul-Islam*, who was in charge of marriage and divorce cases.
5. The *darugheh*, who was in charge of the police.
6. The chaplain of the army, who met the religious needs of the troops and signed the voucher for their pay.

All of the above were appointed by the Shah. Only the first two sadrs and the Molla Bashi received their pay from the treasury. The Divan had charge of the appointments of judges, preachers, and policemen in the provinces, and was presided over by an appointee of the Shah who was called the *divan beg*. He was the executor of the decisions of the Divan. Four days a week he presided over the Divan and two days a week he held court in his house for non-religious *urf* cases. He had a fief and in addition received 10 per cent of all fines.

The administrative affairs of the empire were under the general supervision of the grand vazir, who sat at the right hand of the Shah, signed orders and acted on behalf of the Shah. He was not salaried. His income was from fief and gifts.

Under him the administration branched out into two sections. One had to do with the provinces. These were governed by a hierarchy of four officers. At the top was the Provincial Governor and next to him was the District Supervisor aided by what might be called the County Commissioner (Khan) who had under him local supervisors called sultans. All of these officers had fiefs commensurate with their rank. It was their job to collect taxes, pay the salary of soldiers in their locality and send a specific amount of money each year to the Shah. In addition to money they also sent gifts to the Shah. Each one of these officers had someone close to the Shah who in return for appropriate gifts, spoke well of him and caused him to be favored.

The second section of the administration had to do with running the army, court, and finances of the empire. The main strength of the early Safavids came from the qizilbash tribes. These were represented in the government by two individuals. One was called the Chief Caliph, who headed the caliphs (spiritual leaders of the Sufi order) of the different tribes. In the eyes of the Sufis, the Chief Caliph was assistant to the perfect leader, i.e., the Shah. The second representative of the qizilbash was the *qurchi bashi*, who was the lay leader of the tribes and who paid the warriors. Both of these men received salaries in addition to their fiefs.

Shah Abbas broke the power of the qizilbash and set up three army units with modern weapons. One was the artillery, the second was the rifle corps recruited from among the Persian-speaking population of the villages, and the third was a "slave" corps recruited from among Georgians, Circassians, and Armenians. It is doubtful that these were actual slaves in the ordinary sense. They were almost all Christians whose religion was not interfered with and who prided themselves in being the "slaves of the Shah." Each of these corps had a commander from its own ranks who reported to the Shah and the grand vazir. Each commander received his income through a fief.

The court of the Shah had a bevy of officers, from chief of protocol, private secretary, physician, and astrologer, to gate keeper, valet, stable chief, and a host of others too numerous to be named. The chief chamberlain was in charge of the Shah's harem. The Safavid harems, like those of the Ottomans, were guarded by eunuchs, usually black. Persian women seemed to have had more freedom than their sisters in the Ottoman empire. The Safavids took their wives with them to wars and some of the women were good marksmen and actually participated in battle. In cases of defeat and general or hasty retreat, the eunuchs had orders to behead all the women. Sometimes there was "women's day" at the bazaars. No men except the storekeepers would be allowed. On such days the harem women mingled with the town women. After the boulevard in Esfahan was completed by Shah Abbas, he inaugurated women's evening at the boulevard. There the ladies promenaded up and down the tree-lined streets. The women were also given a special place from whence they could enjoy the frequent fireworks and lamp-lighting ceremonies which were favorite pastimes of the Shahs. One can imagine that such occasions were most eagerly anticipated by the women who otherwise led such secluded and sheltered lives.

Finances were under the supervision of an individual who was responsible to the Shah. There was no distinction made between the expenses of the Shah and those of the government. Everything belonged to the Shah. In the finance department, there was one person in charge of the mint. Silver and gold coins were minted in the capital for the whole country. Copper coins were minted locally and were changed every year.

Another officer connected with the finance section was the man in charge of fair prices. During the Safavid period and on into the twentieth century, there were well-organized guild systems in Iran. Under good administrators, usually every three months and sometimes oftener, the officer in charge of prices met with the leader (*white beard*) of each guild and determined prices. Until the early years of the twentieth century the offenders were put in stocks and paraded in the bazaars.

The main source of income for the Shah and the government was from the tax levied on each province. This was both in cash and in kind, such as silk, horses, slaves, oils, wine, rice, etc. There was also income from the private domains of the Shah. After the destruction of qizilbash power by Shah Abbas, the private lands of these feudal lords were confiscated, and the income realized from them was tremendous. A third source of revenue was from the taxes on income. There was an annual tax of one half of all livestock, one third of all silk and cotton, bridge and road tolls, head tax for non-Muslims, import duties, etc. A very lucrative source of income was the tax on the sale and cultivation of tobacco. The Portuguese introduced tobacco into Iran and it became very popular. Shah Abbas himself did not like to smoke and so no one dared to do so in his presence. After his death, however, smoking became a national habit.

A fifth type of income came from miscellaneous sources, such as confiscation of property, gifts of foreign embassies, and the like. It was also customary for craftsmen to work for less wages when engaged in the construction of the Shah's buildings. It is estimated that the income of the empire was between 700,000 and 900,000 *tomans* every year. The annual expenditure is not known but it was less than the income, and until the beginning of the eighteenth century, the Safavid kings had full coffers.

Among the customs continued by the Safavids was that of bestowing titles such as the "pillar of the realm," "steward of the kingdom," and a host of others. Sometimes these titles were hereditary and sometimes they were taken away from one and bestowed on another. Since most title holders were also important leaders of the state, the historian is always at a loss to distinguish father from son or grandson or from half a dozen others who have been given the same title.

The Safavids had their own historians. One of the most important source for the reign of Shah Abbas is the *History of Abbas*. Such books, however, like their Ottoman counterparts, are daily chronicles of the activities of the Shah and always flattering to the Shah and his policies. Fortunately, some of the many European visitors to Iran wrote about their experiences and have described the life of the people among whom they lived. It is through their reports that it is possible to penetrate the façade built by the official historians.

Most of the men spent their leisure hours in the coffeehouses. Sultan Murad IV, a contemporary of Shah Abbas, had ordered all coffeehouses closed, whereas Shah Abbas encouraged them in Iran. He used to frequent them himself and on several occasions took the foreign visitors to them. These coffeehouses were centers for the dissemination of news. To these also came travelers who recounted their experiences, and dervishes who for a price regaled their audiences with stories of the heroes of Iran from the *Shahnameh*. The Safavids encouraged the observation of many of the pre-Islamic Persian festivities such as those held at the equinoxes and the solstice. The spring equinox, bringing the new year, was and still is the most important festival in Iran. There were also the rose festival and the water festival and others which gave the common man an opportunity to escape from the drudgery of his routine life.

Other pastimes engaged in by the populace were cock, wolf, and bull fights; card games; acrobatics; tightrope walking; puppet shows; and, for the aristocracy only, polo. Formal physical exercise was a common practice in Iran before the Safavid period and has continued to modern times. A brotherhood was formed of those people who spent their leisure in physical exercise and these brotherhoods have existed to the present. Their center was called "house of strength" and they had a hierarchy with special codes of honor. They exercised to the beat of the drum. Usually the drummer was a man with a good voice who sang the story of the adventures of Persian heroes from the *Shahnameh*.

Islam and especially Shi'i Islam did not bring many festive days into the life of its adherents. With the exception of the anniversary of Mohammad's receiving the call and festival of sacrifice (Id al-Adha, enjoined by the Koran and celebrated throughout the Muslim world), the rest were occasions for mourning. There were mourning services for the death of Ali and Hasan and the all important tragic event in Karbala where Husayn lost his life. The Safavids in their zeal for Shi'ism encouraged the observance of these events, and the common people crowded to the mosques to hear and weep at the recounting of the stories by the mollas and to participate in the numerous processions.

The event at Karbala on the tenth of Muharram (the first month in the Muslim lunar calendar) was the most important. Everywhere in the country there were processions. In the cities the districts vied with each other in the excellence of their processions and sometimes even fought against each other. In these processions, they paraded corpses draped in blood-stained shrouds, and a headless body of Husayn. The Umayyad Caliph, Yazid, whose troops ambushed and killed Husayn, was always impersonated in these parades and this gave the onlookers opportunity to curse the Sunnis. Hundreds of individuals were involved in each procession. Some beat their breasts. There were others who beat their bare backs with a cluster of chains. On the tenth, when religious feelings had reached a climax, a new group joined the procession. These individuals were clad in white shrouds and each held a short sword in his right hand while with his left hand he held his companion's belt. They marched sideways inflicting wounds on their heads. In all cases there were dirges and chantings and a chorus of "Ya Husayn, Shah Husayn."

In the late Safavid period "passion plays" came into vogue. Traveling troupes of actors with complete wardrobes and makeup performed in the village and town squares, depicting different episodes, real and embellished, of the scene at Karbala.

From the literary and intellectual point of view, this was a relatively sterile period. Shi'ism was considered a heterodoxy during the Abbasid Caliphs and as such, attracted all types of freethinkers. Unhindered intellectual inquiry was usually found among the Shi'is. During the Safavids, however, Shi'ism became the religion of the state and was transformed into a most rigid and fanatical orthodoxy. It is indicative of the sterility of the intellectual life to note that since 1500 Iran has produced only two philosophers of some note. One is Molla Sadra of Shiraz (d. 1641) and the other Hajji Molla Hadi of Sabzavar.

A SELECTED BIBLIOGRAPHY

Alderson, A. D., *The Structure of the Ottoman Dynasty*. Oxford: Clarendon Press, 1956.

Arberry, A. J., *Classical Persian Literature*. London: George Allen & Unwin, Ltd. 1958.

Browne, E. G., *A Literary History of Persia*. (4 vols.). Cambridge, England: Cambridge University Press, 1964.

Bosworth, C. E., *The Islamic Dynasties*. Edinburgh: The University Press, 1967.

Eversley, G. J. S. and Chirol, Valentine, *The Turkish Empire from 1288 to 1922*. London: T. Fisher Unwin, 1923.

Fisher, Sydney Nettleton, *The Foreign Relations of Turkey, 1481–1512*. Urbana, Ill.: University of Illinois Press, 1948.

Hasluck, F. W., *Christianity and Islam Under the Sultans*. Oxford, England: Oxford University Press, 1929.

Howorth, H. H., *History of the Mongols* (4 vols.). London: Longmans & Green, 1870–1927.

Kritzeck, James, ed., *Anthology of Islamic Literature*. New York: Holt, Rinehart & Winston, 1964.

Le Strange, Guy, *Mesopotamia and Persia Under the Mongols in the 14th Century A.D.* London: Royal Asiatic Society, 1903.

Lockart, Laurence, *Nadir Shah—A Critical Study Based Mainly Upon Contemporary Sources*. London: Luzac, 1938.

Levy, Reuben, *The Social Structure of Islam*. Cambridge, England: Cambridge University Press, 1962.

Merriman, R. B., *Suleiman the Magnificent, 1520–1566*. Cambridge, Mass.: Harvard University Press, 1944.

Runciman, Steven, *A History of the Crusades* (4 vols.). Cambridge, England: Cambridge University Press, 1951–58.

Spuler, Bertold, *The Muslim World, Part II—The Mongol Period*. Leiden, Netherlands: E. J. Brill, 1960.

Sykes, Sir Percy, *History of Persia* (2 vols., 3nd ed.). London: Macmillan, 1951.

Wittek, Paul, *The Rise of the Ottoman Empire*. London: Royal Asiatic Society, 1938.

Wright, Walter, trans., *Ottoman Statecraft*. Princeton, N.J.: Princeton University Press, 1935.

PART THREE

IMPERIALISM
AND AWAKENING

PRECEDING PAGE: *Persian revolutionaries in chains, 1909* (COURTESY OF IRANIAN PRESS
AND INFORMATION). ABOVE, TOP: *Malkom Khan (d. 1907) and Namik Kemal (1840-
1888), intellectual supporters of the Persian Revolution and Turkish nationalism
respectively.* BOTTOM, LEFT TO RIGHT: *Midhat Pasha, author of the first Turkish
Constitution (1876), was exiled by Abdul Hamid II. Sultan Abdul Hamid II (1876-
1909), called "Abdul the Damned," was deposed in 1909. Sayyed Jamal al-Din
Afghani (1838–1897), was a proponent of pan-Islamism.*

CHAPTER 19

STRUGGLE OVER
THE OTTOMAN EMPIRE

At the beginning of the eighteenth century the world of Islam lay sprawled from central Europe and Morocco to central Asia and the Bay of Bengal. Its destiny over 300 years had been in the hands of men of Turkish origin, namely the Ottomans in the west, the Safavids in Iran, and the Moguls in India. The people of these three empires had more in common than Turkish lineage. They all were Muslims, recited the same Koran, prayed toward Mecca, and they honored the religious law of Islam, *Shari'a*. Furthermore, the literate among them loved Persian literature and corresponded mostly in that language; a "cultured" person was judged by his knowledge of the literature, history, art, and mores of the Persians.

And yet these three empires never united or even cooperated in any project. Long distances and lack of communications were partially responsible. The main reason, however, was the fact that Safavid Iran was Shi'i in religion, and her geographical location separated the two Sunni empires of the Ottomans and the Moguls. On the other hand, religious differences aside, there was a good deal of cultural and commercial intercourse between Iran and India, and except for occasional raids from the tribes of central Asia, their borders were quite peaceful.

The fanatical religious enmity between the Safavid and Ottoman empires was heightened by disputes over the control of the Shi'i holy places of Najaf and Karbala in southern Mesopotamia, and over the Shi'i settlements in eastern Asia Minor. Economically, the Ottoman empire lay athwart the traditional trade routes connecting Iran with the Mediterranean and the Straits of Dardanelles and Bosporus. It was to break this barrier that the Safavid Shahs tried to ally themselves with different potentates of Europe against the Ottomans. When that proved impossible, the trading parties bypassed the Ottoman barriers in the Mediterranean and the Levant, and opened up brisk commerce in the Persian Gulf. There is no doubt that the European nations benefited by this intense rivalry, for throughout the seventeenth and part of the eighteenth centuries, the Ottomans and the Persians vied with each other in giving special economic and commercial privileges to the merchants and nationals of Europe.

Language differences were perhaps more important than economic rivalries in keeping the Ottomans and the Safavids at odds. The vast majority of the inhabitants of Azarbaijan and northwestern Iran were Turkish-speaking people. Intermittent wars and religious fanaticism, which made the wars personal, helped separate the two Turkish-speaking peoples and distinguished one as "Persian" and the other as "Turk." If the Shi'is ever had as their goal the expansion of the frontiers of Islam against non-Muslims, the Safavids discouraged it. Instead, they tried to destory the Sunnis, especially Ottoman Sunnis, wherever they could find them, and required the Shi'is to curse the "usurpers" of the Imamate, namely the first three caliphs of Islam.

The eighteenth century, which ushered in the cultural, political and economic rejuvenation of most of the European countries, marked the beginning of stagnation in the world of Islam. The Mogul empire was in an advanced state of decay and fell prey to merchant adventurers of the West. The Safavids were in decline and the Ottomans, though still strong if only because of their size, were not far behind the Safavids.

It must be noted that Europe alone was not the cause of the downfall of the Ottoman empire. The disintegration had already begun and the empire would have fallen apart because of its own weakness. European countries happened to be there to pick up the pieces. Had it not been for the rivalry of European nations, the Ottoman empire would not have lasted the next 200 years. Some of the learned men in the Ottoman empire saw the handwriting on the wal' and gave warning, but no one paid any attention to them.

One of these learned men, Koji Bey, wrote a report on the state of the empire in 1630 when Sultan Murat IV had reached the age of 21. Possibly the sultan himself, a relatively energetic person among a line of incompetent sultans had ordered such a report, or more probably it was the sultan's talented mother In any case Koji Bey in unusually clear language described the degeneration of the empire and enumerated the causes in his report, *Resaleh*. Among other things, he mentioned that the sultan had made himself "invisible," preoccupied, as he was, in his harem life. Because of the influence of the harem "the sultan no longer governs himself and neither is the grand vazir allowed to do so; power is actually in the hands of negro eunuchs and purchased slave girls." He reported further on the economic decline of the empire and blamed it principally on heavy taxation and corruption in the administration. He criticized the organization of the sepahis. These same troops mutinied against Sultan Murat IV and even though the Janissaries helped quell the rebellion Koji Bey did not spare the corps.

About 15 years later, during the reign of Sultan Ibrahim (1640-1648) an unknown author wrote a tract called *Nasihatnameh*, "Words of Advice." He complained about corruption and the sale of taxes to the highest bidder for collection. His advice, presumably to the sultan, is to lower taxes and pay the officials and the army, rather than let them loose among the peasants. His plea was for the imposition of fixed taxes and for the appointment of pious Muslims as tax collectors.

The greatest intellectual luminary of the seventeenth century in the Ottoman empire was the celebrated historian Haji Khalifa (1608–1657). One of his books, *Dastur al-Amal*, "Manual for Action," is very much like the Persian *Mirror to Princes*.[1] He repeated the old familiar maxim, "No state without *rijal*, 'men [of affairs],' no *rijal* without *mal* [wealth], and no *mal* without subjects." Like Avicenna, he likened the state to a body with four pillars—ulama, army, merchants, and farmers. He claimed that the state was sick and diagnosed the reasons for the illness as high taxation, oppression of the masses, and the sale of offices to the highest bidder.

It was during this decaying state that the Ottomans launched their last campaign against Vienna, which had escaped their grasp so often. It was carried out by Mehmed IV and his incompetent court favorite, Kara Mustafa the grand vazir, in 1683. Kara Mustafa laid seige to Vienna in mid-July and for two months bombarded the city. The defenders of the city under the command of Count Starhemberg were greatly weakened and Kara Mustafa expected the city to surrender. Even though he knew of the approach of King John Sobieski of Poland with 70,000 soldiers, Kara Mustafa did nothing to check their advance or prepare his own defenses against them. The fateful encounter occurred on September 12, 1683. The Ottoman army was routed and the Austrians and Poles pursued their victory. By 1687, the Ottomans had lost all of Hungary to the Austrians and Morea, Corinth, and Athens to the Venetians. The Ottomans deposed Mehmed in favor of his brother Suleiman II (1687–1691), who had hardly emerged from the harem for 45 years. In 1688, Belgrade fell. In desperation Suleiman called Mustafa Köprülü, the brother of Ahmed, to be the grand vazir. He was able to hold the line for a while, but the Ottoman empire had lost its resilience and its ability to recoup. The crushing blow was dealt by Prince Eugene of Savoy in 1697 at the battle of Zenta. Two years later the Treaty of Karlowitz was signed.

Karlowitz marks the beginning of the end for the Ottoman empire. It was the first of many dictated peace treaties which the Turks had to sign. European diplomats knew that henceforth the Turks would not threaten the integrity of Europe. The Ottomans, on the other hand, slowly realized that their domain was at the mercy of the countries of Europe. Furthermore, the Ottomans were to realize that Europe considered the rule of the Sultan-Caliph over an empire in which the Christian "minorities" outnumbered the Muslim "majority" an anomaly and were not willing to allow it to continue.

[1] See above, p. 110.

The traditional enemies of the Ottoman Turks in Europe were Austria, Poland, and Venice. In eighteenth-century Europe there was no room for city states. Venice was in a state of decay and soon was absorbed by neighboring powers. Poland was surrounded by the rising powers of Russia, Prussia, and Austria. Before the end of the eighteenth century this hapless country was absorbed by these three powers and did not regain its precarious independence until 1919. Austria remained fairly strong throughout the eighteenth and nineteenth centuries but, like the Ottoman empire it was eager to replace, was made up of so many different nationalities that it remained unwieldy and always in danger of falling apart. Austria would not have had the initiative or the ability to threaten the considerable possessions of the Ottomans in southeastern Europe were it not for the determination and initiative of the Russians.

The Ottomans did not know much about the Russians except as vassals of their distant kinsmen, the Tatars. The Ottoman sultans owned enough territory north of the Black Sea to make the latter a Turkish lake. There was nothing farther north to attract them and they had all but forgotten about the Russians.

The Russian rulers, however, had not forgotten the Ottomans. It will be remembered that the very foundations of the Russian state were laid on Byzantine institutions and values. Russian law, architecture, alphabet, and religion were taken from Byzantium. Before the Mongol domination, most of the Russian trade was with the south. The Russians felt a natural affinity with their coreligionists under the Muslim rule. When the Muscovite Prince Ivan III (1462–1505) married Sophia Palaeologus, the orphaned niece of the last Byzantine emperor, he felt that he had also married the prestige and the religious and temporal authority of Byzantium. In 1547 Sophia's grandson, Ivan the Terrible, who considered himself the heir of the Byzantine emperors, crowned himself as the "Tsar of All the Russias." The Russian church leaders developed the theory that with the "fall" of Rome through heresy and the fall of Constantinople ("the second Rome") at the hands of the Turks, Moscow, "the third Rome," was henceforth the capital of Christianity and was the guardian of all Christians, especially the Orthodox. To the Russians Constantinople was always "Tsargrad." What could be more appropriate than for the Tsar of all the Russians to win back Tsargrad from the "infidel" Muslims and free all the Orthodox from the Turkish yoke?

Religious and imperial traditions were not the only forces driving the Russians southward. A large number of the subjects of the Ottoman empire were Slavs. As the Russian state grew stronger it developed a "big brother" attitude toward the other Slavs who were under foreign domination. During the nineteenth century, Slavophilism became an important nationalist view in Russia and a potent tool of Russian imperialism. So with Orthodoxy and pan-Slavism as the goals, and the desire for warm-water ports as the perennial ambition, every Russian Tsar or head of state, capitalist or communist, from

Peter the Great on, tried, by diplomacy or war, to gain control of the Straits and of Constantinople. This by itself would not have become so significant were it not for the fact that western European nations either singly or in concert blocked Russia's path to the Straits. This, more than anything else, contributed to the long life of the Ottoman empire and kept it alive.

Napoleon refused to give Alexander I of Russia a free hand in the Straits at Tilsit in 1807. France and England joined the Crimean War against Russia in order to prevent Russia from occupying Istanbul. In the twentieth century, Hitler refused to recognize what the Soviet Union called its "legitimate interests" in the Straits and the Persian Gulf area. In 1947, President Truman of the United States promulgated the so-called Truman Doctrine to protect Turkey, and the Central Treaty Organization (CENTO) was established between Pakistan, Iran, Turkey, and Great Britain with the blessings of the United States for the same purpose. There is only one curious exception to the general rule of European nations keeping Russia from obtaining Istanbul. This occurred during World War I in the secret treaty of London in 1915, when England, France, Italy, and Russia, in dividing the spoils of war in case of victory, actually consented to give Russia Istanbul and the Straits.

In the heyday of imperialism in the nineteenth century, England, Germany, and France insisted on protecting the integrity of the Ottoman empire *vis-à-vis* Russia, even though they themselves violated that integrity in North Africa and the Fertile Crescent. They did so because they believed in the theory that the Straits and the Persian Gulf area constituted a "heartland," and whoever controlled that area could influence the destinies of the world. They did not want Russia to have it, but neither would they permit any one country to control the region. Consequently the most complicated game in European diplomacy was how to keep that delicate phenomenon, "the balance of power" in proper relationship in that area.

Most of this, however, occurred during all of the nineteenth and part of the twentieth centuries. In the 1700's, difficulties among the western European countries had prevented them from paying too much attention to Russia. Furthermore, the Ottoman empire was so vast that its existence was not endangered by either Austria or Russia. If Russia and Austria did not succeed in annihilating the Ottoman empire, it was not because the western European countries interfered. In the eighteenth century the Ottoman empire still had some strength and Russia and Austria had not become strong enough. In the attacks on the Ottoman empire, Russia usually took the initiative and Austria followed.

Peter the Great of Russia, who wanted a foothold on the Black Sea, had already captured Azov on the Black Sea. He was not satisfied, however, and attacked the Turks in 1711. He was himself a victim of Russia's propaganda and apparently believed that he would be received by the inhabitants of Bessarabia as a liberator. Rather careless in his military strategy, he was virtually surrounded after he crossed the Pruth river. To escape with his life, he had to accept the peace of Pruth, give up Azov, and relinquish the right of maintaining a navy on the Black Sea. The Truks missed the opportunity of crushing the Russians.

The Ottomans, however, took advantage of the weakness of Venice and reconquered Morea in 1715. The people had been taxed so heavily by the Venetians that they were willing to go back to the Ottomans. The Austrians were alarmed by the Turkish victories and broke the peace with the Sublime Porte. Prince Eugene dealt several blows at the Ottomans and defeated them in the battle of Peterwardine. Hampered by the Spanish policy in Italy, he signed the lenient peace of Passrowitz in 1718. Austria kept all the territory it had won from Venice. The Ottomans lost the rest of Hungary and part of Wallachia, but were permitted to keep the territory they had won from Venice.

In 1736 Russia took advantage of the preoccupation of the Ottomans with the powerful Nader Shah of Iran and invaded Crimea and many fortresses on the Black Sea. Austria joined the fray but the Ottomans had enough stamina to push the Austrians back and hold the Russians at bay. The result was the peace of Belgrade of 1739. Austria lost, but Russia did not gain much more than Azov again and freedom to trade on the Black Sea, provided goods were carried on Turkish vessels.

For 30 years after the treaty of Belgrade the Ottomans enjoyed a period of peace. Nader Shah was assassinated in 1747 and European countries were involved in the War of the Austrian Succession (1740–1748), and the Seven Years' War (1756–1763). The Ottoman Sultans Mahmud I (1730–1754), Osman III (1754–1757), and Mustafa III (1757–1773) did not take advantage of the reprieve to strengthen themselves. Indeed, during the Seven Years' War, Frederick the Great of Prussia endeavored to persuade the Porte to launch an attack on Austria. Raghib Pasha, perhaps the last of the able grand vazirs, actually prepared a draft of a treaty of alliance in 1761, but Sultan Mustafa III, encouraged by the ulama, refused to became involved. A year later, Catherine II became the Empress of Russia and it was too late for the Ottomans to assert themselves.

In 1761, the sultan had refused involvement in European politics, when it might have been to the Porte's advantage. Seven years later the sultan, with the approval of the ulama, joined the "confederation" made up of Austria, France, and Sweden to safeguard the integrity of Poland against Russian aggression. In the end, not only was Poland partitioned, but the only member of the confederation that did not benefit was Turkey.

The Porte had watched with great suspicion the progress of Russian designs on Poland. The main purpose of Catherine the Great was to make Russia a stronger power in Europe and an effective participant in European politics. As a step toward this goal, Catherine attached the greatest importance to Russian domination over Poland. The throne of Poland became vacant in 1763, and this gave Catherine the awaited opportunity for Russian intervention. Through the machination of Catherine and the support of Frederick the Great of Prussia, Count Stanislas Poniatowski, one of Catherine's former lovers, was chosen king. The Russian empress used to say that Poniatowski had "less right than any other candidate [to be king] and therefore should be all the more grateful to Russia." Poniatowski was grateful and helped Catherine and Frederick partition Poland.

Louis XV of France, who was a member of the confederation against Russia and Prussia, persuaded Sultan Mustafa to commit his unprepared army in a war against Russia. Catherine welcomed the opportunity, even though her armies were not prepared either. Her current lover, Gregory Orlov, had a master plan which included the sending of the Russian fleet around Europe to the Mediterranean, and this plan counted upon the uprising of the Greek Orthodox and the Balkan Slavs against the Turks. In the early spring of 1770, a Russian squadron under the command of Alexis Orlov, Gregory's brother, sailed through the Mediterranean and reached the shores of Turkey. The insurrection of the Christian population, however, did not materialize. It should be noted that under the Ottoman millet system the Christian population were relatively autonomous and they were not willing to give this up in exchange for Russian control. In the nineteenth century, when the peoples of the Balkans did rise against the Ottomans, it was not for the purpose of joining the Russians but for their own national independence.

The Russians won great victories at Chios and Chesme and annihilated the bulk of the Ottoman fleet. But even though the fleet was reinforced, the Russians were not able to reach Istanbul. By 1773, Catherine had to admit that "the fleet is doing nothing." The land war was slow and protracted. The Russian advance was so slow that Frederick of Prussia is reported to have quipped that it was a war between "one-legged men against the one-eyed." The Russian advances, however, were great enough to alarm the Austrians, and the latter negotiated a treaty of mutual assistance with the Porte. Then, to prevent war with Austria, Catherine and Frederick agreed to make Austria a partner in the first partition of Poland in 1772. The partition of Poland stiffened the resistance of the Turks, for they believed, and rightly so, that a similar fate was agreed upon by the powers for the Ottoman empire. The war dragged on. The death of Sultan Mustafa in January 1774 weakened Turkish resistance. In the same year a peasant uprising against Catherine, led by Pugachev, assumed alarming dimensions. Both sides instituted direct negotiations and in July 1774 signed the Treaty of Kuchuk Kainarji.

Under the provisions of this famous treaty, Crimea became autonomous and Russia annexed Kerch and the territories between the Bug and the Dnieper rivers, and received the privilege of free navigation on the Black Sea with the right of passage through the Straits. The Porte retained Moldavia, Wallachia, and the Greek Islands but had to pay an indemnity of 4,500,000 rubles.

This treaty is considered particularly significant because of articles VII and XIV. In the latter, Russia was given permission to build a public church in

Istanbul which "shall always be under the protection of the ministers of that [Russian] Empire. . . ." In article VII, Russia received very vaguely defined rights. Later on the Russians used these articles to claim protectorship over the Christian subjects of the Porte. Other than these two articles there is not much new, however, in the treaty. The Ottoman empire was in the habit of giving capitulatory privileges to foreign countries.[2] These were mainly for trade privileges but nearly always religion also was mentioned. The last treaty of capitulation had been obtained by France in 1740, under which all Roman Catholics were put under French protection. Even though the agreement meant to imply the foreign Roman Catholics residing within the empire, the French acted as though they were also the protectors of the Roman Catholic subjects within the Ottoman empire. The difference, however, between the former capitulations and the religious and economic capitulations in the Treaty of Kuchuk Kainarji was that the former capitulations were granted freely by the Porte either to bolster trade or to compete with similar privileges granted by the Safavids of Iran. The capitulations in the Treaty of Kuchuk Kainarji were forced upon the Porte as a penalty of defeat. Even though "the Sublime Porte promises to protect constantly the Christian religion and its churches. . . ," Russia as a victor could use the agreement as a convenient pretext to interfere in the domestic affairs of the Ottoman empire.

During the decade in which the sultan was left in peace, the future of the Ottoman empire dominated the foreign policy of Russia. Potemkin, the latest lover of Catherine, knew the predilection of his imperial mistress for aggrandizement and prepared the notorious plan of conquest known as the "Greek Project." According to this plan, the Ottoman empire would be partitioned. Part of it was to be called the "Kingdom of Dacia" with Potemkin as king, and the major section with Constantinople as capital was reserved for Catherine's newly-born (1779) youngest grandson whom she had appropriately ordered to be named Constantine. Austria, who after the agreement of Kuchuk Kainarji had demanded and received from the Porte the province of Bukovina as "commission" for remaining neutral during the war, now joined the "Greek Project." As a reward Joseph II of Austria was given Serbia, Bosnia, and Herzegovina.

After a series of characteristic maneuverings which combined pleasure, diplomacy, and intrigue, Catherine, in violation of the Treaty of Kuchuk Kainarji, annexed the Crimea in 1784. Three years later she invited her friends, among them Emperor Joseph of Austria, to a spectacular party in the Crimea to celebrate the annexation. The military and naval maneuvers staged by Potemkin alarmed Sultan Abdul Hamid I (1773–1789) and war broke out in 1787 between the Ottomans and the Russian-Austrian alliance.

As usual, Russia was not prepared, but fortunately for her the Ottomans, also as usual, were even less prepared. The initial Russo-Austrian victories

[2] See above, p. 176.

encouraged Catherine to try to execute the "Greek Project." She again hoped that the Balkan Christians would revolt against the Porte. This war also was a protracted one and in the end international complications, such as the French Revolution, forced Catherine to give up the "Greek Project." The death of Emperor Joseph II (1790) weakened the alliance. Pressure from England, Prussia, and Holland persuaded the new Emperor Leopold of Austria to sign the peace of Sistova with the Porte on August 4, 1791, without any gains. A few months later (January 1792) Catherine signed the Peace of Jassy and advanced her territory to the Dniester River, thus confirming the annexation of Crimea.

Catherine did not abandon the "Greek Project" altogether. She mentioned it in her testament of 1792 and included it in the Austrian-Russian Agreement of 1795. Her death in 1796 prevented a new war for the conquest of Constantinople.

CHAPTER 20

WESTERN IMPERIALISM AND THE OTTOMANS

The Ottoman empire entered the nineteenth century in a fairly advanced state of decay. The long ordeal of the eighteenth century had witnessed defeat after defeat without creating an appreciable reaction on the part of the leaders. They neither took remedial steps nor looked for the causes of the malady. The attitude of most of the sultans was "business as usual" and the usual business of the sultan continued to be life in the harem and the sale of offices to pay for that type of living. The few sultans who did care found that the world had rapidly changed. Economic, social, political, military, and international problems were so new and overwhelming that the most intelligent of the sultans could not understand them and not even the strongest could cope with them.

The Ottoman empire remained a military encampment which was strengthened by well-organized levies of troops, supported economically by peasants, merchants, and craftsmen who depended on the army for the safety of the roads, and sustained by the ecclesiastical organization (ulama) which interpreted the Shari'a. The empire was administered by a burgeoning bureaucracy headed by the sultan himself. In the nineteenth century both the organization and methods of administration were hopelessly out of date. In Europe growing liberalism, democratization, industrialization, and secularism had destroyed feudalism, decreased the power of the church, and nationalized the armies. Even though the Ottoman religious, military, and feudal systems were not like those of Europe, nevertheless the Ottoman institutions could not cope with the problems of the century, such as the power of western nations and their aggressive imperialisms, the nationalistic struggles of non-Turkish peoples, and the restless quest of the Turks themselves for progress and change.

In addition to being out of date, the Ottoman institutions were corrupt. The empire was divided into 26 *velayats* (provinces) and these were subdivided into about 160 *livas*. The governor of the velayat and often of the liva was called a *pasha* and the governorship *pashalik*. According to an old Mongolian custom which the Ottomans had perpetuated, the standard of the velayat pashas carried three horse tails, while that of the liva pashas carried two or one, depending on the size and importance of the liva.

The pashaliks were for sale and went to the highest bidder. It was one of the best ways of amassing fortune at the expense of the peasants and provincial merchants. As long as the pashas sent the annual revenue agreed upon to Istanbul, the sultan did not care how the money was obtained. The pashalik, therefore, was the objective of the ambitious men in the empire. The facts that it could only be obtained by cash and that cash was scarce limited the number of buyers. Those who could borrowed money from Greek, Armenian, or Jewish moneylenders and literally mortgaged their pashalik at high interest. In order to insure payment, often the moneylender appointed his agent as "secretary" of the pasha. The secretaries were more merciless than the pashas. They extorted enough from the helpless peasants and merchants to insure income for the sultan, the pasha, the moneylender, and themselves.

Even though the pashas had power of life and death over the inhabitants and maintained a court and harem in imitation of the sultan, they were not all-powerful. There were local strong men who often refused to obey the pashas and in the struggles between the two, the inhabitants suffered even more. In Anatolia there were hereditary warlords known as *dere beys* (lords of the valley), probably descendants of Ghazi leaders who at the zenith of Ottoman power were obedient enough, but who now had taken advantage of the weakness of the central government and revived their old independence.

More notorious than the dere beys were the Greek phanariotes. Under the millet system, the Greek Orthodox Patriarch in Istanbul was the head of all the Orthodox Christians in the empire. Because the offices of the Patriarch were located near the lighthouse (phanar) on the shore of the Golden Horn, the members of the bureaucracy were called phanariotes. These men, who were all Greeks, exploited the Orthodox of the empire who were non-Greek, such as Rumanians, Serbians, Bulgarians, and the rest. Later, when the rule requiring all officials of the empire be Muslims was slackened, these phanariotes became official interpreters in the increasing international involvement of the empire. In these positions they wielded great influence and amassed fortunes for themselves and for their Greek compatriots. All of this adversely affected the economy of the country. The caravan routes were not safe, roads and bridges were in bad repair, and local wars and brigandage had paralyzed commerce.

More destructive to the economy of the empire than internal disorders were the events in Europe. Trade routes had shifted. With the discovery of new ocean routes and progress in shipbuilding, European trade which had been most active in the Mediterranean moved to the Persian Gulf for a few decades and from there to eastern Asia. With the increased number of manufacturing centers in Europe the demand for the handmade products of the Ottomans slackened. Furthermore, the flow of silver and gold from the New World shifted the center of finance from the Mediterranean coastal cities to western Europe. In all this the Ottoman trade suffered and the merchants of the empire, even if they had been free from corruption, would not have been able to compete with the corporations and cartels which had been established in the west.

Decay in the central governmental institutions, the weakness of and defeats of the army at the hands of the Russians, increase in corruption and graft, and the shift in trade had created an atmosphere in which there was no incentive for investment. Those who had the money either did not know how to invest, were afraid to, or did not care to.

The organization of the government, however, remained intact. The sultan, the vazirs, the bureaucrats, the ulama, and the moneylenders used their relatively short terms of office for amassing as much wealth as they could. In the nineteenth century, the Ottoman sultan could no longer depend on the Janissaries who had grown in number and in arrogance. This once-effective force which had guarded the power of the sultans became a club in the reactionary hands of the ulama against any sultan who dared to change the status quo. During the nineteenth century Egypt revolted, the Wahhabis of Arabia challenged the religious authority of the caliph, the Druzes and the Maronites of Lebanon set up autonomous governments, national groups in the Balkans agitated for independence, and the very pashas sent there to quell the rebellions rose against the central government.

Notwithstanding all this, the "sick man of Europe," as Nicholas I of Russia is reported to have called the Ottoman empire, lived another century. Indeed, the house of Osman survived the Romanovs by a few years. To the contemporary observers it seemed that the empire could not last a day longer, but in the process of history it does not seem so amazing that the empire lasted so long. During the centuries, a system had been established which benefited the sultan as the commander in chief and those whom he wished to favor. As long as the sultan was strong and alert, he shifted his favors from one segment of society to the other and, in the long run, all were at peace, relatively secure, and satisfied.

But during the two centuries when the power of the sultanate was at low ebb, the system did not disintegrate. Instead it remained and benefited an oligarchy of which the sultan was often a member. The categories of the beneficiaries became fixed. There were the sultans influenced by the women of the harem, who in turn were under the strong and ambitious hands of eunuchs. There were the military commanders, the ulama, the pashas, the moneylenders, and the influential leaders of the various non-Muslim millets. These profited from the system by exploiting the masses under them, both Muslim and non-Muslim. The fact that they often viciously fought against each other was part of the contest. But as soon as the system was threatened by external force or internal desire for reform, they united and supported each other to ward off the attack. No sooner would the "danger" pass than they would be at it again and also at each other.

The Ottoman system would, nevertheless, have fallen of its own weight and corruption had it not been for the fact that European nations sometimes singly and often together gave the tottering empire enough blood transfusions to keep it alive. The essence of what in European history is called "The Eastern Question," is the western inability to divide the property once the sick man died. No one of the European powers was strong enough to subdue the others and annex the empire. Meanwhile, each was fearful lest another power take the advantage. Ruthlessness, intrigue, secret agreements, duplicity, and war were all part of the diplomatic game. As soon as one country or any combination of countries got the upper hand, the rest came to aid the Ottomans until the "balance" was restored. When it became evident that the empire had to be kept alive in order to uphold the European balance, some of the European countries, such as Great Britain, France, and later Germany, joined the Ottoman oligarchy in the exploitation and perpetuated the system. Austria-Hungary was too unwieldy to be effective and Russia had too much of a Messianic obsession to be practical. Indeed even after world War I the European powers tried to keep the Ottomans alive and they would have succeeded, had it not been for the Turks themselves who practiced euthanasia and buried the corpse.

The major European countries involved in the affairs of the Ottoman empire were six: Austria-Hungary, Russia, Great Britain, France, Germany, and Italy. Austria and Russia were primarily interested in the European holdings of the Ottomans. As such their interests often clashed. The Hapsburgs had borne the brunt of the Ottoman pressure since the fourteenth century and felt that they had the first option in the choice of territory. More especially they wanted control of the Danube and the approaches to the Adriatic and Aegean Seas. They, however, had difficulties which were not unlike those of the Ottomans. The Austrian and Hungarian ruling classes were made up of Germans and Magyars while the population over whom they ruled were predominantly Slavs. The religion of the ruling classes was Roman Catholicism while that of most of the subjects was Orthodoxy. Like the Ottomans, the Austro-Hungarians were not able to weld the diverse groups of the empire into a nation. The spirit of nationalism growing in Europe in the nineteenth century encouraged movements for independence and adversely affected the Austro-Hungarian empire.

The Russians, on the other hand, were more homogeneous. Their spirit of nationalism transcended their boundaries and reached the Slavs of the Balkans who were under either the Ottomans or the Austrians. Furthermore, as the only independent Orthodox country, the Russians had already claimed protection over the Orthodox subjects of the Porte, a fact which was not welcomed by the Hapsburgs, who also ruled over Orthodox people. Economically and politically the Russians felt hemmed in, as the Ottomans controlled the outlets to the great rivers of southern Russia. They continually justified their attempts to expand by ascribing their need for warm-water ports. In all these objectives they clashed with the Austrians. Neither of them alone was strong enough in the eighteenth century to put an end to the Ottomans, nor could they afford to unite in the effort. By the nineteenth century, when the Russians could deal with the Ottomans, the British and the French had become interested in the fate of the Turks and intervened on their behalf.

The main interests of Great Britain and France in southeastern Europe were economic and the upholding of the European balance of power. Any territorial ambitions which they might have had were not of highest priority. Their territorial interests were concentrated in the African and Asian dependencies of the Ottoman empire. The imperial policy of Great Britain was built around the protection of India and the main routes leading to it. In the Middle East this meant the Persian Gulf and the Red Sea and the lands surrounding them.

France was interested mainly in North Africa and the Levant. Inasmuch as the boundaries of the Levant were always in doubt, she and Great Britain clashed. Otherwise the interests of France in the rest of the Ottoman empire were economic and religious. She was one of the first to conclude a commercial treaty with the Ottomans and this was renewed many times in the course of centuries. French businessmen, industrialists, and financiers had invested heavily in the Ottoman empire. In religion, the French had the same interest and claim over the Roman Catholic subjects of the sultan as the Russians had over the Orthodox. Since both the Orthodox and the Roman Catholics wanted control of the Christian shrines in Palestine, Russia and France clashed.

Germany and Italy were late-comers to the scene. German interests were mainly economic and the gaining of influence at the Porte in order to thwart the plans of Russia and England. Italy's role was insignificant, but it managed to gain control of Libya while others were involved elsewhere.

The relationship of the European powers to each other and to the Ottoman empire does not, however, follow a logical pattern. It was dictated by opportunism. France and England joined together against Russia and Austria as readily as France and Austria against Great Britain and Russia.

The leaders of the Ottoman empire, in the meantime, had learned two lessons. One was the necessity of reform, which will be the subject of a separate chapter. The reform on which all Turks agreed was in the military field, even though graft and inefficiency prevented them from doing very much about it. The second lesson was the realization that it was possible to set one European nation against the other. Heretofore, the Ottomans, in the tradition of Islam, considered all non-Muslims as the "abode of war" and potential enemies. As late as the middle of the nineteenth century, if two European countries were at war their subjects residing in the Ottoman empire cooperated with each other, for they saw in the Ottomans a more dreadful enemy. Observing this, the Ottomans were convinced that all Europeans were one in their enmity toward the Turks. From the second half of the eighteenth century on through the nineteenth, European conflicts extended to their nationals who were residing in Turkey, and the Ottomans realized that they could play the one against another. Toward the end of the century the Ottomans, in the person of Sultan Abdul Hamid II, became quite adept at this art. On the whole, however, the Turks did not follow a long-range policy and usually reacted to a crisis rather than acting according to a plan.

The French Revolution at the end of the eighteenth century was a respite for the Ottoman sultans. Later they were strongly affected by it, but for the time being it kept the Europeans too busy to pay any attention to the Ottomans. The emergence of Napoleon, however, changed the situation as he involved the Ottomans and even the Persians in his global plans. When Napoleon invaded Egypt in 1798, the Ottomans were forced to end their long friendship with the French and declare war, but there was no open clash, as the invasion of Napoleon was destroyed by the British. Napoleon was forced to abandon his troops and go back to France.

The same year Napoleon invaded Egypt, the 27-year-old Selim II became sultan (1799–1807). Relatively speaking, he was one of the better educated and took some steps towards reviving the vigor of the empire. He sent some young men to Europe for study and observation, reintroduced the printing press and, most urgent of all, tried to reorganize the army. Not daring to touch the Janissaries, he tried to organize a new corps with new uniforms and modern weapons. His purpose was to encourage the Janissaries to emulate this corps, but they refused and not much was accomplished.

In the meantime, Europe was going through one of her frequent periods of realignment. Russia joined the coalition of Great Britain and Austria-Hungary against Napoleon and demanded that the sultan join the coalition. This pushed the Ottomans closer to France, but Selim was wise enough not to commit himself. He used this friendship, however, to bring in French officers and technicians for the reorganization of his army. After Napoleon's victory at Austerlitz in December 1805, the sultan got closer to the French and more inimical to the interests of Russia. This brought upon him the wrath of both Russia and England. Both of them declared war on the Porte in 1806 and actually sent a small but ineffective fleet to the Straits.

In the midst of this confusion, two events altered the course of Ottoman history. One was that the Janissaries turned their soup kettles upside down, which was a sign of revolt, and persuaded the Shaykh ul-Islam to issue a *fetva* deposing the sultan in May 1807 and elevating his submissive cousin Mustafa IV to the throne. The other event was that Alexander I of Russia and Napoleon met at Tilsit in June 1807 and signed a treaty of friendship. Even though Napoleon did not bow to the Russian demand to be given a free hand in the Straits, such a friendship was a blow to the Ottomans.

The Ottoman armies of the Danube took advantage of the lull in the war with Russia and helped depose Mustafa and chose his younger brother Mahmud II (1807–1839), who was the only male heir left in the house of Osman. Mahmud was also the last effective and forceful ruler in the Ottoman empire, and he is known as the man who inaugurated many reforms of far-reaching consequences in the empire.

The Russians renewed the war with Turkey in 1809 and Napoleon did nothing to stop her. The Russians made their usual slow advance, but by 1811 the European situation had deteriorated. Alexander I wanted to make peace lest he be forced to fight both France and Turkey. Napoleon, on the other hand, tried to persuade Mahmud to stay in the war. Mahmud, who was tired of defeats and disgusted with the duplicity of the French, signed the Treaty of Bucharest, ceding Bessarabia up to the Pruth River to Russia. A month later Napoleon attacked Russia. If the Turks had known the course of events they might have regained a good deal of their empire by becoming allies of Napoleon. Perhaps Napoleon would not have met the fate he did. As it was, Mahmud II executed his emissaries for having ceded territory to Russia. Three years later Alexander I, who was riding the crest of power and popularity after the downfall of Napoleon, might have been able to fulfill the dream of Peter the Great and conquer Constantinople, but he did not. He was too intent on strengthening his pet project, the "Holy Alliance." He was also under the influence of Metternich, who was bent on the principle of "legitimacy," which upheld the right of every despot including the sultan to hold his power against the republican ideas unleashed by the French Revolution.

Alexander I heeded Metternich's advice but the Greeks did not. In 1821 they revolted against their "legitimate" master, the Ottomans, and slaughtered some 30,000 Turks. The Ottomans retaliated by massacring the Greeks in Istanbul. All Europe seemed to be aroused, not by the massacres but by the fact that Greece, the birthplace of democracy, had declared her independence. As was to happen a century later in the case of Zionism, European liberals, classical scholars, and lovers of democracy formed "Philhellene" societies, raised money for the Greek revolutionaries, and encouraged their governments to oppose the sultan in favor of the Greeks. On January 13, 1822 the Greek "National Assembly" met and declared its independence.

The sultan with his ill-equipped army and rebellious Janissaries could not cope with the insurrection and in 1824 reluctantly asked his nominal vassal, Muhammad Ali of Egypt, to quell the rebellion. Muhammad Ali, who must have been waiting for such an opportunity, sent his son Ibrahim to subdue Greece. In 1825, Ibrahim landed in Navarino and in a series of successful campaigns was able to capture Athens. By 1826, the rebellion was almost crushed and Greek independence was considered a lost cause.

While all this was going on, the sultan must have been smarting over the fact that it was the European-trained army of his Egyptian vassal that had accomplished this task while the Janissaries had remained indolent at home. By the beginning of the eighteenth century the Janissary corps had become a heavy burden on the Ottoman empire. With the passage of time it had also become a stumbling block to progress and a threat to the sultanate. The Janissaries had become so powerful, corrupt, and indolent that they deposed and elevated sultans at will, beheaded grand vazirs, and opposed every attempt at reform. Sultan Selim had lost his life in a vain attempt to subdue them. Mahmud, however, prepared the ground before he took the vital step. He formed a new artillery group with modern weapons and brought thousands of these soldiers to Istanbul. Then he ordered the Janissaries to adopt the European form of military drill. The Janissaries, refusing to change their ways, rushed toward the palace whereupon they were mowed down with grapeshot. They took refuge in their barracks and the artillery bombarded the barracks until almost all were destroyed. They were hunted in every city of the empire and were killed mercilessly. Then the sultan issued a decree abolishing the corps. The importance of this event in the history of the Ottoman empire cannot be exaggerated, for it not only opened the way for military reorganization but for all other reforms. The reactionaries of the empire who had depended upon the Janissaries had been rendered impotent.

The exultation of Mahmud was dampened by the realization that the Greek episode was not over. Nicholas I (1825–1855) of Russia, who did not have the scruples of Metternich about "legitimacy," was anxious to turn the Greek revolt to Russian advantage. The British and French were forced to intervene by the great pressure of public opinion in favor of the Greeks expressed by Lord Byron of England and Chateaubriand of France. They were also afraid Russia might use this as a pretext to wreck the Ottoman empire. So the three powers, Great Britain, France, and Russia, jointly asked the sultan to negotiate with the Greeks. This Mahmud refused, whereupon the combined fleet of the three European powers destroyed the Ottoman fleet at Navarino on October 20, 1827, and forced Ibrahim to withdraw.

The sultan asked for indemnity and Russia retaliated unilaterally by declaring war in 1828. As usual the Russians were slow, but the Ottomans had not had time to organize a new army after the destruction of the Janissaries. After a year the Russians had advanced perilously close to Istanbul by capturing Edirne (Adrianople). The European powers intervened and brought pressure upon Mahmud to sue for peace. By the Treaty of Adrianople (September 14, 1829) the Porte recognized the independence of Greece under the "Three Powers" guaranty, granted autonomy to Serbia, and ceded the mouth of the Danube to Russia.

For nearly a quarter of a century after the Treaty of Adrianople the attention of the Porte was directed toward either internal struggle with Muhammad Ali of Egypt or attempts to reform, both of which will be discussed in subsequent chapters. The Porte was relatively at peace with its European neighbors. In the meantime Europe went through the convulsion of a social and economic revolution in 1848 which had repercussions in the Middle East. In the same year, Marx and Engels published the *Communist Manifesto*. In the course of four years, France, through a series of revolutions, changed from a monarchy to the Second Republic and then to the Second Empire, with another Bonaparte, Louis Napoleon, as dictator.

Louis Napoleon, who had helped the Pope in his difficulties and in turn had been assisted by the Vatican in his coup to become emperor, was eager to prove himself a faithful son of the Church. He could do this by reasserting France's interest in the Roman Catholic subjects of the Porte and gain special privileges for the Vatican in the care and administration of the Christian holy places in Palestine. Furthermore, such a move would check the ambitions of Nicholas I, who had not accepted Napoleon III as a "brother" monarch, and would enhance the prestige of France.

There had always been friction between the Roman Catholics and the Orthodox over the right to control the holy places. Ever since the Ottomans came into possession of Palestine, the Porte had made decisions favoring sometimes one group and sometimes the other. To avoid bloodshed, sometimes Muslims were given custody of and the key to these places. There was friction again in 1850 and by 1852 Sultan Abdul Mejid (1839–1861) very reluctantly decided in favor of French control. Tsar Nicholas I, who considered this a great blow to Russian honor, sent Menshikov to persuade and cajole the sultan to change his decision. The sultan, with the open support of the French and the surreptitious encouragement of the British, gave a formal refusal to Russia in 1853.

It is very difficult to determine who started the Crimean War. Russia was committed to upholding her prestige, was "certain" of the neutrality of Great Britain, and was confident of her success. Nicholas I suggested that Russia and Great Britain cooperate in dividing the property of the "sick man" who was about to die. France was committed to holding her gains and apparently did not expect Great Britain to stay neutral. For the Ottomans, this seemed to be the opportunity they had been awaiting, because the sultan was confident that he would have the assistance of both Great Britain and France. In Britain the intense popular dislike for the autocracy of Nicholas I and the fear of the government for the safety of access to India combined to make British involvement in the war a certainty.

The main antagonists in the Crimean War were Russia against the Ottoman empire, Britain, and France. Later, Austria and Prussia made a defensive alliance with each other and the former joined Britain and France in 1854. The Treaty of Paris ending the war was signed in March 1856. The Ottomans who had become involved in the power politics of Europe suffered as a result. They lost even though they were part of the victorious alliance. In the treaty, the interested European powers virtually assumed responsibility for protecting the Ottoman empire by declaring that anything which endangered the integrity of the empire would "be considered a question of European interest." The Europeans demanded reform and got it, at least on paper. The imperial rescript, *hatti humayun*, was issued in 1856 and embodied far-reaching reforms. Until the beginning of World War I, the Ottomans had to exhibit some sort of "reform" as a mark of good behavior in order to be allowed to continue in existence.

The European powers were interested in reforms in the Ottoman empire mainly to promote their own interests, especially in economic matters, but also in order to satisfy their own citizens who were imbued with ideas of liberalism and optimistic about the Enlightenment for the betterment of mankind. The western Europeans were still interested in safeguarding the independence of the Porte from Russian encroachment. Furthermore, western powers had discovered that keeping the Ottoman empire alive was economically very profitable, and the investors of Europe were vying with each other to participate in the loot.

For nearly 200 years the Ottoman empire had been humiliated and defeated, had lost vast territories, but at least the Porte was economically free from foreign domination. The Ottoman sultans had many ways of meeting their deficits. They depreciated currency, they expropriated the wealth of their subjects, and they borrowed money from native moneylenders. They were not in the habit of borrowing money from foreign banks and governments. Insofar as can be ascertained, 1854 was the first time the Porte borrowed money from Britain and France to buy weapons and meet the needs of the Crimean War. Once the door was opened, the sultans continued borrowing. Local bankers and the European investors had such a good profit that they encouraged the practice. Loans with discount rates as high as 55 per cent and rates of interest of 12 per cent were indeed profitable. By the time Abdul Hamid II became sultan (1876–1909), the country was virtually bankrupt. The Ottoman defeat in the war of 1876 against Russia imposed an indemnity of $100,000,000 on the Porte. By 1881, the whole empire went into receivership. The British, French, Dutch, German, Austrian, and Italian creditors set up the Council of Administration of the Ottoman Public Debt and took control of the major phases of the economic life of the empire, in both production and collection of revenue. This council restored credit and encouraged the flow of foreign capital. For the first time, the subjects of the empire began to have a small share in the prosperity, and everyone realized that the institutions of the empire headed by the sultan were not responsible for any of it.

European investors found a gold mine in the vast and underdeveloped territory of the empire, both in raw material and in opportunities for development. The Ottomans needed roads, railroads, city lights, water, and public works of all types. The Europeans were ready to loan money and receive concessions. In 1870, Bismarck did not think that all the Balkans were worth the "bones of a single Pomeranian grenadier." Twenty years later the Germans, under Wilhelm II, were not only selling armaments to the Turks, but were also busy building railroads in Anatolia. In 1898, the Kaiser paid a second visit to Istanbul and this time went to Damascus and Jerusalem. The *Drang nach Osten*, to the east, was inaugurated and the famous Berlin-to-Baghdad railway introduced German imperialism into the Middle East. This frightened the British, the French, and the Russians to such a degree that they forgot their differences and cooperated to block the German push eastward.

During the two decades following the Treaty of Paris, the Europeans were busy with their own struggles, wars of unification, and much else. This should have given the Ottomans some respite, but it was not so. The ideals of the French Revolution and the emergence of national states in western Europe had aroused similar feelings among the subject peoples of the Balkans. Serbs wanted independence, Greeks desired more territory, Bosnia and Herzegovina were seething with revolt, and there were uprisings in Rumania.

The educated liberals in western Europe were aghast at the speed and severity with which the Ottoman soldiers dealt with the revolters and were clamoring for punishing the Turks. The governments and industrialists of western Europe, on the other hand, had profitable investments to protect and did not care for such humane considerations. The Russians and Austrians saw in this a chance to settle accounts with the Turks. Representatives of European powers assembled in Istanbul to reach a solution. The wily Abdul Hamid II, who had just been elevated to the throne by the reformists (August 31, 1876) agreed to constitutional reforms. This pleased the British but not the Russians, who were bent on war. France was still licking her wounds from defeat at the hands of the Germans; Bismarck was not interested in the Balkans; and in Britain public sentiment was too critical of the Turks to permit the leaders to go to war on the side of the Ottomans.

In the war of 1877–1878 the Turks fought bravely but could not hold the Russians, who reached the village of San Stefano (Yeshilkoy), only ten miles from Istanbul. Abdul Hamid signed the Treaty of San Stefano (March 13, 1878), which dismembered whatever was left of the Ottoman empire in Europe. It gave independence to Montenegro, Serbia, and Rumania, and gave autonomy to Bosnia and Herzegovina. The heart of the treaty, however, was the creation of a large Bulgaria, extending from the Black to the Aegean Sea. Furthermore, in eastern Asia Minor the Porte had to cede considerable territory. In addition to all this, the demoralized sultan agreed to an indemnity of some 300,000,000 rubles.

There were immediate protests from the Greeks, who saw an end to their territorial ambitions, from the Serbs who resented seeing so many Serbs become subjects of a large Bulgaria, from the Austrians who felt that their advance to the east was blocked, and from the British who, led by Prime Minister Disraeli, turned against Russia. All of these countries, together with Germany, brought pressure to bear upon Russia and convened the Congress of Berlin (June 13, 1878) to reconsider the Treaty of San Stefano.

The Treaty of Berlin replaced that of San Stefano and was full of double dealing that did not settle the Balkan problems. Bulgaria was divided and part of it was given back to Turkey; Austria attained control over Bosnia and Herzegovina; Serbia and Montenegro became independent; Russia annexed Bessarabia as well as Batum and Kars; Greece gained some territories; and Great Britain got Cyprus.

The nineteenth century came to an end with the Ottomans under the political and economic domination of European powers. Abdul Hamid II used all his cunning to wrest himself free, but the case was hopeless. By the time of World War I the sultan had lost practically all his European holdings, and his control over the Fertile Crescent and North Africa was only nominal.

CHAPTER 21

IMPERIALISM IN THE ARABIC-SPEAKING WORLD

The expedition of Napoleon to Egypt in 1798 is usually regarded as an impor tant landmark in the history of the European penetration into the Arabic speaking world. It acted as a catalyst in arousing the interest of Europeans in what to them must have been, the hinterland of the Ottoman empire, and in opening the eyes of some Muslim leaders to the possibilities of western civiliza tion. Both France and Great Britain had some familiarity with the area. Ever since the time of the Crusades, France had been interested in the Levant both for its flax and silk trade and also because of the Maronites, who were Roman Catholics and had French sympathies. In the intermittent struggles between the Maronite Christians and the Druzes, France always came to the aid of the Maronites. The British, who also had holdings in the Middle East and were rivals of France, took the side of the Druzes. In the seventeenth century, the British East India Company had penetrated the Persian Gulf and had estab lished trade centers in Basra, Baghdad, Damascus, and Aleppo. In 1770 Warren, the governor of the British company in Bengal, sent an expedition to Suez. The purpose was to use it as a base for shipment of goods overland to the Mediterranean. In 1778, the British were able to conclude a treaty with the Mamluk ruler of Egypt to secure the Red Sea shipping.

The rivalry between France and Britain in the Middle East, as well as in India, was heightened by the French Revolution and the rise of Napoleon While the main scene of the struggle between France and England was in Europe, it was part of the grand scheme of Napoleon to harass Britain from all directions. Certainly the trade route to India was one of the most vulnerable Perhaps he also had dreams of building a great empire or of spreading western culture among the peoples of the Middle East. The fact that he took so many nonmilitary personnel with him shows that he was prepared to take advantage of every opportunity to win fame and popularity at home and in the world at large. His expedition was based on fairly accurate knowledge of the social and political situation in Egypt and he took with him scholars and scientists to learn more. In Egypt, Napoleon posed as the liberator of the masses from the tyranny of the Mamluks. He proclaimed himself a friend of Islam and of the Ottoman sultan. But Egypt belonged to the Ottomans and the Sublime Porte did not like Napoleon's intrusion. The British were not slow to point this out and the sultan sent an expedition which, with the help of the British, forced the French army to surrender in 1801.

THE RISE OF MUHAMMAD ALI

Napoleon failed in his attempt to harass the British or even to increase his own fame. He had returned to France long before his army surrendered. Everything probably would have gone back to normal had it not been for two by-products of the Napoleonic expedition. One of these was the fact that the scholars who had accompanied Napoleon discovered the famous Rosetta Stone which furnished a key to the unraveling of the ancient Egyptian civilization. Napoleon's scholars also prepared a wealth of accurate information about the physical, human, and economic geography of Egypt. The second by-product was an accident for which Napoleon was not responsible. It happened that in the expeditionary force sent by the sultan to Egypt was a young man, Muhammad Ali, who changed the history of Egypt. Napoleon's expedition revealed the might of Europe, but Muhammad Ali was one of the few who understood the source of that might and attempted to bring Egypt into the modern world by borrowing from the West.

Muhammad Ali was born in Albania in 1769 and was probably of Persian and Turkish ancestry. Whether he was a tobacco vendor or the son of a tobacco merchant is not certain. What is certain is that he was already an important officer in 1799 when he went with the Albanian contingent to Egypt. After the defeat of the French army in 1801, it was Muhammad Ali who filled the vacuum. By 1805, he was appointed Pasha of Egypt. From then on Muhammad Ali's star shone brighter with the passing of the years. Before long the British suspected that they had saved Egypt from France only to put it into the hands of Muhammad Ali. The French, on the other hand, felt that perhaps Muhammad Ali could accomplish what they had failed to do and gave him every assistance.

Muhammad Ali, however, did not become the puppet of the French. He was shrewd enough to see the supremacy of European arms, technical knowledge, and education. He asked the French to teach his followers. Bringing French naval and military experts to Egypt, he created a new army and navy with the latest weapons. Opening schools on the French model, he also had French books translated into Arabic. He brought in agricultural experts and by 1815 had monopolized trade in cotton, hemp, indigo, and sesame. And he built ships and harbors. It may be surmised that he was not doing these things for the glory of Islam or for the uplifting of the Egyptian masses. There seems little doubt that his ambitions were for himself and his descendants.

He obeyed the summons of the sultan to send an expedition to Arabia and quell the religio-political rebellion of the Wahhabis[1] in 1818. A few years later, in 1824, when the Greeks revolted for independence, the sultan again asked Muhammad Ali for help. Ibrahim, the son of Muhammad Ali, went with 10,000 troops and would have been successful had not European powers intervened and destroyed the Egyptian fleet at Navarino in 1827.[2]

While all this was going on, the British were busy strengthening themselves against the possible power of Muhammad Ali. They occupied Bab al-Mandab and Aden in the Arabian peninsula. They established permanent residency in Muscat on the Persian Gulf and in Baghdad. In Syria they strengthened the hands of the Porte, and in Egypt itself they tried to revive the power of the Mamluks against Muhammad Ali. Both to thwart the British plan and to rid himself of the Mamluks, Muhammad Ali in a series of maneuvers turned two of the important leaders of the Mamluks against each other. When only one leader was left, Muhammad Ali invited him and the other dignitaries of the Mamluks to a grand party at the citadel. There he had them all massacred after dinner. Thus came the end of Mamluk power and misrule. They had come to power by treachery and violence and they were destroyed by the same means.

In 1831, Muhammad Ali decided that the time was ripe to execute his plan of grasping ultimate power by invading Syria. He claimed that the sultan had promised him the pashalik of Syria as a reward for going to the aid of the Porte in the Greek rebellion. Again he sent well-equipped troops under the command of his son, Ibrahim. The Egyptian troops overran Syria without much difficulty and by 1833 were in Asia Minor where they defeated the Ottoman army at Konya. The Ottoman Sultan Mahmud was so alarmed that he asked the aid of Russia. The Tsar, hoping for an opportunity to expand Russian influence, gladly accepted the invitation and sent troops to Istanbul. The French, who had been encouraging Muhammad Ali all along, became apprehensive and asked their protégé to make peace with the beleaguered sultan. Muhammad Ali decided to comply and in return was given the pashalik of Egypt, Syria, and Crete on an annual basis, in return for an annual tribute of £150,000. The Russians, however, before evacuating Istanbul, signed the treaty of Hunkyar Iskelesi, which gave them the right to send troops to Turkey whenever internal conditions warranted.

Thus Egypt and all the Fertile Crescent was drawn into the maze of European power politics. The British were unhappy when the Egyptians in Syria threatened their access to India. The French who had aided Muhammad Ali were alarmed at the turn of events and like the British, feared the consequences of the Hunkyar Iskelesi Treaty. The sultan could not bear defeat at the hand of his vassal and prepared for war. Muhammad Ali was thus thwarted in his attempt to destroy Mahmud II, whom he held in contempt. But for eight years Ibrahim ruled Syria with ability and enlightenment. For the first time in cen-

[1] See below, p. 242.
[2] See above, p. 204.

turies, the Muslims, Christians, Druzes, and Jews lived together in peace. Ibrahim also prepared for war and imposed a much-hated conscription upon the Syrians. Uprisings broke out in several places.

With such universal dissatisfaction, conflict could not be prevented. The sultan's army, which had been trained by the German General Von Moltke, crossed over into Syria in 1839 and was soundly beaten by Ibrahim at Nazib. A few days after that battle, the sultan died, and his death was followed by the surrender of the Ottoman navy to Egypt in Alexandria. The new sultan was willing to accede to Muhammad Ali's demands, and once again the European powers exerted vigorous activity. In the end Britain was able to persuade Russia, Prussia, and Austria to agree to a treaty in 1840, according to which Muhammad Ali would be given the hereditary pashalik of Egypt and life-time control of south Syria. Muhammad Ali refused and British troops landed in Syria. With the aid of their friends, the Druzes, the British took Beirut and defeated Ibrahim. France suffered a diplomatic defeat because it, like Britain, was afraid of Russian intentions, and chose not to oppose the European powers. Muhammad Ali was defeated in his purpose and was content to accept the hereditary pashalik of Egypt. The Hunkyar Iskelesi Treaty was replaced by the "Straits Convention" in 1841 which closed the Straits to the warships of all nations. Thus ended the first major attempt in the long history of the Ottoman empire to unseat the house of Osman. The attempt failed, but it had far-reaching repercussions. It brought Egypt out of its miserable stupor; it opened Egypt and the Fertile Crescent to direct European imperialism; and, perhaps most important of all, it gave the Arabic-speaking world a taste of what European technology could do.

During the last half of the nineteenth century, Great Britain and France, in order to defend their own interests, were committed to safeguarding the integrity of the Ottoman empire against the encroachments of Russia and Austria. They sometimes looked with displeasure at the subject nationalities of the Porte in the Balkans who demanded independence. The above policies, however, did not prevent the same two nations from violating the integrity of the Ottoman empire in the Fertile Crescent, Egypt, and North Africa.

SYRIA-LEBANON

Religious rivalries and wars have been part of the history of Syria-Lebanon for a long time. There were not only Muslims, Christians, and Druzes fighting against each other, but there was strife among the different sects within Islam and Christianity. When Ibrahim and his Egyptian troops entered the region, Lebanon was part of the pashalik of Syria, ruled by Bashir II (1788–1840). He was a scion of the house of Shihab, which had been in power since 1697. In the struggle among the three religions, the dynasty managed to belong to all three. They changed their religion whenever the situation demanded. Bashir II was baptized a Christian, but his mother was a Muslim. At the time of

Egyptian occupation he happened to be a Druze. He cooperated with Ibrahim, even though a number of lesser shaykhs of different religious persuasions remained loyal to the sultan. With the encouragement of Ibrahim, Bashir opened Lebanon to the West. In addition to French businessmen and British ships, French and American missionaries came into the region.

With the defeat of Ibrahim, the rule of Bashir ended and he was exiled to Malta. European rivalry became dominant in the area. On the whole the Maronite Christians sided with the French, the Orthodox with the Russians, the Druzes with the British, and the Muslims with the Ottoman sultan. Since neither the sultan nor the Russians had much power in the Fertile Crescent, the main protagonists were the French and the British acting through their protégés, the Maronites and the Druzes, respectively.

For a time the Porte sent governors to rule the area under the aegis of five European powers. When this scheme failed, the powers developed a dual control, the Maronites in the north and the Druzes in the south. Skirmishes between the two groups led to open war-fare in 1860, when the Druzes massacred some 14,000 Maronites. The French sent an expedition to help the Maronites, but by the time the troops arrived the Ottomans had managed to pacify the area. The French, with the support of Russia, wanted to declare a protectorate over Lebanon. The British, with the support of the Porte, opposed the move. By June 1861, the European powers and the Porte were able to sign the "reglement organique" in Istanbul. According to this, Lebanon was declared autonomous under a Christian governor designated by the Porte. This arrangement lasted until World War I.

EGYPT

The main activity of the Anglo-French rivalry as well as imperialism was centered in Egypt. For all practical purposes Muhammad Ali was the master of Egypt and did not have any interference from Istanbul. By the time of his death in 1848, Muhammad Ali had overhauled the administration and revitalized the economy of Egypt. He created a hierarchy of officials for collection of taxes, control of irrigation, and public security.

He controlled all the land which had been confiscated from the Mamluks. Parts of this he gave to his family and friends. The rest was state property which was leased to tenants. By 1858 these lands were registered in the name of the "owners" and came under the Islamic law of inheritance. This meant that the land remained in the families, thus creating a class of landlords. He organized state monopolies for the export of cotton, tobacco, and other products. The government bought all products at low prices and sold at great profit. In nearly 40 years of his rule the cultivated area of Egypt rose from 3,200,000 acres to 4,150,000; revenue rose from £1,203,500 to £4,200,000; and exports from £200,000 to £2,000,000.

He also built factories, but these generally failed because there were no trained technicians, fuel, or spare parts. The financial loss was staggering, but the iron determination of Muhammad Ali kept these factories going despite the loss. What spelled the doom of Muhammad Ali's industrial empire was the Anglo-Ottoman Commercial Treaty of 1838 according to which monopolies and trade controls were outlawed and the British had the right to buy directly from the people. This treaty was enforced in Egypt and thwarted the plans to industrialize the country. It is doubtful whether the reforms of Muhammad Ali raised the standards of living and health of the masses, but they were a remarkable beginning.

Unfortunately for Egypt, the successors of Muhammad Ali were mostly incompetent and extravagant. His immediate successor, Abbas, was a religious fanatic who refused to receive the French advisers whom Muhammad Ali had brought. His short misrule of six years was of little consequence and his murder in 1854 brought the glutton Sa'id to power.

SUEZ CANAL

Sa'id had many European friends, among them the talented Ferdinand de Lesseps, son of the French political agent in Egypt. Apparently he had been thinking of reopening the Suez Canal, which had been partly dug by the pharoahs. Almost immediately after the accession of Sa'id, de Lesseps came to Cairo and received a concession to dig the canal. While much of the world paid scant attention to the news, a small minority in France became very enthusiastic, and a similar minority in Great Britain was incensed and did everything in its power to stop it. The concession needed the approval of the Porte, who could ill afford to antagonize an ally such as Britain in the Crimean War, which was going on at the time. It was not that England did not appreciate the commercial possibilities of Egypt. Indeed, Egypt traded more with Britain than with any other country. In 1869, British trade totalled 41 per cent of Egypt's imports and 49 per cent of Egypt's exports. England, however, was obsessed with the idea of protecting India. The canal, it was true, would shorten considerably the distance between London and Bombay, but by the same token would make it easier for other powers to threaten the British hold on India, and for rivals to compete with its trade in Egypt and in the area of the Persian Gulf.

But de Lesseps was able to raise the necessary capital in France, the Netherlands, Spain, and Italy. By 1856 he formed the Compagnie Universelle du Canal Maritime de Suez. For giving the concession to the company for 99 years from the date of completion, Sa'id received preferred shares giving him 15 per cent of the net profit. For the building of the canal he promised to provide four fifths of the labor. Founders of the company and influential individuals who could be of assistance to the company received shares which returned 10 per cent of the profit. There were also 400,000 shares of common stock at 500 franks per share. The digging started in 1859 without the permission of the sultan, though by the year of Sa'id's death in 1863, not much had been accomplished.

Sa'id's travels, public works, and high living had incurred a debt of some £3,000,000. This did not bother Sa'id's spend-thrift successor, Isma'il, for these were prosperous times for Egypt. Because of the Civil War in the United States, Egyptian cotton was in great demand, and Isma'il's revenue from cotton rose to five times above normal. Isma'il confirmed the concession and paid the indemnity for not providing all of the agreed-upon forced labor. While the digging of the canal was going on, Isma'il gave vent to his craze for building. He built palaces, including the huge Abdin Palace in Cairo. He erected public buildings, installed gas and water, extended railroads, and built expensive factories which could not be used. He traveled to the capitals of Europe, and everywhere he was lavish in his entertainment and in the giving of expensive gifts. He almost doubled the annual tribute to the Porte and in return received the title of Khedive with the law of succession established in his line.

When the Suez Canal was finished in 1869, Isma'il spent upwards of £1,000,000 for entertainment. The canal was 93.5 miles long, from 96 to 110 yards wide, and 35 feet deep. It began at Port Sa'id on the Mediterranean and continued to Suez on the Red Sea. It had taken 12 years to build. Among the thousands of guests were Princess Eugenie of France, Emperor Joseph of Austria, and the Crown Prince of Prussia. In the opera house which he had built, Verdi's Aïda, a story based on ancient Egyptian history, was performed for the first time in 1871.

The cost of the canal to Egypt was 11,500,000 francs, not counting the tremendous cost in forced labor. The company did not begin to show a profit until 1875. In 1873 an international conference set a schedule of tariffs for the passage of ships through the canal, and agreed that the canal would be open to ships of all countries. In 1888, the Constantinople Convention was drawn up and signed by Austria, France, Germany, Britain, Italy, Holland, Russia, Spain, and Turkey. It stated that the canal should "always be free and open in time of war as in time of peace, to every vessel of commerce or of war, without distinction of flag." Great Britain was to violate the above agreement during World War I, just as it had violated the 1873 canal agreement in 1881 and 1882 by refusing free access to its enemies. The commercial operation of the company, however, remained intact, and worked smoothly until the nationalization of the Suez Canal in 1956. It was the strategic position of the canal and the rivalry for its control and/or protection that was an important factor in placing Egypt under the influence of European powers.

EUROPEAN INTERVENTION AND BRITISH OCCUPATION

Isma'il had fallen into the habit of indiscriminate spending, so when the end of the Civil War in the United States brought cotton prices down, he borrowed large sums of money from unscrupulous bankers of Europe at onerous terms which included high discounts, generous commissions, and exorbitant interest rates. By 1875 the combined foreign and domestic debt reached nearly £100,000,000. The interest charges alone amounted to the burdensome total of £51,000,000 per year. The per capita public debt was £14, with an annual service charge of £1/15s/10d, which was perhaps the highest in the world. Undaunted, Isma'il raised the taxes of the fellahin to pay for his new schemes. When this source was exhausted he sold all of his ordinary shares of the canal stock to Britain for £4,000,000, thereby providing the formerly antagonistic England with economic as well as political interest in the canal.

This money was a paltry sum compared to the indebtedness of the Khedive. The creditors were alarmed and pressed their demands. At the instigation of Bismarck, joined by England and France, the Porte was persuaded to dismiss Isma'il in favor of his mild-mannered son Tawfiq. The account of Isma'il's departure from Alexandria in his yacht foreshadowed the way his great-grandson, Faruq, was exiled from the same port in 1952. The European bankers followed the change of Khedive by foreclosing the mortgage on Egypt and taking control. They acted through two controllers—hence Dual Control—Monsieur de Blignieres, the Frenchman who was in charge of Egypt's expenditures, and Major Evelyn Baring, the Englishman who was to supervise the collection of taxes.

The Dual Controllers, who had become the actual rulers of Egypt, passed the Law of Liquidation in 1880. This law fixed the debt of the country at £98,377,000 and 4 per cent interest. Out of the anual income of the government a certain sum was set aside for the needs of the budget; all the rest was designated for the liquidation of debt. There was nothing left for development. No matter how hard the people worked, their income, beyond subsistence or less, went to pay the debt.

THE FIRST EGYPTIAN REVOLT

The reduction of expenditures meant that a large number of employees, including army officers, were dismissed or retired. But at the same time the foreigners were drawing handsome salaries, and the financial retrenchment did not involve the high army and administrative officers who were either Turks or Circassians. Heavy taxes, incompetence of government officials, the presence of foreigners who seemed to be allied with Turks, all aroused animosity among the Egyptians. For the first time in centuries the junior officers of the army, who were all Egyptians, arose in protest. Their leader, Colonel 'Urabi, a former student of Azhar University and a son of a fellah, headed the resistance movement. The resistance was neither well organized nor well thought out beyond vague ideas concerning a constitution. In its ranks were only some educated Egyptians, theologians, civil servants, and junior army officers. Tawfiq accepted the demands of the officers against the advice of the Dual Control. Due to some unfortunate excesses, riots broke out in Alexandria and some Europeans and Egyptians were killed.

This was used as a pretext for the powers to intervene. The Porte remained neutral and although France demanded armed intervention, it also eventually remained neutral. British historians believe that Great Britain was left alone and reluctantly accepted the responsibility of intervention. On the other hand it is possible to conclude that this was the opportunity Great Britain had been waiting for. Its great rival France, due to a change of government and also out of fear of German designs in North Africa, withdrew as a neutral, hoping perhaps that Great Britain would do the same and then they would try to come to terms with 'Urabi. This left Great Britain in the role of the sole deliverer of Europeans of all nationalities in Egypt who felt themselves in danger. It also made Britain the undisputed ruler of Egypt.

In any case, on July 11, 1882 the British bombarded Alexandria. In September of the same year, in the battle of Tel al-Kabir, north of Cairo, the British contingent defeated 'Urabi's forces and became masters of Egypt. 'Urabi was banished to Ceylon. The revolt failed but, nevertheless, a genuine, even though disorganized, movement had been started which gained momentum until 1952, when another group of junior army officers under another colonel, Gamal Abdul Nasser, forced out the last of the non-Egyptian rulers and took full control.

In sending troops to Egypt the British had promised to withdraw "as soon as the state of the country and the organization of proper means for the maintenance of Khedival authority will permit it." The fact that the British troops stayed on Egyptian soil until 1956 may be defended on, perhaps, admissible grounds. In the mind of the Egyptians, however, as well as most of the Asians, it was another neat trick in the imperialist trade.

EGYPT UNDER THE BRITISH

The direct and indirect British rule which lasted until 1936 (according to some Egyptian historians, until 1952), was a mixed blessing. The Egyptians were under both the Ottomans and the British, but the Ottomans were under the British. In this double deck imperialism, the British were certainly more efficient than the Ottomans. They were anxious to create a viable Egypt for the safety of the route to India, for purposes of trade and, incidentally, for good public relations as well.

The pretense of the Dual Control was abandoned and, as the sole power responsible for Egypt, the British sent the very able and astute Lord Cromer, the former Major Evelyn Baring, as pro-Consul. Nominally the Ottoman sultan was the ruler and his representative was the Khedive, but the actual power was in the hands of Lord Cromer. He ruled through a "legislative" assembly of 30 members—16 elected and 14 appointed—which was, in reality, consultative. For each Egyptian minister there was a British adviser and for each governor a British inspector.

Cromer abolished forced labor, revised taxation in favor of the fellahin, cut down the national debt, and improved irrigation, sanitation, and other services.

These reforms were capable of being carried out by administrative action and Cromer made them in an orderly and efficient manner. He did not concern himself, however, with reforms which had to be carried out through social revolution, such as land tenure, waqf, education, and the like. Under Cromer, Egypt was economically solvent and had a balanced budget. Per capita income rose and with it the standard of living. Furthermore, peace and order advanced Egyptian agriculture and foreign trade. At the turn of the century, cotton prices rose and the terms of trade were in Egypt's favor. On the other hand, the British relied on a one-crop agricultural policy, and ignored the problem of population growth. While they encouraged mining, they were consciously against industrialization. By 1916, the total number of industrial laborers in Egypt did not exceed 35,000.

The positive and negative aspects of the proximity of Egypt with Europe could not help but create collaborationists as well as antagonists, evolutionists in social change as well as revolutionists. It may be safely stated that any manifestation of the spirit of nationalism was frowned upon by the increasingly imperious Lord Cromer. His successors, Sir Eldon Gorst in 1907 and Lord Kitchener in 1911, were more or less of the same opinion, but these men were less efficient. Lord Cromer kept the number of British officials to a minimum, but under Gorst and Kitchener they increased in number and decreased in quality. Great Britain could not afford to relax control. Not only the safety of India was at stake, but also the Suez Canal and heavy economic investments. So the history of Egypt during the first half of the twentieth century is the story of the growing desire of the Egyptians for change versus the reluctance of the British to offer the opportunity.

CHAPTER 22

WESTERN IMPERIALISM IN IRAN

The Anglo-French struggle for supremacy in the Arabic-speaking world was repeated in Iran and for precisely the same reasons. France under Napoleon Bonaparte wanted to reach India, and England was anxious to safeguard the route to that subcontinent. Russian interest in Iran, however, was more basic than that of France. Because of its perennial excuse of needing warm-water ports it was interested in the Caspian Sea and the Persian Gulf region. It is not definitely known whether Russia was seriously considering the annexation of India. If it had such a plan, it could be accomplished either by way of the Persian Gulf or through Afghanistan. Consequently, the cornerstone of British imperial policy was to prevent Russia from taking Iran which, in the early years of the nineteenth century, included Afghanistan. After the defeat of Napoleon, the political interest of France in Iran practically disappeared and the history of western imperialism in Iran became the story of Anglo-Russian rivalry in that country.

Even though the assassination of Nader Shah in 1747 ended the glory of the Persian empire, Iran was still a power to be reckoned with in west Asia during the short-lived Zand dynasty (1750–1794), and was important enough to be wooed by European rivals. During the whole of the nineteenth century, when Europe was in the throes of industrial revolution, imperial expansion, ideological change, and intellectual advancement, Iran, like her neighbor the Ottoman empire, was ruled by monarchs who were almost entirely oblivious of these developments. The Qajar Dynasty, which had come to power in 1794, was perhaps the only dynasty in the whole history of the Middle East whose founder lacked even the vigor and the prowess which founders of dynasties usually possess. Practically every king in the Qajar Dynasty, which lasted from 1794 to 1924, was inept, unimaginative, superstitious, and selfish. Not only were they ignorant of the impact of developments in Europe, but they also neither acted nor lived according to the old traditions of their own country. The result was that they were caught in between the power of Russia from the north and the pressure of England from the south.

Agha Mohammad, a scion of the Turkish Qajar tribe from Mazandaran in northern Iran, was a cruel and shrivelled-up young man whose psychological vindictiveness was perhaps caused by the fact that he had been castrated at the age of five. He was a hostage in the court of Karim Khan Zand in Shiraz and was treated with kindness by the mild-mannered ruler. Upon the death of Karim Khan, Agha Mohammad fled to Mazandaran and after years of warfare, in a confused struggle for power, gained the throne of Iran in 1794 with Tehran as his capital. No sooner had he succeeded in unifying the country when the Russian army by order of Catherine the Great invaded the Caucasus in 1796. But the Empress died the same year and the new Tsar Paul, whose policy was to oppose his mother's policies, stopped the campaign. A year later Agha Mohammad was assassinated by his own servants.

His nephew and successor, Fath-Ali Shah (1797–1834), whose only claims to fame were an unusually long beard and a progeny of some 2,000 princes and princesses, had most of his uncle's bad traits. Almost from the beginning he was called upon to make decisions on international problems for which he was not prepared. The British, who were anxious for the safety of the Afghanistan road to India, wanted the new shah to keep the peace in that region. Tsar Paul and Napoleon, on the other hand, wanted to make an alliance with the shah in order to harass Great Britain.

In 1800, England sent Captain Malcolm on the first of many missions to Tehran, where he induced the shah to agree not to ally himself with France. He also concluded a commercial treaty which exempted British and Indian merchants from paying taxes and allowed the importation of British broadcloth, iron, steel, and lead without duty. In the meantime, France and Russia had one of their periodic quarrels which made Napoleon send a mission in 1805 to Iran, proposing an alliance against Russia provided Iran would repudiate her treaty with England. This the shah agreed to do, and negotiations resulted in the Treaty of Finkenstein in May 1807. Following this, Napoleon sent a very large mission under the leadership of General Gardanne for the purpose of training the Persian army and setting up foundries for making cannons and other weapons. All this came to nought, however, because of the treaty of friendship between Napoleon and Tsar Alexander I at Tilsit in 1807.

The British took advantage of this opportunity and sent a mission under Sir Harford Jones in 1808, and signed a treaty of alliance with Iran against France and Russia. The treaty had provisions to train the Persian army plus a "subsidy" of £120,000 for the shah. This was followed by a large pompous mission under Malcolm, representing the East India Company in 1810. It must be noted that there was rivalry between the British government and the East India Company. Each sent its own mission and the two sometimes worked at cross-purposes. Neither the shah nor any of his advisers was shrewd enough to take advantage of this or of the other rivalries and wars among the Europeans.

Ever since 1804 the Russians had carried on a campaign of expansion at the expense of Iran in the Caucasus. The campaign slackened whenever Russia became involved with the struggle against the Ottomans or with any of the European countries. The Persian army was under the command of Abbas Mirza, the crown prince, who was considered the most able man in the Qajar line. This army was trained along European lines, sometimes by the French and at other times by the British. From all accounts, it seems that the command was not uniform and the soldiers were confused. In any case, the major battle of this prolonged and slow war was fought in 1812 at Aslanduz. Since Great Britain, in its struggle against Napoleon, had once again come to an understanding with Russia, most of the British officers commanding in the Persian army were withdrawn. How much confusion this caused in the Persian ranks is not known, but the Russians gained a great victory. The British used their good offices and the Persians signed the peace treaty of Golestan on October 12, 1813. According to this treaty, Iran lost five cities in the Caucasus and gave up claim to Georgia and Daghestan. On her part, Russia promised to support the claim of Abbas Mirza to the throne.

The crown prince, in accepting the support of Russia, was inviting the latter to interfere in the internal affairs of Iran. Great Britain, not to be outdone, joined Russia in this support. After this every Qajar crown prince, except the last, was accompanied to the capital by the Russian and British ministers when he ascended the throne. The involvement of Russia in the Napoleonic wars did not firmly establish her in the new territory in the Caucasus. It was quite apparent that the Persians did not consider their defeat conclusive and had every intention of regaining their lost territory.

While Russia in 1812 was fighting for her life against Napoleon, Great Britain tried to strengthen its position in Iran. The British representative, Sir Gore Ousley, concluded a "Definitive Treaty" with Iran in 1814. According to this agreement, Iran promised to break her alliance with any European power at war with Great Britain; to prevent any army hostile to Great Britain from entering Iran; and to induce the Khans of Kharazm, Tataristan, Bokhara, and Samarqand (who paid tribute to the Shah) to deny access to an invading army destined for India. On the other hand, Great Britain promised to help Iran settle her boundaries with Russia; to come to Iran's aid in case of war with a European country; not to interfere in any struggle between Iran and Afghanistan; and to pay Iran an annual subsidy of £150,000.

During the decade between 1815 and 1825, Fath-Ali Shah was involved in securing his throne against internal enemies, forcing Afghanistan to pay tribute, and warring against the Ottomans in 1821–1823. This latter was the last campaign in the long and fruitless strife between the two peoples which had started with the battle of Chaldran in 1514. Since the Ottomans had their hands full with a Greek rebellion, the Russians encouraged Abbas Mirza to attack the Turks and regain his prestige, which had suffered at the hands of the Russians. The Turko-Persian War, like so many before it, was inconclusive and ended in 1823 with the Treaty of Erzerum, which involved no territorial changes.

Russia made a major thrust against Iran in 1825 when it occupied Gokcha in the region of Erivan. At first the Persian forces were very successful and regained many of the lost cities in the Caucasus. Fath-Ali Shah, however, whose avarice was as notorious as his long beard, hoarded gold rather than spending it for defense. The arsenal was empty and a good deal of the army disbanded because of lack of pay. The British, who were supposed to come to the aid of Iran according to the treaty of 1814, refused to do so on the claim that Iran was the aggressor. The fact of the matter was that England had just signed a treaty of friendship with Russia. Consequently, the Persians, who nevertheless were waging some successful campaigns, could not sustain a long war and had to retreat. By 1827 even the major city of Tabriz was occupied. The Persians had to sue for peace and signed the Treaty of Turkmanchai in 1828.

The defeat of Iran was complete. It lost all its territory west of the Caspian Sea. The boundary followed the Aras River to the forty-eighth parallel, south to include Lankaran, and east to Astara on the Caspian Sea. Furthermore, duty on Russian imported goods was limited to 5 per cent and Iran accepted the principle of extraterritoriality and the payment of an indemnity amounting to 3,000,000 pounds. The Treaty of Turkmanchai ushered in a new era, because from that date on Iran was not altogether independent. This fact was not lost on the British, who had failed to aid Iran. With the payment of £150,000 to the penniless Crown Prince, the British were able to cancel that portion of the "Definitive Treaty" of 1814 in which Great Britain had promised to aid Iran if the latter were attacked by a European nation.

Abbas Mirza, the Crown Prince, died in 1833 and his father, Fath-Ali Shah, died a year later at the age of 68. The new heir was Mohammad, the son of Abbas Mirza, but there were many other claimants. The young Mohammad Shah marched to Tehran with an army commanded by the British General Sir Henry Lindsay Bethune, and was accompanied by both the Russian and British ministers. This was enough to dishearten most of the rivals, even though some were foolish enough to persist for a time.

The coming of the Russian minister to uphold the right of the young shah was also a significant fact for Great Britain. Heretofore, the British were afraid that the French might attack India. With the elimination of France, the fear was transferred to Russia. Whether or not the Russians planned to take over India is a matter of conjecture, but they certainly proceeded to annex, as opportunities presented themselves, the land east of the Caspian Sea as they had done in the west. Since these territories were in the direction of India, the British were certainly afraid that the Russians might be tempted to want to go all the way. Hence Afghanistan and the territory south of it to the Persian Gulf became of utmost importance to Great Britain.

The Persians, who claimed suzerainty over Afghanistan and the territory east of the Caspian Sea, wanted to strengthen their positions there in order to offset their losses in the west. The British, however, were against this because they did not think that the Persians were strong enough to stop the Russian advance. Furthermore, the British rightly believed that the Qajar kings had

Russian sympathies and might enter into an agreement with them for a campaign against India. Consequently, the main history of Iran from 1828, the date of the Treaty of Turkmanchai, until about 1900, is the story of the slow but sure advance of Russia from the northeast and Great Britain from the southeast. That most of Iran was spared annexation was not because of the strength of Iran but because neither Russia nor Great Britain would allow the other to annex the country.

Mohammad Shah spent most of his 13 years as king trying to strengthen his position in Afghanistan. Once again Britain broke her "Definitive Treaty" of 1814 with Iran, this time by intervening in the dispute. Mohammad Shah was forced to retreat. The Qajar kings, who were not endowed with much ability themselves, could not even endure able grand vazirs for long. Mohammad Shah ordered the death of the very able Abol Qasem Qa'em Maqam, and gave the office to his tutor Haji Mirza Aghasi, whose superstitions, ignorance, fanaticism, and avarice ruined the country even more. One of the important events in the reign of Mohammad Shah was the advent of the Bab, the founder of the Babi religion which will be explained in a later chapter.

Mohammad Shah died in 1848 and his son, Naser al-Din, was escorted from Tabriz to Tehran by both the British and Russian ministers to become Shah. It was the custom of the Qajars to appoint the heir to the throne as the governor of Azarbaijan, of which Tabriz was the capital. Naser al-Din was one of the better of the Qajar kings, but during the 50 years of his reign did not leave much of a constructive legacy. The story might have been different had he not, like his father, ordered the death of his grand vazir, Mirza Taqi Khan Amir Kabir, who was, without doubt, the most able individual in Iran who reached that high office in the nineteenth century.

Naser al-Din was 16 years old when he ascended the throne in 1848. After a series of political maneuvers by both Iran and Great Britian in Afghanistan, Iran occupied the city of Herat. This action was considered serious enough by Great Britain to declare war on Iran the same year. A British army marched on Herat while other British forces, after occupying Bushire on the Persian Gulf, took the city of Mohamareh (later called Khorram Shahr) at the confluence of the Karun and Shat al-Arab rivers. Later a British flotilla went up the Karun and occupied Ahvaz. Apparently most of this was done without much resistance on the part of the Persians and the little resistance they did offer was disorganized.

A treaty of peace was concluded in Paris in 1857. According to this treaty, Iran agreed to evacuate Afghanistan and recognize its independence. Iran also agreed to use the "good offices" of Britain in any future disputes with Afghanistan. A few weeks after the conclusion of this treaty the famous "Indian Mutiny" broke out and the British used their troops in quelling that uprising. Following the "mutiny," the British government took over the formal control of India and the securing of its western and northwestern approaches became all the more important. The defense of India was made easy by the British supremacy in

Afghanistan, which also included the Hindu Kush mountains. It was not necessary for the British to leave the safety of the mountains and to go farther north. This left Central Asia and the land east of the Caspian Sea open for the Russians to do as they pleased.

But after its defeat in the Crimean War and the death of Nicholas I, Russia was in no position to carry on campaigns of expansion. Furthermore, Alexander II was busy freeing the serfs and trying other internal reforms. But the wars of Italian and German unification in Europe, added to a relative stability at home, allowed Alexander to try his hand again in Turkey and, more especially, in the east Caspian area. An account of the campaigns is too tedious to repeat here. Suffice it to say that the Russian troops occupied Bokhara in 1868, Khiva in 1873, and Khokand in 1876. With the capture of Marv in 1884, Russia became master of the territories east of the Caspian and all of Central Asia. Iran was forced to accept the Atrak River as the new boundary, thus ceding to Russia the most fertile land to the north of the river.

The envelopment of Iran by Russia and Great Britain was now complete. Just as Great Britain did not find it necessary to interfere with Russian advance to the Atrak River and the northern borders of Afghanistan, the Russians did not mind the British annexation of Persian territories south of Afghanistan to the Persian Gulf. The British used means other than military capaigns to gain their ends. From 1870 to 1903 there were minor revolts in Baluchestan and boundary disputes with Afghanistan. In all these, Great Britain was there to offer its "good offices." For example, there were the Mokran Boundary Commission of 1871, the Sistan Arbitration Commission of 1872, and the Perso-Baluchestan Boundary Commission of 1892. By the time of the Second Sistan Commission of 1903, the western boundaries of British India had expanded considerably at the expense of Iran. Just as in the northwest of Iran, Azarbaijan had been cut into two parts—Russian and Persian—so in the southeast, Baluchestan was cut into two parts—British and Persian.

The Anglo-Russian rivalry in Iran that had started with the defeat of Napoleon in 1812 ended its annexation phase with the beginning of the twnetieth century. Neither country allowed the other to annex any more territory. Long before the end of the nineteenth century, however, the rivalry had entered its second phase, namely economic, which lasted from about 1870 to 1921. During this long period, Iran was avowedly a buffer state in which Russia and Great Britain wielded political and economic power without having to assume any responsibility for the welfare of the inhabitants.

An immediate cause of what might be called economic imperialism in Iran was the Indian Mutiny. Both in the course of the struggle in India and afterwards when the British government assumed full responsibility for India, speedy communication became of utmost importance. To connect London and Delhi by telegraph, it was necessary to pass through Iran. In 1863, the Overland Telegraph Convention was signed in Istanbul which connected the capital of the Ottomans to Baghdad. In 1864, the British made arrangements with the Shah to extend the line to Kermanshah, Hamadan, Tehran, and Bushire. The Indo-European Telegraph Company was formed in 1870 to extend telegraph services and connected Tehran with Tabriz and Odessa. No doubt the establishment of these lines was a great boon to Iran. It not only made effective control of the provinces possible by the central government, but also ended the isolation of Iran and helped to bring her closer to the ideas and institutions of Europe. At the same time it must be stated that this first concession opened the way for other concessions not only to the British but also to the Russians who demanded equal treatment. The telegraph concession in 1870 was the first of many concessions given to both Great Britain and Russia for a period of 40 years. These concessions and loans gradually put the resources of the country under foreign control and culminated in the most far-reaching concessions of all—those concerning oil—which were given to the British in 1900 and to the Russians in 1911.

In 1872, Baron Julius de Reuter, a naturalized British subject, received a 70-year concession from Naser al-Din Shah for a gigantic monopoly for the building of railroads, exploitation of mines, establishment of a bank, building of water works, regulation of rivers, etc., in exchange for the customs receipts and most of the other resources of the country. The next year, when the Shah made his first trip to Europe, he found out that the Russians were against the concession and, on his return, was forced to cancel it.

The Persian army, trained by the French, then the British, again by the French, followed by the Italians, and then by the Austrians, in 1878 fell into the hands of the Russians. The Russians formed a Cossack brigade commanded by Russian officers, with uniforms similar to the Russian Cossack troops. This remained about the only organized force in Iran until 1921.

In 1888 the British received a concession to develop the lower Karun river for navigation. In the following year the Shah, in partial compensation for the cancellation of the previous concession, gave Baron de Reuter a new one for the establishment of a bank, to be known as the Imperial Bank of Persia, with the right to issue bank notes. This was matched by the founding of the Banque D'Escompte de Perse by Russia. The Imperial Bank printed paper money which was negotiable only in cities designated on the bill. Travelers going from city to city had to pay commission to exchange their money for the money accepted in that city, as though they were in a different country.

The most notorious of all concessions was the Tobacco Regie of 1890, which gave the British monopoly for the production, sale, and export of all tobacco in Iran. In return, the Shah was to receive an annual payment of £15,000 plus one-fourth of the profits. The concessionaires, according to their advertisement for the sale of shares, expected a profit of £500,000 per annum. It is of interest to note that in 1884 the Ottoman empire had given a somewhat similar, but more limited, concession to the French for a flat payment of £630,000 per annum. While the Persian concession was all-inclusive and was to be effective for 50 years, the Turkish concession was for internal consumption and of

30 year's duration. Whereas the French monopoly went almost unnoticed by the populace, this one in Iran aroused a most vehement antagonism among the people. In a country where a large majority of men and women smoked, such an antagonism could not be ignored. The people could not understand why they had to buy from the British the tobacco which they themselves had grown. The ulama, who were against western and non-Muslim encroachments in Iran, took the side of the people and asked the government to cancel the concession. The Shah responded by imprisoning the opponents of the concession. The controversy dragged on until early December 1891, when the respected Shi'i Mujtahid, Haji Mirza Hasan Shirazi, issued a *fatva* from his residence in Samarra, Iraq, making it unlawful for Persian Muslims to smoke until the concession was withdrawn. The obedience to this religious rule was so total that the Shah was forced to cancel the agreement.

The cancellation, however, cost Iran £500,000 in damages, which was borrowed from the newly established Imperial Bank at 6 per cent interest and paid to the company. The customs of the Persian Gulf were pledged for the payment of the interest, and the capital was to be paid at the end of 40 years. This was the first foreign loan contracted by Iran. There were many others to follow, and eventually most of the resources of the country were pledged to the British and Russian creditors.

In 1896, Naser al-Din Shah was celebrating his jubilee, according to the lunar Muslim calendar, as the "King of Kings." On Friday, May 1, 1896, just a few days before the celebrations were to begin, the Shah went to the shrine of Shah Abdul Azim, some 10 miles south of Tehran. There he was shot to death by a certain Mirza Reza of Kerman. The assassin was a disciple of the notorious Sayyed Jamal al-Din al-Afghani, a pan-Islamist agitator, who had been ousted from Iran by the late Shah in 1891. Afghani was residing under the protection of Sultan Abdul Hamid II, whose hope of becoming the caliph of a unified Islamic world was no secret. Pan-Islamism was not a popular movement in Iran and the murder does not seem to have been the result of the unrest caused by the tobacco fiasco. The hope that the Shah would be killed was expressed by Afghani more than once and a devoted disciple, who also had his own personal grudges, carried out the wish.

Thus came to an end the life of the last autocratic king of Iran. In a dynasty of inferior kings he was perhaps the most able. He made three trips to Europe, in 1873, 1878, and 1889. The country did not gain anything by these visits. If he did apprehend the serious movements going on in Europe, he did not think them to be useful for Iran, because he discouraged, with growing harshness, every attempt at westernization. But he liked the short skirts of the ballet dancers of Europe and ordered the women of his palace to adopt them. A short ballet skirt over long and sometimes tight-fitting slacks became fashionable among the women of Iran. The Shah also left behind a superficial tourist diary of his trips to Europe.

The heir apparent, Mozaffar al-Din, who lived in Tabriz, came to Tehran accompanied by the British and Russian ministers, and was crowned king. He was 43 years old and rather sickly. He had been advised to go to Europe for cure and now as Shah he was impatient to make the trip. But there was no money in the treasury and the Belgian customs advisers, headed by M. Naus who had been employed by the late Shah, could not produce the funds soon enough. The Russian bank, however, loaned the Shah £2,400,000 at 5 per cent interest against the customs receipts of the whole country except the Persian Gulf. To make Russia the sole creditor, the loan was made on condition that the £500,000 debt to the Imperial (British) Bank, incurred because of the tobacco fiasco, be paid. After the payment of this debt, discounts, and commission, enough was left for the Shah to depart for Europe in the summer of 1900.

Two years later, the Shah arranged for another loan of a little over a million pounds from Russia at 4 per cent. Attached to his loan was the concession to construct a road from Julfa on the Russo-Persian border to Tabriz, Qazvin, and Tehran. The loan also carried with it a revision of the tariff regulation. The Belgian official, M. Naus, is usually derided for working against the interests of Iran, but evidence does not support this accusation. His revised tariff did produce more revenue for Iran, but it also favored Russia against Great Britain.

The heavy burden of these unproductive loans, the quarrel between the corrupt Russophile Persian officials with the equally corrupt Anglophile officials, the harsh treatment of the people by the grand vazir (Sadr-e A'zam), and the general awakening (which will be discussed in a later chapter) culminated in the demand for a "House of Justice." What the common people understood and demanded was "justice." To the educated ulama, however, it meant the establishment of the Muslim Shari'a, and to the European educated elite it signified a "constitution." Whatever it was, the shah granted it without too much difficulty in a royal rescript on August 5, 1906. This proclamation limited the power of the monarchy and ordered the establishment of an assembly, *majles*, and the creation of regulations for governing.

This was the basis of the Constitution which was prepared that year. Usually revolutions precede the drafting of constitutions, but in the case of Iran, civil war and bloodshed followed the granting of the constitution. In all the struggles, changes of government, and even a change of dynasty, the constitution has remained intact and has become the oldest in all of Asia.

PERSIAN OIL—THE FIRST PHASE

The presence of oil in the Middle East was known to the people in ancient times. Noah's Ark was made seaworthy by the use of pitch, which is an oil product, and the Zoroastrians of Iran built some of their religious fire temples around the ignited natural gas. In certain parts of southwestern Iran, seepage of oil to the surface had formed small pools and the distribution of this crude oil had become a small industry in the nineteenth century. In 1872, when Baron de Reuter was granted the comprehensive concession by the Shah of Iran, oil was one of the many items mentioned.[1] In 1892, Professor Jacques de Morgan, head of the French archeological expedition on the site of ancient Susa in western Iran, wrote an article claiming the existence of oil in that part of the country. Later, Ketabchi Khan, a Persian customs official, was impressed by this article and tried to interest French capitalists in the exploitation of oil. Failing in this, he approached Sir Henry Drummond Wolff, the former British Minister in Iran, with his plan. The latter placed Ketabchi in touch with his friend William Knox D'Arcy, who was an Australian oil prospector.

D'Arcy, whose name has been immortalized in connection with the Persian oil, never went to Iran. He sent geologists there and, after receiving favorable reports, sent his representative Alfred Marriot to negotiate a concession. In 1901, a concession was signed by Mozaffar al-Din Shah for Iran and by Mr. Marriot for D'Arcy. The extent of the concession included all of Iran except the five provinces of the north. The term of concession was for 60 years, after which time all the machinery, buildings, and installations would revert to Iran without compensation. The concessionaire agreed to pay the Persian government £20,000 in cash and £20,000 in paid-up shares, plus an annual royalty of 16 per cent of the net profits.

After seven years of hard work and heavy expenditures, when D'Arcy and his associates were about to abandon the whole project, oil in commercial quantities was discovered in the region of Masjed-e Solaiman, northeast of Ahvaz. The memorable date was May 26, 1908. A year later the Anglo-Persian Oil Company was formed, with a capital of £2,000,000. By this time the Persian Revolution was two years old. The proceedings of the first session of the Persian Paliament reveal that the deputies discussed the oil concession but were not aware of its tremendous importance in the economic and political life of the country. By 1914, the Anglo-Persian Oil Company had drilled some 30 wells, and had built a pipeline to the nearby refinery which had been constructed on the island of Abadan in the Persian Gulf. After 1908, the Company had the assistance of the British government in coming to terms with the Bakhtyari tribesmen who owned land in the oil fields, and with the war lord, Shaykh Khaz'al, who claimed jurisdiction in the area of Abadan.

By the beginning of World War I, the British Admiralty had converted the British Navy from coal to oil. Both for the purpose of obtaining oil at a low price and for preventing other countries from having a share in the rich deposits of Iran, the British Admiralty arranged to purchase enough shares in the Oil Company to become its major and controlling partner in May 1914. A month later the House of Commons approved the agreement. With the investment of £2,200,000, the British government gained control of the Anglo-Persian Oil Company and, through two *ex officio* representatives, had veto power over the policies of the Company and all its subsidiaries. From this date until the nationalization of the Persian Oil in 1951, the British Navy bought oil from the Anglo-

[1] See above, p. 226.

Persian Oil Company at a "special" price. The Company never revealed what this price was nor whether the British Navy paid anything at all for the oil.

The rivalry between Britain and Russia in Iran was the main reason for exempting the five northern provinces from the D'Arcy Concession. Apparently the Russian government, probably because of the Baku oil fields, did not demand a similar concession in northern Iran. In 1916, however, a Russian entrepreneur, A. M. Khoshtaria, with the help of the Russian government, received a concession from Vosuq al-Doleh, then Prime Minister of Iran. The concession was for the exploitation of oil in three of the northern provinces, Gilan, Mazandaran, and Astrabad, for a term of 70 years. The rest of the provisions of the concession were similar to those given to D'Arcy. According to Persian law, all concessions had to be ratified by the Persian Parliament, a condition which did not apply in 1901 when D'Arcy obtained his concession. The Khoshtaria Concession was never ratified and so was considered null and void. Later the Russian Revolution and the Bolsheviks' renunciation of all concessions obviated the whole issue. The Persians thought the matter was closed, but they were mistaken.

CHAPTER 23

TURKISH AWAKENING

The history of the Middle East in the past 200 years, whether it be of Turkey, Iran, or the Arabic-speaking world, is largely the story of the reaction of the governments and peoples of the region to the challenges of western civilization. These challenges have been political, social, religious, economic, literary, and artistic. The peoples have reacted to these in different ways and it is quite likely that the reaction will not be resolved before the end of the twenteeth century.

One thing is certain, however, and that is that the encounter of the peoples of the Middle East with western civilization has created two types of revolutions. Actually these two revolutions are two aspects of the same phenomenon called nationalism. One is revolution for independence from a colonial power and the other is revolution for change. The revolution for independence is relatively short and always spectacular and cohesive. Since the blame for all the ills of society is almost always placed on the outsiders, all elements of society usually unite. The anti-imperialist who has the courage of his convictions and a certain amount of charisma is often a popular hero.

The revolution for change, on the other hand, is long, tedious, and divisive. Since the hero must, of necessity, be a reformer, he must criticize and sometimes destroy the established norm, whether it be political, social, economic, religious, literary, or artistic. Such an activity causes dissension and civil strife. The contending parties try to gain power by any means available and the struggle goes on for a very long time.

Since Turkey and Iran have not been under direct European colonial powers, they have not been involved in the revolution for independence from colonial rule. Instead they have struggled for independence from imperialistic domination. In these two countries this struggle and the revolution for change have gone on hand in hand. The Arabic-speaking countries, however, spent a good deal of their time in the struggle for independence and did not fully succeed until after World War II. This is not to say, however, that the Arabs did not take any step toward modernization while under imperial rule, but that it could not have been a planned and direct attempt.

The fact that the coming of Napoleon to Egypt in 1799 is considered a landmark should not lead students of Middle Eastern history to conclude that westernization was first introduced by his campaign or that western ideas spread all over the Middle East from Egypt from that date. All of the three regions of the Middle East had been in contact with the West before 1800. The westernization of Egypt, on the other hand, may have influenced the process of change in Syria-Lebanon, though it had little effect in the Ottoman empire and almost none in Iran.

TANZIMAT

On November 3, 1839, Sultan Abdul Mejid (1839–1861) gathered the notables of the empire in the *gulhaneh* (rose garden of the palace) and had his foreign minister read a statement which has come to be known as the *hatti sharif*, or the "noble rescript." Twenty-seven years later, on February 18, 1856, the same sultan issued another statement which is known as the *hatti humayun*, "imperial rescript." Both were issued under pressure and were partly made for the purpose of appeasing European governments. Nevertheless, they did inaugurate and endorse an era of reform in the Ottoman empire, which is called *Tanzimat*. It must be noted, however, that Tanzimat was as much the result of upheavals in the eighteenth century as it was the cause of changes in the nineteenth and twentieth centuries.

The Ottoman state was a military encampment for the propagation of Islam. The sultans had not only expanded the *dar al-salam*, the territory of Islam, but they had become powerful because of victorious campaigns, and had enriched the empire through tribute and booty. Steady defeats in the latter part of the seventeenth and early eighteenth centuries shocked the empire, and the Ottomans felt threatened on three fronts: economically, because of loss of revenue; politically, because of loss of power; and psychologically, because of their inability to expand the realm of Islam.

It was then that Ibrahim Pasha, the grand vazir to Ahmed III (1703–1730), attempted reforms. He felt that the West had something to teach the Ottomans in military matters. In 1720, he sent Mehmed Chelebi to France and asked him to visit fortresses and factories and report practical measures for the Ottoman army. One result of the report was the founding of the first printing press. A certain Ibrahim Muteferrika, who was in charge of the press, tried to introduce his readers to the reforms which were going on in Europe. But all this was dangerous for the positions of the ulama and the Janissaries. It resulted in the abdication of Ahmed III and the execution of the grand vazir.

Once the bureaucrats, who had become indispensible for the administration of the country, had a taste of this new knowledge, the movement for reform continued. The bureaucrats were the educated class in the empire and were called *ahl al-qalam*, people of the pen. In the end it was they who were primarily responsible for the Tanzimat. In 1732, the printer Ibrahim Muteferrika published the first book on the superiority of the West, and, in 1734, the first school was founded along western lines for the teaching of mathematics to the military officers. Perhaps the most far-reaching "discovery" of the bureaucracy was stated in a book published in 1774, which said that new methods were at variance with old institutions and that the Ottoman empire needed new institutions to cope with new problems.

Sultan Selim (1789–1807) was the first reform sultan. He asked the "people of the pen" for reports and recommendations. With him the idea of reform was not limited to military matters but also included civil and even religious questions. Whatever other subjects these reports disagreed on, they all agreed that the West should be the model and European trainers should be invited for instruction. Not much, however, was accomplished, because the empire lacked the machinery to implement these reports. In 1795, the *nizam-i jadid*, the new military, was one of the projects initiated. Though most of the "reforms" of Selim were confined to reports, the Janissaries felt threatened enough to depose him in favor of the puppet Mustafa IV. This move, however, availed nothing, for a counterrevolt movement called the "Comrades of Ruschuk" deposed Mustafa and chose Selim's nephew, Mahmud II (1808–1839).

Since the bureaucrats were behind the uprising which brought Mahmud II to power, a document of cooperation, *sanadi itefak*, was signed between them which ignored the ulama and the nobility. Instead of downgrading the religious institutions, Mahmud increased the power of the bureaucracy. His one daring act was the disbanding of the Janissaries, but he did other things also. He put the bureaucrats on salary and made it possible for them to be decorated for distinguished service. He organized a postal system and established a special council. He created the office of prime minister to chair the newly created council of ministers. Perhaps more far reaching in its results was the organization of a Judicial Council which seemed to rob the ulama of their most important monopoly, namely the practice of law. In 1829, when Pertev Effendi, the minister of foreign affairs, was enumerating the four orders of the government, he did not name the ulama.

Mahmud was no liberal. Like some of his contemporaries, he was an enlightened despot, but wanted to be obeyed. He forced the Shaykh ul-Islam to write a book on the necessity of complete obedience to the sultan. In his *Summary of Reasons for Obedience to the Sultan*, the religious dignitary produced no less than 25 hadiths to prove the point. Mahmud II seemed to have abandoned the idea that the Ottoman empire was for the propagation of Islam. He was probably secularized enough to believe that reform was possible in the context of power but not in the context of religion. He is supposed to have said, "From now on I want to know my subjects as 'Muslims' only in the mosque, as 'Christians' only in the church, and as 'Jews' only in the synagogue." All of this culminated in the proclamation of the *hatti sharif* in 1839, which ushered in the Tanzimat.

To say that the two royal rescripts, the *hatti sharif* and the *hatti humayun*,

in the period of Tanzimat were charters of individual liberty is to exaggerate
for both Mahmud (who prepared the way) and Abdul Mejid (who made the
Tanzimat possible) were autocrats. On the other hand, to state that these were
solely for the purpose of complying with the demands of the European power
is to miss the point. Tanzimat contained the germs of individual liberty and
constitutional government. It was used for the purpose of mollifying the liberal
elements among European powers, but it also sprang from intellectual and
administrative ferment which had been going on within the Ottoman empire
for some time. Tanzimat was a "palace revolution" for the strengthening of the
position of the bureaucrats who were in power. Almost all the changes in the
machinery of the government were designed to give more power to the "people
of the pen."

The old system of two institutions, the "Muslim Institution" headed by the
Shaykh ul-Islam, and the "Ruling Institution" headed by the grand vazir, which
had been dying gradually, was discarded altogether. There was a council of
ministers now headed by a prime minister, and the "new" military system was
under the order of the council of ministers. These ministers were served by a
bureaucracy which comprised the secular literate elite in the empire. Some of
the members of the bureaucracy might have been anticlerical, but practically
none were anti-Islamic. They ignored the Muslim Institution as often as they
possibly could. They did not disband the religious schools but opened up
secular schools beside them. The religious schools continued to train religious
lawyers, but the secular schools trained, as well as lawyers, civil servants, doctors, engineers, and army officers. From 1840 to 1879 the judicial system of the
empire was gradually modeled after that of France. By 1869, when the civil
laws were codified, only personal status laws, i.e., marriage, divorce, inheritance
and personal property, were under the Shari'a.

In addition to the above, during the Tanzimat period the government
encouraged the sending of students to western Europe, chiefly to France. The
first high school for girls was opened in 1861. Two years later, the American
Congregationalist missionary, Cyrus Hamlin, opened Robert College. At first
only Christian students of Bulgarian, Greek, and Armenian origin attended
but soon the Muslims patronized the College as well. This institution and the
American College for girls have played great parts in the modernization of
Turkey. In 1862, the Ottoman Scientific Society was formed, and many more
similar organizations followed. In gatherings of this sort, young men who had
returned from Europe discussed their observations, and poets and writers
expressed their thoughts.

The Tanzimat period produced a new school of Turkish writers who transformed Turkish literature in both style and content. Among these writers was
Ibrahim Shinasi, who spent five years in Paris. After a few years in the Turkish
Ministry of Education, he worked on the staff of the *Terjumani Ahval*, the
first nongovernment newspaper, which was founded in 1860. Later, in 1862,
he edited his own paper, *Tasviri Efkar*, which was issued until 1925 when it

was suppressed by Mustafa Kemal Ataturk. He was a forerunner in freeing the language from its pompous style and, through his translations, showed that it was possible to express foreign and sophisticated ideas in simple Turkish. He was followed by Ziya Pasha, who translated Rousseau and Mollière, Ahmad Medhat, the short story writer, and Ahmad Jevdat, who started a movement to scrap Arabic and Persian words from the Turkish language.

In 1839, the *hatti sharif* decreed by Sultan Abdul Mejid had recognized the sovereignty of law, the equality of all subjects, and the universal application of justice. In the enthusiasm of the period, the Turks shaved their beards, wore European tunics and trousers, listened to western music and exchanged the turban for the fez. In 1856, the *hatti humayun* decreed by the same sultan, which was mostly a product of foreign pressure, was more extensive. It eradicated, at least on paper, the differences which existed between the Muslims and the Christians, and extended to the Christians all the rights and privileges which were enjoyed by the Muslims. This meant equality in taxation, military service, and education. It also envisaged the founding of banks, and fiscal and agricultural reforms.

But these reforms and pronouncements were not without their opponents. The ulama did not sit idly by and in many instances were assisted by some of the members of the bureaucracy who had become established and did not want to change any further. The foreign powers, who espoused reforms to satisfy the liberal elements in their own countries, did not help the Turkish reformers. They were more interested in political and economic exploitation of the weak empire than in strengthening it with modern institutions.

The members of the religious hierarchy appointed by the sultan under the millet system were not enthusiastic, for under the new equality they would lose power in their communities. The rank and file of the Christians had to serve in the army for the first time and pay the same tax as the Muslims. A large number of them wanted both equal rights and also wanted to retain the privileges which they enjoyed under the millet system. As a Turkish writer puts it, when the Tanzimat people brought the ideas of democracy and nationalism from Europe, the Turks chose democracy while the Christians chose nationalism. The evidence for this is the series of independence movements by the Greeks, Serbians, Rumanians, etc., which characterized the political history of the empire during the last part of the nineteenth century.

THE YOUNG OTTOMANS

More important than any of the other opponents of Tanzimat were the young Turkish critics who accused the bureaucrats of being more interested in imitating the West than in creating a new Ottoman society. Most of these young men were part of the same bureaucracy and some of them had worked in the translation bureau of the Porte. They were familiar with the West and were anxious to direct the destinies of the Ottoman empire. A number of them formed a secret society in 1865 by the name of "Patriotic Alliance," along the

lines of similar groups prevalent in Europe at that time. They were the fore-
runners of a new breed of young men who were not satisfied with modernizing
the machinery of the state, but wanted to establish a constitutional monarchy
and revitalize Islam. They may properly be called "Young Ottomans" to
distinguish them from the Tanzimat which preceded them and the "Young
Turks" who came after them.

The name is significant because these men, unlike the bureaucrats of Tanzimat, had accepted the principles of nationalism as well as of democracy. The
only "nation" which they knew was the Ottoman empire and they set out to
weld a nation, a task which had been neglected for five and a half centuries. The
problems were insurmountable, especially since the non-Turks in the empire
had already started their independent nationalistic programs. But the Young
Ottomans were undaunted. It was quite natural that they should choose Islam
as a spiritual-ideological base for their nationalism. By emphasizing Islam they
probably knew that they could not attract the non-Muslim populations of the
empire, but most of these peoples were in revolt anyway. On the other hand, they
hoped to gain support among the non-Turkish Muslim subjects of the empire.
They believed in a limited form of pan-Islamism welded together by the power
of the Ottoman empire. Indeed, a considerable number of the literate elite
among the Arabic-speaking subjects of the empire were attracted to them and
for a time, "Ottomanism" was discussed and written about in Arabic literature.
But, as we shall see, it did not last long, for the Arabs had also drunk of the cup
of nationalism and were reluctant to throw in their lot with the Turks.

The Young Ottomans, like many similar intellectual groups of Europe, were
vague about their methods. Some were in favor of terror, others supported infil-
tration into the government, still others voted for converting the sultan. Divergent
as their ideas and their methods were, they managed to meet in secret societies
and work together. The Young Ottomans used an Islamic vocabulary. Whereas
the intellectuals of the medieval Ottoman empire based their ideas on such
diverse works as the Koran, Islamic political philosophers, the *Practical Counsels*, and the Turko-Iranian secular legislation,[1] the Young Ottomans based
their ideas almost entirely on the Koran. Like many Muslim reformers who
came before and after them, they wanted to go back to the time when Islam was
"pure"—i.e., the time of the Medina Caliphate, which was idealized and
used as an illustration time and time again.

Perhaps the most important intellectual, theoretician, and writer of the
Young Ottomans was Namik Kemal (d. 1887). He was an effective critic of
Tanzimat, which in his opinion had achieved a degree of modernization but had
not freed the individual from internal tyranny, nor freed the nation from foreign
domination. This writer and gifted poet was from a family of Baktashi dervishes
and in his youth read Turkish translations of the French *philosophes*. All his life
he tried to blend Islam and the ideas of the Enlightenment. He wrote exten-

[1] See above, p. 110.

ively in the newspaper *Hurriyet,* which was the organ of the Young Ottomans, and which approached problems from the Islamic point of view. Unlike the Young Turks who came after him, he was not interested in the Turks as Turks or in the pre-Islamic Turks of Central Asia. Unlike the Tanzimat bureaucrats who preceded him, he talked about the importance of the Shari'a and the observance of the basic principles of Islam. He was an Ottoman and is credited with having used the words *vatan* (Arabic *watan*), "fatherland," and millet, "nation," in their modern sense. Soon the former was used throughout the Middle East and the latter mostly among the non-Arabic speaking peoples.

The Islamic leanings of the Young Ottomans attracted some of the ulama to their groups, but their number was insignificant. On the whole, the Young Ottomans were suspect in the eyes of reactionaries like Sultan Abdul Hamid II. Their headquarters were raided by the police. Nevertheless Young Ottomans such as Namik Kemal, the liberal statesman Medhat, the journalist Zia, and others, were influential in bringing Abdul Hamid II to the throne in 1876. The wily sultan, in order to rid himself of the Conference of Powers gathered in Istanbul to review the future of the Balkans, ratified the constitution which was drawn up by the Young Ottomans on December 3, 1876. He appointed Medhat Pasha as Prime Minister and promised to appoint Namik as his personal secretary. Almost as soon as the Conference of European Powers adjourned thinking that they had a liberal sultan in Abdul Hamid, the sultan shelved the constitution and exiled Medhat and Namik Kemal. Soon he suspended the assembly, and one by one the rest of the leaders were jailed or went into exile. By 1878, the Young Ottoman movement had come to an end.

The Young Ottomans were perhaps the first ideologists of Islam in modern times who tried to take the "best" of the West and graft it on to Islam. They failed because their picture of the "purity" of the Medina Caliphate was a figment of their imaginations. Furthermore, they overstretched their interpretation of the Islamic theories to fit the concept of democratic popular government. For example, the practices of *baya'h,* allegiance, and *mashwara,* consultation, were applied respectively to the modern concepts of "popular sovereignty" and "government by the people." In Islam the principle of paying allegiance to a newly elected caliph was a prerogative of only a few, and the idea of consultation was to strengthen the government *for* the people and not *by* them. It goes without saying that in Islam, government is most certainly of God and not *of* the people. Hence the principle, "the government of the people, for the people, and by the people" does not fit Islamic teachings. The phrase must be changed to "the government of Allah, by His designated representatives, and for the people."

Even though the Young Ottomans failed to graft western ideologies to the body politic of Islam, they were successful in introducing new values to the Turks. Time and time again, Ottoman writers in imitation of the men before them had counseled the sultans with advice which should be familiar to the reader by now. "No government without an army, no army without money, no money without subjects."[2] Toward the last third of the nineteenth century the Young Ottomans used the same format as the above, but the content was different and replete with new values. They wrote, "No security without free-dom, no endeavor without security, no prosperity without endeavor, no hap-piness without prosperity."

THE YOUNG TURKS

From 1878, when the sultan put aside the constitution, until 1908, when he was forced to reinstate it, Abdul Hamid II was the central figure on the Turkish scene. This man, who was destined to influence events in one of the most critical periods in Ottoman history, was full of contradictory characteristics. The Euro-peans were so attracted to him at first that they predicted that he might become a second Suleiman the Magnificent. Later, however, they called him "Abdul the Damned." His own subjects referred to him as "the hangman," "bloody majesty," or the "Ogre of Yildiz," though some of the same subjects went to kiss his hands in submission. It seems that he was consistent in two things. He was suspicious of everything and everyone. He had a whole army of spies scat-tered all over the empire, and others to watch the spies. He had agents in foreign capitals, not to gather diplomatic information, but to spy on his own subjects His second consistent characteristic was in being autocratic. He was against all movements which in any way limited the power of the sultan. He had not learned from his father's reformist inclinations any more than his fellow monarch Alexander III of Russia had learned from his father.

In 1881, when Alexander III became Tzar, he decided to walk in the foot-steps of his grandfather, Nicholas I, and declared his "faith in the strength of autocracy" and promised to "maintain and defend the autocratic power. . . ." In 1878, when Abdul Hamid sent the constitutionalists into exile, he decided to follow his grandfather, Sultan Mahmud, "who understood that only by force can one move the people with whose guardianship Allah has entrusted me." In an era of change, both Abdul Hamid and Alexander favored the order prevalent in their grandparents' time though they had not themselves experi-enced it.

The autocratic sultan with his network of spies was not able to prevent the new crop of Turkish patriots from meeting in and out of the country, or to stop the rising nationalistic aspirations of the non-Turkish elements within the empire. Among these, the Armenians and Kurds were more troublesome mainly because they were located in eastern Asia Minor in the heart of the empire. Of the two, the Armenians were more menacing because they were Christians and had friends among the European powers. Indeed, there was an article about their protection in the Treaty of Berlin (1878). Like the other millets, the Armenians had their own social classifications. The more wealthy

[2] See above, p. 152, p. 191.

among them chose the patriarch of the Armenian church and had a vested interest in the preservation of the Ottoman system.

The majority of the Armenians were influenced by nationalism and demanded an autonomous state of their own. From 1880–1890, they had their own secret nationalistic societies with different approaches to the common goal of independence. In 1890, all of the Armenian societies were federated into one nationalist movement known as Dashnaktzoutun. The Roman Catholic and American Protestant missionaries had gained converts among the Armenians and they were probably the only millet in the Ottoman empire who had advocates among the Greek Orthodox, Roman Catholic, and Protestant powers of the West. Abdul Hamid was afraid of them, and with good reason. He set the restless Kurds against the Armenians and their unchecked excesses resulted in the massacre of 1894. The Armenian leaders retaliated and seemed needlessly to expose their coreligionists in order to attract the attention of Europe. During three years, some 100,000 Armenians lost their lives and Europe did not intervene. On the contrary, in 1898, Kaiser Wilhelm paid his second visit to the Ottoman Sultan. On his way to Palestine he laid a wreath at the tomb of Saladin and, in the garb of an Arab shaykh, promised to defend Islam. One can imagine that the picture was not so amusing to the Kaiser's grandmother, Queen Victoria, who herself had over 100,000,000 Muslim subjects.

In the meantime, the ideological heirs of the Young Ottomans had banded together and were plotting the overthrow of the sultan. In 1889, a group of students in the medical college under the leadership of Ibrahim Edhem (Temo) formed a society by the name of the "Committee of Union and Progress," which was destined to grow and wield great influence. By 1892, the sultan's spies discovered the plot and the members fled into exile. One group went to Egypt where one of their members, Murad Bey, published the newspaper called *Mizan*. Another group went to Paris, where one of them, Ahmad Reza, published another newspaper, *Meshveret*. Eventually these two papers represented two points of view. Murad Bey was closer to the ideas of the Young Ottomans. He was of pan-Islamist persuasion and felt that Islam was a liberal enough entity to unite all the Muslims under one roof. His solution was to remove the sultan, restore the constitution, make Islam the cornerstone of the empire, and bring the nationalities under the aegis of the Ottoman empire. About this time, Abdul Hamid met the pan-Islamic agitator Afghani and became aware of the broader possibilities of pan-Islamism with himself as sultan-caliph. Whether Afghani, who was living in Istanbul at the time, was or was not responsible is uncertain, but Murad Bey and a number of his followers defected from the revolutionary ranks and made their peace with the sultan in 1897.

Ahmad Reza, however, had different ideas. Although he never rejected Islam, he was a disciple of Auguste Comte, and did not think in terms of pan-Islamism. The positivistic philosophy of Comte led him toward secularism and the espousal of Turkish rather than Ottoman nationalism. A number of his followers were freemasons and they established lodges in Turkey.[3]

The revolutionaries in Paris were aided by the escape of Damad Mahmud Pasha, the brother-in-law of the sultan, and his two sons Sabah al-Din and Lutfullah. The arrival of the royal fugitives in Paris in 1899 created quite a commotion in both Turkey and Europe. Damad Mahmud Pasha did not live to see the fruits of his labors, but his son Sabah al-Din, together with Ahmad Reza, called the first congress of Ottoman liberals in Paris in 1902. The 47 members present were Albanians, Arabs, Armenians, Circassians, Greeks, Jews, Kurds, and Turks. Sabah al-Din presided. The only point on which they all agreed was the deposing of the sultan. The national minorities wanted attachment to foreign powers, the non-Muslims did not care for the dynasty, and even the non-Turkish Muslims had become nationalistic. Sabah al-Din was for a federal union, while Ahmad Reza was for Turkish nationalism. It was the latter who won.

Perhaps because of Reza's influence, but independently of him, a group of graduates of the military school formed a society by the name of *vatan* in 1906. Among the members was a young officer named Mustafa Kemal who, after World War I, became Ataturk, the first President of modern Turkey. But at the time, leadership was in the hands of Talat Bey, Enver Pasha, and Jemal Bey. They spread their revolutionary ideas through student groups, masonic lodges, and dervish orders. In 1907, the different societies which had been formed merged under the old name of Committee of Union and Progress. In 1908, they led a successful coup d'etat against the sultan. The people accepted the coup not only because of the misrule of Abdul Hamid, but also because they were afraid of what Russia and England might do. Their traditional enemy, Russia, had joined the Triple Entente in Europe and had divided Iran into spheres of influence with Great Britain in 1907.[4] The Turks were afraid lest their turn come next.

The wily Abdul Hamid, however, was not ruffled by the coup. He welcomed it and reinstated the constitution of 1878. For a few weeks there was much rejoicing. Muslims, Christians, and Jews rejoiced together, Muslim ulama and Christian priests embraced, and Enver Pasha proclaimed the equality of all. Perhaps the Young Turks would have been able to build a viable nation had they been given a chance, but they were not. In the same year, Austria-Hungary annexed Bosnia, and Ferdinand of Bulgaria proclaimed himself king. On April 13, 1909, the counterrevolution which had been organized by Abdul Hamid proclaimed the supremacy of the sultan and the Shari'a. The army, however, stood by the revolution and on April 27, Abdul Hamid was deposed in favor of his brother Mehmed V, who "had not read a newspaper in twenty years."

This was not all. Albania revolted in 1910, and Italy occupied Tripoli in

---

[3] At about the same time, freemasonry was also introduced in Iran. See below, p. 256.
[4] See below, p. 259.

911. Turkey fought against Italy and lost. In 1912, Bulgaria, Serbia, Montenegro, and Greece united against the Ottomans and started the First Balkan War. The defeat of the Ottomans in 1913 did not end the war, for the victors ought against each other. This involved the Ottomans once again in the Second Balkan War. Peace came late in 1913, and all that was left of the Ottoman Empire in Europe was a little under 11,000 square miles of territory. A year ater World War I began, which involved the Ottomans once again and annihilated the empire.

And yet it is doubtful whether the Young Turks could have succeeded had they had peace after 1908. The parliament which convened after the abdication f Abdul Hamid was presided over by Ahmad Reza, who had been called from Paris to preside. The country was dominated by a triumvirate made up of Talat, Enver, and Jemal. Ottomanism of the older generation and federalism f Sabah al-Din had given way to the Turkish nationalism of Reza. The Young Turks wanted to unite the empire on the basis of the Turkish language and the ideal of pan-Turanianism, which connected the Turks with the Tatars of Central Asia and the great Chengiz Khan. They started the program of Turkification and established Turkish Ojak (hearth), where intellectuals and writers like Ziya Gökalp, Helide Edib, and others lectured on the history of Turan and the irtues of the Turks. This program, however, was oppressive to non-Turks and was doomed to failure. The non-Turkish elements, mainly Arabic-speaking, who as Muslims still had some sympathy with the empire, lost it altogether in the face of the pressure to give up their language in favor of Turkish. The great var of 1914–1918 ended the dream. Jemal Bey went to Afghanistan to become military advisor, Talat Bey was assassinated by an Armenian in Germany, and Enver Pasha, a pan-Turanian to the end, was killed for the cause in Turkestan.

The development of Turkish awakening, which had started in the Tanzimat, went through the successive steps of Ottomanism, pan-Islamism, and pan-Turanianism. It was left for Mustafa Kemal, the soldier-reformer, to reject them all and succeed with the simple Turkism of the Turks of Asia Minor.

CHAPTER 24

THE AWAKENING OF
THE ARABIC-SPEAKING PEOPLES

Ideas and events stirred the Arabic-speaking peoples during the nineteenth century. They were influenced by the West directly through Egypt and the activities of American and French missionaries in the Levant, and indirectly through the Young Ottoman and Young Turk movements. Antedating the influence of the West, however, and entirely independent of it, was the indigenous Wahhabi movement in the Arabian peninsula. This movement in both its purpose and method was so much like the movement started by Muhammad in the seventh century that some have called it the "second coming of Islam." It is not possible to understand the reaction of Islam to the West without considering the Wahhabi movement. Even though Wahhabism did not take hold outside of the Arabian peninsula, its religious ideas influenced pan-Islamism and its basically Arab nature contributed to the pan-Arabism of the middle twentieth century.

Muhammad ibn-Abd al-Wahhab (d. 1792) traveled in different parts of the Ottoman empire and observed a tottering and sick society. Some years later an Ottoman intellectual named Zia Pasha also traveled in Europe and the Ottoman empire. He wrote, "I roamed in the lands of the infidels and have beheld their cities and mansions. I also traveled in the realm of Islam and all I saw was ruins." While later Muslims were to compare the world of Islam with Europe and find the former wanting, Ibn-Abd al-Wahhab, on the other hand, compared the world of Islam with what it should have been according to the Koran and found it wanting. He did not go to Europe because he was sure the "infidels" had nothing to teach Islam. Instead he went back to the Koran and the time of the Prophet and denounced every influence, religious, social, and intellectual, which did not have its justification in the Koran. These influences according to Ibn-Abd al-Wahhab, included the Sufi belief in the immanence of God, the rationalism of the intellectuals, and the practices of the common people in visiting the tombs of saints and asking the intercession of the Prophet and the Imams. He was a strict Muslim in that he thought that innovations such as belief in the power of saints, shrines, tombs, rosaries, trees, and jinns were against Islam. He was an Arab in that he preached that Islam had been polluted by the non-Arabs, especially the Persians and the Turks. He was also the first to challenge the legitimacy of the Sultan-Caliph.

His followers called themselves *Muwahhidin* (unitarians) in contrast to the rest of the Muslims, whom they called "polytheists." They idealized the times of the Prophet and his early companions and advocated the strict observance of the laws of the Koran and the Sunna of the Prophet according to the Hanbali School of Law.[1] Quite in keeping with the tradition of early Islam, they took to the sword and went about converting the "polytheists." In 1765, a tribal chieftain by the name of Muhammad ibn-Sa'ud accepted this message and dedicated his sword to the new cause. By 1773, the city of Riyad was captured and by the beginning of the nineteenth century the Wahhabis, as others called them, took Mecca and Medina in the west and were threatening Karbala and Najaf in the north. To them the Arabs had fallen into a second period *jahiliyya* (ignorance) and they were set to revive Islam in its purity and save the Arabs.

The Sultan-Caliph could not let the challenge go unnoticed, but at the same time did not have the power to quell such a rebellion in a remote corner of the empire. Consequently he appealed to Muhammad Ali of Egypt, who responded to the call in 1811. Through a series of campaigns which lasted several years, Ibrahim the son of Muhammad Ali subdued the Wahhabis in 1818 and recaptured Mecca and Medina. Throughout the nineteenth century, the Wahhabis fought against the representatives of the sultan until 1891, when Muhammad ibn-Rashid took Riyad and drove Ibn-Sa'ud's family into exile in Kuwait. It was from here in January 16, 1902, that 20-year-old Abd al-Aziz ibn-Sa'ud, the Shaykh of the Wahhabis, stole his way into the Rashidi palace in Riyad, killed the governor, and from there went on to eventually become master of all Arabia.

The definitely articulated ideology of the Wahhabis, their singleness of purpose, and their faith in the method used starkly contrasted with the confusion which reigned in the minds of the Arabic-speaking peoples of the Fertile Crescent and Egypt. The latter had conflicting loyalties. Religiously, there were Christians of different persuasions and Muslims of different sects, Druzes, and a small minority of Jews. Politically, some were for the Ottoman empire, some for independence, and a few for some sort of autonomy under the Ottomans. Even though they all spoke Arabic, many of them, especially the Egyptians, did not consider themselves "Arabs," for the idea of an "Arab nation" was not to take shape until the middle of the twentieth century. Consequently, it is not possible to determine, and neither is it important, which movement came first.

[1] See above, p. 105.

PAN-ISLAMISM

We have already mentioned that some of the Young Ottomans, such as Namik Kemal and others, thought in terms of a limited form of pan-Islamism within the Ottoman empire. Abdul Hamid II encouraged the idea partly to gain loyalty among the non-Turkish elements of his own realm and partly to neutralize the pressure from European powers, some of whom had large Muslim populations of their own. Since the Arabic-speaking peoples were the largest Muslim group in the Ottoman empire and, because of their language, were best suited for the propagation of pan-Islamism, the sultan gathered a number of these around him.

One of the most important of the pan-Islamists invited by Abdul Hamid was Shaykh Abul-Huda of Aleppo, who gained a great deal of influence in the Ottoman court. He was against Wahhabism and believed that the institution of the caliphate was essential in Islam and the person of the caliph was the executor of God's decrees. The faithful should be "thankful if he [the caliph] does right, patient if he does wrong." Abul Huda's pan-Islamism was limited to the Muslims of the empire and his main purpose was to strengthen the claims of Abdul Hamid.

JAMAL AL-DIN AL-AFGHANI

Without doubt the most famous pan-Islamist of the nineteenth century, one whose horizon was not limited by the confines of the Ottoman empire, but included the whole umma of Islam, was Jamal al-Din al-Afghani (1839–1897). His life was so tumultuous, his writings so flamboyant and incendiary, and his projects for the revival of the glory of Islam so varied and sometimes contradictory that the last word has not been written on him by the scholars. He claimed to be from Afghanistan, though he actually was a Persian. He paraded as a Sunni though he was a Shi'i. There are those who believe that he was the forerunner of the Persian Revolution, but it is evident that he was not a constitutionalist. All his life he was looking for a strong Muslim ruler as whose prime minister he could revive and unify Islam. He wrote vituperatively against the British empire and considered it to be the main enemy of Islam. Nevertheless, there are those who believe that he was a British agent.

Be this as it may, Afghani, or Asadabadi, as he is known in Iran, was an able, effective, and restless agitator. He was much more interested in philosophy than in theology and more interested in politics than in philosophy. In politics, he was an activist rather than a theoretician. Like most activists, he had a tendency to oversimplify his concepts and set right against wrong. Like the Wahhabis, he idealized the period of the first four caliphs and believed in transcendentalism. Unlike the Wahhabis, Afghani believed in the importance of reason in Islam. According to him the Koran contained hidden references to modern scientific discoveries such as the steam engine and electricity as well as o modern political and social institutions.[2] All man had to do was to apply is reason to truly understand the word of God. But more importantly, to him slam was power and only incidentally a faith.

A favorite phrase of his was "Islam needs a Martin Luther" and perhaps he elieved that in himself Islam had found one. But the sword of the crusader ,as more to his liking than the pen of the reformer. To bring about the union f Islam he wanted the shah of Iran to recognize the Ottoman sultan as caliph. n turn, the sultan should recognize the "independence" of Iran and cede the hi'i holy cities of Karbala and Najaf to that country. Having done this, he ·anted all Muslim countries to send their "political" leaders for a conference 1 Istanbul for the purpose of declaring jihad against the European powers. (o wonder the shah of Iran threw him out of the country. Not long afterward, owever, the shah was assassinated by one of the disciples of Afghani.

It was evident that Afghani, as an activist agitator, was willing to use any nd all means to attain his purpose. He preached the unity of Islam, he argued >r its supremacy over all other religions, and he endorsed the death of those ,ho he thought stood in the way. For a time he actually tried to gain the coop-·ation of the British and later he sought the assistance of the Russians. Since is Shi'ism was a hindrance, he claimed to be from Afghanistan so that everyone ,ould take it for granted that he was a Sunni (most of the Afghanis are of that ersuasion). He went to Paris, London, and Petersburg in the hope of enlisting he aid of any of these empires in the rejuvenation of Islam. In the Islamic ,orld he searched for a strong political ruler, anyone strong enough to unite slam. He went to the Khedive of Egypt, the Shah of Iran, and the Sultan of 'urkey. Each one used him for a while and then let him go. He was more ttracted to Abdul Hamid than to anyone else. He went to Istanbul again but nce Afghani's ultimate loyalty was to Islam and not to the Osmanli Dynasty, 1e wily sultan kept him in honored house arrest where he died of cancer in 897.

1UHAMMAD ABDUH

Another pan-Islamist of great influence was Muhammad Abduh (1849– 905). He was a disciple of Afghani, but more of a thinker, and he had greater 1fluence. Unlike his vagabond teacher, Abduh was rooted in the life and cul-1re of Egypt. Even though he was drawn for a time into the orbit of political ctivities of Afghani, his heart was not in it and he spent his fruitful years in ducation and reform. He agreed with his teacher that there was aggression gainst Islam but disagreed with him that the aggressive force was the Chris-:an religion. He believed Islam was misunderstood mostly because of the con-uct of the Muslims themselves. Abduh believed that Islam should respond to

---

[2] In the middle of the twentieth century, the spiritual heirs of Afghani claimed that the .oran contained references to the radio, television, atomic energy, and rocketry in outer space.

the challenge of the West not so much through a return to political power, but through reform within Islam. Consequently, Abduh founded the first benevolent social service society in the modern Muslim world and spent his energies in educational reform in Azhar University, and in social and religious reform in Islam. He rejected the purely political road of intrigues which Afghani was following in the capitals of the Muslim world and instead angered his former teacher by suggesting that he should persuade the rulers to inaugurate educational reforms.

He also followed the Wahhabis in idealizing the "purity" of Islam in the first century, but unlike them accepted modern science, new methods of education and even modern patterns of philosophy in expounding Islam. He was opposed to *taqlid*, imitation of the past writers, and believed that the door of *ijtihad* interpretation of the Koran, was not closed. This last was a heretical belief in Sunni Islam. But neither was he for the imitation of European aims of education. He felt that the Muslims must borrow European methods and go through the same sacrifices as the Europeans had in the evaluation of their aims. He held Islam to be a universal religion and his important commentary on the Koran is tolerant, moral, and pragmatic. It is inclined toward both a voluntarist and an activist ethic.

Most of his life he had to defend himself against attacks from orthodox Muslims who were devoted to the tradition passed down to them. "What sort of a shaykh is this," they complained, "who speaks French, travels about in Europe translates western books, quotes from western philosophers, holds discussions with their scholars, issues fatwas on things that not one of the ancients would have known about, takes part in benevolent organizations and collects money for the poor and the unfortunate? If he is a doctor of religion, let him spend his life between his home and the mosque. If he belongs to the secular world, we are of the opinion that he is more active in that sphere than all the rest of the Muslims."

Abduh was an Egyptian and took part in the nationalist 'Urabi rebellion against the Khedive and the foreign powers. He was proud of the glories of ancient Egypt and as such his ideas may be a slight modification of the supranationalism of the Muslim umma. He considered the unity of Muslims in one country as a strong link in the chain of the unity of all Muslims. This was orthodox pan-Islamism, but the modification introduced by Abduh was that when both Muslims and non-Muslims belonged to the same nation there should be unity between them regardless of differences in religion. On the other hand, he was critical of doctrinaire nationalistic thinking.

For Abduh, as for countless Muslim thinkers after him, there was always a tension between the demands of Islam that men should live according to the dictates of God, and the irresistible demands of modern civilization, which virtually forced them to live in a certain different way. He maintained that the two were not incompatible. Whenever they did differ, he believed that the moral and doctrinal imperatives of Islam could not be compromised. Never theless, the tension was ever-present, and in time he was rejected both by the orthodox because he had gone too far, and by the modernists because he had not gone far enough.

THE BEGINNINGS OF PAN-ARABISM

Despite the genuine universalism of Islam, there is an abiding link between it and Arabism. Certainly Umar, the second caliph, considered the Arabs to be above all other Muslims, who were considered to be only "clients." The Umayyads intensified this sense of Arab superiority and imposed the Arabic language on all who became Muslims. As the political power of the Arabs waned, Arabism as a political phenomenon disappeared, but Arabism insofar as it was connected with the language remained. Strict Muslims have generally believed in the proposition that "whoever loves the Prophet loves the Arabs, and whoever loves the Arabs loves the Arabic language in which the best of the books was revealed." It is a common saying among the Muslims everywhere that 'Arabic is the language of the angels." However, the revival of Arabic language and literature in the nineteenth century, and its use as a base for the political movement of pan-Arabism which developed in the second half of the twentieth century, were mainly due to the activities of the Christians of the Fertile Crescent and the encouragement of American Protestant missionaries.

Most of the Christians of Syria-Lebanon, unlike their Muslim neighbors, did not feel loyalty to the Ottoman empire. To gain the support of the Muslims to his program of pan-Islamism, Abdul Hamid completed the building of the Hijaz railroad to make pilgrimage easier, repaired the buildings of the holy cities, appointed Arabs to high office and chose Arab soldiers for his body guards. The Christians, however, were left out of such generous considerations. Precisely because of their lack of loyalty, the Christians were more receptive to western ideas and institutions. The religious interests of the French Catholics in the Maronites of Lebanon and the missionary zeal of American Protestants brought the benefits of western civilization. In religious matters, neither mission proved very successful, but their cultural, social, and indirect political influence was of utmost importance.

There was an unspoken rivalry between the Catholic and the Protestant missions. Both opened schools and hospitals, both established printing presses, and both founded universities with faculties in medicine, engineering, and other branches of knowledge. The French influence was more limited in that the Roman Catholics were most interested in educating and strengthening the Maronite Christians. Furthermore, being interested in the propagation of the French culture, they stressed French language and literature. The American Protestants, on the other hand, used the vernacular to preach the Christian Gospel to all of the Arabic-speaking peoples. In 1834, they established the first Arabic press in Beirut and set about, as all pioneering Protestant missionaries have done, translating the Bible into Arabic. Cornelius Van Dyke, who became a great Arabic scholar, was in charge of the project and was assisted by two

Lebanese, Butrus al-Bustani (1819–1883), and Nasif al-Yaziji (1800–1871). Yaziji wrote on Arab history and literature and exalted classical Arabic in his poetry. It was he who, in 1868, perhaps for the first time, announced that they should work for freedom from the Ottoman yoke. Butrus became a school-teacher and a very productive writer. In 1870, he founded the first Arabic periodical al-Jinan, which for 16 years provided reading material on modern themes in the Arabic-speaking world.

The students and alumni of the Syrian Protestant College, later called the American University of Beirut, spearheaded a renaissance, nahda, which not only rediscovered the versatility of the Arabic language but also introduced the religious, social, scientific, and political thought of the West. These pioneers started literary and scientific societies and in these societies the Arab national movement was launched.

Of the two most influential periodicals published in the last half of the nineteenth century, one was al-Muqtataf, founded in 1876 by two graduates of the Syrian Protestant College, Ya'qub Saruf and Faris Nimr, and the other was al-Hilal, founded by Jurji Zaydan in 1892. The editors of both of these, as well as of other publications, later fled the heavy hands of Abdul Hamid's agents and went to the freer atmosphere of Cairo. These men and a host of others, among them Shibli Shumayyil (1850–1917) and Farah Antun (1874–1922), were in general agreement on certain points.

First and foremost was western science. This was believed to have a universal value all its own and to hold the key to the secrets of the universe. It was the basis for the unity of all being. To express this unity they used tawhid, the same awe-some word which in Islam denotes the oneness of God. Most of them were impressed by social Darwinism and the idea of progress was as much a reality to them as it was to the writers of Europe whose works were being translated into Arabic.

Second, they believed in the unity of the nation and equality of all its citizens regardless of religious differences. For nation they sometimes used watan (fatherland), sometimes qawm, (people), or sometimes umma, the word used by pan-Islamists to denote the whole Muslim community. Those words were to be specifically defined in the twentieth century. But what mattered then was that Muslims, Christians, Jews, and Druzes were members of the same umma, qawm, or watan.

Third, they believed that the new science embodied in itself new laws and new relationships. Complete subjugation to the laws of the past, be they the Shari'a of Islam or the canon law of Christianity, was regressive. Furthermore it would divide the people and create inequality and strife.

Fourth, they believed in the separation of religious institutions, Muslim or Christian, from the temporal. Any mixture of the two would corrupt both and putting religion at the basis of nationality would curb the freedom of thought and the liberty of the individual. Most of them, not all, were religious people and some of them, even though they were Christians, went so far as to say that Islam, as an historical expression of the Arabs, should be given an honored place.

By demanding the creation of a secular state, the Christians were asking not only for equal rights with the Muslims but also for an equal and active share in the social and political responsibilities of society. For the Muslims, on the other hand, acceptance of the same principle meant giving up the preferred position which they had enjoyed all along. For the pan-Islamist, even for a person as tolerant and moderate as Abduh, it was the denial of the supremacy of Islam over all religions.

But as more Muslims came into contact with the ideas and institutions of the West, and as they became disenchanted with the policies of the Ottoman sultan, they became more receptive to such ideas. The Young Turk revolution of 1908 and its Turkification program forced the Arabic-speaking Muslim youth to make common cause with the Christian. Some joined the existing Christian organizations, and others founded Muslim groups such as the al-Fatat, which demanded complete independence. Still others, who could not go quite that far, championed a dual monarchy, Arab and Turk, like that of Austria-Hungary. These societies grew in number and had their meetings in secret or in Cairo or in Europe. During World War I the British took advantage of this desire for independence for their own ends.

LOCAL NATIONALISM

The Ottomans governed most of the Fertile Crescent as a unit, with the exception of Lebanon and parts of the Arabian Peninsula under separate governments. Egypt, as we have seen, was distinct both geographically and politically. The advent of Muhammad Ali and the subsequent history of Egypt widened the gap between the Egyptians and the peoples of the Fertile Crescent. Thus it was easier for the intellectual elite and the political activists of Egypt to think of themselves as a separate nation. The European contacts which the reforms of Muhammad Ali provided made it easier for them to adopt the European nationalism. The cry, "Egypt for the Egyptians," was raised in Egypt of 1882, though there was no corresponding cry, "Syria for the Syrians," or "Iraq for the Iraqis."

On the other hand, Al-Azhar University in Cairo, as the largest center of Islamic studies, was very influential and its teachers, like Afghani and Abduh, were proclaiming the demands of Islam. Furthermore, because of the fact that there was more freedom in Egypt than in the other parts of the Ottoman empire, many of the writers from Syria and Lebanon moved to Cairo and published their papers and books there. Hence, Egypt became the center of all sorts of movements prevalent in the Ottoman empire. Pan-Islamists were there as well as pan-Arabs. There were the Muslim traditionalists as well as secularists. There were also Egyptians who thought of themselves as a "nation" and did not have anything to do with the others, though they spoke Arabic or were Muslims or both. To make the picture more confusing was the fact that in each of the three groups, i.e., pan-Islamists, pan-Arabs, and Egyptian nationalists, there were different degrees of relationships and/or loyalty to the Ottoman sultan.

The economic collapse of Egypt and subsequent supremacy of foreign creditors brought different elements together in the national party, *hizb al-wataniyya*, which resulted in the 'Urabi revolt. Even though Abduh was not happy with the principles underlying the revolt, he nevertheless joined it. They were banded together not as Ottomans, or as Arabs, or even as Muslims, but as Egyptians. A Muslim (Abdullah Nadim), a Christian (Adib Ishaq), and a Jew (Ya'qub Sanu), emphasized "national," i.e., Egyptian, unity.

Later on, when the British won and established order, many joined the new civil service, while others, like Abduh, devoted their time to the development of education and other reforms. A new generation came into being that had not known the condition of Egypt before the arrival of the British. To them Britain was not the savior of Egypt from bankruptcy, but a foreign country imposing its rule. It is quite likely that the British attitude goaded these young men into action. The British, through Lord Cromer and others, stated that Egypt was not a nation and consequently the idea of a patriot, whether a Muslim or not, was not capable of realization. On the other hand it was possible, said Cromer, for the diverse elements in Egypt to be fused together into "one self-governing body." But such an ideal would take "years—possibly generations—to achieve. . . ." It was, of course, implied that the British would remain for years—possibly generations—until it was achieved.

To the challenge that Egypt was not a nation, Mustafa Kamil (1874–1908) answered that it was. He was a controversial figure, to some a hero, and others an impostor. His premature death at the age of 34 has made him a hero in the eyes of his countrymen. He believed that Egypt was a nation, but part of a larger whole which was at once Ottoman, Muslim, and eastern. For the time being, however, the last three had to wait until Egyptians had asserted their nationality. For a time he sought the aid of the French to oust the British and did not oppose the annexation of Algeria by the French. He and many other Egyptians denounced Arabism and especially disliked the Syrians. He believed that the basis for nationality was neither language nor religion nor tribal descent but land. Egypt would be a nation when the Egyptians could say, "Egypt my country."

At the beginning of the twentieth century, there were three parties in Egypt. First was the Peoples' (umma) Party to which belonged Abduh and his friends, who, as pan-Islamists, were Muslims first, Egyptians second, and perhaps Ottomans and/or Arabs third. The second was the Constitutional Reform Party, founded by the friends of the khedive with the blessings of the British, for the safeguarding of the status quo. The third was the National Party led by Kamil, for whom Egypt came first and Islam and Ottomanism took less significant positions. It was the spirit of the National Party which prevailed. Egyptianism was the driving force of Egyptian nationalism until the second half of the twentieth century.

CHAPTER 25

THE PERSIAN AWAKENING

In the history of the Middle East, the Persians were the only major group conquered by the Arabs, who kept their identity as a people. As we have seen, the Persians almost always kept themselves apart. Rightly or wrongly, they thought that they were different from the rest of the Muslims and consistently aroused the hostility of others by thinking themselves superior. This sense of identity as a nation or a people was sometimes expressed religiously, as in the revolts of the "Black Shirts," "White Shirts," and "Red Shirts" during the early Abbasid period.[1] Sometimes it was expressed through literature, as in the Shu'ubiyya movement and in the poetry of Ferdosi.[2] It was also at times expressed politically, in, for example, the partially successful revolts of the Saffarids, Samanids, and others, who established autonomous principalities. Sometimes it was expressed culturally, as during the Mongol period, when the Persians developed a culture of their own distinct from the Arabic-speaking Muslims.

Even though the Persians thought of themselves as special or unique, they were at least in and part of the Muslim world. They participated in the various activities of the community (umma) of Islam. The Persians wrote the first complete grammar for the Arabic language, even though they refused to speak it. They had a large share in writing a systematic theology of Islam, even though eventually they refused to follow it. They made a good deal of the history of Islam and wrote it for posterity—but somehow did not feel part of it. Much of what is commonly known as "Islamic," and erroneously as "Arab," culture in the fields of art, literature, philosophy, medicine, mathematics, astronomy, physics, chemistry, history, geography, and theology, was contributed by the Persians. Their poets and architects were invited to India and their art adorned the mosques and buildings of the Ottomans. From the thirteenth century to

[1] See above, pp. 79, 81.
[2] See above, p. 82.

251

the end of the sixteenth century, from Istanbul to Delhi, most art was Persian and the sign of culture was the ability to speak Persian.

The purpose of the preceding paragraph is to state not only that the Persians were different from the Arabs or the Turks but also that they were very conscious of these differences and made themselves obnoxious and were shunned by boasting about them. During the Safavid period, the establishment of Shi'ism as the official religion isolated the Persians even more. Notwithstanding the very extensive commercial and political relationship between Iran and various European countries during the Safavid period, there was no intellectual interaction. Culturally Iran was isolated from the non-Muslim world and by espousing Shi'ism it was separated from the rest of the Muslim world. Iran was in the world of Islam but certainly not one with it. As the power of the Safavid and other kings decreased and the influence of the Shi'i ulama increased, the isolation of Iran became more complete. Various movements in the nineteenth and twentieth centuries in Iran can best be understood in the light of this isolation. These movements attempted to destroy the wall surrounding the Persians. The purpose of the very insignificant pan-Islamist group in Iran, encouraged by Afghani, was to destroy the inner wall which separated the Persian Shi'is from the rest of the Muslims. The aim of the "constitutionalists" was to raze the wall which isolated Iran from the rest of the world. In all cases the vast majority of the Shi'i ulama and their followers tried to prevent both of these walls from crumbling.

The strong sense of identity which the Persians had developed became very useful in the process of nation-building in the 1900's. As early as the tenth century Ferdosi expressed the sentiment, "If there is no Iran, then let me not be." While the students of nationalism in the Middle East credit the Turkish writer of the nineteenth century, Namik Kemal, with the use of *vatan*, fatherland, in the modern sense, we find the Persian poet Sa'di (d. 1291) using the phrase "love of fatherland," *hobb-e vatan*, to criticize a sentiment which is quite modern. He says "O Sa'di, love of *vatan* is a noble sentiment. But one just can't die miserably [for it] because one is born there."

It is considered erroneous to identify these sentiments as "nationalism," although one is at a loss to know what to call them. But the fact of the matter is that the Persians built their modern nationalism which they borrowed from the West on the consciousness of their own national and cultural identity. The Turks and the Arabic-speaking peoples had difficulty in adapting the concept of nationalism to such concepts as Islam, Ottomanism, Arabism, and Turanianism. The Persians did not have such difficulties. It is important to note that while the Turks and Arabs were, and in a sense the Arabs still are, in search of identity, the Persians had a fairly developed one.

BABI-BAHAISM

In the previous chapter we discussed Wahhabism as an indigenous reform movement in Sunni Islam. Babi-Bahaism was an indigenous reform movement n Shi'i Islam and did much to destroy the wall of isolation. Babism was a genuinely Persian and Shi'i movement with no influence from abroad, while Bahaism showed foreign influence.

Babi-Bahaism was an offshoot of the Shaykhi sect within the twelve Imamate Shi'a. According to this school, the twelfth Imam, who is hidden and shall someday appear, keeps in touch with the believers through one person, who is called the *bab* or gate. In 1844, the leader of the Shaykhi group, Mirza Ali Mohammad (1821–1850), of Shiraz in south Iran claimed to be the *Bab*. Later he said that he was the "Point of Revelation" and the hidden Imam himself. It is not so certain that he really did claim to be the hidden Imam because in his book *Bayan*, the Bab uses mystic terms, calling himself a mirror, and speaks of "Him whom God shall manifest." It seems certain that he thought he was inaugurating a new age and a new kingdom with a new calendar, in which the numbers 9 and 19 have mystical qualities.

The fact that these claims gained ready following in all parts of the country is perhaps indicative of the opposition of the people toward the power of the ulama and toward conditions in general. Typical of most Islamic movements, the Babis, as they were called, took up arms and set out to establish the new kingdom. Soon Kerman and Yazd in south Iran became centers. It was not a movement of the southerners against the north, as one historian claims, for there was one stronghold in Barforush on the Caspian and another in Zanjan in northwest Iran. The shah forbade it, and the ulama preached against it, but the movement grew. Fighting broke out in many parts of the country and the Babis of Zanjan resisted a siege for a year.

The Bab himself was arrested and eventually executed in Tabriz by a Persian government firing squad. Soon after the execution of the Bab, two of his followers made an attempt on the life of the Persian monarch, Naser al-Din Shah. In retaliation, there was mass arrest and severe persecution. The courage, fortitude, and selflessness which the Babis exhibited as they went to their deaths reciting poetry was by far more effective in spreading the faith than the teachings of its leaders.

Among the leaders of the Babis after the execution of the Bab were two half-brothers from Mazandaran in north Iran. One of them, Yahya, was designated by the Bab as the leader of the group and was given the title *Sobh-e Azal*, the Morning of Eternity. The other, Hoseyn Ali, was given title Bahaullah, the Splendor of God. Both brothers and a number of Babis were exiled to the Ottoman empire. In 1866, Bahaullah claimed that he was "Him whom God shall manifest," as foretold by the Bab. Yahya did not submit to his authority and the ensuing conflict between the two groups caused the Ottoman government to separate the two brothers. Sobh-e Azal was sent to Cyprus and Bahaullah to Acre in Palestine.

Bahaullah, however, won the struggle and Babism was replaced by Bahaism. The further dissension among the Bahais after the death of Bahaullah in 1892 and the eventual growth of the "Bahai World Faith," with centers in many parts of the world, is not part of this story.[3] Whether Babism could have become a national religio-political movement in Iran is not certain. Bahaism, however, under Bahaullah and especially his son Abdul Baha, became too devoted to internationalism to be in sympathy with the constitutional movement in Iran or to be attractive to the Persian nationalistic revolutionaries. The Shi'i religious leaders who were opposed to Bahaism and westernization identified the two with each other. They denounced Bahaism because it was preaching new doctrine, and they rejected everything new from attire to ideas by charging that they were "Bahai." Even though the Bahais were not particularly interested in westernization, they were accused of it, and all modern concepts were attributed to them. There is no doubt that the Persian Bahais were more receptive to the new ideas even though they were not the originators of them. By the end of World War I, however, Bahaism lost its "new look" and ceased to be a modernizing influence. It is difficult to estimate the number of Bahais in Iran, as they were being persecuted as late as 1954, and had no legal status.

AFGHANI IN IRAN

Pan-Islamism, with all its religious and political connotations, was unpopular in a Shi'i country like Iran and was unacceptable to the Persian ulama, who wanted to keep their own brand of Islam isolated from the contaminating influences of the Sunnis. The pan-Islamist Afghani, however, being a forceful and charismatic person, had a small number of followers in the lay circle close to the shah of Iran. During his active adult life, Afghani went to Iran only two times. Both times he was the guest of an important merchant in Tehran and most of his visitors were laymen and not the clergy. Both times he had an audience with Naser al-Din Shah.

Afghani's first visit to Iran was in 1886. His vituperous utterances so infuriated the shah and his courtiers that his host, Haji Amin al-Zarb, was asked to take him out of the country. The latter took Afghani with him to Russia. In 1889, during his third trip to Europe, the shah saw Afghani in Munich. Afghani claims that he was sent on a special mission to Russia and the shah asked him to return to Iran after that. According to Afghani's own account, he went to Petersburg in behalf of the notorious Amin al-Sultan, the Prime Minister, to assure the Russians that the recent concession for the Karun river navigation and bank given to Great Britain would be matched by corresponding concessions to Russia. The fact that Afghani would consent to go on such a mission, which was detrimental to Iran, perhaps reveals his opportunism as a political agitator. The fact that the shah, who had known Afghani, would invite him once again to visit Iran, perhaps reveals the confusion in the mind of the monarch.

The second visit was not much different from the first. Perhaps Afghani once

---

[3] The center of the faith in the United States is in Wilmette, Illinois, where their nine-sided temple is a well-known landmark.

again insisted on his plan for the union of Islam, with autonomy for Iran under the Ottoman caliph. This time the shah was so infuriated that Afghani, to save himself from expulsion, took sanctuary, *bast*, in the nearby shrine of Shah Abdul Azim. Shortly afterward he was forcibly expelled from Iran.

The year 1890, in which Afghani was expelled, was also the year in which the notorious Tobacco Concession was granted to a British Company.[4] Perhaps because most Persians smoked, this concession aroused the hostility of the whole country without Afghani having to do anything. To the ulama, this concession was another breach in their isolationist wall. They had led sporadic riots against the concession, unassisted by Afghani. Only after Afghani was rebuffed by the shah did his hatred for the monarch become so complete that he made common cause with the ulama whom he had attacked until then. He wrote letters against the shah and the concession to the Mujtahids in Samarra and Shiraz. Since one of the letters was addressed to Haji Mirza Mohammad Hasan-e Shirazi, who had issued the famous fatva against smoking, Afghani has been credited with having played an important role in the tobacco strike and in the awakening of the Persians which subsequently resulted in the revolution of 1906. The defeat of the concession showed that the Persians could, with concerted action, control the activities of the king. As such it was an important step toward the establishment of a constitutional monarchy.

Afghani, however, went to Istanbul and continued his anti-shah activities. The pan-Islamic group in Iran was very small and was led by Shaykh Ahmad Ruhi, a poet from Kerman. His poetry denouncing Naser al-Din Shah and praising Abdul Hamid as the "Sultan of Islam," leaves no doubt about the plan of Afghani for the union of Islam and the position of Iran in such a union. Eventually one of Afghani's pan-Islamic disciples, Mirza Reza of Kerman, assassinated Naser al-Din Shah in 1896.

INFLUENCES FROM THE WEST

The isolation of Iran was broken directly by encounter with the West and indirectly through Turkey and India. As in the case of the Ottoman empire, the first borrowing was in military equipment and training. During the reign of Fath-Ali Shah (1797–1834) and during the Russo-Persian wars, foreign officers commanded Persian troops, but it was Mirza Taqi Khan, the astute grand vazir under Naser al-Din Shah, who put modernization on a sound basis.

This remarkable man, who is commonly known by the title Amir-e Kabir, was the son of a cook and a protégé of Qa'em Maqam, the able vazir under Mohammad Shah. When Naser al-Din was Crown Prince and governor of Azarbaijan, Amir-e Kabir was his chief officer and close enough to him to marry the Prince's sister. When Naser al-Din was crowned in 1848, Mirza Taqi Khan was made the grand vazir. During his three short years in office he did more than any other individual to direct Iran toward modernization.

---

[4] See above, p. 226.

He was familiar with the Tanzimat of the Ottoman empire and had observed much on his visit to Petersburg. He was convinced that the salvation of Iran was to reform along western lines.

He reorganized the government, facilitated commerce with Europe, built bazaars and warehouses, and reorganized the army. Perhaps his greatest accomplishment was the establishment in 1851 of the *Dar al-Fonun*, Institute of Arts and Sciences, which became an important center of learning. To this center were brought teachers from Europe who taught western science, history, and technology. But Amir-e Kabir was not allowed to continue in office. His most powerful enemies were the ulama, who had found an effective ally in the person of the Queen Mother. She had great influence over her son and was a mortal enemy of her son-in-law. By the end of 1851 Mirza Taqi Khan was dismissed from office and a year later was executed in Kashan. About the only person who stood by him until the end was his devoted wife, the Shah's only sister.

Western influence came to Iran also through students, who as early as 1815 had been travelling to Europe. They returned to become teachers, newspaper publishers, translators, and authors. The first newspaper in Iran was published by the Amir-e Kabir, as a weekly government gazette. Because of censorship, papers were published abroad and smuggled in. Of the two most important papers, one was *Akhtar* [star] published in Istanbul from 1875. For a while it advocated pan-Islamism under the influence of Ruhi,[5] but later became a proponent of westernization and was very popular in Iran. The other paper was *Qanun* (law) published in London in 1890. Its editor, Malkom Khan, was very close to Naser al-Din Shah and acted as his envoy to England. But Malkom's progressive ideas could not be tolerated by the shah, who saw westernization as a danger to his position and wanted to keep his people so ignorant of Europe that they would not know whether, to quote the king himself, "Brussels was the name of a city or a kind of cabbage." Malkom Khan wrote on social and political subjects in simple Persian, always emphasizing the necessity of the rule of law. He also tried to revise the alphabet and introduced freemasonry *faramush khaneh*, the "house of forgetfulness," in Iran.

Publication of books played an important role in introducing western ideas. The Institute of Arts and Sciences became the center for translation and publication of books on scientific, technical, and social subjects. Two authors who had more direct influence on the revolution are Abdul Rahman Talebof and Zeynul Abedin Maragheyi, both merchants from Azarbaijan. Talebof, who had long sojourns in the Caucasus, was interested in chemistry and physics and wrote extensively on these as well as social and political subjects. A book of his which became very popular was *Ahmad*. It is a dialogue between a father and his little boy, Ahmad. In a child's simple language the father discusses the progress of Europe and the backwardness of Iran.

Even a more popular book than *Ahmad* was the *Travels of Ebrahim Bey* by

[5] See above, p. 225.

Maragheyi. Ebrahim was the son of a Persian merchant residing in Cairo who went to see what Iran was like. His varied experiences and involvements reveal the misery of the people, the deceitfulness of the clergy, and the cruelty of the officials. This book caught the imagination of the people, was read by those who could, and was read aloud to the illiterate, as was the custom, in tea houses.

Schools also played an important role in the awakening of Iran. Dar al-Fonun was about the only important school opened by the government in the nineteenth century, but liberal merchants in Azarbaijan, Gilan, and other provinces opened schools along western lines. The models for these were the schools which had been established by the American, British, and French missionaries. The French Lazarite mission established a school in Tabriz in 1839 and later opened schools in other parts of the country. The Americans began their work in Urumiyeh (later Rezaiyeh), Azarbaijan, in 1839 and the British in Esfahan in 1870. Both established hospitals as well as schools. One of these schools, Alborz College in Tehran, became an especially important educational institution in the country. Its long-time and beloved President, Dr. S. M. Jordan, is the only American, perhaps the only foreigner, in all the Middle East whose statue was erected by an appreciative people. The Americans were the first to establish schools for women. They were also the first to publish a magazine for women. *The World of Women*, edited by Mrs. Arthur Boyce with the assistance of the graduates of the American girls' school in Tehran, continued publication for 12 years and was the forerunner of many similar modern magazines for women.

The Persian Revolution is perhaps unique among the revolutions of the twentieth century Middle East in that the military did not have much to do with it. No strong man, military or civilian, had complete or even partial charge of it. The revolution was directed, somewhat haphazardly, by the merchants, the educated elite, and the moderate-to-liberal ulama. The merchants and the business community in the bazaars were very vital to the Persian revolution. From 1860 onward Persian merchants, especially from Azarbaijan and Gilan, went north to Russia. The annual fair at Nizhni Novgorod had many Persian visitors. Furthermore, the shortest route to Europe was through Russia. Toward the end of the nineteenth century, thousands of Persians worked in the oil fields of Baku and in other industries in Russia. All of these came back impressed not only with the progress of Russia compared to that of Iran, but also with the ideas which led to the Revolutions of 1905 and 1917 in Russia.

THE PERSIAN REVOLUTION

It has been noted that no one man or party directed the revolution or brought the various elements together. The ulama had their own particular purpose in all this and the Europeanized elite had their own. The merchants caught between the two were perhaps more often with the westernizers than the clergy. This was not a planned revolution. It simply happened.

The accession of Mozaffar al-Din Shah in 1896 did not change the situation in Iran. The opportunist grand vazir, Amin al-Sultan, was in charge and sided with the British or the Russians as situations demanded. The sickly and weak-willed shah was obsessed with the desire to go to Europe, both for cure (he was suffering from a kidney ailment) and also to be wined and dined by the crown heads of Europe. The heavy expenses of the two trips which the shah took increased the indebtedness of Iran to both Russia and Britain. The new pro-Russian tariff agreements arranged by the Belgian director of customs had raised the price of sugar. On December 11, 1905, a group of merchants called a strike in protest and closed the bazaars. The government retaliated by flogging the merchants. On December 13, some two thousand clergymen and merchants headed by two moderate Mujtahids, Sayyed Mohammad Tabataba'i and Sayyed Abdullah Behbahani, took sanctuary at the nearby shrine of Shah Abdul Azim. There they demanded a "house of justice."

On January 12, 1906, the shah issued a rescript promising to comply with the wishes of the people. When the statement was read in the court of the mosque there was much rejoicing and the cry of "Long live the Persian nation" was much heard. But the shah was persuaded by his reactionary ministers to forget about the promise.

In July 1906, a large number of the ulama and their followers took sanctuary in the important shrine of Qom some 60 miles south of Tehran. At the same time, 13,000 westernizers, merchants, tradesmen, and others took sanctuary in the grounds of the British Legation in Tehran. The taking of sanctuary, *bast*, was an honored institution in Iran, but the usual places of sanctuary were shrines, mosques, the palaces or stables of the shah, and, of late, the provincial telegraph office, which presumably had a line connecting it to the shah's palace. Taking sanctuary in a foreign legation was an innovation, but it was done with the consent of the British. In the rivalry between Russia and Great Britain the revolutionaries sided with Great Britain because of its liberal and democratic institutions. Great Britain on its part joined the revolutionaries because such a policy would hurt Russia. On August 5, 1906, Mozaffar al-Din Shah finally granted a constitution and a parliament, *Majles*. The election to the first Majles was based according to membership in different sections of society, such as princes, ulama, nobles, landlords, merchants, and guilds. The first Majles was represented by all segments of society except the peasants. Almot its first act was to reject a joint Anglo-Russian loan of £400,000, and this action was followed by compelling the shah to dismiss the Belgian customs officials.

The death of the shah on January 8, 1907, placed the young revolutionary movement in grave jeopardy. The new shah, Mohammad Ali, was known to be a puppet of Russia and against the revolution. Even though at his coronation he swore to uphold the constitution, practically everything he did was against it. One of his first acts was to recall the reactionary Amin al-Sultan and name him Prime Minister.

The granting of the constitution had brought with it freedom of the press. The number of newspapers increased by the month, and by 1911 had reached over 400. As the new shah increased his anti-majles activities the newspapers lampooned the shah and the reactionaries in poetry, prose, satire, humor, and cartoon. Songs were written on the love of country, freedom, equality, justice, and democracy. Everywhere in the country the troubadors who played at weddings sang these songs, which spread the message and encouraged the people to oppose the reactionaries.

Perhaps the best evidence that the constitutional movement was not the monopoly of a "very small European-educated elite" is the appearance of the *Anjomans*, councils. All over the country there arose literally hundreds of *Anjomans* to carry out some aspect of the revolution. These *Anjomans* each had from half a dozen to 100 members. Some were religious groups, others supported education and conducted literacy classes, still others became pamphleteers, and a few were terroristic, assassinating a number of antirevolutionary leaders. There was no central committee of the revolution to direct the activities of the *Anjomans*. Each had its own rules. The terroristic *Anjomans*, which were similar to the contemporary nihilist and social revolutionary groups in Russia, chose its own victims. A leader with imagination and a program could have welded them together, but one did not appear.

The return of Amin al-Sultan and the need for money revived the question of loans. The Majles was against borrowing from Russia or England, while Amin al-Sultan was for it. On August 31, 1907, as the Prime Minister was leaving the Majles, he was shot dead by a terrorist, who immediately committed suicide. On the assassin's body was found a paper bearing the inscription "Abbas Aqa, money changer of Azarbaijan, member of the *Anjoman*, national devotee, *feda'i*, no. 41." The name of the *Anjoman*, however, did not appear on the paper. There were several of these secret terroristic societies and in subsequent years they killed many.

On the same day as the assassination, an Anglo-Russian convention was signed which had far-reaching influence on the fate of the Persian Revolution. The convention was a result of the Eastern Question, which, in essence, was the inability of the Western powers to get along among themselves. With the advent of a unified Germany on the European scene and with the avowed interest of Kaiser Wilhelm in the problems of the Middle East, Russia and Britain wanted to show a "united front" against the newcomer. They came to an agreement concerning Iran, Afghanistan, and Tibet. In the case of Iran, in which both Great Britain and Russia were interested, they designated "spheres of influence." Territory north of a line drawn from Yazd going northeast to the Irano-Afghan border east of Mashhad, and another line going northwest to the Irano-Turkish border west of Kermanshah was under Russia's influence. In contrast to the Russian area, which included most of the large cities of Iran, the British got as their sphere of influence only the southeast corner adjacent to "British" Baluchestan. The rest of the country, i.e., most of the southwest, was designated neutral. Such an uneven division shows that Britain was still obsessed with the defense of India and that the oil in southwest Iran had not yet been discovered. The Persians quite correctly viewed the agreement as a violation of the independence of their country. The Persian revolutionaries, who had hoped for so much from "democratic" Britain, believed they had been betrayed. This belief was also true, as they were to learn more fully in 1911.

In the summer of 1907, however, the revolutionaries did not have much time to brood over the betrayal, for the reactionary shah was closing in on them. After a series of moves and countermoves, a Cossack regiment, under the command of Colonel Liakhanov, bombarded the Majles by order of the shah. A large number of revolutionaries were arrested, their leaders were executed, and the rest fled the country. It seemed that the constitutional movement was over, but the movement had supporters among the people. Three centers rallied in defense of the constitution: Tabriz, Esfahan, and Rasht.

The Tabrizis, under the leadership of Sattar Khan and Baqer Khan,[6] refused to allow the government forces to enter the city and were besieged by the shah's and Russian troops for over nine months. Mr. Howard Baskerville, a young American teacher at the mission school in Tabriz, resigned his post and joined the revolutionaries. He trained some of his own students and led a sortie to bring food for the starving population. He was killed on April 21, 1909, and his grave became a shrine of the revolution.

The gallant resistance of Tabriz gave time and encouragement to the nationalists in other centers. The Bakhtyari tribe under their chief, Sardar-e As'ad, declared for the constitution and moved toward Tehran. Later on it became evident that the Bakhtyaris were interested not so much in the ideas of the revolution as in their own power, but at the time their assistance was a boon to the constitutionalists. In Rasht in the north, an army of volunteers including a large number of Armenian nationalists, *Dashnaktzoutun*, also moved toward Tehran. The Rasht contingent was under the nominal command of Sepahdar and the actual command of Sardar Mohi and the Armenian Yefrem Khan. The two armies from the north and south converged on Tehran and took the capital on July 13, 1909. The shah was deposed and his young son Ahmad was declared king on the next day.

The siege of Tabriz was lifted and constitutionalists were in power again, but they were faced with many problems. With the intervention of the Russians and the British, the ex-shah was reluctantly pensioned and gladly sent to Europe. Furthermore, neither Sardar As'ad, the Bakhtyari chieftain, nor Sepahdar of Rasht was seriously constitutionalist. In addition to this, the differences between the ulama and the European-trained nationalists came to the surface. When the second Majles opened on November 15, 1909, there were two distinct groups, one revolutionary and the other evolutionary. The former were known as Social Democrats, and these believed in the separation of temporal and religious powers, land reform, compulsory conscription, universal education, division of land, etc. The other group, called Social Moderates, included

---

[6] "Khan" is not a surname but an honorific title assumed by practically all Persians. Its use was forbidden in 1934, when all titles were abolished.

the ulama and most of the nobility and landlords, who were against only the excesses of Mohammad Ali Shah.

This division was seen at the outset in the Supplement to the Constitution which was passed October 7, 1907. While the nationalists wanted a constitutional government, *mashruteh*, based on laws passed by the elected representatives of the people, the ulama wanted *mashru'a*, or the rule of the Muslim Shari'a. The two were poles apart but the compromise they reached is apparent in the Supplement to the Constitution. Article II of this document requires that five representatives of the ulama be present in the Majles with veto power over any legislation which they consider to be against the tenets of Islam. The fact, however, that Article II was never implemented shows that the secular nationalists were not without influence.

During the second Majles, the rift between the two groups was open and fierce. The ulama from Najaf excommunicated the Social Democrats while, on the other hand, a number of moderates were assassinated by secret *Anjomans*. Most of 1910 was spent by the Majles in looking for money to run the country. Since they were against borrowing from Russia and Britain and were unable to borrow from Germany, the Majles authorized an internal loan. This was received with enthusiasm by the population and women sold their jewels to provide the money.

In the meantime, the Majles realized that they needed expert financial advice from abroad. To ask for such aid from Russia and Britain was unthinkable. Their experience with other European nationalities had not been satisfactory. But the influence of the American missionaries, the martyrdom of Baskerville, and the general policy of the United States made it natural for the Persians to seek such aid from America. Morgan Shuster, together with a number of assistants, arrived in Iran as Treasurer-General and was invested with very extensive powers.

Shuster was very popular among the Persians and in sympathy with the aims of the Social Democrats in the Majles. This probably disappointed the Bakhtyaris and the moderates, who wanted to use him for their own purposes. Shuster realized that the country would have sufficient revenue if taxes were paid regularly. One method employed by some landlords in not paying taxes was to declare themselves "under the protection" of Russia or Britain. The treasury forces, however, confiscated the properties while the owners were taking refuge in the foreign legations. The Russians protested, and it was evident that the British sympathized with them.

A series of incidents resulted in the Russian government sending its first ultimatum on November 29, 1911, asking the Persian government to dismiss Shuster. A second ultimatum followed, requiring Iran not to employ foreign advisers without the sanction of Russian and British governments. A third came soon afterward, demanding indemnity for the troops which Russia had dispatched to Iran. The British, to whom the Persians had appealed, not only advised compliance with the Russian ultimatum but brought Indian troops to occupy south Iran. Many of the people responded by boycotting Russian and British goods, closing the bazaars, and demanding resistance. The finest hour of the revolution came when the members of the Majles, in a roll-call vote, unanimously rejected the ultimatum.

The cabinet, however, under the leadership of Samsam al-Saltaneh Bakhtyari, closed the Majles and dismissed Shuster on December 24, 1911. Aref Qazvini, the popular songwriter of the revolution, composed a song which continued to be sung long after Shuster's departure.

> *"Shame on the host whose guest unfed doth from the table rise*
> *Rather than this should happen, make thy life his sacrifice*
> *Should Shuster fare from Persia forth, Persia lost in sooth*
> *O let not Persia thus be lost, if ye be men in truth."*[7]

Thus came to an end this phase of the Persian revolution. It failed because of the rift between the ulama and the nationalists, lack of unity among the nationalists, and lack of experience in government and administration. It also failed because of the interference of Russia and Great Britain. During World War I, the Persians were afraid that in case of an Entente victory, Iran would certainly be divided between Russia and Britain. So they sided with the Central Powers. The Entente won, but Iran was not divided mainly because Russia was temporarily taken out of the rivalry by the Communist Revolution.

[7] Translation by the late E. G. Browne.

A SELECTED BIBLIOGRAPHY

Adams, C. C., *Islam and Modernism in Egypt*. London: Oxford University Press, 1933.

Ahmed, Jamal M., *The Intellectual Origins of Egyptian Nationalism*. New York: Oxford University Press, 1960.

Anderson, M. S., *The Eastern Question*. New York: The Macmillan Company, 1966.

Antonius, George, *The Arab Awakening: The Story of the Arab National Movement* (4th ed.). Beirut: Khayyat's, 1961.

Berkes, Niyazi, *The Development of Secularism in Turkey*. Montreal: McGill University Press, 1964.

Browne, E. G., *The Persian Revolution*. London: Frank Cass, 1966.

Curzon, George, *Persia and the Persian Question*. London: Frank Cass, 1966.

Earle, Edward Mean, *Turkey, the Great Powers and the Baghdad Railway: A Study in Imperialism*. New York: The Macmillan Company, 1923.

Emin, Ahmed, *The Development of Modern Turkey as Measured by Means of Its Press*. New York: Columbia University Press, 1968.

Herold, J. C., *Bonaparte in Egypt*. London: Hamilton, 1962.

Hoskins, Halford L., *British Routes to India*. New York: Longmans, Green & Co., 1928.

Hourani, Albert, *Arabic Thought in the Liberal Age, 1798–1939*. London: Oxford University Press, 1963.

Hurewitz, J. C., *Diplomacy in the Near and Middle East* (Vol. I, 1535–1914). Princeton, N.J.: D. Van Nostrand Co., 1956.

Issawi, Charles, ed., *The Economic History of the Middle East, 1800–1914*. Chicago: University of Chicago Press, 1966.

Jach, Ernest, ed., *Background of the Middle East*. New York: Cornell University Press, 1952.

Keddie, Nikki R., *Religion and Rebellion in Iran, The Iranian Tobacco Protest of 1891–1892*. London: Frank Cass, 1966.

———, *An Islamic Response to Imperialism: Political and Religious Writing of Sayyid Jamal al-Din "al-Afghani."* Berkeley, Calif.: University of California Press, 1968.

Kedourie, Elie, *Afghani and 'Abduh: An Essay on Religious Unbelief and Political Activism in Modern Islam*. London: Frank Cass, 1966.

Landes, David S., *Bankers and Pashas, International Finance and Economic Imperialism in Egypt*. Cambridge, Mass.: Harvard University Press, 1958.

Lerner, Daniel, *The Passing of Traditional Society: Modernizing the Middle East*. Glencoe, Ill.: The Free Press, 1958.

Mardin, Serif, *The Genesis of Young Ottoman Thought—A Study in Modernization of Turkish Political Ideas*. Princeton, N.J.: Princeton University Press, 1962.

Marlowe, John, *Arab Nationalism and British Imperialism: A Study in Power Politics*. London: The Cresset Press, 1961.

Puryear, Vernon J., *Napoleon and the Dardanelles*. Berkeley, Calif.: University of California Press, 1951.

Ramsaur, Ernest E., *The Young Turks*. Princeton, N.J.: Princeton University Press, 1957.

Rifaat, Mohammed, *The Awakening of Modern Egypt*. London: Longmans, Green & Co., 1947.

Saunders, J. J., ed., *The Muslim World on the Eve of Europe's Expansion*. Englewood Cliffs, N.J.: Prentice-Hall, 1966.

Shuster, Morgan, *The Strangling of Persia*. New York: The Century Co., 1912.

Von Grunebaum, G. E., ed., *Unity and Variety in Muslim Civilization*. Chicago: University of Chicago Press, 1955.

Yale, William, *The Near East*. Ann Arbor, Mich.: University of Michigan Press, 1958.

Amin, Osman, *Muhammad 'Abduh* (trans. C. Wendell). Washington, D.C.: American Council of Learned Societies, 1953.

Young, C. T., ed., *Near East Culture and Society*. Princeton, N.J.: Princeton University Press, 1951.

Zeine, Zeine N., *Arab-Turkish Relations and the Emergence of Arab Nationalism*. Beirut: Khayat's, 1958.

———, *The Struggle for Arab Independence*. Beirut: Khayat's, 1960.

PART FOUR

MODERN MIDDLE EAST

PRECEDING PAGE: *President Gamal Abdul Nasser of the United Arab Republic distributing land deeds to peasants* (COURTESY OF THE ARAB INFORMATION CENTER). ABOVE, TOP TO BOTTOM: *A bazaar in modern Istanbul, Turkey, on a Monday morning* (WIDE WORLD PHOTOS). *Jewish immigrants arriving in Israel* (COURTESY OF THE ISRAEL OFFICE OF INFORMATION). *Literacy corpsmen teaching in a Persian village* (COURTESY OF IRANIAN PRESS AND INFORMATION).

CHAPTER 26

THE NEW TURKEY

It was perhaps inevitable that the Ottoman empire should enter World War I on the side of the Central Powers. Russia was an old enemy and experience had shown the Turks that they could not always depend on the British and the French, especially when they were allies of Russia. On the other hand, Germany was a new power with whom they had not had adverse experiences. The Germans had extensive commercial enterprises in the empire, and the Kaiser's trips (1889 and 1898) had made favorable impressions. Furthermore, the triumvirate, Jemal, Enver, and Talat, who were running the empire, were pro-German and many a Turk believed that the coming of Germany would neutralize the power of Russia and Britain.

The war, however, brought the Ottoman empire to the verge of destruction. The bravery of the Turkish troops in numerous battles and their victory at Gallipoli were not enough to overcome the inner weaknesses of the empire. Long before Germany came to its knees the defeat of the Ottomans was a certainty. The term "verge of destruction" is used advisedly, because after the Armistice of Mudros, October 3, 1918, the Allied powers, especially Great Britain, did not want to utterly destroy the Ottoman empire. A weakened and subservient Ottoman state would serve the same purpose and would be just as effective a buffer against the new designs of a Russian state with communist ideology. The "sick man of Europe" was still useful and was to be kept alive in a nursing home administered by the western powers. It was during the struggle for independence between 1919–1923 that the Turks decided to destroy the sick man altogether and start anew. Consequently, the four years after World War I are more significant to the modern Turks than the four years of the war itself.

For the defeated Ottomans, there was only President Woodrow Wilson's word that "The Turkish portions of the present Ottoman empire should be assured a secure sovereignty." In secret agreements during the war (1915–1917) the Allies, without the knowledge of the United States, had divided Asia Minor among themselves. The only territory left for the Ottoman state was northern Anatolia. For the first time in history, the western European Powers agreed to Russia's control of the Straits. Perhaps to compensate for this, Great Britain had insisted, and France and Italy had reluctantly agreed, on giving the western end of Asia Minor south of the Dardanelles to Greece.

When the Bolsheviks took over the government of Russia, they annulled all agreements entered into by the previous governments and embarrassed their former allies by publishing the secret agreements. This, however, did not change the situation drastically, as is seen in the peace imposed upon the Ottomans by the Treaty of Sèvres on August 10, 1920. About the only difference was the new arrangement made for the territories given to Russia in the secret agreements. In the west, the Straits were internationalized under the League of Nations, but Istanbul remained under Turkish sovereignty. In the east, almost exactly the same territory which had been given to Russia was declared the independent state of Armenia. Furthermore, local autonomy was granted to the Kurds with a provision of a plebiscite and possible independence within a year.

In addition to the territorial dismemberment, the Turkish army was limited to 50,000 and subject to the advice of the Allied or neutral states. A financial commission representing Britain, France, and Italy was given control of all financial affairs of the state. Extraterritoriality was continued and the Turks had to give assurance as to the rights and privileges of the minorities within their boundaries. Humiliating as this treaty was, some historians believe that the Turks might have accepted it had not the Greeks been given a share of the spoils. Greece had been under the Ottoman rule for nearly three centuries. To see them brought back as masters was too bitter a pill for the Turks to swallow. Not only did the prospective gains of the Greeks arouse the Turks, but also the creation of Armenia, Kurdish autonomy, capitulations, and financial control, all of which were included in the Treaty of Sèvres. All of this, however, might have been forced upon them had it not been for one person. He was Mustafa Kemal Pasha, later known as Ataturk, who united the Turks and led them to victory.

Mention has already been made of Mustafa Kemal, who as a young officer had joined the Committee of Union and Progress. He did not have an active part in the coup d'etat of 1908 and at no time was he identified with the policies or practices of the Young Turks who had control of the government. He had his disagreements with the triumvirate but he was too good an officer to be pushed aside. His defense of Gallipoli won him national acclaim. Toward the end of the war, however, he was a disillusioned officer on the Syrian front. Whether it was by accident or by design will probably never be known, but in May of 1919 he was appointed inspector of the Third Army in Anatolia. On May 19, 1919, he landed on the Black Sea port of Samsun in northern Anatolia. This date became a national holiday in all Turkey.

Almost immediately after landing, he began to arouse the nation against the severe limitations which, thanks to the Bolshevik disclosure, everyone knew would be imposed on Turkey. In two conferences, one in Erzerum in July 1919, and the other one in Sivas in September of the same year, he organized the Committee for the Defense of Eastern Asia Minor. He sent a telegram to the sultan asking him to dismiss the Prime Minister and to call for a new election to the Ottoman Parliament. This the sultan proceeded to do. It must be remembered that Mustafa Kemal was a well-known hero. More important than this, the Third Army of Anatolia was intact and the Ninth Army under General Bekir, which had been carrying on successful campaigns in the Caucasus, had joined the nationalist cause. Mustafa Kemal was strong and the sultan was cognizant of this.

The result of the elections was a clear victory for the supporters of Kemal, and deputies from different parts of the country converged upon Istanbul. The British realized that it would be hard to cope with the decisions of such a Parliament and so they arrested the deputies and sent some of them to Malta. The sultan was forced to denounce the nationalists. The Shaykh ul-Islam, in what was to be the last *fetva* of any Shaykh ul-Islam, declared that the whole nationalist movement was against Islam. Not to be outdone, Mustafa Kemal gathered the clergy of Anatolia and then issued a counter fetva denouncing the Shaykh ul-Islam. In place of the disbanded Ottoman Parliament, the nationalists established the Grand National Assembly in Ankara, April 23, 1920.

With the creation of the Grand National Assembly, there were virtually two governments in Turkey, but the more powerful and popular one was the nationalist government in Ankara. Mustafa Kemal made excellent use of the opportunities which presented themselves. One of these was a quarrel among the Allies. After the war, the British and the French had serious misunderstandings in the Fertile Crescent, which led to recrimination and hostility. Furthermore, the French had much larger economic investments in Turkey than the British. French bond holders were afraid that the Turkish nationalists might cancel all debts the way the Bolsheviks had done. The Italians were not satisfied with the coming of the Greeks. Furthermore, Count Sforza, the Italian Commissioner in Istanbul, predicted a nationalist victory. Both France and Italy wanted to gain as much as they could without going to war and they did not mind wounding Britain in the process. Thus Italy and France made agreements with Mustafa Kemal, ceding their territories in return for economic concessions.

Perhaps the most important ally of Mustafa Kemal was the Soviet Union. Even though the doctrinaire Marxists among the Bolsheviks looked to Europe for the predicted proletarian revolution, there were enough "Asia firsters" among them to pay some attention to Iran and Turkey. As early as November 8, 1917, the Bolsheviks annulled all of the annexations of Tsarist Russia. In 1919, the Bolsheviks were very friendly to Mustafa Kemal and his revolution. Some of them went so far as to write that there was not much difference between the red flag of Turkey and the red flag of Russia. Mustafa Kemal was never a Communist, but he played along with them. In 1919, the Turkish Communist,

Shefi Degmer, founded the Socialist Workers and Peasants Party, which in 1922 became the Communist Party. In the World Communist Congress of 1922 there was one Turk in the executive committee. But when Mustafa Kemal became master of the situation in Turkey, he outlawed the Communist Party and arrested many, including Degmer.

The Bolsheviks were involved in a civil war of their own and were not in a position to give military assistance to Mustafa Kemal. But friendship with Lenin's government was good for Turkish morale and secured them from attack from the east. When the nationalist army under General Kiazim Bekir captured Kars from the Armenians, the Bolsheviks welcomed it. On December 3, 1920, they officially ceded Kars, Ardahan, and a large portion of eastern Asia Minor to the Turks. On March 16, 1921, Mustafa Kemal signed a treaty of friendship and collaboration with Russia against the western powers.

THE GRECO-TURKISH WAR

The Greeks were the protégés of the British and were used by them as agents to defeat the plans of the nationalists. The Greeks, furthermore, were overjoyed by the fact that their ancient enemy, the Turks, had been subdued and humiliated. In this they saw a great opportunity to establish their power in Asia Minor and perhaps even take control of Istanbul as the rightful heirs of the Byzantines. The Greeks landed in Smyrna on the western shore of Asia Minor on May 15, 1919.

British plans for the control of the Ottoman state were blocked by the resistance of Mustafa Kemal. Many of the British people, who had just finished a long and bloody war, were in no mood to fight against the nationalists in Turkey. Besides, informed and liberal public opinion in England did not support fighting against a people who were demanding self-determination. Under the circumstances, the best that Prime Minister Lloyd George could do was to help the Greeks to destroy Mustafa Kemal. The Greeks were only too eager to take advantage of this opportunity.

In June 1920, the Greek army moved eastward from Smyrna and won several victories. Brusa, the capital of the early Ottomans, was captured. These victories were not won easily and it was March 1921 before the Greeks were ready to start another offensive. Again they were successful and captured Kutaia, close to Ankara. The first check to Greek advance was at the battle of Sakarya (August 24 —September 16). A year later, August 1922, the Turks were able to launch an offensive which swept everything before them and within two weeks the Greeks were thrown back to the sea. Atrocities were committed by both sides, by the Greeks as they were retreating and by the Turks when they took Smyrna. The Greek dream was shattered and Mustafa Kemal went toward Istanbul.

TREATY OF LAUSANNE

Lloyd George sent a plea to his former allies to help defend the Straits against the Nationalists. But France and Italy responded by withdrawing their forces from the Straits. Great Britain was not in a position to fight and fortunately Mustafa Kemal did not want to provoke the western powers. Consequently, the convention of Mudania was signed, according to which eastern Thrace and Adrianople were ceded to Turkey, and Mustafa Kemal accepted the international control of the Straits.

By this time the Treaty of Sèvres was obsolete. Another conference met in Lausanne in 1922 to write a second treaty of peace. The chief antagonists were Lord Curzon for the British, and General Ismet Pasha, later known as Inönü, for Turkey. The imperious Curzon was reluctant to accede to the wishes of Turkish nationalists. Ismet Pasha, on the other hand, felt that time was on his side and was persistently patient. The main issues were the oil-rich province of Mosul which the Turks demanded, and the principle of extraterritoriality, which Lord Curzon did not want to relinquish. The conference was at last suspended, resuming again in July 1923. This time Lord Curzon was not there, and the Treaty of Lausanne was signed. Turkey was recognized as master of all of Asia Minor, the Straits, and eastern Thrace. Extraterritoriality was abolished. The Straits were internationalized under the League but the chairman of the commission was to be a Turk. The Straits were also demilitarized, but Turkey was allowed to keep a garrison of 12,000 in Istanbul. The Turks and the Greeks agreed to an exchange of population with the exception of the Greeks of Istanbul and the Turks of western Thrace. The question of Mosul was left to arbitration by the League of Nations. Mustafa Kemal and his associates had achieved their goal after four years of perseverance, sacrifice, diplomacy, and war. Kemalist Turkey was much smaller than the Ottoman empire, but it was more homogeneous and manageable and a strong viable state.

THE TURKISH REFORMS

For Mustafa Kemal, independence from foreign interference was not an end but only a means to give the Turks the opportunity to build a new Turkey. This could be done by far-reaching reforms in practically every aspect of life. Most of the reform programs launched by the nationalists under Mustafa Kemal had been proposed and discussed by scores of Turkish intellectuals and reformers from Tanzimat on. The most important contribution of Mustafa Kemal was not so much originality of ideas but the ability to choose a set of interrelated, consistent, and relevant ideas and build them into a practical program. He was more a child of the Young Turks than of the Young Ottomans and more a Turkist than a pan-Turkist. His idea of Turkification was not the imposition of Turkish language and culture on non-Turks, but getting rid of non-Turkish elements, including territories with non-Turkish populations.

Some of these ideas had been systematized by the famous sociologist Ziya Gökalp (1876–1924), whose writings influenced many a Turkish nationalist, including Mustafa Kemal. Gökalp separated culture and civilization and proposed to "graft western civilization in its entirety" to the Turkish national culture. The mistake of all past reformers, according to him, was their attempt to reconcile western civilization with that of the east. Civilizations, according to

Gökalp, are incompatible with each other and do not mix. The thing for the Turk to do was to divest himself of eastern civilization, revive his Turkish culture, and then graft western civilization to his culture. To Gökalp, "Turkish culture" is a combination of somewhat idealized folk mores, Islam, and some modern concepts, provided they are all expressed in Turkish. Turkism in religious matters meant reading the Koran and giving the call to prayer and praying in Turkish. In law it meant establishing "modern law," and in morality it meant going back to the early "democracy" of the Turks. Turkism was defined as a "scientific, philosophical, and literary movement," but not as political movement. Turkism, however, supported the "Peoples' Party . . . of our great Mustafa Kemal . . ." because he "delivered the country from invasion and, at the same time, called our state, nation, and language by their real name, . . ." that is, Turkish. Gökalp may be called the philosopher of a latter-day Turkish nationalism of which Kemal Ataturk was the executor and inspirator.

The Committee for the Defense of Eastern Asia Minor which, in 1919, had called the conferences at Erzerum and Sivas, gradually developed into the Peoples' Party, *Halk Firkasi*, in September 1923. This party had a six-point program which came to be known as the "Six Principles of Kemalism." It was not until 1937 that these were incorporated into the Turkish Constitution. All reforms, however, before the proclamation of the six principles and after, were based on them. These principles were:

1. Republicanism, which asserted the idea that sovereignty was vested in the people.
2. Nationalism, which claimed Turkey for the Turks and rejected jurisdiction over territories with non-Turkish population.
3. Populism, which did away with the millet system and proclaimed the equality of all classes of people before the law.
4. Statism, which accepted the necessity of the constructive intervention of the state in the national economy.
5. Secularism, which established the principle of the separation of religion and state.
6. Reformism, which emphasized the determination to change and bypass tradition and precedent if they do not serve national purpose.

It is important to note that notwithstanding violent vicissitudes, the death of Ataturk in 1938, and World War II, the above principles have remained without much modification. Furthermore, these and all the reforms carried out under them have been directed toward one major objective, namely the replacement of an eastern civilization with that of a western one. While the other countries of the Middle East have tried to reconcile the two civilizations, the Turks have attempted to turn their backs to the East and think of themselves as members of the European community.

Since Islam rejected the principle of the separation between spiritual and temporal, it penetrated all aspects of life and controlled all things by laws Not only prayer and pilgrimage, but government and commerce, peace and war, sex, marriage and divorce, and even food and attire were regulated either by the Koran and the hadith or by mores and customs which had become almost as binding. Consequently, all of the reforms which are discussed have some relationship to Islam. From 1922 to the death of Ataturk in 1938, the major activities of the government and people of Turkey consisted of abolishing institutions or laws or ways of life and substituting others in their place.

  1. *The Abolition of the Sultanate.* Soon after the military victory against the Greeks and the political victory against the British, the Grand National Assembly, on November 1, 1922, deposed Sultan Mehmed V. Perhaps in the mind of Ataturk the sultanate was doomed from the beginning, but he did not reveal this. In the Erzerum and Sivas Conferences in 1919, the delegates sympathized with the sultan and said that he was a "prisoner" of the Allies. As late as April 1921, even after the nationalists had been denounced by the Shaykh ul-Islam, the National Assembly, gathered in Haji Bayram Mosque in Ankara, prayed for the "holy" person of the sultan. Even though Mehmed V was gathering troops against them, the nationalists were asking the people to "liberate" the sultan-caliph from "captivity." These remarks were probably not made to induce a false security in the sultan, although they might have had that effect. The fact of the matter was that many of the nationalists in Ankara did not want the dissolution of the Ottoman Dynasty, but only a different sultan subject to a constitution. Even as the sultan and his family were boarding a British ship into exile, his cousin, Abdul Mejid, was designated caliph. Almost a year later, on October 29, 1923, the Grand National Assembly declared Turkey a Republic and chose Mustafa Kemal as its first president.

  2. *The Abolition of the Caliphate.* If the abolition of the sultanate offended many a Turk, the abolition of the caliphate offended all Sunni Muslims everywhere. This decision also was reached cautiously. Ataturk studied Islam and used to impress the Ankara clerics with his knowledge of it. He even tolerated the calling of a pan-Islamic conference at Sivas in February 1921. One fifth of the members of the Grand National Assembly were clerics. Many of Ataturk's associates wanted a liberal but Islamic state. Perhaps Ataturk, who had the reputation of being an agnostic, believed that if the state was Islamic it could not be liberal. In the public mind, however, Abdul Mejid the caliph could not be distinguished from Abdul Mejid the sultan. It had always been that way. To those who had some knowledge of Islam, the office of the caliph without the power of the sultan was an anomaly. The question was debated in the Assembly and, on March 3, 1924, the office of caliph was abolished. Abdul Mejid and the other members of the family of Osman, the founder of the Ottoman empire, were banished from Turkey. The Ottomans had ruled 625 years. The institution of the caliphate was not replaced by anything.

  3. *The Abolition of the Islamic Law.* The abolition of the sultanate and the caliphate did not affect the daily life of the average Turk. The end of the caliphate, however, marked the beginning of far-reaching reforms which affected every individual and rocked the country. One of the most important of these was the abolition of Islamic law, Shari'a. The judicial reforms of 1926 swept aside the religious courts and replaced them with Swiss civil and Italian penal

codes. This act disqualified the ulama, who had had virtual monopoly of the legal profession. Only those who had studied western law could pass the bar examination. Practically all of the schools for the teaching of Islamic law were closed. The department of Islamic Theology in the University of Istanbul was so small that it was combined with the department of literature. The office of Shaykh ul-Islam was abolished and in its place all religious matters were administered by two bureaus attached to the office of the Prime Minister. One of them was the Bureau of Religious Affairs, which licensed preachers, censored sermons, and gave occasional advice on the intricacies of the Shari'a. The second was the Bureau of Religious Foundation, *evkaf*, which administered all religious endowments.

The Islamic law was replaced by European law, and it probably was the hope of some of the leaders to replace the religious attitude of the intellectuals with scientific positivism. Not only was theocracy rejected as a method of government, but the religious character of the nation was abandoned. Ataturk stated, "We now admit science and civilization as principles of life and strength" and regard the principles of secularism as the "single factor of existence."

4. *The Abolition of the Islamic Calendar.* In the same year (1926) that Shari'a was put aside, the Muslim calendar was replaced by the Christian calendar. For many years Turkish business firms were in the habit of using both Muslim lunar dates and the western solar dates. All Muslim festivals and religious dates were according to the Muslim calendar. The state, however, adopted the western calendar and ordered the citizens to use it exclusively, this was another step away from the east and closer to the west. With the change of calendar came also the change of the capital. Istanbul was too Ottoman and "foreign" to suit the new mentality. Ankara was located in Anatolia where the "real" Turks lived. Istanbul had numerous mosques, but in the new city built next to the old town of Ankara, no mosques were erected. Furthermore, since Ankara's location was in the center of a farming district, the officials of the government could not, like the old Ottomans, avoid the Turkish peasants who lived all around them.

5. *The Abolition of the Arabic Alphabet.* Even though all Muslims had not adopted the Arabic language as was hoped by the early conquerors, all Muslims, no matter what their language, adopted the Arabic alphabet. The main purpose of education was to be able to read the Koran even though they could not understand the words. The Turkish Assembly in 1928 replaced the Arabic alphabet with Latin symbols adapted to suit the needs of Turkish language Ataturk ordered the Koran to be translated into Turkish and published it in the new alphabet. He also ordered the call to prayer to be given in Turkish and tried to persuade the people to pray in Turkish. Not all of the Muslim were persuaded to pray in Turkish, but with the change of alphabet the new generation of Turks could not read the Koran in Arabic. Only the very devout took the trouble to teach their children the rudiments of the Arabic alphabet

The purpose of Ataturk in changing the alphabet was not to prevent the Turks from reading the Koran. He wanted to reduce illiteracy and develop a uniform and logical Turkish language. He rightly concluded that it was easier for a Turk to learn to read and write with the use of the Latin alphabet. He and the members of the Assembly each took a blackboard to the villages and towns and proved that the Latin alphabet was an easier medium. The introduction of a new alphabet was a staggering undertaking in the printing of books for the growing schools of the country, but it was done. Turks everywhere knew for the first time how a word was to be pronounced by the way it was written.

6. *The Abolition of Titles.* The continuation of titles, such as bey, pasha, and others, was against the principle of populism, which asserted the equality of all classes of people before the law. In later Ottoman times, titles had been sold to the highest bidder and created a false class stratification. In 1934 all titles were abolished and Turks were ordered to choose family names. No two families were allowed the same name unless the one who had chosen it first gave his consent. Many were encouraged to choose purely Turkish names. It was in conformity with this law that Mustafa Kemal was given the name Ataturk, Father of the Turks, by the Assembly.

7. *The Abolition of Turkish Attire for Men.* Like Peter the Great in Russia earlier, Ataturk, in his program of westernization, forced the Turks to wear European clothes. No doubt both men thought that a change in attire might change the outlook of a person. If a person wore a European hat, he might be persuaded to think like a European. The Turks might not have minded the change to European coats and trousers if they had been allowed to wear the fez, but Ataturk insisted on the use of the hat. The Turks had forgotten that the fez itself was introduced in the nineteenth century as a sign of modernization. The fez, however, was compatible with Muslim practice in a way which the hat was not. In prayer the Muslims cover their heads. Since one of the postures of prayer is prostration and touching the forehead to the ground, European hats presented a problem. But the Turks changed, the faithful learned to pray with bare heads or with a cap turned backwards.

8. *The Abolition of the Veil.* If a modest Muslim woman wanted to follow the general directions of the Koran she would be dressed somewhat like a Roman Catholic nun. The origin of the veil which covers the face of the woman is obscure. But, un-Koranic as it is, the custom has been identified with Islam and followed it wherever it went. As the first step toward the emancipation of women, the veil was abolished and Turkish women began to take part in all aspects of national life. In 1934 they were given the right to vote. Polygamy was abolished and soon women were seen as teachers, lawyers, doctors, office workers, and even members of the Grand National Assembly.

9. *The Abolition of Mosque Schools.* In the Ottoman empire, all education had been under the control of the ulama. Beside each mosque there was usually a school. In small towns, the mosque was used as a school in which the main purposes were to learn to read the Koran, to pray, and to perform the basic rituals of Islam. Those who wanted to go further attended special schools for the train-

ing of the ulama. From Tanzimat days in the middle of the nineteenth century, European-type schools began to appear, though their number was not large. Under the Republic, education was taken away from the ulama. The government built western-type schools and education was proclaimed to be universal and free. It was easy to make education free but to make it universal would take decades to accomplish.

10. The Abolition of Friday as a Day of Rest. This was accomplished in 1935. The rationale for it was theological, cultural, and economic. It was argued that the main purpose of the three main religions of the Middle East, Judaism, Christianity, and Islam, was the same, namely that there should be one day of rest during the week. The fact that Jews had Saturday, Christians Sunday, and Muslims Friday was pure accident and irrelevant to the main issue. Furthermore, since all of the western nations had Sunday and the Turks wanted to be like the Europeans, they might as well adopt Sunday. Keeping Friday as a holiday, it was pointed out, had dire economic consequences. Most of the business of Turkey was with Europe, which was closed on Sunday. If Turkey insisted on closing on Friday, she would then lose three days in a week, since the Saturday in between would also be sacrificed. Turkey could not afford so much leisure. Turkey has remained the only Muslim country in which Friday is not a national holiday.

11. The Abolition of Non-Turkish Words. The Turkish language had borrowed heavily from Arabic and Persian. Turkish writers and intelligentsia had written and spoken for each other. The bulk of the population, who did not know Arabic or Persian, could not understand them. In a genuine desire to reach the masses and in a surge of understandable nationalism, the nationalists threw away as many Arabic and Persian words as they could and replaced them with "Turkish" words. Almost every week newspapers published a list of these words. In many cases where they could not find a Turkish word, they preferred a European word to an Arabic or Persian one. In the same spirit, they also changed many place names, such as Izmir for Smyrna and Edirne for Adrianople.

One of the most important programs, and one which caused the Turkish Republic more trouble in later years, was in the field of economics. Many of the above reforms were not popular among the Turks, but the principle of government's interference in economic matters was even less popular. In the Ottoman days, most of the commerce was in the hands of Greeks and Armenians. With the exchange of population with Greece, and the general flight of Armenians during World War I, the Republic was faced with a great shortage of trained businessmen. It was deemed all the more necessary for the government to intervene.

In the 1930's, French experts advised the government in all aspects of economic life. New banks were established to help in agriculture, industry, mining, commerce, and finance. The government took control of all planning and state monopolies were established in tobacco, salt, liquor, matches, playing cards, munitions, etc. Roads were built, factories were established, and foreign invest ment and trade were encouraged. A gradual nationalization of railroads was accomplished. The purpose was to make Turkey economically independent, and to do this the Turks were required to work and sacrifice.

None of these reforms, religious, social, or economic, was easily accomplished. If it had not been for the power and popularity of Ataturk, not much would have been achieved. In the constitution adopted in 1924, democracy was proclaimed and it was declared that sovereignty was vested in the nation. In practice, however, Ataturk was a dictator whose word was law. Some of his associates criticized him on his dictatorship. There were others who objected to some of the reforms. In the purge of 1926, some of them lost their lives and others, like General Kiazim Bekir, the hero of the war against the Greeks, and Halide Edib, the novelist and perhaps the first Turkish woman to serve as a soldier in the front lines, were banished. In the general election of 1927, when Ataturk's Peoples' Party had won, partly for encouragement and partly in self-justification, he gave a speech which lasted six days. He began with, "On May 19, 1919, I landed at Samsun," and ended with, "Our nation cannot die; if that ever happens, the world cannot support the bier."

Ataturk was a benevolent dictator, one who was not aloof. His dictatorship was similar to the dictatorship of a coach training his athletes. In 1930, he asked one of his friends to organize an opposition party, but the venture failed. The Peoples' Party remained the only party, but in 1935, 16 independent deputies were elected. Without the use of power, the reforms would have failed. Perhaps the effectiveness of Ataturk's dictatorship can be shown by the fact that in 1926, had there been a free choice, most of the reforms would have been rejected. In 1947, however, when there was a free election, most of the reforms were endorsed.

In foreign policy, Turkey followed a cautious and peaceful attitude. Its relation with Russia remained correct, but the issue of communism drew them apart. Ataturk was closer to the countries of western Europe and the United States. He had to compromise on the Mosul question. Turkey was given 10 per cent of the oil royalties for giving up its claim on that territory. He was successful in his negotiation with the French on the port of Alexandrata (Iskandrun) on the Mediterranean; the French ceded it to Turkey over the opposition of the Syrians. The question of the Straits eventually was settled to the satisfaction of Turkey. On July 20, 1936, the Montreux Convention was called, in which the Soviet Union was also a participant. The spector of Hitler and the growing friendship between him and Mussolini persuaded Britain and France to accommodate Turkey. In peacetime and in a war in which Turkey was neutral there would be freedom of passage for all. If Turkey was belligerent, only vessels of countries not at war with Turkey enjoyed freedom. More important than these and other provisions were the abolition of the International Straits Commission, which restored the jurisdiction to the Turks, and the permission for the Turks to militarize the Straits.

On November 10, 1938, Ataturk died of cirrhosis. His death was premature and aggravated most likely by overwork, overdrinking, and overindulgence. He had created a strong and viable state out of the ruins of the Ottoman empire. A grateful people mourned him sadly. For almost the first time in 500 years, power in Turkey passed to a successor, Ismet Inönü, without bloodshed and according to the rules laid down in a constitution.

CHAPTER 27

EGYPT—STRUGGLE
FOR INDEPENDENCE

On December 18, 1914, a few months after the beginning of World War I, Great Britain declared openly what had been a reality for decades. It announced that Egypt was a protectorate of Great Britain and no longer under the control of the Ottoman empire, nominal as that had been. Fortunately for Great Britain, Khedive Abbas Hilmi, who was anti-British, was in Istanbul at the time. He was deposed in absentia and his uncle Husayn Kamal was chosen in his place. The new ruler was not called a Khedive but was promoted to "sultan."

The British took great pride in their record in Egypt. They had brought peace to a country ridden with strife and prosperity to a bankrupt people. They had also given the Egyptians an efficient administration. But there were also failures, and the younger generation of Egyptians saw only these. There was practically no social change to match the efficient administration. Turko-Egyptians still constituted the ruling class. It was they and their relatives who owned most of the land. The *fellahin*, or peasants, still lived in squalor, paid the taxes, and supplied forced labor. The ulama administered the sacred law, which seemed to have less and less to say about either the struggle of the poor or the idleness of the rich. Banking, business, shipping, and finance were in the hands of foreigners, British, French, Italians, Greeks, Armenians, and others who, because of their foreign passports, enjoyed capitulatory (extraterritorial) rights and had all the advantages but ran practically none of the risks. Indeed, the British government was there to safeguard their interests.

Egypt was relatively prosperous and orderly and the more so it became, the more did the British become reluctant to relinquish their hold. The famed British Commissioner, Lord Cromer, and his successors had a condescending attitude toward the Egyptians, believing that they had a "tendency to shirk their responsibility" and could not be trusted with the administration of Egypt. Under Cromer the administration was efficient and paternal, but just. His successors, however, Gorst and Kitchener, did not impress the Egyptians with either their efficiency or their justice. Positions that were filled by Egyptians under Cromer were given to Englishmen, and with bigger salaries. Foreign concession seekers, profiteers, and usurers flooded the country and took advantage of capitulation privileges. The pan-Islamists and the ulama in general bemoaned the British "Christian rule." Educated civil servants, professors, lawyers, and newspapermen took pages out of the books of European liberal writers and politicians and used them against the British. For the Egyptian nationalists, it was an exhilarating experience to quote British authors against British imperialism.

Almost all of the Egyptians who were politically aware joined the anti-British movement. They did not have a united purpose except to oust the British. They were journalists, small landlords, older bureaucrats who hated to work under young Englishmen, pan-Islamists, frustrated politicians, and nationalists who hoped for an independent Egypt. Khedive Abbas Hilmi was demanding independence and, for a time, worked hand-in-hand with some nationalists against the British. A younger generation had appeared which had not experienced the condition of Egypt before the British occupation in 1882 and did not appreciate what the British had accomplished. Furthermore, they did not have the patience of the older generation and were more aggressive in their attitudes.

The war years, however, were relatively peaceful. There were thousands of British, Australian, New Zealander, and Indian troops in Egypt. Martial law was proclaimed and the army was supreme. Throughout the war Rushdi Pasha was Prime Minister. If the Egyptians were on the side of the Central Powers, they did not show it. But though the presence of so many foreign soldiers must have wounded the pride of the nationalists, they did not try to sabotage the British war machine. With so much military spending there were severe shortages and rocketing inflation, but no riots. The British commandeered forced labor for the Western Front in France, but no one objected openly, least of all the peasants for whom forced labor was a daily occurrence. Sultan Husayn Kamil of Egypt died in 1917 and his brother Fuad succeeded him.

THE WAFD PARTY

The eruption which started after the conclusion of the war shocked the British out of a peaceful slumber. In their state of shock and surprise, however, all they did was tighten their grip and give a negative answer to all the Egyptians' demands. A foundation for Egyptian nationalism had been laid, but what sparked the movement for independence was Woodrow Wilson's Fourteen Points, especially his principle of self-determination. The latent influence of the United States on the minds of leading nationalists of the Middle East through the liberal views of President Wilson, cannot be exaggerated. All of them wanted to send delegations to the Paris Peace Conference in the hope that Wilson's presence and influence would gain them a hearing and recognition.

The Egyptians also wanted to go, and the person who assumed leadership ,as Sa'd Zaghlul Pasha (1857–1927). He was a friend of Abduh and one-time :udent of Afghani. As a judge he was active in reforming the laws of Egypt ccording to modern needs. In 1906 Zaghlul was made Minister of Education nder Cromer, with whom he was on good terms. Perhaps because of his dis- ke for Gorst and Kitchener, Zaghlul resigned and was elected a deputy to the .gyptian Assembly. In November 1918 he sought permission of the British uthorities to lead a delegation (*wafd*) to the peace conference. He was not per- nitted to do so. Then he asked to go to London and put Egypt's case before the ·ritish authorities, but this was also denied. The British argued that Zaghlul ad not been "elected" by the Egyptians to represent them, which was true, ut they failed to recognize that he was voicing what was in the mind of most of 1e nationalists. Zaghlul persuaded the Prime Minister Rushdi Pasha to ask to o to Paris. Rushdi also was refused permission and he resigned the premier- 1ip. In the meantime, during the first months of 1919, Zaghlul had formed the Vafd Party and, with this backing, he tried to prevent the sultan from appoint- 1g a new Prime Minister. The British responded by arresting Zaghlul and a ·w of his associates. Zaghlul was exiled to Malta. By this time, the idea of :nding a delegation, *wafd*, had become a *cause célèbre*, and thousands rushed to)in the Wafd Party. Zaghlul's exile ignited a conflagration. Riots, general :rikes, burning of foreigners' houses, and the killing of British soldiers became 1e order of the day. This was the first of many riots which were to shake Egypt ntil well after World War II.

The British reacted by tightening their grip even more closely. But the leaders f the general strike insisted on the "Delegation." Lord Allenby, the conqueror f Jerusalem, was sent to Cairo to maintain order. In the end there was no ther way out but to free Zaghlul and let him lead his delegation to Paris. Ie did not accomplish much in Paris or later in London. But he had become ery popular at home and returned in triumph.

'ARTIAL INDEPENDENCE

The British came to the conclusion that some sort of a compromise was ecessary. In December 1919, they did what became a habit of theirs in periods f unrest between the two great wars—they sent a commission to study and eport. The Wafdists, on the other hand, set an example which was followed by 1ost of the Arab leaders in Palestine until World War II—they boycotted the ommission.

Lord Milner, the head of the commission, finished his investigation in March 920 and reported his recommendations. The British government was asked to ive up the protectorate for a treaty of alliance with an "independent" Egypt, ·ith the following conditions. Egypt was to have a constitutional monarchy. 'he British were to have the right to defend Egypt, "guide" its foreign relations, nd control the Suez Canal. Negotiations broke down because Zaghlul did not accept the terms. The British tried to reach an agreement without Zaghlul and that also failed. In 1921 there were more riots and bloodshed. Zaghlu and some of his associates were exiled again, this time to Aden.

On February 28, 1922, the British unilaterally terminated the protectorate and declared Egypt's independence. Sultan Fuad assumed the title of King Malik. (Sultan also means king but it was discarded perhaps because of its association with the Ottomans). Thus Egypt became the first Arabic-speaking state to achieve at least partial independence. Not much had actually changed under the new arrangement. The four points "absolutely reserved to the discretion of His Britanic Majesty's Government" were (1) the security of the Imperial communication in Egypt, (2) defense of Egypt, (3) protection o foreign interests and minorities, and (4) control over the Sudan.

In 1923, King Fuad promulgated a constitution that provided for a bicamera legislature, which granted great power to the king. He could dissolve the Parliament, appoint and dismiss ministers, or rule by decree if he wished. He had vete power, which could only be overruled by two thirds majority. He was com mander in chief of the armed forces and could appoint two fifths of the member of the senate. At the same time the constitution was proclaimed there was also an announcement of general elections. Under the general amnesty proclamation Sa'd Zaghlul returned to Egypt and in the election of January 1924, the Wafd Party won a landslide—199 seats against 27. Zaghlul was made Prime Minister and immediately pressed for the revision of the unilateral declaration of indepen dence. He called for complete sovereignty in Egypt and the Sudan.

The Wafd Party dominated the political scene in Egypt until 1952. It had a wide base of support and was very popular. The Wafd not only negotiated but also led in strikes, riots, and even terroristic activities. During most of the years before 1952, it dominated the Parliament. The Premiership, the appoint ment to which office was a prerogative of the king, usually went to an anti Wafdist. Consequently, the cabinet and the Parliament were at loggerheads and the winner of this conflict was usually the king or the British or both. There were other political parties in Egypt. One was the Liberal Constitutional Party founded in 1922, by Muhammad Mahmud Pasha. It usually represented the aristocracy and landlords. Another was the Union (Ittihad) Party founded in 1925 by Yahya Ibrahim Pasha. It represented the interests of the palace. A third was the Peoples' (Sha'b) Party, founded in 1930 by Isma'il Sidqi. This wa formed on the founder's personality and did not have much mass following. In 1932, the Wafd Party split and the insurgents formed the Sa'di Wafd Party under Ahmad Maher and Nukrashi Pasha. All of these parties were more mod erate than the Wafd and were willing to collaborate with the British or the king or both.

Nationalists in general neglected economic and social conditions because they spent all their energies in trying to oust the British. Indeed, they tended to blame everything on the British and to believe that if the British went out o Egypt by one door, progress and prosperity would come in by the other. Grea

Britain, on the other hand, was still interested in controlling the road to India, and in safeguarding foreign economic interests in Egypt. Aside from the needs of the empire, the British did not assume much responsibility except in maintaining "law and order." Taxes were heavy on the masses and small landowners. Since Egyptian long staple cotton was the best in the world, more and more land went into cotton plantations to supply the need of British textile industries. In 20 years, from 1917 to 1937, the population of Egypt rose by a staggering 25 per cent, but land under cultivation remained constant and consequently the level of living went down.

There were more riots in 1924, and on November 19 of the same year Sir Lee Stack, the British Commander in Chief of the Egyptian army and Governor General of the Sudan, was assassinated. The British met this rebellion with strong reprisals and demanded punishment of the culprits, an apology, and an indemnity of $1,500,000. Furthermore, they forbade political demonstrations and ordered the withdrawal of Egyptian troops from the Sudan. They also demanded that British advisors be retained in the Finance, Justice, and Interior departments. Perhaps most stringent of all was the threat that the area of cultivation in the Sudan's Gezira would be extended. Such an act would channel the Nile water for irrigation and decrease the flow of water into Egypt. Without the Nile there would be no Egypt. Since the flow of water in the Nile can be controlled from the Sudan, Egypt has always had a great interest in the government of the Sudan.

ANGLO-EGYPTIAN SUDAN

During 1881, a certain Muhammad Ahmad had claimed to be the Mahdi (messiah) sent to deliver the Muslims. This started the famous Mahdi movement which embroiled the Sudan for a number of years. The situation in Egypt was too chaotic, because of the 'Urabi revolt, for anyone (British or Egyptian) to bother about the Mahdi. Consequently, his power grew and the Anglo-Egyptian garrison in Khartoum was in danger. In 1884, Lord Cromer sent General Gordon to evacuate Khartoum, but the latter delayed the operation and was cut down by the Mahdi's forces. For over a decade, the Mahdi had control of all the Sudan. In 1896, Lord Kitchener took Dongola, the headquarters of the Mahdi, and two years later routed him in the battle of Omdurman. This led to an agreement between Britain and Egypt which is commonly called the "Condominium." According to this document, which was signed on January 19, 1899, the Sudan was ruled by a governor-general chosen by the British but appointed by the Khedive. Laws of the Sudan were made by the governor-general and the laws of Egypt were not valid in the territory. While Egyptian goods were free from import duties, no power was allowed to establish a consulate in the Sudan without permission of the British government. Slavery was abolished and the Brussels Act of 1890 governed the import, sale, and the manufacture of munitions and liquors. Henceforth, the region was called

"Anglo-Egyptian Sudan," but as might be expected the voice of Egypt wa even weaker in the Sudan than it was in Egypt.

Since the Condominium had already recognized the legitimacy of the Egyp tian interest in the Sudan, Zaghlul considered the British demand of 192 that Egypt withdraw its troops from the Sudan outrageous. Many leading Egyp tians looked upon the further threat of diverting the Nile's waters for the irriga tion of the Gezira as an act tantamount to a declaration of war. In rejecting th ultimatum, Zaghlul resigned and Ziwar Pasha became Prime Minister. H then accepted the ultimatum. The British, however, implemented all the point of the ultimatum except that concerning the irrigation of the Gezira. As result of the riots of 1924, the British got a stronger hold on Egyptian affairs and Egypt lost all voice in the affairs of the Sudan.

Sa'd Zaghlul died in 1927, and leadership of the Wafd Party went to Naha Pasha. The change of leadership, however, did not make negotiation betwee the British and the Wafd any smoother. Basic problems remained. The Britis wanted a bilateral agreement which continued British dominance and th Wafd wanted evacuation of British troops from Egypt, and control of the Sudan Negotiations ended in 1930 and were not resumed until five years later. Th position of the Wafd was weakened by the death of Zaghlul, the existence c other parties, and the open hostility of the king. Despite this weakened position the Wafd won the elections again in 1929. King Fuad, rather than appoint Wafdist Prime Minister, dissolved the Parliament, appointed Sidqi Pasha, th leader of the Peoples' Party, as Premier, and revoked the constitution of 1923 In the new constitution which Fuad promulgated in 1930, he gave himself mor power and introduced a two-grade indirect voting system. As a result of thes measures, he and Sidqi Pasha ruled without effective opposition until 1934

EGYPTIAN INDEPENDENCE

The Italian invasion of Ethiopia in 1935 changed the complexion of Anglo Egyptian relationships. The British were all the more intent on the defense o the Suez, because they were afraid of Italian propaganda in Egypt against th British. On the whole, the British were anxious to reach some sort of a bilatera agreement with the Egyptians. The strong man, Sidqi Pasha, had resigned th year before because of ill health, and the Wafdists, together with the othe parties, did not hide their dislike of the constitution of 1930. In 1935, followin the advice of the British, King Fuad suspended the 1930 constitution, but agains their advice he reinstated the 1923 constitution. Accordingly, elections wer held in 1935 and the Wafd won again. Fuad died in April of 1935, and hi 16-year-old son, Faruq, was proclaimed king. The Egyptians mourned Fua sincerely and received Faruq very enthusiastically, thereby presenting a parado to the observers of the Egyptian scene. On the one hand, the Egyptians showe a high regard for the institution of monarchy and the person of the king but, o the other hand, they repeatedly defeated the palace party and elected the anti monarchical Wafd.

By 1936, the Wafd Party was older, mellower, and corruptible. The four years of Sidqi "dictatorship" had taught Nahas Pasha and the Wafd Party that politics was the art of the possible and not the demand of the absolute. Moreover, Egyptians of all parties were also apprehensive about the Italian threat and did not think that Italians as masters were preferable to the British. Events had prepared both the British and the Egyptians for negotiations.

The British entered negotiations with Nahas Pasha, the new Prime Minister, and on August 26, 1936, signed a treaty of alliance recognizing Egypt as a sovereign state. After solemnly stating in the first Article that "the military occupation of Egypt by the forces of His Majesty the King [of England] and Emperor is terminated," it goes on in sixteen additional articles to define the nature of Egypt's independence. On the positive side, as far as the Egyptians were concerned, were provisions such as the appointment of ambassadors between the two countries, possibility of Egyptian membership in the League of Nations, abolition of capitulations, return of Egyptian troops to the Sudan, and unrestricted Egyptian immigration to the Sudan. On the negative side, however, there were articles which limited the sovereignty of Egypt. These were the implication that Great Britain was responsible for the defense of Egypt, the responsibility of Egypt to put at the disposal of Great Britain in time of war "all the facilities and assistance . . . including the use of . . . ports, aerodromes, and means of communication." Furthermore, Great Britain was permitted to station not more than 10,000 troops and 400 pilots in the Suez Canal area for its defense. The agreement was for 20 years.

Britain had not given up much, but the Egyptians had received more than they expected. Consequently, the Wafd Party accepted the treaty and the Egyptian Parliament ratified it on December 22, 1936. On May 8, 1937, capitulations were abolished, and on May 26 of the same year Egypt was admitted to the League of Nations. For a time, Nahas Pasha, as Prime Minister and regent for the minor king, had absolute control of the country. But Faruq came of age in 1937 and once more the old rivalry between the palace and Wafd started. The king dismissed Nahas Pasha and chose the non-Wafdist Mahmud Pasha, who had to cope with a Wafdist Parliament. The Wafd Party had lost a good deal of its virility and influence in the course of years. Nahas Pasha did not have the charisma of Zaghlul. Among the leaders of the Wafd who had enjoyed positions of leadership, and had developed personal vested interests, some had become corrupt and others just old and tired. Furthermore, they had lost the anti-British zeal which had made them so popular. Later, young nationalists were to denounce the Treaty of 1936 as a "shotgun marriage" and blamed the Wafd for it.

SOCIAL AND INTELLECTUAL ATMOSPHERE

Egyptian men of affairs were understandably preoccupied with the British between the two wars and did not pay much attention to social reform. Neither were the British interested in social or economic reform any more than they had been before the war. Indeed, the British had relinquished responsibility for the development of Egypt unilaterally in 1920 and by agreement with Egypt in 1936, while continuing the occupation of the country. Nevertheless, changes did occur by force of circumstance and without conscious planning on the part of anyone in particular.

During World War I, inflation and shortage of consumer goods hurt the villagers and small-town people, but in Cairo and Alexandria and other cities where the soldiers were stationed, there was a business boom. The urban population made huge profits and the farmers in search of work and food rushed to the cities. Land prices rose in the cities and housing rents rose from 60 per cent to 100 per cent. Cotton was in great demand and construction in the cities was going on at a rapid pace. All of this brought a nouveau riche class into being, which joined the old wealthy class and developed a political front made up of landlords, businessmen, and professionals. These were united to protect their economic gains and, at the same time, to wrest power from Great Britain.

The war needs brought some industrialization. In 1920, the Misr Bank was established and this bank gradually developed an industrial combine with subsidiaries in cotton, silk, woolens, cigarettes, soap, shipping, insurance, motion pictures, and other enterprises. In 1922, the Egyptian Federation of Industries was established and by 1937 it had some 430 members. A new commercial middle class was created which prospered and allied itself with the less prosperous but more articulate middle class made up of white-collar workers, intelligentsia, and civil servants. This commercial class did not try to destroy the landed gentry but married into it and formed a governing class which comprised about 20 per cent of the population. The remaining 80 per cent of the people lived in the rural areas; 90 per cent of these were illiterate.

The new industries created new needs and the satisfaction of these needs changed the mode and values of life. The press, radio, and telephone, as well as the new industries, demanded a new type of education. Between the two wars and up to the revolution of 1952 there were two types of education, each independent of the other and each performing in a closed circuit of its own. There was the venerable Azhar University which, oblivious of the world outside its walls, represented the older, religious type of education. Most of the Shaykhs of Azhar rejected modernism and did not see any need for change. Even men like Muhammad Abduh, who believed in the necessity of institutional change to fit new situations, did not intend any basic theological reconstruction. The Azharites did not debate doctrine. The modern schools, on the other hand, were hostile to Azhar and developed a system of values all their own. It is not that they rejected Islam, but they imported both content and method of education from the West and were insulated from the influences of Azhar and the latter's insistence on the Shari'a. Thus western ways were not too slow in coming to Egypt. Men wore European clothes, women came out without the veil, European laws became popular, and child marriage was abolished. As the nouveaux riches became more westernized, the Shaykhs became more rigid and people like Abduh, who were trying to steer a middle course, were forgotten.

At the time of the independence of Egypt in 1936 there were, intellectually and religiously speaking, four distinct groups. With two of these groups, namely the ultraconservatives of Azhar and the moderate reform school of Abduh, we are already familiar. The third was the militant Muslim groups and the fourth, the proponents of a secular state.

THE MUSLIM BROTHERHOOD

At least three factors brought into being the militant Muslim groups which wielded great influence in Egypt until well after World War II. One was the presence of the British and the humiliation devout Muslims felt in being ruled by Christians. Another was the rapid secularization of the Egyptian educated and middle classes, and the corresponding deterioration of Muslim laws and institutions. A third was the threat of Turkey and, as it appeared to Egyptian eyes, the complete de-Islamization of that country. The abolition of the caliphate by the Turks so alarmed the Shaykhs of Azhar that they called a conference on the caliphate in May 1926. Of the 38 delegates, one third were Egyptians. The conference was inconclusive, but it revealed the seriousness of the situation to Egyptians and other Muslims.

The militant Muslims were spiritual heirs of the fundamentalist Wahhabis of Arabia[1] and the militant Jamal al-Din al-Afghani.[2] By far the most important, influential, and largest of the militant groups organized between the two wars in Egypt was the Muslim Brotherhood, *Jam'iyat al-Ikhwan al-Muslimin*. It was started in the city of Ismailia on the Canal in 1928 by a 22-year-old school teacher, Hasan al-Banna. He and six young companions started the movement with nothing but a strong faith in the sufficiency of Islam and complete dedication to the cause. In a relatively short time it had become a very strong force in Egypt and other Muslim countries, and was still a power to be reckoned with 40 years after its founding. In its missionary zeal and organization it was similar to the medieval Ismai'li group called the Brethren of Sincerity.[3] In its militancy and method it had copied another Ismai'li organization, the Assassins.

The energetic and capable young leader of the Brotherhood was not a Shi'i like the Isma'ilis but a strict Sunni brought up in a family which belonged, like the Wahhabis, to the fundamentalist Hanbali school. He borrowed, however, the Isma'ili table of organization. Hasan al-Banna as the absolute leader of the Brotherhood was called *Murshid al-'Am*, or "Guide General." A select group of missionaries who worked under him were called *da'i*, or devotees, the same name used by the Isma'ilis. The general headquarters of the movement in Cairo was called *dar*, and from these modern offices the supreme leader administered the varied programs of the Brotherhood.

The Muslim Brotherhood was a militant group which believed in the sufficiency and supremacy of Islam and in the literal interpretation of the Koran

[1] See above, p. 242.
[2] See above, p. 244.
[3] See above, p. 110.

and the Sunna. It worked for the revival of the principle of jihad, holy war. Unlike the Wahhabis, however, it believed in reform and in the utilization of certain western methods. Unlike Abduh, the Brotherhood did not think that a restatement of Islamic doctrine was necessary. It was strongly against the secularization of Muslim life and worked for the reinstatement of the laws of the Koran. It was pan-Islamic and preached military preparedness on the part of all Muslims. "A strong army," the Brotherhood proclaimed, "is more important than prayer or fasting." It emphasized government by Allah for Muslims, with Koranic tolerance for the minorities, provided they stay loyal to the government of Islam.

The above objectives and ideas were implemented and taught through diverse means. Branches of the Brotherhood in different cities and towns of Egypt conducted evening schools for adults and lectured on Islam. They also opened day schools for both boys and girls. In contrast to the ultraconservatives, the Brotherhood believed in education for women, though never in coeducation. They did charitable works in towns, had dispensaries for the care of the sick, and distributed free food for the needy. Their missionaries preached in mosques. Each member was enjoined to forswear evil in his own life as well as forbid it in others. This important injunction of the Shari'a, covers such things as gambling, dancing, theater and movies, drinking, etc. The Brotherhood also had a youth organization. Boys up to the age of about 16 joined the *Kashshaf*, which was something like scouting and had some of the same activities. After that, young men joined a para-military organization with secret drills and war games.

The membership of the Brotherhood was kept a secret and there are no accurate statistics available. It is estimated that by 1939 the Brotherhood had about 500 branches with a membership of about 500,000. By 1953, the estimate was 2,000 branches and 2,000,000 members. Equally secret was the Brotherhood's source of income. The early members were mostly poor students, but in six years they were able to move their headquarters to Cairo and widen their base of membership. They operated a printing press and other enterprises, such as the Islamic Transaction Company, the Ikhwan Spinning and Weaving Company, and the Commercial and Engineering Company.

The slogan of the Muslim Brotherhood was "God is most great, thanks be to God," and their emblem was a Koran between two swords. Between the two wars, the Brotherhood was like an iceberg in that a good deal of its activities were underground. After World War II it became more open and clashed head-on with other revolutionaries. The consequences of this clash will be discussed in a later chapter.

PROPONENTS OF SECULARISM

Those in Egypt who favored the establishment of a secularist state did not have an organization such as the Muslim Brotherhood. Perhaps they did not feel the need of it because they were in the majority. Furthermore, the proponents of secularism were individualistic enough not to be doctrinaire and would not undergo the discipline of forming an ideological organization. Some were agnostics and did not care about Islam or any other religion. Others were devout Muslims who believed that religion was a personal matter and should be separate from government. Whether agnostics or believers they had two things in common. First, they believed in the separation of religion and state and the freedom of religion within the state. Second, they believed in the importance of "Islamic Culture" in the life of Egypt. Even the Christian Copts adhered to this concept. The identification of Islam with all other aspects of life was so complete that for an atheist to say he was not a Muslim was tantamount to confessing that he was not an Egyptian. The religious and the secularist groups cooperated. Some of the secularists ignored Islam altogether, and some practiced it privately but did not believe in imposing it on the nation.

In the period between the two wars, perhaps the person most influential in articulating the ideas of the secularists was Taha Husayn (b. 1889). This blind genius, educator, and humanitarian was educated at Azhar and in France. In a sense, he rejected both the religious fundamentalism of Azhar and the desire of the West to dominate the East as witnessed in France. For the culture and the civilization of the West, however, his love and admiration knew no bounds. His love of western culture made him appreciate the culture of the East. While in France, he wrote about the North African historian Ibn-Khaldun. In 1919 he went back to Egypt with a French wife and spent his energies in education.

He wrote novels, histories, biographies, and treatises on education. His most important books, however, were *Pre-Islamic Poetry*, published 1926, and the *Future of Culture in Egypt*, published in 1938. The first shocked the Muslim world and branded him a heretic. The second laid some of the intellectual foundation of the modern Egyptian secularist state.

In his *Pre-Islamic Poetry*, Taha Husayn applied modern critical methods of scholarship to a number of poems known as the *mu'alliqat*,[4] and doubted whether they were pre-Islamic at all. This caused a great uproar and opposition. The religious community was afraid that application of critical methods to any ancient text might encourage critical study of the Koran and Hadith and cast doubt on the authority of the scriptures. Furthermore, the place of the Arabic language is considered so holy and is so sacrosanct in the study of the Koran that any tampering with it might destroy the faith. Many books were written in opposition, and Husayn's book had to be withdrawn. But Taha Husayn was perhaps the first Muslim to encourage the application of the critical method to the study of the Koran.

The *Future of Culture in Egypt* was written to present a set of goals for the country which had won its independence in 1936. Taha Husayn idealized the agreement of 1936 as a sign of European trust in Egypt and an Egyptian promise to

[4] See above, p. 29.

follow in the footsteps of Europe. Western civilization, according to him, reached a high pinnacle when it set reason free to direct man's actions, and set religion free to inspire man to action. Egypt must use its independence as a means to achieve this high goal. He believed that Egypt was part of Europe by its connection with the Greco-Roman civilization. He was very much like the Turkish sociologist, Ziya Gökalp,[5] when he said that Egyptians should take the European civilization, but not its religion, and graft their Egyptian culture to it. It is evident that language is a very important foundation of nationalism. The Turks, as we have seen, rejected Arabic and Persian, and the Persians rejected Arabic and Turkish. Taha Husayn, exalted Arabic not for the sake of religion but for the sake of the nation. He went so far as to volunteer to help improve the poor Arabic which the Christians used in their ritual so that Egyptian Christians might worship in good Arabic.

The Egyptians went through World War II with a limited political independence and with varied ideologies. The concerned and articulate among them, from the agnostic secularist to the fundamentalist Muslim, thought in terms of loyalty to Egypt or to Islam or to both. They did not consider themselves "Arabs" and therefore many did not involve themselves in the affairs of the people of the Fertile Crescent. The events in the last years of the war, the specter of Zionism, and the anti-isolationism of the young Egyptian leaders changed the situation considerably and placed Egypt at the center of "Arab nationalism."

[5] See above, p. 271.

CHAPTER 28

IMPERIALISM IN
THE FERTILE CRESCENT

The entry of the Ottoman empire into World War I on the side of the Central Powers threatened the British imperial line of communication to India. Consequently, from their bases in Egypt and the Persian Gulf, the British tried to secure that lifeline. The Germans, on the other hand, who were the main advisers of the Ottoman armies both in the field and on the general staff, wanted to harass the British in their holdings all the way to India. They advised the Turks to curtail shipping through the Suez Canal and proclaim a *jihad*, holy war, against the Entente. The main purpose of the jihad was to insure the allegiance of the Arabic-speaking Muslims of the Ottoman empire and to arouse feelings of animosity against the British among the Muslims of India. Jihad was proclaimed in all its solemnity by the sultan-caliph on November 23, 1914, without effect. With the exception of Yaman, a few tribal shaykhs in south Arabia, and several Indian pan-Islamists, the bulk of the inhabitants of the Fertile Crescent reacted to the jihad by doing nothing. Some actually took up arms against the caliph.

In a previous chapter we discussed the evolution of nationalism among the Arabic-speaking peoples of the Fertile Crescent. By the beginning of the war the Ottomanism of the Arabic-speaking peoples of the Crescent had been dealt great blows. The Young Turk revolution of 1908 had reasserted the supremacy of Turks over non-Turks. Arabic-speaking peoples were not adequately represented in the Ottoman parliament. Furthermore, they were not willing to give up Arabic in favor of Turkish. Consequently, a number of Muslims began to be attracted to the pan-Arabist ideas of their Christian friends. At first they formed purely Muslim societies; later they established mixed groups in which Muslims, Christians, and Druzes joined in advocating the formation of a secular state with freedom of religion. There were more than a dozen of these societies from Baghdad to Beirut and some of them were formed by Arab officers in the

Ottoman army. In 1913, 24 representatives of secret nationalist societies held a congress in Paris, in the wake of the Balkan wars, and called for independence from the Ottoman rule. During the early years of the war Jemal Pasha, a member of the Turkish triumvirate, was commander of Turkish forces in Syria. His ruthlessness against the Arabs increased the popularity of the secret societies.

The British knew about these movements, and naturally took advantage of their anti-Turkish feeling. Furthermore, the British campaign under General Allenby in the Sinai was not going well in 1915, and a British army of 13,000 men under General Townsend surrendered in Mesopotamia on April 25, 1916. The Ottomans did not expect revolt on the part of the Arabs, but the British desired to foment one. The secret societies in different cities of the Fertile Crescent were not strong enough to offer armed resistance to the Turks who controlled the cities. There were, however, two Arab leaders who at the time had enough influence and freedom to lead a revolt against the Turks. One of these was Ibn-Sa'ud, the leader of the Wahhabis, who had regained his patrimony and was ruling Najd, the eastern section of the Arabian Peninsula on the Persian Gulf. The other was Husayn, appointed sharif of Mecca by the sultan in 1908. He was the scion of the clan of Hashim, the same to which the Prophet Muhammad belonged, and was, virtually, ruler of Hijaz, the western part of the Arabian peninsula on the Red Sea.

In our discussion of imperialism in Iran, we have mentioned the rivalry which existed between the British East India Company, which was the virtual ruler of India, and the British government in London. After the Indian Mutiny of 1857, the British government abolished the company and itself assumed control. Because of India's importance, it was governed through a separate department and was not part of the colonial office. There was a secretary for India in the British Cabinet, and in the course of years those Englishmen who administered India developed a special point of view which examined every policy in the light of the defense of India. A main interest of Great Britain in the Middle East was to safeguard the route to India. Because the British government personnel in India were on the spot and claimed special knowledge of Indian problems, they believed that they knew much better than the "London government" how to deal with the "natives." London, however, was reluctant to relinquish policy matters to New Delhi. There was rivalry between the London government and the "India government" until the disbanding of the latter in 1947, when India became independent. Sometimes this rivalry pertained to British policy in Iran and the Fertile Crescent.

At the beginning of World War I there was a difference of opinion between London and New Delhi over policy to be pursued in the Fertile Crescent. Indian Muslims had great respect for the caliph of Islam, who happened to be the Ottoman sultan and at war with Great Britain. The India government expected Muslims of the Fertile Crescent to have the same respect for the person of the caliph as the Indian Muslims had. So they were against instigating a revolt among the Arabs. They concluded treaties of friendship with the shaykhs of the

Persian Gulf, and recognized Ibn-Sa'ud as king of Najd. They paid subsidies to all of them and kept them friendly throughout the war.

The London government, however, knew about the nationalistic sentiments of the Arabs against the Turks and pursued the policy of fomenting open revolt. The British were aware of the anti-Ottoman feeling of Husayn and also of his personal ambitions. His second son, Abdullah, had visited Lord Kitchener, the British pro-consul in Egypt, before the war to sound out the British position. In 1915 Lord Kitchener, as secretary of war, advised Sir Henry McMahon, the high commissioner in Egypt, to approach Sharif Husayn of Mecca. In the meantime, Sharif Husayn sent his pro-Ottoman third son, Faysal, to Damascus to assure the Turks of his loyalty and also obtain the opinion of the Syrian leaders. It was on this trip that Faysal was converted to the cause of Arab nationalism without distinction of religion. He became a member of the Fatat secret society and discussed with its leaders the feasibility of revolt against the Turks and the possibility of British assistance. These leaders gave Faysal a document, known as the "Damascus Protocol," which contained the conditions under which such a revolt should be launched. The subsequent negotiation between Sharif Husayn and Great Britain was based on the contents of this Protocol.

From July 14, 1915, to March 10, 1916, Sharif Husayn, representing the Arabs of the Crescent, and Sir Henry McMahon, representing Great Britain, exchanged ten letters which are known as the "Husayn-McMahon Correspondence." This correspondence, in the nature and often in the language of an alliance, dealt with two principal points. In one, Husayn promised to recruit soldiers and fight against the Ottomans, and Great Britain promised, in case of victory, to "support the independence of the Arabs." In his correspondence, Husayn reveals the secular influence of the Syrian nationalists when he insists that "there is no difference between a Moslem and a Christian Arab, they are both descendents of one forefather." Furthermore, the term "Arab" or "Arab nation" in the view of Husayn or the Syrian nationalists did not include the populations of Egypt, North Africa, or possibly south Arabia and Najd.

The second point of the correspondence dealt with the boundaries of the "independent Arab Nation." On this point the correspondence, especially on the side of McMahon, is very ambiguous. Great Britain limited the boundary of the Arab nation by saying that "portions of Syria lying to the west of the district of Damascus, Homs, Hama, Aleppo cannot be said to be purely Arab, and should be excluded from the limits demanded." Sharif Husayn understood this to mean the area of modern Lebanon and the coastal region to the north of it, especially in the light of the fact that McMahon had mentioned the interest of France in that region. In his reply, Husayn stated that his acceptance of the above limitations was only temporary and expressed the hope that after the war Great Britain would help him in his negotiations with France.

After the war, the Husayn-McMahon Correspondence and especially the geographic meaning of the above limitation became a subject of bitter controversy. The main issue was whether the description "west of the district of Damascus . . ." included Palestine or not. The Arabs have forcefully maintained that Palestine was to be part of the Arab nation and successive British governments since 1922 have repeatedly affirmed that the above sentence meant the whole Mediterranean coast from Sinai to Turkey, which includes Palestine. Sir Henry McMahon himself, as late as 1937, said that he had not "intended Palestine to be included in his pledge to King Husain." This celebrated controversy was perhaps settled in 1964 by the "Westermann Papers," opened for research by the Hoover Institute at Stanford University. The collection contains two documents prepared by the intelligence department of the British Foreign Office for use by the British delegation at the Paris Peace Conference. These documents fell into the hands of William Westermann, Professor of History at Columbia University and a member of the American delegation at Paris. He gave the papers to the Hoover Institute with instructions that they were not to be opened until after his death. The documents state categorically that Palestine was included as part of the British pledge to the Arabs.

As a matter of fact one did not have to wait until 1964 to be convinced that the British had indeed broken their pledge to the Arabs. Six months after the close of the Husayn-McMahon correspondence the British government discarded its entire pledge to the Arabs by signing the Sykes-Picot Agreement. But this was part of the Triple Entente secret agreements and the Arabs did not know about it. On the strength of McMahon's pledge the Arabs declared war on the Ottomans on June 5, 1916. Arab troops under the command of Prince Faysal with the advice of the famous Colonel T. E. Lawrence fought against the Turkish garrisons and conducted guerilla activities all along the Turkish lines of communication. Most of the Arab officers were members of the Fatat secret society of Syria, and the Ahd society of Iraq. They took the port of Aqaba in July 1917, which made it easier for General Allenby to capture Jerusalem in December 1917. Faysal and his troops made a triumphant entry into Damascus on October 1, 1918. Remembering the Sykes-Picot agreement, the British government ordered General Allenby to go to Damascus and counteract the activities of Faysal and Lawrence. Faysal, however, proclaimed the formation of an "Arab Constitutional Government, fully and absolutely independent." He then went in pursuit of the Turks, and captured Homs and Hama in the north. On October 29, 1918, the Turks surrendered on the plain of Marj Dabiq, the same place where sultan Selim had conquered Syria in 1508.

SYKES-PICOT AGREEMENT

During World War I, there were three secret agreements among the members of the Triple (Britain, France, and Russia) Entente which dealt with the Ottoman empire. One was the Constantinople Agreement of March 18, 1915, which divided parts of north Syria and Asia Minor among the member countries. The second was the London Agreement of April 26, 1915, which was arranged when Italy joined the war and demanded its share of the spoils. In these two agreements, the Fertile Crescent was left to Great Britain and France.

On October 21, 1915, the British informed the French about the Husayn-McMahon Correspondence and suggested that they get together and discuss their interests in the Fertile Crescent. Accordingly, Sir Mark Sykes of Britain and Charles Georges-Picot of France reached an agreement by February 1916. Later this agreement was ratified by Russia and Italy. Without regard to the pledge to the Arabs, the Fertile Crescent was divided into three parts. At the insistence of Russia, Palestine, because of its holy places, was made international. The rest was divided by a line extending from the Mediterranean coast north of Haifa in a northeasterly direction to the Persian border south of Mosul. The region north of this line was to go to France and south of the line to Great Britain. Furthermore, the northern region was divided into two parts, one under direct French control and the other under its "influence." Similarly the southern region was divided into two parts, one under the direct British control and the other under its "influence."

The Sykes-Picot agreement was secret, but the Bolsheviks made it public property in November 1917. Jemal Pasha of Turkey sent the agreement to King Husayn and proposed a separate Turko-Arab Peace. Husayn asked the British for explanations and they, on three occasions, assured him that they would help in the establishment of an Arab state. The Arabs believed these assurances, perhaps because they wanted to believe them. With the Ottomans losing on practically all fronts, a Turko-Arab treaty did not have any meaning. The Arabs could not do much else but to hope for the best.

ZIONISM AND THE BALFOUR DECLARATION

The fledgling Arab nationalism of the Fertile Crescent faced many problems from the beginning. In addition to the formidable imperialistic power of Great Britain and France, Faysal and his Arab nationalist advisors had internal adversaries. The Christians of Syria-Lebanon, especially the Maronites, wanted separation from the Muslims and the protection of a foreign power. There were pan-Islamists encouraged by the local ulama who were against the "Arabism" of the liberals and wanted an Islamic state. There were the Bedouins in both Hijaz and the Fertile Crescent who were basically nomadic and did not particularly care for any kind of state. No doubt Arab nationalism, given peace and time, could have solved some of these problems were it not for the fact that it had to deal with a new and strong rival—Jewish nationalism—which appeared on the scene toward the end of 1917.

Jewish nationalism, or Zionism, had its roots in Hebrew religious history. Of the three religions—Judaism, Christianity, and Islam—that have theological and historical ties with each other, Judaism alone was exclusive. It believed its people were different from all other peoples by birth, by heritage, and by virtue of a special covenant which God had made with them through Abraham and Moses. Furthermore, God had designated a particular territory, known in ancient times as Canaan and in modern times as Palestine, to be the special land where this people could live and practice their religion without danger of intermarriage with others. Notwithstanding the promise of God, the Jews were never the exclusive settlers of Canaan. The original inhabitants, who were defeated by the army of Joshua, were not wiped out but remained in the land.

In the course of centuries, two trends developed in Judaism. One was the priestly trend, which was ritualistic and usually segregationalist and literal in its interpretation of the law of Moses. The other was the prophetic trend, which was against ritualism and usually integrationalist and spiritual in its interpretation of the law. Beginning with the Babylonian captivity, 586 B.C., and especially in the later Roman period, the Jews gradually were scattered to all parts of the world. Wherever they went, they carried these two schools of thought. The prophetic school of thought followed the admonitions of Jeremiah, Isaiah, Micah, and other prophets, who had advised the dispersed Jews to "build houses . . . plant gardens . . . take wives and beget sons and daughters" in the lands they had settled "for in the peace thereof shall you have peace." But the priestly school followed the admonitions of people like the author of Psalm 137 who had said, "If I forget you, O Jerusalem, let my right hand wither, let my tongue cleave to the roof of my mouth, if I do not remember you, if I do not set Jerusalem above my highest joy." The prophetic school considered the Temple as a "house of prayer for all people," while to the priestly party it was exclusively for the Jews. According to one group, the Messiah would establish the Kingdom of God, while according to the other group he would establish the Kingdom of David.

What is relevant to this discussion is the fact that the followers of the priestly school were in the majority. Generations of Jews were taught to consider themselves "strangers" in the land where they were living. All of the Jewish festivals, with the exception of *Yom Kipur*, Day of Atonement, are quasi-national festivals. Jewish families at the end of Friday evening prayers drank a toast, "Next year in Jerusalem," and every Jew turned toward Jerusalem when he prayed. But the festivals, the toast, and the direction of prayer did not mean that the majority of Jews wanted to go to Canaan or Palestine to live, any more than a Muslim praying toward Mecca desired to live there. Some went to Jerusalem for pilgrimage and came back, but the city and the land were not forgotten. Whenever there were persecutions, and there were many, the desire for the "Return" and the "Kingdom of David" would come to the surface.

POLITICAL ZIONISM

The Age of Englightenment in Europe, the political and social revolutions, and the separation of church and state affected the position of Jews in western Europe. Ghettos disappeared and religious Jews, who had come under the influence of scientific thought and method, revived the prophetic school of interpretation and introduced Reformed Judaism. The Reformed Jews of the nineteenth century in Europe and the United States spoke of the "Kingdom of Truth" and considered themselves "no longer a nation, but a religious community, and therefore expected neither a return to Palestine, nor the restoration of a sacrificial worship under the Sons of Aaron, or of any of the laws concerning the Jewish State." In the nineteenth century, however, the majority of the Jews lived in the ghettos of eastern Europe and Russia where the ideas of Enlightenment had not penetrated. They were victims of Christian fanaticism and periodic pogroms. Even though a number of them had come under the influence of Marxian socialism, the bulk of them were strictly orthodox Jews who expected that someday the Messiah would lead them to Palestine, the Promised Land, and would once again establish the Jewish state.

In 1894, Theodor Herzl, a Jewish intellectual and journalist, was covering the famous Dreyfus trial for his Vienna newspaper. A crime committed by a member of the French aristocracy was blamed on Captain Alfred Dreyfus of the French army chiefly because he was a Jew. The conviction of Dreyfus and his imprisonment in a penal colony created a wave of anti-Semitism throughout France. Even though some of the liberals exposed the fraud and fully cleared Dreyfus of any guilt, the lesson was not lost on Theodor Herzl. If in France, the center of Enlightenment, in spite of all its stress on liberty and religious freedom, there was such an undercurrent of anti-Semitism, then the only hope for the Jews was to leave Europe and organize a state of their own. He embodied this idea in his book *Der Judenstaat* (*The Jewish State*) and launched the modern Zionist movement.

Zionism, from the beginning, was the merging of two trends of nineteenth century Jewish thought. One was the religious longing for the "return to the Promised Land," intensified because of the anti-Jewish pogroms and the urgency of escape from persecution. The other was the nineteenth century liberal and romantic nationalism which exalted "statehood" and saw in it a panacea for the ills of humanity. The secular Jews, following the current thinking of the late nineteenth century, concluded that only by the creation of a Jewish state could anti-Semitism be destroyed. This also appealed to some non-Jewish liberals of the day who were as ashamed of anti-Semitism as the Jews were afraid of it.

There were bitter conflicts between orthodox and liberal Jews in the early days of Zionist organization. To the orthodox Jews, the return to Palestine was all-important, while to the secularists, statehood was essential and not the locality. Theodor Herzl, who belonged to the secularists, and some of his associates suggested Argentina, Australia, Africa, or anywhere else that was available. In the first World Zionist Congress held in Switzerland in 1897, the delegates reached the conclusion that Palestine had an emotional appeal to the devoutly religious Jew and Christian alike, which another locality would not have. Once Palestine was decided upon, religious and agnostic Jews worked together for the realization of the common goal.

JEWISH COLONIZATION

Palestine was part of the Ottoman empire and its conversion into a Jewish state did, of necessity, require the colonization of the land by mass transplantation of Jews from Europe. Colonialism and imperialism were accepted institutions in late nineteenth century Europe. It is not surprising, therefore, to find the Zionists having the same general attitudes and using the same methods as the rest of their fellow Europeans. For example, for the purpose of financing and supervising the colonization of Palestine, the Zionists formed commercial and political organizations such as "Jewish Colonial Trust," "Colonization Commission," "Jewish National Fund," "Palestine Office," and "Palestine Land Development Company." Having heard of the bankruptcy of the Ottoman empire, Herzl arranged an interview with Sultan Abdul Hamid II and proposed that a Jewish financial syndicate would assume all the foreign debts of the empire if the sultan would grant a charter for Jewish colonization of Palestine. Abdul Hamid refused the offer although he said he would allow a limited number of Jews to settle in Palestine, provided they became Ottoman citizens. Herzl and his friends appealed to practically every government in Europe and offered Jewish loyalty in return for Zionist colonization of Palestine.

Toward the end of the nineteenth century, it became evident to the Zionists that Great Britain was the power to deal with. Herzl tried to persuade Cecil Rhodes in 1899 and Joseph Chamberlain in 1902, without result, Herzl died in 1904, and a few years later the mantle of Zionist leadership fell on the able shoulders of Dr. Chaim Weizmann, a chemist and a naturalized British citizen. While Herzl and his associates had failed to entice a number of British governments to accede to their requests, developments during World War I set the stage for an alliance between the Zionists and Great Britain. The first announcement of this alliance was in the form of a letter by the Foreign Secretary, Lord Balfour, to Lord Rothschild, a Jewish financier, on November 2, 1917. This letter is known as the "Balfour Declaration."

In the course of two short years, from November 1915 to November 1917, Great Britain had solemnly made agreements with three different parties which were contradictory to each other. It is probably incorrect to assume that Great Britain did this out of either stupidity or willful malice. Neither is it possible to dismiss the whole matter as an "unfortunate mistake" in the confusion of war. Each step was calculated to strengthen the British empire. But when unforeseen complications arose, changes were made which best served the empire and without regard to the anguish it might cause others. This was a rule of the game of imperialism.

In 1915, it was the British policy to supplant the Ottoman empire by an independent Arab state in the Fertile Crescent in which Britain had special privileges. If the situation had not changed, it is quite likely that Great Britian would have honored its promise. But there were pressures from other European powers, especially France, who insisted in sharing the control of the Fertile Crescent. The only way that Britain could control the southern part of the area was to give the northern section to France. This was the essence of the Sykes-Picot agreement in 1916. Russia complicated the matter by insisting on the internationalization of Palestine because of the Russian Orthodox Church's interest in the area. Internationalization involved the French, who also had an interest in the holy places. This alarmed the British policy makers, especially the India government, who did not want the French so close to the Suez Canal. The Zionists had been arguing all along that a Jewish national home in Palestine required the presence of Great Britain in the area, and a grateful Zionist government in Palestine would always remain an ally of the British empire.

The strongest opposition to this convenient alliance with the British government came from the anti-Zionist Jews of Britain, France, and the United States. This becomes clear by examining the text of the Balfour Declaration. "His Majesty's government view with favor the establishment in Palestine of a national home for the Jewish people, and will use their best endeavors to facilitate the achievement of this objective, it being clearly understood that nothing shall be done which may prejudice the civil and religious rights of existing non-Jewish communities in Palestine, or the rights and political status enjoyed by Jews in any other country."

The last phrase was inserted to allay the fears of anti-Zionist Jews, who saw the solution to the Jewish problem as integration rather than self-segregation and did not want the creation of a Jewish state to prejudice their nationality status in the countries of their birth. "National home" in the first sentence was understood by the Zionists, and perhaps by Balfour, to be the same as "national state." The first World Zionist Congress in 1894 had decided to use "home" instead of state, "in the interest of opportunism," to quote Dr. Max Nordau, one of the famous leaders of Zionism. Perhaps the Zionists believed that they could settle in Palestine without prejudice to the civil and religious rights of the Palestinians. The later Faysal-Weizmann agreement confirmed their belief.

King Husayn was perplexed when he learned about the Balfour Declaration. Great Britain sent Commander Hogarth of the Arab Bureau to Cairo on January 4, 1918, to assure him that a Jewish settlement in Palestine would be allowed only if it were "compatible with the freedom of the existing population, both economic and political." The British also advised King Husayn to accept the Zionists because "the friendship of world Jewry to the Arab cause is equivalent to support in all states where Jews have a political influence." A few days later, a joint Anglo-French proclamation promised the Arabs a government "freely chosen by the population." Both King Husayn and Faysal were encouraged by these assurances and accepted them as they had done in the case of the Sykes-Picot agreement.

THE PARIS PEACE CONFERENCE

At the end of World War I there were three groups which were contending for supremacy in all or part of the Fertile Crescent. The first and the most powerful was the Anglo-French group. Great Britain and France, together with Italy and the United States, formed the "Big Four" and dominated the peace conference. But Britain and France were not in agreement. Since France had not done any of the fighting in the east, British troops occupied all of the Fertile Crescent and they were reluctant to leave. On the other hand, France insisted on carrying out the Sykes-Picot agreement. They landed some 20,000 French troops in Lebanon and demanded British evacuation. The British, on their part, wanted modifications in the agreement concerning the oil-rich province of Mosul and the "internationalization" of Palestine. While speeches to determine the peace of the world were going on, the intense in-fighting between the two imperialistic rivals led to accusations and recriminations.

The second group which was contending for a part of the Fertile Crescent was the Zionist organization. The Zionists were more powerful than the Arabs because they had men of influence in the countries of the "Big Four" to advance their cause. They did not want the Balfour Declaration to remain a private agreement between themselves and Great Britain. They wanted to incorporate it in all of the policies pertaining to the Middle East. There were Jews, however, who strongly opposed the Zionist plan. Some 300 leading American Jews sent a letter to President Wilson against Zionism. There were leading Jews in Europe who believed that Zionism was endangering their status and causing more anti-Semitism.

The third and the weakest contenders for the Fertile Crescent were the inhabitants of the area represented by Faysal. The Arabs wanted the independence promised to them by Great Britain. They also pinned their hopes on Woodrow Wilson and his principle of self-determination—a principle which both the Anglo-French coalition and the Zionists wanted to discard except for themselves. The weak Arabs were further weakened by disagreements among themselves. The Christians in general and Maronites in particular were afraid to be a minority in a predominantly Muslim state. France, as an old-time protector of the Maronites, organized a group called the "Syrian Commission" which went to Paris and opposed Faysal and the union with the Muslim Arabs. Furthermore, there was rivalry between the Arab leaders of Baghdad and Damascus. Some wanted a united kingdom and others, perhaps more realistically, preferred a federation of two states.

Faysal went to London and for the first time became fully acquainted with the Sykes-Picot agreement. The British told him to accept the French, and the Zionist leaders gave a banquet in his honor. Faysal continued to talk about self-determination, freedom, and justice, but he had become aware that the realities of politics did not pay much attention to such ideals. Perhaps it was this realization which induced him to sign an agreement, in January 1919, with Weizmann, the head of the Zionist Organization. In this document Faysal accepts "the immigration of Jews into Palestine on a large scale," provided "the Arab peasant and tenant farmers shall be protected in their rights." For their part, the Zionists agreed "to send to Palestine a commission of experts to make a survey of the economic possibilities" of Palestine as well as "the Arab state." Faysal's signature is conditioned upon the creation of the "Arab state" which was not created. This agreement might have averted a great deal of subsequent bloodshed had it not been for the Sykes-Picot agreement which was against the creation of an Arab state.

In the meantime, President Wilson took the view that the great powers, in accepting his fourteen points, had automatically nullified their secret agreements. To minimize tension, a compromise was reached in the introduction of the mandate system of the League of Nations. This was based upon the idea that the Arabs were not ready for self-government and would be tutored in the art by a mandatory power. President Wilson accepted this principle because it was not a rejection of the principle of self-determination, but only a postponement of it. But difficulties arose on the question of which powers should have mandatory rights over what specific areas. Wilson proposed to send a joint commission to the Fertile Crescent to ascertain the wishes of the people. France refused to join, Britain abstained, and the Zionists opposed the proposal. But President Wilson sent the King-Crane Commission to the area in August 1919. By the time the commission was ready with its report, Wilson was a defeated and sick man. Every one of his fourteen points, save one, had been modified or rejected or its enactment postponed. The one remaining point, the League of Nations, became a reality but was rejected by his own country. The report of the commission was not published until three years after.

By the end of the Peace Conference, Britain and France had come to an understanding on the Sykes-Picot agreement, Palestine, and the mandates. The Zionists had succeeded in turning the Balfour Declaration into an international proclamation. The Arabs, however, found themselves serving two European Christian masters in place of the one Turkish Muslim master against whom they had rebelled.

CHAPTER 29

FERTILE CRESCENT
UNDER MANDATE

One of the ideas behind the mandate was to enable some European powers to carry out the same imperialistic activities under a new name. It was the extension of the "white man's burden" with the blessing of the League of Nations. The mandate system did not change the nature of the Sykes-Picot agreement. Britain and France had two difficulties with it; one concerned Palestine and the other was the oil-rich Mosul. Both of these problems were solved outside the Paris Peace Conference and were eventually settled at San Remo on April 24, 1920. Great Britain was recognized as the mandatory power over Palestine. Thanks to Zionist efforts, the League instructed Great Britain to implement the Balfour Declaration. Because of the presence of oil in the Mosul region, Great Britain was trying to persuade a reluctant France to revise the Sykes-Picot agreement on this point. The fact that Turkey claimed the territory further complicated the problem.

THE IRAQ PETROLEUM COMPANY

In ancient times oil was known to exist in northern Iraq, as it was in southwestern Iran. In the late nineteenth century the Ottoman empire was advised of the presence of oil in commercial proportions. In a special decree, Abdul Hamid II, the Ottoman sultan, transferred the concessions of the provinces of Mosul and Baghdad to the "Civil List," that is, himself.

A succession of foreign prospectors, from 1904 to 1912, showed interest in acquiring concessions. The Germans were involved through the Deutsche Bank that had been established in Istanbul. The British had an interest through D'Arcy's Anglo-Persian Oil Company. The Royal Dutch Shell Company was interested through its subsidiary, the Anglo-Saxon Oil Company. Finally, the Americans had begun negotiating through the so-called Chester Group. For the purpose of keeping the Americans away from Middle East oil, British,

German, and the Dutch entrepreneurs formed the Turkish Petroleum Company in 1912. The British controlled 50 per cent of the shares of this company while the Germans and the Dutch each held 25 per cent. Negotiations were started with the Ottomans in 1914, and on June 28 Grand vazir Sai'd Halim in a letter to the German Ambassador said that his government "consents to lease these [Mosul and Baghdad] to the Turkish Petroleum Company, and reserves for itself the right to determine . . . the general condition of the contract." The outbreak of World War I stopped further action on the matter. The company did not have a contract, only a letter of consent. The legality of this was disputed in later years.

The Americans, who were left out, were represented by the Chester Group. In 1909, a retired United States naval officer, Admiral Colby M. Chester, had acquired a concession from the Porte to construct railroads in eastern Asia Minor and northern Mesopotamia. Included in the railroad agreement was a concession for mineral rights, including oil, for 20 kilometers on both sides of the rail line, which passed through Kirkuk and Mosul to the Persian border. The Turkish Minister of Public Works signed the agreement and sent it to the parliament in 1911 for ratification. But the Balkan wars prevented ratification and a second attempt in 1914 was interrupted by World War I. The fact that it was not ratified made the concession invalid, but this concession also was disputed in later years.

Apparently neither Sykes nor Picot was aware of these negotiations in 1914, so that their division of spoils did not take oil into consideration. British officials, however, who knew about oil took it for granted that the concession to the Turkish Petroleum Company was valid. But it was awkward to hold a concession for oil in a territory that was assigned to France. The British Foreign Secretary, Sir Edward Grey, introduced the difficulty to the French Ambassador in a secret letter dated May 15, 1916. In December 1918, when the French Premier Clemenceau visited London, the subject was brought up again. It was tentatively agreed that in return for a share in the Mosul oil and British support for French demands in the Ruhr, France might be willing to accommodate Great Britain. This became the basis of later negotiations between the two countries. According to the new agreement, France relinquished the province of Mosul to Britain in return for 25 per cent of the shares in the Turkish Petroleum which originally were to go to Germany. A new map was prepared to show the change, and the whole plan was incorporated as part of the San Remo agreement of April 24, 1920.

The San Remo agreement, however, did not altogether solve the oil problem. The interest of American oil companies in the oil of the Middle East and the claim of the Tutkish nationalists over Mosul complicated the issue. An American observer at San Remo reported on the oil concession, and the United States government demanded a share in the enterprise for the American oil companies. The American argument was based on the fact that the United States had paid for the war against Turkey even though it had not officially declared war.

Furthermore, the monopoly of an oil concession by Britain and France was against the American Open Door Policy. Later, the United States introduced the Chester concession and argued that it was as valid as the one given to the Turkish Petroleum Company.

The argument dragged on until 1923 and was an issue at the Lausanne Conference. At this conference, Ataturk demanded the province of Mosul. For a time, the Turks and the Americans discussed an arrangement through which the Turks would give the Mosul oil to the Americans if they in turn would help the Turks to acquire Mosul. In the meantime the British became convinced that they could not keep the Americans out of the oil enterprise in Iraq as they had done in Iran.[1] Because the Council of the League had resolved the Mosul question in favor of Great Britain, the Turks decided to come to terms with the British. So, with minor border adjustments and a 10 per cent share in the royalty payments from the Mosul oil, the Turks withdrew their claim to Mosul. The story of the final settlement of the Mosul oil is too complicated to relate here. Under a new formula, the Iraq government gave a concession for 24 plots of land to the Turkish Petroleum Company, subsequently renamed Iraq Petroleum. The British, French, Dutch, and American groups each received 23.75 per cent and the remaining 5 per cent went to Sarkis Gulbenkian, the broker for the original 1914 concession, who somehow had had a hand in all subsequent negotiations. Because this arrangement was for only 24 plots and the Iraqi government could offer the remaining territory for competitive bidding, the competition was very keen and wrangling over rights was prolonged.

FAYSAL AND THE FRENCH

As we have seen, the Paris Peace Conference adjourned without reaching firm agreements about the Fertile Crescent. Faysal and a small number of Arab leaders pinned their hopes on President Wilson's King-Crane Commission. The commission toured the area and recommended that two mandates be set up, one in Iraq and the other in Syria; that Britain be given the mandate for Iraq and the United States the mandate for Syria; that Syria not be divided; and that Faysal be the constitutional monarch of Syria. It correctly predicted that there would be war if France was given mandate over Syria. But no one paid any attention to the report and it was not even published until three years later.

The hopes of the Arabs, however, were shattered by the Anglo-French Agreement of September 1919, which showed that the Sykes-Picot agreement still was official policy. French troops replaced the British and the protests of Faysal resulted in nothing. To counteract the Anglo-French policy, the Syrian Congress, led by the Fatat society, met in Damascus on March 20, 1920, and announced the independence of Syria (which included Lebanon and Palestine). They offered the crown to Faysal, and he accepted it. The British and

[1] See below, p. 334.

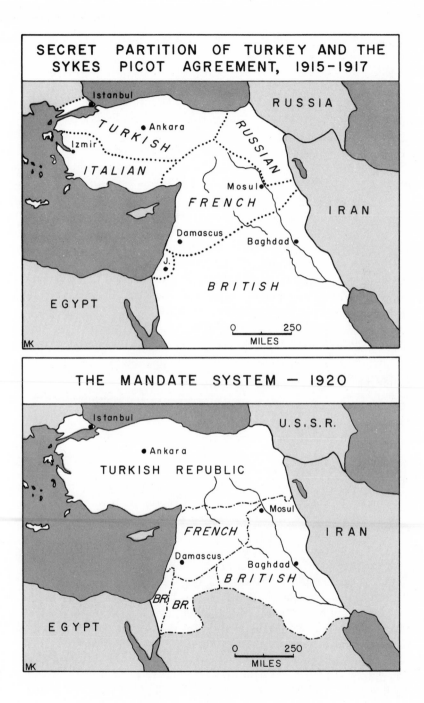

SECRET PARTITION OF TURKEY AND THE
SYKES PICOT AGREEMENT, 1915–1917

Istanbul
RUSSIA
TURKISH
Ankara
Izmir
RUSSIAN
ITALIAN
Mosul
FRENCH
IRAN
Damascus
Baghdad
J.
BRITISH
EGYPT
0   250
MILES
MK

THE MANDATE SYSTEM — 1920

Istanbul
U.S.S.R.
Ankara
TURKISH REPUBLIC
Mosul
FRENCH
IRAN
Damascus
Baghdad
BRITISH
BR. BR.
EGYPT
0   250
MILES
MK

French governments repudiated the action of the Congress and continued their preparation for the San Remo Conference, which decided the fate of the Fertile Crescent.

The French and the Syrians were getting ready for war. General Gouraud, the French high commissioner for Syria, sent an ultimatum to Faysal demanding the immediate acceptance of the French mandate, French paper currency, French occupation of Aleppo, reduction of the Syrian army, abolition of conscription, and punishment of those responsible for anti-French demonstrations. The Syrians wanted to resist, but their army had ammunition for only a few hours. Faysal accepted the ultimatum, which must have surprised the French general for he presented eight more stringent demands. It was evident that the French wanted to occupy all of Syria. War could not be averted. The battle of Maysalun, on July 24, 1920, lasted half a day, and the French army of Africans, Algerians, Moroccans, and Senegalese advanced toward Damascus. They entered the city on July 25, and Faysal left Damascus 22 months after his triumphal entry, on October 1, 1918. The British had ties with the French and they did not want to break them for the sake of the Arabs. But they did receive Faysal in their territory with high honor.

The French mandate over Syria-Lebanon, and the British mandate over Palestine and Iraq were approved by the Council of the League of Nations in July 1922. The United States recognized the mandates in 1924.

MANDATE OVER SYRIA-LEBANON

It is naïve to think that the French had gone through so much trouble to gain the mandate solely in order to help educate the Syrians and Lebanese for self rule. Perhaps here and there some French officials thought in those terms, but the main purpose was political and cultural domination. Among the imperialistic countries perhaps France alone had a strong sense of mission; as had been true in the past, it wished to bestow the blessings of the French culture on the nonwestern world. France had indeed sacrificed economic and political advantages for the sake of cultural supremacy, something Great Britain never did. The best example is to be found in the Middle East, where in countries like Egypt and Iran Britain had the political and economic advantages, but French language and culture were paramount.

In the Levant, French interest was of long standing. It was the French Prime Minister Clemenceau who assured President Wilson that if France did not stay in Syria it would be a "national humiliation, as the desertion of a soldier from the battlefield." It is significant to note that General de Gaulle, exhibiting the same spirit, had to be driven out of Syria-Lebanon in 1946.

With such a national as well as imperial purpose, France was against Arab nationalism and in favor of strengthening those groups who potentially might support France. These were to be found among minorities such as the Christians, Alawis, Kurds, Armenians, etc. Adopting the time tested policy of divide and rule, General Gouraud, the French high commissioner, divided the little territory into five parts. These were: (1) Greater Lebanon, which included the Lebanon and Anti-Lebanon mountains and the sea coast from north of Tripoli to Palestine; (2) Latakia, the Alawi seacoast territory north of Tripoli; (3) Aleppo; (4) Damascus; and (5) Jabal Druze, or the territory of Druze mountains to the south of Damascus. This division proved impractical from the beginning. Different French high commissioners suggested federations of one sort or another, but in the end two separate administrations evolved, one for Greater Lebanon and the other for the combination of the remaining four sections, which was called Syria. Of these two, Lebanon was easier for France to administer, chiefly because of the Maronites who had always favored the French.

The history of Syria from the ousting of Faysal in 1920 until independence in 1946 is a story of riots, uprisings, and war. For this there were two main reasons. One was the fact that in comparison with any other part of the Arabic-speaking world, Arab nationalism was and remained strongest in Syria. It was in Syria-Lebanon that Arabism had its start and it was the Syrian Fatat society that proposed the idea of a united Arab kingdom as early as the Husayn-McMahon correspondence. Under the Ottoman administration, the term "Syria" included Lebanon and Palestine. The Syrians were never willing or able to adjust themselves to the separation. Furthermore, the Syrians feel a special responsibility for Arab unity because of the fact that Damascus was the capital of the first and only united Arab empire, that of the Umayyads.

A second reason for Syrian resentment was poor administration by the French. On the whole, the French were proud, narrow-minded, inept, condescendingly paternalistic, and harsh. The division of the people according to religion was basic policy, but the military high commissioners, who probably did not share the traditional anti-clericalism of the French, went out of their way to aid the propagation of Roman Catholicism and favor the Catholic Christians over the rest.

The imperialism of France, on the one hand, and the desire of the Syrians for independence, on the other, led to the revolt of 1925. The immediate cause of it was the tactlessness of Captain Carbillet in introducing changes not sanctioned by the Druze chief Sultan al-Atrash, and the harsh handling of the whole matter by General Sarrail, the high commissioner who invited the Druze leaders to a banquet and then arrested them. Atrash, who had not attended the banquet, attacked a French garrison in the Druze area. This was the signal for uprising in Damascus, Homs, Hama, and other places. There was collusion between the Druze leader and the nationalists in these cities. General Sarrail was replaced by General Gamelin and he moved with armor and planes against Damascus in October 1925. He took the city but the insurrection dragged on, with great loss of life, until 1928. A lull came when France sent a civilian high commissioner who started negotiations. Syrian nationalist parties formed a Nationalist Block, *Al-Kutla al-Wataniyya*, and demanded autonomy and unity of all the separate administrative areas except Lebanon. For eight years, interspersed by strikes and uprisings, the nationalists and the French wrangled over the contents of a constitution, form of government, and degree of independence.

The same considerations which induced Great Britain to come to terms with the Egyptians, namely the rise of Hitler and the campaign of Mussolini in Ethiopia, forced the French to accommodate the Syrians. A treaty was signed between the two countries on September 9, 1936, with provisions similar to the Anglo-Egyptian treaty of the same year. The nationalists won the elections and chose Hashim al-Atassi as President and Jamil Mardam as Prime Minister. Apparently France was not serious, for it resumed its mandatory regime in Syria as though no agreement had been reached. The French Parliament never ratified the treaty. The approach of World War II ended the short-lived independence of Syria.

The situation in Lebanon, because of the presence of the French army headquarters and because of the French proclivities for the Maronites, was not as volatile as in Syria. There were nationalists in Lebanon, Christians, Muslims, and Druzes, who were members of the Syrian National Party and wanted union and independence. On the whole, however, the initiative for nationalist agitation was in Syria. As a result of the war of 1925 in Syria, the Lebanese gained some measure of independence. They established a republic and chose Charles Dabbas as president, but the French emphasized the fact that Lebanon was independent but not sovereign. It was not long before the French took away the "independence" and revoked the constitution. In 1936, a treaty similar to the Franco-Syrian one was arranged with Lebanon, and the constitution of 1926 was restored. But the French did not deal any better with the Lebanese than they had with the Syrians. They simply were not able to let their mandates go free and let the "civilizing mission" of France take its own course.

MANDATE OVER IRAQ

The British mandate over Iraq was peaceful compared to the French mandate over Syria. This was owing partly to the British experience in the area. From the second half of the nineteenth century, the Persian Gulf region had become a preserve of Great Britain and British agents had political and economic influence in lower Mesopotamia. Furthermore, a number of British officers had fought side-by-side with Arab officers in the Hijaz army in the war against the Ottomans, an experience which most of the French officers did not have. The Iraqi political parties were not dominated by extremists as were the parties of Syria. For the Syrians the motto was "all or nothing," a policy which the Arabs used time and again in dealing with the question of Zionism. For the Iraqis the motto was "take and ask for more." This is not to say, however, that Iraq did not have its share of extremists and coups d'etats.

The British had difficulties in the beginning mainly because the affairs of Iraq were under the control of the government of India. As early as 1918 the "Anglo-Indians" were so sure that they were going to have control of Iraq that they moved in with their families and took over the administration as though they were going to stay forever. The British high commissioner, Sir Arnold Wilson, conducted a "plebiscite" which showed that the Iraqis preferred Great Britain.

Of course the Iraqis actually did not prefer the British, as the rebellion of July 1920 proved. The announcement of the San Remo agreement of April 1920, coupled with the attitude of the Anglo-Indians, caused the outbreak of July 1920. It is significant that at this same time Egyptian nationalists were challenging the authority of the British, Kemalists were resisting the "peace" imposed by the Entente, and the Syrians were fighting against the French. After landing some 65,000 troops, spending about $1,000,000 and suffering casualties on both sides, the British government in London took control. Sir Percy Cox, a man known and respected in the area, was made high commissioner. He announced the British intention of establishing a national Iraqi government.

The Cairo Conference in 1920, under the chairmanship of the then colonial secretary Winston Churchill, had a delicate problem in its hands. In the implementation of the Sykes-Picot agreement the general consensus was that Faysal would become king of Syria and his older brother Abdullah king of Iraq. Indeed, the Syrian National Congress, in choosing Faysal as king of Syria, had designated Abdullah as king of Iraq. Great Britain was not opposed to this. The French government, however, complicated the situation by expelling Faysal, which meant that the British had two "kings" on their hands. Of the two brothers, Faysal was the more popular, so Great Britain decided that he should be king of Iraq. Sir Percy Cox saw to it that there was an invitation from the leaders of Iraq to Faysal to become their king. He was enthroned on August 23, 1921. As for Abdullah, he was given the Amirate of "Transjordan," a region conveniently created by the British on the west bank of the Jordan River, extending southward to the Gulf of Aqaba.

The idealistic nationalism of Faysal received several severe jolts during the three years after his decision to fight against the Ottomans in 1918. He tried to steer a course between the extreme nationalism of the Syrians and complete subservience to the British. Great Britain, having freed its Middle East policy from the influence of the India government, also became less rigid. Between 1922 and 1930 several treaties were negotiated and discarded. There was a tug of war in which the Iraqi nationalists demanded more than the British imperialists were willing to give. As an Arab, Faysal was not totally trusted by Great Britain and as a protégé of the British, he was not beyond suspicion by the nationalists. But he did keep a balance between the two sides until 1930, when a treaty was signed giving Iraq its independence. The treaty was a prototype for the Anglo-Egyptian treaty six years later and a model for the French as well. Great Britain was allowed to maintain a naval base in Basra on the Persian Gulf, and a base at the Habbaniya Airfield near Baghdad. In time of war Iraq agreed to put its resources at the disposal of the British. Iraq was declared independent and the last semblance of the mandate came to an end.

By 1932, both Great Britain and Iraq ratified the treaty and Iraq became the first Arab state to be admitted to the League of Nations.

Iraqi nationalists were not satisfied with the Treaty of 1930. In their eyes, Iraq was not fully independent as long as it had ties with Great Britain. They also wanted to make common cause with the nationalists of Syria. On the other hand, the discovery of oil in Iraq and the conclusion of oil concessions made Iraq affluent. The concession was granted for 75 years and Iraq received a royalty of four gold shillings per metric ton of crude oil. There were those among the Iraqis who were reluctant to share this wealth with the rest of the Arabs. Furthermore, the Iraqi currency was secure as a member of the "sterling block" and a far cry from the fluctuating Syrian currency which was tied to the French franc.

The ruling body in Iraq was divided into political factions, each built around influential individuals whose fortunes rose and fell with the number of votes they could muster in parliament. On the whole, they were divided into two groups, one in favor of alliance with Great Britain and the other against it. In the former were the National Party, the Progressive Party, and the old Ahd Party of the premandate days dominated by the personality of General Nuri al-Sa'id. Individuals who opposed Great Britain had formed the National Brotherhood, *Ikha al-Watani* Party, which was dominated by Yasin al-Hashimi and Rashid al-Gailani.

Lack of homogeneity in the people of Iraq made the solution of political and social problems more difficult. This was true of many countries in the Middle East and colonial powers were not responsible for it. The vast majority of the 5,000,000 inhabitants of Iraq were Muslims, but they belonged to three hostile camps, Shi'a, Sunni, and Kurd. The Sunni minority, which ruled the Shi'i majority, were never sure of the latter's loyalty because of their Persian proclivities. The Shi'is and the Sunnis spoke Arabic, but the Kurds, who were Sunni in religion, spoke Kurdish. Furthermore, they were part of the seminomadic Kurds who lived in Iran and Turkey and who aspired to national autonomy. Perhaps the most tragic group in Iraq were some 90,000 Assyrian Christians who spoke Syriac. They lived in the mountains of western Asia Minor. The British held before them, as they had done with the Armenians, the hope of national autonomy and had encouraged them to rise against the Turks. After the withdrawal of the Russian troops caused by the Bolshevik revolution, the Assyrians were pushed south to Mesopotamia. In the struggle of 1920, the British enlisted Assyrian soldiers to fight against the Iraqis, causing enmity between the groups. In the subsequent peace negotiations the Turks did not permit the Assyrians to return to their homes, which meant that the bulk of them were stranded in Iraq. In addition to these, there were 100,000 Jews who had settled in Mesopotamia from before the Christian era, a smaller number of Armenians, and sundry groups known as Sabbeans and Yazidis.

After Iraq had gained its independence in 1932, Faysal wanted to transform the various ethnic and religious groups into a nation. He wanted to strengthen the armed forces of the country, bring a rapprochement between the Sunnis and the Shi'is, open schools, encourage industries, solve the land problems, and reform the administrative system. For this purpose he tried to bring about a coalition government. He asked Nuri al-Sa'id to resign the premiership and eventually offered it to Rashid al-Gailani of the National Brotherhood Party. This party dominated the parliament from 1932 to 1936. Perhaps Faysal would have succeeded had he lived, but he died in 1933. His 21-year-old son, Ghazi, was proclaimed king, but had neither the experience nor the prestige to check the dictatorial actions of the National Brotherhood under Rashid al-Gailani and Yasin al-Hashimi.

In 1936, two widely divergent groups joined together and overthrew the government by a coup d'etat, the first of several in the history of Iraq subsequent to Faysal's death. One of these groups was the *Ahali* party, made up of young intellectuals who professed a kind of socialist democracy. The other group was made up of army officers who advocated nationalism while preferring their own brand of dictatorship. The two groups got together through Hikmat Sulayman of the Ahali and General Bakr Sidqi of the Army, and overthrew the government in October 1936. The inexperienced young intellectuals were no match for the army, and the latter took over control under General Sidqi. Then the army leaders turned against each other, which led to the assassination of General Sidqi in 1937 and another coup d'etat. After a year, a third coup brought back once again General Nuri al-Sa'id. The jockeying for power was only one of Iraq's problems; there were others. One was a new controversy with Great Britain over oil-rich Kuwait. Britain held a protectorate over the area while Iraq claimed ownership. The fate the Palestine in the struggle with the Zionists was another problem which involved the Iraqis. There were also problems of reform and the question of Iraqi nationalism versus the larger Arab nationalism.

In the midst of this, the young king Ghazi was killed in an automobile accident on April 4, 1939. Since he was popular and on the reformist nationalist side on all questions, it was difficult for many to believe that his death was only an accident. His four-year-old son, Faysal II, was proclaimed king with Abdul Ilah, his maternal uncle, as regent. Nuri al-Sa'id was Prime Minister, holding anti-British nationalists at bay, when World War II started.

MANDATE OVER TRANSJORDAN

The territory of Transjordan, over which Abdullah was asked to be the Amir, was mostly desert inhabited by some 200,000 people, most of whom were Bedouins. To make it palatable for Abdullah to rule over the empty land, the British arranged for a monthly stipend of 5,000 pounds. From 1921 until after World War II the influence of Great Britain in the area was not challenged. In the confines of this same preserve the British could observe and hope to control the restlessness of Iraq, the struggle for power in Palestine, and the passage through the Persian Gulf. Through a subsidy of 100,000 pounds per year, which by 1940 had grown to two million, the British organized an army which became the best trained and equipped army in the Fertile Crescent. The Arab Legion, as the army was called, was commanded by Captain F. G. Peake until 1939 and from then on by the legendary Glubb Pasha (Sir John Glubb). The army was made up of volunteers from all parts of the Fertile Crescent, dominated by young men from the Bedouin tribes.

The nature of government in Transjordan was simple. The powers of legislation and administration were vested in the Amir who, in turn, had an executive council to assist him. Membership in the legislative council was based on proportional representation among the Bedouins and other groups. The British residents stationed in Amman (Philadelphia of Roman times) supervised the administration and controlled the budget, army, and foreign affairs. After the death of King Faysal of Iraq, Abdullah was the head of the Hashimite family which ruled Iraq and Transjordan. Abdullah tried to identify his ambitions for the family of Hashim with the desire for unity on the part of the Arabs of the Crescent and supported a program called "The Greater Syria Movement." The idea was a revival of the contents of the Husayn-McMahon Correspondence, which envisaged a United Fertile Crescent under the rule of the Hashimites. Against the plan were Saudi Arabia and Egypt, as well as the Christians of Lebanon, aided by some political parties in Syria and Iraq.

SAUDI ARABIA

In the confusion of the war, claims and counterclaims in the Paris Peace Conference, and the revolts connected with the mandate regimes, perhaps the reader has forgotten about King Husayn who had started the whole chain of events. Actually everyone else seemed to have forgotten and abandoned the venerable Sharif of Mecca. He who had proclaimed himself "King of the Arab countries" in 1916 and had provoked the enmity of other hopeful claimants to such a title was reduced to being a king without a country. He kept up the pretence for some time without doing anything to secure his position. Events and developments passed him by while he insisted on being king. He did not clarify his relation with the British under changed circumstances, and paid no attention to international meetings such as Versailles, San Remo, Lausanne, and the League of Nations. He had already aroused the hostility of Muslim groups in India by drawing sword against the caliph of Islam. His anger, pride, and frustration led him, on March 7, 1924, to assume the title of "caliph of all Islam."

This announcement gave his rival, King Ibn-Sa'ud of Najd, the pretext he had been waiting for. We have already stated that the latter was a protégé of the India Government and had treaty relationships with the British. On August 24, 1924, Ibn-Sa'ud led his Wahhabi fighters against Husayn, who was friendless and had no funds to raise an army. Husayn's sons, Faysal and Abdullah, probably were not in a position to help him, and he had served his usefulness to the British. The Wahhabis swept everything before them and by January 1926, Ibn-Sa'ud was master of the holy cities and of the major portion of the peninsula. Husayn fled to Cyprus, where he was received with great honor by the British and was invested in the Order of St. Michael.

It can probably be stated that ever since the rise of the Prophet Muhammad no such powerful and astute leader as Abd al-Aziz ibn-Sa'ud had arisen in the Arabian peninsula. But the supremacy of the Wahhabis over the holy cities of Mecca and Medina created a very serious problem in the world of Islam. The Wahhabis were puritan fanatics and were opposed to the liberal practices of the rest of the Muslims whom they called "polytheists." But revenue from pilgrimage was the highest income of the Arabian government and Ibn-Sa'ud did not propose to sacrifice this income. So on June 7, 1926, he called an Islamic conference in Mecca. His purpose was to allay the fears of the Muslims and to provide an opportunity for his Wahhabi ulama to meet others. The Muslim delegations were captivated by the personality and wisdom of the tall monarch. Pilgrimages, which had been sporadic during the war, resumed on a regular basis.

Next, Ibn-Sa'ud clarified his relationship with Great Britain, who had direct or indirect control of territories along the southern coast and parts of the eastern coast of Arabia in addition to Palestine, Transjordan, and Iraq to the north. A basic difficulty concerned Transjordan, partly because it was an expedient creation of the British to find a place for Abdullah, and partly because Ibn-Sa'ud had a feud of long standing with the Hashimite family to which Abdullah and Faysal belonged. These and other questions were resolved by two treaties, one in the agreement of Hadda, November 2, 1925, which settled the boundaries with Transjordan. The other was the treaty of Jidda, May 20, 1927, in which Great Britain recognized the independence of Saudi Arabia, and Ibn-Sa'ud acknowledged the special interest of Great Britain in the Persian Gulf Shaykhdoms. In reality, Saudi Arabia was the first relatively independent Arab state, as there were no special clauses for political privileges or any military bases. British trade had always been paramount on both the Red Sea and the Persian Gulf and continued to be for some time to come.

The main task for Ibn-Sa'ud, like that of the Prophet Muhammad, was to break up the tribal system and the rivalries and wars among them. He organized the Wahhabis in small Brotherhoods, *Ikhwan*, and settled them on oases across the land. He provided each settlement with agriculture, mosques, and schools. These settlements were very much like the military towns of the second caliph Umar. They were socioeconomic as well as military units and all were loyal to the king. It took him years of fighting, firm administration, and justice to accomplish his task.

In the unification of Arabia the most instrumental factor was the discovery of oil. Oil had been found on the island of Bahrain in 1932. A year later, on July 29, King Ibn-Sa'ud gave a concession to the Standard Oil Company of California, which was to be effective for 60 years. The company was to start operation immediately and the king was to receive a royalty of four gold shillings per ton of crude oil produced. Even though the exploration at first did not produce oil in commercial quantities, the company showed good sense by advancing Ibn-Sa'ud a much-needed £30,000 to replace the slackening of pilgrimage revenue due to world depression. By 1938 oil in great quantities was found in Dhahran on the Persian Gulf. Because the Texas Oil Company had joined Standard, the new partnership was named Arabian American Oil Company (Aramco). With the importation of equipment and foreign personnel, and the building of roads, ports, and refineries, the young men of the tribes were attracted to centers of labor and training. This marked the beginning of the end of roaming and feuding among tribes in Arabia.

CHAPTER 30

THE STRUGGLE FOR PALESTINE

The Balfour Declaration and its eventual ratification by the League of Nations and other international bodies dealing with the Middle East initiated a bitter and prolonged contest between two nationalisms, one Arab and the other Zionist. Both claimed the same territory, commonly known as Palestine. The Palestinian Arabs wanted it because they lived there. The Zionists demanded it because the land had been promised them by their God, Yahweh, which promise was later confirmed by Balfour, ratified by the League of Nations, the Congress of the United States, and finally, by the United Nations. For the Zionists, it was a "return" full of mystical significance. For the Arabs, it was simply another invasion. Both sides believed in the use of power to reach their ends. The Zionists were able to muster the religious, moral, political and economic power of the West and combine it with their own ability, as westerners, to make use of the modern weapons of war. The Arabs, on the other hand, who were in the early stages of development, were not close to the centers of power and could not obtain and were not familiar with the modern weapons of warfare. All they seemed able to do was to carry on sporadic uprisings, engage in flamboyant oratory and, out of weakness, cry out for "justice." It was easy for the Zionists, most of whom did not live in Palestine, to accept at different stages of the struggle whatever anyone was willing to concede to them. The Palestinians, however, who believed the land belonged to them, were not willing to compromise. They had the motto "all or nothing," while the Zionists followed the policy "take and ask for more."

By 1967, the fiftieth anniversary of the Balfour Declaration, the Zionists were masters of all Palestine and the Sinai Peninsula, but the end of the struggle was not in sight. The history of these 50 years was full of stories of courage, cowardice, compassion, tyranny, fear, prejudice, achievement, frustration, terrorism, war, political bickering, propaganda, and bitter controversy. Most of the points of difference in the struggle have not been settled and, in spite of hundreds of volumes written on the subject, all the sources are not available to the historians.

It is difficult to give a full and impartial account. All that a contemporary historian can do is to sketch the main moves, but even then he will be criticised by one side or the other or, often, by both.

We have already mentioned that, for the Zionists, the term "national home" in the Balfour Declaration meant a national state. In 1919, and repeatedly afterwards, Dr. Chaim Weizmann, head of the Zionist organization, and others, stated that they wanted Palestine to be "just as Jewish as England is English." For the achievement of such an aim two things were essential. One was to transfer Jewish populations from Europe and other countries to Palestine, and the second was to secure land for the immigrants to settle. Even before the Balfour Declaration, Zionists aimed to settle Jews in the countryside and discourage as much as possible emigration to crowded cities. All through the years between the two wars, the Zionists tried to implement these two goals. Their success in both programs alarmed the Palestinian Arabs.

The King-Crane Commission sensed the importance of these two points and recommended "serious modification of the extreme Zionist Program for Palestine of unlimited immigration of Jews, looking finally to make Palestine distinctly a Jewish state." The reason for the modification was the fact that the "anti-Zionist feeling in Palestine and Syria is intense and not lightly to be flouted." But as we have seen, the peacemakers did not pay much attention to the report of this commission. On April 25, 1920, the San Remo Conference gave the mandate over Palestine to Great Britain, and two years later, the Council of the League of Nations confirmed it. Not only was the Balfour Declaration included in the text of the mandate, but also a number of points which the Zionist delegation had presented to the Peace Conference. It recognized the Jewish Agency, which was to work with the administration in all "matters as may affect the establishment of the Jewish national home." It also recognized the Zionist organization "as such agency." Furthermore, the administration of Palestine was instructed to facilitate Jewish immigration and encourage them to settle on the land, "including state lands and waste lands not required for public purpose." The Jewish Agency was like a government within the administration of the mandate with wide responsibilities and powers. It is important to note that no such provision was made for the Palestinian Arabs. Indeed the mandate articles do not refer to Arabs, except a few times indirectly, as the "non-Jewish" or "other sections of the population."

Soon after the San Remo Conference, Great Britain appointed Sir Herbert Samuel, a prominent British Jew, as the high commissioner. He was the first Jewish ruler of Palestine in more than 2,000 years. Whether or not the British authorities wanted to impress the Arabs with that is not known. What is certain, however, is that Sir Herbert, perhaps because he was a Jew, leaned over backwards to be fair and just to the Arab population. It is part of the irony of history that it was Sir Herbert who appointed Haj Amin al-Husayni as Mufti of Jerusalem. The latter claimed descent from the Prophet, was educated in Azhar, and fought on the Turkish side during the war. As Mufti, he was in charge of the religious endowments, *waqf*, which amounted to about $300,000 a year. He became the head of the Supreme Council and later headed the intensely anti-British, anti-Zionist Palestine Higher Committee. The British put a price on his head during World War II while he was broadcasting anti-Allied and anti-Jewish speeches from Berlin.

The first anti-Zionist uprising broke out in Jerusalem in 1921. A local commission under the chairmanship of Sir Thomas Haycraft, Chief Justice of Palestine, reported that the Arabs had instigated the riots because of their fear of Zionist programs. Winston Churchill, however, as head of the Colonial Office, issued a lengthy statement which was designed to please both sides. He emphasized that it was not the aim of Great Britain "that Palestine should become as Jewish as England is English." He also stated that "the Jewish People will be in Palestine as of right and not on sufferance." During the 30 years of the life of the mandate, Great Britain tried to carry out the two diametrically contradictory purposes of the Balfour Declaration, namely, to help establish a national home for the Jews and to safeguard the civil and religious rights of the Arabs. Since they could not do both at the same time, they first did one and then the other, depending upon the situation. Zionists, however, insisted that Great Britain did not have dual obligations "of equal weight." They claimed that the safeguarding of the rights of the non-Jewish people was a "secondary and subordinate clause" and should not be given the same importance as the main purpose of the document, which was the establishment of a national home.

After the initial riots of 1921 there followed some eight years of calm. The mandate government allowed the formation of the Palestine Arab Executive Committee which acted as an unofficial spokesman for the Arabs. This committee did not have the official sanction or the powers of the Jewish Agency, which was active in bringing in Jewish settlers and acquiring land. The Jewish Agency also introduced new industries into Palestine, and by 1939 some 90 per cent of all industries in Palestine were owned by Jews. But industrialization did not cause as much friction as did immigration and the acquiring of land.

The Palestinian Arabs were apprehensive lest excessive and rapid immigration of Jews cause the Arabs to become a minority in what they considered their own country. This, of course, was precisely what the Zionists planned to do. In 1922, the year in which the first census was taken, the estimated population of Palestine was about 744,000, of which 83,000 were Jews. Between 1922 and 1930 the Arab population increased by 23 per cent, while the Jewish population increased by almost 100 per cent. The contrast in the rate of increase from 1931 to 1940 is even more striking. The Arab population grew about 30 per cent while the Jewish population more than tripled. In 1920 the Jews formed about 9 per cent of the population of Palestine but in 1940 the ratio had increased to about 30 per cent.

From the above summary statistics and other sources we can safely deduce a few points. In the first place, the rate of Jewish immigration from the date of the mandate to 1932 was not large. In the second place the bulk of Jews migrating were from Poland and Russia. In the third place, the majority of these migrants, in spite of inducements offered by the Zionists, did not want to go to Palestine but to the United States and other western countries. In the fourth place, it was usually only when there were persecutions and other discriminations that the Jews thought of going to Palestine. For example, in 1925, the restrictive immigration laws of the United States reduced Jewish immigration to that country from 50,000 in 1924 to only 10,000 in 1925, which explains the sharp rise of immigration to Palestine in that year. Finally, one may surmise that were it not for Hitler's rise to power and his wanton and systematic annihilation of the Jews of Europe, Palestine might have remained a peaceful national home for the Jews rather than a turbulent national state.

The large and rapid increase of population in Palestine naturally caused economic crisis and widespread unemployment among both Jews and Arabs. The Zionists, however, had funds from outside and well-organized groups in Palestine to take care of their members. The most important economic and social organization created by the Zionists was the Jewish Federation of Labor, *Histadrut*, which was not merely a trade union but also controlled rural and industrial cooperatives for production and marketing, hospitals, schools, banks, and insurance. The Arabs did not have similar organizations and felt the economic dislocation more severely. No doubt the activities of Histadrut in behalf of labor helped the Arab laborers, especially on the railways and in the ports of Palestine, but these were not enough to offset the fact that in Zionist-owned industries, which were about 90 per cent of the total, Arab laborers did not feel welcome.

Immigration did not arouse the indignation of the rural Arabs as much as the land policy of the Jewish Agency. The question of "land transfer" became a thorny issue between the two groups. The Zionists had rightly concluded that they could not build a viable Jewish state without Jewish rural and agricultural settlements. Inasmuch as the mandate government did not put the state lands at their disposal, the Zionists bought land from the Arab owners at high prices. In an arid land like Palestine farmers were, of necessity, huddled together in villages where there was a spring. Often the land surrounding the village belonged to an absentee Arab landlord who lived in Jerusalem, Beirut, or Damascus. Even though the landlord held title to the grazing land and water, these were used by all the village. The village was a social as well as an agricultural unit. The Arab landlord who sold the land made a good profit, but it was the Arab farmer who bore the brunt of this transaction.

It was the Zionist plan to purchase farmlands and encourage Jewish immigrants to settle on the land and learn to become farmers. In the majority of cases, the purchase of land by Zionists meant that Arab farmers had to be evicted. Lands bought by the Jewish National Fund, a subsidiary of the Jewish Agency, was declared "national land" and was not transferable to non-Jews. Furthermore, the Jewish cooperatives, or whoever else received the land for cultivation, were not allowed to use Arab labor. The dislocated Arab farmer who went to the cities to find work faced difficulties partly because the Zionist industries were reluctant to employ him and those that did paid him lower wages. It must be mentioned, however, that most of the Arab workers were unskilled and had a hard time adjusting to modern industrial methods. Those Arab farmers who stayed on the land soon witnessed the rise of modern settlements next to their villages, against which they could not compete. The people in these new settlements not only spoke a different language and followed a different religion, but used different methods of agriculture and held different social values. It is not surprising that the Arabs could be readily aroused to try to expel the strange invaders.

One of the strange phenomena in the Jewish settlement of Palestine was the fact that the funds were contributed largely by the Jewish capitalists of western Europe or the United States, who were firm believers in free enterprise, while the recipients of these funds were socialist or Marxist idealists of Poland and Russia, who had definite tendencils toward collectivism. Chief among these collective settlements were the *kibbutz* and the *moshav*. The kibbutz combined collective farming and collective living, with a common mess hall and common nursery. All profits went to the group and individuals received weekly spending money from the treasury. The moshav, on the other hand, was a regular cooperative where each family had its own apartment and retained a good deal of freedom socially as well as economically.

In spite of all the encouragement given by the Zionist organization for the return to the land by 1943 only about 13.2 per cent of the Jews were engaged in agriculture. Their efforts were more marked in the field of industry. By 1944, the Jews owned over 2,000 industries employing some 45,000 workers. Chief among these were the Palestine Electro Corporation, for harnessing the Jordan and Yarmuk rivers, and the Palestine Potash Company on the Dead Sea.

The Zionists established a complete Hebrew school system comprising elementary and secondary schools, trade, art and music schools as well as a technical college and the Hebrew University. One of the most impressive achievements of the Zionists in Palestine was the revival of Old Testament Hebrew and the use of it in a modern industrial and technical society.

The Jews in Palestine had their own communal organizations composed of elected assemblies and enjoyed certain degrees of self-government. There were numerous political parties represented among the Jewish settlers of Palestine, from communism to capitalism and from the religious to the secular. There were parties within parties. For example, a religious socialist and a secular socialist formed two parties although they agreed on economic issues.

Of even greater significance was the division of Jews in their ideas concerning the future of Palestine. Zionists were in favor of establishing a Jewish state in cooperation with the mandate administration. In their planning the Zionists ignored the Arabs. Herzl, the founder of modern Zionism, in his book *The*

Jewish State, does not mention the Arabs at all. In an official report to the Anglo-American Commission of 1946, the Jewish Agency stated that the rights of the non-Jewish population of Palestine would be safeguarded "so far as might be compatible with" the establishment of a Jewish national home. David Ben-Gurion, the first Prime Minister of Israel, in his book *Rebirth and Destiny of Israel*, stated that "The State of Israel is a part of the Middle East only in geography. . . ." The unfortunate (because it was not true) but enduring motto of the Zionists was Israel Zangwil's phrase "a land without people for a people without land."

A group of Zionists who went by the name of Revisionists were opposed to the policy of moderation pursued by the main body of Zionists. They opposed the British mandate and wanted to create a Jewish state over the whole area which had been originally demanded by the Zionists at the Paris Peace Conference in 1919. The map which they had submitted at that time included most of Transjordan and a major part of Syria and Lebanon. Still another group among the Zionists organized the *Ihud* (Union) Party. Its purpose was union with the Arabs. The proponents of this program were Judah Magnes, President of the Hebrew University, Martin Buber, the philosopher, and other intellectuals who favored the formation of a bi-national state in Palestine.

The Jewish Agency, which had organized vast agricultural, cultural, economic, political, and social enterprises, also commanded its own armed forces. In the late nineteenth century small Jewish settlements in Palestine as well as Arab villages did not enjoy the best of security. Each Jewish settlement had its own guardsmen. In 1907, these guardsmen formed an organization called *Hashomer*, which continued into the mandate period as an elite guard. In World War I, Jewish veterans in the British army who returned to Palestine formed a defense corps called *Haganah* to protect Jewish settlements during the numerous disorders. They trained clandestinely and kept arms illegally. They were financed by the Histadrut and the Jewish Agency. By 1936 the Haganah had tacit British recognition and some of its members were accepted in the police force. Another para-military organization was the *Irgun*, the fighting force of the Revisionist Party, which fought the British and the Arabs alike. Even more nationalistic than the Irgun was the *Stern Group*, or "Fighters for the Freedom of Israel." They engaged largely in terroristic activities. The Jewish Agency criticized both the Irgun and the Stern and disavowed any relationship with them until the war with the Arab states in 1948, when all fighting forces came under one command.

Compared with the complete and efficient Jewish organization, the organized activities of the Arab community were insignificant. There were practically no comparable Arab groups in any field. There was the Supreme Muslim Council which had charge of the Muslim religious courts and the religious endowments, but it was not concerned in political or social questions. The political activities of the Arabs were channelled through the union of several parties called the Arab Higher Committee, but they were sporadic and ineffective. Both the Muslim Council and the Higher Committee were headed by the Mufti, Haj Amin al-Husayni, who was extremely anti-British and anti-Zionist. The Arabs depended upon schools opened by the mandate, did not receive any aid from outside and could not boast of all the things which the Zionists had accomplished. In their frustration and in the face of growing Zionist power about the only thing they did do was protest and start riots.

The first major Arab action against the Jews, starting in August of 1929 in Jerusalem, Hebron, and other centers, resulted in casualties on both sides. Sir Walter Shaw headed a commission of inquiry and his report, one of the first among many similar reports in the coming years, appeared in March 1930. It condemned the Arabs but explained that their anger was caused by their frustration and suggested that the government should "issue a clear statement of policy on such matters as immigration, land purchase, and land transfer in order to alleviate the fears of the Arabs." The Zionists attacked the implications of the Shaw Report, whereupon Great Britain sent another mission under Sir John Hope Simpson to study the land problem. This report, which was the basis of the Passfield White Paper issued by the British government, upheld the legality of land purchase by the Zionists, but criticized the provisions which forbade non-Jewish labor on the purchased land, and also banned its resale to non-Jews. On other points, the Passfield White Paper rejected both extremist Zionist and Arab views and asked all to cooperate.

The White Paper caused such resentment among the Zionists that Weizmann resigned as President of the Zionist Organization and the Jewish Agency. The voices of protest from the Zionists in Europe and the United States were so strong that Prime Minister MacDonald of Great Britain wrote a letter to Weizmann to allay his fears on immigration and land purchase. Then it was the Arabs' turn to protest against the Prime Minister's "black letter," and attack the Balfour Declaration once again.

From 1933 to 1936 there were numerous Arab uprisings, most of them directed against the British mandate. In 1936, the different Arab political parties united in the Arab Higher Committee under the leadership of the Mufti of Jerusalem, Haj Amin al-Husayni, and called a general strike. Bombing, sabotage, destruction of Jewish property, and widespread violence accompanied the strike. Trapped by its own hypocrisy in making contradictory promises, Great Britain could do nothing better than to send another fact-finding commission, under Lord Peel in the autumn of 1936. The Peel Commission came to the conclusion that Great Britain could not "both concede the Arab claim to self-government and secure the establishment of the Jewish National Home." It recommended, therefore, that the country be partitioned into Jewish and Arab states with Jerusalem and Bethlehem under the direct administration of the mandate.

The reaction to this first proposal of partition was mixed, both among the Zionists and the Arabs. There were a number of Zionists, among them Weizmann, who favored it because it recognized the aspiration of the Zionists for independent statehood. The Twentieth Zionist Congress in 1937, however, rejected the plan as infringing upon the guarantees made in the Balfour Declaration, but left the door open for further study. Among the Arabs only Abdullah, the Amir of Transjordan, counseled acceptance. The Arab High Committee was against it and a Pan-Arab Congress held in September of 1937 in Syria rejected the plan outright, demanding the withdrawal of the Balfour Declaration.

Soon after the Syrian conference, Arab rebellion broke out again and continued sporadically until the beginning of World War II. The British ordered the arrest of the Mufti of Jerusalem and other extremist members of the Arab Higher Committee, but they fled to Lebanon, from where they directed the rebellion. In 1938, Great Britain, now seemingly acting by force of habit, sent the Woodhead Commission to report on the partition plan, but its report was rejected by the government. The Zionists, on the other hand, were under great pressure because of the rise of Hitler and the rising demand on the part of German Jews to immigrate to Palestine. There was virtual civil war in Palestine. The Haganah received permission from the mandate government to bear arms and the underground, Irgun, became active in terrorism.

Instead of sending another commission, Great Britain convened a round table conference of Arabs and Zionists in London on February 7, 1939. In addition to the moderate and extremist Palestinian Arabs, representatives from Egypt, Iraq, Saudi Arabia, and Transjordan were also invited. For the first time non-Palestinian Arabs were invited to take part in the solution of the Palestine problem. On the other side, both Zionist and non-Zionist Jews were invited, as well as Jewish leaders from Europe and the United States. The conference did not even succeed in making the delegates sit together around one table, owing to Arab refusal, and of course failed to narrow the gap between the two opposing views.

War clouds were, once again, gathering on the European horizon and Britain had to think of the German threat. It did not want the Arabs to side with the Germans. The Egyptians and the Arabs of the Crescent were outwardly friendly but unhappy over Palestine and there was no guarantee what effect concentrated German propaganda might have. Taking the possibility of a second world war into consideration, Great Britain issued a white paper on May 17, 1939. There was a definite reversal of policy in favor of the Arabs. It proposed the creation of an independent bi-national state of Palestine in ten years. It provided for about 75,000 immigrants to enter Palestine in the course of five years, after which further immigration would be conditional on Arab consent. Land sale was allowed in some parts, restricted in others, and forbidden in most of Palestine. Both sides rejected the proposal, though the Zionists were more vehement than the Arabs. There were Zionist demonstrations all over Palestine, and Ben-Gurion, Chairman of the Jewish Agency executive, promised Zionist resistance to British policy.

Strange as it may seem, World War II calmed the strained nerves in the Middle East. For the Zionists the choice was clear. In a war between Great Britain and Hitler's Germany there was no question which side the Zionists would support. In the words of Ben-Gurion, "We shall fight the White Paper as if there is no war; and we shall fight the war as if there is no White Paper." The Zionists wanted to have the opportunity to organize a totally Jewish unit, but the British organized a Palestine Pioneer Corps and opened it to both Arab and Jewish volunteers. By 1944, however, the British relented and allowed the formation of a Jewish brigade with their own insignia and flag. The Arabs, not having the same incentive to fight against Germany as the Zionists, were reluctant. Not more than 9,000 volunteered.

Both the Zionists and Arabs knew that the war between the great powers would eventually determine their fate. The difference was that the Zionists tried in every way possible to assist fate to decide in their favor while the Arabs were prone to leave everything in the hands of Allah.

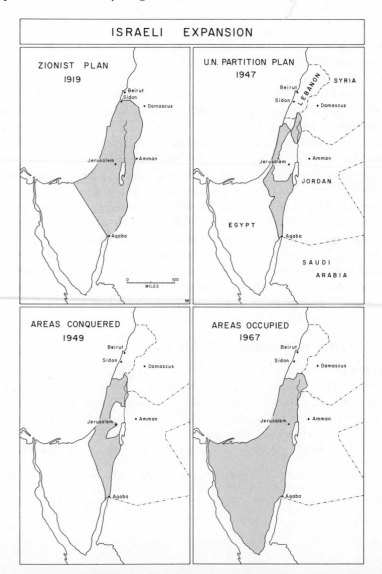

ISRAELI EXPANSION

CHAPTER 31

IRAN—THE PAHLAVI ERA

During World War I, Iran was the scene of numerous battles between the Entente and the Central Powers, even though it had declared its neutrality. Russians and Turks fought in Azarbaijan; the British formed a Persian militia in the south known as the South Persia Rifles; and the Germans tried to arouse the tribes against the Entente through adventurous agents such as Niedermayer and Wassmuss. In the meantime, the young monarch, Ahmad Shah, having come of age, was crowned in July 1914 and Iran began to have some semblance of parliamentary life. The government was in the hands of a coalition of political moderates, tribal gentry, and landed aristocracy, a large number of whom had been against constitutional government a few years before. Ever since the closing of the Majles in 1911 when Shuster was dismissed, the liberal Democrats had been scattered. Since the liberals believed that in case of an Entente victory, Iran would surely be divided between Russia and Great Britain, their sympathies were with Germany and Turkey. Most of those who had fled to Europe gathered in Berlin, from where Hasan Taqizadeh of Tabriz, one of the foremost liberal revolutionaries, edited a paper called *Kaveh*[1] until 1921. Some of the liberals who had remained in Iran made the long trek to Istanbul to make common cause with the Ottomans.

THE SOVIET REPUBLIC OF GILAN

Neither in Berlin nor in Istanbul did the Persian liberals affect the course of events in Iran. There were, however, a few liberals who took matters into their own hands, gathered a small number of armed men, and set up revolutionary governments in Azarbaijan, Gilan, and Khorasan, the northern provinces of Iran. Perhaps the most important of these was the one led by Mirza Kuchek Khan in the province of Gilan south of the Caspian Sea. He and his

[1] Kaveh was the name of the legendary Persian blacksmith who, by raising his leather apron, led a revolt against the tyranny of the non-Persian Zahhak. Kaveh's leather apron became a symbol of Persian freedom and was carried as a standard in war. It was called *Darafsh-e Kaveyani*.

followers had vowed not to shave or cut their hair until foreign troops had withdrawn from Iran. Living as they did in the forests of Gilan, they came to be known as *Jangali*, jungle men, and supported themselves in Robin Hood fashion. For a time, German and Turkish officers trained the Jangali volunteers to harass the British and Russian lines of communication. After the Russian revolution, the Bolsheviks got in touch with the Jangalis through Ehsanullah Khan, a Communist agent from Azarbaijan and a friend of Kuchek Khan.

The relationship between the Jangalis and the Communist Central Committee in Moscow was never stabilized. On the one hand, the Bolsheviks were not sure whether Iran was ideologically "ready" for revolution. On the other hand, only Ehsanullah was a radical Communist among the Jangalis, and the leader Kuchek Khan could not bring himself to cooperate wholeheartedly with the Bolsheviks. Nevertheless, in the spring of 1920 he did accept the aid of the Bolsheviks in forcing the British soldiers, who had occupied northern Iran after the Russian revolution, to evacuate Gilan. A Soviet Republic of Gilan was established in Rasht, the provincial capital, but soon there was a rift among the Jangalis. Kuchek Khan, as a Persian nationalist, would not allow Gilan to become part of Russia, and as a moderate socialist, would not agree to the complete dispossession of Persian landlords and merchants.

It has been mentioned that Moscow was not certain as to what policy to follow. At the same time that a Soviet Republic was being formed in Gilan, Moscow was negotiating a treaty of friendship with the Persian government in Tehran. Eventually Lenin decided to let the situation in Iran develop until it was ready for a Marxist revolution. He withdrew his support from the Jangalis and recalled the Soviet troops. Mirza Kuchek Khan, thus left alone, could not cope with the Persian government forces. His troops were defeated and disbanded and he died of exposure as a fugitive in the mountains of Gilan.

The reasons Moscow refused to annex the Soviet Republic of Gilan and with it perhaps the whole northern littoral are too conjectural and detailed to be elaborated here. The following might be considered.

1. There was doubt among the Bolsheviks whether Iran was advanced enough to accept the Marxist ideology.
2. The Bolsheviks were still idealistic enough to be against annexation as an act of imperialism.
3. There was difference of opinion between Moscow and the Soviet of Azarbaijan which had arranged the Gilan adventure.
4. The Soviet Union was too weak after the civil war and was not certain whether Great Britain would allow it to penetrate into northern Iran.
5. Perhaps Moscow believed that through friendship and propaganda it could someday have the whole country rather than just a province or two.
6. Perhaps the Soviet Union simply made a mistake in not annexing the territory. A quarter of a century later, Ja'far Pishevari, who had a hand in arranging the Gilan project, led a separatist movement in the Persian province of Azarbaijan. Once again Moscow, this time under Stalin, decided to withdraw its troops and allow the Communist rebellion to be crushed by the Persian government.

THE ANGLO-PERSIAN AGREEMENT

The Bolshevik Revolution in Russia affected Iran in diverse ways. One of them was that it, at least temporarily, ended the Anglo-Russian rivalry over the country. The revolution had rendered obsolete the Anglo-Russian Convention of 1907 by which the two countries had divided Iran into spheres of influence. With the absence of Russia it was only natural for Great Britain to fill the vacuum and bring all of Iran under its influence, thereby controlling the land and sea approaches to India as well as the newly discovered oil wells. It was the dream of Foreign Secretary Lord Curzon to create a "chain of vassal states stretching from the Mediterranean to the Pamirs" in which Iran was the "most vital link." In 1919, the veteran British diplomat, Sir Percy Cox, was minister in Tehran and he was given the task of implementing the above policy.

The year 1919 also was the year of the Paris Peace Conference to which Woodrow Wilson's doctrine of self-determination had attracted so many small nations. Iran had also sent a delegation with a set of demands. The British were against admitting Iran to the conference. Wilson was for admitting all delegations, and in the case of Iran, France and Italy were favorable, but Great Britain would not consent. By August 1919 it was announced that Great Britain and Iran had signed an agreement, negotiation for which had been going on secretly for some time. Representing Iran in this ill-famed agreement were Prime Minister Hasan Vosuq al-Doleh and Prince Firuz who had been appointed Foreign Minister by his cousin the Shah.

The agreement was so obviously on the side of Great Britain that it aroused the wrath not only of Persian liberals but also of countries like the United States and France. After the usual promise to respect absolutely the independence and integrity of Persia, the agreement went on to stipulate the following:

1. Great Britain would provide advisors for as many Persian departments as considered necessary. Iran would agree to pay the cost and to endow the advisors with "adequate powers."
2. Great Britain would organize and train a Persian army at the expense of the Persian government.
3. A loan of £2,000,000 at 7 per cent was arranged to pay for the above, and collateral was to be "all the revenues and customs receipts" of Iran.
4. Great Britain would improve communication in Iran by "means of railway construction and other forms of transport."

The agreement was designed to bring Iran under the tutelage of Great Britain and in many ways it was similar to the unilateral agreement imposed upon Egypt in 1922.

The reaction to the agreement was immediate and negative. Not so much by the opposition of the Persians, as by that of the United States, the agreement was abandoned. It must be stated that combined with the idealism of Woodrow Wilson was the desire of American oil companies to gain concessions in Iran. The companies did not like the monopoly which such an agreement gave to

Great Britain. The British, on the other hand, were so sure of themselves that even before the agreement was ratified by the Majles (it never was), they dispatched three chief advisors to Iran, Armitage-Smith for finances, General Dickson for the military, and Sir Herbert Smith for customs. The scuttling of the agreement was a blow to British prestige, but soon they found another scheme to regain their influence in Iran. In view of the impossibility of direct control, a strong anti-Russian government in Iran, friendly to Great Britain, would serve the purposes of the empire. They proceeded to bring about such a change.

THE COUP D'ETAT OF 1921

Iran was in a state of hiatus in 1920. The Constitutional Monarchy was neither strong nor constitutional. The cabinet changed hands from one member of the landed gentry to another. The failure of the agreement had left a vacuum and the establishment of the Soviet Republic of Gilan had made the Persian leaders apprehensive of Bolshevism. This hiatus was broken by a coup d'etat in the early hours of February 21, 1921. Some 2,500 Cossacks under the command of Colonel Reza Khan, accompanied by newspaper editor Sayyed Ziya al-Din Tabatabai, moved to Tehran from Qazvin, 60 miles to the west, and took control of the capital. There was practically no opposition. In the morning, a number of well-known individuals from different economic and political groups were arrested. The frightened Shah was forced to appoint Sayyed Ziya as Prime Minister and to give the title of *Sardar-e Sepah*, Commander of the Army, to Reza Khan.

Sayyed Ziya was a moderate nationalist and editor of the middle-of-the-road newspaper *Ra'd* (Thunder), which was known for its pro-British editorials. He was suspect among the liberals because of his pro-British attitude and was not prominent enough socially to be a confidant of the landed gentry. His political activity was centered in the *Pulad* Committee, which was founded by the British in Esfahan. His only official connection with the government was membership in the Persian delegation of 1919 to the Caucasus to sign treaties of friendship with some of the states who hoped to be independent of Bolshevik Russia.

Reza Khan, on the other hand, was a military man, tall, with a commanding personality, and with little education. He had risen to a position of command in the Russian-dominated Cossack force by dint of courage and initiative. When the Bolshevik Revolution left the Russian officers of the Persian Cossack regiment stranded, Reza Khan was the leader of a group of Persian officers who ousted the Russians and took control of the regiment themselves. Because of his military upbringing, his brand of nationalism envisaged the glory of Iran under a unified military regime. Because of his harsh experience under Russian commanders he was generally anti-foreign and especially anti-Bolshevik and anti-Russian.

So far as can be ascertained these two men, Reza Khan and Sayyed Ziya, who were opposite each other in temperament, education, and almost everything else imaginable, did not know each other. They had met, probably for the first time, on the night of the coup d'etat in Shahabad, a few miles outside Tehran. Furthermore, their plans after the success of the coup were not coordinated. A large number of men were arrested but it was evident that a list had not been prepared in advance. They arrested liberals, moderates, conservatives, rich and poor seemingly without discrimination. Sometimes Reza would free a person whom Ziya had ordered arrested. Sayyed Ziya did not even have his cabinet picked before the coup d'etat. A third group must have made the preliminary arrangements; all evidence seems to point to the British.

Of Ziya's friendship with Colonel Smythe, the military representative, and Howard, the political representative of Great Britain, there is no doubt. His frequent visits with these men and others during the days before the coup, and his nocturnal meetings with British friends for the purpose of "reciting and explaining modern Persian poetry to them" are also attested. Furthermore, the Cossack troops, who had ragged uniforms in Qazvin, were well-clad and wearing British military boots when they entered Tehran. The Tehran government, which was advised of the Cossack move toward the capital, sent a small delegation to Shahabad to see what was happening. Oddly enough, two representatives of the British legation went with them and, even more odd, they happened to have enough money along to be distributed among the troops. Furthermore, the British Information Services in World War II issued a statement acknowledging that Great Britain had a hand in the coup d'etat.[2]

To say that Sayyed Ziya and Reza Khan were aided by the British in taking control of the Persian government does not mean that they had made the interests of Iran subservient to those of Great Britain. Such a charge could probably be made against Vosuq al-Doleh who signed the agreement of 1919, but not against Ziya or Reza. The government of Sayyed Ziya did not last more than three months. His arrests had made him enemies among liberals and reactionaries alike. He was highhanded with all types of people from the Shah down, but he did not have the power to back up his pretensions. The military was loyal to his rival, Reza Khan. On April 25, 1921, Reza Khan was admitted to the cabinet as Minister of War. The immediate issue between the two was the fate of the Gendarmerie, a military force under the Minister of Interior, and also the British military advisors who were still around. Reza Khan wanted to unify the armed forces and dismiss the British. Sayyed Ziya opposed both moves and was defeated. On May 24, 1921, he was forced to leave Iran. He lived in Palestine and did not return until World War II, when the British and Russian forces were once again in Iran and his rival had abdicated the throne. Sayyed Ziya did not think that anything substantial could be

---

[2] There is no biography of Reza Khan, who later became the Shah of Iran. Sayyed Ziya has not published his complete memoirs. This event is important for the study of the nature and methods of imperialism. Students would do well to read the pro-British book, "Modern Iran," by Peter Avery of Cambridge University (Praeger, 1965) on this and other issues.

accomplished in Iran without the aid of a foreign power. Among the big powers, he consistently preferred Great Britain.

Reza Khan was different. He believed that nothing could be accomplished without a strong central military government which was free of foreign intervention. He used the British to come to power and then tried more than once to get rid of them. In his career he was forced to employ foreign advisors, though he was not at ease in their presence, and never kept them on a project more than a few years. Such xenophobia was not healthy, but one wonders whether, in the second decade of the twentieth century, any other attitude would have convinced the Persians that they could build an army without a foreign advisor and construct a railroad from the Caspian Sea to the Persian Gulf without floating a foreign loan.

IRAN-SOVIET TREATY OF 1921

Five days after the coup d'etat, a Russo-Persian Treaty which had been negotiated between the previous Persian Cabinet and Moscow, was signed. The immediate results of the treaty were the withdrawal of Soviet troops from Gilan, which caused the eventual destruction of the Soviet Republic of Gilan. Mirza Kuchek Khan became a fugitive in the mountains of Gilan and died from exposure. The text of the treaty, which was published widely by the Russians, was ostensibly a declaration of anti-imperialist and anti-colonialist policy of the Bolshevik government and was a pleasant contrast to the Anglo-Persian Agreement of 1919 which had just been officially repudiated. By this treaty, the Russians gave all the Russian assets, concessions, and properties to Iran provided that Iran promise (Article 13) not to cede any of these to a third power, but to "retain them for the benefit of the Persian people." The treaty, however, retained some vestiges of Tsarist imperialism and some provisions for future Russian proletarian imperialism.

For example, the Caspian Fishery Concession of 1867 and the tariff regulation of 1902 remained unchanged. Fish were necessary for the food supply of Russia and the tariff was favorable to the Soviet Union. In 1927, a new Irano-Soviet Fisheries Company was set up with a concession to operate for 25 years. But the tariff was not revised and Persian trade suffered as a result. Iran tried to set up state monopolies in order to compete with Soviet trade monopolies. On the whole, the growing rigidity of the governments of the Soviet Union and Iran, under Stalin and Reza Shah, was not conducive to freedom of trade.

What caused Iran a good deal of trouble in later years was Article 6, which stated that if a third power attempted "to use Persian territory as a base of operation against Russia . . . Russia shall have the right to advance her troops into the Persian interior . . . ." This article was used by the Soviet Union to invade Iran in September 1941 and at other times to object to Iran's security agreements with non-Communist countries after World War II.

PERSIAN OIL: THE SECOND PHASE

The Soviet Union had an opportunity to invoke Article 13 of the treaty almost immediately. When Sayyed Ziya went into exile in May 1921, Reza Khan did not seize the premiership, but freed all those who had been arrested. One of these, Qavam al-Saltaneh, brother of Vosuq al-Doleh, became the Prime Minister. Qavam belonged to that school of Persian diplomacy which believed that a third power was needed to neutralize the powers of Great Britain and Russia. Qavam's name in modern Persian history is connected with the northern oil and American financial missions.

On November 22, 1921, the Persian government signed a contract allowing Standard Oil Company to exploit the northern oil for fifty years. The Anglo-Persian Oil Company filed a protest on the ground that the concession for northern oil was given in 1916 to Khoshtaria.[3] The British had bought the rights for £100,000 and had formed a company called the North Persia Oil. They claimed that the Persian government had no right to grant concessions for the same territory to two parties. The Russians, on the other hand, who did not want American interests to be in northern Iran, protested that according to Article 13 of the treaty, Iran had promised not to cede to a third party a concession which the Soviet government had given up. Iran's answer to both was that since the Khoshtaria agreement had not been ratified by the Majles, as the constitution required, it had become null and void and could not be considered valid.

The wrangling over this matter, especially between the British and Americans, continued for some time. The British had the advantage because the A.P.O.C. had the exclusive right of oil transportation in the Persian Gulf area and would not allow Standard to pipe oil to any port in the south, which is the best outlet for the northern oil. On February 28, 1922, the British and American companies agreed to a partnership in which the Americans would have voting control. The Persians, however, did not agree for the British company to have a hand in the north and rejected the whole project.

At this time, the Sinclair Oil Company became interested in the project. Sinclair's advantage over Standard was that it had received oil concessions on Sakhalin Island from the Soviet Union and also the rights to market Soviet oil in the world. It was believed that the Soviet Union would permit Sinclair to export the northern oil via its territory. The Persian Majles had already passed a law permitting the government to grant a concession for the northern oil to "any independent and responsible American company." One of the conditions was that the concessionaire float a loan of $10,000,000 for the Persian government. The question of the loan was not an easy problem, but Sinclair came to Iran with the blessings of the Soviet Union, so it seemed, and started negotiations.

[3] See above, p. 230.

The Sinclair oil negotiation and the events connected with it have all the ingredients for international intrigue, scandal, arson, and murder. To begin with, in March 1924, when the Majles ratified the Sinclair Concession, part of the Majles building caught fire, reportedly at the hands of an arsonist. In April, the American Blair and Company sent a certain James Forbes to study Iran's security for a loan, but the British emphasized that they would not allow the pledging of southern customs for a loan in the United States. Then in the summer of 1924, when the Sinclair representative was in Iran, Tehran was rocked by two events. First, a bizarre religious revival occurred, which culminated in the report that a miracle had been wrought at one of the water fountains of the city. Hundreds of the sick and afflicted went to this place for cure and thousands of others went to watch. Second, Major Imbrie, the United States vice consul, at the instigation of an American employee of the Anglo-Persian Oil Company, went to photograph the place of the miracle. He was murdered by the mob, while his companion was not harmed. The official investigation seems to indicate that the police looked the other way and did not try to rescue the American. The summer of 1924 was also the date of the American Teapot Dome Scandal, which involved the Sinclair Company. How much each of these events contributed to the failure of the project is conjecture. What is important, however, is that the question of northern oil did not come up again until after World War II.

REZA SHAH PAHLAVI

The Persian government's attempt to involve the Americans in northern Iran failed, but it succeeded in employing Dr. Arthur Millspaugh, the economic advisor to the American Department of State, as financial advisor in Iran. Dr. Millspaugh and his party arrived in Iran in 1922 and for five years served Iran well. Thanks to Millspaugh's financial and economic policies, the Minister of War, Reza Khan, had enough money to organize and train the army. Reza Khan used it to subdue rebellion, disarm the tribes, and bring every corner of the country under the authority of the central government. Ruthless methods were used, but the roads were safe from brigands and for the first time in almost a century well-laden caravans could travel in all parts of the country without molestation. To a people who had been at the mercy of outlaws for a lifetime, security was more important than freedom to vote.

In October 1923, Reza Khan became Prime Minister, the first time since the revolution that a military man had become the head of government. Indeed, at this time most of the governors of the provinces were military men and those who were not were under the power of the military commanders of the areas. Election for the fifth session of the Majles was held, mostly under the influence of military governors or commanders. In many ways it was one of the most eventful sessions in the modern history of Iran. It was also the last one, until 1942, in which the deputies dared to speak their minds.

It may be safely stated that Reza Khan was to the Persian Revolution what Napoleon was to the French Revolution. Reza was a child of the revolution and was also its critic. He believed in many of the goals of the revolution, but not in its method, which was envisaged to be democratic. In the fifth Majles there were three factions: the Reformers, made up of individuals who approved of both the program and the method of Reza Khan; Socialists, who supported him but hoped to influence him in the line of democracy; and the "minority" of half a dozen deputies under the cleric Modarres, who for diverse reasons were opposed to Reza Khan. The rest were independent.

Soon after Reza Khan became prime minister, Ahmad Shah went on one of his frequent trips to Europe. In February 1924, there was talk of establishing a republic and telegrams came from many parts of the country, instigated by military commanders, asking the Majles to depose the Qajar dynasty. Criticism against the Qajar was fairly common, but there was sharp disagreement over the establishment of a republic. In the Majles and out, the proponents of a republic were the liberals, moderates, military, and other individuals who had hitched their wagons to Reza Khan's star. The opponents of the idea were the clerics and the shopkeepers of the bazaars, who generally followed the clerics. Allied to the clerics were a small number of intensely anticlerical liberals who were ideologically in favor of a republic, but whose devotion to the principles of democracy and civilian rule made them oppose this particular movement because it was led by a "dictator and a cossack."

The masses of Tehran were under the influence of the clergy, so they demonstrated against the republic and Reza Khan. The murder of the young anticlerical poet, Eshqi, who had lampooned the dictatorship of Reza Khan and his "synthetic republic," added fuel to the fire. Reza Khan was shrewd enough to see the hadwriting on the wall. He hurried to the shrine city of Qom south of Tehran, consulted with the chief religious dignitaries, and issued a proclamation stating that since the defense of Islam was the foundation of the program of the Persian government, he and the religious dignitaries had decided to ask the people "to stop [mention of] the republic and instead spend their energies helping me to . . . strengthen the foundations of Islam and the independence of the country."

The failure of the republican movement did not save the Qajar dynasty. From Paris, the Shah dismissed Reza Khan as prime minister and asked the Majles to recommed another person. The Majles ignored the wishes of the Shah and recommended Reza Khan, who almost immediately took steps to assume complete sovereignty. Deputies were called to his house to sign a resolution asking the Majles to depose Ahmad Shah, make Reza Khan the provisional head of the state, and call a constituent assembly to choose a permanent one. Most of them signed the document. On October 31, 1925, the Majles deposed the unlamented Qajar Dynasty and called for a constituent assembly.

Only four deputies had the courage to oppose the resolution. Of these, Yahya Dolatabadi, left public life, while Dr. Mohammad Mosaddeq went into political banishment within Iran for a while and assumed great power after World War II; Taqizadeh and Ala served the new Shah in important posts. It is important to note that in their speeches none of them defended the pleasure-loving Ahmad Shah or his brother the crown prince. All of them opposed the resolution because it was "against the constitution." Only Dr. Mosaddeq, a constitutional lawyer, explained that it was to the advantage of the country to have Reza active as Prime Minister rather than inactive as a constitutional monarch. If Reza Khan were to became an active monarch, he would then become a dictator rather than a constitutional monarch.

The liberal and the socialist factions of the Majles who had signed the resolution agreed with Dr. Mosaddeq, but they thought they had taken care of the problem. In return for their signature, Reza Khan had agreed to make the kingship elective. They thought they had arrived at a republican form of government through the back door and were quite satisfied. In December, however, when the Constituent Assembly convened, there was no mention of an elected shah but instead a permanent dynasty was established. Sulaiman Eskandari, the leader of the socialists, was outraged, but it was too late. On December 12, 1925, Iran had a new king, Reza Shah Pahlavi.

REZA SHAH AND REFORM

Reza Shah was popular among the masses because his military power had brought security to the country. The villagers no longer needed to carry guns to defend themselves against the brigands. The ruthlessness of the Shah was directed against tribal chiefs and the grandees, not against the peasants. He was also popular among the educated classes and among liberals because he was a reformer with an open determination to westernize Iran. The reforms began almost as soon as he became prime minister and continued for over 15 years.

All his life the army remained the object of his special devotion. Oil royalties were spent to supply its needs for weapons, and compulsory military service was enacted to meet its needs for men. It was through the army that most of his reforms were channelled. He built roads, constructed wireless service, and took over from the British the management of the telegraph company. His crowning glory in the field of communication was the building of a railway from the Caspian to the Persian Gulf. This bold project, which was started in 1927 and completed in 1938, was financed by a special tax on sugar and tea, with no loan from foreign governments. Reza Shah did not abolish private enterprise, but organized foreign trade monopolies and subjected all commerce to strict governmental control. In 1928, he established the National Bank of Iran and withdrew the privilege of issuing banknotes from the British Imperial Bank. In 1927, he had abolished extraterritoriality.

Almost as soon as he became king he curbed the powers of the ulama. Religious endowments were taken out of their hands, Islamic law was partially set aside in favor of western law, and Islamic education was abandoned in the public schools. The Islamic lunar calendar was abolished and gave place to the old Persian-Zoroastrian solar calendar with its Persian names for the months of the year. The month-long mourning for the death of Husayn, the grandson of the Prophet, was reduced to three weeks, and carried on without religious processions. Some mosques were "modernized" by the introduction of chairs, and some old shrines were changed into museums. The call to prayer was frowned upon, and going to Mecca for pilgrimage was discouraged.

Reza Shah abolished all titles and asked the people to select family names; he himself chose the name of Pahlavi, honored in pre-Islamic Persian history. He introduced modern education and established schools, in 1934 founding the University of Tehran. He prohibited the use of Persian attire and hats for men, in favor of European costume. He took away the divorce privileges of men and in 1935 abolished the use of the veil by women. He established the Persian Academy, whose main task was to rid the Persian language of borrowed Arabic words. In all these and other reforms he used force. In order to silence the critics of the reforms all criticism was banned, the number of newspapers dwindled to a handful, and the handpicked deputies of the Majles eulogized His Majesty the Shahanshah.

PERSIAN OIL: THE THIRD PHASE

After the failure of the Persian government to involve the Americans in the oil of northern Iran, the Anglo-Persian Oil Company had a virtual monopoly for the exploitation of the country's oil. With the exception of technical experts, most of the administrators of the company in Iran were recruited from members of the Government of India. These individuals brought their paternalistic attitude of superiority with them and dealt with Persians as they had dealt with the Indians. For a long time, all the accounts of the company were in Indian rupees and the laborers were paid in that currency.

The establishment of a strong nationalistic government in Iran under Reza Shah could not allow the old order to last in the administration of the oil company and its relation with the government. In 1928, when the Shah went to Khuzestan to open a new road, he did not accept the invitation of the company to visit the oil installations. Instead he sent them a message saying that he was not satisfied with the "pittance" which Iran was receiving from the large profits of the company and wanted to revise the D'Arcy Concession. While prolonged negotiations were going on in 1931, the oil royalties showed a sharp decline and the Persian government refused to accept payment. On November 27, 1932, Taqizadeh, the Minister of Finance, in a letter to the Company, announced the cancellation of the D'Arcy Concession on the grounds that the government could not be bound by a concession granted prior to the establishment of constitutional regime. The letter further stated that the government was willing to negotiate a new concession. The British government objected and the matter went to the League of Nations. In the end, however, it was settled out of court by the untimely intervention of the Shah in 1933. He became impatient and personally negotiated a new agreement which, on the surface, was a victory for Iran, but in the long run was worse than the D'Arcy Concession. The Shah was unaware of the implications of the agreement and no one dared oppose him.

The Concession of 1933 had two superficial advantages for Iran which no doubt pleased Reza Shah. The area of the concession was reduced considerably, but the company had gathered considerable geological data and saw to it that almost all of the oil was within the 100,000 square miles left to it. Secondly, the royalty on the basis of per ton production guaranteed Iran a fixed income in time of depression, but in times of prosperity all that Iran received was 20 per cent of the dividends distributed to ordinary stockholders. The most serious losses to Iran in the new agreement were twofold. In one article the company was exempted from all taxation, and in the other the duration of the concession was set at 60 years from 1933, which extended the time of the concession by 30 years.

EVALUATION OF REZA SHAH'S REFORMS

Many writers compare Reza Shah's reforms with those of Ataturk, and there are those who believe that Reza Shah emulated the Turkish reformer. On the surface it appears that he did, and it may be likely that he was influenced by the Turkish dictator. But this should not obscure the differences between the two individuals and especially the two countries. Reza Shah had practically no education, no knowledge of the world, and no well-defined program. He did not form a party, did not make speeches, and had no ideology to expound. His choice of reforms was based on the suggestion of his advisors, his own desire for power, and his personal attitude which had tendencies of superficiality and xenophobia.

Furthermore, Reza Shah had an insatiable thirst for wealth, especially in real estate. When Reza Shah died, he was not only the largest landowner in the history of the country, but he also owned factories and hotels. No doubt he rationalized that he was developing all this for the good of the country. This was partly true, but for the acquisition and management of these lands he had to depend on others, who in the process acquired land and business monopolies for themselves. Reza Shah's pampering of the army made tyrants of a large number of his officers, who suppressed the masses, especially in the provinces, for their own gains. When war clouds began to gather in the later years of the 1930's, the very army which had been the object of his devotion had become the most important single reason for the disaffection of the masses against him. To strengthen himself and to make his dictatorship more efficient he sought help from Hitler, who was glad to send him advisors. Throughout his life, perhaps as a result of his experience in the Cossack Brigade, he was wary of the Russians. He had his quarrels with the British over oil and other subjects, but managed to solve them amicably. Under Reza Shah, Iran and Turkey, which had been old foes, started a friendship which has continued. In 1937, Afghanistan, Iran, Iraq, and Turkey signed the Sa'dabad pact which became a forerunner of CENTO after World War II.

Nevertheless, Reza Shah was a reformer whose lack of education made him a devotee of the glitter of western civilization rather than of its substance. He accepted the suggestion of his advisors by sending scores of students to Europe to study, but did not allow them to express themselves when they returned. The outward facade of democracy was maintained and the handpicked members of the Majles went through the motions of decision-making. There were improvements, however, in communication, commerce, industry, and education. A new group had risen and became the entrepreneurs and contractors of the new era. The old titles were abolished and some of the holders of those titles left public life. Their places were taken by the members of the emerging middle class who, because of their education, held the new titles of "doktor" or "mohandes" (engineer). These people eventually took the leadership in Iran when Reza Shah was forced to abdicate in 1941.

CHAPTER 32

MIDDLE EAST IN WORLD WAR II

The Middle East was the scene of fewer battles during World War II than during the previous world war. Nevertheless, its strategic location and oil resources made the area as tense as ever.

TURKEY

Turkey declared its neutrality and was able to maintain it almost until the end. The Turks did not take part in the ideological conflict which divided Europe during the years before the outbreak of the second world war. They were not communists or fascists, nor were they socialists or capitalists. The rulers of Turkey were military men, bureaucrats, and intellectuals who were intensely nationalistic. Turkish attitudes toward the major countries of Europe can be explained under three heads. Historically the Turks were conditioned not to trust Russia, economically they favored Germany and valued its trade, and culturally they were attracted by the institutions and mores of Great Britain and France.

When the Russo-German treaty was signed in 1939, the Turks were apprehensive over the fate of the Straits. Shukru Sarajoglu, the Foreign Minister of Turkey, went to Moscow but came back empty-handed because the Russians wanted Turkey to close the Straits and promise not to participate in a war against Germany. Turkey could not accept this and instead signed a treaty of mutual assistance with Great Britain and France, under which Turkey was under no obligation to open hostilities against the Soviet Union. Even though Turkey was under obligation to assist Britain and France in case war spread in the Mediterranean, it saw fit to ignore its treaty obligations and remain neutral when Mussolini entered the conflict.

When Germany attacked Russia in 1941, a situation somewhat similar to that in World War I was created for Turkey, in that Great Britain, France, and Russia were allied against Germany. Hitler's armies had control of the Balkans, and Turkey was hard-pressed by Germany to cancel its treaty with

Britain and France. Rather than risk the displeasure of an apparent victor of World War II, Turkey unashamedly signed a pact with Germany in June 1941, thereby breaking its agreement with Britain and France. There was also a trade agreement for the sale of raw materials, especially chrome ore.

During most of the war, Turkey was the center of spying and intrigue, as citizens of all the belligerent nations were free to come and go. Economically the war was a strain. All the products of Turkey, such as chrome, oil, mohair, tobacco, etc., had ready customers among the antagonists. Indeed, one side would buy the above materials at high prices in order to prevent the other side from purchasing them. There was a large supply of foreign exchange in the country, which could not be used for imports. This caused inflation and budgetary deficits. Furthermore, Turkey had to maintain a large army and in order to raise money levied a special tax based on the income of individuals. Special committees in each province were given power to determine the amount. On the whole, the Greeks, Armenians, Jews, and foreigners bore the brunt of this taxation and the harsh treatment which followed noncompliance with assessment. The increased taxes did not last more than a year, but they left a bad impression upon the non-Turkish citizens of Turkey who had been victimized in conditions of emergency.

Turkish leaders had shown good sense, patience, and perseverance in keeping Turkey out of the war. By 1944 it was evident which side was going to win and the Turks could afford to relax. In February 1945 they declared war on Germany, Italy, and Japan in order to become charter members of the United Nations.

EGYPT

In 1939, three years after the Anglo-Egyptian treaty, Great Britain had not evacuated Egypt as it had promised. When the war came in September, the British used the provisions of the treaty and sent more troops into the country. During the war, the Egyptians did nothing to sabotage the British war effort. But neither did the government bow to the British demand to declare war against the Axis. They believed that the Axis powers were going to win and did not want to do anything to antagonize the victors. This passive resistance was not acceptable to the British. It is one of the ironies of history that in 1942 the British surrounded the royal Abdin Palace in Cairo with tanks and told King Faruq either to appoint the Wafdist Nahas Pasha, an old anti-British protagonist, as prime minister, or leave the country. If Faruq had rejected the British ultimatum he probably would have become the greatest hero in modern Egyptian history. But he surrendered, and appointed the formerly anti-British Nahas Pasha. The latter then chose to cooperate with Great Britain.

Nahas Pasha held office until 1944 but apparently nothing was done to check the corruption within the government or to ease the tension between the king and his prime minister. When the danger of German victory was lifted by the defeat of General Rommel at al-Alamayn and the landing of Americans in North Africa, Nahas Pasha had served his usefulness to the British. King Faruq took advantage of the situation and dismissed him. He chose the anti-Wafd leader of the Sa'd Party, Ahmad Maher, to form a government. On February 24, 1945, Maher was assassinated by a young Egyptian. Nukrashi Pasha, who was second in command of the Sa'd Party, succeeded him. Two days later he declared war on Germany and Japan. Egypt also later became a charter member of the United Nations.

IRAQ

In 1939, the prime minister of Iraq was Nuri al-Sa'id, who had come to power as a result of the last in a series of five coups d'etats. He was inclined to cooperate with the British and had received £7,000,000 from Great Britain and the Iraq Petroleum Company in loans and advance royalty payments. Nevertheless he merely broke diplomatic relations with Germany and did not declare war. Anti-British feelings in Iraq and the possibility of German victory were too strong to permit even the Iraqi "pro-British" government to go very far in committing themselves.

Local politics in 1940 forced Nuri al-Sa'id to resign the premiership in favor of the nationalist Rashid al-Gailani. Iraq had become involved in the struggle in Palestine, partly because a "sister Arab state" was being "invaded" by an alien people, and partly because the "Greater Syria Movement" which envisaged the unity of the Fertile Crescent under the Hashimites, to which the royal family of Iraq belonged. It will be recalled that Great Britain had invited Iraq to participate in the 1939 conference to find a solution to the Palestine problem. Furthermore, Haj Amin al-Husayni, the Mufti of Jerusalem and leader of the anti-British Arab Higher Committee, who had fled to Lebanon, was given asylum in Baghdad. With Syria and Palestine under foreign control, Iraq had become the center of pan-Arabism. Haj Amin received a generous subsidy from the Iraqi government and began his activities for the independence of Palestine.

The nationalist prime minister, Rashid al-Gailani, quite naively tried to entice the British into discarding the Balfour Declaration and declaring the independence of an Arab Palestine. In return, Iraq would formally join the Allies and declare war against the Axis. The refusal of Great Britain to comply with such a request strengthened Gailani and his fellow nationalists in their hope that cooperation with the Axis might help them achieve their goal. Haj Amin was already in touch with the Germans. Gailani joined hands with him and established contact with Von Papen, the German Ambassador in Ankara.

The British could not tolerate such activities, and asked the regent, Abdul lah, to dismiss Gailani. The premier refused to resign and there was confusion in the Iraqi Parliament. Political pressure, however, forced Gailani out of office in favor of General Taha al-Hashimi. On April 4, 1941, Gailani executed a coup d'etat with the help of four army colonels.[1] Regent Abdul Ilah and a number of moderate leaders including Nuri al-Sa'id escaped, taking the infant king with them.

Even though the Germans had a hand in the coup, they were too busy in Greece to be able to take advantage of it. The British landed troops in Basra while the Iraqis had surrounded the Habbaniya Airfield. The Germans were able to land 50 planes in Iraq via Syria which was under the pro-Axis French Vichy government, but it was too late. The Arab Legion from Transjordan came to rescue the British. The "Thirty Day War" ended in disaster for Rashid al-Gailani, the Mufti, Haj Amin of Jerusalem, and a number of their supporters. They fled to Iran and from there they found their way through Turkey to Germany. During the rest of the war they, especially the Mufti, worked for the Axis. After the war Gailani escaped in disguise on board a French ship to Beirut and from there across the desert to Riyad, capital of Saudi Arabia, where King Ibn-Sa'ud gave him asylum. The Mufti was in house arrest in Paris after the war. In May 1946, he also escaped in disguise on board an American military craft to Cairo, where he was given asylum by King Faruq.

For the remainder of the war, Nuri al-Sa'id was Prime Minister. By declaring war against the Axis, Iraq was the first Middle Eastern country to become a member of the United Nations. Iraq played a part in the transportation of war supplies to the Soviet Union. Like other countries in the Middle East, Iraq was rich in foreign exchange but a scarcity of consumer goods caused inflation.

SYRIA-LEBANON

The puppet Vichy government which the Germans had created in France claimed suzerainty over the French colonial empire. Before the Vichy government sent General Dentz to Syria-Lebanon as high commissioner in November 1940, a number of French officers and soldiers had escaped to Palestine to join the Free French forces. With the arrival of General Dentz, Syria-Lebanon became an open field for Axis espionage against the British.

Syrians and Lebanese considered the fall of France as an opportunity to press for their immediate independence. The collapse of the French franc, and the economic hardship which resulted, gave the Syrians and the Lebanese occasion to carry on strikes, organize political demonstrations, and demand independence. The measures which General Dentz took to satisfy the nationalists were not effective.

British experience with the revolt in Iraq made them realize all the more the potential dangers of German concentration in Syria and Lebanon. Consequently, in June 1941, British and Free French forces, under General Wilson and General Catroux respectively, entered Lebanon and Syria. General Dentz offered a stiff resistance but could not prevent the Allies from entering Beirut

---

[1] Colonels Sabbagh, Sa'id, Salman, and Shabib. Some refer to them as the "Four Colonels" and others as the "Golden Square."

and Damascus. In July, the Vichy French forces surrendered; those who wished were allowed to leave for France, and those who so desired were allowed to stay.

General Catroux, as representative of General de Gaulle, head of Free France, appointed new governors for Lebanon and Syria. This did not satisfy the nationalists, who clamored for national independence. In the meantime, the British, who had to supply the economic needs of Syria-Lebanon through their Middle East Supply Center in Cairo, revised the currency and brought the two regions under the sterling block. It was an open secret that the British were encouraging the nationalists in their demand for independence. In May 1943, the Syrians conducted an election and chose nationalist leader Shukri al-Quwatly as president of the new republic. The Lebanese followed the same procedure in August and chose their nationalist leader Bishara al-Khuri as president.

The Free French under General de Gaulle proved no different from other Frenchmen who had had jurisdiction over the territories. They were reluctant to relinquish power. This led to strikes and uprisings. The French arrested the President of Lebanon and the Lebanese countered by repealing all French rights in the country. Great Britain and the United States supported the Lebanese and the Syrians. The United States and the Soviet Union recognized the two republics and and they, in turn, by declaring war against the Axis in 1945, became charter members of the United Nations. Nevertheless, General de Gaulle insisted upon "French prerogatives" and the French army did not fully evacuate Syria until April 1946, and remained in Lebanon until December of the same year.

PALESTINE

During World War II the Jews of Palestine were wholeheartedly with the British in the prosecution of war and against them in the implementation of the 1939 White Paper. All that can be said about the Arabs of Palestine is that they did not do anything to antagonize the British or to sabotage the war effort.

Perhaps the most important single event affecting Palestine occurred in the United States. The occassion was an extraordinary Zionist conference in 1942 at the Hotel Biltmore in New York City. In this conference the Zionist program was reformulated to meet the changing situation and has since been called "the Biltmore Program." The conference urged the fulfillment of the "original purpose" of the Balfour Declaration which was interpreted to be the creation of an independent Jewish state. It rejected the 1939 White Paper, supported the creation of a Jewish army under its own flag, favored unlimited immigration of Jews to Palestine, and urged that the Jewish Agency be given power and facilities to develop the state lands in Palestine for the use of Jewish refugees.

Most of the Biltmore Program was not new although some of the points, especially those on statehood, had not been previously emphasized so clearly.

Heretofore, the talk was of a "Jewish national home" and not of a state. What was new and significant, however, was that the Biltmore Conference signified a change in the attitude of Zionism from dependence upon Great Britain to dependence upon the United States. Nearly 30 years of vacillating and uneasy British-Zionist cooperation was coming to an end. The entry of the United States into the war and its tremendous economic and military power were realities which the Zionists could not ignore. In the 1920's and 1930's the British empire had partially served the Zionists' purposes. In the next decade the situation demanded that they look to the United States for support. As a result of this change of attitude at the Biltmore Conference, Zionist activity increased in the United States. Jewish and non-Jewish organizations in that country urged the implementation of the Biltmore Program, resolutions to this effect were introduced in both houses of Congress, and a pro-Zionist plank was part of the platform of both major parties for the election of national, state, and even local offices.

There were dissenting voices against the plan among the Jews. In Palestine, the opposition was voiced by members of the *Ihud* Party, mostly intellectuals led by Judas Magnus, President of the Hebrew University in Jerusalem, the philosopher Martin Buber and others, who opposed the idea of a pure Jewish State. Instead, they were for reconciliation with the Arabs and supported the creation of a binational state. In the United States the Biltmore Program was opposed by the American Council for Judaism whose members, all of Jewish faith, believed that Judaism was not a nationality for a political end but a faith for spiritual rejuvenation. Among the non-Jews, the Arabs of Palestine, Christians and Muslims alike, were against the Biltmore Program. They, however, did not have a spokesman, especially when their leader, the Mufti, had become a Nazi Amir Abdullah of Transjordan appealed to President Roosevelt in 1944. A year later, after the meeting with King Ibn-Sa'ud of Arabia, President Roosevelt wrote the Arabian monarch essentially what he had written Amir Abdullah, that the United States would make no decisions which would be hostile to the Arabs.

No discussion of wartime Palestine should fail to mention the plight of the Jews in Europe. The diabolical and systematic policy of the Nazis to exterminate European Jews stirred both Jews and non-Jews in many parts of the world While it is true that the free countries of the West did not automatically open their doors to receive these victims, it is also true that Zionists used the plight of the refugees to advance their aim for statehood. Underground groups, some Jewish and some non-Jewish, smuggled Jewish refugees out of Europe and into Palestine. The British, who could have modified their stand, found themselves in the unenviable position of having to resort to violence in order to prevent Jewish immigration. Thousands of these refugees were arrested by the British and placed in camps in Cyprus, which must have reminded the victims of the Nazi concentration camps.

THE LEAGUE OF ARAB STATES

It will be recalled that the traditional British policy to maintain the independence of the Ottoman empire had a triple purpose. One was to use it as a buffer state against the southward expansion of Russia, a second was to use it for the safeguarding of the route to India, and a third was to maintain the balance of power in Europe. By the middle of the twentieth century, the protection of the vast oil reserves of the Middle East perhaps outweighed all these considerations. During World War I, Great Britain decided to continue its previous policy by replacing the defunct Ottoman empire by a united or federated Arab state in the Fertile Crescent. An agreement embodied in the so-called Husayn-McMahon Correspondence was a direct result of such a policy. The Sykes-Picot agreement and the Balfour Declaration, however, prevented the implementation of this policy. Instead of a united or federated Arab state in the Fertile Crescent, five different states came into being, excluding Sa'udi Arabia and the Persian Gulf Shaykhdoms.

During World War II, because of the defeat of France, British troops controlled all of the Fertile Crescent as they had done in 1917. The British still needed a buffer to stop the expansionist plans of the Soviet Union and they still needed friendly people along the route to India. It was not surprising, therefore, to see Great Britain revive the old policy.

As early as 1939, the British government called a conference on Palestine and for the first time involved representatives of Arab states. On May 29, 1941, Anthony Eden, British Foreign Secretary, announced the need for Arab unity and spoke of their desire for "a greater degree of unity than they now enjoy." In the same speech he also promised that "His Majesty's government for their part will give their full support to any scheme that commands general approval." The idea of pan-Arabism was in the ascendency among the Arabic-speaking peoples of the Fertile Crescent, so that the remarks of Eden fell on receptive ears. In direct response to this invitation, Nuri al-Sa'id of Iraq in 1942 proposed a union of Iraq, Palestine, Transjordan, Syria, and possibly Lebanon, with the possibility of others joining later on. This sounded very much like the "Greater Syria Movement" under the Hashimite family and was not acceptable. Nahas Pasha of Egypt, who had not previously shown enthusiasm for pan-Arabism, invited one Arab government after the other to "consultations on Arab unity." In consultations which lasted more than a year, Syria and Iraq were for a federative scheme, Transjordan championed union with Palestine, Syria, and possibly Lebanon within a greater Arab Union, and Egypt, Lebanon, Saudi Arabia, and Yaman favored a confederation of states.

How much the Biltmore Program spurred the Arabs toward union or encouraged the British to bring it about cannot be determined, but it probably did have some effect. On October 7, 1944, the eight states mentioned above signed the Protocol of Alexandria in which they agreed to form an Arab League.

The final pact of the League of the Arab States was signed in Cairo on March 22, 1945. It favored a confederative scheme and was inspired mostly by the Covenant of the League of Nations. Each state was sovereign and the decisions of the League were not binding. One of three annexes to the agreement dealt with Palestine. It considered Palestine "legally" an independent Arab state which could not as yet exercise its rights, and gave the League the right to choose a representative for Palestine until the time that it could do so. By the end of the war, Arab nationalism had, for the first time, a legally though loosely constituted body to represent it against the Zionist nationalism in Palestine.

IRAN

It will be recalled that Reza Shah in his later years found the efficient dictatorship of Hitler to his liking. He probably thought that he could use the Germans to free himself from British influence. In any case Iran availed itself more and more of the technical services and economic opportunities readily provided by Germany. By 1939 over 41 per cent of the foreign trade of Iran was with Germany, and German engineers and technicians came to Iran in great numbers. With these came Nazi propaganda, and good-will tours by men like the Nazi youth leader Von Schirach. For the first time, the Persian army discriminated against conscripts who belonged to minority religious groups, and the Persian Boy Scout movement began to resemble the Nazi youth movement. At the outbreak of the war, a large number of the Persian ruling circles, especially army officers, were pro-German, and there was brisk commerce with Germany through the Soviet Union.

The German invasion of Russia changed the situation of Iran drastically. The Soviet Union needed supplies to fight against Germany, and of the three routes open for sending such aid, namely Iran, Murmansk, and Vladivostok, Iran was the only all-weather route. In the summer of 1941, Great Britain and the Soviet Union asked Iran, who had declared its neutrality, to permit the transportation of lend-lease material through its territory. Reza Shah's refusal changed the request into an ultimatum. In 1941, Reza Shah and his military subordinates were expecting a German victory and were not ready to be persuaded otherwise. When the ultimatum was also refused, Great Britain and the Soviet Union simultaneously invaded Iran and the army of Reza Shah crumbled like a house of cards. The Russians and the British occupied Iran and Reza Shah abdicated under pressure in favor of his 20-year-old son, Mohammad Reza Pahlavi. The ex-shah was taken to the island of Mauritius and later to Johannesburg, where he died on July 26, 1944.

The departure of Reza Shah created a reaction the like of which has had few parallels in the history of the country. The Shah had not yet left the country when the members of the Majles, the old hand-picked eulogists of his ex-majesty, began abusing him. People in general reverted to their old ways as if 20 years of Reza Shah's rule had not happened. Newspapers which had been suppressed years before started publishing their next number as though no interruption had occurred. In the same way, here a man raised his voice to call the faithful to prayer, there a woman put on her veil, and the clerics donned their turbans and walked in the streets mumbling their prayers.

Even the Allies acted as though nothing had intervened since the days of World War I. The Soviet troops occupied the northern provinces and the British occupied the south. Both countries rushed their troops to Tehran. Later, when the United States entered the war, its troops shared the south with the British and established a base in Tehran. From 1941 until 1945, Iran was the only country where the soldiers of the three major allies were together.

The coming of the Allies in 1941 and the abdication of the dictator ushered in a period of freedom and a new effort on the part of some to establish a constitutional government. But the Allies were more interested in winning the war than in democracy for Iran. They preferred to do business with the known and tried older men rather than the hot-headed and unpredictable younger nationalists. So the older men stayed and carried on their business in the old way. In 1942, Qavam al-Saltaneh once again became prime minister after a lapse of 20 years. He was a believer in involving a third power to neutralize the Anglo-Russian rivalry. Just as he had done 20 years before, he arranged for the coming of an American financial adviser. Early in 1943, Dr. Arthur Millspaugh, who had the same position from 1922 to 1927, came to Iran. Oddly enough, Dr. Millspaugh also tended to forget that a Reza Shah had ruled Iran, and started where he had left off in 1927. He got into all sorts of difficulties and in the end was forced to resign in 1945.

The younger men, however, would not be denied. The year 1942 produced a bumper crop of political parties, each with permits to publish two or three newspapers, so that if one was suppressed one day, the other could be published the next. Most of the parties did not have a national base but represented either personal ambitions or interest groups. About the only exception to the rule was the *Tudeh* (masses) Party, which had a good organization and a broad base of support. It was Marxist but had enough nationalists in it to make pronouncements which were not entirely to Moscow's liking. At no time did it claim to be communist or ask for the nationalization of property. The party was strongest in the north. It edited six newspapers and organized demonstrations, mass meetings, and strikes. In the election of 1943, about the only significant change in the Majles was the fact that there were eight Tudeh members in it. The rest were old-timers.

To counteract Soviet political activity directly in the north and through the Tudeh Party, the British brought back the 1921 coup d'etat prime minister, Sayyed Ziya, who had been living in Palestine. He organized the anti-Communist National Will Party with a platform of justice, distribution of public domain lands, and defense of Islam and religious education in public schools.

While these political activities were going on, the presence of foreign troops handling war supplies to Russia, and their immense expenditure created a rocketing inflation. Entrepreneurs and contractors supplying the Allies became wealthy, land prices and house rentals went up, and in general the gap between the rich and poor widened. Poor crops caused near-famine and Persians, even in Tehran, had to stand in long lines to buy bread.

To appease Persian sensitivities, the British and the Soviet Union concluded a Tripartite Treaty of Alliance with Iran on January 29, 1942. It claimed that the presence of allied troops in Iran did not constitute occupation and provided for the withdrawal of foreign troops within six months after the end of hostilities. Later, American troops came to Iran on the strength of this treaty. At the end of the Tehran Conference in December 1943, President Roosevelt suggested that he, Churchill, and Stalin issue a communique honoring the territorial integrity and independence of Iran, acknowledging Iran's services in behalf of the war, promising economic assistance, and invoking the principles of the Atlantic Charter. The Persians, fearful that the old Anglo-Russian rivalry would start all over again at their expense, pinned their hopes on the presence of a third power, the United States. This new relationship went through many happy and sad vicissitudes in the postwar period.

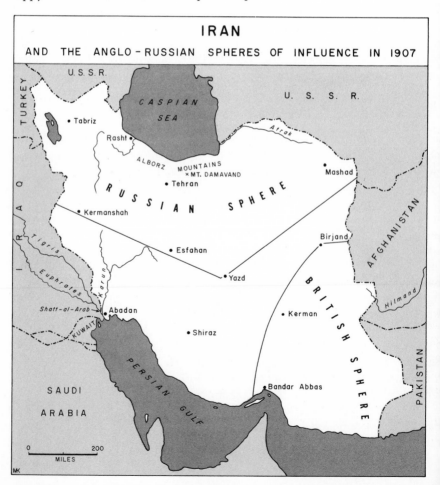

IRAN

AND   THE   ANGLO – RUSSIAN   SPHERES   OF   INFLUENCE   IN   1907

CHAPTER 33

IRAN—THE WHITE REVOLUTION

From the time of the Persian Revolution in 1906 until nearly the end of World War I, Tsarist Russia was on the side of Persian reactionaries who preferred the status quo, while Great Britain appeared to be on the side of the revolutionaries who desired change. During World War II, when the two countries occupied Iran, their positions were reversed. The Soviet Union was on the side of the revolutionaries who demanded change while Great Britain sided with reactionaries who were satisfied with the status quo. The British who supported the revolutionaries of the earlier years did so for their own ends and not for the sake of democracy or freedom. They did not hesitate to betray the Persian Revolution by signing the Anglo-Russian Convention of 1907 or by advising the Persian Majles to accept the Russian ultimatum to dismiss Shuster. Similarly, the Russians who sided with the Persian communists and radicals in the 1940's and early 1950's did so for their own ends and not for the sake of the people or of the revolution. They also betrayed their comrades in 1946 and abandoned them altogether in 1953.

PERSIAN OIL: THE FOURTH PHASE

It will be recalled that during the war two important political parties were organized in Iran. One was *Tudeh* which was supported by the Soviet Union and was founded by some of the young men whom Reza Shah had sent to Europe and who had been imprisoned after their return on the charge that they were "communists." The other party was the National Will, founded by Sayyed Ziya and supported by the British. For a time, the rivalry between these two parties had all the earmarks and the promise of a genuine two-party system which was divided along ideological, social, and economic lines. There is no telling what the outcome would have been had the parties had the opportunity to fight it out. But Iran had oil. The oil in the south was under the control of the British and it was no secret that the Soviet Union, like Tsarist Russia, wanted similar privileges in the north.

Toward the end of the war, there were indications that American oil companies wanted to renew their attempt, which had failed in 1924, to gain oil concessions in the north. The Anglo-Persian Oil Company[1] was not friendly to American "intrusion" in 1944 any more than it had been in 1924. As the Soviet Union was in occupation of northern Iran, however, it was in a good position to drive its rivals out of the field. There were long and heated debates on this question in the Persian Majles. Dr. Mohammad Mosaddeq, an independent deputy, was able to persuade the Majles to pass a law forbidding the Persian government to grant or negotiate oil concessions to any foreign country without approval of the Majles. The Tudeh Party, however, was in favor of giving the northern oil concession to the Soviet Union on the principle of "positive neutrality." This was based on the argument that because Great Britain had the oil concession in the south, the Soviet Union should be given the oil concession in the north.

On September 2, 1945, the day of Japan's surrender and the end of the war, there was antigovernment uprising in the northwest province of Azarbaijan and demands for its autonomy. It soon became evident that the Soviet Union was using its predominance in the north to outmaneuver the Anglo-American rivals and receive the oil concession in the north. By December, the Tudeh Party was split three ways. The nationalists in the party, under the leadership of the brilliant theoretician, Khalil Maleki, repudiated Tudeh's subservience to Moscow and formed a socialist party of their own, sometimes called the Third Force.

On December 12, 1945, the Azarbaijani members of the Tudeh formed a party of their own called "Demokrat," deposed the governor at Tabriz, and proclaimed the Autonomous Republic of Azarbaijan. They had the Red Army's full protection. When a contingent of the Persian Army was dispatched to Azarbaijan to quell the rebellion, the Red Army refused to allow them to enter the province. The leader of the Azarbaijan Demokrats was the notorious Ja'far Pishevari, who had been active in the establishment of the Gilan Autonomous Republic in 1920. He and his associate took control of the province and started social, economic, and property reforms along communist lines. At the same time, the Kurds of Iran, at the instigation of the Soviet Union, formed a republic of their own with Mahabad as their capital.

According to the Tripartite agreement of 1942, signed by Great Britain, Iran, and the Soviet Union and adhered to by the United States, foreign troops were to evacuate Iran within six months after the end of hostilities. By March 2, 1946, American and British troops were out of the country but the Red Army refused to leave. Iran appealed to the United Nations. Pressure of world opinion and the demands of Great Britain and the United States were certainly factors in the ultimate Russian decision to evacuate Iran, but it withdrew only after it was assured of an oil concession.

---

[1] Later the name was changed to Anglo-Iranian Oil Company (A.I.O.C.).

In March 1946, Ahmad Qavam, the Persian prime minister, led a delegation to Moscow for talks with Stalin. Qavam agreed to the formation of an Irano-Soviet Oil Company for the exploitation of oil in northern Iran. Iran was to have 51 per cent of the shares and the Soviet Union 49 per cent. The term of the concession was to be 25 years. Qavam promised Stalin that he would persuade the new Majles, yet to be elected, to ratify the agreement provided the Russians evacuate Iran. Stalin agreed and Qavam proceded to make good his promise. He asked Hosayn Ala, the Persian ambassador to the United Nations, to withdraw Iran's complaint. Ala, however, refused to comply and the complaint remained on the agenda.

On May 9, 1946, the Red Army evacuated Iran. The Persian army took possession of Azarbaijan and Kurdestan, and severely punished the Communist rebels of those two provinces. Some of the leaders, among them Ja'far Pishevari, escaped to Russia. The Soviet Union, whose declared policy was and continued to be to help "national liberation movements" anywhere in the world, betrayed one which it had helped instigate in exchange for oil concession in northern Iran.

Prime Minister Qavam, who could not persuade Ala to withdraw the Persian complaint from the United Nations, was more powerful at home. He arrested the anti-Communist Sayyed Ziya and disbanded the National Will Party. Then he proceeded to organize a party of his own, called the *Iran-e Demokrat.* It was a coalition of all parties, including the Tudeh. This party had extensive organization and its own uniformed "Guard of National Salvation." To further show his good faith, Qavam appointed three of the Tudeh leaders to his cabinet.

The fifteenth Majles was elected during the summer of 1947, with Qavam in power and his party in the majority. He presented the Irano-Soviet oil concession to the Majles and on October 22, 1947, the Majles defeated it almost unanimously with only two dissenting votes. Qavam resigned, his Party was disbanded, and Tudeh was discredited.

The evaluation of Qavam's role in this episode is a subject of controversy among Persian historians. There are those who believe that he acted cleverly by deceiving the Russians and saving the province of Azarbaijan for Iran. There are also those who think that Qavam did not see anything wrong in the establishment of the Irano-Soviet Oil Company as a price of saving Azarbaijan. After all, there was an Irano-Soviet Fisheries Company that had been in operation for some time. The pressure which the United States brought to bear on the Soviet Union to evacuate Iran cannot be exaggerated. This was done in special letters to Stalin and protests in the United Nations. The most provocative statement was made by Mr. George Allen, American Ambassador in Iran, a few weeks before the Majles was to vote on Qavam's Irano-Soviet oil proposal. He said that Iran was free to dispose its resources in any way it desired and assured patriotic Persians "that American people will support fully their freedom to make their own choice." The role of the Shah was that of constitutional monarch. He showed courage and determination by refusing to go along with compromise plans in dealing with Azarbaijan insurrectionists. He also accompanied the army into Azarbaijan and received the plaudits of the population.

THE AFTERMATH OF THE WAR (ECONOMIC, RELIGIOUS, AND SOCIAL UNREST)

The physical removal of the Red Army from the northern provinces and the failure of the separatist movement in Azarbaijan removed the danger of the dismemberment of Iran. But it did not open the door for reform so badly needed in the country. The going of the dictator, Reza Shah, did not free the country, but freed the hands of the oligarchy to reclaim their lost prestige and property and to continue their paternalistic rule. The oligarchy, sometimes referred to as the "one thousand families," buttressed by the clergy and supported by the old army officers, paid lip service to the constitution and the democracy it envisaged, and ruled without regard to the changing times.

As the Majles, composed mostly of the members of the oligarchy or their supporters, could not be expected to change the status quo, there were groups clamoring for change outside the halls of parliament. The evacuation of foreign troops had brought in its wake economic depression and unemployment. Bankruptcy became a frequent occurrence and, for the first time, Iran had an army of educated unemployed. The high school and university graduates and even those students who had returned from Europe aimlessly walked the streets. The radical groups of both right and left, who led in the seemingly endless demonstrations and rioting, were recruited mostly from the educated unemployed.

Some radical groups were religiously oriented. After the abdication of Reza Shah, governments and individuals reestablished those religious practices which the ex-shah had tried to destroy. Women were permitted to put on their veils; the clergy donned their religious garbs; religious processions came into vogue; the Koran was chanted on the radio; religious education became compulsory in the schools; the old discontinued religious school of Sepahsalar Mosque was revived as the Faculty of Theology under the University of Tehran; and thousands were given passports to make the pilgrimage to Mecca.

The radical religious activity, however, was in the formation of political activist groups. One of these was the *Feda'iyan-e Islam*, "Devotees of Islam," under the leadership of Navvab Safavi, an unknown cleric who imitated the organization and methods of the Muslim Brotherhood of Egypt. In fact, there is evidence that he was in touch with them. A second group was the *Mojahedin-e Islam*, "Warriors of Islam," under the leadership of Ayatollah Abul-Qasem Kashani, an important member of the *ulama*, who later became a member of the Majles and eventually its Speaker. These two groups separately and sometimes jointly used every means in their power, especially assassination and terrorism, to gain political control. An important nonreligious group on the right was the Fascist pan-Iranist Party, which espoused extremist racist nationalism of the German National Socialist variety.

On the left, in addition to the well-organized Tudeh Party which, even after the setback over the oil and Azarbaijan, was still strong and active, there were two others. One was the Toilers Party, attached to the person of an intellectual deputy, Dr. Baqa'i. The other was the previously mentioned Third Force Party led by Khalil Maleki. Both of these were anti-Stalinists but had as members Marxists and socialists of different varieties. At the center was the Iran Party, made up of a group of young intellectuals, businessmen, lawyers, doctors, and teachers. Its nominal leader was Allahyar Saleh, a former minister of Finance and a deputy in the Majles.

The position of the young Shah in the early postwar period was rather ambivalent. He was close to the old army officers and the nonpolitical but conservative clergy. His youth and the presence of foreign troops in Iran during the war years united the country behind him. His courageous stand on the Azarbaijan separatist movement *vis-à-vis* the Soviet Union and the Persian appeasers made him popular. Perhaps these experiences gave him confidence and enabled him to be more active after the Azarbaijan incident and he began to take more part in the affairs of the country. One of the first things the Shah did was to implement, for the first time, a constitutional provision for the organization of a senate. In it the Shah was entitled to appoint 30 senators. Even though his appointees were mostly older army officers and conservative intellectuals, the Shah was beginning to have some influence in the affairs of the country.

The Americans were willing to help but did not know how. In July 1948 the United States gave Iran a credit of $10,000,000 for the purchase of surplus war materials. The Persian government employed the American firm, Overseas Consultants, to prepare a seven-year development program. The result was one of the most comprehensive plans of development produced for underdeveloped countries. The plan provided for the expenditure of $650,000,000 and encompassed social, educational, economic, and technical problems. It was expected that the plan would be financed by royalties from the Anglo-Iranian Oil Company and economic aid from the United States. The government was negotiating with the British Oil Company for a revision of the terms which, added to the aid from the United States, was deemed sufficient to start the development program.

Perhaps it was indicative of the effective activities of the Shah that the first of several attempts on his life was made on February 4, 1949. On the occasion of the Shah's visit to the University of Tehran, a man in the guise of a news photographer fired five shots at him at close range. Fortunately the shots only grazed his majesty and he was able to address the nation by radio from the hospital. The would-be assassin was killed and those who searched his room made the allegation that he had connections with both the Tudeh Party and radical Muslim groups. As a result, the Tudeh Party was outlawed and several of its leaders imprisoned. This, however, did not end the unrest. The Soviet Union, deflated on the Azarbaijan and the oil ventures, carried on a radio campaign against the Shah and the Americans in Iran.

The seven-year development plan needed money, and negotiation with the officers of the A.I.O.C. was not fruitful. The Shah decided to come to the United States and to make a personal plea for economic aid. He arrived on November 16, 1949, and made a good impression across the country. But the United States government was not willing to involve itself so deeply in the development of Iran. Perhaps the sad experience in China contributed to such a decision. Lack of knowledge of the Middle East on the part of American leaders made them wary lest Iran prove to be another China and the Shah another Chiang Kai Shek.

In any case, the disappointed Shah went back empty-handed. But he did not give up the idea of reform. The year 1950 marks the beginning of the direct involvement of the Shah in reforms. He started by transforming the large land holdings inherited from his father into the Imperial Organization for Social Welfare, to be distributed among the peasants at convenient terms. In June 1950 he appointed an enlightened young military general Razmara as prime minister. Razmara appointed young men to the cabinet and suspended many officials who either were inept or had a reputation for corruption. The Shah backed such improvements because he believed them necessary and also because he wanted to show the Americans that he meant business.

The American response to these efforts was a loan of $25,000,000 from the Export Import Bank. In the light of generous aids which the United States was giving to the former Axis countries, this small sum infuriated the Persians, and, for the first time, there were anti-American demonstrations in the country. The Soviet Union was not slow in taking advantage of this, and arranged a $20,000,000 trade agreement.

OIL NATIONALIZATION

It will be recalled that the seven-year development plan expected to use oil royalties for its implementation, and the Anglo-Iranian Oil Company was not responsive to Persian demands. The chairman of the Majles committee for oil was Dr. Mohammad Mosaddeq, who had a reputation for honesty and nationalism.[2] Lack of sensitivity on the part of the British and lack of response on the part of the Americans led Dr. Mosaddeq to say that it was beneath the dignity of Iran to send its king begging to America when it had all the required money in oil. He introduced the idea of nationalization. Eight members of the Majles, a number of them from the Iran Party, formed a coalition by the name of National Front under the leadership of Dr. Mosaddeq and pushed for nationalization. They espoused the principle of "negative neutralism." "Now that we have refused to give the northern oil to the Russians," they argued, "we should take away the southern oil from the British."

By January 1951 it was reported that Aramco, Arabian American Oil Company, had revised its arrangement with Saudi Arabia and had agreed on

[2] See above, p. 332.

a 50–50 profit sharing plan. This news advanced the cause of nationalization. By the time the British Company brought itself to report to Prime Minister Razmara that it was ready to make a similar arrangement, it was too late. General Razmara had already expressed himself against the practicality of nationalization and was a target of great criticism. On March 7, 1951, he was murdered in the Sepahsalar Mosque by a member of the Devotees of Islam. On March 15, the Majles approved the principle of nationalization. On April 30, the Majles passed a nine-point enabling law which included provision for compensation to the company. The British government protested the nationalization and insisted that under the 1933 agreement Iran should submit to arbitration. Hosein Ala, who had been appointed a caretaker prime minister, replied that the British government had no right to interfere in a matter between Iran and an oil company. On April 15, the British closed the Abadan Oil refinery and on April 27, Ala resigned. On April 28, Mosaddeq was appointed prime minister and on the same day the Majles voted unanimously to seize the company's properties in Iran.

Events occurred swiftly and surprised practically everyone concerned with the crisis. The British were surprised to see that Iran was not intimidated by threats, the freezing of Persian assets, or even the sending of gunboats to the Persian Gulf. Western observers were surprised that Iran was not brought to its knees when the oil refinery in Abadan closed down and royalties stopped coming in. The Persians were pleasantly surprised that they were twisting the British lion's tail and getting away with it. Perhaps the most surprised of all was Dr. Mosaddeq when he realized how popular he was with the people. It has been suggested that Mosaddeq's greatest mistake was that he did know the extent of his own popularity.

In the course of the crisis, which lasted two years, half a dozen alternative proposals were made, most of them accepting the principle of nationalization, but they all failed to bring about a solution. The British complained to the United Nations. In September 1952 Mosaddeq went to New York to defend Iran's case, contending that nationalization was an internal matter and not subject to international jurisdiction. The Security Council referred the question of jurisdiction to the World Court and the Court decided in favor of Iran, stating that the problem was an internal question and outside of the competency of the World Court or of the United Nations.

The intervention of two American presidents, Truman and Eisenhower, and the World Bank failed to solve the problem. Mosaddeq took over the oil installations in Abadan and broke diplomatic relations with Great Britain. But he was in political and financial trouble at home. It will be recalled that the National Front was a coalition of parties, interest groups, and individuals with diverse opinions joined together for the purpose of nationalization. When the failure to find a solution dragged on, disagreement developed. At the opening of the seventeenth Majles in July 1952, Mosaddeq demanded extraordinary powers for six months. When some of the deputies balked, he threatened to resign. Such threats were usually followed by mass demonstrations in which the members of the Tudeh Party and fanatical Muslim groups participated.

As the crisis worsened, Mosaddeq demanded more power. The more power he sought, the more friends he lost and, in the end, he had to rely more and more upon Tudeh members. In the summer of 1953, communication between the Shah and his prime minister, and between the prime minister, his cabinet, and the Majles had broken down. Even then, Mosaddeq was so popular that it took the combined efforts of the Shah, the Persian army, and the American C.I.A. to oust him. On August 13, 1953, the Shah issued an order dismissing Mosaddeq from office and another one appointing General Fazlollah Zahedi as prime minister. Mosaddeq refused to comply and arrested the messenger who had brought him the order. On August 16, the Shah and empress Sorayya left the country in order to "prevent bloodshed." For three days Tehran was in the hands of Mosaddeq's followers, over whom he did not have control. One of the curious aspects of these turbulent days was Moscow's attitude. The mobs in the streets at the initial instigation of the Tudeh Party were breaking the statues of both the Shah and his father. The members of the Tudeh Party could probably have taken control of the government, but on strict orders from Moscow they stayed home. They paid heavily for their inaction, because under the new regime soon to come to power, they were hunted all over the country and those of their leaders who were not executed or imprisoned fled the country and continued to live precarious lives in Communist countries.

By August 19, General Zahedi entered Tehran and was able to arouse pro-shah sentiment. His soldiers surrounded and partially demolished Mosaddeq's house. By nightfall, he published the Shah's letter appointing him prime minister. On August 22, the Shah returned to Tehran in triumph. Mosaddeq was arrested and later tried. Even Zahedi's ruthlessness was not able to suppress the followers of Mosaddeq. It took years before the people were reconciled, so that his death in March 1967 created little comment.

EVALUATION OF MOSADDEQ

There is little doubt that in Dr. Mohammad Mosaddeq the Persians had found what they had been unconsciously looking for—an honest, charismatic, popular leader they could follow. In the modern history of Iran the nationalization of oil ranks higher in popular support than the strike against the tobacco monopoly in 1890, the granting of the constitution in 1906, the rally in support of Morgan Shuster in 1911, and the early years of the change of dynasty in 1924. It is doubtful whether the British and other westerners understood the Persian point of view. The British, at first, tried "gunboat" diplomacy to bring the Persian government to its knees. Having failed in that and in the World Court, the British froze Persian assets, and persuaded Europeans to boycott Persian oil and Americans to withhold economic aid, still to no avail.

The British looked at the Anglo-Iranian Oil Company as a business venture which had to bring profits. In all the plans which were submitted, the British not only wanted payments for the assets of the company, which the Persian government acknowledged, but they also wanted to be compensated for all the profits they would have made until 1993. All along, the British Company felt that they had done Iran a great service by exploiting the oil and were genuinely surprised when the Persians were not grateful. In the light of such an attitude the company's huge profits, which in some years reached 150 per cent, were not relevant. What was pertinent in their minds was that the oil income of the Persian government would not exist at all were it not for the effort and industry of the British.

Persians, on the other hand, wanted a larger share of the profits; were rebuffed at the constant refusal of the company to open its books to Persian inspectors; were frustrated at the slowness of the British to replace foreign technicians with Persians; and were angry when they realized that the company violated the political independence of the country. Because most of the oil royalties had gone to support the Persian army and had not trickled down to the people, the small merchants, the bureaucrats and the students who supported Mosaddeq did not care if the whole company was shut down.

Dr. Mosaddeq was responsible for the sense of hope and pride which the Persians exhibited during most of the crisis. But he was also responsible for the partial failure of the movement, and for letting the Persians down. Mosaddeq was woefully ignorant about the oil industry. He either did not read all the excellent reports which were prepared for him or if he did, he did not heed or investigate, both of which are severe shortcomings in a leader. For example, he believed that Europe's need for Persian oil was so great that countries would vie with each other to buy it from him. He should have known that Great Britain and the United States could tap, as they did, the vast reserves of oil in Bahrain, Kuwait, and Saudi Arabia. Furthermore, Iran did not have a single oil tanker to transport oil. He was shown several charts indicating the interrelatedness of the major oil companies of Europe and America and the control they exercised on shipping and market. Even if the British company had not challenged nationalization, Iran had to depend upon the existing companies to market the oil.

In the second place, Mosaddeq allowed his personal hatred for the British to cloud his judgment as a responsible leader. Among the several plans which were offered, perhaps the one presented by the World Bank was the best. It adhered to all the points of Persian nationalization law. And yet Mosaddeq rejected it because the Bank insisted on the freedom, as a neutral world body, to use British as well as other personnel in its operations.

Perhaps, Mosaddeq's greatest shortcoming was that he was not a revolutionary. He was so immersed in nationalization that it had become an end in itself rather than a means toward reform. He was reluctant to touch upon internal reforms for fear of offending members of his coalition, National Front. He even prevented the Shah from distributing his own lands, lest landlords in the coalition be hurt. Nevertheless, Dr. Mosaddeq's name will go down in Persian history as the leader who stirred the Persians to the depths.

General Zahedi reached an oil agreement in August 1954. A consortium of eight major oil companies in the United States, Great Britain, Holland, and France would extract, refine, and market oil for the national Iranian Oil Company on a 50–50 basis. This was not as good as some of the proposals which Mosaddeq had rejected but even this would not have been forthcoming were it not for Mosaddeq's efforts.

THE SHAH AND THE WHITE REVOLUTION

In August 1953, when Mohammad Reza Shah Pahlavi returned to Tehran from his self-exile, he had made a definite resolve. For 12 years he had reigned as a constitutional monarch but neither he nor the country had made much progress. In 1953, when he was given the opportunity to come back, he resolved to rule instead. He had repeatedly said that he did not find any glory in being king over millions of poverty-stricken and disease-ridden people. He had divided part of his lands among the peasants and therefore was dubbed "The Bolshevik Shah" by the landlords. The same landlords dominated the Majles in 1953, the reactionary clergy had their old power back, and the young educated nationalists who had been frustrated by the defeat of Mosaddeq were negative in their outlook.

The corruption and the reactionary attitude of some of the old army officers had driven a number of young officers to join the Tudeh Party. Nevertheless, the bulk of the army was still loyal. The Shah moved with caution. He started out by straightening Iran's relations with its neighbors. In June 1954, Iran signed a commercial treaty with the Soviet Union. The new Soviet leadership after the death of Stalin was anxious to win friends. Next, Iran joined the Baghdad Pact, an area defense treaty signed by Iran, Iraq, Pakistan, Turkey, and the United Kingdom. The Pact came under heavy criticism by the Persians because of British membership in it, and the Russians sent notes of protest. But Iran remained a strong member even after the name was changed to CENTO, when Iraq left the organization.

It will be recalled that successive Persian governments since the turn of the century had tried to remain neutral between contending great powers. The shah broke this tradition and joined the "American Block." Over the protest of the Soviet Union, an American military mission was established in Iran and Iran received not only tremendous amounts of economic aid but great quantities of military equipment under a mutual defense agreement. The Irano-American alliance, however, did not prevent the Soviet Union from inviting the Shah and the empress to visit Moscow and other parts of the country as official guests. Iran and Turkey showed that with post-Stalinist Russia, one did not have to be neutral in order to be in its favor.

The Shah continued the division of his lands among the peasants. Under his encouragement, successive Persian cabinets with American aid, inaugurated five-year programs. Recognizing the agricultural nature of the economy, the government built dams, irrigation systems, and power plants. The oil industry expanded and the foreign exchange received from that was used for financing the development projects.

By 1961, the Shah was popular among the peasants and had gained the confidence of some of the former members and followers of the National Front and the Tudeh Parties. The army was entirely loyal and the Shah believed he was ready. At his urging, a bill was sent to the Majles which limited the amount of land a person could own. The excess had to be sold to the government in order to be distributed among the peasants. The Majles, still made up of landlords, attached so many amendments to the bill that it became meaningless. To put it in the Shah's own words, "I became convinced that being an example, giving advice . . . or even using the usual parliamentary methods would not be useful." So he used his power. On May 6, 1961, he dissolved the Majles and, in effect, suspended the constitution by not calling for an election. A new liberal cabinet implemented a royal decree for land reform. All land, in excess of 400 irrigated and 800 unirrigated hectars, had to be sold to the government. The price of land was determined according to income tax statements filed by the landlords themselves. As there was hardly a landlord who had not devalued his land in order to pay less taxes, a cry of "foul" was raised, but there was nothing the landlords could do. The Shah, however, was shrewd enough not to press the point too strongly.

The Shah of Iran was perhaps the first monarch in history to become the leader of a peasant movement. In January 1963, on the occasion of the opening of a conference on rural cooperatives, he unfolded a six-point revolutionary program, to which three more points were added later. In a national referendum, the "White Revolution" of the Shah was endorsed by a landslide. The nine objectives of the revolution were: distribution of land, nationalization of forests, sale of shares in government-owned factories to underwrite land reform, participation of workers in the profits of factories, electoral reform and enfranchisement for women, creation of literacy corps, formation of health corps, creation of extension and development corps, and the opening of the houses of equity. The literacy, health, and development corps were primarily carried out by educated young men who spent their time in these creative services in lieu of two years in the army. The Houses of Equity were local courts to settle disputes, thereby saving the villagers from the expense of going to provincial towns to seek justice.

These were far-reaching reforms. The implementation of land reform and the enfranchisement of women aroused the combined wrath of landlords and reactionary clerics. There were uprisings and bloodshed, but the Shah remained adamant, and many of the opposition leaders, including important clerics, were sent to jail or exiled. The election of 1965 brought almost entirely a new group to the Majles, the majority of whom were committed to a program of modernization and to the Shah's White Revolution. In the new Majles the Shah worked through a newly formed New Iran Party. Even though other parties were in existence and had deputies in the Majles, New Iran became the executor of His Majesty's will.

The problems of Iran are not solved and it has a long way to go. There may be pitfalls, but a beginning has been made. Ever since the young Shah succeeded his father in 1941 many wondered why he was not crowned. He is reported to have said that he had inherited the throne, but wanted to earn the crown. The coronation took place on his forty-eighth birthday, October 26, 1967. On that day he also crowned Empress Farah, a ceremony which had no precedence in Muslim Iran. The jubilant enthusiasm of the Persians certainly proved to the Shah that he had earned the crown.

CHAPTER 34

TURKEY—THE ORDEAL
OF A DEMOCRACY

The rich and varied legacy of Kemal Ataturk for his people may be divided in two parts. One has to do with the way Turks looked upon themselves in relation to the other nations of the world. The second pertains to the way the Turks looked upon themselves as a nation independent of other nations. President Ataturk left his deep impress upon the Turks in both of these questions. To perpetuate his ideas and policies, he organized the Republican Peoples' Party in 1923. The party was both the symbol of "Kemalism" and the instrument to implement his principles.

Our discussion of modern Turkey thus far has tried to establish the fact that Ataturk saw the salvation and progress of Turkey in teaching the Turks to think of themselves as Europeans. A number of his reforms had the expressed goal of forcing unwilling and stubborn Turks to turn their backs to the East and espouse the culture, mores, and attitudes of western man. When the Communist ideology caused a great rift in the western world, Ataturk and his followers did not hesitate to reject the Communist interpretation of western civilization and turn to the institutions and attitudes of western Europe. It must be borne in mind that as Russia, the traditional foe of the Turks, was Communist, this made Communism less palatable than it otherwise might have been.

THE TRUMAN DOCTRINE

During World War II, Turkey, due to geographical and political circumstances, was able to maintain its neutrality until nearly the end of the war. Immediately after the war, however, Turkey found itself practically cut off from Europe. All of the Balkans, except Greece, were under the direct or indirect rule of Moscow. The success of the separatist movement in Persian Azarbaijan, with possible autonomy for the Kurds, would have resutled in Turkey being almost completely surrounded by the U.S.S.R. The Turks did not have any reason to believe that the policies of the Soviet Union towards modern Turkey would be much different from the policies of Tsarist Russia toward the Ottoman empire.

Indeed, the Turks did not have to wait too long to find this out. In 1945, before the war was actually over, the Soviet Union demanded Kars and Ardahan, mountainous regions in eastern Turkey. They coupled this with demands for bases on the Straits. Such demands by Russia were not new in Turkish history and the Turks had always resisted. Selim Soper, the Turkish Ambassador in Moscow, did not think it necessary to consult his government to find out the answer. He refused both demands outright and then reported to his government.

But the Russians tried to reach the same perennial goal in another way. Article 29 of the Montreux Convention on the governing of the Straits, held in 1936, provided that each signatory was entitled to initiate a revision of the agreement at the end of five-year intervals. Inasmuch as 1946 marked the end of the second five-year interval from the signing of the treaty, the three powers (the Soviet Union, the United States, and the United Kingdom) agreed to revise it. Consequently, the United States, in agreeing to participate in the revision of the Montreux Convention, proposed four points for consideration. These were that merchant ships of all nations be permitted passage through the Straits; that warships of Black Sea nations be permitted passage at all times; that except with the consent of Black Sea nations, the warships of other countries not be allowed passage; and that necessary revisions be made to bring the treaty up-to-date.

All of the countries concerned accepted these changes. The Soviet Union, however, in a note of August 1946, accepted the American proposal but added two points of its own for consideration. These points were that the regime of the Straits be controlled by a committee made up of Black Sea powers; and that the defense of the Straits be a responsibility of the Black Sea powers. Once again Russia was playing its oft-repeated game of trying to get a foothold on the Straits. The Black Sea powers consisted of Turkey, Bulgaria, Rumania, Ukraine S.S.R., and U.S.S.R. This would mean four votes against one and, if accepted, Russia would control the Straits. As usual, Turkey was apprehensive, and Great Britain did not have the strength or the means to aid Turkey in refusing Russian demands. To withstand Soviet pressure Turkey was obliged to keep almost a million men under arms. The Soviet Union, in its plan to encircle Turkey, also exerted pressure on Greece. On March 12, 1947, the American Congress proposed an historic resolution which came to be known as the Truman Doctrine. It appropriated $400,000,000 to strengthen Turkey and Greece to resist Russian pressure. For the majority of American congressmen the main purpose was to "contain Communism," but in the context of Middle East history, the United States had replaced the weakened western European powers and was ready to prevent Russia from controlling Istanbul and the Straits.

American aid, which by 1958 had reached $2.5 billion, was put to work in mechanizing the Turkish army, building roads, improving communication systems, and, in general, helping Turkey to withstand Russian threats.

TURKEY AND THE WEST

The Truman Doctrine provided the security which Turkey needed and, at the same time, opened the way for it to join the western nations as a "European" power. In 1950, when the United Nations formed an international army to defend the Republic of South Korea from Communist aggression from the north, Turkey was one of the first to dispatch 5,000 soldiers to fight under the command of General MacArthur. The gallantry of Turkish soldiers in battle gained them world acclaim and took them a step farther into the European camp. Indeed, the Turkish desire for identity with Europe was so strong that the government declined an invitation by Prime Minister Nehru of India to send delegates to an "Asian Conference." When the western European countries and the United States formed the North Atlantic Treaty Organization (NATO), Turkey applied for membership. There were those among the NATO countries, however, who did not want Turkey, on the grounds that it was not an Atlantic country. But neither was Italy, who was also a member. Turkish insistence was fruitful, for in 1951, along with Greece, it was admitted to membership. Izmir became the eastern headquarters for NATO, and important naval and air bases were built in Turkey along the perimeter of the Soviet Union.

Only after Turkey joined western European alliances such as NATO and the Council of Europe did it enter into agreements with the countries of the East. Perhaps it was doing so as a "European" power who had common regional and defense problems with its neighbors to the east. In April 1954, Turkey entered into a mutual cooperation agreement with Pakistan, and on February 24, 1955, filled the defense gap by joining Iran in the Baghdad Pact. This pact was one of a series of mutual defense agreements encouraged by the United States. The members were Iran, Iraq, Turkey, Pakistan, and the United Kingdom. As we have noted, after Iraq's withdrawal from the Pact the name of the agreement was changed to Central Treaty Organization (CENTO), and there was a line of defense on the "Northern Tier" of the Middle East from Turkey to Pakistan.

THE MULTI-PARTY DEMOCRACY

A second aspect of the legacy of Ataturk to his people had to do with the internal development of the nation. This legacy was expressed in the Six Principles of Kemalism, which became the main guide of the Republican People's Party which ruled Turkey. These principles were: republicanism, nationalism, populism, statism, secularism, and reformism.[1] They formed the under-

[1] See above, p. 272.

structure of Turkish government and society. At different times one or another of the principles was emphasized but none was repudiated.

During the lifetime of Ataturk the principle of "populism," which included the concept of democracy, was reiterated but not practiced. Reforms were considered essential, but given the level of education in Turkey, no reform could have been enacted had the people been consulted in a democratic way. President Ataturk experimented by allowing the formation of another party to act as "loyal opposition" to the government and debate issues with the Republican People's Party, but this did not work. The concept of loyal opposition was new and debate soon degenerated into diatribe. Ataturk had to abandon the idea and ruled through the one party. Soon after his death in 1938, Turkey had to face the dangers of war and experience the economic difficulties of a war-torn world.

The cost of Turkish neutrality during the war was high. Citizens were subjected to shortages of food, inflation, and badly administered taxation. They blamed the party in power, even though it was Ataturk's party. The mantle of leadership had fallen on Ismet Inönü, and he was not as strong as Ataturk had been in checking corruption. When the war was over, President Inönü was liberal enough to allow the formation of political parties to contest in the election of 1946. Four of the leaders of Ataturk's Republican People's Party, namely Celal Bayar, Adnan Menderes, Fuat Köprülü, and Refik Koraltan, left the Party to form a new Democratic Party. There was not enough time for much discussion of issues in the election of 1946. The Democrats won only 60 seats out of the 487. During the next four years there was freedom for the opposition parties to organize. Some of the dissidents from the Democratic Party formed a political party of their own called the Nation Party. There was healthy political activity in the country. To the surprise of many observers of the Turkish scene, and in one of the rare occurrences in history, a one-party dictatorship was allowing open criticism of its policies and taking the chance of being defeated at the polls.

The Republican Party had been in power for such a long time that it attracted a great deal of criticism. In addition to reports of real and imaginary corruption in the government, the businessmen of Turkey were dissatisfied because of wartime controls; the urban people were unhappy because of high prices; the non-Muslims felt the injustice of the confiscatory taxes of 1942; and the peasants felt neglected because the country was being industrialized at their expense. The major issues, however, which divided the nation concerned two of the six principles of Ataturk. These two were statism, which dealt with economic policies, and secularism, which had to do with religion.

The opposition parties whose leadership had aided Ataturk in the revolution were not against these principles but claimed that the Republican Party had misinterpreted them. The Republican Party was criticised as having made statism and secularism ends rather than means toward prosperity and the progress of the nation. The business-men in urban centers wanted more private enterprise than they enjoyed and less restrictive laws imposed by the bureaucrats in Ankara. The Democratic Party accused the government of misinterpreting the principle of secularism and of espousing a program of "enmity toward religion." In 1947, there were doubts within the Republican Party whether they had not gone too far in implementing secularism and alienated the peasants who were concerned with the question. Consequently, the government permitted religious education in schools upon written request of the parents. It further allowed a limited number to make the pilgrimage to Mecca, organized special courses for the training of *imams*, established a theological faculty at the University of Ankara, and opened the mausoleums of Ottoman sultans and other religious and political leaders of the Ottoman era. These measures, however, did not save the Republican Party. In the election of 1950 the Democrats won by a landslide, 416 out of 487 seats, and the government changed hands in an orderly manner.

TURKEY UNDER THE DEMOCRATIC PARTY

The new National Assembly elected Celal Bayar, the head of the Democratic Party, as President, and Adnan Menderes as prime minister. The new government had the cooperation and good will of the western European democracies and was held as a model to the emerging nations. Here was proof that a nation had been educated in the ways of democracy and had become mature enough to change governments without coups and bloodshed. There are those who believe that such confidence and enthusiasm were premature because of the subsequent military coup d'etat of 1960. But in the context of Turkish history it may be equally premature to announce the failure of democracy in Turkey.

The Democratic Party was able to poll decreasing but nevertheless impressive majorities in the elections of 1954 and 1957. During the decade of its rule, between 1950 and 1960, its main preoccupation was the reinterpretation of secularism and statism and the implementation of the new interpretation. Of the other four principles, republicanism and nationalism were so entrenched that no one, except perhaps a small number on the fringes of Turkish society, challenged them. The principle of populism, which was to advance representative democracy and which was neglected during the Republican People's Party regime, had come to its own by the will of the same party. It must be remembered, however, that part of the mounting opposition to the Democratic Party, which had come to power on the principle of populism, was its repeated attempt to destroy it. In the light of the multiparty system developed after the election of 1946 the principle of reformism, i.e., the right of government to inaugurate reforms by force, was both unnecessary and impractical. Henceforth, it was probably impossible, except in emergency cases, to. force change in Turkey the way it was done in the days of Ataturk. The two questions which have generated national debate and are likely to do so for sometime to come are the questions of religion and economics.

TURKISH SECULARISM

Secularism was one of the most important principles of Ataturk's revolution. To Ataturk, the term meant the virtual exclusion of religious influence from public life. Even though a number of Ataturk's associates were against the interference of religion in public questions, they did not approve Ataturk's measures, which made it difficult for individuals to practice their religion. In 1924, Ataturk allowed the formation of the Progressive Republican Party as a "loyal opposition." But he disbanded it mainly because this party criticised the government for going "too far" in limiting individual religious freedom. Perhaps the most contentious debate in Turkey for a long time to come will be where to draw the line. If complete religious freedom is granted, then there is fear of the resurgence of the ulama, Islamic law, and a general return of all the institutions and practices which the Turkish reform movement had abolished. To Ataturk the solution was simple—he tried to prevent the corporate and private practice of religion in public. Even Ataturk could not forbid people from praying in mosques nor prevent them from giving the call to prayer (adhan). But he virtually forbade the adhan by ordering that it be given in the Turkish language, penalizing those who used (as Islamic usage prescribes) Arabic.

After the advent of the multiparty system in the election of 1946, the Republican People's Party, which had held fast to Ataturk's interpretation of secularism, felt the pressure of dissent, especially in the rural areas, so they relaxed the laws and allowed religious education in schools, pilgrimage to Mecca, and other practices, to go on unmolested. The Democratic Party, however, in the election of 1950 had as one of its main planks the recognition of "religious freedom . . . as a sacred human right." During the election the Democrats had discovered that the issue of religion was one of the grievances of the rural population against the government.

Almost the first act of the new government under the Democratic Party was to abolish the penalty on the use of Arabic in the call to prayer. This was followed by celebration of fasting in the month of Ramazan, publication of religious books, the liberalization of laws concerning religious orders, increasing the number of schools for the training of imams, and the building of mosques. It is estimated that during the decade of its rule the Democratic Party government built 5,000 mosques and also about the same number of public schools. To the adherents of Ataturk's interpretation of secularism, who were against the building of mosques, the equality of school and mosque construction was tantamount to abdication of the principle altogether. What angered and alarmed Turkish secularists most was that the government reversed the previous ruling about religious education in schools. It established the teaching of religion in all schools and parents who did not want such education for their children had to request it in writing.

Nevertheless, it was not the intention of Democratic Party leaders to abandon the principle of secularism or to bring back the situation which existed before the formation of the Turkish Republic. When groups and individuals tried to voice such ideas, the government tried to suppress them. The criticism of the secularists was precisely that relaxation of laws restricting religion would encourage return to the old ways. Indeed the Nation Party, which was organized in 1948, went further than the Democratic Party in this matter. It advocated respect of the religious tradition of the nation and demanded freedom for everyone to worship in any language. It also asked that the religious endowments, *vaqf*, be turned over to the ulama. Religious orders that had gone underground came out in public, some wrote and spoke against westernization and nationalism. Some even advocated that Turkey should fight on the side of the Arabs in Palestine. Most of these people and groups were suppressed, but the debate continued. No one was sure what this "resurgence" of religion signified: utilitarian use of religion by the political parties, or a restoration of the old system, or an expression of religious freedom, or betrayal of the tenets of secularism, or a renaissance of a new and reformed Islam.

THE NEW STATISM

More immediate and more complex than the issue of secularism was the economic policy of the new government. The shortage of consumer goods, inflation, and lack of economic expansion in the decade before 1950 brought about conditions which made people desire change. Furthermore, during a quarter century of stable government there had emerged in Turkey a new class of businessmen, entrepreneurs, capitalists, industrialists, and managers who welcomed the economic changes promised by the Democratic Party. The postwar situation of Turkey, the Truman Doctrine, and the promise and expectation of massive economic aid made the leaders of Turkey use this unprecedented opportunity to develop the country by rapid industrialization.

The nature of American economic aid in the Middle East, especially in Turkey and Iran, was military and for the purposes of the cold war. Moreover, most of the American organizations administering the aid in both countries were controlled and advised by American military personnel. The Congress of the United States appropriated funds annually and it was known that failure to spend appropriated funds one year would result in smaller appropriations the next. The temptation, therefore, was to spend the money building factories and expanding industrialization. For the American agencies such expansion insured renewed appropriations from a congress whose sole purpose was to "stop communism in the Middle East"; for the Turkish public the factories signified "development"; and for the party in power it meant more votes.

Development, however, is a long-term process. Under favorable economic circumstances it takes at least five years to realize the capital invested in the building of a factory. In many cases the Turkish government did not have enough capital to start production after the construction was over. So, in the expectation of foreign aid, the Menderes government embarked on a program of deficit spending. By 1960 it had incurred a debt of $1,354,604,636. This is not to say, however, that no good was done. Roads were built, agricultural methods were advanced, and a great deal of infrastructural projects were carried out. But on the whole, the rapid industrialization and excessive construction program overtaxed the economy. Prime Minister Menderes did not like planning, ignored economic realities, invested in nonproductive projects, carried on construction for political gains, and brought the country to the brink of economic disaster. Students of the Turkish economy have stated that some of the guilt, at least, should be borne by those who continued providing him with the necessary funds.

THE COUP D'ETAT OF 1960

Turkish secularists were alarmed at the resurgence of religious power, businessmen were frustrated at the disparity between external and internal prices, which made it unprofitable for them to export and expensive for them to import, and the Turkish public was angered at the shortage of consumer goods which had caused inflation. These problems were enough to defeat any government, but what caused the coup d'etat was the suppression of the principle of populism, through which the Democratic Party had come to power. No sooner had that party come to power than it started, by a gradual process, to make itself the only party in the country. The party in power had not become used to the idea of a loyal opposition. In 1953, the government retired all judges who had served 25 years or more, providing opportunity for political appointments. It also banned political activity on the part of university professors and confiscated the assets of the Republican People's Party. In the election year of 1954, the government banned "political propaganda," established censorship, and suspended opposition newspapers for "damaging public confidence" in the government. In the election year of 1957, the government passed a law forbidding the coalition of parties and gave any party winning the majority vote in a given province all the deputies allotted to that province. Even with such tactics they did not win more than 47.7 per cent of the votes, while the Republican Party polled 40.9 per cent.

The disintegration of the economic situation in Turkey encouraged the Menderes government to stay in power through repression. In 1959, the first violence took place when former president Ismet Inönü, the leader of the Republican People's Party, was hit on the head. This and similar incidents caused the government to bring in an army detachment to prevent an uprising. In February 1960, the opposition party questioned the government on a number of irregularities. On April 2, police tried to stop Inönü from entering the city of Keyseri. He tore up the order and remained on the train. When people heard about this they came and kissed his hands. At another occasion soldiers stopped his car at a bridge. Inönü got out of the car and walked to the soldiers who stood at attention, letting him pass.

The first student riots took place at the University of Istanbul on April 28–29 and soon spread to Ankara. Students built barricades, hurled stones, and shouted "freedom, freedom, Menderes resign." NATO was meeting in Istanbul in May and students increased the tempo of demonstration to embarrass the government. On May 20, Prime Minister Nehru of India had come on a state visit and the crowd in Ankara jeered Menderes. The actual coup d'etat, sometimes called a revolution, took place on May 27, 1960, and lasted for only four hours. Strategic buildings in the capital were occupied and President Celal Bayar and Prime Minister Menderes were arrested. The coup was led by the army under the command of General Cemal Gürsel, former commander of Land Forces. He was head of a junta known as the National Unity Committee. One of their first acts was to commission a number of political science and law professors from the Universities of Istanbul and Ankara to write a constitution. The junta appointed a 17-man cabinet, 15 of whom were civilians, and announced a 15-point program which dealt with all kinds of subjects, including economic matters, religion, freedom of the press, the importation of coffee, ease of foreign travel, property transfer, and financial transactions.

During the 17 months of its rule, the National Unity Committee retired 5,000 officers and 147 university professors, and brought to trial some 600 members of the Democratic Party. The trial lasted 11 months. The Court passed death sentences on 15, gave life imprisonment to 31, acquitted 138, and gave jail sentences of different lengths to the rest. The death sentences of all except Prime Minister Menderes, Foreign Minister Zörlü, and Finance Minister Polatkan were commuted to life. The purpose of the trials was to impress upon the Turks that crimes of any regime would not be allowed to go unpunished. Observers believe that the trials had both positive and negative results, but they did not diminish the popularity of Menderes and the Democratic Party, especially among the peasants. Some of the new political parties did not hide their adherence to the principles of the defunct Democratic Party in order to capture the votes of its followers.

The constitution was ready and in January 1961 the Constituent Assembly met to approve it. On July 9, the new constitution was put to a general referendum and over 60 per cent of the people approved it. The 1924 constitution was for a republic in which power was invested in the National Assembly. It did not have enough checks and balances. In the new constitution, the Turks have tried to close the loopholes which permitted individuals to become strong. It provides for a multiparty system and more checks and balances. Of the six principles of Ataturk, the new constitution mentions only four. Revolutionism and statism are not mentioned. The constitution declares that "The Turkish Republic is a nationalist, democratic, secular, and social state." Among the fundamental rights, the controversial religious education in schools is "subject to the individual's own will and volition." Some believe that even though statism is ignored, it nevertheless appears in the provisions for a state planning organization. As with any other constitution, its effectiveness will be determined after it has been put to the test of experience.

THE SECOND TURKISH REPUBLIC

While the trials were in progress and the constitution was being written, new political parties were being formed and they were preparing for the promised elections. Some 11 parties registered and carried on a lively campaign. In the election on October 12, 1961, only four parties were able to win seats in the Assembly. The Republican People's Party won 173 seats, the Justice Party 158 seats, the New Turkey Party 65 seats, and the Republican Peasants' National Party 54 seats. Inasmuch as the Republican People's Party did not have a majority, it arranged a coalition with the Justice Party. The Assembly elected General Gürsel as President and Ismet Inönü as Prime Minister. A year later internal disagreement in the coalition caused the People's Party to arrange coalition with the other two parties and leave the Justice Party out of the government.

No one was surprised that the Republican People's Party got more votes than any other. Aside from being Ataturk's party, it spearheaded opposition to the excesses of the Democratic Party. What surprised the observers, however, was the strength shown by the Justice Party. Generally it was composed of conservatives who believed in lower taxes and the transfer of state monopolies to private industry; the party was for the abolition of governmental controls and against all state planning. On the whole, the Justice Party captured the votes of the followers of the Democratic Party.

The New Turkey Party was made up of economic, liberal, and political progressives who someday might be the chief opponents of the Republican People's Party. They were strong secularists and advocated the rights of labor to strike. The Republican Peasants' National Party advocated social conservatism and had antisecularist tendencies. It and the Justice Party generally appealed to the rural areas while the Republican and the New Turkey parties had their followers among the urban dwellers.

On the question whether Turkey is a western country or eastern, it is safe to say that the rural peoples pull the country to the east while the urban dwellers go toward the west. Perhaps the question which decides the issue is religion. The secularists want to follow Ataturk, which means no religious education in school and no use of the Arabic language in religious observances. The clericalists, on the other hand, want religious education in shcools, demand the use of Arabic in worship and want all the religious endowment funds turned over to the ulama. Between these two are the moderates who believe in the "partial" restoration of Islam. But when it comes to translating this restoration into action, most of the moderates are afraid that freedom of religious instruction will reinstate the use of Arabic letters, veil, polygamy, caliphate, etc. So the final decisions will be made, not by fiat, but by the process of education and the rapidity with which the rural areas westernize.

CHAPTER 35

THE CREATION OF ISRAEL

The defeat of Germany in 1945, coupled with the victory of the British Labor Party at the polls, gave new hope to the Zionists. Members of the Labor Party were generally "pro-Zionist" and had attacked the conservative government for issuing the White Paper of 1939, which had limited Jewish immigration in Palestine. The Zionists, however, were disappointed. As a member of the opposition party, the socialist Ernest Bevin had defended the rights of the Zionists, but as the new Foreign Secretary of the British government he became sharply aware of the existence of the Arabs. With the pressure which the Soviet Union was exerting on Turkey and Greece, the separatist movement in Persian Azarbaijan, the Kurdish autonomy bid, and the independence movement in India, Great Britain could ill afford anti-British uprisings among the Arabs. Consequently, Bevin continued the policies of his predecessor.

In August 1945, President Truman asked Prime Minister Clement Atlee for the immediate admission of 100,000 Jewish refugees into Palestine. Atlee countered by inviting American participation in the solution of the Palestine problem. The United States accepted and an Anglo-American Commission was dispatched to London, Germany, Austria, and Palestine to study the matter. In the meantime, the plight of the Jewish refugees in central Europe and West Germany was getting worse. The Zionists were accused, not without justification, of using the plight of the Jewish refugees as a weapon to further their political ends. Five years later, in much the same way, the Arab states were accused of using Arab refugees to put pressure on Israel.

If the attitude of the British Labor Government disappointed the Zionist leaders, it angered the Jewish Irgun and Stern terrorist forces in Palestine. The terrorists were able to receive money from the United States to buy weapons and coordinate their activities with the semiofficial Zionist force, Haganah, while the Zionist political leaders publically donounced their terrorism. In any case, terroristic activities by these underground Jewish groups had started against the British as early as 1944. They bombed British police stations and killed civil and military officials. In November 1944, a member of the Stern group assassinated the British Minister of State, Lord Moyne, in Cairo.

THE ANGLO-AMERICAN COMMISSION

The Anglo-American Commission carried on its investigation in an atmosphere of hostility and general insecurity. By the fall of 1945, even the Haganah-trained commandos (Palmach), were involved in anti-British activities. In October, they attacked a camp and freed over 200 immigrants who had been illegally smuggled in against the provisions of the 1939 White Paper. Later that month, they sank three British ships. During the rest of 1945, the Irgun and Stern underground groups tore up rails, blew up oil refineries, raided arms depots, robbed banks, destroyed bridges, and ambushed British soldiers. The British retaliated but were not able to do much, mainly because the Jewish population helped the underground groups. The most famous Irgun feat was the bombing of British military headquarters in the King David Hotel in Jerusalem, killing over 90 people.

The Anglo-American Commission presented its report on April 30, 1946. Its conclusions were not drastically different from the reports of previous commissions. It recommended that Palestine be neither a Jewish nor an Arab state, warned against partition, and favored a binational, bilingual state, safeguarding the rights of Arabs and Jews alike. It did not find the situation ripe for independence and recommended that "Palestine be continued as at present under mandate pending the execution of a trusteeship agreement under the United Nations." In order to alleviate the suffering of the Jewish refugees in Europe, the commission recommended the admission of 100,000 Jews. On the evening of the day that the report was published, President Truman, singling out the one recommendation which interested him the most, asked that 100,000 Jews be admitted immediately. Prime Minister Atlee refused the request, stating that the report "must be considered as a whole in all its implications."

The British invited Arab and Zionist representatives to a conference in London in September 1946, to see if they could reach a solution. There was no expectation of any agreement in the conference, but circumstances afforded Foreign Secretary Bevin an opportunity to blame the United States for the failure. It will be recalled that 1946 was an election year in the United States, and one of the most important campaigns for the Democratic Party was the gubernatorial contest in New York. President Truman, despite a British request for silence, spoke in New York and demanded that 100,000 Jews be admitted to Palestine. The next day Republican gubernatorial candidate, Thomas Dewey, did one better and said that 150,000 was a more realistic figure. A few days later, Republican Senator Robert Taft raised the figure to 175,000.

The British were caught in a dilemma. Perhaps the only friend they had among the Arab leaders was Abdullah of Transjordan, whom they had elevated to the position of king of the sovereign state of "Hashimite Kingdom of Jordan" on January 17, 1946, when they had terminated the British mandate. The Irgun and Stern groups were in open warfare against the British in Palestine. Furthermore, at the world Zionist Congress, that met in Basle in December 1946, the pro-British Chaim Weizmann almost lost the presidency of the congress. The American Zionists, headed by Rabbi Hillel Silver, denounced British rule in Palestine as "illegal," and called Weizmann a "gradualist," an "appeaser," and even a "demagogue." Weizmann was elected president by a slim majority, but the American Zionists captured the leadership and cooperated with the more radical members of the Jewish Agency, led by Ben Gurion.

THE UNITED NATIONS COMMISSION

In such an atmosphere of distrust, recrimination, sabatoge, and murder, it had become clear that the British were not able to solve the problem, if indeed anyone could. The hypocrisy and the inconsistencies of the promises of the First World War had eventually caught up with the British policy makers. On February 18, 1947, Foreign Secretary Bevin announced the decision of the British government to submit the Palestine problem to the United Nations. The General Assembly appointed a commission to study the situation and report in September. The United Nations Special Committee on Palestine (UNSCOP) was composed of representatives of 11 states, Austria, Canada, Czechoslovakia, Guatemala, India, Iran, the Netherlands, Peru, Sweden, Uruguay, and Yugoslavia. When the committee was in Palestine, the Irgun staged a daring attack on the prison at Acre and freed many Jewish prisoners. Perhaps also for the benefit of UNSCOP, the Zionists timed the arrival of the SS Exodus with about 4,500 Jewish refugees on board. It was seized by the British and sent back to France from where it had sailed.

UNSCOP was not able to present a unanimous report. Three countries, India, Iran, and Yugoslavia, presented a minority report, recommending a federated Palestine. The rest proposed partition of Palestine into Arab and Jewish states. The Zionists favored partition, while the Arabs rejected both plans. Consequently, the political committee of the United Nations considered the partition plan. It divided Palestine into six parts, three for the Arabs and three for the Jews. Even though the division was according to the concentration of each group in a given area, there were 100,000 Jews (1 per cent) in the Arab state and nearly 500,000 Arabs (48 per cent) in the Jewish state. Fifty-six per cent of the area of Palestine was given to the Jews, who constituted about 30 percent of the whole population, and 43 per cent was given to the Arabs. The remaining one per cent, the area of Jerusalem and Bethlehem, was to be under international control.

The naïvete of the proponents of partition was further shown by attaching a condition of a ten-year economic union to the plan. In this economic union, the Jewish state was obligated to assist the Arab state. But in the heat of the debate which followed, the economic union, which was a major justification for partition, was forgotten. At the United Nations, it was by no means certain that the partition plan would receive the two thirds majority necessary for any recommendation of the General Assembly. Some countries were against the plan, especially the Philippines, whose representative, General Carlos Romulo, spoke eloquently against it. The final vote was scheduled for November 26, 1947, but there were delays partly because November 27 was Thanksgiving Day in the United States. During the delay great pressure was brought to bear, reportedly by American officials, on the countries who had planned to cast negative votes. One by one the reluctant countries were brought into line, and even the Philippines delegation received instruction to change its vote. The fact that three of the five permanent members of the Security Council were in favor of the plan helped the Zionist cause. The other two, Great Britain and China, abstained.

When the Assembly convened on November 29, it was evident that the partition plan would pass. It was then that the Arab delegation proposed consideration of the minority report which they had rejected earlier. This sort of conduct became a regular habit of the Arabs in the years to come. They would vehemently oppose a resolution or an arrangement and then would support it after all hope for its approval had disappeared. The partition plan was accepted by a vote of 33 to 13, with 11 abstentions. Great Britain announced that it would terminate the mandate on May 15, 1948, and would evacuate Palestine before August 1.

CIVIL WAR IN PALESTINE

Almost immediately after the vote of the United Nations, civil war began between Palestinian Arabs and the Zionists. The British troops did not intervene. They were interested mainly in their own orderly withdrawal and in the progressive abandonment of strong points. The Arabs were armed by the neighboring Arab states and the Zionists procured arms in the United States and Czechoslovakia. The Haganah, Irgun, and Stern groups continued raiding British depots for more arms. It is estimated that the Arabs had about 5,000 men with little experience, under the distant direction of the ex-Mufti of Jerusalem, who was in exile in Cairo. The Zionists, on the other hand, were better armed and better trained. A large number of their officers and men were veterans of World War II.

There were acts of violence on both sides. In January 1948, the Irgun blew up the Arab-owned Semiramis Hotel in Jerusalem and the Arabs retaliated by blowing up the Jewish-owned *Jerusalem Post* building. In February, a bomb exploded in the crowded market place of Ramleh. Two days later, the Arabs countered with an explosion in the crowded center of Tel Aviv. The most shocking incident was the massacre at the Arab village of Deir Yassin. It was captured by the Haganah on April 29 and turned over to the Irgun-Stern for policing. But the Irgun-Stern groups butchered 254 Arab men, women, and children. A few days later, the Arabs retaliated by ambushing a Jewish convoy bound for the Haddassah Hospital in Jerusalem and killed nearly 80 doctors, nurses, and students. There was panic among the noncombatants, both Arabs and Jews, but Jews were not allowed to leave their homes without the express permission of the Haganah, while the Arabs did not have such protectors. By the time of the termination of the mandate on May 15, there were already about 150,000 Arab refugees who had fled the scenes of battle and bloodshed.

In the midst of all this bloodshed, two incongruous events were taking place thousands of miles apart from each other. In the halls of the United Nations in New York, the United States had an apparent change of mind. It proposed that in view of the difficulties in implementing the partition plan, the United Nations should take over the Trusteeship of Palestine. A special session of the General Assembly sat between April 16 and May 15 to consider this proposal amid the harsh criticism of the Zionists and their supporters. While the delegates in the United Nations were discussing the fate of the partition plan, Ben Gurion and the members of the National Council of the Jewish State in Palestine gathered in Tel Aviv on May 14, 1948, and proclaimed the creation of the State of Israel. In a matter of minutes, President Truman announced United States recognition of the new state, while his country's representatives were still debating trusteeship in the United Nations. Dr. Chaim Weizmann was chosen as the first president of the new republic and David Ben Gurion as its first Prime Minister.

ARAB-ISRAEL WAR

On the morning of May 15, six Arab states (Egypt, Iraq, Jordan, Lebanon, Saudi Arabia, and Syria) attacked Israel. When one considers that a nation with a population of 650,000 defeated the combined Arab states with a population of 40,000,000, the result seems nothing short of a miracle. But when actual fighting forces are taken into consideration, a different picture emerges. The combined fighting force of the six Arab states did not exceed 70,000. Of these only about 10,000 had adequate training and this included the 6,000 men in Jordan's Arab Legion. Facing the Arab armies were the Israelis with a minimum of 60,000 fighting men of the Haganah. In this army there were 300 British-trained officers, some 20,000 veterans of World War II, and 3,000 specially trained commandos (Palmach). The active combatants in the Irgun and Stern groups were not more than a thousand men. One should not in any way minimize the courage and tenacity of the Israelis, who had high morale and were fighting for their very existence. The Arabs, on the other hand, had neither the singleness of purpose nor a unified command. Most of the Arab soldiers did not know what they were fighting for, and their leaders were not without their national and personal vested interests.

Both armies were poorly equipped at the start, but the Israelis were supplied with necessary arms by Zionists, in America and Europe, and airplanes piloted by Jewish volunteers from England, America and South Africa. Nevertheless, the Arabs made considerable headway at the beginning. The Egyptians occupied the Negev; Jordan controlled Old Jerusalem; and Iraqi soldiers were within 15 miles of Haifa. When the first truce was arranged on June 11 by the United Nations, the opposing forces were occupying roughly the territories assigned to each side by the United Nations. By the terms of the cease fire, the contending armies were to hold their positions and were not supposed to reinforce their armies by men or arms. Both sides ignored the second part of the agreement. The Arabs, however, were not able to circumvent the arms embargo to the whole area. But the Israelis were able to purchase great quantities of first class armaments from Czechoslovakia. Flying fortresses from the United States and Beau-fighters from Britain were smuggled into Israel.

Count Folke Bernadotte of Sweden was sent by the United Nations as a truce mediator. He made proposals of his own for an armistice based on economic union of both Palestine and Jordan and autonomy for a Jewish state. Under this plan, Jerusalem and the Negev would go to the Arabs while the whole of Galilee would belong to Israel. Both the Arabs and Israelis rejected the plan and fighting started on July 9. In the ten days of fighting which followed, the Israelis made considerable gains. The second truce was imposed by the United Nations on July 19. Old Jerusalem was occupied by the Arab Legion and New Jerusalem by the Israelis. Count Bernadotte was still trying to find a solution to the problem when he was felled by a Sternist's bullet on September 17, 1948.

The second truce was very much like the first. The Israelis built up their forces and toward the end of September launched two attacks on the Negev and Galilee. By October 31, the Israeli armies with air superiority had pushed the Egyptians out of the Negev and the "Arab Liberation Force" out of northern Galilee. In the meantime, the United Nations debated the Palestine question. Ralph Bunche of the United Nations Secretariat was chosen as acting mediator. At his headquarters on the Island of Rhodes he gathered the Arab and Israeli representatives in different rooms (the Arabs refused to sit with the Israelis in one room) and went back and forth between the rooms until he obtained the first armistice between Israel and Egypt on February 24, 1949. Others followed: with Lebanon on March 23, with Jordan on April 3, and with Syria on July 20. A truce was achieved and Ralph Bunche received a well-deserved Nobel Peace Prize for his efforts, though there was no peace.

Three important problems were left unresolved. The first was the question of boundaries. In every armistice agreement, there was a phrase similar to Article V of the Egypt-Israel armistice, which stated that "The Armistice Demarcation Line is not to be construed in any sense as a political or territorial boundary, and is delineated without prejudice to rights, claims, and positions of either party to the Armistice as regards ultimate settlement of the Palestine question." The fact that the United Nations did not insist that Israel go back to the original partition lines shows that perhaps many responsible United Nations officers did not think they should. The rapidity with which the Israelis "settled" their new borders with Jews shows that they did not expect to move back when and if an "ultimate settlement" was arranged. The most important criterion for designating the "temporary" boundaries was the position of the opposing troops. Demilitarized zones were created to avoid further clashes. Consequently, the Gaza Strip was given to Egypt; no appreciable change was made on the border with Lebanon; and all of the Sea of Galilee and upper Jordan River went to Israel except the Lake Hulah marshland, which was demilitarized. King Abdullah of Jordan was allowed to annex the territory west of the Jordan River, which his armies occupied. This included Old Jerusalem. The ex-Mufti, Haj Amin al-Husayni, who was in Cairo, did not accept this annexation of Palestinian territory by King Abdullah, but he was not in a position to implement his opposition. Thus, the "temporary" settlement of boundaries gave Israel over 20 per cent more Palestinian territory than it had been given in the Partition plan.

JERUSALEM

The second unsettled problem was the question of Jerusalem, Old and New. The city, together with nearby Bethlehem, was envisaged by the United Nations to be under international control. The war changed the status of the city from an international one to a divided one with barbed wires. The Jordanians had control of Old Jerusalem and Bethlehem, where most of the shrines holy to Christianity, Islam, and Judaism are located. The Israelis had occupied the greater part of New Jerusalem. Although the United Nations had not abandoned the idea of an international Jerusalem, the peacemakers allowed the demarcation formula which had been followed in armistice agreements to apply to Jerusalem also. Consequently, the area occupied by Israel and Jordan became separate territories and Jerusalem remained a divided city.

The internationalization of Jerusalem remained on the agenda of the United Nations and every year during the first 20 years of Israel's existence, the delegates passed resolutions concerning the status of Jerusalem, but neither Israel nor Jordan paid any attention to them. As early as 1949, Israel proclaimed Jerusalem as its capital and moved the *Knesset*, parliament, as well as many of the ministries there. Diplomats assigned to Israel, however, did not recognize this fact and kept their embassies at Tel Aviv. Furthermore, Israel ignored the fact that Jerusalem was supposed to be demilitarized and held annual commemorative military parades in the city. After the "six day war" of June 1967, and the annexation of Old Jerusalem by Israel, the question of internationalization of the city in all likelihood became a dead issue.

ARAB REFUGEES

The third and the most vexing problem following the cease-fire agreements between Israel and the Arab states was the fate of Arab refugees. By the end of the fighting early in 1949, there were approximately 750,000 Arab refugees scattered in Egypt (Gaza Strip), Jordan, Lebanon, and Syria. There have been conflicting reasons advanced as to why there were so many refugees. The Israelis and their supporters usually claim that the Arabs were encouraged, via radio, by the Arab states to leave their homes, join the invading armies, and defeat Israel. This does not explain why they took their women and children along, except to say that they did not want to leave them among their enemies. The Arab writers claim that the Israeli soldiers "drove" Arab men, women, and children out at bayonet point in order to make room for the Jewish refugees who were coming into the country. Although careful study of radio monitors of the European countries in Palestine does not substantiate the Israeli claim, one can safely assume that a number of Arabs who heard the overoptimistic reports of Arab "victories" on their radios thought that they had better leave and come back with the victors. On the other hand, it has been substantiated that in Haifa and other large cities Jewish loudspeakers encouraged the Arabs to leave; that in some villages Israeli soldiers destroyed Arab houses and at other places Arabs were expelled. Nevertheless, the bulk of the Arabs, like so many people in countless wars, were afraid for their lives and sought refuge from war hoping to return when the shooting was over. At the end of the war, however, the Israeli forces did not allow them to return. Their homes were occupied by tens of thousands of Jews, who poured in from Europe, and their farms and orchards were harvested by the conquerors.

Practically every year the United Nations reiterated the principle of the right of Arab refugees to return to their homes but Israel, which considered the Arab refugees as potential fifth columnists, did not allow them to return. Neither did Israel offer to compensate them for the expropriation of their lands and properties unless the Arab countries were willing to sign a comprehensive peace treaty. Most of the refugees lived in camps and were supported by the United Nations Relief and Work Agency (UNRWA), Friends Service Committee, World Church Service, and other charitable organizations. Egypt confined most of the refugees to the Gaza Strip and discouraged them from swelling this already overpopulated country. In Syria-Lebanon, the refugees were technically aliens but the educated among them managed to get jobs and gain citizenship. A number of educated refugees went to Kuwait and Saudi Arabia as teachers. Only in Jordan, which had annexed what was left of Palestine, were the refugees given the right of full citizenship. Nevertheless, those who were in camps carried on an aimless existence and in the course of years became a sad piece in the general mosaic of the Fertile Crescent.

A ZIONIST STATE

Israel is perhaps unique among the states of the world, in that it was established intentionally as a refuge. In a sense, the United States, Canada, Australia, and some other countries which have built upon immigration could be considered as places of refuge. But what makes Israel unique is that it is a place of refuge for a particular group, the Jews, and for no one else. Because Zionism had labored for a Jewish home and then a Jewish state, it was inevitable that Israel should prepare for the "ingathering" of all the Jews of the world. The State of Israel never denied admission to non-Jews, but its "Jewishness" was so emphasized that non-Jews found themselves out of place. Not only did the Zionists invite the Jews, but they also helped transport them, house them in the new state, and find them jobs. Any Jew from any part of the world can go to Israel, and in as long as it takes to fill out the proper papers, gain citizenship. Non-Jews cannot do this.

Consequently, one of the burning questions in Israel was and remains "Who is a Jew?" The Israelis are more or less agreed that, at least legally, belief, faith, or ideology have nothing to do with being a Jew. There are in Israel devout believers in God and in the Torah, and also agnostics and atheists, but all are Jews. The most important (perhaps the only) criterion for being considered a Jew is birth. The courts of Israel have decided that a person whose mother was of "Jewish blood" can be considered a Jew. This emphasis on "Jewishness" is consistent with the claim and program of Zionism, but appears anachronistic when applied to a modern state. Regardless of belief, immigrants into Israel who cannot prove their Jewish descent are not considered Jews and therefore are not participants in the privileges and perquisites of the laws of the "ingathering." Such a state is likely to appear to its critics parochial, exclusive, and self-centered.

The classic Zionist ideology was expressed by Prime Minister Ben Gurion to the twenty-fifth Zionist Congress in December 1960. While the Jew in the diaspora is "subordinate to a non-Jewish authority in all his material and political life," only in Israel, "—the soil we walk upon, the trees whose fruit we eat . . . the schools where our children are educated . . . the landscape we see and the vegetation that surrounds us—all of it is Jewish." With such an all-pervasive Jewishness of the state, it is doubtful whether non-Jews, even with the existing democracy, can ever feel at home. There seems to be an attitude of "anti-Gentilism" in Israel which is rather similar to anti-Semitism in other countries.

ISRAELI GOVERNMENT

This is not saying that there is not democracy or freedom for the citizens of Israel. It has been stated, with considerable truth, that Israeli society is "one of the most egalitarian in the world." The government of Israel is based on democratic principles. The early Jewish immigrants brought with them the political diversities of eastern Europe and have combined these with British parliamentary procedures. In the first election of 1949, 21 parties competed for the 120 seats of the *Knesset*. People vote for a party and not for an individual. Parties send representatives to the Knesset in proportion to the number of votes they receive. Of the 21 parties in 1949, only nine had enough votes (5 per cent) to occupy at least one seat in the Knesset. Among the important parties are the Mapai, Mapam, General Zionists, Herut, and Mizrachi.

The Mapai, or Israel Workers' Party, is the most influential party in the country and has controlled the premiership ever since 1948. It is a labor party with Marxian socialist ideas. Some of its leaders, men like Ben Gurion, were members of the Jewish Agency during the mandate. Perhaps its domination of great labor and industrial organization, Histadrut, explains its power among the electorate.

To the left of the Mapai is the United Workers' Party or Mapam. It is doctrinaire Marxist and makes Zionism subservient to socialism. It advocated a binational (Arab-Jewish) state and was against the Biltmore Program.[1] The party is mostly rural, collectivist, anti-capitalist, and neutralist in its orientation.

To the right of the above parties is the Liberal Party, which is a coalition of different groups. They do not espouse any ideology except Zionism, and are sometimes called General Zionists. The party has its strength among the urban businessmen and is inclined toward private enterprise. During the early days of the republic, this was the second largest party in Israel, but it has given its place to the Herut Party, which is a right-wing offshoot of the General Zionists. The Herut Party is led by some of the leaders of the Irgun and is the heir to the Revisionists who were against the separation of Transjordan from Palestine in 1923. The party is chauvinistic and preaches Israeli expansionism and preventative war against the Arab states.

Important among the religious parties are the Mizrachi and the Mizrachi Workers. They believe that Zionism is rooted in Jewish religion and therefore Jewish religion should not be separated from Jewish nationalism. They are strong advocates of religious education and practices. Because no party in Israel has ever gained a majority in the Knesset, it has been necessary to form coalition governments. Perhaps because the religious parties do not challenge the economic principles of other parties, they have usually been part of every coalition government in Israel. To obtain the cooperation of the religious parties, the Mapai has acceded to their demands for religious education, observance of dietary and Sabbath laws, control of marriage and divorce, and a ban on pig raising, etc.

SOCIAL INTEGRATION

Because of the nature of the State of Israel and the circumstances under which it was established, it is beset by special social, economic, and political problems. The population of Israel in 1948 was about 650,000. Within the first 18 months of its existence, the population was swelled by over 300,000. As almost all the immigrants were refugees without financial resources, the problems of providing housing, jobs, and general social integration were staggering. After 1950, when immigration of European Jews (Ashkenazim) slackened, special efforts were made to bring in "Oriental" Jews (Sephardim) from the Arabic-speaking countries, Iran, Turkey, India, and elsewhere. Operation "Magic Carpet" brought in 45,000 Yamani Jews, and operation "Ali Baba" trans-

[1] See above, p. 341.

ported 114,000 Jews from Iraq. By 1962, Oriental Jews comprised 55 per cent of the population of Israel.

Immigrants brought with them different cultures, languages, prejudices, religious beliefs, and even appearances. They had to learn a new language and live and work together as one nation. In their native countries, they were known as "Jews," but in Israel they were Germans, Poles, Rumanians, Iraqis, Yamanis, Egyptians, or Americans. The Germans disliked the Poles, and the Europeans looked down on the Orientals. For the purpose of integration the Israeli government established mixed cooperatives, but these were given up because social differences led to quarrels and even shooting.

On the whole, the Oriental Jews, because they are late-comers, less educated, less skilled, and simply "Oriental," are discriminated against both intentionally and accidentally. Almost all the better paying jobs are held by Europeans. The European Jews are conscious of the fact that they were the ones who established the state through years of work and sacrifice. They believe, therefore, that the Oriental Jews should go through some of the same experiences and should not expect to be treated equally. This may be logical to the European Jews, but to the struggling Orientals it is a bitter pill to swallow. Consequently, a number of Jews from non-Arab and non-European countries have left Israel.

The Israeli army, to which both men and women are conscripted, is the best amalgamator. Also, war with the Arab states tends to bring the different elements in Israel together. Nevertheless, social integration, especially in a limited geographical space, is a long and hard process.

ISRAELI ECONOMY

The economy of Israel has always been in a precarious state. The country is uninviting physically and economically. If enough water were available, either through discovery of new sources or the desalinization of sea water, a maximum of 5,000,000 acres could be cultivated. This is not considered enough for a potential population of 4,000,000 people. In the 20 years of its existence, the imports of Israel have usually been two and one half times its exports. Israel has depended upon loans and gifts from the outside. These have come from United States and United Nations grants, "reparations" from West Germany for the losses of Jewish property, contributions from American Jews, and sales of bonds. United States aid to Israel has been the highest per capita of any country, and the United Jewish Appeal has an annual goal of $250,000,000. But there is no guarantee that such aids will continue indefinitely.

To offset such tremendous economic difficulties, the Israelis have taken bold steps and have made great progress. They have diverted water from Lake Galilee and carried it in 108-inch pipes to the Negev. They have built some 9,000 industries employing about 100,000 persons. They have developed the port of Eilat on the Gulf of Aqaba for trade with Asia and have built an oil pipeline from there to Haifa on the Mediterranean. They export citrus fruits, tomatoes, olives, and cucumbers to markets in Europe. They have developed tourism, and with the annexation of the west bank of the Jordan River in 1967, they have practically monopolized the tourist trade to the "Holy Land." They have many projects for the future, but nevertheless, Israel will have a precarious economic existence at least as long as it is at war with Arab states.

ISRAEL AND THE ARAB STATES

The social and economic problems of Israel are closely tied in with its relation to the Arab states. The problems of passage through the Suez, or use of the Gulf of Aqaba, or the status of the refugees are symptoms of the basic issue, which is the establishment of Israel against the will of the non-Jewish inhabitants. Perhaps if the Arabs could view Israel as a "tiny nation," friendly and without design on its neighbors, a reconciliation could be worked out. But Israel's relationship with world Jewry and the expressed hope of Zionists to bring "all" the Jews to Israel, transforms the state into a colossus in the eyes of the Arabs. To the Arabs, World Zionism is more dangerous than Communism. So they fight it, they boycott it, and they are afraid of it. When, as a result of three wars in 20 years, Israel is master of all Palestine, the Sinai Peninsula, and a strategic district of Syria, it is understandable why the Arabs cannot regard it as a "tiny" nation. On the other hand, the fact that Israel is surrounded by the Arabs on three sides produces a precarious political existence which contributes to an already uncertain economic life.

Israel, with its techniques of modern civilization, can be a great blessing to the neighboring Middle East countries as its technical aid missions have been to many emerging African states. Perhaps two conditions will have to be met before such a hope can be entertained. One is a modification in Zionist ideology which will transform Israel from an exclusively Jewish state into a pluralistic secular state where "race" or religion are not considered criteria for citizenship. The second is the abandonment of the attitude of superiority which Israel, as a European transplant, has shown toward the "Oriental" Arabs.

CHAPTER 36

THE NEW EGYPT

A new Egypt came into being as a result of the revolution of July 23, 1952. For the first time since the conquest of Egypt by Rome, Egyptians—not Arabs, Mamluks, Turks, or British—controlled the affairs of the country. After years of struggle for independence, the 1952 revolution achieved far-reaching social and economic reforms. For the first time in modern Egyptian history a revolution was launched not principally on antiforeign slogans but on an anti-corruption basis. This revolution, carried out by a small band of young officers, sons of lower middle class Egyptians, was in the context of Egyptian history and had its roots in events which have been described in previous chapters.

SOCIAL AND POLITICAL CONDITIONS

The small but growing middle class in Egypt was increasingly dissatisfied with the rulers of the country after World War II. Throughout the century between 1850–1950, the main spokesmen for Egyptian nationalism were the approximately one half of one per cent of the population, who owned 37 per cent of the cultivable land. These people were served by the small land owners and their families, who were educated enough to work in the bureaucracy. They did so by control of the parliament and all domestic and foreign policies. They also formed the various political parties which were different more because of personal ambition than because of programs of reform or ideology. The peasants, small shopkeepers, and minor officials, who comprised nearly 80 per cent of the population, were asked to work and left to shift for themselves.

Egypt, like all victims of imperialism, had to go through two revolutions, one for independence and the other for social reform. It is understandable, therefore, why during the last half of the nineteenth century the cry for national independence became the hallmark of all self-respecting nationalist groups and the most important plank in the program of every political party. What neither these political parties nor the king, who was engaged in a private struggle against them, perceived was the growing number of educated but landless

Egyptians who wanted reform while they were struggling for independence. This was increasingly true between the two great wars, when the level of education and sophistication had risen, and the people, especially in urban centers, were dissatisfied with their lot. They had reason to be dissatisfied. The population of Egypt was increasing much faster than the means available to feed it. This increase had been going on rapidly since 1913, and yet the landed aristocracy, who had the power to do something about it, did not seem to be concerned. In 1913, the average annual income of the Egyptian peasant was about $60. At constant prices, that income had fallen by 1951 to about $35. After World War II, there was general unemployment in urban centers.

In the face of these difficulties, the political parties were still talking only about independence. The Wafd Party, which had come to power and popularity on the program of national independence, had become middle aged and content without adding any planks for reform to its program. There was corruption, graft, and high living among the privileged who succeeded each other in forming governments. The king's preoccupation was to set one political group against the other and reap the lion's share of power and privilege for himself. Among his ancestors, King Faruq had persons like Khedive Ismai'l, who was an extravagant spender, and Sa'id, who was a glutton, and it seemed that he had inherited the weaknesses of most of his ancestors. He was an extravagant spender, a glutton, a chaser after women, a fancier of expensive yachts, and a collector of rare postage stamps and pornography. In a world which had experienced a most devastating war, and in an Asia and Africa, which were experiencing so much social and political change, the young educated Egyptians believed that they deserved something better than what the king or the ruling oligarchy represented.

FREE OFFICERS CLUB

A number of such young Engyptians were in the army. In 1936, when Egypt became partially independent, the army, which had been the exclusive preserve of the privileged class, was opened to the sons of the lower middle class. Young men were attracted to it because the army provided a good education and opportunity for advancement. Among the young men who attended the military school was Gamal Abd al-Nasser, the son of a postal clerk, born in 1918. As a student in high school he had taken part in numerous demonstrations for independence. As a young officer, he had gathered a number of his officer friends for discussion of Egypt's problems. These young men were the heirs of the ordeals which Egypt had experienced for a century. They had read about Muhammad Ali, had discussed the rise and fall of 'Urabi, Zaghlul, and other nationalists, had studied the ideas of Muhammad Abduh, and had been influenced by the revolution in Russia. Among these officers, at least two were communist-oriented, four or five were members of the Muslim Brotherhood, and the rest were ardent nationalists uncommitted to any particular ideology.

THE SIEGE OF FALUJA

It is quite likely that these young officers would have spent their time in discussion groups had it not been for the war against Israel in 1948. It will be recalled that Egypt occupied the Negev and planned to push north to make contact with Jordan's Arab Legion. During the second truce, the Israelis, with their recently acquired weapons and airplanes, pushed the Egyptians back and surrounded a large number of them at Faluja. The Egyptians also had received supplies of weapons, but due to corruption and graft from the king down, the weapons were faulty, old, and useless. Nasser and a number of his friends were in Faluja. There they discussed not the war in Palestine but the predicament of Egypt, "which was then a prey to the wolves that ravaged it." The last words of one of his friends who died in battle were, "Egypt is the field of our supreme war effort." It was the defeat in Palestine which convinced the young Egyptian officers that the first order of business was to cleanse Egypt from corruption and graft. When they returned to Egypt, Nasser formed the Secret Free Officers Society, whose purpose was not merely discussion but action.

WAFD AND THE BRITISH

While the young officers were planning their revolution, the Egyptian government under Nahas Pasha, the veteran leader of the Wafd, was pressing the British to evacuate the Suez Canal zone and to cede the Sudan to Egypt. The British, as usual, were moving so slowly that to Egyptian eyes they were not moving at all. Great Britain claimed that the Treaty of 1936, according to one of its articles, could be revised in 20 years, which meant that they had to wait until 1956. On the question of the Sudan, the British believed that the Sudanese had to be consulted before any decisions could be reached. Negotiations dragged on until 1951, when Nahas Pasha, perhaps encouraged by the examples of Dr. Mosaddeq of Iran, unilaterally cancelled the Treaty of 1936 and proclaimed Faruq "King of the Sudan." He then encouraged the mob to harass and kill British soldiers in the canal zone and everywhere else in Egypt. Egyptian laborers in the canal zone went on a general strike and guerrilla attacks against British forces became worse by the day. When the British retaliated in January 1952 by fighting the police and declaring martial law in villages under their control, the mob in Cairo was incensed and moved toward the center of the town. The government allowed them to proceed to where western businesses and buildings were concentrated. They burned and looted theaters, hotels, restaurants, and shops. By that time, there was no discrimination in burning and when it was finished some 12,000 Egyptians were homeless. It was reported that the Muslim Brotherhood had a major role in this anti-European program. The Wafd Party's strategy had backfired. Nahas Pasha resigned and new unstable governments followed each other for some months.

THE COUP D'ETAT

In the meantime, the Free Officers were laying plans. Faruq became suspicious and ordered the closing of Cairo's Officers' Club, of which most of the young conspirators were members. On July 23, 1952, the young officers struck. Because they were all young (average age 34) and unknown, they had arranged with a respected and popular older officer, General Muhammad Nagib, to act as leader. The General was appraised of the plans rather late and tentatively accepted the offer. It is said that in the early hours of July 23, Nasser telephoned Nagib and asked him to go to the revolutionary headquarters. "If we fail," Nasser is supposed to have said, "you have suppressed us. If we succeed, you are the leader of the new Egypt." Between one o'clock in the morning and noon, Nasser took the capital without resistance. Faruq hoped for British interference but nothing happened. For the first time in the modern history of Egypt, a new government had come to power not with anti-British or antiforeign slogans, but with a promise to purge corruption and graft in Egypt.

It is evident that the young officers did not have a prearranged plan of social and political revolution. They wanted to purge corruption and believed that an energetic civilian rule would somehow be established. The chief among corrupt leaders, in their view, was the king, who was forced to abdicate in favor of his infant son on January 26. Faruq left Egypt permanently, and a year later Egypt was proclaimed a republic. What disappointed Nasser and his friends was the fact that people did not rise in enthusiasm. "The vanguard performed its task," says Nasser in his *Philosophy of the Revolution*, "it stormed the walls of the fort of tyranny . . . and stood by expecting the mass formations to arrive at their ultimate object." But all they got was chaos, dissention, and idleness. Then it was that they decided to stay in power and improvised policies as they went along.

THE ANGLO-EGYPTIAN AGREEMENT

The young officers had not come to power and popularity chiefly because of anti-British slogans. Perhaps because of this they were able to negotiate with the British in an objective atmosphere. Concerning the Sudan, the British had been saying all along that the Sudanese had to choose their future for themselves. With the able assistance of General Nagib, who was half Sudanese himself, the Egyptian government was able to bring all the Sudanese factions together into the same camp as Egypt. The Sudanese were willing to cooperate, because the new Egyptian government was flexible and more understanding of Sudanese nationalism. On February 12, 1953, Egypt and Britain agreed to grant self-government to the Sudan and a plebiscite was to be held within three years to determine the Sudan's relation to Egypt. The agreement was a great accomplishment for the new Egyptian government, because it had achieved accommodation with Great Britain and close cooperation with the Sudanese nationalists.

The next problem was the occupation of the Suez Canal zone. Here, too, negotiations were carried out in a relaxed atmosphere. A number of factors had finally convinced the British that it was no longer worthwhile for them to maintain a base at the Suez Canal zone. For one thing their experience in Palestine had shown them that it was very expensive to maintain a base in a hostile area. Furthermore, violence brought the subject to the attention of the British public, who had a history of turning against their own government in such matters. India, which had attained independence, was no longer an issue, and the atomic bomb had probably made the maintenance of such bases superfluous. How much American pressure was brought to bear is not certain, but in 1954 Great Britain agreed to evacuate the canal zone. The only condition was that they were allowed to reoccupy the zone in case of an attack on Turkey or on any of the Arab countries.

The amicable solution of the Anglo-Egyptian conflict over the Sudan and the Suez Canal zone made it possible for the young officers to direct their attentions to the internal problems of Egypt. It was the intention of the young officers to purge the government and establish an "honest" civilian rule. In good faith they chose a former prime minister, Ali Maher, who had a reputation of honesty and progressivism, to form a government. But this did not prove satisfactory. The older men were too conservative to condone radical change. As most of them had tremendous vested interests in land holdings, they could not be expected to act as social revolutionaries. So, willy-nilly, the young officers formed the Revolutionary Command Council (R.C.C.) and took over the government, with General Nagib as prime minister. The R.C.C. dismissed some 800 civilians from important posts in the government and retired 100 older military officers. They banned all parties but the Muslim Brotherhood.

THE R.C.C. AND REFORM

Having purged the government of undersirable personnel, the R.C.C. felt its way, rather gingerly at first, in the role of social revolutionaries. The *sine qua non* of social change in the Middle East was land reform. Except for the landlords themselves, practically everyone was in favor of it. The more conservative Muslim Brotherhood believed that maximum land holding should be limited to 500 *feddans*, or acres, and everything in excess should be divided among the peasants. The radical groups in Egypt wanted the maximum to be set from 50 to 100 feddans. The R.C.C. settled on 200. In Egypt, where yield per acre is high, 200 feddans were more than adequate, hence only very large landowners were affected. As the vast land holdings of the king were expropriated and all of the land was not distributed, the government became the largest landlord in Egypt.

THE STRUGGLE FOR POWER

The new regime was not without enemies and its decision to become revolutionary gained them some more. The enemies of the regime may be divided

into four categories. First, the old politicians, who were denied the right of political activity. Second, the Muslim Brotherhood, in whose eyes the R.C.C. was
too secular and radical. Third, the Communists, in whose eyes the R.C.C. was
neither radical nor doctrinaire enough. Fourth, the rich landlords, who were
dispossessed by the land reform law of 1952. These groups had money and the
support of young Egyptians who believed more in the ideals of parliamentary
democracy, which the R.C.C. had violated, than they did in social and economic reform. The only thing, however, that prevented these opposition groups
from moving against the regime was the lack of a common issue. This issue
was provided in February 1954.

General Nagib, it will be recalled, had been brought in to be the figurehead
of the new regime. Actual power was in the hands of the R.C.C., headed by
Nasser. But General Nagib had become extremely popular among the Egyptians and was recognized as the real leader of the revolution. He wanted more
power as prime minister of the country than the single vote allotted to him in
the 13-man R.C.C. would allow. The most important factor which caused a
rift between Nagib and the R.C.C. was age. The young officers of the R.C.C.
believed that the politicians were old, corrupt, and unimaginative. The 51-
year-old Nagib, however, remembered the same politicians when they were
young firebrands with initiative and imagination. Nagib respected these men
of his own generation and it is possible that these men encouraged Nagib to
seek more power. In any case, Nagib demanded more power in order to establish parliamentary democracy, which meant that most of the same old politicians would come to power.

In February 1954, the R.C.C. announced the resignation of General Nagib.
This created an uproar which the R.C.C. did not expect. The opposition groups
rallied around the General and demonstrated on his behalf. The R.C.C. did
an unorthodox thing—perhaps the only way open to it—by reinstating General
Nagib. The next few months were very tense in the history of contemporary
Egypt and also very confused. General Nagib proceeded to undo some of the
reforms of the R.C.C. and announced that by July a full-fledged civilian government would be established.

Meanwhile, Nasser was working behind the scenes to isolate Nagib and to
reinstate the power of the R.C.C. By April, a general strike materialized in
support of the R.C.C., the army staged a strike, demonstrations took place in the
streets and the R.C.C. "elevated" General Nagib to the presidency and made
Nasser the Prime Minister of Egypt. In October 1954, a member of the Muslim
Brotherhood made an unsuccessful attempt on the life of Nasser. This gave the
R.C.C. the necessary excuse to outlaw the Brotherhood, put General Nagib
under house arrest, and to purge its own organization of Communist and Brotherhood members. By the end of 1954, Nasser was the acknowledged leader of
the revolution, and he promised that by 1956 he would present the country with
a new constitution.

NASSER AND THE ARAB WORLD

Any nation involved in a serious program of economic, political, and social revolution needs a certain degree of isolation and noninvolvement in external affairs in order to put its house in order and establish the foundations of its revolution. In the Middle East, the Arabic-speaking countries have difficulty concentrating their thought and limiting their activities to a specific country. As we have seen, it was relatively easy for Turkey to limit its nationalism to the Turks only. Their language was different from the countries of the Middle East. They were, however, Muslims, but with the principle of secularism they severed official religious affiliation with their neighbors and were able to concentrate on their own affairs. It was even easier for the Persians to avoid the temptation of dissipating the vigor of their nationalism in neighboring countries. By language and religion they were already isolated from their neighbors to the west, and they did not interfere in the affairs of Afghanistan, in which Persian is an official language.

It was not so easy for Egypt. While it is true that the Free Officers had planned the revolution to free Egypt, it must be remembered that part of the planning was done while they were fighting in Palestine in defense of the "Arab cause." By language and religion, they were tied to the countries of the Fertile Crescent and North Africa. While it is true that Egyptian nationalists, until the beginning of World War II, did not consider themselves "Arabs," the situation had changed drastically since the war. After all, Great Britain did use Nahas Pasha to establish the League of the Arab States, Cairo did become the headquarters of the League, and the Egyptians did fight in Palestine against Israel.

It was not only nationalism, however, which caused Egypt to become involved in the affairs of other Arabic-speaking countries. Economic and historical factors played an important role in shaping Nasser's policy. From the time of the pharaohs, the commercial and cultural route connecting Egypt with the outside world was through Sinai and the Fertile Crescent. The fate of the Crescent in a large measure determined the fate of Egypt. Israel, established athwart this route, cut this historic link and was considered to be a threat to Egypt. The moderate General Nagib spoke as though he would not have any objection to the existence of Israel provided a link was established between Egypt and the Fertile Crescent through the southern Negev.

In addition to the above considerations, Egypt was drawn into the affairs of the Arabic-speaking countries by the popularity of Nasser among the nationalists of these countries. Indeed, Nasser could not remain indifferent even if he so wanted. Egypt was the first Arab country after the defeat in Palestine to purge itself and to stand on its own feet. Nasser was at the center of this revolution and was a hero to the nationalists of the Arabic-speaking countries. Egypt became the model country and Nasser the model leader.

In his *Philosophy of the Revolution*, Nasser sees the role of the Egyptian revolution in three circles. The first is the Arab circle, which is "as much a part of us as we are a part of it. . . ." Second is the African circle, "in which fate has placed us. . . ," and the struggle which it is going through "will affect us whether we want or not." The third is the Islamic circle, "with which we are tied by bonds which are not only forged by religious faith but also tightened by the facts of history." Nasser is perhaps the first Egyptian nationalist leader who has tried to fuse together the concepts of pan-Arabism and pan-Islamism, which were antithetical in their origin. Pan-Arabism rejected Islamic faith, or any faith for that matter, as a basis for nationalism, while pan-Islamism refused to identify Islam with Arabism. The enmity between the pan-Islamic Muslim Brotherhood, which is not without strength in the Arab world, and the secular pan-Arabists makes it premature to judge whether such a fusion is workable or not.

Nasser is also the first Egyptian leader to connect the destiny of Egypt with the continent of Africa. This is an uncharted course without much historical precedence. What is important in Nasser's "circle" thesis, however, is the circle which he has omitted, namely the *Egyptian circle*. During the Palestine War in 1948, Nasser and his friends "were fighting in Palestine but [their] dreams were in Egypt." By 1955, Palestine, Egypt, and the other Arab countries had merged into one "Arab Nation" in the thinking of pan-Arabists like Nasser. Nevertheless, *The Philosophy of the Revolution* implies, and Nasser's subsequent actions leave no doubt, that the center of all the circles is Cairo. Perhaps the Africans and non-Arab Muslims have not paid too much attention to such an implication, but the point was not lost to the Arabic-speaking peoples in general. The Iraqis and Syrians were particularly incensed, because each group considers its own capital, Baghdad or Damascus, the center of pan-Arabism and/or pan-Islamism.

ENTER THE SOVIET UNION

The events which led to the nationalization of the Suez Canal Company in 1956 were partially forced upon Egypt by the outside. Perhaps one of the first was the creation of the Baghdad Pact in 1955. The fact that Iraq was a member of it was considered both an afront and a threat to Nasser. Nasser believed that the Baghdad Pact was a new form of western imperialism. The fact that Iraq was being armed by the United States alarmed Egypt. Not only was there nationalistic rivalry between the two countries, but Iraq, with its monarchy, landed aristocracy, and conservativism also could become a center of opposition to Nasser. So he directed the full force of his propaganda against the Pact.

Furthermore, a number of Israeli raids across the Egyptian border were costly to the Egyptian army and increased Nasser's desire to strengthen his army. He tried to procure arms from the West but was not successful. The United States would not sell him arms partly because of Israel and partly because of Egypt's neutralism and its recognition of the Peoples' Republic of

China. Nasser, like other Arab leaders, was apprehensive of Israel's intentions and believed that Egypt should build its defenses. After repeated rebuffs from the western powers, Egypt arranged with Czechoslovakia in September 1955 for the delivery of arms. Western control over the supply of arms in the Middle East was broken and opened the way for the other countries of the area to purchase arms from the Soviet bloc.

THE ASWAN DAM

Notwithstanding these developments, the major emphasis of the Revolutionary Command Council was still on internal reform. The formulation of the main problem of Egypt was quite simple, even though its solution was well-nigh impossible. Egypt needed more food for its teeming population, more land to raise food, and more water to irrigate the additional land. Water could be had by enlarging the high Aswan Dam in upper Egypt, but over a billion dollars was necessary to build the dam. Egypt looked to the United States for this money and the United States arranged to provide the necessary funds with the help of Great Britain and the World Bank.

Egypt, however, delayed the signing of the agreement, perhaps because it believed it could get a better deal by using the rivalry of the cold war between the United States and the U.S.S.R. Nasser claimed that the Soviet Union was willing to loan him more money "with no strings attached," a claim which the Russians denied. Nasser negotiated trade and cultural agreements with China and engaged in diatribes against "American imperialism," which did not please American congressmen. Furthermore, he began training special commandos (Fedayi'in) to raid Israel. The case dragged on until July 1956. Nasser was then ready to accept the American offer, but Secretary of State John Foster Dulles abruptly cancelled the whole project. Dulles gave Egyptian economic inability as reason for the cancellation, but it seems that he wanted to humiliate Nasser in the process. A week later, on July 26, 1956, Nasser retaliated by nationalizing the Suez Canal Company.

THE NATIONALIZATION OF THE SUEZ

It will be recalled that the Suez canal was operated by the Suez Canal Company, founded in 1854. It was registered in Egypt and France and was not involved in all the political and military negotiations carried on between Egypt and Great Britain. The Company had the concession to operate the canal for 99 years and was to hand it over to the government of Egypt in 1968. In the Anglo-Egyptian agreement of 1936, the canal was recognized as belonging to Egypt and in 1954, Egypt was solely responsible for its defense. That the nationalization of the canal announced by Nasser on July 26, 1956, was a direct reaction to the cancellation of the Aswan loan by the United States, there is no doubt. But it is doubtful whether a nationalist government under Nasser would have allowed the company to operate until 1968.

The reaction of the West to the nationalization of the Suez Canal Company was impulsively negative and revealed an attitude which imperialism had cultivated among the Europeans toward the people of the East. The West showed the same attitude toward Egypt that it had revealed toward the Persians when they had nationalized the Anglo-Iranian Oil Company in 1950. This attitude like a two-pronged spike was directed against the easterners' ability and their honesty. It was said that the Egyptians had neither the mechanical ability nor knowledge to operate the canal. Furthermore, the Europeans believed that the Egyptians could not be trusted with the control of the canal. With more than half of the European oil needs passing through the canal, Egypt would have its "thumb on Europe's wind pipe" and could not be trusted, it was pointed out, to act responsibly in the company of nations.

Great Britain and France tried to use every means in their power to stop Egypt. They froze Egyptian assets, called their reserve forces to arms, ordered their navies into the Mediterranean, and strengthened their army and air bases in Cyprus. They also withdrew their pilots from the service of the Canal Company and encouraged other non-Egyptian pilots to resign. They called a conference of 18 nations who used the canal and proposed a "users' company" to "cooperate" with Egypt in the operation of the canal. British and French ships refused to pay the regular dues to the nationalized company. The counsels of the United States were divided on this matter. The Americans took part in these meetings and protests but did not join them wholeheartedly. On October 5, 1956, the case was taken to the Security Council of the United Nations, but in the light of what had happened in the Persian case, few expected that the United Nations would intervene. The Security Council, however, issued a set of six principles governing the affairs of the canal, which were accepted by all parties concerned.

ISRAELI INVASION OF EGYPT

Apparently, the Anglo-French acceptance of the principles recommended by the United Nations was a ruse. On October 29, 1956, with the full knowledge of France and Britain, Israel invaded Sinai. By the next day, Israel had advanced 75 miles. On the same day, France and Britain sent an "ultimatum" to both sides to stop fighting and withdraw their troops a distance of ten miles from either side of the canal. As Nasser refused to comply, Anglo-French air and naval forces attacked Egypt and occupied Port Said. The Anglo-French-Israeli alliance had planned well and expected a quick occupation of the canal and the fall of Nasser from power.

They expected the U.S.S.R. to object, but what surprised the invading forces was the severe remonstrance from the United States. It is quite likely that the attack was scheduled just one week before the American presidential elections in the expectation that no candidate in his right mind would jeopardize five million Jewish votes and censure Israel. President Eisenhower, who was a candidate for reelection, severely censured Israel and its allies, perhaps against the advice of his political advisers. A union of the United States and the U.S.S.R. was too strong to ignore. By December, the Anglo-French forces evacuated Egypt and by March 1957, the Israeli troops evacuated Sinai, the Gaza Strip, and the Strait of Tiran. A United Nation's peace-keeping force was dispatched to guard both sides of the Israeli-Egyptian borders and the approaches to the Strait of Tiran. Israel refused to allow United Nations forces on its soil but Egypt offered no objection.

By April 1957, the Suez Canal was cleared of the ships that Egypt had sunk to block passage. The Egyptians operated the canal efficiently and indeed arranged for widening it to permit two-way traffic. Egypt lost greatly by the destruction of Port Said, defeat in Sinai, and loss of revenue from the canal. But these losses were "compensated" by political gains. The Arabs were impressed that Nasser had challenged both France and Great Britain, who only a few years before were masters of all Egypt and the Fertile Crescent, and had won. He was looked upon as the leader of true Arab nationalism and the savior of Arab peoples from foreign encroachment and internal corruption.

CHAPTER 37

UNITY AND DIVERSITY
IN THE ARAB WORLD

THE MYTH OF ARAB UNITY

The Arabic-speaking peoples are searching for identity. Ever since World War II, they have talked of unity while remaining as separated as ever; they have spoken of one "Arab Nation" while acting as a dozen different nations. The only things which they have in common are language and religion. These entities have not united the English-speaking peoples, nor have they created a desire among the Spanish-speaking peoples to declare themselves as one nation. Indeed, Latin American countries have much more in common than the Arabic-speaking countries of the Middle East, but it is the latter that speak of being one nation.

One of the factors which separates the Arabic-speaking countries is the form of government. There are monarchies, republics, dictatorships, para-democracies, and small shaykhdoms on the Persian Gulf which defy classification. Other, more important differences are such things as degree of education and general attitude toward the modern world. Countries like Lebanon and Egypt, which have numerous universities and attitudes which embrace the virtues and vices of Europe, have more in common with France and Italy than they have with Saudi Arabia and Yaman, which still live in fifteenth century circumstances. Perhaps the most important difference is in the field of economics. The "have" countries such as Saudi Arabia, Kuwait, and Iraq do not see why they should share their wealth with the "have not" countries such as Egypt, Syria, and others. To these factors should be added the intense rivalries between Egypt, Syria, and Iraq for the leadership of the "United Arab Nation," if and when it is established.

It is difficult to determine how deep into the masses this idea of unity has penetrated, but there is no question that the literate population seems to be obsessed with it. Consequently, it is difficult to narrate the history of each Arabic-speaking country separately. They belong together. After World War

II, two factors, one negative and the other positive, kept the possibility of unity alive among the Arab countries.

The negative factor was Israel. Its establishment enraged all of the Arabic-speaking countries, its presence frustrated them, its real and imaginary expansionist policies frightened them. But anger, frustration, and fear did not unite the Arabs much beyond the talking stage. Often hatred or fear of a common enemy has united countries even though they believe in antithetical ideologies, forms of government, and policies. The union of the U.S.S.R. and the United States against Hitler is a case in point. The Arabs may all have fear and hatred for Israel, but such sentiments were not able to unite them against Israel. One must conclude that their hatred and fear of Israel were not as deep as some of the differences which separate the Arab countries from each other.

The positive factor for the unity of the Arabs was the appearance of a popular and charismatic leader in the person of Gamal Abd al-Nasser. The Fertile Crescent and Egypt probably had not seen a more popular or potentially powerful leader since Saladin defeated the Crusaders and captured Jerusalem. Photographs of Nasser could be seen in practically every Arab marketplace, home, and tent from Yaman to Morocco. He arranged for British troops to leave Suez, he rid Egypt of a corrupt king, he withstood the combined attacks of the Anglo-French-Israeli alliance, he was courted by the United States and the U.S.S.R., and he was the hope of Arab unity. Notwithstanding all this, Nasser failed to unite the Arabs because he could not rise above the differences which separated them.

SYRIA AND ARAB UNITY

The history of the Arabic-speaking countries of the Fertile Crescent during the quarter of a century after War II is in part the story of the reaction of each country to Israel and to the leadership of Nasser, carried on in a context of an inter-Arab cold war. Syria is one of the best examples of the Arabs' desire for unity and their difficulties in achieving it. Syria can rightly claim to be the home of modern Arab nationalism. The division of Ottoman "Syria" into four independent countries (Syria, Lebanon, Jordan, and Israel), with one of them an alien implant, has never been accepted by ardent Syrian nationalists. Nevertheless, Syrians have not been able to speak with one voice, for they are divided by religious, ethnic, and sectional differences. The 85 per cent Muslim population is divided into Sunnis, Shi'is, Alawis, Druzes, Isma'ilis, and Yazidis. The smaller Christian population is divided into a dozen denominations. About 10 per cent of the population is non-Arabic-speaking, including Kurds, Turkomans, and Circassians. Another 10 per cent are roaming Bedouins, who cause more divisiveness than their number indicates. Sometimes political and economic interests are centered in each of the four major cities—Damascus, Homs, Hama, and Aleppo.

During a given week, a Syrian as a Sunni could be against the rest of the

Muslims; as a Muslim, against the non-Muslims; as a pan-Arab secularist, against the religious communalists; as a Damascene against all other sections of Syria; and as a Syrian against other Arab countries. If some of the Syrians somehow transcend all these barriers, their intense individualism will hinder their cooperation. Syria is the Arab world in microcosm; anyone who can rule Syria can unite the Arabs.

During the two decades since independence in 1946, Syria has had nearly ten coups d'etats and about as many constitutions. Each government undid whatever the previous government had done or wanted to do. During 1949–1950, perhaps as a reaction to the defeat in the Palestine War, three military coups d'etats rapidly followed one another. The last one, by Colonel Adib Shishakli, lasted long enough to permit a constitution to be written and a foundation laid for a welfare state with far-reaching social and economic legislation. As a result of opposition from the landlords and conservatives, Shishakli staged a second coup in 1952, dissolving parliament and outlawing political parties, trade unions, and student organizations. He wrote a new constitution, organized his own Arab Liberation Party and got himself elected president and prime minister for a five-year term. In February 1954, however, Shishakli was ousted by a coalition of all dissident groups.

In the relatively free elections which took place after the coup of 1954, the Ba'th (Resurrection) Party gained 15 seats. This was not very much in a 142-member parliament, but in the light of the role the party played in Syria, this was significant. The Ba'th Party was created in 1953 from a fusion of two parties which had been pan-Arab and socialist in their orientation. It advocated nationalization of industry, distribution of land and extensive social reforms. The party was led by Michel Aflaq, a Christian, and Salah al-Bitar, a Muslim. As true secular pan-Arabs, they believed in "one Arab nation with an eternal mission." Between 1954 and 1958, Ba'thists became influential and organized branches in Lebanon, Jordan, and Iraq. The main rival of the Ba'th in Syria, in organization, ideology, and influence, was the Communist Party.

THE UNITED ARAB REPUBLIC

The ouster of Colonel Shishakli and the coming to power of a civilian coalition government did not solve Syria's problems. The leftist groups, both Ba'thists and Communists, undermined the stability which the conservatives and moderates were attempting to establish. In 1956, the Syrian conservative and moderate politicians had come under the influence of Nasser and hoped that he might save them from leftist domination. There was a split within the leftist camp; the Communists favored collaboration with the Soviet Union and the Ba'thists were for independent action. The Communists gained increasing influence in the army and brought General Afif Bizri, chief of staff of the Syrian Army, to a pro-Soviet position. The more powerful the Communists became, the more the Ba'thists thought of union with Egypt, which would save Syria from Communism and would be a step toward the ultimate union of all Arabs.

In the beginning, Ba'thists considered Nasser as a military dictator and looked down upon the Revolutionary Command Council of Egypt as a group without ideology. But after the nationalization of the Suez Company and the Sinai war, Nasser had emerged with new ideas. The slogan of the R.C.C.—discipline, unity, work—was changed to democracy, socialism, and cooperative society. Nasser "Egyptianized" all foreign industry and property and at the same time nationalized many Egyptian-owned private industries. This endeared him to Ba'th's socialist eyes. They thought they would add an ideological dimension to Nasser's pragmatism and use his popularity and power for the union and socialization of all the Arab world.

In January 1958, the Ba'thists, who were afraid of a Communist coup, went to Cairo and asked for union. The United Arab Republic was established after a remarkably short negotiation. Having been disappointed with the confederation of the League of Arab States, the two countries set up an extremely opposite model—that of a totally centralized union. The union was hailed as the first step toward the unity of all Arabs. Nasser as the first President of the U.A.R. was the idol of all Arabs. Not to be outdone, the Hashimite kings of Jordan and Iraq announced a federal union, but it did not impress even the citizens of those countries. The U.A.R. became the hope of Arabs for the future. But this hope was short-lived.

LEBANON AND ARAB UNION

It will be recalled that the almost even division in the population of Lebanon between Christians and Muslims gave it a peculiar position in the Arab world. The Maronites were usually pro-European, while the Muslims were for closer ties with the Arab countries. The orthodox and other Christians tipped the scales in favor of Arabism. Nevertheless, the Christian minority was apprehensive about its life in a unified Arab Muslim country. When Lebanon became independent, first in 1943 and finally in 1946, President Bishara al-Khuri proposed a National Pact in order to ease the tension between Muslims and Christians. All government positions, from clerk to director general, were distributed among the various religious communities on a fixed ratio based on the census of 1932. The number of seats in the Chamber of Deputies, even though fluctuating, was always a multiple of 11—a ratio of six Christians to five Muslims.

In the course of years this unwritten National Pact began to wear thin. Muslims complained of "second-class citizenship" and demanded a new census which, they were sure, would show a Muslim majority in Lebanon. By 1956, when Nasser had become an Arab hero, the Muslims of Lebanon identified themselves with him, while the Maronites became more pro-European. President Chamoun of Lebanon was accused by Muslims and by some Christians of discrimination against non-Maronites. At the time of Nasser's visit to Damascus, as the first president of the U.A.R., hundreds of thousands of Lebanese went there to welcome him, and the desire to have Lebanon join the union was very strong. This, added to the general dissatisfaction concerning the Chamoun government and the rumors that Chamoun wanted to ammend the constitution in order to be able to serve another term, caused the Muslims to riot.

There were violent clashes between the government and the opposition. The Lebanese government charged that the rebels had received military supplies from Syria and took the matter to the Arab League. As the League did not take any action, Lebanon took the matter to the United Nations Security Council. The Security Council's team of observers, however, did not find anything to substantiate the charge. By midsummer of 1958, there was a virtual civil war in Lebanon but it was not between Christians and Muslims. In this case, the Maronite patriarch was against Chamoun's policies, believing that they might endanger the position of all Christians in the Arab world.

On July 14, 1958, there was a military coup d'etat in Iraq which destroyed the Hashimite rule in that country. As it was reputed to be a pro-Nasser revolt, Chamoun became alarmed lest Lebanon be next and appealed to the United States to invoke the Eisenhower Doctrine. This controversial doctrine passed by the United States Congress in 1957 was to help Middle Eastern countries to defend themselves against outside aggression. President Eisenhower complied with the request and American troops landed in Lebanon.

THE IRAQI REVOLUTION

It will be recalled that the government of Iraq was in the hands of an oligarchy of landlords, tribal shaykhs, military officers, and elder politicians presided over by the young king Faysal II. Even with the lush flow of oil royalties, the dismal poverty of the people was appalling. In 1951, thanks to the Persian nationalization of the oil industry, the Iraq Petroleum Company arranged a 50–50 sharing of profits with the Iraqi government. But not much of this sum trickled down to the masses. There was a Development Board to use the oil income for public projects, but most of these projects profited the landlords.

Egyptian land reforms created unrest among Iraqi peasants, and the 1956 Egyptian war made Nasser a hero in the eyes of the Iraqis. Insofar as coups were concerned the Iraqis were no match for the Syrians, but they were a close second. From 1934 to 1958 the Iraqis had eight coups with varying degrees of violence. The 1958 coup d'etat was a collaboration of several nationalist and leftist groups, with the army under the leadership of General Abd al-Karim Qasim. It differed from the Egyptian revolution in that it was not all military and was also much more violent. In July 1958, the mobs were let loose in the streets of Baghdad, killing and looting. The leaders of the revolution did away with King Faysal, Crown Prince Abdul Ilah, and Prime Minister Nuri al-Sai'd. Ba'thists, Communists, and members of a couple of other parties formed the civilian component of the revolution.

After overthrowing the Hashimite kingdom, the new Iraqi government under

General Qasim seceded from the federation with Jordan, broke all ties with the Baghdad Pact, and recognized both the Soviet Union and Red China. Nasser sent his congratulations and the Syrian Ba'thists urged their fellow party members in Iraq to join the U.A.R. This was the closest the Arabs have ever been to union. The union of Syria and Egypt was a reality, a seemingly pro-Nasser group had come to power in Iraq, there was a pan-Arab uprising in Lebanon, and even Yaman had tied itself with special arrangement to the U.A.R.

THE FATE OF JORDAN

Surrounded as it was by revolutionary forces, Jordan seemed to have no choice but to join. Under the circumstances, Jordan could not join the U.A.R. without first ousting the Hashimite King from the country. The position of the Hashimite family in Jordan had always been precarious, because Jordan itself was an artificial creation of the British government to solve a special local problem. After the incorporation of parts of Palestine into the Hashimite Kingdom of Jordan, the position of the king became even more precarious.

Two thirds of the population of Jordan were Palestinians who were better educated and more politically aware than the Bedouins who inhabited the east bank of the Jordan River. These Palestinians, who were most bitter over the creation of Israel and frustrated by defeat, came to consider King Abdullah of Jordan as the main cause of their plight. They accused him of undermining the cooperative effort of the Arabs in the war against Israel in 1948. In July 1951, one of their members assassinated King Abdullah as he was attending the Mosque of Aqsa in Jerusalem.

Abdullah's son Talal succeeded him but had to abdicate, because of illness, in 1953 in favor of his 18-year-old son, Husayn. Resolute and courageous as Husayn proved to be, he had a difficult time balancing the Palestinian and Bedouin elements in the country. The rise of Nasser was a beacon of hope for the Palestinians who saw in him the sure way of defeating Israel and reoccupying their lost lands. Husayn was in a difficult position. He could not join the U.A.R. or make peace with Israel without losing his throne. If he were attacked by the U.A.R., then Israel might occupy the west bank of the Jordan River as a "preventive" measure.

The fact that Husayn received military and economic aid from the United States did not make him popular with the Palestinian nationalists, but helped him stay in power. After the Iraqi revolution of 1958, Husayn was in real danger, so he appealed to Great Britain and some 2,000 British troops were brought in to protect Jordan against its Arab neighbors.

QASIM AND NASSER

Qasim of Iraq did not prove to be the pan-Arab revolutionary that people thought he was. Neither was he the reactionary that he was accused of being by Nasser. He came to power at the head of a coalition of Communists and pan-

Arab Ba'thists. He was, however, an Iraqi nationalist who, along with the non-pan-Arab elements of Iraq, did not want to share their sovereignty and wealth with Nasser. He used the Ba'thists and Communists to come to power and then used the Communists to get rid of the Ba'thists. One of the leading pan-Arab nationalists, Colonel Abd al-Salam Arif, was in Damascus two days after the 1958 revolution with Nasser, receiving the cheers of the population; three months later he was in a Baghdad jail under sentence of death.

For nearly three years the Communists were free in Iraq. They had good organization and numerous front groups. They established a field "people's court" in which they tried members of the former government. In these trials, sarcastic remarks were made against President Nasser of the U.A.R. In 1959, a U.A.R.-supported uprising against Qasim in Mosul was brutally suppressed. A few months later, an unsuccessful attempt on Qasim's life was attributed to Nasser's Egypt. The animosity between the two became stronger by the day. At the time when the pan-Arab nationalists were at the verge of attaining their goal of union, the ascetic-looking and ascetic-living General Qasim, helped by the Communists, raised the cry of "Iraq for the Iraqis."

SETTLEMENT IN LEBANON

The year of 1958 was a crucial year for Arab unity. In that year, the pan-Arabists experienced the joy of achievement in the creation of the U.A.R., and also the dismay of failure in the breaking up of that union. One of the first to resume normalcy was Lebanon. The American troops did not engage in any fighting but their presence quieted the opponents in the civil war. On July 31, 1958, the parliament elected the popular General Fuad Shehab to succeed Chamoun. The new president chose Rashid Karami, the Muslim leader of opposition in the civil war, as Prime Minister. A new "salvation cabinet," made up of an equal number of Christians and Muslims, carried on the work of rebuilding and pacification.

Events had probably convinced the majority of the Lebanese that it was better for their country to resume its role of "neutrality" in the inter-Arab cold war. The Arabs of the Middle East needed a "neutral Switzerland" and Lebanon was qualified, both by the beauty of its landscape and by the aptitude of its people, to be such a place. The Lebanese, who pride themselves on being the descendants of ancient Phoenicians, are better off as financial managers of the Arab world than as participants in inter-Arab rivalries. Almost all Arab countries have accounts in the numerous banks of Lebanon, and the banks in turn finance many industrial developments in these countries. Lebanon enjoys many advantages. It is accessible by sea and air to trade centers in Europe, and it has practically no commercial or monetary encumbrances often found in other Middle Eastern countries. Consequently, almost all foreign enterprises that have invested in all the countries of the Middle East, save Israel, have their offices in Lebanon.

The rival politicians of the Arab countries need a neutral Lebanon. As long as the coups and countercoups continue, as they seem to, in Syria, Iraq, Yaman, and even in Saudi Arabia, the defeated need safety and the rivals need a neutral ground to iron out their differences. The oil-rich shaykhs of the Persian Gulf and Saudi Arabia find Lebanon as beautiful and more convenient than Switzerland. They build their palaces in the cool mountains of Lebanon and enjoy the virtues and vices of Europe without the handicap of needing an interpreter. Beirut enjoys over a dozen daily newspapers, almost all of them subsidized by one Arab country or another. All one has to do is to read the editorials in order to know the current policy of each of the Arab countries. The number of seats in the Lebanese parliament and Muslims in the cabinet denoted equality of opportunity for the leaders of these groups.

DEMISE OF THE U.A.R.

Lebanon is not a typical Arab country and its method of return to normalcy could not be a model for others to follow. Because General Qasim of Iraq was not a pan-Arab nationalist, the Ba'thists of Syria were disgruntled and confused. The natural partner for union with Syria, both geographically and historically, should have been Iraq, not Egypt. The Syrian Ba'thists had appealed to Egypt because the Hashimite rulers of Iraq were ideologically unacceptable. The fall of the Iraqi monarchy did not bring about union and the Syrians found themselves hemmed in by Egypt. Now they began to have second thoughts about the wisdom of their union.

Other groups in Syria, such as the moderates, conservatives, military, and small businessmen, gradually realized that Syria was becoming a province of Egypt rather than an equal partner in a union. Businessmen and shopkeepers suffered under economic restrictions which were based on Egyptian needs. The army was disgruntled because it had come under the control of the U.A.R. Vice President Hakim Amer, who acted as Nasser's proconsul in Syria. The Ba'thists, as the enthusiastic proponents of union, had suffered the most. They had accepted the disbanding of all political parties, including their own, confident that they would be given a free hand in building the new National Union Party of the U.A.R. But Nasser refused to give them that opportunity. Indeed, in the first election in 1959, the Ba'thists were pushed out of the government altogether. Perhaps the severest blow came when Nasser began to collaborate with such former enemies as Jordan and Saudi Arabia, against which both Nasser and Ba'thists had poured so many vindictives.

For whatever reasons, Nasser did not take into account the existing agricultural, economic, and social differences between Syria and Egypt and forced upon Syria his "Arab socialism," which was devised for Egyptian needs. For their part, the Ba'thist ideologists of Syria did not take into account the pragmatism of Nasser, who introduced and discarded ideological principles as he went along. Nasser could not allow Qasim to continue imprisoning Iraqi Nasserites without challenging him. And he could not very well challenge him without the aid of Jordan and Saudi Arabia. In the summer of 1959, Nasser restored diplomatic relations with Jordan and received King Sa'ud of Arabia as an honored guest in Cairo. Furthermore, it looked as though the Soviet Union were aiding Qasim against Nasser, and this drove the latter into closer ties with the United States.

A climax came in June 1961, when the British protectorate over Kuwait, established in 1899, was lifted and the oil-rich territory was declared independent. Qasim used the occasion by declaring that Kuwait belonged to Iraq and prepared to annex it. The ruling Shaykh of Kuwait immediately invoked the treaty agreement with Great Britain and arranged for British troops to defend his country against Iraq. Ideologicaly, the U.A.R. should have welcomed the annexation of a reactionary shaykhdom by a radical Arab, but Qasim was a sworn enemy of Nasser and could not be allowed to do this. Consequently, the Arabs witnessed the unusual spectacle of Nasser cooperating with the British to save Kuwait from the hands of Qasim. By mid-September, the British troops had left, and it was a combination of troops from Egypt, Jordan, and Saudi Arabia who stood guard over Kuwait against another Arab country.

The Syrians had had enough. On September 28, 1961, Syrian officers staged a coup and ordered vice president Amer and other Egyptian officials to leave. Nasser did not try to quell the rebellion and accepted the separation of Syria and Egypt. The leaders of the coup called an election; almost all the old parties won seats (though the Ba'thists won only 18), and undid most of what the U.A.R. had done. Syria had not changed much in its desire for Arab unity. It signed a National Unity Charter in which it advocated the creation of a "voluntary" Arab union. Neither had it changed much internally for there was another coup in March 1962, which tried to reinstate some of the reforms of the U.A.R.

In the meantime, the Iraqi branch of the Ba'th party staged a coup against Qasim on February 8, 1963. The leader of the coup, Abd al-Salam Arif, whose death sentence had been reprieved by Qasim, ordered the death of Qasim and his leftist supporters. Nasser sent his congratulations to Arif. Michel Aflaq, the Syrian theoretician of the Ba'th party, held long meetings with his Iraqi colleagues. On March 8, 1963, Syria had another coup which brought to power a number of military leaders, who, although not Ba'thist, were sympathetic to its ideas. Once again the three countries, Iraq, Syria, and Egypt, held meetings for union and every meeting ended in recriminations. In spite of all this, the Egyptian, Iraqi, and Syrian leaders still spoke of union and approved a flag design with three stars on it.

NASSER AND ARAB SOCIALISM

Nasser had spent a good deal of his energy in the cause of pan-Arabism and all he had to show for it was the name "U.A.R.," which he insisted on continuing as a symbol of a goal to be achieved. He had not, however, neglected reforms at home. He and his friends assumed power without a well-defined ideological program. Consequently, he was not bound to a preconceived ideology and was free to try different programs and shift position as he went along. Perhaps because of his meeting with Nehru of India, his friendship with Tito of Yugoslavia, his visit to the Soviet Union, his association with the Ba'thists of Syria, and the general needs of all developing nations, he followed programs which were socialist in nature. Land reform, which he started in 1952, was the beginning. In 1956, when the Suez Canal Company and many other foreign enterprises were nationalized, the government formed an Economic Organization which was to manage the industries. In a short time, the Economic Organization was operating industrial, commercial, financial, and agricultural concerns. Indeed, the acquisition of the foreign concerns demanded the formation of the Economic Organization.

Because 50 per cent of national income was in the hands of one and a half per cent of the population, Nasser ordered the nationalization of all important concerns such as banks, cotton, fertilizer, insurance, iron, public utilities, steel, and textiles. Only small industries were left for private enterprise. Salaries were restricted and all income above 10,000 Egyptian pounds was taxed 90 per cent. The maximum acreage of landholding was decreased from 200 to 100 feddans. There were laws for the benefit of laborers. In forbidding persons to hold more than one job, many positions were opened up for the large number of the educated unemployed.

Indeed, in the first ten years of the Nasser regime, Egypt could boast of building more houses, schools, hospitals and infirmaries, social service centers, and agricultural cooperatives than it had during the half century before the R.C.C. came to power. In 1959, Egypt and the Sudan reached an agreement on the use of the Nile and the Soviet Union agreed to extend a $300,000,000 loan to build the high Aswan Dam. The R.C.C. was the first government in Egypt to pay serious attention to the problem of population and to establish family planning centers. Given the lack of education, the increase in population, and the difficult odds, perhaps these reforms, even after the completion of the Aswan Dam, will not make too much difference in the standard of living. But the psychological effect of these reforms on the population was tremendous, and Egypt to the Egyptians was a country on the move.

THE YAMAN INCIDENT

Because of the position of leadership which it enjoys in the Arab world and Nasser's popularity, Egypt has had to be concerned about events in the whole Arab world. In 1962, there was a coup d'etat in Yaman which brought a revolutionary government into power. Nasser felt that he had to support the revolutionary government. To say that Nasser's "interference" in Yamani affairs was nothing but imperialism on Nasser's part may be misleading. Perhaps self-aggrandizement was involved, but given the idea of Arab unity, which most educated Arabs hold as a "fact" to be desired, then it becomes incombent upon a progressive Arab country to aid all progressive movements everywhere in the Arab world.

Yaman was a hermit country, closed to outside influence for over 1,000 years. It was ruled as a theocracy by hereditary Imams of the Zaidi Shi'a sect. In 1945, Yaman joined the League of Arab States and in 1947 became a member of the United Nations. In 1958, Yaman joined the U.A.R. under a federal arrangement. In 1961, when the U.A.R. was dissolved, Nasser terminated the federal union with Yaman. A year later there was a revolution in Yaman and Nasser was accused of fomenting it. Civil war developed in Yaman, with Egypt siding with the revolutionary government and Saudi Arabia helping the ousted Imam. The war lasted for six years and Egypt was forced to dissipate its energies and millions of dollars in Yaman. The case went before the United Nations, which sent observers to prevent Egypt and Saudi Arabia from interfering with the civil war, but the end had not come even with the truce in 1967, when Israel attacked the Arab countries.

THE ARAB-ISRAELI WAR

After the second attempt toward union failed in 1963, Egypt and the Arab countries of the Fertile Crescent returned to their traditional ways. This generally meant coups in Syria and Iraq and cold war among the Arab leaders. About the only thing these countries could agree on was their opposition to Israel. Syrians as usual were at the forefront, claiming to be more ardent Arabs and better opponents of Israel than anyone else. The Soviet Union was arming Egypt and Syria; France was selling arms and airplanes to Israel; and the United States was providing some military equipment to Jordan and Saudi Arabia.

Israel, in the meantime, had developed the port of Eilat on the Gulf of Aqaba. It built an oil pipeline from Eilat to Haifa, through which Persian oil flowed for the use of Israeli industries. Egypt broke diplomatic relations with Iran for being willing to sell oil to Israel. Israel also defied an injunction of the United Nations and diverted Jordan River water for agricultural purposes in the Negev.

These and the unsettled problems between Israel and its Arab neighbors caused periodic clashes. Because the borders between Israel and Egypt were guarded by a United Nations Peace Keeping Force, there were not many incidents. The vulnerable position of Jordan did not allow it to cause too much trouble for Israel. Syria was in a better position to attack both Israeli settlements and Israeli encroachment on land designated by the United Nations as neutral or demilitarized zone. Israel retaliated periodically, not against Syria but against innocent Jordan villages on the border. Jordan's inability to retaliate against Israel gave Egypt and Syria an excuse to attack Husayn for his "pro-Israeli" policies.

It is difficult to determine why Israel punished Jordan for the sins of Syria. Since there was a mutual aid treaty between Syria and Egypt, perhaps Israel was afraid that attacking Syria might involve Egypt in the conflict. Furthermore, the Palestinian refugees had formed a government in exile and a "Palestine Liberation Army," which had training camps in Syria and the Gaza Strip. Israeli attacks on Jordan might bring this army into Jordan, in which case Israel would have an excuse to wage a "defensive war" and occupy the west bank of the Jordan River, a goal which the Herut Party had been advocating for a long time.

In any case, the situation grew very tense. On May 15, 1967, Israel celebrated its nineteenth anniversary of independence with military parades in "demilitarized" Jerusalem against United Nations objections. Prime Minister Eshkol of Israel reminded the Israelis of the gravity of the situation and said that Israel "will be forced to take suitable retaliatory measures" to counteract increasing Syrian agitation against Israel. The various commando groups which had been training in Syria and the Gaza Strip under the direction of the Palestine Liberation Organization increased their maneuvering activities. The Syrians taunted President Nasser for hiding behind the United Nations forces. On May 17, the U.A.R. requested that all United Nations forces evacuate Egyptian soil. Secretary General U Thant complied with the request, permitting Egyptian troops to replace the U.N.E.F. and occupy Sharm al-Shaykh, which controlled the approach to the Gulf of Aqaba and the Straits of Tiran.

On May 22, the U.A.R. closed the Gulf of Aqaba to Israeli ships and all non-Israeli ships carrying strategic material to Israel. Israel considered the closing of an international waterway an act of war and started to mobilize. On May 30, Egypt and Jordan signed a military alliance to repel an attack on either nation. On June 3, Libya joined the Egyptian army, and the next day Iraq joined the Egyptian-Jordanian alliance. The ring around Israel was complete.

The great powers did not want war in the Middle East. But the Soviet Union was sympathetic with the Arabs; the United States and Great Britain agreed with Israel that the Straits of Tiran were international; and France declared its neutrality in the conflict. It is even doubtful whether Egypt wanted war, but Israel could not gamble on that.

On Monday morning June 5, 1967, Israeli air and land forces attacked and fighting began from Sinai to Syria and along the Jordanian border. In about two hours the Israeli planes destroyed the Egyptian, Syrian, and Jordanian air forces. Then, with complete air superiority, the Israeli ground forces advanced on all fronts. In six short days Israeli soldiers stood along the Suez Canal in the south, the Jordan River in the east, and the Syrian heights overlooking the Lake Galilee in the northeast. They had captured nine Egyptian generals, over 300 officers, thousands of prisoners, and millions of dollars' worth of Russian-made military equipment, most of it undamaged. The "six day war" exposed once again the disunity and the ineptness of the Arabs as well as the audacity and the solidarity of the Israelis. Israel had dealt a severe blow to the Arabs with American money, French airplanes, and the courage and ability of the Israeli pilots.

A SELECTED BIBLIOGRAPHY

Agwani, M. S., ed., *The Lebanese Crisis, 1958: A Documentary Study.* New York: Asia Publishing House, 1965.

Avery, Peter, *Modern Iran.* New York: Frederick A. Praeger, 1965.

Banani, Amin, *The Modernization of Iran, 1921–1941.* Stanford, Calif.: Stanford University Press, 1961.

Ben-Gurion, David, *Rebirth and Destiny of Israel.* New York: Philosophical Library, 1953.

Binder, Leonard, *Idealogical Revolution in the Middle East.* New York: John Wiley & Sons, 1964.

Campbell, John C., *Defense of the Middle East.* New York: Frederick A. Praeger, 1960.

Cottam, Richard W., *Nationalism in Iran.* Pittsburgh: University of Pittsburgh Press, 1964.

Davis, Helen Miller, *Constitutions, Electoral Laws, Treaties of States in the Near and Middle East.* Durham, N.C.: Duke University Press, 1947.

Dickson, H. R. P., *Kuwait and Her Neighbours.* London: George Allen & Unwin Ltd. 1956.

Frye, Richard N., ed., *Islam and the West.* The Hague, Netherlands: Mouton, 1956.

Haim, Sylvia G., ed., *Arab Nationalism.* Berkeley, Calif.: University of California Press, 1962.

Harris, Christina Phelps, *Nationalism and Revolution in Egypt.* The Hague, Netherlands: Mouton, 1964.

Harris, George L., *Iraq, its People, its Society, its Culture.* New Haven, Conn.: Human Relations Area Files Press, 1958.

Hay, Sir Rupert, *The Persian Gulf States.* Washington, D.C.: Middle East Institute, 1959.

Hitti, Philip K., *History of Syria.* London: Macmillan, 1951.

————, *Lebanon in History.* London: Macmillan, 1962.

Hourani, Albert H., *Syria and Lebanon: A Political Essay.* London: Oxford University Press, 1946.

Hurewitz, J. C., *The Struggle for Palestine.* W. W. Norton, New York: 1950.

————, *Diplomacy in the Near and Middle East* (Vol. II, 1914–1956). Princeton, N.J.: D. Van Nostrand, 1956.

Issawi, Charles, *Egypt in Revolution: An Economic Analysis.* New York: Oxford University Press, 1963.

Khadduri, Majid, *Independent Iraq: A Study in Iraqi Politics Since 1932.* London: Oxford University Press, 1951.

Kinross, Lord, *Ataturk.* New York: William Morrow, 1965.

Lacqueur, Walter Z., *The Soviet Union and the Middle East.* New York: Frederick A. Praeger, 1959.

——, *Middle East in Transition*. New York: Frederick A. Praeger, 1958.

Lebkicher, Roy, Georg Rentz, and Max Steineke, *The Arabia of Ibn Saud*. New York: Russell F. Moore, 1952.

Lewis, Bernard, *The Emergence of Modern Turkey*. London: Oxford University Press, 1961.

Lewis, Geoffrey, *Turkey*. New York: Frederick A. Praeger, 1955.

Lilienthal, Alfred, *What Price Israel*. Chicago: Henry Regnery, 1953.

Marlowe, John, *The Persian Gulf in the Twentieth Century*. London: The Cresset Press, 1962.

Nasser, Gamal Abd al-, *The Philosophy of Revolution*. Cairo, 1954.

Neguib, Mohammed, *Egypt's Destiny*. London: Victor Gollancz, 1955.

Pahlavi, Mohammed Reza Shah, *My Mission for My Country*. New York: McGraw Hill, 1961.

Patai, Raphael, *The Kingdom of Jordan*. Princeton, N.J.: Princeton University Press, 1958.

Peretz, Don, *Israel and the Palestine Arabs*. Washington, D.C.: Middle East Institute, 1958.

Rivlin, Benjamin, and Joseph Szyliowicz, eds., *The Contemporary Middle East*. New York: Random House, 1965.

Sayegh, Fayez A., ed., *The Dynamics of Neutralism in the Arab World*. San Francisco: Chandler Publishing Co., 1964.

Shwadron, Benjamin, *The Middle East Oil and Great Powers*. New York: Frederick A. Praeger, 1956.

Smith, Wilfred C., *Islam in Modern History*. Princeton, N.J.: Princeton University Press, 1957.

Sparrow, Gerald, *Modern Jordan*. London: George Allen & Unwin Ltd., 1961.

Upton, Joseph M., *The History of Modern Iran*. Cambridge, Mass.: Harvard University Press, 1960.

Warriner, Doreen, *Land and Poverty in the Middle East*. New York: Oxford University Press, 1948.

Wenner, Manfred W., *Modern Yemen*. Baltimore: Johns Hopkins University Press, 1967.

Weiker, Walter F., *The Turkish Revolution, 1960–1961*. Washington, D.C.: Brookings Institution, 1964.

Weizmann, Chaim, *Trial and Error*. New York: Harper, 1949.

Winder, R. Bayly, *Saudi Arabia in the Nineteenth Century*. New York: St. Martins Press, 1965.

Ziadeh, Nicola A., *Syria and Lebanon*. New York: Frederick A. Praeger, 1957.

EPILOGUE

During the second half of the twentieth century, the countries of the Middle East had won their struggle for independence and were in different stages of social and economic change. The progress of the Arabic-speaking peoples was impeded by their preoccupation with the State of Israel which had emerged as a most powerful military force in the Middle East. Israel occupied all the area of Palestine, plus the whole Sinai peninsula and the Jawlan district (Golan heights) in Syria overlooking Lake Galilee. It annexed "old" Jerusalem and the heights of Golan as integral parts of Israel. It was willing to discuss the fate of the rest of the occupied territory directly with the Arabs, but only after the Arabs were willing to recognize the existence of Israel. The Arabs, on the other hand, declared their willingness to do that which they had refused to do for nearly 20 years, namely to recognize Israel, if the latter withdrew its troops to the pre-June 1967 boundaries. This the Israelis refused to do. Even though the administration of Arab populations in the conquered territories was a constant source of trouble, it was doubtful whether Israel would abandon any of the occupied territories. In doing so, it would be giving up shorter and more defensible borders such as the Suez Canal and the Jordan River for longer and less defensible borders in the Negev and west of the Jordan River.

Among the Arab countries, Jordan lost the most in territory, in economic potential, and in tourist revenues. It was reduced to the old territory of Trans-jordan, which is practically devoid of any economic potential. It had the added burden of hundreds of thousands of Arab refugees who had fled from the west bank of the Jordan River. Economically, Jordan had become more dependent on the largesse and loans given by Saudi Arabia and especially Kuwait.

In addition to the losses sustained by Egypt in territory, men, and war material, Nasser suffered loss of personal prestige. There was open criticism of him in Egypt and opposition in some of the Arab countries. Egypt lost the revenue of the Canal, as Israel would not allow its opening without being allowed free passage. Furthermore, the construction of "jumbo" oil tankers, which could transport oil from the Persian Gulf to the ports of Europe via the Cape at cheaper prices, had minimized the economic potential of the Suez Canal.

The economic plight of Egypt made it almost totally dependent upon the Soviet Union. The fear of Israel forced Egypt to allow the Soviet naval forces to be stationed at Port Said and Alexandria. Perhaps it was the price demanded by the Soviet Union for the tremendous military and economic aid to Egypt. In any case, the result was the same—foreign conquerors occupied Sinai, Egypt's gateway to the Fertile Crescent, and Russian warships were docked in Egyptian ports, where during the first half of the twenteeth century British warships were stationed.

The struggle for independence and social change did not bring greater unity among the Arabs. They were adamant in refusing to sit at a "conference table" with Israel, but their unity against Israel had not diminished the mutual suspicions and incriminations among the Arab leaders. In spite of their differences, the Arabs believed that time was on their side. There would come a time, they insisted, when the Arabs would learn the use of modern weapons and defeat Israel as Saladin had defeated the Crusaders in the twelfth century.

The social and political struggle in the Middle East, as well as the world situation, had altered the relative roles of the great powers in the Middle East. The power and influence of Great Britain had decreased steadily. It could not afford the economic burden of the occupation of Aden or the maintenance of naval forces in the Persian Gulf. Nevertheless, it had treaty relations with Jordan, Saudi Arabia, and the Shaykhdoms of the Persian Gulf and would likely exert some influence.

France shifted back and forth between Israel and the Arab countries, depending upon circumstances. After the alliance with Israel against Egypt in 1956, France remained a staunch ally of Israel, providing it with arms. Immediately after the "six day war," France suddenly changed its allegiance and denounced Israel for not withdrawing its troops to the prewar borders. This move by President de Gaulle disgusted some and puzzled many, but in the long run it might be useful for maintaining the balance of power between the U.S.S.R. and western Europe in the Middle East.

The United States had become all but paralyzed among the Arabic-speaking countries of the Middle East. Because of its internal politics, the United States was so committed to supporting policies of Israel that it was not able to take an impartial stand, let alone a strong one.

The decrease of American influence in the Middle East has usually, though not always, meant a corresponding increase in the prestige of the Soviet Union. One of the constantly recurring themes in the history of Russia, Tsarist or communist, has been the desire of the governments of that country to get a foothold in the Mediterranean and the Persian Gulf area. To achieve this goal, Russia has incessantly tried to control the Turkish Straits and to dominate Iran. The Russians, however, failed to accomplish their purpose not only because of the resistance of Turkey and Iran, but also because of the opposition of western European powers to Russian design. The Truman Doctrine was the continuation of this historic western European policy.

Russian penetration into the Arab world began in 1956 and continued to be strengthened, especially in Egypt and Syria. For the first time in history, Russian warships were based in the Mediterranean. The U.S.S.R. did not gain control of the Straits or domination over Iran, but both Turkey and Iran, perhaps conscious of the shadow of the U.S.S.R. leapfrogging over them into the Mediterranean, followed a policy of rapprochement with the Soviet Union.

In the last analysis, the inner strength of the countries of the Middle East does not depend so much on the power play among the western powers in the Middle East but on the quality of the synthesis which the Middle Eastern countries are able to make out of their past culture with the modern western civilization. Islam has a major role to play in this synthesis, though not to the same degree in every country. Psychologically, Turkey resolved to turn its back on the East and accept the West. After some 40 years, it found that it was not possible to reject all of the past. Perhaps in the next 50 years it will try to adopt and/or reinterpret those values of the past which have survived.

While Iran has not shown much hesitancy in accepting the West, it has been reluctant to turn its back to the East. East and West have been going on hand-in-hand in Iran, sometimes as compatible and sometimes as incompatible values. It will be a process of trial and error, sometimes consciously and often unconsciously, until a definite synthesis is developed.

It is difficult to establish simple classification for the Arab world, for it has neither political unity nor ideological agreement. Islam has a special position with Arabism which it does not have with Turkish or Persian nationalism. After all, Muhammad was an Arab, the Koran was revealed in Arabic, and the pan-Arab nationalists identify Muslim culture as "Arab" culture. It is too early even to conjecture what kind of synthesis will result.

The peoples of the Middle East, Arabs, Persians, and Turks, are caught in a fast-changing world and they themselves are involved in a renaissance, religious reformation, economic overhauling, political change, and social revolution—all at the same time. They are like a family which is in the process of completely remodeling their house inside and out but want to live in it and entertain friends, and are anxious for their friends to admire the architecture of the house they are remodeling and praise the beauty of the furniture they are discarding—all at the same time. Perhaps because of this and other reasons they bring into the world scene attitudes, expectations, and conduct which seem to the outsider as impractical, naïve, arrogant, rigid, innocent, reasonable, and inconsistent—all at the same time.

A CHRONOLOGY
OF IMPORTANT EVENTS

570 Birth of Muhammad.
622 Hijra.
632 Death of Muhammad.
634 Beginning of Muslim wars of expansion.
635 Conquest of Syria. Battle of Qadesiya.
639 Conquest of Egypt.
640 Conquest of Iran.
653 Recension of the Koran.
656 Muslim Civil War. Battle of the Camel.
659 Assassination of Ali.
661 The Umayyads come to power.
680 Death of Husayn at Karbala.
711 Conquest of Spain and Sind.
750 Fall of the Umayyads and rise of the Abbasids.
754 Murder of Abu Muslim Khorasani.
767 Death of Abu Hanifa, founder of the Hanifite School.
795 Death of Malik ibn-Anas, founder of the Malikite School.
813 The establishment of the Translation Bureau by Ma'mun.
820 Death of Muhammad ibn-Idris al Shafi'i, founder of the Shafi'i School.
833 The coming of the Turks.
850 Death of Ahmad ibn-Hanbal, founder of the Hanbali School. The beginning of the period of principalities.
910 The Fatimids established in Egypt.
950 Death of Farabi the philosopher.
956 Death of Mas'udi the historian.
972 Azhar University founded in Cairo.
1037 Death of Avicenna the physician and philosopher.
1048 Death of Biruni the mathematician.
1055 The coming of the Saljuqs.
1071 The battle of Manzikert.
1099 Crusaders in Jerusalem.
1137 Fall of the Saljuqs.

1171   Fall of the Fatimids.
1187   Battle of Hittin, Saladin defeats the Crusaders.
1220   The advance of Chengiz Khan.
1252   Beginning of the Mamluk rule in Egypt.
1258   Fall of Baghdad. End of the Abbasids.
1260   The Mamluks defeat the Mongols.
1273   Death of Jalal al-Din Rumi the mystic.
CA. 1300   Beginning of the Ottoman Empire.
1324   Death of Marco Polo.
1369   Advent of Tamerlane.
1389   Battle of Kossova.
1402   Tamerlane defeats Bayezid.
1406   Death of Ibn-Khaldun the social historian.
1453   Fall of Constantinople.
1500   Beginning of the Safavid Empire.
1507   The Portuguese come to the Persian Gulf.
1514   The Battle of Chaldran.
1517   Conquest of the Fertile Crescent by the Ottomans.
1591   The British enter the Persian Gulf.
1599   Persian embassy to European capitals.
1656   Mehmed Köprülü becomes grand vazir.
1657   Death of Haji Khalifa the Turkish historian.
1683   The Turks advance to Vienna.
1699   Peace of Karlowitz.
1718   Peace of Passrowitz.
1722   Fall of the Safavids.
1739   Capture of Delhi by Nader Shah.
1757   Advent of Wahhabism.
1774   Treaty of Kuchuk Kainarji.
1780   Rise of the Qajars in Iran.
1789   Napoleon in Egypt.
1795   The nizam-i jadid in Turkey.
1811   The end of the Mamluks.
1814   The Anglo-Persian Definitive Treaty.
1826   The end of the Janissaries.
1828   Treaty of Turkmanchai.
1831   Conquest of Syria by Egypt.
1839   Hatti Sharif in Turkey.
1840   The house of Muhammad Ali established in Egypt.
1844   The Advent of the Bab in Iran.
1851   Opening of the Dar al-Fonun School in Iran.
1853   The Crimean War. Founding of the Suez Canal Company.
1856   Hatti Humayun in Turkey.
1860   Druze-Maronite War.
1862   Ottoman Scientific Society, Ibrahim Shinasi
1869   Suez Canal completed.
1882   The British occupy Egypt.

1887   Death of Namik Kemal of Turkey.
1888   Constantinople Convention on the Suez Canal.
1889   Committee of Union and Progress in Turkey.
1890   The Tobacco Concession in Iran.
1894   The Armenian Massacre in Turkey.
1897   The first World Zionist Congress.
1898   Assassination of Naser al-Din Shah Qajar.
1906   Granting of Constitution in Iran.
1907   Anglo-Russian agreement dividing Iran.
1908   The Young Turk Revolution.
1911   The ousting of Shuster from Iran.
1915   Husayn-McMahon correspondence.
1916   Sykes-Picot agreement.
1917   The Balfour Declaration.
1918   Faysal's army enters Damascus.
1919   The secret Anglo-Persian Agreement. The landing of Ataturk in Samsun.
1920   San Remo Agreement. Faysal ousted from Syria. Treaty of Sevres.
1921   Coup d'etat by Reza Khan in Iran. Faysal becomes king of Iraq. Creation
       of Transjordan. First anti-Zionist uprising in Palestine.
1922   Turkish victory over the Greeks. Millspaugh mission in Iran.
1923   Treaty of Lausanne. Reza Khan becomes prime minister of Iran. The Re-
       public of Turkey.
1924   Rise of Ibn Sa'ud of Arabia. End of the caliphate.
1925   Reza Pahlavi becomes Shah of Iran.
1923–1939   Reform movement in Iran and Turkey.
1933   New Anglo-Persian oil agreement.
1936   Montreaux Convention on the Straits.
1937   Sa'dabad Treaty between Afghanistan, Iran, Iraq, and Turkey.
1938   Death of Ataturk. Completion of trans-Iranian railway.
1939   British White Paper on Palestine.
1941   Allied entry into Iran. Abdication of Reza Shah. Gailani coup in Iraq.
       British occupation of Iraq, Syria, and Lebanon.
1942   Zionist Biltmore Program.
1944   League of Arab States.
1945   Azarbaijan separatist movement.
1946   Red Army evacuates Iran. Anglo-American Commission on Palestine.
1947   Creation of Israel. Truman Doctrine.
1948   Arab-Israeli war.
1950   End of one party rule in Turkey.
1951   Turkey becomes member of NATO. Nationalization of oil in Iran.
1952   Nasser coup in Egypt.
1953   Fall of Dr. Mosaddeq in Iran.
1954   British evacuate Egypt.
1956   Nationalization of Suez Canal Company. Anglo-French-Israeli attack on
       Egypt.
1957   Eisenhower Doctrine.
1958   Union of Egypt and Syria. End of the Hashimite rule in Iraq.

1960   Military coup in Turkey.
1961   Second Republic of Turkey. End of the Syria-Egyptian Union.
1962   Coup in Yaman.
1963   Inauguration of White Revolution in Iran.
1967   The Arab-Israeli War. Coronation of the Shah of Iran.

INDEX

Abbas (uncle of Muhammad), 76, 79
Abbas Aqa, 259
Abbas Effendi (Abdul Baha), 254
Abbas Mirza (Qajar Prince), 222, 223
Abbas I (Khedive of Egypt), 215
Abbas I the Great (Safavid Shah), 162, 165–68,
   171–77, 180–84
   destruction of qizilbash by, 166, 182, 183
   Europeans and, 167, 171, 173–77, 183
   History of Abbas about, 184
   treatment of Armenians by, 167, 172, 182
Abbas II Hilmi (Khedive of Egypt), 279–80
Abbas II (Safavid Shah), 162, 175
Abbas III (Safavid Shah), 162, 168
Abbasa (sister of Harun al-Rashid), 82
Abbasids, 64, 76–95, 99, 113, 114
   architecture of, 118
   end of rule by, 131–32
   poetry by, 116
   religious dogma and, 119
Abd al-Aziz, 67
Abd al-Malik (Umayyad Caliph), 64, 68, 70,
   72, 76, 96
Abd al-Rahman (Caliph of Andalusia), 90
Abd al-Rahman ibn Khaldun, 20, 27, 71,
   142–43, 289
Abd al-Rahman I ibn Mu'awiyah (Caliph of
   Damascus), 67, 76
Abduh, Muhammad, 245–47, 249–50, 286,
   288, 382
Abdul Baha (Abbas Effendi), 254
Abdul Hamid I (Ottoman Sultan), 196
Abdul Hamid II (Ottoman Sultan), 298
   abdication of, 240–41
   Afghani and, 227, 239, 245, 255
   Armenians and, 238–39
   Europeans and, 202–3, 208–9, 302
   pan-Islamism of, 227, 239, 244
   Treaty of San Stefano and, 208
   Young Ottomans and, 237–38

Abdul Hamid II and, 227, 239, 245, 255
   as pan-Islamist agitator, 227, 234, 244–45,
   249, 252, 254
   in Russia, 254
Abdul Mejid (Ottoman Sultan), 206, 232,
   234–35, 273
Abdul Muttalib, 30, 79
Abdullah (Abd-Allah ibn-Abd-al-Muttalib),
   30
Abdullah (King of Jordan; Amir of Trans-
   jordan), 293, 312–13, 322, 370, 375,
   397
Abdullah (son of Abbas), 79
Abdullah ibn-Maymun (Ismaili leader in
   Iran), 92
Abdullah ibn-Zubayr, 74
Abraha (ruler of Yaman), 32
Abraham, 28, 32, 37, 40, 42, 295
Abu-al-'Ala'al-Ma'arri, 92
Abu al-Atahiya, 83, 116
Abu Bakr (1st Caliph), 60, 165
   as follower of Muhammad, 32, 34–35
   Islam ruled by, 48–53, 56, 65
   as "usurper," 101
Abu Hanifa, Imam, 105
Abu Lahab, 33
Abu Lolo Firooz, 55
Abu Muslim Khorasani (Behzadan), 76,
   79–81
Abu-Nasr al-Farabi, *Opinions of the Citizens
   of the Virtuous City*, 109
Abu Nuwas, 83, 116
Abu Sufyan, 37–39, 59, 65
Abu Talib (uncle of Muhammad), 30, 33
Abul Abbas (al-Saffah; Abbasid Caliph),
   76, 79, 82, 95
Abul Hassan Ali al-Ash'ari, 99–100
Abul-Huda, Shaykh, 244
Adam, 32, 41, 42
Aden, 212

413